STUDIES IN
LANGUAGE LEARNING
AND
SPANISH LINGUISTICS

IN HONOR OF
TRACY D. TERRELL

TRACY D. TERRELL
1943–1991

STUDIES IN
LANGUAGE LEARNING
AND
SPANISH LINGUISTICS

IN HONOR OF
TRACY D. TERRELL

EDITED BY

PEGGY HASHEMIPOUR   RICARDO MALDONADO

MARGARET van NAERSSEN

McGraw–Hill, Inc.

New York St. Louis San Francisco Auckland Bogotá Caracas Lisbon London Madrid
Mexico City Milan Montreal New Delhi San Juan Singapore Sydney Tokyo Toronto

Studies in Language Learning and Spanish Linguistics in Honor of Tracy D. Terrell

 This book is printed on recycled, acid-free paper containing a minimum of 50% total recycled fiber with 10% postconsumer de-inked fiber.

1 2 3 4 5 6 7 8 9 0   DOC DOC   9 0 9 8 7 6 5 4

ISBN 0-07-064488-8

Publisher: Thalia Dorwick
Editor: Richard Wallis
Production supervisor: Tanya Nigh
Design manager: Francis Owens
Text and cover designer: Deborah Chusid
Compositor: Chris de Heer Design
Printer and binder: R. R. Donnelley, Inc./Crawfordsville

Library of Congress Cataloging-in-Publication Data

Festschrift : studies in language learning and Spanish linguistics in honor of Tracy D. Terrell /
    edited by Peggy Hashemipour, Ricardo Maldonado, Margaret van Naerssen.
        p.   cm.
    Includes bibliographical references.
    ISBN 0-07-064488-8
    1. Language and languages—Study and teaching.   2. Second language acquisition.
3. Spanish language.   I. Hashemipour, Peggy.   II. Maldonado, Ricardo.   III. van
Naerssen, Margaret.   IV. Terrell, Tracy D.   V. Title: Studies in language learning and
Spanish linguistics in honor of Tracy D. Terrell.
P51.F47 1994
418'.007—dc20   94-27451
                                                                                                            CIP

CONTENTS

PART 3   Spanish Language Studies

A SOCIOLINGUISTICS

FOREWORD

McGraw-Hill is pleased to offer this volume in honor of the vast contributions to the fields of second-language teaching and research made by Tracy Terrell over the course of his professional career. The language textbooks that he coauthored—*Dos mundos, Kontakte,* and *Deux mondes* at the college level and *¡Bravo!* at the secondary level—continue to have a lasting influence on second-language instruction in this country and abroad. The articles in this volume, written by his colleagues from around the country, are a tribute to the scope of Terrell's research activities, which he never separated from his keen interest in learning and teaching.

We at McGraw-Hill had the privilege of knowing Tracy Terrell and working with him in creating his textbooks and disseminating them to the educational community. He was a friend and mentor to many, and he has left an extraordinary legacy. His generosity was boundless. With this volume, we hope to repay him for all he taught us.

Dr. Thalia Dorwick
Publisher, Foreign Languages
and ESL
McGraw-Hill, Inc.

PREFACE

Early in 1990, it became clear to Tracy Terrell's friends and colleagues that he was seriously ill. We began thinking about what we could do to let him know how much we cared about him and to honor him for his contributions. A number of professional organizations held presentations to honor him, and, at the same time, his friends in language-teaching methods and research and those in Spanish linguistics began talking of a festschrift volume. Hearing of each other's efforts, we decided to pool our contributions. Then came the practical matter of funding. Thalia Dorwick, Publisher of Foreign Languages and ESL at McGraw-Hill, heard of the festschrift project. She had worked closely with Tracy for nearly ten years on the publication of his college textbooks and was then working with him on his new high school Spanish series. Out of her close friendship with and respect for Tracy, she proposed that we do this collection of essays for McGraw-Hill.

We began working with Thalia on the project, first identifying who among his colleagues and friends, past and present, would submit a paper in one of Tracy's major areas of professional interest: language acquisition, sociolinguistics, and Spanish mood and tense. We talked with Tracy about our proposal to make sure we had contacted everyone he thought might want to contribute. While it was awkward in one way to be talking with him about a volume in his honor, he truly appreciated knowing that so many people wanted to keep his ideas alive and build on them in their own ways.

When Tracy made plans to go on sabbatical from the University of California, San Diego, at the end of spring quarter 1991, the linguistics department planned a luncheon in his honor. At that event, we presented him with the initial table of contents for this volume, and we kept in touch with him about our progress throughout the rest of the year. We hoped, of course, to be able to present him with a published book, but his health continued to deteriorate. Tracy died on December 2, 1991.

In the months to come we experienced setbacks in our progress due to professional and personal changes in our lives. Richard Barrutia, Tracy's longtime friend and colleague at the University of California, Irvine, unfortunately had to withdraw as one of the original editors, and we want to take this opportunity to thank him for all his efforts on this project. We also realized that much more work was involved in the publishing process than we had anticipated and than our individual schedules permitted. Thalia again came to the rescue by providing us with a managing editor, Richard Wallis, who took over the day-to-day responsibilities. As an experienced editor, he was also able to keep us on track and provide professional editing advice to the individual contributors. We appreciate the patience of all involved during these delays and editing procedures.

We regret that Tracy did not live to see this volume. It is our hope, however, that we—together with the individual contributors and the publisher—have produced a collection worthy of his memory. But even more lasting will be our memories of what Tracy gave to us.

Peggy Hashemipour
Ricardo Maldonado
Margaret van Naerssen

INTRODUCTION

Tracy Terrell's work and life were extraordinarily rich, and his creative energies were a source of inspiration to students, teachers, colleagues, and friends around the world. The material in Part 1 brings together the personal and scholarly aspects of his life as background for the diverse collection of essays that follow.

What's in a Name?
Tracy (Terry) Dale (David) Terrell:
A Son and a Brother, a Scholar and a Teacher, a Friend

Jane Terrell
Lyndon B. Johnson High School and Austin Community College

Tracy Dale Terrell was born on June 23, 1943, during World War II. Our parents, Tracy L. Terrell and Alma N. Duncan Terrell, had married the previous year before my father was shipped out with his navy unit. We were classic children of the baby boom era. Having lived through a depression and a world war, our parents dreamed of a better world for their children. And education was the key to that world.

There was never a question as we were growing up that we would both go to college. My brother Dale (as he was called in his childhood) was always one of the smartest in his class. Teachers adored this gifted child. He especially excelled in math and science. His weakness was spelling. (He later was thankful for the invention of the word processor, spell-checking, and talented editors.)

He attended Harveytown Elementary School, a very small rural school in Huntington, West Virginia. My parents then moved to a more middle-class neighborhood, where he attended Cammack Junior High School. His first exposure to languages came at this time; he took Latin during the ninth grade. He always credited his study of Latin with giving him a good foundation for language study. Next, he attended Huntington High School, the same school our parents had attended. There he was introduced to Spanish, to fulfill his college entrance requirements like everyone else. He excelled at learning a second language, but then he excelled at all of his studies. He was a member of the National Honor Society, editor of the school newspaper, and a straight "A" student. He continued to major in math and science.

Due to financial reasons, he attended Marshall University, the local college in Huntington. It was from this institution that he received his bachelor's degree (BA), graduating *cum laude* in 1965 with majors in Spanish and in mathematics. During his college years his love of language developed. I had been placed in an experimental program in junior high school that offered French. He took my French book and began to study it, teaching himself. I would try to help with pronunciation and practice speaking with him. In turn, he began to teach me Spanish. I suppose I was his first Natural Approach student. I would give him a phrase in French and he would teach me the Spanish equivalent. He soon surpassed me in ability and knowledge. Most college students spend their money on cars and partying. My brother spent his money buying Harcourt Brace's ALM French books and records. Next, he tackled German, again studying the language on his own. Later, he took courses at the university to refine his knowledge of German.

Tracy made some important decisions during those years at Marshall that were instrumental in his success. One summer he decided to work abroad. He participated in a program that helped college students find jobs in Europe and worked as a waiter in Switzerland at a resort hotel. The maitre d' was German-speaking and many other waiters spoke only Italian. Tracy would frequently be called upon to translate. He also was required to help guests in ordering their meals and paying their bills. On their days off and for the last few weeks of summer, a group of students rented Vespas and traveled throughout Europe. They stayed in youth hostels or slept in fields. That summer he learned Italian and became more proficient at Spanish, French, and German.

In parts of the United States, Spanish is commonly heard because of a high population of Hispanics. Huntington, West Virginia, is not one of them. There wasn't even a Mexican restaurant there until the 1980s, when Mexican food became popular nationally. Realizing that his pronunciation was less than accurate and that his opportunities to become fluent in Spanish were limited, Tracy decided to study Spanish at the University of Mexico one summer. He and a friend boarded the train in Huntington in June bound for an adventure that would change their lives. He used the train ride as an opportunity to learn. Rather than remain with the other English-speaking passengers, Tracy sat among the Mexican families. He talked and played with the children and asked questions of the adults. It was a practice that he retained throughout his travels. While in Mexico City, he lived with a Mexican family. He immersed himself in the language and culture and his interest in the people and language grew. He remained in touch with the family for many years, and we visited them a few years later during a family vacation to Mexico.

After Tracy graduated in January 1965, he accepted a temporary position with the Baltimore School District teaching junior high school mathematics. His career as a public school teacher was short-lived, however. He had applied for a graduate fellowship at the University of Texas in applied linguistics. For admission, they required a tape demonstrating spoken Spanish. They agreed to accept him, but they recommended that before entering graduate school, he needed to improve his Spanish speaking skills. He decided to postpone graduate school and applied for a Fulbright instead. The next fall, after teaching for one semester in Maryland, Tracy was offered a Fulbright Fellowship to study at the University of Guatemala. Rather than take more courses in Spanish, Tracy enrolled in economics, history, biology, chemistry, and sociology. He knew he would learn the language by being immersed in a world where Spanish was the only language spoken. He told me later that this was vital to his success in obtaining a Ph.D. After a year in Guatemala, he resubmitted his tape and was offered a full fellowship to study at the University of Texas at Austin. (He was offered fellowships at two other universities, but I don't remember where.) So, in 1966, he came to Texas.

Our whole family brought him to UT and took an extended trip to Mexico as our last family vacation together. We were in Austin one fateful morning, deciding whether to go to the university that day to get him registered or to go on to Mexico and register later. Fortunately, we decided to postpone registration and go on with our trip, because on our way out of town, the radio announcer reported that Charles Whitman had opened fire on the students on campus from the University Tower. Had we decided to go to UT that day, our family would have been sitting in the area where all of the people were shot, since the administrative offices are in the Tower building in the center of campus. Fate was not ready for us that day.

At the University of Texas, he majored in applied linguistics. He was accepted into an accelerated program that allowed him to earn a Ph.D. in three years. He skipped the master's program entirely. His primary interest was scientific: he was interested in how language worked, how people acquired language skills, and what rules governed that process. It was at UT that he developed his fascination for Spanish dialectology. He was only twenty-seven years old when he earned his doctorate in August 1970.

In his summers while studying at UT, Tracy worked with the Peace Corps teaching volunteers Spanish. He lived in La Jolla and it was then that he began his love affair with San Diego. It would always be the city in his heart. He felt very fortunate that he had the opportunity eventually to live there. Even at the end of his life when his illness required moving back to Texas to live with me, he would grow very homesick for San Diego.

Perhaps my brother's influence led me to major in Spanish when I entered college. After two years at Marshall University, I had the opportunity to come to the University of Texas to live in Austin with my brother and to complete my degree. Marshall had not prepared me for the rigorous curriculum offered at UT, so I was forced to change my major. But I never lost my love of the language and continued to practice speaking with my brother and learning from him. We shared a duplex for nine months while he worked as a teaching assistant. He was loved as a teacher even then; he always had a natural talent for teaching. I'll never forget Lucy, one of his first-year students. She developed a crush on Mr. Terrell. She made him cakes and cookies and left them on our doorstep anonymously. She once left a cold six-pack of Coors (then impossible to get in Texas) on his car in the parking lot. Naturally, he maintained a professional relationship with her, and she never knew that he had figured out she was the one leaving presents; however, our other roommate and I loved the goodies he received. He was always a professional and students really learned in his classes; he truly cared about teaching. Learning and teaching were always primary in importance to him, and "academics" were secondary. Please don't misunderstand. He enjoyed academics and studying new theories, but he was practical. He knew that teaching skills were necessary to be an effective college instructor.

In fact, he had been a teacher all his life. As my big brother, he taught me how to ride a bicycle when I was six. He taught me how to swim when I was eight, and he taught me algebra when I was eleven. Most of what I learned as a child I learned from him. Unlike most older brothers, he liked having a kid sister to teach. He also helped me with my homework, especially essays. He offered to take me places with him and included me when his friends planned outings. We would watch "American Bandstand" together and practice the newest dance steps. He was an excellent dancer and always enjoyed music. He collected 45s for years and read *Billboard* magazine every week.

He loved to swim. During college he earned his American Red Cross Certification to be a life guard and a swimming instructor. One summer he worked as a counselor at a camp and taught the swimming classes. He also swam one-half to one mile almost daily until he earned the Red Cross fifty-mile patch. His love of swimming and the beach led him to California when he began his job search.

He also collected fish as a hobby. Like all his hobbies, he had to study his subject thoroughly. He researched the fish that he owned and studied their feeding and breeding habits. He had aquariums all over the house—even in my room. He also built ponds (three of them) in our yard so the fish could go outside during the summer. Later in California he decided to become a bird breeder. He built aviaries along one side of the house (at least ten of them). He raised parakeets, finches, cockatiels, and a few exotic types of small parrot. Again he researched the best techniques and became actively involved in a local bird-breeder's organization. He would spend end-less hours with his birds.

Bridge was another one of Tracy's outlets for fun. He taught me how to play bridge when I was in junior high school. He and my mother would want to play on Sunday afternoons and needed at least a third, and he often would include me with his friends when they needed a fourth and I was convenient. It was with love that we continued to enjoy playing bridge together. He was fortunate to find a group of friends in San Diego who also loved bridge, and they had a regular bridge club.

Travel was always a joy for Tracy. He loved learning about the culture and history of a people. He was fortunate to be able to travel all over the world. After that summer working in Europe, he visited the Netherlands often. He taught himself Dutch during those visits and practiced with a Dutch friend, Roan van Twist, at home. He later used his knowledge of Dutch in his lectures on the Natural Approach to demonstrate the technique. Besides Spanish, Dutch became his favorite language.

Wherever he traveled, he often stayed in local hotels rather than large American-owned chains just so he would have a more natural experience. He was also very thrifty by nature and never saw the point in wasting money on expensive hotels. He spent time talking with the people, always learning what textbooks and travel brochures fail to mention. It was fun to travel with him because he knew so much about each country and he had such a sense of adventure.

As a side interest to his travel, Tracy learned the differences among all of the types of aircraft used by commercial airlines. He could tell you the seating configura-tion of all and he knew the manufacturer of the various types and the years they were produced. He also loved looking up flight schedules and working out connections. He knew most of the airports in the world and something about their histories as well. Again, he was never content with just a little knowledge; he had to know everything about the field that he could. His fascination with airplanes was so extensive that the last house he bought in San Diego was a penthouse condominium overlooking down-town San Diego and its airport. He would sit in the living room and tell me, "That's a 727 probably headed for San Francisco. That's a DC10 going to Paris." He could even recognize a plane by the sound of its engine.

My brother's name was often a matter of some confusion that I would like to clarify. His birth certificate says Tracy Dale Terrell. My parents called him "Dale" for his entire life. When I joined him at the University of Texas, I had to adapt to calling him "Tracy," because that is what his friends called him. When he moved to California, people meeting him for the first time often called him "Terry," probably combining his first and last names. He never corrected them, so it stuck. To many friends there he is "Terry Terrell." He never liked either of his names, especially after Tracy became a popular girl's name in California. He decided to change his middle name to David, and my daughters grew up calling him Uncle David. Also, our last name is frequently mispronounced. We pronounce our name ['terəl], not [tə'rel]. Again, he felt rude if he corrected anyone, so he just allowed people to mispronounce his name.

Perhaps Tracy and I inherited our talent and interest in public speaking from our grandfather. He was a Pentecostal minister in our hometown. We attended his church every Sunday morning and often went to our grandparents' house for Sunday dinner. Sometimes we would spend Saturday night with them, when our grandfather would be preparing his sermon. He would discuss his work with us. Although religion was not an important part of Tracy's adult life, during his teenage years he was a Sunday school teacher in our grandfather's church. Tracy was always a gifted public speaker and a natural performer, and he brought these talents into the classroom. And it is with these traits that the Natural Approach is most successful. The classroom teacher who can be physical, enthusiastic, and dynamic presenting language will be more successful. We often talked about public speaking, because that became my own major after an unsuccessful semester in calculus. I went on to get my bachelor of science degree from the School of Communications at UT and later a master's degree in speech communications. I, too, became a teacher. I teach high school speech and honors English and I teach speech at the local junior college. Tracy was very aware of how to keep an audience's involvement and interest. We often talked of new approaches for both teaching and performing.

As a teacher, I would have summers off. My two daughters and I would take a month's vacation visiting "Uncle David" every summer. It was during those summers that he had begun to write *Dos mundos*. He would rise every morning by 6:30. After eating breakfast and feeding the birds, he would be hard at work at the computer by 7:00. He would write all morning, only taking small breaks occasionally. He would usually work until 3:00 or so, then he would quit for the day. He was very organized and dedicated and worked with discipline. The first edition took many years to write. Since I taught high school, he would often ask me questions about students' interests or activities. He talked with his nieces to gain insight into children's language awareness—always testing his theories and trying to come up with interesting topics for exercises for the book. His work and research were meticulous, just like everything else that he did. I remember the summer when the first galleys came in the mail. It was so exciting to help proofread the pages, looking for errors. The book went through several revisions and proofreadings before the first edition was finally published. Although this was not the first book Tracy had published, it was the one he valued the most and was most excited about.

The book really is the work of hundreds of people. All of the people Tracy had met and known, students in his classroom, colleagues at the university, Peace Corps volunteers, his family—we all were his inspiration and we all were his materials. But it was his genius to choose Jeanne Egasse, Miguel Muñoz, and Magdalena Andrade as a team of co-authors and to lead them in creating a teaching program through *Dos mundos*. I think that Tracy always instinctively taught Spanish using the Natural Approach, but when he heard Steve Krashen speak at a conference on a theoretical concept of language acquisition, something just "clicked." After this night of revelation, he began to develop his own theory that eventually led to the Natural Approach. Again, Tracy was always practical. He was not content only to theorize about language acquisition; he had to develop those theories into practical teaching skills. He became the director of the teaching assistants, training them to use the Natural Approach first at the University of California at Irvine and then at the University of California at San Diego. Both programs became very successful due to his skills in inspiring and developing young teachers.

Tracy was rarely idle during the summer months when most teachers rest. He spent his last few summers teaching in a special program sponsored by the government. These were language programs developed to teach diplomats and government personnel as part of their preparation for foreign service. He lived in Morocco in 1988 and he was in Turkey in 1989. That was the last year, however. The weather was too hot and he became increasingly ill. He was unable to finish the program and had to return home. He spent the last two years of his life commuting between San Diego and Austin. He had retired from active teaching and was no longer able to attend conferences or hold workshops.

The last year of his life was dedicated to working on three final projects. He finished work on the second edition of *Deux mondes* and the third edition of *Dos mundos*. The other project was very dear to his heart—the development of the high school Spanish series entitled *¡Bravo!*. He was instrumental in putting together the team of writers and remained actively involved in the development of the material despite his illness. I believe that he would be very pleased with the outcome.

During the summer of 1990 he was hospitalized for the first time. Cards, letters, and flowers arrived from all over the world. I especially remember one packet of letters that arrived in a large manila envelope. One teacher with whom Tracy had worked and corresponded had told her class how ill he was. She had the students in her class write to him. The honest testimony from these kids who had never met my brother was incredible. They had been part of a special program, in which some classes in their school used the Natural Approach and others used traditional methods of teaching. The students could clearly tell a difference in their level of comprehension and ability to speak the language. It was so moving to have these students appreciate what Tracy had done for the teaching profession and their lives. It's what teachers really work for: to be immortalized in the lives and minds of their students. As many have said, "They don't do it for the money; they do it for the love of the kids."

Tracy was always curious about how things worked. When he was diagnosed with the HIV virus, he read every article he could find. He studied it as he studied everything. Aside from his personal interest, he had a scientific interest in what was happening inside his body. He was able to maintain his health longer because of his extensive knowledge of the disease.

Tracy died December 2, 1991. We had enjoyed a wonderful Thanksgiving holiday. His companion of ten years, David Gravely, our aunt and uncle, Ruth and Ray Mays, my daughters Rebecca and Rachel Eichen, and I were all with him. He wanted a traditional meal with turkey and dressing and all of the special treats we had enjoyed as children. It was his last wish to be close to his family and loved ones one last time. He seemed to know that he would not be alive for Christmas. We held memorial services in his honor in both Texas and San Diego. Friends and colleagues gathered and gave eulogies filled with the love and respect he had earned in his life. The Faculty Center at the University of California at San Diego was filled to capacity with a fraction of the people whose lives he had touched. We ended the service with a candlelight ceremony and a moment of silence. It was Tracy's wish that we also have a party in his honor, since he loved socializing with friends.

Teaching was Tracy's life. He dedicated his life to the pursuit of knowledge and to sharing that knowledge with others. He felt a thrill every time he saw that light of understanding that would illuminate a student's face. His immortality rests in those of us who were fortunate enough to be his students. We learned from him more than facts and vocabulary words; we learned a love of the quest. I am a teacher. Every day I can only hope that I can touch someone's life as richly as my brother touched students' lives. It is a legacy I carry on proudly. It is a legacy he passed on to all of the teachers in the world who share with him a love of language and of people from all over the world. He is missed but not forgotten.

A Selected Listing of Published Works of Tracy D. Terrell

Beginning in 1971, Terrell published nearly 100 works in the form of books, research articles, and book reviews. In addition, he delivered dozens of papers and keynote addresses at academic conferences around the world. Listed below is a representative sample of his publications.

Books

with M. S. de Cargill. *Lingüística aplicada.* New York: Wiley. 1979.

with R. Barrutia. *Fonética y fonología españolas.* New York: Wiley. 1982.

with S. D. Krashen. *The Natural Approach: Language Acquisition in the Classroom.* San Francisco: Alemany; London: Pergamon. 1983.

with E. Hesse and H. Orjuela. *Spanish Review.* Boston: Heinle and Heinle. 1984.

with M. Martini, E. Marino, and C. Ralley. *The Rainbow Collection.* New York: Santillan Publishing. 1984.

with E. Tschirner, B. Nikolai, and H. Genzmer. *Kontakte: A Communicative Approach.* 2nd ed. New York: McGraw-Hill. 1992. (1st ed. 1988)

with M. B. Rogers, B. K. Barnes, and M. Wolff-Hessini. *Deux mondes: A Communicative Approach.* 2nd ed. New York: McGraw-Hill. 1993. (1st ed. 1988)

with M. Andrade, J. Egasse, and E. M. Muñoz. *Dos mundos.* 3rd ed. New York: McGraw-Hill. 1994. (1st ed. 1986; 2nd ed. 1990)

with E. M. Muñoz, L. Paulus, M. B. Rogers, B. Snyder, E. Cabrera, and K. L. Kirk.*¡Bravo!* Books 1 and 2. Evanston, Ill.: McDougal, Littell & Co. 1995.

Research Articles and Reviews

Review of *Problemas y métodos en el análisis de preposiciones,* by María L. López. *Hispania* 54:980-81. 1971.

Review of *Spanish for Communication, Level II,* by William Bull et al. *Hispania* 56:327-28. 1973.

with J. Hooper. A Semantically Based Analysis of Mood in Spanish. *Hispania* 57:484-94. 1974.

Functional Constraints on the Deletion of Word-Final /s/ in Cuban Spanish. *Journal of the Berkeley Linguistics Society* 1:431-37. 1975.

La nasal implosiva y final en el español de Cuba. *Anuario de letras* 13:257-71. 1975.

Review of *Semantic Structures in Spanish,* by Frances Aid. *Modern Language Journal* 59:297. 1975.

with J. Hooper. Stress Assignment in Spanish: A Natural Generative Analysis. *Glossa* 10:64-110. 1976.

Assertion and Presupposition in Spanish Complements. In *Current Studies in Romance Linguistics,* ed. M. Luján and F. Hensey, 221-45. Washington, D.C.: Georgetown University Press. 1976.

Constraints on the Aspiration and Deletion of Final /s/ in Cuban and Puerto Rican Spanish. *The Bilingual Review* 4:35-51. 1977.

A Natural Approach to Second Language Acquisition and Learning. *Modern Language Journal* 61:325-36. 1977.

La aportación de los estudios dialectales antillanos a la teoría fonológica. In *Corrientes actuales en la dialectología del Caribe hispánico*, ed. H. L. Morales. San Juan, P.R.: Editorial Universitaria de la Universidad de Puerto Rico. 1978.

with B. Tranel. Parallelisms between Liaison in French and /s/ Aspiration and Deletion in Caribbean Spanish Dialects. In *Etudes linguistiques sur les langues romanes*, 31-50. Montreal: Montreal Working Papers in Linguistics, vol. 10. 1978.

A Natural Approach to the Teaching of Verb Form and Function in Spanish. *Foreign Language Annals* 13:129-36. 1980.

The Problem of Comparing Variable Rules across Dialects: Some Examples from Spanish. In *Festschrift for Jacob Ornstein*, ed. E. Blansitt and R. Teschner, 303-13. Rowley, Mass.: Newbury House. 1980.

Review of *Contemporary Studies in Romance Linguistics*, ed. by M. Suñer. *Language* 56:492. 1980.

Review of *Spanish Phonology and Morphology: A Generative View*, by W. Cressey. *Language* 56:882-86. 1980.

La marcación de pluralidad: evidencia del español dominicano. In *Homenaje a Antonio Rabanales. Boletín de filología*, 923-36. Santiago, Chile. 1981.

Current Trends in the Investigation of Cuban and Puerto Rican Phonology. In *Spanish in the States: Sociolinguistic Aspects*, ed. J. Amastae and L. Elías-Olivares, 47-70. Cambridge: Cambridge University Press. 1982.

The Natural Approach to Language Teaching: An Update. *Modern Language Journal* 66:121-31. 1982.

The Natural Approach in Bilingual Education. In *Schooling and Language*. Sacramento, Calif.: California State Department of Education. 1982.

Review of *The Notions of Simplification, Interlanguages, and Pidgins and Their Relation to Second Language Pedagogy*, ed. by S. P. Corder and E. Roulet. *Language*. 1985.

Recent Trends in Research and Practice: Teaching Spanish. *Hispania* 69:193-202. 1986.

Acquisition in the Natural Approach: The Binding/Access Framework. *Modern Language Journal* 70:213-227. 1986.

Review of *Beyond Basics: Issues and Research in TESOL*, ed. by M. Celce-Murcia. *Modern Language Journal*. 1986.

Functional Constraints on Phonological Rules. In *Language and Language Use: Studies in Spanish Dedicated to Joseph H. Matluck,* ed. T. Morgan, J. Lee, B. VanPatten. Lanham, Md.: University Press of America. 1987.

Avoiding Fossilization in Communicative Approaches. *Dialog on Language Instruction* No. 4. Monterey, Calif.: Defense Language Institute. 1987.

Review of *Communicating Naturally in a Second Language,* by W. Rivers. *Studies in Second Language Acquisition* 8. 1987.

with C. Silva-Corvalán. Notas sobre la expresión de futuridad en el español del Caribe. *Hispanic Linguistics* 2:191-208. 1989.

Foreigner Talk as Comprehensible Input. In *Linguistics, Language Teaching, and Language Acquisition,* ed. J. E. Alatis, 193-206. Georgetown University Round Table on Languages and Linguistics. Washington, D.C.: Georgetown University Press. 1990.

Trends in the Teaching of Grammar in Spanish-Language Textbooks. *Hispania* 73:201-11. 1990.

The Role of Grammar Instruction in a Communicative Approach. *Modern Language Journal* 75:52-63. 1991.

with A. Koch. Affective Reactions of Foreign Language Students to Natural Approach Activities and Teaching Techniques. In *Language Anxiety: From Theory and Research to Classroom Implications,* ed. E. Horwitz and D. Young. Englewood Cliffs, N.J.: Prentice-Hall. 1991.

LANGUAGE LEARNING AND TEACHING

The Natural Approach is one of the most important developments in language acquisition research and methodology of the past twenty years. It is also the aspect of Tracy Terrell's work that is most closely associated with him. The papers in Part 2 reflect a wide range of interpretations and applications of the Natural Approach. They also serve to demonstrate the wide-ranging influence of Terrell's impact on the language teaching community.

LANGUAGE LEARNING AND TEACHING

he papers in Part 2 relate in a variety of ways to the basic features of the Natural Approach and its ongoing development in the language teaching and research communities. Tracy Terrell first articulated the basic principles in "A Natural Approach to Second Language Acquisition and Learning," a 1977 *Modern Language Journal* article:

a. consideration of affective factors

b. creation of meaningful opportunities to convey messages

c. providing comprehensible input.

These were refined in his 1982 *MLJ* paper, "The Natural Approach to Language Teaching: An Update," and then further developed and applied in the book that he and Stephen Krashen coauthored, *The Natural Approach: Language Acquisition in the Classroom* (1983). Chapter Two of that book reflects a close relationship between Natural Approach principles and those in Krashen's model of second language acquisition.

One of Tracy Terrell's strengths was that throughout the development of the Natural Approach, he was always eager to listen to the suggestions of others. He continued to listen, improving on the approach and refining his ideas about second language learning and the implications of his theories. In fact, in his last published paper (1991) Terrell was beginning to explore the relationship between explicit grammatical instruction and acquisition. At that time, he saw no direct influence but concluded that there may be an indirect relationship.

Overview

The overview section begins with Terrell's 1982 paper, in which he acknowledged that not all of the ideas in the Natural Approach were new. However, he believed that a combination of all of them resulted in an approach that was strikingly different from current notions of language teaching. He believed that comprehension promotes acquisition and, therefore, should precede speech production. Furthermore, production emerges in stages. In the Natural Approach, comprehension and production are achieved through a series of affective acquisition activities that promote acquisition by: (1) providing comprehensible input, (2) lowering anxieties, and (3) creating opportunities to convey messages.

The second paper, "Two Mad, Mad, Mad Worlds: Notes on Natural Approach and the Writing of *Dos mundos*," is a warmly written paper by Magdalena Andrade, Thalia Dorwick, Jeanne Egasse, and Elías Miguel Muñoz. They reflect on their experiences with Terrell in the process of codifying an approach that then existed only in their classrooms into a textbook for much wider use in college-level Spanish classes. Terrell's coauthors describe the birth of a textbook and the adaptations required to make an idealized model acceptable to a wider audience of teachers.

In the final overview paper, "On Breaking with Tradition: The Significance of Terrell's Natural Approach" (a reprint of a 1992 article), Armando Baltra looks at Terrell's work in terms of the degree of acceptance or rejection that his pedagogical views have received since he first presented them in 1977. Baltra concludes that Terrell's major contribution was that he based "foreign language teaching methodology on research in second language acquisition" and thus contributed "to raising the field of applied linguistics to the level of an academic specialty in the eyes of literature-oriented members of many foreign language departments."

The Growth of the Natural Approach and Related Issues

The remaining papers in Part II describe applications of the Natural Approach, extensions of its principles, and issues related to or consistent with its three main principles.

1. Applications and extensions of the natural approach

Patricia Richard-Amato's *Making It Happen: Interaction in the Second Language Classroom* is widely used in teacher training and as teacher's reference. It contains a chapter rich in teaching ideas entitled "The Natural Approach and Its Extensions." This was one of the first published efforts—beyond Terrell's own—to translate the principles of the Natural Approach into a collection of classroom activities. Her present contribution is an update of that chapter as well as a reflection on some of the limitations of the approach.

Stephen Krashen notes in "What Is Intermediate Natural Approach?" a limitation of comprehension-based beginning methods such as the Natural Approach and Total Physical Response: the inability of students to use the conversational abilities already developed for more cognitively demanding tasks. He suggests extending the principles of the Natural Approach to the intermediate level through Sheltered Subject Matter Teaching and Free Voluntary Reading.

2. Affective factors

Many in language teaching and research recognize that unless the learner is open psychologically and emotionally to the language and wants (or needs) to learn it, language teaching will not be effective and language acquisition will not take place—or will progress slowly. Three contributors specifically emphasize the importance of these affective factors in language learning and teaching. Dolly Young's 1988 interview with Tracy Terrell, entitled "Perspectives on Language Anxiety," provides the fullest and most recently published record of his views on this topic. Of particular importance are Terrell's comments on the positive aspects of anxiety, indicating the importance of distinguishing between anxiety and attention (the latter involves "effort"). In making this distinction, he apparently differed with Krashen on the automaticity of acquisition.

Robert Hammond and Diane Ringer Uber report on studies of affective factors among Spanish-speaking immigrants in the United States. Hammond, in "Attitudes, Variables, and the Affective Filter in the Acquisition of Second Language Sound Systems," reports on a study of the perceptions of immigrants of their own pronunciation in English, of the roles of effort and intelligence in eliminating foreign accent, and of the relationship between job success and foreign accent. He also expresses concern about the generally undefined status of pronunciation in communicative teaching models. Ringer Uber, in "On Achieving Competence in Two Languages: The Role of Necessity for the Cuban Mariel Entrant," notes how such global affective factors as motivation and social and psychological distance influence language learning choices and proficiency.

3. Meaningful communication opportunities   While the learner may be motivated and open to learning a language, it is argued that language learning will not be successful if there are no opportunities to use the language—in or out of the classroom—in situations that are meaningful. A "meaningful" situation is one that engages the learner's individual ideas and communication needs or interests; the lack of meaningful opportunities might interact negatively with affective factors. Although other papers in this volume also speak to a concern for meaningful communication, one author has this focus as a primary concern.

The early French immersion programs in Canada, which pre-dated the Natural Approach, have long provided meaningful communication opportunities. Merrill Swain, in "French Immersion and Its Offshoots: Getting Two for One" (a reprint from 1989), describes two other programs that have made foreign and second language learning meaningful: the late immersion programs beginning with twelve-to-fourteen year-olds and the university-level sheltered program. The initial program at the University of Ottawa, with which Krashen was involved in its first year, influenced his suggestion of Sheltered Subject Matter Teaching as an extension of the principles of the Natural Approach.

The contribution of Peggy Hashemipour, entitled "Intermediate Natural Approach beyond the Classroom," introduces a range of additional opportunities for meaningful language study. She proposes service learning within language-community settings as a rich source of experience for language learners.

4. The role of input   In this group of five papers, the role of input is explored from different perspectives: cognitive processing, the reading/writing relationship, discourse analysis, and the adjustments made in several types of foreigner talk (input) and their possible relevance to second language acquisition. Terrell agreed with Krashen on the importance of comprehensible input for acquisition. However, as noted above, he did not feel that acquisition was automatic, for learners need to pay attention at some level. For this reason, he was interested in the direction that Bill VanPatten was following in investigating input processing and examining how it relates to the acquisition of a non-native language. In his paper, "Cognitive Aspects of Input Processing in Second-Language Acquisition," VanPatten focuses on two hypotheses: that learners process input for meaning before they process it for form; and that to process form that is not meaningful, learners must be able to process informational or communicative content at little or no cost to attention.

Ann Johns, in "The Reading-Writing Relationship: Implications for ESL Teaching," examines the relationship between input and output (specifically between comprehension and production of written language), focusing on second language learners in academic settings. As Krashen has argued in his paper in this volume and elsewhere, students who read widely improve their chances of acquiring both reading and writing proficiency. Extensive reading provides input, which leads to acquisition and production in the form of writing. Johns argues forcefully for the integration of these two skills in ESL courses and for further research in this area. Johns further notes that Terrell was interested in this reading-writing relationship in his work at UCSD.

Discourse analysis is a tool for investigating written or oral input. Researchers, teachers, and materials developers can use this tool to identify language patterns that might help students access written and oral input (making it more comprehensible) and produce comprehensible output. Marianne Celce-Murcia, in "The Role of Discourse Analysis in Curriculum Development," uses concrete programs to show how discourse analysis can be used in a range of roles: in a peripheral role in an English for science and technology reading course; in a shared role in a university-level ESL course; and in a central role in an EFL teacher in-service program.

The authors of the next two papers in this grouping examine the role of foreigner talk as a form of input for learners. The first is a reprinted article by Barbara Freed, "Foreigner Talk, Baby Talk, Native Talk" (from 1981), one of the early detailed, empirical studies of Foreigner Talk (FT). She argued that native speakers make adjustments in their speech when interacting with non-native speakers in response to a combination of factors such as age, communicative purpose, perceived cognitive ability and linguistic proficiency, relative status, and the relationship between speakers. Much ESL research has been devoted to Teacher Talk and FT, often in ESL classroom contexts. Terrell, building on Freed's work, noted in his last public presentation (1990) that such contexts are not representative of interactions in daily life. In that paper, "Foreigner Talk as Comprehensible Input," he reported on an ongoing pilot study in which he was examining adjustments made by a native speaker who was not accustomed to talking with non-native speakers. His preliminary findings suggested that some of the features generally assumed to be useful for second language acquisition might not always be present in FT. This also led him to question the assumption that FT automatically provides good input (Barbara Freed, personal communication with the editor, 1993).

Two papers in Part 3(b) of this volume are also concerned with input: specifically, with the appropriateness and authenticity of classroom input. Klein-Andreu writes on the teaching of the subjunctive; van Naerssen traces the authenticity of future tense forms in Spanish textbooks beginning in the 1970s and continuing into the period of greater communicativity in foreign language texts.

The final paper in Part 2, "Recognition, Retention, Retrieval: The Three Rs of Vocabulary Use" by Wilga Rivers, is an examination of the underlying processes of language acquisition in the classroom. In it, the author addresses the affective and cognitive aspects inherent in the acquisition of vocabulary and suggests creative approaches to motivate students to process and retain words in a new language.

The Natural Approach to Language Teaching: An Update

Tracy D. Terrell

In 1977 I outlined a proposal for a "new" philosophy of language teaching which I called the "Natural Approach" (NA).[1] My suggestions at that time were the outgrowth of experience with Dutch and Spanish classes in which the target languages were taught to beginners whose native language was English. Since then the NA has been used in primary, secondary, and adult ESL classes, as well as in secondary, university, and adult Spanish, French, and German classes. During these five years of experimentation we have concentrated on the development of teaching techniques to implement the original proposals.

This paper has two purposes: (1) to discuss the underlying assumptions of the 1977 paper in light of recent research in second language acquisition and learning, as well as from personal experience in the classroom; and (2) to suggest specific techniques for implementing the NA in second or foreign language classrooms.

 ## GENERAL CONSIDERATIONS

The Natural Approach is not the only means of language teaching that results in students who can communicate with native speakers of a given target language. Any approach in which real communication is the basis of class activities will produce students who, within a very short time, can function in communicative situations with native speakers of that language.[2] The professional literature has positive reports on numerous communicative approaches to foreign language teaching.[3]

For most students, approaches that do not normally result in the ability to communicate are grammar-translation, audiolingual, and the various eclectic cognitive-based methods. They produce skills that match exactly what is taught. In the case of grammar-translation, students can translate from the target language to Ll and usually have a good knowledge of the grammar of the target language—especially if asked

Reprinted, with permission of The University of Wisconsin Press, from *Modern Language Journal*, Vol. 66 (Summer 1982):121–32.

to perform on grammar tests. They normally neither speak nor understand the spoken language, nor should they be expected to do so. Students in an audiolingual approach usually have excellent pronunciation, can repeat dialogs and use memorized prefabricated patterns in conversation. They can do pattern drills, making substitutions and changing morphemes using various sorts of agreement rules. What they very often cannot do is participate in a normal conversation with a native speaker. Students using the various cognitive approaches now in vogue can usually do well on grammar exams and can often even produce new sentences, although slowly and laboriously. This result undoubtedly stems from the fact that they have concentrated on a cognitive understanding of the rules and must therefore apply them consciously when speaking.[4]

Although I make no claims for the NA which another communicative approach could not match, one can demonstrate informally that communicative-based approaches generally produce results superior to any cognitive or habit-drill based approach.[5] In the original NA proposal I suggested three principles on which to base language teaching: (1) the classroom should be devoted primarily to activities which foster acquisition (activities which promote learning might be assigned as homework); (2) the instructor should not correct student speech errors directly; and (3) the students should be allowed to respond in either the target language, their native language, or a mixture of the two.[6] Experience has shown that, by far, the most important principle is that acquisition activities be provided in the class. Such activities allow the development of communicative abilities through natural acquisition processes in addition to fostering the kind of knowledge that results from conscious cognitive learning exercises. The other two suggestions are only particular examples of possible techniques which encourage an acquisition-rich environment. In order, then, to understand how the NA functions in the language classroom, we must examine in some detail the acquisition process and its implementation.

 ## ACQUISITION

Available research in second language study strongly supports the hypothesis that the processes Krashen and others have called acquisition (the unconscious formulation of grammatical principles) and learning (the conscious cognitive-based study of grammar) represent two systems for internalizing knowledge about language.[7] My original proposal was that both are important ways to gain linguistic proficiency. However, since in most cases of foreign language (and often even in second language) study, the student has little chance for acquisition outside the classroom, the instructor must provide this kind of experience. Learning, on the other hand, being of secondary importance in the development of communicative competence, should be more restricted, perhaps to outside-the-class activities. The important point is that activities promoting acquisition are indispensable for all students. Learning activities are more limited in their usefulness to beginners.

On the other hand, some observers evidently believe that the acquisition process is not relevant in a language classroom. Strevens states, for example, that "first language acquisition and LL/LT (language learning and language teaching) belong in different universes of discourse which overlap in only limited ways. To see language teaching as applied psycholinguistics is to misunderstand the relationships between a predominately intellectual activity and a predominately practical one."[8] In my opinion teaching languages as an *intellectual* activity is, to a great extent, responsible for the failure of the educational establishment to impart even the most fundamental communication skills to normal students in foreign language classrooms.

Overwhelming research evidence and informal reports point out that students who wish to communicate must acquire this ability in much the same way that speakers, adults or children, acquire it in natural situations. Krashen provides strong evidence that learned, rather than acquired, rules are of limited use to the student; for some, they serve as a "monitor," i.e., primarily an "editor" to make minor changes or corrections in utterances which for the most part are initiated by acquired knowledge. Research supports Krashen's hypothesis that this "monitor" can be activated only under restricted circumstances. The speakers must: (1) know the rule; (2) be focused on the form of what they are saying; and (3) have time to apply the rule.[9]

Most speakers meet conditions for monitoring regularly and systematically only on cognitive grammar tests. Most of us are not able to monitor to an appreciable degree in normal communicative situations. Thus, even if rules are learned by the students through explanation, drill, and practice, and even if they demonstrate that they can produce correct forms and syntax on grammar exams, such (cognitively based) knowledge is usually not very helpful in normal communicative situations, particularly in beginning stages.[10] Krashen's monitor theory thus explains that oral proficiency in communication is not necessarily related to the ability to achieve high scores on standard grammar tests, a fact usually overlooked by language teachers who claim to have communicative competence as a goal but continue to evaluate progress only in the learning of grammar rules.[11]

Krashen claims that the monitor theory also accounts for the tremendous variation in grammatical accuracy among adults. There are "under-users," those who rarely use their learned competence or perhaps those whose learned competence is low. ("Under-users" might still achieve very high levels of communicative accuracy entirely through acquisition.) "Over-users" spend so much time and effort on correctness that it often seriously interferes with communication. "Optimal-users" are those who are able to monitor their speech and improve their level of grammatical accuracy, but not to such an extent that it interferes with smooth communication. A fourth category was suggested by Carlos Yorio at the 1978 TESOL convention in Mexico City: "super-users," those who are consciously able to apply learned rules quickly and efficiently so that a listener would not notice the monitoring at all. Many language instructors fall into this category, and although most have acquired the relevant rules through subsequent experience and no longer need to monitor their speech consciously, they often feel that this mode of production (super-monitoring) is the most efficient way to learn another language. Unfortunately, many, perhaps most, students are not capable of performing with the mental gymnastics of their super-monitor instructors.

Some assert that learned rules are acquired through practice. This assumption seems to underlie most cognitive approaches in which a three-part technique is used: explanation, practice, and application. Advocates of cognitive approaches, Chastain notes, believe that comprehension of the rule *must* precede its use. The learning of a grammatical principle *can* precede its acquisition. Whether it facilitates acquisition probably depends on the learning style of the acquirer.[12]

Fortunately, a conscious understanding of grammar rules is not prerequisite to their acquisition. Most adults are not very good at learning grammar, but they acquire rules readily, although usually imperfectly, given the chance to interact in communicative situations with native speakers of the target language.

If the monitor theory of second language competence and performance is correct, activities that foster acquisition must assume a central role in any approach having communicative abilities as its goal. Research indicates that acquisition takes place under certain conditions. In a communication situation: (1) the focus of the interchange is on the message; (2) the acquirer must understand the message; and (3) the acquirer must be in a low anxiety situation.

The claim that the focus must be on the message in a communicative situation is a strong one and has immediate implications for the classroom.[13] If this claim is correct, and so far we have no contradictory evidence, it means that, for the most part, acquisition will not take place during traditional grammar exercises or drills since they provide no opportunity for meaningful communication.[14] For this reason the syllabus of a NA course consists of communication goals.[15] For example, a possible goal might be to talk about what the students did over a weekend. In the activities which are used to achieve a particular goal, the necessary tools (vocabulary and structure) are supplied. However, the focus of the student during the activity must be maintained on the semantic content (in this case, the weekend activities), not the grammatical form (here, the past tense).

The second condition is that the student understand the message. Acquisition does not take place by listening to speech that is not understood by the student. Therefore, the input supplied by the speech of the instructor must be made comprehensible. That does not mean, however, that speech need be simplified to the extreme of using only lexical items, grammatical forms, and structures already studied by the student, a practice common to the audiolingual approach.

Language acquirers in natural situations regularly receive comprehensible input. In first language acquisition we call it "caretaker speech," in second language acquisition "foreigner talk."[16] The characteristics of this sort of simplified speech have been studied in some detail and are of interest to teachers because they seem to be useful to the learner. Hatch summarizes the most important characteristics of simplified input: *slower rate* (clear articulation, diminished contractions, long pauses, extra volume, and exaggerated intonation); *understandable vocabulary* (high frequency vocabulary, less slang, few idioms, high use of names of referents instead of pro-forms); *marked definitions* (explaining a term that the speaker doubts the learner will know, repetitions, gestures, pictures); *simplification of syntax vis-à-vis the meaning* (simple propositions, focus on topics, repetition and restatement, less proverb modification, helping the learner complete utterances); *discourse techniques* (giving a possible answer within the question, yes-no question, tag questions).[17]

The remarkable thing about simplified input is that the techniques to produce it are easily acquired. Native speakers do not necessarily give immediate input at the correct level for all acquirers in all situations; but, for most adults some experience talking with acquirers will result in the ability to make the above sorts of changes automatically and unconsciously.

The third condition is that the students receive comprehensible input in a low anxiety environment.[18] I have previously (1977) asserted that affective factors are the most important in language acquisition (but not necessarily in language learning). I am even more convinced that the lowering of affective barriers must be the overriding concern in classroom activities if acquisition is to be achieved. "Student attitudes," Stevick says, "take chronological priority [over course content] . . . . The linguistic material presented during the first week . . . is only a vehicle for getting acquainted and for finding and reducing anxieties."[19]

A low-anxiety situation can be created by involving the students *personally* in class activities. Specific techniques for lowering affective barriers will by necessity vary from group to group because of the different personalities, interests, and aims of students and instructors. The goal is that the members of the group become genuinely interested in each other's opinions, feelings, and interests, and feel comfortable expressing themselves on the topics of discussion in class. From these observations it follows that no text can supply more than suggestions for the activities which actually involve students.[20]

In summary, then, affective acquisition activities rather than cognitive learning exercises form the core of NA.[21] An activity that promotes acquisition must allow for comprehensible input in which the focus is on the communication of messages in a low-anxiety environment.

Let us now turn to the sorts of activities we use in the NA classroom. I will describe the activities which correspond to three stages of language instruction for beginners: (1) comprehension (pre-production); (2) early speech production; (3) speech emergence.

 ## COMPREHENSION (PRE-PRODUCTION)

Since the ability to comprehend novel sentences in the target language is a necessary condition for acquisition to take place, we have tried to develop a series of techniques which provides listening comprehension experiences in initial stages of language acquisition. These activities do not require the students to speak in the target language. The use of a preproduction period is not an innovation of the NA, but with the exception of Asher's Total Physical Response, it is one of the few approaches which uses it extensively.[22] Children acquiring their first language learn to comprehend before speaking.[23] Indeed, for all speakers, competence in comprehension outpaces competence in production. Winitz and Reeds estimate that in first language acquisition "comprehension antedates sentence generating by about a year. This sequence of development—comprehension first, production second—is a functional property of the human brain which should not be violated in language instruction."[24] Strong research evidence suggests that a pre-speaking phase is beneficial to students in the classroom.[25]

Comprehension in a new language, whether of spoken or written materials, is achieved in early stages primarily by learning how to make intelligent guesses. The major components are: (1) a context; (2) gestures and other body language cues; (3) a message to be comprehended; and (4) a knowledge of the meaning of the key lexical items in the utterance.

Grammatical signals are not usually crucial to the comprehension task of beginning students. Snow notes that "children figure out rules underlying syntactic structure by using the cues provided by the meaning of the adult's utterance" and that this implies that "children must be able to determine what an utterance means on the basis of nonsyntactic information since the syntax is precisely what is to be learned." Following Macnamara, Snow describes the process for children exactly as I have suggested for adults: "Knowledge of the meaning of important lexical items plus knowledge of what is likely to be said about those entities or actions given the situation must enable the child to guess correctly what the utterance means. This implies of course that the child must be a good guesser, but also that the adult must say the kinds of things the child expects to hear."[26]

In his famous guide, *Teaching and Learning English as a Foreign Language* (one of the most important theoretical precursors of Audiolingualism), Fries takes the opposite view: "In learning a new language, then, the chief problem is not at first that of learning vocabulary items. It is, first, the mastery of the features of arrangement that constitute the structure of the language."[27] Neither informal observations of second language acquisition nor formal studies of the same have supported this view of the priority of phonology and grammar over the lexicon. As Bolinger so clearly put it, "The lexicon is central, . . . grammar is not something into which words are plugged but is rather a mechanism by which words are served. . . . The quantity of information in the lexicon far outweighs that in any other part of the language, and if there is anything to the notion of redundancy it should be easier to reconstruct a message containing just the words than one containing just the syntactic relations."[28]

Brown's comments on caretaker children interaction constitute excellent advice for the classroom teacher in teaching listening comprehension. He notes: "I do think parents are exclusively concerned with communication. I do think they continuously monitor the child for signs of distraction or incomprehension, and when they see them promptly act . . . to correct the situation."[29]

In the following paragraphs, I will mention only a few of the techniques we have used to develop listening comprehension; imaginative instructors can easily develop others. The important point for beginners is that they not be required to produce utterances in the target language until they feel comfortable with comprehension.

Asher's Total Physical Response (TPR) techniques have proved to be very useful in the NA. In these activities the instructor asks the students to perform certain actions or act out events. Simple commands (*Sit down! Raise your hand! Close your book!*) are a part of many methodologies. TPR can be used in many other ways, however. Parts of the body and clothing lend themselves easily to TPR (*Put your left hand on your right leg. Point to a blue sweater.*). Classroom objects (or any object easily portable) work well with TPR. (*All those with pencils, point to something red. Walk to the blackboard and write your name on it.*). These commands may become quite complex and after appropriate practice in an affectively positive situation, individualized: *Kevin, please pick up the large glass sitting in front of the woman wearing a red sweater and put it on the desk in back of the student with the beard.*

Another technique, which is useful in the first few days of class, makes use of the students' names and descriptions. The following is an example of "teacher talk," that is, comprehensible input: *What is your name? (Barbara.) Everyone look at Barbara. Barbara has long, blond hair* (using context and gestures to make meaning of *hair, long, blond*). *What is the name of the student with long, blond hair?* (Class responds with name only.) *What is your name* (selecting another student)*? (Mark.) Look at Mark. Does Mark have long hair?* (Use gestures to contrast long-short.) (Class responds, *yes.*) *Is his hair blond? (No.) Is it brown* (use context and gestures)*? (Yes.) Mark is the student with short, brown hair. What is the name of the student with long, blond hair? (Barbara.) And the student with short, brown hair? (Mark.)*

This activity can be continued using physical characteristics (*positive* attributes only) and clothing, including colors and some simple descriptions. This activity serves not only as comprehensible input (key words are easily interpreted from context), but also serves as a means for the instructor and students to learn each other's names.

Another technique we use extensively from the first contact hour makes use of pictures and focuses on the learning of names. The instructor introduces pictures by describing what is in the pictures emphasizing only key lexical items in each one. *In this picture there are two women. One is standing and the other sitting. The woman who is standing has a cup of coffee.* Each student is given a different picture. The questions addressed to the class consist of information about the picture which can be answered with the name of the student who is holding the picture. *Who has the picture with the two women? Who has the picture with a woman holding a cup of coffee in her hand?* Naturally such questions will be taken from a variety of pictures: *Who has the picture with the woman talking on the telephone? What is the name of the woman with the picture of the two men washing the dog?*

An additional technique uses learning personal details about each student in the class. For example, the purpose of the lesson might be to learn which classes other students are taking and the teacher supplies for the entire class the target language equivalent. The idea is that the target language word for a particular course is associated with a particular student in the course. As the activity proceeds the instructor asks questions like: *Who is studying psychology? Which two students are enrolled in both English literature and music appreciation?* Other possibilities for early topics which lend themselves easily to association are sports, games, birthplaces, birthdates, work experiences, etc.

The prespeaking stage should last as long as the students need it to last. In 1977, I insisted that the individual students must decide when to begin speaking. Experience has proven this suggestion to be feasible. In my experience with NA classes, elementary age students need comprehensible input for several months to begin the acquisition process. Secondary students usually begin to speak comfortably after a month or so. University level students are normally all speaking voluntarily after four or five class hours.

 ## EARLY SPEECH PRODUCTION

The transition to early speech production is simple if students have developed a reasonably extensive passive vocabulary. I recommend a recognition level of 500 words before extensive early production is attempted. In early production we want to encourage the use of acquired knowledge and to avoid as much as possible the use of "L1 plus Monitor" mode. Early opportunities for speech should therefore consist of questions which require only single word answers. *Either-or* questions are especially valuable and evolve easily from the listening comprehension activities described in the previous section: (looking at a picture) *Is this woman standing or sitting? Is this car red or green?*

NA students go through production stages similar to those of an acquirer in a natural environment (these are not completely discrete steps): yes and no answers (*Is he eating a salad? Yes.*); one word answers from either-or questions (*What color is this blouse? Blue.*); lists (*What do you see in this picture? woman, hat, yellow*, etc.); two words strung together (*big hat, at home, no have, me go, see nothing*, etc.); three words and/or short phrases; longer phrases; complete sentences; connected discourse and dialog. As with children learning their first or second language, the stages overlap. Some sentences may be complex, while other ideas are still being expressed with single words.

Several activities other than question-answer encourage early speech production via the acquisition mode. Most are traditional techniques which I have simply given labels. The frame itself is unimportant, but the possibility for interesting follow-up with spontaneous conversation is crucial.[30]

The *Open Sentence* model provides a sentence frame with a single word missing: *My mother is _____. The class I like best is _____.* The *Open Dialog Frame* consists of short interchanges with key elements missing: *Hi, where are you going? I'm going to the _____. Would you like to _____ with me tonight?* The *Open Interview* is good for early production, especially if the frames are given for responses: *What is your name? My name is _____. His/Her name is _____. Where do you live? I live at _____. He/She lives at _____.* I have described another early production model, the *Association Model* elsewhere in some detail.[31]

Early speech production of all students will contain errors. This reality is inevitable since grammar rules are acquired over long periods of time and proficiency with any particular grammar rule will occur only after considerable experience with real communication. For this reason, in the original NA paper I proposed that direct correction of speech errors be avoided. This point deserves some extended comment before proceeding with the third stage of the NA.

ERROR CORRECTION

My earlier proposal to avoid correction of student speech errors was seen as quite "radical" and has proved to be a "bone of contention" for many who are interested in the NA. I suggested then that "there is no evidence which shows that the correction of speech errors is necessary or even helpful in language acquisition."[32] This statement is still valid. Five years of experience in classes in which speech errors are not corrected have convinced me that the practice of correcting speech errors directly is not just merely useless, but actually harmful to progress in language acquisition.[33]

I believe that the problem language teachers have accepting ungrammatical speech from students stems from two misunderstandings. First, I claim that direct correction of speech errors is not helpful for acquisition. I have never claimed that the correction of errors is unnecessary for the conscious, cognitive-based learning of grammar rules and structures. I proposed that no student errors be corrected during acquisition activities in which the focus by definition must remain on the message of the communication. Correction of errors would focus the students on form thereby making acquisition more, not less, difficult. Correction of speech errors may lead to *learning*, but not to *acquisition*. Since the NA classroom consists almost completely of acquisition activities, it follows that student speech errors are not normally corrected directly. On the other hand, traditional classrooms where cognitive exercises and/or audiolingual drills form the central component of the course, not to correct speech errors would be counterproductive. It would certainly be a waste of time to perform an item-substitution drill which focused on subject-verb agreement, for example, if the student were allowed to ignore agreement. Or, if the instructor wished to check the answer to a cognitive grammar exercise in which the student had filled in the blank with correct verb forms, it would be equally ludicrous to accept an erroneous answer without correction. The non-correction of errors in the NA stems directly from the hypothesis that acquisition is the central component in language competence and performance and that the correction of speech errors, in general, does not play a role in the acquisition of language by children or adults.

Second, misunderstanding results from the fact that teachers (and parents!) feel intuitively that the correction of errors is responsible for the students' improvement toward the form of an adult grammar; that only through the use of language and constant feedback with error correction do the students advance in their ability to express themselves in the target language. Five years of experience with several thousand students who have successfully completed language courses using the NA without overt correction of speech errors and who continue to progress and improve throughout the course is strong evidence, albeit informal, that error correction is not a prerequisite for improvement in competence and performance.[34]

If error correction of student speech is not the source of improvement and progress, then what is? Monitor theory predicts that given continued exposure to comprehensible input in the target language used in affectively positive situations, the student continues to improve both in fluency and accuracy. According to monitor theory, this improvement is the result of the nature of comprehensible input. When students hear a communication and understand the message, they do not necessarily understand all of the lexical items, grammatical structures, or forms used by the speaker. At a given level of lexical and structural complexity, students can understand speech containing lexical items, structure, and forms which is slightly more advanced than the acquirers' current competence, but not so far advanced as to interfere crucially with comprehension. As the acquirer advances and improves, so does the level of the input. This difference between comprehensible input and the current production abilities of students accounts for improvement.[35]

On the other hand, speech errors in the NA are not passed over without any sort of response. We use the same conversational techniques with our students that caretakers use with children and that native speakers use with foreigners in real communication. If the students' speech is extremely garbled, the instructor tries to reconstruct a possible sequence. *What are you going to do after class today? I no go do eat cafeteria, no have money.* The instructor would respond, *Oh, you aren't going to eat in the cafeteria because you don't have any money. Why don't you have money? Did you forget it? Is it at home?* If the speech contains only minor errors, they are normally corrected indirectly by simple expansion: *What's the baby doing? Baby playing. Yes, the baby's playing. What's he playing with?* Almost any response can be commented on and expanded into more conversation.

One should not think that these expansions have immediate effects for all students. The usefulness depends on the readiness of each particular student. Hatch, discussing the conversation of a Spanish-speaking adolescent learning English, makes this point clearly: "It seems unlikely that this particular learner attends to the corrections included in the replies of the native speaker. More likely, he 'hears' them only as signals that his listener understands what he is trying to tell him. Perhaps at some later stage he will hear them and match them to his own performance."[36]

I believe that three solid reasons exist for avoiding direct correction of speech errors: (1) correction of speech errors plays no important role in the progress toward an adult's model of grammar in any natural language acquisition situation; (2) correction of speech errors will create affective barriers; and (3) correction of speech errors tends to focus the speaker on *form* promoting learning to the expense of acquisition.

 ## SPEECH EMERGENCE

Classroom activities in the third stage will depend to a great extent on the goals of the course, both in terms of the situations and functions for which the language will be used, and in terms of the particular language skills desired, oral skills, reading and writing skills. I will orient the remainder of this discussion to a description of activities which foster oral skills by means of acquisition. However, it should not be thought that NA excludes in any way reading and writing skills. Four sorts of activities promote acquisition by virtue of the fact that their focus will always be on the content of communication rather than on its form.

1. Games and recreation activities   Games have always been used by language instructors, but mostly as a relaxation activity rather than as a core component of the language course. Games, by their very nature, focus the student on what it is they are doing and use the language as a tool for reaching the goal (participating in the game) rather than as a goal itself. No instruction hour, even with adults, should be without an activity in which the target language is used for some sort of fun.

2. Content   The target language may be used to explore some content area. In language classrooms this area has been traditionally dedicated to cultural similarities and differences or to some aspect of the history of the language or peoples who speak the language. Immersion programs such as those in Canada make use of content to teach academic subject matter.[37] The important point is that content activities, if they are interesting to the students, qualify as an acquisition activity since they use language as a tool for learning something else. Focus is necessarily on the information being transmitted rather than the means (the target language). Popular activities in this category include: slide presentations, movies, reports, show and tell sessions, panels, photographs, guest speakers, and so forth.

3. Humanistic-affective activities   These include activities which appeal to the student on a personal level. Affective-humanistic activities explore the students' values, ideas, opinions, goals, and feelings as well as their experiences. They qualify as an acquisition activity because the focus is on the message being conveyed rather than the form of the language used to convey the messages. Christensen, Galyean, and Moscowitz have developed this sort of activity and we use them extensively in the NA in the third stage.[38]

4. Information and problem-solving activities   The student must determine a solution or an answer to a specific question or problem. These activities are especially useful in preparing students to function in the country in which the language is spoken. For example, working with clothing advertisements from the newspaper, the instructor asks questions like: *How much does a suit cost? What is the price reduction on underwear this week? What time does the store close? If you had only 350 to spend in this store, what would you buy?* Or the student could be given an advertisement from a grocery store and asked to plan a meal. Charts of information are useful and many newer English as a Second Language texts use this technique extensively.[39] A chart of daily chores for the Green family might include indications on what is done, by whom, and when. Questions center around information. *Who does the dishes in the Green family? What are the duties of the youngest child? Does the father ever wash the car?*

There are, of course, activities in which more than one of the categories is relevant. One can construct with the class, for example, a chart of daily activities of the students themselves. This activity is both problem-solving and affective. Or, a problem-solving activity can be used as a game. The important point is that each activity provides the students a chance to use language for what it was intended: a tool in communication. Focus in all acquisition activities is on the messages being exchanged, not the form.

 ## CONCLUSIONS: BASIC PRINCIPLES

Although the basic principles of the NA have not changed, its focus has expanded considerably. If the goal of the course is the ability to communicate using the target language, grammar rules must be acquired, since rules which have been learned are available only for monitoring. Comprehension is the basic skill which promotes acquisition and therefore should precede speech production. Production (speech and writing) is not taught directly, but rather emerges in stages from response by gestures to complete discourse. Both comprehension and production experiences are provided by a series of affective acquisition activities, the main purpose of which is to promote acquisition by: (1) providing comprehensible input; (2) lowering anxieties; (3) creating opportunities to convey messages. NA posits three stages of language acquisition with various techniques used in each stage.

I. Comprehension (pre-production)
   a. TPR
   b. Answer with names—objects, students, pictures
II. Early speech production
   a. yes-no questions
   b. either-or questions
   c. single/two-word answers
   d. open-ended sentences
   e. open dialogs
   f. interviews
III. Speech emerges
   a. games and recreational activities
   b. content activities
   c. humanistic:affective activities
   d. information:problem solving activities

Roger Brown attempted to answer the question "How can a concerned mother facilitate her child's learning of language?"[40] Despite the numerous differences between first and second language acquisition, his answer is just as applicable to the classroom situation with adults as with children: "Believe that your child can understand more than he or she can say, and seek, above all, to communicate. To understand and be understood. To keep your minds fixed on the same target. In doing that, you will, without thinking about it, make 100 or 1000 alterations in your speech and action. Do not practice them as such. There is no set of rules of how to talk to a child that can even approach what you unconsciously know. If you concentrate on communication, everything else will follow." Teachers of a second or foreign language can be given no better advice.

Notes

1. See T. D. Terrell, "A Natural Approach to the Acquisition and Learning of a Language," *Modern Language Journal*, 61 (1977), pp. 325–36. Kelly and Titone make it apparent that there are no new approaches to language teaching: only rearrangements of ideas which have gone in and out of style since man began speculating on language teaching and learning. L.G. Kelly, *25 Centuries of Language Teaching* (1969; rpt. Rowley, MA: Newbury House, 1976); Renzo Titone, *Teaching Foreign Languages: An Historical Sketch* (Washington, DC: Georgetown Univ. Press, 1968). Theodore Higgs, "Some Pre-Methodological Considerations in Foreign Language Teaching," *Modern Language Journal*, 63 (1979), pp. 335–41, implies that I "rediscovered" the Natural Approach. This implication is, in a sense, true; during the audiolingual period, when I studied language teaching methodology, we paid very little attention to methods other than grammar-translation, which we had set out to replace, and audiolingualism, its replacement. Leonard Newmark, "How Not to Interfere with Language Learning," reprinted in Mark Lester, *Readings in Applied Transformational Grammar* (New York: Holt, Rinehart, 1970), made suggestions very similar to mine in 1963.

2. I am fully aware of the difficulties in defining these two terms. I defined communicative competence in my 1977 article and it is relatively clear despite the criticism in Higgs (note 1 above), p. 335. A "very short time" must remain vague because of the many factors which determine rate of acquisition. In any case, I see no reason to accept the radical view that the ability to communicate messages cannot be achieved in a classroom or even that many, many years of language study is unfortunately hidden by the almost universal practice of testing *only* grammatical competency. Students often do well with complicated grammar manipulations on written tests and one assumes (although probably not really believes) that if the proper situation arose, they could use this knowledge for communication. Since such situations rarely arise in the classroom (because the instructor is busy teaching the next grammar point), the student's ability to transmit messages is never put to the test and the failure of the course is hidden. For a similar point of view see Karl Conrad Diller, *Generative Grammar, Structural Linguistics and Language Teaching* (Rowley, MA: Newbury House, 1971), pp. 1–2.

3. Language teachers should be familiar with at least the following "new" approaches to language instruction: Lozanov's Suggestopedia, see E.W. Stevick, *Teaching Languages: A Way and Ways* (Rowley, MA: Newbury House, 1980), pp. 229–59; William Grabe, "Three Methods for Language Learning: Community Language Learning, the Silent Way, Suggestopedia," *Ohio University Working Papers in Applied Linguistics*, No. 5 (1979); Curran's Community Language Learning, see E. W. Stevick, "Review of Curran," *Language Learning*, 23 (1973), pp. 259–71; E. W. Stevick, *Teaching Languages*, pp. 85–226; Grabe, "Three Methods . . ."; Asher's Total Physical Response, see J. J. Asher, *Learning Another Language Through Actions: The Complete Teacher's Guide* (Los Gatos, CA: Sky Oaks Productions, 1977); Gattegno's Silent Way, see C. Gattegno, *Teaching Foreign Languages in Schools: The Silent Way* (1972; rpt. New York: Education Solutions, 1974); Stevick, *Teaching Languages*, pp. 37–82; Grabe, "Three Methods . . ."; Magnan's Focus Approach, see Sally Magnan, "Reduction and Error Correction for Communicative Language Use: The Focus Approach," *Modern Language Journal*, 68 (1979), pp. 342–48; Beverly Galyean's Confluent Learning, see Beverly Galyean, "A Confluent Approach to Curriculum Design,"

Foreign Language Annals, 12 (1979), pp. 121–27. See also David P. Benseler & Renate A. Schulz, "Methodological Trends in College Foreign Language Instruction," *Modern Language Journal,* 64 (1980), pp. 88–96, for a brief summary of these approaches.

4. See S. Krashen, "Individual Variation in the use of the Monitor," *Principles of Second Language Learning,* ed. W. Ritchie (New York: Academic Press, 1978), pp. 175–83. Krashen has called this strategy the "L-1 plus Monitor mode" of speaking. It consists primarily of using native language word order, target language lexical items and as much "patchwork as possible using target language rules that have been explained and practiced. Although this production strategy works for certain individuals (those who have a "knack" for grammar) in restricted circumstances, it is an extremely inefficient mode of speech and must at some point be replaced by normal modes of speech production.

5. Given the large number of variables difficult to control in any experiment of comparative methodology, it is unlikely that any hard evidence for this claim will be produced in the near future. There are some minor sorts of evidence similar to that reported by Asher, Hauptman, Villani, and Savignon. See J. J. Asher, "The Strategy of Total Physical Response: An Application to Learning Russian," *IRAL,* 3 (1965), pp. 292–44; Sergio Villani, "Communication in an Experimental Foreign Language Class," *Canadian Modern Language Review,* 33 (1977), pp. 372–78; S.J. Savignon, *Communicative Competence: An Experiment in Foreign Language Teaching* (Philadelphia: CCD, 1972). See also Stevick, *Teaching Languages* for impressive personal accounts of successes with various communicative approaches.

6. I use the now accepted "research" definitions of *acquisition* as an unconscious process of constructing grammar rules, also referred to as "creative construction" or commonly as "picking up a language, and *learning* as a conscious attempt to internalize grammar rules; the latter usually includes focused study and practice with various sorts of exercises.

7. See S. Krashen, "The Monitor Model of Adult Second Language Performance," *Viewpoints on English as a Second Language,* ed. M. Burt, H. Dulay & M. Finocchiaro (New York: Regents, 1977); Insup Taylor, "Acquiring versus Learning a Second Language," *Canadian Modern Language Review,* 34 (1978), pp. 455–72; for similar views see Bialystok, who uses the terms "implicit and explicit knowledge." E. Bialystok, "A Theoretical Model of Second Language Learning," *Language Learning,* 28 (1978), pp. 69–83; E. Bialystok, "The Role of Conscious Strategies in Second Language Proficiency," *Canadian Modern Language Review,* 35 (1979), pp. 372–94; rpt. *Modern Language Journal,* 65 (1981), pp. 24–35; E. Bialystok, "An Analytical View of Second Language Competence: A Model and Some Evidence," *Modern Language Journal,* 63 (1979), pp. 257–62.

8. Peter Strevens, "The Nature of Language Teaching," *Understanding Second and Foreign Language Learning,* ed. Jack Richards (Rowley, MA: Newbury House, 1978), pp. 179–203.

9. For research support for this claim see: S. Krashen, "The Monitor Model for Second Language Acquisition and Foreign Language Teaching," *Second Language Acquisition and Foreign Language Teaching,* ed. R. Gingras (Arlington, VA: CAL, 1979); S. Krashen, "A Response to McLaughlin, The Monitor Model: Some Methodological Considerations," *Language Learning,* 29, i (1979), pp. 151–68; S. Krashen, "The Theoretical and Practical Relevance of Simple Codes," *Research in Second Language Acquisition,* ed. R. Scarcella & S. Krashen (1980), pp. 7–18; D. Larsen-Freeman, "The Acquisition of Grammatical Morphemes by Adult ESL Students," *TESOL Quarterly,* 9 (1975), pp. 409–19; S. Krashen, J. Butler, R. Bernbaum & J. Robertson, "Two Studies in Language Acquisition and Language Learning," *IRAL* (1978), pp. 73–92; E. Bialystok (note 7 above) and "Explicit and Implicit Judgements of L2 Grammaticality," *Language Learning,* 29, i (1979), pp. 81–104.

10. Bialystok (note 7 above) presents strong evidence that general exposure to the language in communicative situations is relevant to performance requiring attention to either meaning or form, but that additional formal practice after a particular point no longer facilitates performance. Rivers' comment from her diary account of learning Spanish is revealing. "You cease to think in the language when the exercises make you say things which are contradictory or do not apply to you"; see W. Rivers, "Learning a Sixth Language: An Adult Learner's Daily Diary," *Canadian Modern Language Review*, 36 (1979), pp. 67–82. Both formal and informal evidence thus points to the centrality of conveying meaning in messages, not of formal practice.

11. See Karen A. Mullen, "Direct Evaluation of Second Language Proficiency: The Effect of the Rater and Scale in Oral Interview," *Language Learning*, 28, ii (1978), p. 303; T.D. Terrell, C. Perrone & B. Baycroft, "Teaching the Spanish Subjunctive: An Error Analysis," *IRAL* (forthcoming).

12. K.D. Chastain, *Developing Second-Language Skills* (Chicago: Rand McNally, 1976), p. 135.

13. The importance of focus on content for children has long been recognized, but holds equally for adults. See H. Dulay & M. Burt, "Should We Teach Children Syntax?" *Language Learning*, 23, ii (1973), pp. 245–58; H. Dulay & M. Burt, "Remarks on Creativity in Language Acquisition," *Viewpoints on English as a Second Language*, ed. M. Burt, H. Dulay & M. Finocchiaro (New York: Regents, 1977), pp. 95–126.

14. I do not claim that no acquisition can take place in learning activities. For example, in any exchange in which the attention is focused on verb tenses, other structures (word order, noun-adjective agreement, gender, etc.) may be acquired if the other conditions posited are met. Unfortunately, most cognitive grammar-based exercises are boring to all but the most dedicated of students. I would omit them entirely, but am convinced they are helpful to at least a few students. On the other hand, their failure as a basis for a language course is painfully obvious.

15. Notional-functional syllabuses, in use in Europe now for some time, are based on a similar philosophy of language teaching. See, for example, C.A. Wilkins, "The Linguistic and Situational Content of the Common Core in a Unit/Credit System," *System Development in Adult Language Learning: A European Unit/Credit System for Modern Language Learning by Adults* (Strasbourg: Council of Europe, 1973), pp. 136–37; Keith Johnson, "The Adoption of Functional Syllabuses for General Language Teaching Courses," *Canadian Modern Language Review*, 33 (1977), pp. 667–80; B.D. Kennedy, "Conceptual Aspects of Language Learning," *Understanding Second and Foreign Language Learning*, ed. Jack Richards (Rowley, MA: Newbury House, 1979). The difference is that when I use the term communication goals, I refer principally to the sorts of personal messages a beginner would need to communicate (information about himself, his family, his friends, daily activities, hobbies, likes, dislikes, and so forth). The notional-functional syllabus focuses also on messages, but from the point of view of what the speaker wishes to do: greeting, inviting, giving directions, expressing agreement, etc.

16. An excellent collection of papers on speech to children and its significance for the acquisition process is available in C. Snow & Ferguson, *Talking to Children: Language Input and Acquisition* (Cambridge: Cambridge Univ. Press, 1978).

17. See Evelyn Hatch, "Simplified Input and Second Language Acquisition," unpubl. paper presented to the annual meeting of the Linguistic Society of America, Los Angeles (1979).

18. I use the term "low anxiety" to mean "affectively positive." A certain level of "tension" may be good for learning, but probably not very helpful for acquisition. Schumann classifies factors in second language acquisition in some detail using a nine-way classification: (1) social; (2) affective; (3) personality; (4) cognitive; (5) biological; (6) aptitude; (7) per-

sonal; (8) input; (9) instruction. See John H. Schumann, "Affective Factors and the Problems of Age in Second Language Acquisition," *Language Learning*, 25, ii (1975), pp. 209–36. My use of affective covers his categories (1), (2), (3), and (7)—i.e., factors such as motivation, attitude, self-esteem, anxiety, and so forth.

19. E. Stevick, *Memory, Meaning and Method* (Rowley, MA: Newbury House, 1976), p. 62; see also R. C. Gardner & W. E. Lambert, *Attitudes and Motivation in Second Language Learning* (Rowley, MA: Newbury House, 1972).

20. Particularly good suggestions are found in Christensen, from whom I take the term Affective [Acquisition] Activities: Clay B. Christensen, "Affective Learning Activities," *Foreign Language Annals*, 8 (1975), pp. 211–19; Clay B. Christensen, *Explorando: Affective Learning Activities for Intermediate Practice in Spanish* (Englewood Cliffs, NJ: Prentice Hall, 1977). See also B. Galyean, *Language From Within* (Long Beach, CA: Prism, 1976); G. Moskowitz, *Caring and Sharing in the Foreign Language Classroom* (Rowley, MA: Newbury House, 1979) and "Effects of Humanistic Techniques on Attitude, Cohesiveness, and Self-Concept of Foreign Language Students," *Modern Language Journal*, 65 (1981), pp. 149–57; A. Papalia, "From Manipulative Drills to Language for Real Communication," *Canadian Modern Language Review*, 32 (1976), pp. 150–55.

21. Compare this position to the opposite one of a cognitive approach such as that proposed by Nahir (somewhat misleadingly called a "practical approach"), who states that "our first premise, then, is that second-language learning must, at least in the early stages, be based on basic structures and rules, introduced following careful programming and followed first by thorough exposition, discussion, and association of the grammatical units and lexical items, and then by well planned drills, exercises, and other types of practice." See M. Nahir, "A Practical Progression in the Teaching of a Second Language," *Canadian Modern Language Review*, 35 (1979), p. 595.

22. See note 3 above for references to TPR; see also Norman F. Davies, "Receptive versus Productive Skills in Foreign Language Learning," *Modern Language Journal*, 60 (1976), pp. 440–42.

23. See C. Fraser, U. Belluzi & R. Brown, "Control of Grammar in Imitation, Comprehension, and Production," *Journal of Verbal Learning and Behavior*, 2 (1966), pp. 121–35.

24. See Winitz & Reeds, "Rapid Acquisition of a Foreign Language (German) by the Avoidance of Speaking," *IRAL*, 11 (1973), pp. 295–317.

25. Asher (note 4 above); see also J. J. Asher, Jo Anne Kusudo & Rita de la Torre, "Learning a Second Language Through Commands: The Second Field Test," *Modern Language Journal*, 58 (1974), pp. 24–32; Kenneth F. Ruder, Patricia Hernamm & Richard L. Schefelbusch, "Effects of Verbal Imitation and Comprehension Training on Verbal Production," *Journal of Psycholinguistic Research*, 6 (1977), pp. 59–72; V. A. Postovsky, "Effects of Delay in Oral Practice at the Beginning of Second Language Learning," *Modern Language Journal*, 58 (1979), pp. 229–39.

26. See Catherine Snow, "Conversations with Children," ed. P. Fletcher & M. Garman (Cambridge: Cambridge Univ. Press, 1979), p. 369.

27. Unfortunately, too many in the profession have accepted this extreme position and, even worse, Fries' definition of what constitutes learning a foreign language: "A person has 'learned' a foreign language when he has thus first, *within a limited vocabulary* mastered the sound system . . . and has, second, made the structural devices matters of automatic habit" (p. 3). Such a view of language competence is both restricted, i.e., the learner will not be able to participate in many normal communicative contexts, and unrealistic, i.e., many second and foreign language learners never learn to control the phonology and grammar as a matter of automatic habit. See Charles Fries, *Teaching and Learning English as a Foreign Language* (Ann Arbor: Univ. of Michigan Press, 1945), p. 3.

28. Dwight Bolinger, "Getting the Words In," *American Speech*, 45 (1970), pp. 257–62.

29. Roger Brown, "Introduction," *Talking to Children: Language Input and Acquisition*, ed. E. E. Snow & C. A. Ferguson (Cambridge: Cambridge Univ. Press, 1977), p. 15.

30. Many of the examples are adapted from Christensen (note 20 above).

31. T. D. Terrell, "A Natural Approach to the Teaching of Verb Forms and Function in Spanish," *Foreign Language Annals*, 13 (1980), pp. 129–36.

32. T. D. Terrell (note 1 above), p. 330; John F. Lalande, II, "An Error in Error-Correction Policies?" *ADFL Bulletin*, 12, iii (1981), pp. 45–47.

33. J. Hendrickson, "Error Correction in Foreign Language Teaching: Recent Theory, Research, and Practice," *Modern Language Journal*, 63 (1978), p. 389, devotes a great deal of space to the "when, which, how, and who" of error correction. However, his discussion of the central question, "Should learner errors be corrected?" is predictably short. In fact, his evidence in support of an affirmative answer is weak. He argues that "students unable to recognize their own errors need assistance of someone more proficient in the language than they are." This assertion is true, but correct input can be supplied in many ways without direct correction of speech errors. I believe the other arguments advanced to be so weak that they are not worth extended comment. When Hendrickson paraphrases Krashen & Seliger, "Error correction is especially helpful to adult second language *learners* because it helps them to learn the exact environment in which to apply rules and discover the precise semantic range of lexical items" (my emphasis), this assertion cannot be used as evidence for the use of error correction in the *acquisition* of language rules and structure but only in *learning* easy rules for monitoring. See Krashen & Seliger, "The Essential Contribution of Formal Language Instruction in Adult Second Language Learning," *TESOL Quarterly*, 9 (1975), pp. 173–83.

34. Students who have studied a second language using the NA do make errors when engaging in normal communication in the target language; however, my claim is that they do not make *more* speech errors than students using other methodologies.

35. See Krashen as listed above in notes 7 & 9.

36. Hatch (note 17 above), p. 66.

37. M. Swain, "Bilingual Education for the English-speaking Canadian," *Georgetown University Roundtable on Languages and Linguistics*, ed. James Alatis (1978), pp. 141–54.

38. All are listed in note 20 above.

39. See, for example, R. C. Yorkey et al., *Intercom: English for International Communication* (New York: American, 1977).

40. Roger Brown (note 29 above).

Two Mad, Mad, Mad Worlds: Notes on Natural Approach and the Writing of "Dos mundos"

Magdalena Andrade
University of California, Irvine, and
Irvine Valley Community College

Jeanne Egasse
Irvine Valley Community College

Thalia Dorwick
Publisher, Foreign Languages
and ESL, McGraw-Hill, Inc.

Elías Miguel Muñoz

The co-authors and publisher of the first Natural Approach text (*Dos mundos*) describe the ideas and circumstances that led Tracy Terrell to undertake this new project in 1981. Terrell's beliefs about language pedagogy, his dissatisfaction with existing methodologies, and the growing interest in Natural Approach techniques encouraged him and his co-authors to gather their materials into book format. Here all four recount the problems they encountered in addressing the issues of syllabus, vocabulary, grammar, and activities and learning about the realities of textbook publishing. The four conclude by describing the success of the first edition of *Dos mundos* and the decision in 1987 to begin work on a second edition.

1 THE EARLY PICTURE

Natural Approach arose from a general dissatisfaction with the methodologies preceding it, such as Grammar-Translation, Audio-Lingual, Direct, and Cognitive Code. Tracy Terrell had experience with all of these methodologies, either as a student learning Spanish via Grammar-Translation or as a teacher using ALM (in Peace Corps Training Classes), Direct, or Cognitive Code (at UC Irvine 1970–1976).

Another contributing factor that led to the development of Natural Approach was the very low foreign language enrollments of the 1970s. It seemed clear to Tracy and others in the field that changes would have to be made in foreign language classes to encourage more students to begin foreign language study and continue on to more advanced courses. Tracy soon became convinced that a major part of the problem was the fact that, while students spent years mastering grammatical rules, perfecting their pronunciation, and memorizing dialogues and vocabulary lists, their ability to function in the target language was almost nonexistent.

Tracy's interest in psycholinguistics and, especially, in language acquisition gradually led to Natural Approach. Jeanne Egasse recalls when, while studying Spanish linguistics in 1976 under Tracy at UC Irvine, she joined him in attending a lecture by a guest linguist from USC, Stephen Krashen.

JE: Krashen talked about something he called "monitor theory" and compared learning a foreign language to playing tennis. I was unimpressed, but Tracy was excited. He tried to recap it for me afterwards, but it would take a good many more lectures, conferences, and some classes on child language acquisition before I would understand what Krashen was trying to say.

Tracy began to delineate formally the tenets of Natural Approach in 1975, but he had been developing theories long before that. He had gone to Europe in 1973 and found that, with much context and caretaker speech, he could understand some Dutch.

JE: It took him a couple of summers to acquire Dutch, and he insisted on speaking Dutch to me everywhere we went. I was not a willing student. I did not want to learn that language; I wanted to practice my French. But I had to admit that, with a clear context or referent, I did understand Dutch. Gradually I began to use Dutch to answer back. Tracy kept trying to show me how this fit in with Natural Approach; I was *acquiring* Dutch.

In its most basic form, Natural Approach consisted of lengthy periods of listening to comprehensible input (relevant subject matter, caretaker speech), no overt error correction, a non-threatening classroom environment (low affective filter), encouragement of guessing at global meaning, and second-language acquisition proceeding in stages similar to first-language acquisition. Jeanne was a strong Direct Method advocate when she was first learning about Natural Approach. She liked a lot of what she saw, but she was wary of not correcting her students' errors.

JE: I was loath to let errors pass, which was surprising since my own Spanish still contained many, and I would have been irritated if native speakers had corrected my every utterance. As I continued to teach, I relaxed and saw that my students progressed just as well, if not better, free from the worry of error correction. I started using pictures (laminated photos) in my high school Spanish classes to break up the monotony and sometimes to teach grammar. I noticed how much more interested my students were in communicating to me in Spanish when we talked about famous people or actions that they could see in color. The use of photos gradually became one of the most basic activities in Natural Approach.

In 1977 Tracy and Jeanne started giving workshops to ESL and foreign language teachers in Southern California. Initially the foreign language profession was skeptical and, at times, even hostile to Natural Approach. The idea of no error correction was anathema to many, and the concept of comprehensible input was *in*comprehensible. "How can I talk to my students in Spanish," foreign language teachers would ask, "when they do not know any Spanish? They do not even know the most basic sentence structures!" Foreign language teachers were also reluctant to adopt the approach due to the amount of work involved in redoing entire curricula, amassing picture files, and writing affective activities. "As far as many people were concerned," Jeanne recalls, "Tracy and I were just crazy."

It was the ESL profession that gave Natural Approach its first big break. Sandra Anderson, then the bilingual education coordinator for the Irvine Unified School

District, was one of the first to see the value in what Natural Approach had to offer, and it was through her support that workshops started to be given in much of Orange County. ESL teachers were the most willing to listen because their students had an immediate need to communicate. Foreign language teachers knew that most of their students would never use the target language, and seemed to rely on this fact to bolster their support for the "rules first, communicate later" philosophy.

ESL teachers and program directors constantly encouraged Tracy to prepare Natural Approach materials for Spanish. Many of them had been students in very traditional Grammar-Translation or ALM classes and then had tried unsuccessfully to use their learned Spanish with their own Hispanic students. Tracy had indeed considered the possibility of doing a Natural Approach text in Spanish, but the amount of work it would have entailed discouraged him. In addition, it was work that the UC system would not count as solid research and would probably not consider scholarly. He would continue, he thought, to supervise the lower division classes at UCI using *Spanish: A Short Course*, by Zenia Sacks da Silva, augmenting it with his own material: hundreds of acquisition activities such as open dialogues, interviews, preference-ranking activities, and charts.

2 THERE IS A TEXTBOOK IN THE PICTURE

Elías Miguel Muñoz started his graduate studies at UCI in 1977; Magdalena Andrade started one year later. As teaching assistants, they were under Tracy's supervision and soon became enthusiastic supporters of his Natural Approach methodology. Tracy was confident enough in their teaching skills to delegate some of his supervising responsibilities to Magdalena and Miguel, pointing them out as model NA teachers to be observed by the other TAs. Miguel, however, had not "bought" the Natural Approach when he first heard about it from Tracy during the TA orientation.

> EMM: I had studied English in Cuba through Grammar-Translation, and I was convinced that in order for a person to learn a language, he or she should be familiar with its grammar first. (It didn't matter that after four years of high school English grammar instruction in my native country, all I could say upon arriving in the U.S. was: "Water, pleeese!").
>
> My initial opinion of Tracy's way of teaching, shared by other graduate students in the department, was rather negative. We saw the Natural Approach as just game-playing, *un juego infantil*, nothing to be taken seriously. But my doubts about the method were dispelled once I had a chance to see its results. After just five sessions of TPR (Total Physical Response) and student-centered input, my students were understanding a vast number of Spanish words. And we were having fun at it!

Magdalena played a vital role in the shaping of *Dos mundos*. More than anyone else, she kept reminding Tracy of the urgent need for a textbook. She knew only too well that precious time was being spent on creating, preparing, and photocopying communicative materials to supplement the text in use at UCI. A new textbook could combine Krashen's Monitor Theory with Tracy's research in second-language acquisition. Both Magdalena and Miguel thought at the time that such a text had already been virtually written. Putting it together would simply entail gathering and polishing the activities that Jeanne and Tracy had already created and developed (Magdalena was willing to lend them a hand with this), writing some passages for reading, and preparing a brief outline of the theory—sort of a teacher's manual—as it applied to the teaching of Spanish. Tracy could adapt the latter from *The Natural Approach: Language Acquisition in the Classroom,* by Krashen and Terrell. Miguel could write the reading passages, since he had a strong interest in creative writing.

> EMM: I will never forget the day Tracy saw the possibility of my writing the reading component for his textbook. We were attending a faculty meeting (since I was the TA representative, I was expected to attend these meetings). The chairperson was discussing what seemed to be a serious matter, when suddenly Tracy started laughing loudly and wholeheartedly. All heads in the room turned as he looked at me and pointed excitedly to the manuscript he had just read: it was a copy of a story I had written, "Mi querida cuñada." Not long after that he approached me and asked me if I would contribute as co-author to a textbook he was thinking of writing. He had seen in the piece elements he wanted for some of the reading material in his book: lively and eccentric characters, fairly simple language, a sense of humor, and a surprise ending. "Mi querida cuñada" would eventually appear in *Dos mundos.* Needless to say, that story has a very special meaning for me.

In the summer of 1981, Tracy asked Jeanne, Magdalena, and Miguel to bring to an upcoming meeting copies of all of their acquisition activities and ideas for new ones. The four of us would attempt, he said, to organize the activities into a skeletal syllabus based on fifteen semantic areas: (1) students talking about themselves: clothing, colors, physical characteristics, personal data (age, address, telephone, birthdate), family, school, and classes; (2) seasons and weather; (3) sports and leisure-time activities; (4) holidays; (5) daily routine; (6) house and neighborhood; (7) job and career; (8) plans, preferences, and obligations; (9) past activities; (10) childhood; (11) foods and restaurants; (12) travel in Hispanic countries; (13) health and emergencies; (14) shopping and buying; (15) current events.

Once the activities were organized, the newly formed team outlined the basic pedagogical tenet for their textbook: students need opportunities to acquire Spanish by listening to and using language that is comprehensible, relevant, and interesting. The oral activities would need to hold the students' interest and, at the same time, provide comprehensible input in areas that would be useful for them in interacting with native speakers. The focus of the activities should be on the message and on having fun. The book would stress student interest and involvement in two sorts of activities: those relating directly to the students and their lives, and those relating to the Hispanic world. (Thus the text would be divided into two parts, or "worlds," and would most likely be entitled *Dos mundos*). Vocabulary would be of major importance and would be acquired through active listening and participation in class, as well as through assignments with taped materials, written activities (not grammar exercises), and extensive reading. Grammar (and grammar exercises) would play a supportive role to the semantic themes that formed each chapter.

We began to collect our notes and fashion them into textbook format using the syllabus and approach outlined above. Word spread among instructors in Orange County and Los Angeles that our Spanish text had a broader appeal, and we had calls and visits from many language teachers. Eventually, other local schools asked to test the materials in their own classrooms. Thalia Dorwick, then an editor in San Francisco, came to observe our efforts first hand.

> TD: This primitive version of the Natural Approach Spanish textbook was used initially in classes at UC-Irvine and at some other institutions in the area. We first heard about it through our sales representatives in the area, who said that people in southern California wanted to use only Tracy's materials. For this reason, I decided to look into the materials and the approach.
>
> I had never met Tracy or talked with him. So I called him and asked if I could visit the campus to see what they were doing in foreign language instruction. He was most cordial, setting up a morning of class observations for me. By the end of the morning, my head was spinning. I had seen some wonderful things in the classroom in terms of what students were doing with Spanish, but I had serious reservations about the materials that I had seen and about the practicality of the method for the average professor. Sitting in the John Wayne Airport and waiting for my flight back to San Francisco, I started what eventually would become quite a lengthy letter to Tracy that said, in essence, that I did not feel the approach had commercial potential. I'm glad that being right one hundred percent of the time is not part of my job description!

Tracy mailed the manuscript to several publishers and two looked at it seriously, which seems amazing when we look back at the rudimentary form of the activities. Tracy chose Eirik Børve's group at Random House (now McGraw-Hill); he perceived Eirik to be a supportive publisher and Thalia Dorwick to be a superb editor.

> TD: Eirik and I had reservations about the project that Tracy brought to us. But the team was willing at least to listen to our questions and to discuss most of them. They believed very strongly in what they were doing, and I had strong memories of how well students had performed in the classes I had seen. If the approach was responsible for that, then there was something to this Natural Approach. In the end, we agreed to publish the materials because we believed they deserved a chance, not because we thought they would be a commercial success or even have much of an impact at all.

Thalia spent the next four years hammering away at the *Dos mundos* team about how the materials and their organization needed to change in order to be publishable and marketable. We were inflexible in many areas until it became clear to us that it did no good to publish a text if no one would use it. We were initially adamant about keeping the grammar modules in a separate book, as a side-reference grammar only, but Thalia cautioned strongly against this. Determined as we were not to give the impression that the grammar was an integral part of the language-acquisition activities, we finally agreed to include some in each chapter, but separate from the activities. There were Natural Approach enthusiasts who would be disappointed with the inclusion of grammar in the body of the text, but we felt we had made an acceptable compromise—one that would ensure that Natural Approach and *Dos mundos* would appeal to instructors across the country, not just those in southern California.

We insisted on having no drill exercises in the listening-comprehension portion of the workbook. Instead, students would hear simulated real conversations between native speakers, or simulated radio ads and announcements, complete with sound effects and different accents for each character from a different Hispanic region. This was a costly and difficult proposition, but our publisher was supportive. For the second edition four years later, McGraw-Hill worked even harder to make the tapes sound like real-life interchanges and still be comprehensible to students.

3 LOOKING BACK AT A FUZZY PICTURE

Our major initial writing mistake (and something that delayed the second draft) was our refusal to construct a detailed outline and teaching syllabus before we fleshed out our ideas. We had a very compelling reason: we were already teaching with the materials at UC-Irvine, Irvine Valley College, and the Orange County Department of Education. In fact, we would spend entire summers cutting and pasting clip art to make various versions of the manuscript more attractive and less like a hand-out.

The advantage for us was that we were immediately able to field-test activities in many classrooms, so by the time the second draft was done we had a fairly good idea of what worked in class and what did not and of the kinds of material we needed to develop. We quickly learned that we wanted many illustrations, more than clip art could provide. Even with a good picture file, a Natural Approach teacher could not possibly illustrate all the semantic areas and situations that we wanted to explore. We suggested photos and drawings (later supplied by the publisher) for over a thousand small scenes. We worked on expanding the grammar explanations and providing exercises that were more contextual. We knew the workbook needed more writing activities, and we added a pronunciation and orthography section to the taped portion of the workbook. The original comprehension activities had been taped by TAs at UC-Irvine and consequently were not of studio quality. Hoping for a more professional recording, we wrote directions for regional native-speaker dialects and sound effects.

The disadvantage early in the project was that we often worked in the dark, not knowing the general direction of the text, unsure what grammar/vocabulary had been presented and therefore what grammar/vocabulary could be used in writing a new activity. This initial, haphazard writing process was disconcerting to Thalia as she oversaw our efforts. When we look back now, we see how much easier it would have been to work from a well-developed outline for each chapter and lesson.

4 THE PICTURE COMES INTO FOCUS

As it turned out, the basic organization of each chapter in the main text of *Dos mundos* was as follows:

Oral Activities (four to six themes plus some readings)
Vocabulary Lists
Additional Readings
Grammar

The text had five preliminary *pasos* and fifteen chapters. Each *paso* or chapter had from four to six topics loosely unified semantically. Each topic was presented with art to illustrate vocabulary and/or structure, followed by three to six acquisition activities. The Physical Response and work with the photo file preceded many sections as a general introduction to vocabulary. The acquisition activities were intended to be done in class with the guidance of the instructor. Some of these were whole-group activities, others pair activities. Because we viewed grammar as occupying a supportive role rather than a central one, it was to be the last section and was determined by the themes in the chapter. A chapter on sports and leisure, for instance, necessitated the introduction of the *me/te/le gusta* + infinitive structure (but no discussion of indirect object pronouns). Some readings were included in the body of the activities, as they related to theme; others were in the Additional Readings section.

> EMM: The reading component was to be a major feature of *Dos mundos*, since it would serve as an important source of input for the students and would reinforce the vocabulary being acquired and the cultural topics being discussed. "Readings should be fun, varied, interesting and appealing to the students," Tracy told me. He envisioned his book having more reading material than any other textbook on the market, which it did—eventually. With much valuable help from the team and our editor, I ended up writing (and *re*writing) short stories, newspaper articles, interviews, cultural notes, and other types of texts and learning a great deal from all the work. In fact, as I look back on the process of writing *Dos mundo*s, I realize that it was one of the most challenging projects I have faced in my writing career. And I've written three novels!

The basic organization of each chapter in the workbook was as follows:

Listening Activities (eight to twelve listening activities)
Pronunciation and Orthography
Writing Activities

The workbook had five *pasos* and fifteen chapters, correlated thematically with the text. Each *paso* or chapter had from eight to twelve listening activities, such as dialogues, radio ads, or announcements, and corresponding true/false, multiple-choice, or fill-in questions; a section on pronunciation and orthography with vocabulary tied to the chapter; and a section with writing activities (also tied thematically to the oral activities of the text). The latter were not grammar exercises but writing activities for which there was not one correct answer.

The amount of vocabulary in *Dos mundos* presented a real problem in vocabulary control. We wanted to be able to tell instructors what vocabulary was new in each activity, but the sheer quantity of words made it seem an impossible task. Magdalena and Jeanne started trying to keep track of vocabulary on note cards, but they gave up halfway into the text. Tracy then hired someone to write a program for us that would sort vocabulary on computer. The sorting process entailed the following: (1) Someone types in the first activity and asks the program what words are new. (They are all new, so one creates a file for words in Chapter A, Activity 1.) (2) The words from the next activity are then typed and compared to the first activity. (3) By the time one gets to Chapter 15, one is comparing a new activity to a file of thousands of words from all the previous activities in the text.

The process was mind-boggling, and even with a computer many human errors were made. To date we are not sure how to control the vocabulary more accurately in a Natural Approach text. In any case, we were not willing to do what other texts do, which is to establish the vocabulary list first, then write activities using only that vocabulary.

A unique aspect of *Dos mundos* is the Instructor's Manual included at the back of the teacher's edition. It is a complete presentation of Natural Approach and the various aspects of using the program. Furthermore, within the text itself there are extensive marginal notes to the instructor beside each introduction of a theme and beside most activities. Tracy wrote both the manual and the marginal text notes, making sure that users understood how the display art, photo file, dialogues, open dialogues, chart activities, narration series, ads, and readings were used in Natural Approach. Also featured in the Manual are ideas for activities that instructors can include, time and interest permitting. We now realize that producing this Instructor's Manual entailed much more than just a simple adaptation of the original Krashen/Terrell method. But, in retrospect, no single aspect of the book seems, as we had initially thought, to have been "virtually written already."

5 THERE WOULD BE A SECOND PICTURE

All we ever expected from publishing our text was to be able to use our own materials in a professional format in our classes. We would be forever free from the photocopy version of *Dos mundos* and the mountains of supplementary activities we were used to bringing to class. We were thus surprised and gratified to find that there were so many other teachers who wanted to use a text with lots of interesting and affective activities.

JE: At any rate, it was far more work than Tracy had anticipated and certainly more than I had ever dreamed. But when we got into it there were areas where we saw so much room for improvement. Tracy was an incredibly creative person and would come up with wonderful last-minute ideas which we would all try to implement, regardless of what stage of the writing we were in. Even our editor, Thalia, had a hard time keeping current with the latest version of the text. Word processors worked overtime, and we all got more than a little crazy.

TD: What was close to the last straw for me happened at the end of December (the manuscript was scheduled to go to our production department in early January). Before leaving on a business trip, I called Tracy just to check in and make sure that he was going to mail the manuscript as promised. When he answered the phone, he was quite animated and quickly began to tell me about a wonderful idea he had just had and that he was going to "put into the manuscript."

The wonderful idea was a cast of characters, the forty-or-so people from the Spanish-speaking world, each with distinct personalities, lifestyles, families, and the like. Adding this material became one of the biggest editorial nightmares I've ever had to deal with, but it also ended up being one of the most delightful features of *Dos mundos*.

EMM: When you worked with Tracy, you had to be willing to start your job over again, sometimes from scratch, even when you thought your job was done and you had given it your best shot. He was a demanding, highly creative person, a tough critic, and he would not accept the fact that a project had been completed if there was at least one more good idea that could go into it. Tracy had the ability to see the global picture. And he could detect the gaps, the missing pieces. He might not always tell you exactly what he wanted, and you had to settle for a "This doesn't work yet!" or "This is boring!" from him, comments that undoubtedly made your task all the more challenging. Working with Tracy, I learned not to regard the writing of a book as a project to be completed by a certain date, but rather as an ongoing process, an activity that must defy strict deadlines and time factors in order for it to be accomplished in the best possible way.

We remember Thalia saying, when the manuscript was finally going into production, that by the time we received our first royalty check, plans for the second edition would be well under way. But the second edition seemed like a distant mirage, a bridge to be crossed in the faraway future. We had just spent five years working intensely on the book, and the thought of going through that process again was not very appealing. But sure enough, our textbook had barely been out for a year when we received a "2nd ed." memo from our editor. And, believe it or not, by then we were ready to go at it again. We were quite aware of areas that needed work. In fact, as the first edition was being completed, we were already preparing a long list of things to delete, change, and add. Also, questionnaires sent out to users of the book in that first year had given us new ideas for improvement.

TD: In spite of our initial low expectations for sales of *Dos mundos*, the text was an immediate success, with sales increasing every year and wonderful feedback from instructors and students. Natural Approach, people told us, was liberating; it allowed instructors to do all of the things they enjoyed doing in the classroom and knew intuitively were the right things to do. It is a wonderful experience when a book written for all of the right reasons also becomes a commercial success. It couldn't have happened to a nicer group of authors! So successful was *Dos mundos* that McGraw-Hill commissioned Tracy to develop additional Natural Approach college texts for German (*Kontakte*) and French (*Deux mondes*), both now in second editions. In 1994, McGraw-Hill and McDougal, Littell & Co. co-published a Natural Approach Spanish series at the high-school level developed by Tracy and entitled *¡Bravo!*

We ended up deleting many dialogues in the second edition and providing more narration series, art, interviews, authentic readings, and writing activities. Thalia had tried to encourage us to use more realia the first time around, but it was not until the second edition that we heeded her advice and based acquisition activities on realia. And we practically rewrote the entire workbook, making the dialogues sound more like natural conversations and adding a new feature, the *radiodrama*, at the end of each chapter.

Some users of the text asked for more grammar, but we chose to keep essentially the same amount as in the first edition. Although we attempted to contextualize the exercises more, we felt that the grammar was sufficient and, in some ways, excessive for a first-year student. After all, our original intent was to have a *reference* grammatical component; we wanted to make clear that grammar would not be the focus of *Dos mundos*. We did, however, spiral the grammar entry more, augmenting the re-entry of items. Present tense (regular, irregular, and reflexive) is spiraled throughout seven chapters; preterite is distributed throughout four; object pronouns throughout eight. Of course, these grammatical areas are also present in many other chapters as a by-product of natural communication activities.

◆ ◆ ◆

Recently, the team members got together in San Diego and relived "the good old days," remembering team anecdotes such as the time Miguel thought that his Apple computer had gobbled down one week's worth of work. (Miguel has learned a couple of things about computers since then.)

Each of us has a different memory of how and where the first serious talk of writing *Dos mundos* took place. Jeanne remembers Tracy's pool, and indeed several meetings happened there, in the city of Orange, as the four authors listened to Tracy's canaries and Jeanne tried to protect herself from the sun. Miguel remembers the conference room in the humanities building at UCI, surrounded by poster-sized pictures of eminent Spanish and Latin American writers. And it is true that at least one of the meetings took place there: the four potential coauthors sat around the large conference table, listing the few colleges and universities in California that would use their textbook, cutting and pasting activities *ad infinitum*, while Miguel wondered, in bewilderment, "What am I supposed to be doing?"

Working together on *Dos mundos* has been a rewarding if exhausting experience. We have gained an appreciation for the amount of work that goes into publishing a foreign language text and we marvel that any single author can produce a comprehensive text. We continue to enjoy teaching with our own materials and receiving feedback from other instructors using our textbook. Although each of us played an important role in bringing *Dos mundos* to life, it was Tracy Terrell whose creative spark initiated a unique approach to foreign language teaching and guided the development of *Dos mundos*.

Gracias a ti, Tracy!

Afterword from the Publisher

While writing their reminiscences in "Two Mad, Mad, Mad Worlds," the team was already preparing the third edition of *Dos mundos*. Tracy Terrell was actively involved in planning the new edition, and his three co-authors continued to work on the manuscript following his death at the end of 1991. Published in December 1993, *Dos mundos*, Third Edition is available from McGraw-Hill, Inc.

On Breaking with Tradition: The Significance of Terrell's Natural Approach

Armando Baltra
California State University, Fresno

In this paper, written originally at the invitation of this volume's editors but first published in 1992 in *The Canadian Modern Language Review*, reactions to Tracy Terrell's work on language-teaching methodology are examined and his influences on the community are reassessed. With its theoretical underpinnings and "humanistic" goals, the Natural Approach is shown to have had a lasting impact on foreign-language and second-language classrooms since Terrell formulated it in 1977.

 INTRODUCTION

It would be difficult to find today a book on foreign and/or second language teaching methodology that does not mention Tracy Terrell's Natural Approach (NA) as one of the methods proposed in the past two decades. In fact, I have yet to meet a teacher of Spanish who is unaware of the existence of *Dos mundos*, the text first coauthored by Terrell in 1986.[1] When I ask teachers their impressions of *Dos mundos*, I notice that most of them have been influenced by the collection of classroom activities described in that textbook. In fact, many teachers tell me that they are using the activities as a supplement in their classes because they provide a refreshing look at the teaching of Spanish. The following example illustrates a typical reaction from these teachers.

> My school was using another Spanish textbook so I could not fully apply the Natural Approach with my students. But every time I could, I used some of the classroom activities proposed by Terrell. My supervisor heard about my class, came to see what I was doing, and was very impressed with the results. Now I

Reprinted by permission, with changes, from *The Canadian Modern Language Review/La Revue canadienne des langues vivantes*, Vol. 48 (April/avril, 1992):565–93.

think we are going to adopt *Dos mundos* for the whole school! (Oliveira, personal communication)

Terrell's work has received this widespread interest because he recognized and helped to popularize the need to increase student interaction in the foreign language (FL) class through intrinsically motivating and challenging tasks. He has provided FL teachers with a collection of carefully selected and well-designed activities that can readily be used in the language classroom to create a magic, game-like atmosphere whereby students interact in a language not yet their own. And they are successful because these activities are an embodiment of two crucial concepts in communicative methodology: students use the language in order to do something that is meaningful and interesting to them, and activities are not centered on manipulating the grammatical system of the language. These are two of Terrell's major contributions to foreign language teaching.

There is little doubt that in the NA Terrell succinctly put together a curriculum that is comprehensive and includes the current principles and practices of the communicative movement. The degree of his success can be witnessed by the growing number of publications in which teachers describe using the NA in the teaching of languages as varied as Arabic (Magrath 1987), ESL (Mayer 1985), French (Schneider 1989), German (Voge 1979; Whitman 1986; Jappinen 1986), Italian (Lafford 1987), Russian (Meyer and Tetrault 1984), Spanish (Rosales 1986; Conway 1986), and Thai (Brown and Palmer 1988). In addition to Terrell's own account of his Dutch experience (Terrell 1977), I am also aware of unpublished work on Japanese, Hebrew, and Chinese that has been strongly influenced by the NA.

The Natural Approach has apparently caught the attention of scholars representing a wide range of interests. The various stages of acquisition in the NA have even been compared to the process of internalizing a language that is unique to epic verse-making among unlettered singers of Yugoslavia and other South Slavic regions (Worth 1990). It also seems that the NA principles have become more widely adopted than some other innovative teaching proposals (Asher 1979; Curran 1972; Gattegno 1963, 1976; Lozanov 1978). One possible explanation for this latter point is that Terrell's position is an outgrowth of Krashen's well-known theories of second-language acquisition (Krashen 1981, 1982, 1985). Teachers who are acquainted with (and like) Krashen's views find in Terrell's NA a completely outlined set of methodological procedures that follow Krashen's theories and can readily be put to use in the classroom. The NA has been described as "an effort to reconcile the research findings in second-language acquisition with the classroom practices" (Lafayette and Strasheim 1984:569).

Krashen's support has proved to be a bit of a double-edged sword. One of Terrell's arguments was that his method is effective because it is fully supported by a large amount of conclusive research on second-language acquisition. The trouble with this argument is that important studies in the literature seriously question the empirical validity of Krashen's theories and conclusions (McLaughlin 1978, 1987; Munsell and Carr 1981; Taylor 1984; Gregg 1984; Krahnke 1985; Ellis 1986). This evidence does not help promote the scientific claims of the NA; all the criticism, however, is at the level of theoretical research on second-language acquisition and should not directly affect what intuitive teachers believe will work in the classroom. It should never be forgotten that teaching is also an art. Jenkinson's twenty-year-old statement seems just as valid today:

> My quarrel is that because the empirical method has proved so effective in scientific enquiry, we in education have allowed this to influence us too exclusively. Educational evidence which is not labeled "research" or does not present evidence in what is often a pseudo-scientific manner is usually suspect. (Jenkinson 1969:28)

Despite Jenkinson's wise warning, Terrell's work and the reaction it has produced are almost exclusively wrapped in the positivistic framework. The literature uses empirical arguments to attack or support the NA and contemptuously rejects teachers' feedback as merely "impressionistic," "anecdotal," or "informal" evidence with no serious value.

The above discussion, however, is not meant to leave the reader with the impression that since teaching is also an art, research is unimportant. Research has provided significant support to the hypothesis that students acquire a new language through practice in communication and in meaning-focussed problem solving in L2. The NA provides an example of such practice, and it should not be too heavily faulted because Krashen's is not the perfect theory. Savignon (personal communication) puts it succinctly: "Criticisms of aspects of Krashen's theories are not necessarily criticisms of the NA."

Let us now look at the degree of recognition the Natural Approach has received. In his review of the seminal 1983 book by Krashen and Terrell, Krahnke (1985) praises the recommendations on error correction and the way in which theory and practice are integrated. He questions, however, the lack of a theory of language to accompany the theory of learning, and suggests that the energy spent arguing against grammar teaching might be better spent defining and showing what the new role for grammar should be.

To the best of my knowledge, only *Modern Language Journal* has published reviews of Terrell's textbooks (*Dos mundos, Deux mondes,* and *Kontakte*[2]). Surprisingly, *Hispania* has ignored *Dos mundos.* Joiner (1989) admires the taped materials that accompany *Deux mondes* but at the same time regrets that the input the students get is too simplified to be considered authentic. Finnemann (1989) says little about *Dos mundos.* Besides noting that the book does not have an English-Spanish glossary, he proposes a better sequence of verb-tense presentation and concludes his one-page review saying that *Dos mundos* is "a sound teaching program." If one were to say that the two previous reviews are rather bland and non-committal, Alter's reaction to *Kontakte* is certainly the opposite. In short, she does not approve of the NA mainly because it does not have what the traditional teacher expects to find in a German foreign language textbook: "There is no recapitulation of grammar nor are there any chapters with an overall review of grammatical points" (1989:92-94).

The authors of books on teacher-training principles and practices have been more receptive. One of the first books on methodology to give serious prominence to the NA was by Blair (1982). Since that time there has been a growing body of literature on the NA. Celce-Murcia and McIntosh (1979) say nothing about it; however, in a more recent collection edited by Celce-Murcia (1991), there are five articles in which the NA is cited and described. Both Rivers (1981) and Stern (1983) mention Terrell's 1977 paper in a couple of footnotes. Long and Richards (1987) say merely that the informed teacher should be acquainted with the NA; they do not include any article that directly presents it to the reader. Although it was not acknowledged at first by Brown, it is included in his second edition (1987). Oller and Richard-Amato (1983) reprint Terrell's complete 1982 paper. Also, Savignon (1983) supports Terrell's efforts to place due emphasis on communication. Larsen-Freeman (1986) dedicated a whole section of her book to the NA, and Richard-Amato (1988) wrote an entire chapter, a version of which appears in this volume. Omaggio (1986) thoroughly argues against Terrell's work, while Chastain (1988) just as strongly argues for it.

In their book on methods in language teaching, Richards and Rogers describe the NA as follows:

> What characterizes the Natural Approach is the use of familiar techniques within the framework of a method that focuses on providing comprehensible input and a classroom environment that cues comprehension of input, minimizes learner anxiety, and maximizes learner self-confidence. (1986:136)

They examine the NA in the context of their well-accepted approach-design-procedure framework and use the word *familiar* to describe Terrell's classroom techniques because they find that the activities, which have made the NA so popular among FL teachers, are all well known and widely used in the EFL/ESL world. It is true that there is nothing new under the sun, and Terrell himself was the first to acknowledge this (Krashen and Terrell 1983:128). One brief look at the ESL literature will reveal the enormous number of communicative activities available in English (e.g., Byrne 1976; Olsen 1977; Brumfit and Johnson 1979; Ur 1981; Christison and Bassano 1981; Bassano and Christison 1981, 1982; Klippel 1984; Nunan 1989). In fact, Terrell and his colleagues have also produced a very interesting collection of ESL activities for young learners that follow the second-language acquisition stages as proposed by the NA (Marino, Martini, Raley, and Terrell 1984). It is important to point out, however, that what Terrell and his colleagues did in *Dos mundos* was a great deal more than translate classroom activities from English to Spanish. They were careful to design a communicative syllabus that follows Krashen's views on second-language acquisition and does so within the Spanish cultural and situational contexts.

I propose to look at Terrell's work in terms of the degree of acceptance or rejection his pedagogic views have had since he first presented them in 1977. I discuss two issues which have been more or less generally accepted among language teachers: the classroom application of Krashen's notion of comprehensible input and the teacher's role in lowering the student's affective filter in the classroom. I then examine two issues that have been highly controversial and have, in a way, helped propagate Terrell's communicative approach: the teaching of grammar and the correction of errors. I also address the controversy over the lack of evidence that the NA is more effective than other methods. In the last section of this paper I compare the evolution of educational materials and classroom practices in English as a foreign and/or second language with that of their equivalents in FL teaching in the United States. I show that, in general, the latter has been following the developments of the first by about a decade. Once the apparent reasons for this situation have been outlined, the contribution of Terrell toward bridging the gap acquires a new dimension.

2 REACTION TO TERRELL'S PROPOSAL AND ITS UNDERLYING THEORY

Generally Accepted Principles of the Natural Approach

Terrell found support as soon as his views became known (Barrutia 1977; Goldin 1977; Teschner and Cox 1977). As the popularity of Krashen's theories gained impetus and the communicative-competence movement grew stronger all over the world, the ranks of NA supporters likewise increased. Effective language teachers in general had already been aware of the need to encourage comprehension in a friendly environment.

1. The promotion of comprehensible input in the classroom   Of all of Krashen's hypotheses, the one that states that acquisition can only occur if students comprehend the message is perhaps one of the most practical and sound contributions to the development of classroom activities. Krashen (1982) argues that it would be very difficult to acquire a foreign language by watching television programs in that language because the input would not be comprehensible; it would just be "noise." A beginner can do much better by taking a course in the foreign language, where the teacher provides him with plenty of *comprehensible input.*

Terrell applied this hypothesis by insisting on a pre-speech stage in which students just listen and are not required to speak, a sharp contrast to the traditional "listen and repeat" approach of the audiolingual methodology (Terrell et al. 1984). This feature, known as the *silent period,* has been supported by many (Postovsky 1974; Ervin-Tripp 1974; Hakuta 1974; Gary 1975; Huang and Hatch 1978; Asher 1979; Winitz 1981; Burt and Dulay 1981; Littlewood 1984) but has also been questioned by some. There are those who, while agreeing that second-language learners naturally begin by listening, question the claim that all learners should go through a silent period since this would deny the evidence of individual learning styles (Stevick 1982; Daniels 1986; Ellis 1986; Brown 1987; Long and Richards 1987). Furthermore, the evidence presented as support for the silent period phenomenon has been critically questioned with arguments that (1) the observed initial silence might be better described as a period of silent incomprehension and (2) if prolonged, the silent period may represent psychological withdrawal rather than language acquisition (Gibbons 1985). Teachers, however, have understood that the practical classroom implications of this silent period proposal are to refrain from the "listen and repeat" trend and to allow students to remain silent until they are comfortable and ready to speak (Terrell 1982c). Closely following Krashen's position and led by his own pedagogic experience and intuition, Terrell argued that very few FL texts take the teaching of comprehension skills seriously. He suggested that there was an urgent need for materials focusing on the development of comprehension strategies (Terrell 1986a).

Terrell did not hesitate to borrow from earlier sources as long as they were consistent with second-language acquisition theories. Asher also maintained that listening comprehension is crucial for language acquisition; Terrell adopted Asher's *total physical response* (TPR) techniques since they provide a very effective way of supplying comprehensible input during the very early stages of language instruction (Asher 1965, 1966, 1979). In a TPR activity, students demonstrate comprehension by acting out the various commands given by the teacher in the target language. Because of the need to provide as much comprehensible input as possible, teachers are strongly encouraged to speak only in the target language in the classroom. TPR, furthermore, supports the silent-period principle since students do not have to say anything while physically responding to what they hear.

TPR, however, is not devoid of critics. Omaggio wonders if the criteria for choosing commands in a rigorous TPR environment will always have a communicative intent. She observes that the imperatives usually selected in the lesson tend to be actions that can easily be reproduced in a classroom situation or can be fun because they are "bizarre." She warns teachers that, unless this mode of instruction is supplemented with other types of practice, students will have little opportunity to internalize natural language used for authentic purposes (Omaggio 1986).

I think it is fair to say that TPR cannot be successfully implemented by all teachers or enjoyed by every student. I have seen a video demonstration showing an excellent, young, vigorous, and enthusiastic teacher jumping on a chair, beating her chest and screaming like Tarzan in front of twenty-five adults who unhesitatingly follow her, totally captivated with the experience (Rosales 1986). But can you imagine dear old Mrs. Brown attempting a similar feat? And even if there are some energetic teachers willing and ready to go through the TPR commands, some of their students might still feel uncomfortable or embarrassed.

Even Terrell himself at times questioned the universal advisability of TPR, especially toward the end of his teaching career. He and other recent researchers understood that both TPR and the silent period did not automatically produce comprehensible input. Instead, these are simply two means by which comprehensible input can occur (see, for example, Gass 1993). Nevertheless, when the teacher has managed to create the right kind of classroom atmosphere, TPR can help to establish a very effective group dynamic which will be critical for more high-risk social activities later in the course (Wolfe and Jones 1982). And, as Teschner writes, "The chief virtues of TPR are that it gives students an immediate sense of accomplishment and participation while keeping the affective filter miraculously unclogged" (1986:180).

2. The affective domain: Coping with anxiety in the classroom

Another important and widely accepted component of Krashen's views on second-language acquisition is that comprehensible input is seriously hindered if there is great stress and anxiety. Terrell's use of TPR in the early stages of the Natural Approach thus becomes doubly valuable, not only providing comprehensible input, as was shown, but also reducing stress. Psychological tension can be diminished by ensuring that students enjoy their first experience with the foreign language. Thus, the initial TPR activities can effectively break the ice at the beginning of the course since the individual student sees everybody else in the class directly and personally involved in the activity. When asked about being self-conscious or not practicing TPR, a student of Spanish at the University of California, Irvine, said that he had been apprehensive at first about those strange commands in Spanish, but he jumped right in when he saw "everybody making a fool of themselves" (personal communication).

There are various reasons why the FL classroom can easily generate stress and anxiety. That most of the instruction is in the target language can be a source of stress to many students. Furthermore, in most traditional methodologies the students are expected from the first day to produce utterances in the new language and are held responsible for the errors they might make. This attitude can easily lead to a growing feeling of frustration when they fail to perform accurately (Teschner 1986). The fact that in the NA students are clearly told that they are not mandated to speak from the very first day of class is a powerful source of stress reduction. Hesitant or shy students can relax, knowing that their grades will not be affected by remaining silent until they feel they are ready (Terrell 1982b).

Krashen and his colleagues were by no means the first to assert that affective factors are extremely important variables in an educational situation. Good language teachers have always been intuitively concerned with the affective domain. Sauer, for example, is reported to have created anxiety-free environments in Spanish classes in the early 1970s (Hanzeli and Love 1972). It is only recently, however, that this has been strongly promoted as a philosophy of learning (e.g., Christensen 1975, 1977; Moskowitz 1979; Brown 1987; Baltra 1988). Stevick (1976) says that the linguistic material presented during the first week is only a vehicle for getting acquainted and for reducing anxieties. Brown (1987) has pointed out that anxiety can be seen as positive or negative. A certain degree of anxiety may be necessary to reach the state of alertness required for productive learning; however, many researchers have found a strong correlation between lower anxiety levels and effective academic achievement (Carroll 1963; Gardner et al. 1976; Chastain 1975; Brown 1987).

Self-esteem is directly related to self-confidence: "We may perform well because our attitude toward self is positive; we may have a positive attitude toward self because we perform well" (Richard-Amato 1988). Although it is not easy to define self-esteem operationally, various researchers have suggested ways of analyzing it and evaluating its role in education (Coopersmith 1967; Gardner and Lambert 1972; Brodkey and Shore 1976; Heyde 1977). Although the findings have not been conclusive, they have not only confirmed our intuitions but shown the importance of cross-cultural factors in second-language learning.

Following these principles and using the support of Krashen's research on the *affective filter hypothesis*, Terrell insists that the teacher must create a non-threatening and friendly atmosphere in the classroom; otherwise, acquisition will be either impossible or severely hampered. To lower anxiety is to make the activity intrinsically motivating and fun. "No instruction hour, even with adults, should be without an activity in which the target language is used for some fun" (Terrell 1982a:281). Terrell has given teachers many suggestions on how to reduce stress and anxiety in the classroom. He strongly recommends creating an environment designed to counteract those negative, defensive emotions so frequently found among FL learners and so vividly described by Savignon in "A Letter to My Spanish Teacher" (1981). Because they tend to put students at ease in the classroom, humanistic activities such as gaming and simulation permit the creation of "a safe space" where the students can experiment freely and learn from trial-and-error: "I like Mr. Corvalan's class because it's OK to make mistakes" (18-year-old student of Spanish, personal communication, in Baltra 1990).

Another way in which Terrell contributed to the creation of a non-threatening atmosphere in the classroom is by encouraging the teacher to promote a sense of being together and helping one another. While encouraging this willingness to share, the NA tends to support the contemporary tendency toward a change of emphasis from individual production and competition to a cooperative learning framework, from a teacher-centered to a student-centered approach (Johnson and Johnson 1984; Kagan 1985; Baltra 1987).

Issues in the NA That Have Been Questioned

Critiques of Terrell's Natural Approach have basically been an extension of the long-standing "accuracy versus fluency" battle with some interesting twists derived from interlanguage theory. Because all communicative approaches tend to favor fluency (and Terrell's method is not an exception), the objections come from those who think that accuracy should not be so heavily undermined. We will examine the two areas where the NA has received the most criticism: the role it assigns to grammar and its treatment of students' errors. This section ends with a discussion of a third issue: the lack of empirical evidence that the NA is more effective than other methodologies.

1. The treatment of grammar in the classroom   Probably the most controversial contribution of the Natural Approach to foreign-language teaching has been the proposition that the entire class time should be devoted to communicative activities. Following Krashen's emphasis on *language acquisition* (as opposed to *language learning*), Terrell maintained that classroom activities must encourage the student to focus on the meaning, rather than the form, of the utterances. Consequently, in the Instructor's Manual to the first edition of *Dos mundos*, the authors wrote: "We suggest that you avoid detailed grammar explanations in the classroom whenever possible. They rarely help more than a few students and invariably take away valuable time from acquisition activities" (Terrell et al. 1986, as well as subsequent editions). This is not to say, of course, that verb forms should not be taught. In fact, Terrell described in great detail a radically different approach to classroom presentation of verb forms in which the students are involved in what he calls *affective acquisition activities* (1980; see also section 3 below).

The impact of this view has been substantial among FL teachers, since historically the general tendency has been to do exactly the opposite. The most frequently quoted reaction against Terrell's communicative orientation is that of Higgs and Clifford (1982). They state that extensive practice in developing communicative strategies in early stages of second-language learning will lead students to acquire permanent and irreversible errors in their interlanguage. Furthermore, they argue that these students will stop improving and will fossilize at the 2/2+ level in the FSI 0-5 scale of oral proficiency. They strongly advise teachers that grammar must be directly taught and learned by the students *before* they start practicing communicative activities in the classroom. Omaggio, in her commitment to the proficiency movement in the United States and its great concern for grammatical accuracy, has written extensively in support of Higgs and Clifford's fossilization hypothesis (Omaggio 1984, 1986). Influenced by Omaggio's latest work, Mowry (1989) wrote a somewhat biased account entitled "A Semester's Flirtation with the Input Hypothesis," in which he clearly displays his strong grammar-oriented perspective while trying to handle communicative fluency activities.

In 1987 Terrell refuted Higgs and Clifford's fossilization charges, arguing that there is no solid evidence to show that this problem would occur. As for the claim that the communicative movement would force premature production, Terrell responded that, in the NA, students will progress through gradual stages of target-language production, something which has exactly the opposite effect. Furthermore, he felt that premature, forced production is really an issue to take up with the "listen and repeat" advocates and not with the NA, which by overtly allowing a silent period, is not forcing anything but stressing listening comprehension.

What Terrell did not mention in his 1987 article to support his argument was Savignon's earlier study showing that students who had practiced communicative fluency performed just as well as accuracy-oriented learners in a grammar test, and easily surpassed the control group in a series of unrehearsed communicative tasks (Savignon 1971). Years later, in a similar study, Hammond (1988) tested the grammatical accuracy of two groups of students who had just completed their first semester of foreign language. Group A had had one semester of grammar-translation, while group B had been taught using the NA. The NA group, concentrating on practicing communicative skills, did not score significantly lower in grammar than the other group. This is not surprising, since there is a significant grammatical component inherent in the NA materials.

Omaggio (1984) brings up another issue to support the accuracy-first movement. She believes that grammatical accuracy should be emphasized because of studies (Ervin 1977; Albrechtsen et al. 1980; Ensz 1982) which concluded that native speakers judge grammatical errors quite negatively. There is, on the other hand, evidence that learners' errors in grammar and morphology are less of a social problem than Omaggio suggests (Guntermann 1978; Chastain 1980; Galloway 1980; Ludwig 1982; Gynan 1984; VanPatten 1986).

Without directly mentioning their names (but clearly referring to them), Celce-Murcia and Hilles qualify the work of Krashen and Terrell as having "intuitive appeal" but providing only "anecdotal evidence." They then contrast this comprehensible-input view with Higgs and Clifford's fossilization argument, which is said to have "equally appealing and convincing evidence" (Celce-Murcia and Hilles 1988:1-2). Their point in placing these two opposing views side by side is to remind us of the lack of empirical evidence for or against the use of grammatical explanations in the classroom. On the question of whether or not lack of emphasis on grammar will cause morphosyntactic fossilization, there is not yet unequivocal evidence that communicative approaches cause fossilization. In fact, research evidence to date does not suggest that a focus on form is either necessary or beneficial to early stage learners (Balcom 1985; VanPatten 1986; Hammond 1988).

Cross, in his 1985 discussion of Krashen's *monitor theory* and its practical implications for the language teacher, takes the middle-of-the-road view that students' utterances should be assessed on the basis of both communicative effectiveness and formal accuracy. He states that the movement away from behavioral goals and linguistic artificiality is particularly relevant in the multilingual European context.

It seems that, as James (1983) states, the issue is not whether or not to teach grammar, but how much grammar to teach and how. Savignon (1985) expresses reservations about the tension between the communicative and the structural perspectives. She recognizes that without some degree of grammatical ability no meaningful interaction can take place; however, she regrets the excessive grammatical emphasis in the ACTFL guidelines. Another appealing recommendation is proposed by Celce-Murcia (1985), who discusses all the educational variables (age, educational background, course objectives, learning styles, learners' needs, and so forth) that should be taken into consideration before determining the role of grammar in the curriculum. Celce-Murcia and Hilles (1988) bring forth a practical argument in favor of teaching grammar: they suggest it be taught to all students who are required to take official language examinations, which of necessity have a large grammatical component.

One of the problems that seems inherent in most language methods is the underlying assumption that there is only one way of teaching and learning; the debate about grammar in the NA is apparently the result of such an attitude. More important, however, is the fact that Terrell's proposal has made teachers re-examine practices that, through a long unquestioned tradition, have had the status of dogma. Terrell asked, "How many instructors believe that the mastery of Spanish lies along the path of a "new" explanation for *ser* and *estar?*" (1986b:195). Graham Thurgood quite correctly points out that Terrell's key word is *explanation* and that, although the NA indeed deals with the distinction between *ser* and *estar,* it focuses not on explanations but rather on ways to encourage the students to deal with the distinction communicatively (personal communication).

2. Students' errors: To correct or not to correct?   Rigorous error correction has been the standard practice of foreign-language teaching methodologies for a long time. Support for this position was found in the stimulus-response-rein-

forcement behavioristic model of the late fifties, which maintained that any performance that deviated from the target had to be eradicated at once (Skinner 1957; Lado 1964). This concept, which in 1977 was recognized to be in full swing in the teaching of Spanish (Barrutia 1977), seems to have gained a new impetus with Higgs and Clifford's reservations in 1982 about communicative approaches.

Using the support of Krashen's well-known *acquisition/learning distinction*, Terrell strongly defended a position contrary to the model above. He claimed that "the practice of correcting speech errors directly is not just merely useless, but actually harmful to progress in language acquisition" because (1) this would force the student to focus on the linguistic system and not on the communicative message and (2) it would raise the affective filter (Terrell 1982a).

It is important to understand that Terrell's contribution to foreign-language methodology was not a total departure from error correction. In fact, even Krashen, while criticizing the emphasis on accuracy and on learning, has argued that "this is not to say that error correction is useless and that learning is of no value. Learning has a role to play, and error correction may be of use in certain situations" (Krashen 1982:59). Following Burt (1975), Terrell and Krashen distinguished between those errors that hinder communication (*global*) and those that do not (*local*). They advised that, as long as the errors are not of the global type, students should not be directly corrected (Krashen and Terrell 1983:20). They provided specific guidelines on how to correct indirectly, that is, by the *expansion technique*, whereby the instructor includes the correct form in his/her response to the student's ungrammatical statement (Terrell et al. 1982). Teachers have readily adopted this technique because it is intuitively very appealing and seems to reflect the kind of interaction that would occur naturally outside the classroom.

Terrell's recommendations on error correction have had enormous impact on FL teachers because he seriously questioned what had long been an educational tradition. The behavioristic position maintained that errors had to be avoided because they provided negative feedback in the stimulus-response-reinforcement process. This theory of learning provided the psychological basis for the audiolingual method which enjoyed so much popularity all over the world. Ever since Corder (1967), however, many scholars have argued against rigorous, direct error correction since errors are now understood as evidence for the various stages in the process of acquiring a second language. These stages of gradual improvement toward the target language, which Selinker in 1972 called "interlanguages," have been the subject of numerous studies. Thus, Terrell was not the only one to question the whole issue of errors. In fact, there are fourteen other authors mentioned in Hendrickson's excellent 1978 review of error correction in the classroom.

Chastain (1988) states that more important than error-free speech is the creation of an atmosphere in which the students want to talk. Other teachers have expressed their concern much more strongly. Sutherland (1979), for example, regrets that some teachers, regarding themselves as "guardians of the linguistic norm," feel that their main reason for being in the classroom is to ensure correctness. Nevertheless, there is significant evidence to maintain that direct error correction does not promote linguistic accuracy, nor does a lack of error correction hinder the development of linguistic accuracy (Chun 1982; Kelly 1982; Day et al. 1984; VanPatten 1986). Terrell reinforced these ideas in his 1987 reply to Higgs and Clifford. However, there are studies indicating that some students want to have their oral mistakes corrected (Cathcart and Olsen 1976). Gainer says that "those of us who are attempting to learn a second language realize that, at times, a simple correction can help reformulate a rule in our minds and consequently help us speak more accurately" (Gainer 1989:47).

Part of the controversy is that, although there are numerous studies on error correction in the classroom (Holley and King 1971; Allwright 1975; Fanselow 1977; Chaudron 1977), FL instructors apparently had not had very many specific guidelines on what to correct and how to correct. And this is another of Terrell's contributions to the teaching of foreign languages. He claimed that it is time to revise some basic educational views about error correction: (1) by listening to the message instead of looking for errors; (2) by making a distinction between global and local errors; and (3) by correcting global errors indirectly through expansion.

3. Comparing methodologies

We have been looking at various aspects of the impact of Tracy Terrell's work on methodology, and we have discussed the central issues that have been so widely debated. Another topic, however, frequently emerges in the literature, with skeptics demanding solid evidence that the Natural Approach is in fact a better method than established ones. Statements such as "Instructors ... can affirm that their students have made great gains ..." (Terrell 1987:2) and "Informal evidence from students who have successfully completed NA courses suggests that ..." (Terrell 1987:14) are viewed as "anecdotal evidence" and tend to raise eyebrows among those who would like to see control-group studies where researchers bring hard and conclusive data to support the claims made (Richards 1985). The assumption here, however, is that such a conclusive study is possible. The literature contains many attempts to prove the superiority of one method over another, but the results have invariably been doubtful and inconclusive (Chastain 1969; Otto 1969; Smith 1970; Hauptman 1971; Mueller 1971; St. Pierre 1979; Mayer 1985; Shaffer 1989). Hosenfeld attributes these results simply to poor research procedures. She specifically observes that "a review of current research in FL education reveals a plethora of studies marred by inadequate problem development, lack of control of extraneous variables, invalid criterion measures, and inappropriate statistical techniques" (1979).

Politzer (1970), in an effort to obtain better results, tried to reduce the scope of the material under scrutiny. He concentrated on the techniques used by the teachers in the classroom and found that it is still very difficult to talk in absolute terms due to the large number of variables involved and the high complexity of the teaching process. Long (1980) pointed out that the problem with the early studies was that they typically evaluated students before and/or after having instruction with a given method. He called this approach "the black box" syndrome; that is, the investigator treated the classroom as an impenetrable black box and studied only what went into and came out of the classroom. Long maintains that a better way to understand teaching and learning is to get inside the black box (the classroom), and describe what goes on there. This relatively new and rapidly growing field of inquiry—classroom oriented research—is opening vast horizons in the study of classroom interaction (Allwright 1975, 1983, 1988; Gaies 1983; Seliger and Long 1983; Chaudron 1988; Ellis 1988; Van Lier 1988; Peck 1988).

In summary, it is virtually impossible to identify successful foreign language acquisition in the classroom by comparing only teaching methods, since method, per se, is only a small part of a large jigsaw puzzle. To satisfy those who ask for empirically validated proof that Terrell's NA is an effective method would require evaluating the NA in action, that is, a close examination of a language program using the NA. This task would involve looking not only at the method, but also the way it is implemented, including teacher training, students' acquisition processes, and classroom interactions. Furthermore, such a highly complex study would presuppose that there are valid and reliable ways to measure all of those factors.

3 DISCUSSION

The debate that Terrell's Natural Approach has produced in the FL teaching community in the United States was foreshadowed by what occurred in the teaching of English to speakers of other languages (TESOL). There are many comprehensive reviews of this evolution (Roberts 1982a, 1982b; Stern 1983; Howatt 1984; Breen 1987a, 1987b; Alexander 1990). Here I merely wish to look at some central points to justify the statement above. Some twenty years ago, scholars concerned with the teaching of English as a Foreign Language (EFL) reached the conclusion that language teaching should move away from the teaching of sentences as self-contained grammatical units; there was plenty of evidence that a knowledge of how the language functions in communication does not automatically follow from a knowledge of sentences (Widdowson 1972; Wilkins 1972; Brumfit and Johnson 1979; Savignon 1983).

Working with the Council of Europe, Wilkins and his colleagues pointed out the strong structural base of almost every EFL approach up to the late 1960s. They proposed a syllabus which would be constructed on neither grammatical patterns nor frequently encountered social situations, but would rather emphasize the communicative functions of the language (Wilkins 1972, 1976). The idea was that students would be taught how to do things with words (Austin 1962). Following the publication of specific guidelines for the preparation of materials along these lines (Van Ek 1975), there was a proliferation of technical literature on communicative course design and EFL methodology; there were also many new EFL textbooks published.

The swing of the pendulum then went to the other extreme: from textbooks built exclusively around grammar (Hornby 1954; Alexander 1967; O'Neill et al. 1971) to textbooks with no grammar at all (Abbs and Freebairn 1975; O'Neill and Snow 1976; Jones 1977; Castro and Kimbrough 1979). It soon became clear, however, that grammar could not be totally ignored and that a list of communicative functions is no more communicative than a list of grammatical items. In subsequent generations of ESL/EFL materials, writers gradually began to establish a balance between the emphasis on grammatical accuracy and the stress on communicative fluency (Harmer and Surguine 1987; Bodman and McKoy 1988; Richards, Hull, and Proctor 1989; Ferreira 1989). I think it would be difficult to find an EFL textbook published in the last few years that does not reflect this balance.

Changes in foreign-language teaching in the United States apparently mirrors the above sequence of events for EFL. Until very recently, Spanish-language textbooks ignored the communicative movement and were almost totally structure based. As with the EFL books of the 1960s, the emphasis was on mastering the grammar of Spanish rather than providing the student with authentic discourse (Chastain 1987). In 1986 Terrell provided examples of exercises taken from current Spanish textbooks in which students were asked to practice unrealistic language exchanges or transform lists of unrelated sentences into the negative or the interrogative form. "That such nonsense appeared in textbooks in the 1920s or 1930s is lamentable; that it appears in one dated 1980 is inexcusable" (Terrell 1986b:200). Most recently he introduced a framework for describing methodological trends in current beginning-level Spanish texts for colleges and universities, where he showed a clear tendency to increase students interaction through more meaningful and more contextualized activities. Terrell concluded this study saying that while in 1985 it was difficult to find a communicative-oriented Spanish textbook, a teacher five years later had many fine books from which to choose (Terrell 1990).

In the materials accompanying the first edition of *Dos mundos*, Terrell and his colleagues told teachers not to emphasize grammar unduly but to concentrate on communicative activities. The flurry of criticism that this view generated was not ignored, judging by the more explicit grammar explanations that were included in the second edition of *Dos mundos* (1990). Terrell in fact went on to write about *explicit grammar instruction* (1991), and there is now EGI in all the language texts which he coauthored, in the form of clearer grammar explanations, more grammar exercises, and a spiral approach to grammar topics. The swing of the pendulum, which at its most extreme has gone from no communicative teaching to no grammar teaching, will eventually stop in the middle when, just as in the EFL/ESL experience, leaders in FL methodology and textbook writers find a compromise between accuracy and fluency in the classroom. This phenomenon is already beginning to take place. In his analysis of twenty-one currently used Level 1 Spanish textbooks, Terrell reported that the pedagogical orientation of the average text is about one-third communicative and two-thirds grammatical. He also found that "no one advocates the use of communicative activities to the complete exclusion of all grammar-focused exercises" (Terrell 1990:207).

With the exception of the work of Savignon, who in the early 1970s was already proposing a more communicative methodology for the teaching of foreign languages (Savignon 1971, 1972a, 1972b, 1983, 1990), the foreign language profession in the United States has lagged behind EFL; materials and classroom practices have not kept up with trends in research and methodology. It would not be an exaggeration to say that there has been a delay of about a decade between developments in the teaching of English to speakers of other languages and those in foreign language teaching in the United States. We can find evidence for this if we compare the pedagogical orientation of the articles published in *Modern Language Journal* with those in *TESOL Quarterly* in the same year. In 1977 Terrell first suggested in *Modern Language Journal* a departure from grammatical accuracy and a move toward communicative fluency. In that same year *TESOL Quarterly* included an article that already questioned the communicative syllabus and suggested a trend toward the delicate balance between accuracy and fluency (Stratton 1977).

I believe that the reasons for this delay can be found in the fact that most departments of foreign languages in the United States are concerned primarily with literature and not with the teaching of the language itself (Stern 1981; Di Pietro, Lantolf, and Labarca 1983). Evidence for this situation can be found in a report on a decade of research on foreign-language teacher education which revealed that only seventy-eight articles were published on this topic in the United States between 1977 and 1987 (Bernhard and Hammadou 1987).

FL instruction in universities and colleges is often relegated to the junior faculty and to graduate students, but those junior faculty members are hired for the research they have done in literature or theoretical linguistics. This can lead to the kind of situation where a newly appointed assistant professor, hired for her expertise in the dialectology of an obscure village, finds herself assigned as supervisor of all the teaching assistants and director of elementary language courses—despite the fact that her only training as a teacher was when she was a TA herself or, perhaps, only an observer of someone similarly trained. Unfortunately, even in academia the myth still remains that if a person can speak the language, she can teach it (Altman 1979; Di Pietro 1983; Rivers 1983; Chastain 1986; Bernhard and Hammadou 1987).

Advancement and tenure in some of these departments are based largely on how much prestigious academic research the aspirant has been able to publish. Teaching ability, research, and publishing on teaching methodologies are in many cases considered second-class activities and gain the investigator little or no credit from colleagues or from the members of the promotion and tenure committees.

> Faculty members deeply committed to literary scholarship may find pedagogical research and publication somewhat different from that of the writing to which they have long been accustomed, and they may feel uncomfortable judging the quality and quantity of work outside their own area of expertise. In fact, such procedures may lead to questions in the mind of the candidate regarding the validity of the tenure decision. (Chastain 1986:175)

The long-term result of this emphasis on literary scholarship is triply negative for language learning: little new is developed in methodology; those who plan to teach the language learn only out-of-date techniques; and those who want to learn the language are inadequately served (Alatis, Stern, and Strevens 1983). It also has another and less obvious negative consequence. We have seen that, with a few exceptions, most FL classroom activities have not kept up with modern trends in pedagogy. Students, however, are well acquainted with more effective ways of delivering information and better ways of internalizing new knowledge. Subconsciously or not, they have recognized the absence of these features in the FL classes. As a result, foreign languages have failed to capture the interest of the students. This can be seen in the continuous reduction in the number of both classes and languages currently being offered in high schools and universities.

One would assume that students usually study a foreign language in order to speak and to understand speakers of that language. However, a study revealed that 87% of first-year students taking a foreign language at one university did so primarily to satisfy a requirement (Thogmartin 1971). Another report shows that well over 50% of those students who began FL study at the college level did not continue into the second year of such study (Benseler and Schultz 1980). Brewer argues that successful FL acquisition is embarrassingly rare; indeed, he states that many students have acquired foreign languages in spite of being taught them. He claims that the FL requirement of universities in the United States means that most learners are in the foreign-language classroom only because they have to be. And he observes that, what is worse, the initial experience with the language fails to create the motivation to continue beyond the bare requirements (Brewer 1988).

Fully aware of this crisis, Chastain reflects on the need to re-examine teachers' familiarity with the current state of the art in second-language learning and teaching and to evaluate their commitment to the profession and to the students as evidenced by teachers' knowledge and attitudes:

> Staying abreast of emerging ideas stimulates us and encourages us to try new approaches in our classes. Without new ideas we tend to become listless and unenthusiastic, and we become less and less receptive to experimentation and change. Long-held traditions and long-practiced techniques often move subconsciously and imperceptibly from subjective opinion to unchallenged assumptions. As one writer has said, the greatest obstacle to change is not ignorance but the illusion of knowledge. (Chastain 1986:173)

In this context Tracy Terrell's work acquires an even more powerful dimension. By basing foreign-language teaching methodology on research on second-language acquisition, he contributed to the raising of the field of applied linguistics to the level of an academic specialty in the eyes of the literature-oriented members of many FL departments. It is to be hoped that foreign language teaching will continue to follow the path that EFL/ESL methodology has pioneered and that more research on the subject will be forthcoming from the FL departments of our universities.

4 CONCLUSION

The popularity of Terrell's Natural Approach in foreign language teaching has grown substantially in the last few years. The reasons for this are many. Terrell's principles have made teachers re-examine practices that, through a long-unquestioned tradition, had reached the status of dogma. Young teachers welcome the challenge and the opportunity to teach a foreign language in ways that are very different from the traditional methods they experienced. Terrell succinctly put together in the NA a curriculum that is comprehensive and addresses the current issues and practices of the communicative movement. He developed communicative activities that are not centered on the mere manipulation of a language's grammatical system. Furthermore, he revised some basic educational views about error correction by providing more specific guidelines on what to correct and how to correct. Fully aware of the "humanistic" movement, Terrell contributed to the creation of a non-threatening atmosphere in the classroom by encouraging teachers to promote a sense of cooperation. As a result, teachers and students are discovering that it is possible to make progress while having fun in the classroom. Finally, by linking foreign-language teaching methodology with language-acquisition research, Terrell's work lent new respectability to applied linguistics as a legitimate field within university departments of foreign languages.

A successful FL class can be said to be one that produces students able to use the new language effectively. If this happens, they will retain interest and continue to progress. At the same time, the Natural Approach makes the process enjoyable for both teachers and students. It promotes all this at the elementary level and has profound implications for intermediate-level teaching as well.

Notes

1. Terrell's coauthors on *Dos mundos* were Magdalena Andrade, Jeanne Egasse, and Miguel Muñoz, all of whom worked with him as graduate students at the University of California, Irvine, in the mid-1970s. Their account of the genesis of the Natural Approach and *Dos mundos* is included in this volume in "Two Mad, Mad, Mad Worlds." The second edition of the text appeared in 1990 and the third in 1994; each subsequent edition has included additional communicative activities as well as more extensive grammar explanations and exercises.

2. The latter two texts built on the success of the initial Spanish book. The first edition of *Deux mondes* was published in 1988 and the second appeared in 1993, with Terrell joined by coauthors Mary Rogers, Betsy Barnes, and Marguerite Wolff-Hessini. *Kontakte* was the third Natural Approach text developed by Terrell, with coauthors Erwin Tschirner, Brigitte Nikolai, and Herbert Genzmer; it appeared in 1988, with the second edition in 1992. All three books are published by McGraw-Hill. A new Natural Approach text for high school Spanish, *¡Bravo!*, was developed by Terrell and published in 1994 by McGraw-Hill and McDougal, Littell.

References

Abbs, Bryan, and Ingrid Freebairn. 1975. *Strategies.* London: Longman.

Alatis, James, ed. 1990. *Linguistics, Language Teaching and Language Acquisition: The Interdependence of Theory, Practice and Research.* Washington, D.C.: Georgetown University Press.

Alatis, James, H. Altman, and Penelope Alatis, eds. 1981. *The Second Language Classroom.* New York: Oxford University Press.

Alatis, James, H. H. Stern, and Peter Strevens, eds. 1983. *Applied Linguistics and the Preparation of L2 Teachers: Toward a Rationale.* Washington, D.C.: Georgetown University Press.

Albrechtsen, D., B. Henriksen, and C. Faerch. 1980. Native Speaker Reactions to Learners' Spoken Interlanguage. *Language Learning* 30:365-96.

Alexander, Louis. 1967. *First Things First.* London: Longman.

Alexander, Louis. 1990. Fads and Fashions in English Language Teaching. *English Today* 6:35-56.

Allwright, Richard. 1975. Problems in the Study of Teachers' Treatment of Learner Errors. In *New Directions in Second Language Learning, Teaching, and Bilingual Education*, ed. Marina Burt and Heidi Dulay, 127–38. Washington, D.C.: TESOL.

———. 1983. Classroom-Centered Research on Language Teaching and Learning: A Brief Historical Review. *TESOL Quarterly* 17:191–204.

———. 1988. *Observations in the Language Classroom*. London: Longman.

Alter, Maria P. 1989. A Review of *Kontakte*. *Modern Language Journal* 73:92–4.

Asher, James. 1965. The Strategy of the Total Physical Response: An Application to Learning Russian. *International Review of Applied Linguistics* 3:291–300.

———. 1966. The Learning Strategy of the Total Physical Response. *Modern Language Journal* 50:79–84.

———. 1979. *Learning Another Language Through Actions: The Complete Teachers' Guide*. Los Gatos, Calif.: Sky Oaks Productions.

Austin, John. 1962. *How to Do Things with Words*. Oxford: Oxford University Press.

Balcom, Patricia. 1985. Should We Teach Grammar? Another Look at Krashen's Monitor Model. *Bulletin of the Canadian Association of Applied Linguistics CAAL* 7:37–45.

Baltra, Armando. 1987. Communicative Software and Cooperative Learning. *MUESLI* 3:12–5.

———. 1988. On Learning How to Learn. *C.A.L.L. Digest. Computers and Language Learning* 4:3–4.

———. 1990. Language Learning Through Computer Adventure Games. *Simulation and Gaming. ISAGA* 21:443–50.

Barrutia, Richard. 1977. Metodo Nuevo?—Pues Natural. *Hispania* 60: 498–9.

Bassano, Sharon, and Mary Ann Christison. 1987. Developing Successful Conversation Groups. In *Methodology in TESOL*, ed. Michael Long and Jack Richards, 210–18. Rowley, Mass.: Newbury House.

———. 1982. *Purple Cows and Potato Chips*. Englewood Cliffs, N.J.: Alemany Press.

Benseler, David, and Renate A. Schultz. 1980. Methodological Trends in College Foreign Language Instruction. *Modern Language Journal* 64:88–96.

Bernhard, Elizabeth and Joann Hammadou. 1987. A Decade of Research in Foreign Language Teacher Education. *Modern Language Journal* 71:89–299.

Blair, Robert. Innovative Approaches. In *Teaching English as a Second or Foreign Language*, ed. Marianne Celce-Murcia . Boston, Mass.: Heinle and Heinle.

Blair, Robert W, ed. 1982. *Innovative Approaches to Language Teaching*. Rowley, Mass.: Newbury House.

Bodman, Jean, and Judith McKoy. 1988. *Spaghetti Again*. New York: Macmillan Publishers.

Breen, Michael. 1987a. Contemporary Paradigms in Syllabus Design. Part 1 *Language Teaching* 20:81–92

———. 1987b. Contemporary Paradigms in Syllabus Design. Part 2 *Language Teaching* 20:157–74.

Brewer, William Benjamin. 1988. Are Foreign Language Requirements Defensible in the Light of Recent Findings in SLA? *Hispania* 71:155–9.

Brodkey, D., and H. Shore. 1976. Student Personality and Success in an English Language Program. *Language Learning* 26:153–9.

Brown, H. Douglas. 1980–87. *Principles of Language Learning and Teaching*. 2nd ed. Englewood Cliffs, N.J.: Prentice Hall.

Brown, H. Douglas, Carlos Yorio, and Ruth Crymes, eds. 1977.*On TESOL '77*. Washington, D.C.: TESOL.

Brown, Marvin J., and Adrian Palmer. 1988. *The Listening Approach. Methods and Materials for Applying Krashen's Input Hypothesis*. New York: Longman.

Brumfit, Christopher J., and Keith Johnson, eds. 1979. *The Communicative Approach to Language Teaching*. London: Oxford University Press.

Burt, Marina K. 1975. Error Analysis in the Adult EFL Classroom. *TESOL Quarterly* 9:53–64.

Burt, Marina, and Heidi Dulay, eds. 1975. *New Directions in Second Language Learning, Teaching, and Bilingual Education*. Washington, D.C.: TESOL.

Burt, Marina, and Heidi Dulay. 1981. Optimal Language Learning Environments. In *The Second Language Classroom*, ed. J. Alatis, H. Altman, and P. Alatis. New York: Oxford University Press, 177–92.

Byrne, Donn. 1976. *Teaching Oral English*. London: Longman.

Carroll, John. 1963. The Prediction of Success in Intensive Foreign Language Training. In *Training, Research and Education*, ed. R. Glaser. Pittsburgh, Penn.: University of Pittsburgh Press.

Castro, Oscar, and Victoria Kimbrough. 1979. *In Touch*. New York: Longman.

Celce-Murcia, Marianne. 1985. Making Informed Decisions About the Role of Grammar in Language Teaching. *Foreign Language Annals* 18:297–301.

Celce-Murcia, Marianne, ed. 1991. *Teaching English as a Second/Foreign Language*. 2nd ed. Rowley, Mass.: Newbury House.

Celce-Murcia, Marianne, and Lois McIntosh, eds. 1979. *Teaching English as a Second or Foreign Language*. Rowley, Mass.: Newbury House.

Celce-Murcia, Marianne, and Sharon Hilles. 1988. *Techniques and Resources in Teaching Grammar*. Oxford University Press.

Chastain, Kenneth. 1969. The Audio-Lingual Habit Theory vs the Cognitive-Code Learning Theory: Some Theoretical Considerations. *IRAL* 7:34–38.

———. 1975. Affective and Ability Factors in Second Language Learning. *Language Learning* 25:153–61.

———. 1980. Native Speaker Reaction to Instructor-Identified Student Second Language Errors. *Modern Language Journal* 64:210–15.

———. 1986. On Methods, Theory, and Practice: Response to Ms. Losiewicz. *Hispania* 69:173–5.

———. 1988. *Developing Second-Language Skills: Theory and Practice*. 3rd ed. Harcourt Brace Jovanovich.

Chaudron, Craig. 1977. Teachers' Priorities in Correcting Learners; Errors in French Immersion Classes. *Working Papers on Bilingualism* 12: 21–33.

Chaudron, Craig. 1988. *Second Language Classroom Research on Teaching and Learning*. Cambridge: Cambridge University Press.

Christensen, Clay B. 1975. Affective Learning Activities. *Foreign Language Annals* 8:211–219.

———. 1977. *Explorando: Affective Learning Activities for Intermediate Practice in Spanish*. Englewood Cliffs, N.J.: Prentice Hall.

Christison, Mary Ann, and Sharon Bassano. 1981. *Look Who's Talking*. Englewood Cliffs, N.J.: Alemany Press.

Chun, Ann E., Richard R. Day, A. Chenoweth, and S. Luppescu. 1982. Types of Errors Corrected in Native-Nonnative Conversations. *TESOL Quarterly* 16:537–548.

Cross, David. 1985. The Monitor Theory and the Language Teacher. *British Journal of Language Teaching* 23:75–78

Conway, Diana. 1986. Theme Courses for Community Colleges. *Hispania* 69:409–12.

Coopersmith, Stanley. 1967. *The Antecedents of Self-Esteem*. San Francisco: W.H. Freeman.

Curran, Charles A. 1972. *Counseling-Learning: A Whole-Person Model for Education*. New York: Grune and Stratton.

Daniels, Henry. 1986. Playing It by Ear: Things That Happen Inside a Silent Period. *System* 14:47–57.

Day, Richard, Ann Chenoweth, Ann Chun, and Stuart Luppescu. 1984. Corrective Feedback in Native-Nonnative Discourse. *Language Learning* 34: 19–45.

Di Pietro, Robert. 1983. Real Life in the Preparation of Language Teachers. In *Applied Linguistics and the Preparation of L2 Teachers: Toward a Rationale*, ed. J. Alatis, H. H. Stern, and P. Strevens, 124–33. Washington: Georgetown University Press.

Di Pietro, Robert, James Lantolf, and A. Labarca. 1983. The Graduate Foreign Language Curriculum. *Modern Language Journal* 67:366–73.

Ellis, Rod. 1986. *Understanding Second Language Acquisition*. New York: Oxford University Press.

———. 1988. *Classroom Second Language Development*. Englewood Cliffs, N.J.: Prentice-Hall Regents.

Ensz, Kathleen. 1982. French Attitudes Toward Speech Errors. *Modern Language Journal* 66:133–39.

Ervin, G. 1977. A Study of the Use and Acceptability of Target-Language Communication Strategies Employed by American Students of Russian. Ph.D. dissertation, The Ohio State University.

Ervin-Tripp, Susan. 1974. Is Second Language Learning Like the First? *TESOL Quarterly* 8:111–27.

Fanselow, John. 1977. The Treatment of Error in Oral Work. *Foreign Language Annals* 10:583–93.

Ferreira, Linda. 1989. *Express English*. Rowley, Mass.: Newbury House.

Finnemann, Michael. 1989. A Review of Terrell et al., *Dos Mundos. Modern Language Journal* 73:106.

Gainer, Glenn. 1989. Clozing in on Oral Errors. *ELTJ* 43:45–9.

Gaies, Stephen. 1983. The Investigation of Language Classroom Processes. *TESOL Quarterly* 17:205–18.

Galloway, Vicki. 1980. Perceptions of the Communicative Efforts of American Students of Spanish. *Modern Language Journal* 64:428–33.

Gardner, R., and W. Lambert. 1972. *Attitudes and Motivation in Second Language Learning*. Rowley, Mass.: Newbury House.

Gardner, R., P. Smythe, R. Clement, and L. Gliksman. 1976. Second Language Learning: A Social-Psychological Perspective. *Canadian Modern Language Review* 32:198–213.

Gary, John. 1975. Delayed Oral Practice in Initial Stages of Second Language Learning. In Burt and Dulay, eds., 89–95.

Gattegno, Caleb. 1963. *Teaching Foreign Languages in Schools: The Silent Way*. New York: Educational Solutions.

———. 1976. *The Common Sense of Teaching Foreign Languages*. New York: Educational Solutions.

Gibbons, John. 1985. The Silent Period: An Examination. *Language Learning* 35:255–67.

Glaser, R, ed. 1963. *Training, Research and Education*. Pittsburgh, Penn.: University of Pittsburgh Press.

Goldin, Mark. 1977. Who Wouldn't Want to Use The Natural Approach? *Modern Language Journal* 61:337–9.

Gregg, Kevin. 1984. Krashen's Monitor and Occam's Razor. *Applied Linguistics* 5:79–100.

Guntermann, Gail. 1978. A Study of the Frequency and Communicative Effect of Errors in Spanish. *Modern Language Journal* 62:249–53.

Gynan, Shaw. 1984. Attitudes Toward Interlanguages: What Is the Object of Study? *Modern Language Journal* 68:315–21.

Hakuta, Kenji. 1974. Prefabricated Patterns and the Emergence of Structures in Second Language Acquisition. *Language Learning* 24:287–98.

Hammond, Robert. 1988. Accuracy versus Communicative Competency. *Hispania* 71:408–17.

Hanzeli, Victor, and William Love. 1972. From Individualized Instruction to Individualized Learning. *Foreign Language Annals* 5:321–30.

Harmer, Jeremy, and Harold Surguine. 1987. *Coast to Coast*. London: Longman.

Hauptman, P. 1971. A Structural Approach versus a Situational Approach to Foreign Language Teaching. *Language Learning* 21:235–244.

Hendrickson, James M. 1978. Error Correction in Foreign Language Teaching. *Modern Language Journal* 67:41–45.

Heyde, A. 1977. The Relationship Between Self-Esteem and the Oral Production of a L2. In Brown, Yorio, and Crymes, eds., 226–40.

Higgs, Theodore, and Ray Clifford. 1982. The Push Toward Communication. In *Curriculum, Competence and the Foreign Language Teacher*, 57–80. Lincolnwood, Ill.: National Textbook Co.

Hornby, A. S. 1954. *Oxford Progressive English for Adults*. London: Oxford University Press.

Hosenfeld, Carol. 1979. A Learning-Teaching View of Second Language Instruction. *Foreign Language Annals* 12:51–4.

Howatt, Anthony P. R. 1984. *A History of English Language Teaching*. London: Oxford University Press.

Huang, J., and Evelyn Hatch. 1978. A Chinese Child's Acquisition of English. In *Second Language Acquisition: A Book of Readings*, ed. Evelyn Hatch, 118–31. Rowley, Mass.: Newbury House.

James, Carl. 1983. Two Stage Approach to Language Teaching. In *Perspectives in Communicative Language Teaching*, ed. K. Johnson and D. Porter, 109–117. New York: Academic Press.

Jappinen, Ilona. 1986. A Natural Approach to Teaching the German Subjunctive. *Unterrichtspraxis* 19:84–94.

Jenkinson, M. D. 1969. Sources of Knowledge for Theories of Reading. *Journal of Reading Behavior* 1:11–29.

Johnson, D.W., R. Johnson, E.J. Holubec, and P. Roy. 1984. *Circles of Learning: Cooperation in the Classroom*. Association for Supervision and Curriculum Development.

Joiner, Elizabeth. 1989. A Review of Terrell et al., *Deux Mondes*. *Modern Language Journal* 73:364–6.

Jones, Leo. 1977. *Functions of English*. Cambridge: Cambridge University Press.

Kagan, Spencer. 1985. *Cooperative Learning. Resources for Teachers*. 27402 Camino Capistrano, Suite 201, Laguna Niguel, CA 92691.

Kelly, Kathryn. 1982. An Error Analysis of the Spoken Spanish of Twelve American College Students. Manuscript, University of California, Irvine.

Klippel, Friederike. 1984. *Keep Talking. Communicative Fluency Activities for Language Teaching*. Cambridge: Cambridge University Press.

Krahnke, Karl J. 1985. A Review of Krashen and Terrell, *The Natural Approach: Language Acquisition in the Classroom*. *TESOL Quarterly* 19:591–604.

Krashen, Stephen. 1981. *Second Language Acquisition and Second Language Learning*. Englewood Cliffs, N.J.: Alemany Press.

———. 1982. *Principles and Practices in Second Language Acquisition*. Englewood Cliffs, N.J.: Alemany Press.

———. 1985. *The Input Hypothesis*. New York: Longman.

Krashen, Stephen, and Tracy Terrell. 1983. *The Natural Approach: Language Acquisition in the Classroom*. Englewood Cliffs, N.J.: Alemany Press.

Lado, Robert. 1964. *Language Teaching. A Scientific Approach*. New York: McGraw-Hill.

Lafayette, Robert C., and Lorraine A. Strasheim. 1984. The Standard Sequence and the Non-Traditional Methodologies. *Foreign Language Annals* 17: 567–74.

Lafford, Barbara. 1987. Providing Comprehensible Input for Advanced Conversation Classes in University Settings. *Italica* 64:278–97.

Larsen-Freeman, Diane. 1986. *Techniques and Principles in Language Teaching*. New York: Oxford University Press.

Littlewood, William. 1984. *Foreign and Second Language Learning*. Cambridge: Cambridge University Press.

Long, Michael H. 1980. Inside the "Black Box": Methodological Issues in Classroom Research on Language Learning. *Language Learning* 30:1–42.

Long, Michael H., and Jack Richards, eds. 1987. *Methodology in TESOL. A Book of Readings*. Rowley, Mass.: Newbury House.

Lozanov, Georgi. 1987. *Suggestology and Outlines of Suggestopedy*. New York: Gordon and Breach.

Ludwig, Jeannette. 1982. Native Speaker Judgement of Second Language Learners' Efforts at Communication: A Review. *Modern Language Journal* 66:274–83.

Magrath, Douglas R. 1987. A Topical Interactive Approach to Arabic. ERIC doc. ED296597 (ERIC Document Reproduction Service).

Marino, E., M. Martini, C. Raley, and T. Terrell. 1984. *A Rainbow Collection: A Natural Approach to Teaching ESL*. Los Angeles: Santillana.

Mayer, Robert. 1985. Use of the Natural Approach in a Beginning-Level EFL Class in Barcelona, Spain. ERIC doc. ED306769

Mazur, Gertrude, ed. 1979. *Proceedings of the Pacific Northwest Council on Foreign Languages*. Portland, Ore.: Portland State University Press. Volume XXX, Part 2.

McLaughlin, Barry. 1978. The Monitor Model: Some Methodological Considerations. *Language Learning* 28:309–32.

———. 1987. *Theories of Second Language Learning*. London: Edward Arnold.

Meyer, Renne, and Emery Tetrault. 1984. The Joy of Text: A Comprehension Approach to Intermediate Russian. *Russian Language Journal* 38: 39–50

Moskowitz, Gertrude. 1979. *Caring and Sharing in the Foreign Language Class*. Rowley, Mass.: Newbury House.

Mowry, Robert. 1989. A Semester's Flirtation with the Input Hypothesis. *Hispania* 72:439–43.

Mueller, Theodore. 1971. The Effectiveness of Two Learning Models: The Audiolingual Theory and the Cognitive Code Learning. In *The Psychology of Second Language Learning*, ed. Paul Pimsleur and Terence Quinn, 113–22. Cambridge: Cambridge University Press.

Munsell, Paul, and Thomas Carr. 1981. Monitoring the Monitor: A Review of Stephen Krashen's Second Language Acquisition and Second Language Learning. *Language Learning* 31:493–502.

Nunan, David. 1989. *Designing Tasks for the Communicative Classroom*. Cambridge: Cambridge University Press.

O'Neill, T., and P. Snow. 1976. *Crescent English Course*. London: Oxford University Press.

Oller, John, and Patricia Richard-Amato, eds. 1983. *Methods That Work*. Rowley, Mass.: Newbury House.

Olsen, Judy Winn-Bell. 1977. *Communication Starters and Other Activities for the ESL Classroom*. Englewood Cliffs, N.J.: Alemany Press.

Omaggio, Alice C. 1984. The Proficiency-Oriented Classroom. In *Teaching for Proficiency: The Organizing Principle*, ed. Theodore Higgs, 43–84. Lincolnwood, Ill.: National Textbook Co.

Omaggio, Alice C. 1986. *Teaching Language in Context: Proficiency-Oriented Instruction.* Boston, Mass.: Heinle and Heinle. (2nd ed. 1993)

O'Neill, Robert, Roy Kingsbury, and Angela Yeadon. 1971. *Kernel Lessons— Intermediate.* London: Longman.

Otto, Frank. 1969. The Teacher in the Pennsylvania Project. *Modern Language Journal* 53:411–420.

Peck, Anthony. 1988. *Language Teachers at Work.* Englewood Cliffs, N.J.: Prentice-Hall.

Pimsleur, Paul, and Terence Quinn, eds. 1971. *The Psychology of Second Language Learning.* Cambridge: Cambridge University Press.

Postovsky, Valerian. 1974. Effects of Delay in Oral Practice at the Beginning of Second Language Learning. *Modern Language Journal* 58:229–39.

Richard-Amato, P. 1988. *Making it Happen: Interaction in the Second Language Classroom.* New York: Longman.

Richards, Jack. 1985. *The Context of Language Teaching.* Cambridge: Cambridge University Press.

Richards, Jack, and Theodore Rogers. 1986. *Approaches and Methods in Language Teaching.* Cambridge: Cambridge University Press.

Richards, Jack, Jonathan Hull, and Susan Proctor. 1989. *Interchange.* Cambridge: Cambridge UP.

Rivers, Wilga M. 1981. *Teaching Foreign Language Skills.* 2nd ed. Chicago: The University of Chicago Press.

———. 1983. Preparing College and University Instructors for a Lifetime of Teaching: A Luxury or a Necessity?. *ADFL Bulletin* 10:17–24.

Roberts, J. T. 1982a. Recent Developments in ELT. Part I. *Language Teaching* 15:94–110.

———. 1982b. Recent Developments in ELT. Part II. *Language Teaching* 15:174–94.

Rosales, Elsa. 1986. The Natural Approach. Video portion of master's thesis, Department of Spanish and Portuguese, University of California, Irvine.

St. Pierre, R.G. 1979. The Role of Multiple Analyses in Quasi-Experimental Evaluations. *Educational Evaluation and Policy Analysis* 1:5–10.

Savignon, Sandra. 1971. A Study of the Effect of Training in Communicative Skills as Part of a Beginning College French Course on Student Attitude and Achievement in Linguistic and Communicative Competence. Ph.D. dissertation, University of Illinois, Urbana-Champaign.

———. 1972a. Teaching for Communicative Competence: A Research Report. *Audio-Visual Language Journal* 10:153–62.

———. 1972b. *Communicative Competence: An Experiment in Foreign Language Teaching.* Philadelphia: Center for Curriculum Development.

———. 1981. A Letter to My Spanish Teacher. *Canadian Modern Language Review* 37:746–50.

———. 1983. *Communicative Competence: Theory and Classroom Practice.* Reading, Mass.: Addison-Wesley.

———. 1985. Evaluation of Communicative Competence: The ACTFL Provisional Proficiency Guidelines. *Canadian Modern Language Review* 41:100–7.

———. 1990. Communicative Language Teaching: Definitions and Directions. In *Linguistics, Language Teaching and Language Acquisition: The Interdependence of Theory, Practice and Research*, ed. J. Alatis, 1–11. Washington, D.C.: Georgetown University Press.

Schneider, Judith. 1989. The Apartment House: An Experiment in Simulation and the Natural Approach. Focussing on Cultural Competence. *Canadian Modern Language Review* 45:625–30.

Seliger, Herbert, and Michael Long, eds. 1983. *Classroom Oriented Research in Second Language Acquisition*. Rowley, Mass.: Newbury House.

Selinker, Larry. 1972. Interlanguage. *IRAL* 10:209–31.

Shaffer, Constance. 1989. A Comparison of Inductive and Deductive Approaches to Teaching Foreign Languages. *Modern Language Journal* 73:395–403.

Stern, H. H. 1981. Language Teaching and the Universities in the 1980s. *Canadian Modern Language Review* 37:212–25.

———. 1983. *Fundamental Concepts of Language Teaching*. Oxford: Oxford University Press.

Stevick, Earl W. 1976. *Memory, Meaning and Method*. Rowley, Mass.: Newbury House.

———. 1982. *Teaching and Learning Languages*. Cambridge: Cambridge University Press.

Stratton, Florence. 1977. Putting the Communicative Syllabus in Its Place. *TESOL Quarterly* 11:131–41.

Skinner, B.F. 1957. *Verbal Behavior*. Appleton-Century Crofts.

Smith, P.D., Jr. 1970. *A Comparison of the Cognitive and Audiolingual Approaches to Foreign Language Instruction*. Philadelphia: Center for Curriculum Development.

Sutherland, Kenneth. 1979. Accuracy vs. Fluency in the Second Language Classroom. *CATESOL Occasional Papers* 5:25–9.

Taylor, G. 1984. Empirical or Intuitive? *Language Learning* 34:97–105.

Terrell, Tracy. D. 1977. A Natural Approach to Second Language Acquisition and Learning. *Modern Language Journal* 61:325–336.

———. 1980. A Natural Approach to the Teaching of Verb Form and Function in Spanish. *Foreign Language Annals* 13:129–136.

———. 1982a. The Natural Approach to Language Teaching: An Update. *Modern Language Journal* 66:121–32. [reprinted in this volume]

———. 1982b. The Natural Approach in Bilingual Education. In *Schooling and Language Minority Students: A Theoretical Framework*, 117–46. Sacramento, Calif.: California Office of Bilingual Education.

———. 1982c. Teaching Comprehension Skills in the Natural Approach. *CATESOL Occasional Papers* 8:1–6.

———. 1986a. Acquisition in the Natural Approach: The Binding/Access Framework. *The Modern Language Journal* 70:213–227.

———. 1986b. Recent Trends in Research and Practice: Teaching Spanish. *Hispania* 69:193–202.

———. 1987. Avoiding Fossilization in Communicative Approaches. *Dialog on Language Instruction DLI* 4:1–35.

———. 1990. Trends in the Teaching of Grammar in Spanish Language Textbooks. *Hispania* 73:201–11.

———. 1991. The Role of Grammar Instruction in a Communicative Approach. *Modern Language Journal* 75:52–63.

Terrell, Tracy, Jeanne Egasse, and Wilfried Voge. 1982. Techniques for a More Natural Approach to Second Language Acquisition and Learning. In *Innovative Approaches to Language Teaching*, ed. Robert Blair, 174–75. Rowley, Mass.: Newbury House.

Terrell, Tracy, Madeline Ehrmann, and Martha Herzog. 1984. A Theoretical Basis for Teaching the Receptive Skills. *Foreign Language Annals* 17: 261–275.

Terrell, T., E. Tschirner, B. Nikolai, and H. Genzmer. 1992. *Kontakte: A Communicative Approach*. 2nd ed. New York: McGraw-Hill. (1st ed. 1988)

Terrell, T., M. Rogers, B. Barnes, and M. Wolff-Hessini. 1993. *Deux mondes: A Communicative Approach.* 2nd ed. New York: McGraw-Hill. (1st ed. 1988)

Terrell, T., M. Andrade, J. Egasse, and E.M. Muñoz. 1994. *Dos mundos.* 3rd ed. New York: McGraw-Hill. (1st ed. 1986; 2nd ed. 1990)

Teschner, Richard. 1986. Which Method and for How Long? *Hispania* 69:180–1.

Thogmartin, Clyde. 1971. A Survey of Attitudes Toward Foreign Language Education Among 247 First Year Language Students at Iowa State University. *ACTFL Bulletin* 3:39–45.

Ur, Penny. 1981. *Discussions That Work: Task-Centered Fluency Practice.* Cambridge: Cambridge University Press.

———. 1988. *Grammar Practice Activities: A Practical Guide for Teachers.* Cambridge: Cambridge University Press.

Van Ek, Jan. 1975. *The Threshold Level.* Council of Europe.

Van Lier, Leo. 1988. *The Classroom and the Language Learner: Ethnography and Second Language Classroom Research.* London: Longman.

VanPatten, Bill. 1986. Second Language Acquisition Research and the Learning/Teaching of Spanish: Some Research Findings and Implications. *Hispania* 69:202–16.

Voge, Wilfried. 1979. The Role of Listening Comprehension in L2 Acquisition. In *Proceedings of the Pacific Northwest Council on Foreign Languages*, Volume 30(2), ed. Gertrude Mazur, 23–34. Portland, Ore.: Portland State University Press.

Whitman, Charles. 1986. Using Natural Approach Teaching Techniques. *British Journal of Language Teaching* 24:87–91, 115.

Widdowson, Henry G. 1972. The Teaching of English as Communication. *English Language Teaching* 27:15–9.

Wilkins, D. 1972. Grammatical, Situational, and Notional Syllabuses. In *Proceedings of the Third Congress of Applied Linguistics*, 34–47. Heidelberg: Julius Groos Verlag.

———. 1976. *Notional Syllabuses: A Taxonomy and Its Relevance to Foreign Language Curriculum Development.* London: Oxford University Press.

Winitz, Harry, ed. 1981. *The Comprehension Approach to Foreign Language Instruction.* Rowley, Mass.: Newbury House.

Wolfe, David E., and Gwendolyn Jones. 1982. Total Physical Response Strategy in a Level 1 Spanish Class. *Foreign Language Annals* 14:273–80.

Worth, Frederick R. 1990. On Fixed and Fluid "Texts": The Singer of Tales and the Natural Approach of Tracy Terrell. *Hispania* 73:522–25.

The Natural Approach: How It Is Evolving

Patricia A. Richard-Amato
California State University, Los Angeles

This article, adapted from the second edition of the author's book, *Making It Happen*, focuses on the Natural Approach and its classroom usefulness. The four basic principles explicitly laid down by Krashen and Terrell in 1983 are examined: (1) comprehension precedes production, (2) production must be allowed to emerge in stages, (3) the course syllabus must be based on communicative goals, and (4) the activities and classroom environment must work together to produce lowered anxiety. Also discussed are the stages that language learners appear to go through when their second language is allowed to develop normally through the process of communication. Activities extending the Natural Approach are described at each level to promote language-rich environments and an integration of skills.

The essence of language is human activity: activity on the part of one individual to make himself understood, and activity on the part of the other to understand what was in the mind of the first.

O. Jespersen

 AN OVERVIEW

Tracy Terrell was careful to make no claim for the Natural Approach that other methods could not match if they relied on real communication as their modus operandi. Like Asher (1982), he reminded us that students must acquire the second language in much the same way that people acquire language in natural situations (therefore the term "*natural* approach"). Some argue that what was being recommended is not really a method at all but is, in a more general sense, an approach. However, Krashen and Terrell (1983) developed the Natural Approach as a method, and so, for the purposes of discussion, that is the way it will be presented here. They based their method on four principles.

The first principle states that *comprehension precedes production.* As in the total physical response, the teacher observes the need for a silent period. During this time, the teacher uses the target language predominantly, focuses on communicative situations, and provides comprehensible input which is roughly tuned to the students' proficiency levels. Second, *production must be allowed to emerge in stages.* Responses will generally begin with non-verbal communication, progress to single words, then to two- and three-word combinations, next to phrases and sentences, and finally to complete discourse. Students speak when they are ready, and speech errors are generally not corrected directly. However, a teacher focused on communication will give many indirect corrections as part of the natural process of checking for meaning. Thus, the student's interlanguage is allowed to develop normally as the student begins to incorporate such corrections into his or her own utterances. The third principle asserts that *the course syllabus be based on communicative goals.* Grammatical sequencing as a focus is shunned in favor of a topical/situational organization. Discussion centers on items in the classroom, body parts, favorite vacation spots, and other topics of interest. It is felt that the grammar will be acquired mainly through the relevant communication. Fourth, *the activities themselves must be planned so that they will lower the affective filter.* A student who is engrossed in interesting ideas will be less apt to have anxiety than one who is focused mainly on form. In addition, the atmosphere must be friendly and accepting if the student is to have the best possible chance for acquiring the target language.

Natural Approach "extensions" can be used in conjunction with many other methods and activities with which it is compatible (total physical response and the audio-motor unit, jazz chants, music, games, role play, storytelling, affective activities, and so forth). In fact, combining several of these methods and activities can produce extremely rich environments where concepts are reinforced through a variety of ways. The Natural Approach and all the methods with which it is used should blend to form a well-integrated program if it is to work. Although recycling is not emphasized in the Natural Approach literature, it is important that concepts be recycled in many different ways in order for them to be mastered.

Because the focus of the Natural Approach is on real communication, many demands are made upon the time and energy of the teacher. He or she must present a great deal of comprehensible input about concrete, relevant topics, especially at beginning levels. It is not unusual to see the Natural Approach language teacher trudging across campus with sacks filled with fruits to talk about and eat, dishes with which to set a table for an imaginary dinner, oversized clothes to put on over other clothes, and additional paraphernalia to demonstrate the notions involved. This teacher can no longer just ask students to open their books to a certain page, say "repeat after me," or assign the students to endless exercises in rule application. According to Krashen and Terrell, the teacher's chief responsibility during class hours is to communicate with the students about things that are of interest and relevance to them.

Even though other topics might be more appropriate depending upon the goals of the students, the following outline adapted from Krashen and Terrell (1983:67-70) may be useful in planning units for beginning to low intermediate students who appear to be mainly interested in improving personal communication skills.

Preliminary Unit: Learning to Understand

Topics

1. Names of students
2. Descriptions of people
3. Family members
4. Numbers
5. Clothing
6. Colors
7. Objects in the classroom
8. Parts of the body

Situations

1. Greetings
2. Classroom commands

Unit I. Students in the Classroom

Topics

1. Personal identification (name, address, telephone, age, sex, nationality, date of birth, marital status)
2. Description of school environment (identification, description, and location of people and objects in the classroom; description and location of buildings)
3. Classes
4. Telling Time

Situations

1. Filling out forms
2. Getting around the school

Unit II. Recreation and Leisure Activities

Topics

1. Favorite activities
2. Sports and games
3. Climate and seasons
4. Weather
5. Seasonal activities
6. Holiday activities
7. Parties
8. Abilities

Situations

1. Playing games, sports
2. Being a spectator
3. Chitchatting

Unit III. Family, Friends, and Daily Activities

Topics

1. Family and relatives
2. Physical states
3. Emotional states
4. Daily activities
5. Holiday and vacation activities
6. Pets

Situations
1. Introducing, meeting people
2. Visiting relatives
3. Conversing on the phone

Unit IV. Plans, Obligations, and Careers

Topics
1. Future plans
2. General future activities
3. Obligations
4. Hopes and desires
5. Careers and professions
6. Place of work
7. Work activities
8. Salary and money

Situations
1. Job interviewing
2. Talking on the job

Unit V. Residence

Topics
1. Place of residence
2. Rooms of a house
3. Furniture
4. Activities at home
5. Household items
6. Amenities

Situations
1. Looking for a place to live
2. Moving
3. Shopping for the home

Unit VI. Narrating Past Experiences

Topics
1. Immediate past events
2. Yesterday's activities
3. Weekend events
4. Holidays and parties
5. Trips and vacations
6. Other experiences

Situations
1. Friends recounting experiences
2. Making plans

Unit VII. Health, Illnesses, and Emergencies

Topics
1. More body parts
2. Physical states
3. Mental states and moods
4. Health maintenance
5. Health professions
6. Medicines and diseases

Situations

1. Visiting the doctor
2. Hospitals
3. Health interviews

4. Buying medicines
5. Emergencies (accidents)

Unit VIII. *Eating*

Topics

1. Foods
2. Beverages

Situations

1. Ordering a meal in a restaurant
2. Shopping in a supermarket
3. Preparing food from recipes

Unit IX. *Travel and Transportation*

Topics

1. Geography
2. Modes of transportation
3. Vacations

4. Experiences on trips
5. Languages
6. Making reservations

Situations

1. Buying gasoline
2. Exchanging money
3. Clearing customs

4. Obtaining lodging
5. Buying tickets

Unit X. *Shopping and Buying*

Topics

1. Money and prices
2. Fashions

3. Gifts
4. Products

Situations

1. Selling and buying
2. Shopping
3. Bargaining

Unit XI. *Youth*

Topics

1. Childhood experiences
2. Primary school experiences

3. Teen years experiences
4. Adult expectations and activities

Situations

1. Reminiscing with friends
2. Sharing photo albums
3. Looking at school yearbooks

Unit XII. *Giving Directions and Instructions*

Topics

1. Spatial concepts (north, south, east, west; up, down; right, left, center; parallel, perpendicular; etc.)
2. Time relationships (after, before, during, etc.)

Situations

1. Giving instructions
2. Following instructions
3. Reading maps
4. Finding locations
5. Following game instructions
6. Giving an invitation
7. Making appointments

Unit XIII. *Values*

Topics

1. Family
2. Friendship
3. Love
4. Marriage
5. Sex roles and stereotypes
6. Goals
7. Religious beliefs

Situations

1. Making a variety of decisions based on one's values
2. Sharing and comparing values in a non-threatening environment
3. Clarifying values

Unit XIV. *Issues and Current Events*

Topics

1. Environmental problems
2. Economic issues
3. Education
4. Employment and careers
5. Ethical issues
6. Politics
7. Crime
8. Sports
9. Social events
10. Cultural events
11. Minority groups
12. Science and health

Situations

1. Discussing last night's news broadcast
2. Discussing a recent movie, etc.

Students move through three basic, overlapping stages in the Natural Approach: (1) comprehension, (2) early speech production, and (3) speech emergence. Beyond speech emergence is a fourth stage later recognized by Terrell and others as *intermediate fluency*. According to Natural Approach advocates, the length of time spent in any one stage varies greatly depending upon the individual, upon the amount of comprehensible input received, and upon the degree to which the affective filter has been lowered. Some students begin speaking after just a couple of hours while others need several weeks. Children may need several months. The second stage, early speech production, may take anywhere from a few months to one year or longer. The third stage, speech emergence, can take up to three years but usually the student is reasonably fluent long before that if the input has been of high quality, if it was given in sufficient quantity, and if the student has been receptive to it. Generally the teacher does most of the talking to provide the needed comprehensible input. However, as the students become more proficient, they take over and the teacher's role becomes predominantly that of an organizer and a facilitator.

THE COMPREHENSION STAGE

During this first stage the students are allowed to go through a silent period. They receive comprehensible input usually from the teacher or, in some classrooms, from peer teachers and lay assistants. Often the total physical response or versions of it are used. Although the students' main goal is to develop listening skills, many of the activities overlap into the next higher level, early speech production. Simple responses to the comprehensible input may be made by gesturing, nodding, using the L1, answering yes or no, giving names of people or objects as answers to questions such as "Who has on a yellow dress?" (Kim) or "Do you want an apple or an orange?" (apple). A lot of visuals, explanations, and repetitions are used. The teacher's speech is a little slower than usual. The intonation is reasonably normal except that key words receive a bit of extra emphasis. Students are not called upon to respond individually. Instead, questions are directed to the whole group, and one or several can respond. Key terms can be written on the board, perhaps on the second or third time the students are exposed to them. If the student is exposed to written forms of the words too soon, he or she may experience a cognitive overloading which could interfere with acquisition.

Total physical response (TPR) activities may be used to get the students into some basic vocabulary. For example, students can acquire names ("Give the book to Hong"), descriptions ("Take the pencil to a person who has short hair"), numbers ("Pick up three pieces of chalk"), colors ("Find the blue book"), and many other concepts. Notice that aspects of the total physical response will be involved to some degree in almost every activity suggested for this level. From my experience with the Natural Approach, I found that at this stage it is important that new concepts be introduced gradually and that frequent checks for understanding be made before adding other new concepts. In the sample dialogue that follows, the teacher is teaching four colors (red, blue, green, yellow) and has a strip of construction paper for each color.

Notice that the language is very simple for beginners as they are first exposed to the relevant concepts. However, the language will quickly become much richer as the teacher begins to build on these concepts.

> **Teacher:** (*Holding up the red strip*) This is red. This is red. (*The teacher then points to a student's red sweater.*) Is this red? (*The teacher begins to nod her head, softly uttering:*) Yes.
> **Students:** (*Nodding their heads*) Yes.
> **Teacher:** (*Pointing to a student's red skirt*) Is this red?
> **Students:** (*Nodding their heads*) Yes.
> **Teacher:** (*Pointing to a green sweater*) Is this red? (*She begins to shake her head, softly uttering*) No.
> **Teacher:** Good. (*The teacher points to the red strip again.*) Is this red?
> **Students:** Yes.
> **Teacher:** Yes. This is red. (*Again points to the red strip*)
> **Teacher:** (*Holding the blue strip*) This is blue. This is blue. (*The teacher points to a student's blue scarf.*) Is this blue?
> **Students:** Yes.
> **Teacher:** (*Pointing to a blue door*) Is this blue?
> **Students:** Yes.
> **Teacher:** Good. Yes, this is blue. (*The teacher points to the red strip.*) Is this blue?
> **Students:** No.
> **Teacher:** No. (*Pointing to the blue strip*) This is blue and this (*pointing to the red strip*) is red.

And so the teacher continues, adding one color at a time while returning to check for understanding of the colors already introduced. After working through the four colors, the teacher then gives the strips to various students, with the following requests: "Give me the red one" (the teacher reaches for the red one), "Give me the blue one", and so on. The students may not understand all of the teacher's words at first, but chances are they will remember the key concepts that were emphasized and they probably will note (perhaps subconsciously at first) other elements (usually function words) in the utterances. Gradually they will begin to comprehend and then use the concepts in many different meaningful contexts.

It is important not to introduce too many new concepts at once; in addition, it is important to reinforce those introduced immediately. For example, the teacher may want the students to cut out of magazines objects of each of the four colors, paste those of the same color on a sheet of paper, and label the sheet with the name of the color. Or the teacher may ask the students to draw and color with crayons various objects in different colors. A day or so later the teacher may bring in pieces of clothing that are of the same colors taught to see if they are remembered. At that point, the pieces of clothing themselves may be the new concepts to which the students are introduced in a similar manner. One word of caution: the teacher should take care to use fairly normal intonation without using undue stress on key words. It is important that the teacher not be perceived as talking down to students.

Once the students can identify simple concepts, then the teacher can reinforce these and introduce some new ones by using a stream of comprehensible input: "Look at Maria's feet. She is wearing shoes. Look at Jorge's feet. He is wearing shoes, too. His shoes are brown. Look at his hair. His hair is brown. How many students have brown hair?" (nine) "What is the name of the student with red hair?" (Carolina) "Who is behind the person with the red shirt?" (Yung) "Does Yung have on a shirt or a sweater?" (sweater) "What color is the sweater?" (yellow) The teacher can carry on in this fashion about a wide variety of concrete subjects stimulated by a picture, an object, a map, and so on.

The following are additional sample activities, most of which are extensions of the Natural Approach.[1]

Where Does It Belong?
On a chalkboard, sketch and label the rooms of a house. Then briefly talk about the house and the various rooms in it. (*Look at the house. It is big. It has many rooms. Here is the kitchen. Food is kept in the kitchen. People eat in the kitchen.* and so forth.) A few typical household items including furniture can be roughly drawn in each of the rooms to help the students correctly identify them. Other household items can be cut from heavy paper, to be placed in the appropriate rooms. Pieces of scotch tape can be rolled up and placed on the backs of the pictures to make them stick to the chalkboard. (Later the tape can be removed for reuse of the pictures.) Commands such as "Put the stove in the kitchen" or "Put the dresser in the bedroom" can be given. An alternative might be to use a large dollhouse with miniature furniture for the same kind of activity. Items typical of other places can be incorporated in similar activities. Simulated settings such as zoos, farm yards, hospitals, libraries, various work sites, cafeterias, and university campuses can be the focus.

Put It On!
Bring in a variety of oversized clothes. Talk about the clothes. (*These are pants. They are blue. Here is the pocket. Point to the pocket.*) Have the students put the clothes on (over their own) according to the directions you give. The oversized clothes can be taken off using a similar procedure. A camera can come in handy for recording the highlights of this activity. The photos can be displayed in the classroom and used at a later stage to stimulate discussion. A follow-up might be to provide the students with clothing catalogs, scissors, paste, and blank sheets of construction paper.[2] Then demonstrate the activity for the students. Take articles of clothing (which you have previously cut out) as well as a cut-out head, arms, and legs. Show the class how easy it is to create a figure by gluing these items to the construction paper. The figure will probably look very humorous, especially if you have chosen such things as enormous shoes, a little head, and a strange assortment of clothing. Have the students make their own funny figures. Through a cooperative effort, students locate the items each needs to complete a creation. In the process, the same

words are repeated over and over, and a great deal of laughter is generated, lowering anxiety.

Guess What's in the Box![3]   Have a box filled with objects whose names are already familiar to the students. Describe a particular object and have the students guess which object is being described. Once the object has been correctly named, remove it from the box and give it to the student temporarily. Once all the objects have been handed out, you can then ask that the objects be returned: "Who has the rubber band?" and so forth.

Getting Around for ESL Students   Make a large map of the campus or school using strips of butcher paper taped together (an alternative might be to block off the various locations with masking tape placed on the floor). The total area should be large enough so the students can stand on it and walk from place to place. Label rooms, buildings, or whatever is appropriate. Make sure it is clear what the various rooms and buildings are. For example, you might place a picture of medicines in the clinic or pictures of food in the cafeteria. Using TPR, have students move around to various places. Take a tour of the campus or school itself, pointing out these same places. When the students feel familiar with the area, ask them to act as guides to new students of the same L1 backgrounds. In order to survive the first few days, new students need to know where things are before they are fluent enough to ask about them.

The People in Our School   Take photos of personnel within your school. Show them to your students and talk about the job that each one does. You may want to act out the various roles: custodian, cafeteria helper, secretary, nurse, counselor, teacher, orchestra director. Have the students point to the picture of the custodian, the principal, and so on. Now ask volunteer students to act out the roles. See if the others can guess which roles are being acted out.

Classifying Objects   Have each student make a classification booklet. Any categories can be used, depending upon the objectives you have in mind. For example, one page could be for household items, another for clothing, a third for sports or camping equipment. Give the students several magazines or catalogs and have them cut out pictures to be categorized. Then ask them to glue the items to the appropriate pages. You can provide comprehensible input about the pictures and do some individual TPR with each student. (*Point to the _____. Name two objects that belong in a kitchen,* etc.) Previously acquired concepts can be reinforced by this means.

Following a Process   Through a series of simple commands, students can learn to make things to eat (guacamole, onion and sour cream dip, sandwiches), items for play (kites, puppets, dolls, pictures), fascinating projects such as papier-mâché maps or miniature cities. You need to demonstrate first before taking the students through the step-by-step processes. Students are not expected to speak; they simply carry out the commands in TPR fashion.

Matching   Students can match pictures of objects with words placed on heavy paper and cut into puzzle pieces. Thus, the student can use the kinesthetic matching as a clue if necessary and the word itself will be more easily acquired. Or the student can use the word only and the matching of the puzzle pieces will simply reinforce the choice.

The above represent just a small sampling of the many activities that can be used with students at this stage. Of course, some are more applicable to certain ages than others. However, it has been my experience that activities that one might consider "childish" for older learners are often enjoyed by children and adults alike. A lot depends upon the degree of comfort the students feel in the setting that has been established.

Success in internalizing concepts is strongly influenced by a freeing environment and made possible through continued recycling. In addition, the teacher needs to make optimal use of manipulative visuals; to act out, model, or demonstrate expected responses; to make full use of body language in order to clarify meaning; to use high-frequency vocabulary, short sentences, yes/no questions, either/or questions, and other questions that require only one-word answers; and to rely heavily on getting the students physically involved with the target language in order to facilitate its acquisition. At the same time, types of activities need to be varied within any given time period for two reasons: students' attention spans are often short and the teacher's stamina is limited.

 ## THE EARLY SPEECH PRODUCTION STAGE

Getting into Speaking

The transition into the second stage generally begins with an extension of many of the activities used in the comprehension stage. The teacher gradually begins to see changes in the length of the responses. For example, to a question such as "Who has on a blue dress?" the teacher might get the answer "Ashwaq has dress" instead of just "Ashwaq." Once the expansions begin to appear, they come naturally and abundantly, especially if the students are feeling comfortable with the teacher and the ambiance of the classroom. The speech at first will contain many errors which should be dealt with *only* indirectly. To the omission of words in the student's utterance above, the teacher might respond with "Yes, Ashwaq has on the dress" instead of "No, you should say, 'Ashwaq has on the dress'" (emphasizing *on* and *the*). It is felt that if allowed to develop their interlanguage naturally, the students will continue expanding their utterances to include a wide variety of structures and eventual complex language.

Some of the activities that can be added to the teacher's repertoire at this stage (or earlier) are the following:

Charts and Other Visuals   Krashen and Terrell (1983) recommend the use of charts and other visuals that will make discussion easier and will serve as transitions into reading. The following can be written on the board as aids to conversation.

Numbers
  How many students in the class have
     rings _____
     tennis shoes _____
     belts _____
     glasses _____

Follow-up questions: How many students are wearing tennis shoes? Are any students wearing glasses? How many? and so forth.

Clothing

Name of Student	*Clothes*
Carlos	jeans
Sung Hee	dress

Follow-up questions: Who is wearing jeans? What is Sung Hee wearing?

Month of Birth

Month	**Thang**	**Lammathet**	**Ellen**	**Franco**
January				
February		X		
March				
April				
May			X	
June				
July				
August				
September	X			
October				
November				X
December				

Follow-up questions: Who was born in February? When was Ellen born?

Group Murals   Each student can be given a space on a huge piece of butcher paper that has been strung across a wall or two in the classroom. The students, who have been given pencils, rulers, wide felt-tip pens, paints, and brushes, can use their spaces to draw any pictures they wish. They are to put their signatures at the bottom of their pictures. The butcher paper is displayed for a week or two, then rolled up and saved. As the students progress in the target language, the butcher paper can be brought out for different kinds of activities. At first simple questions can be asked about each picture: "Look at Juan's picture. What color is the wagon?" (It's green) "How many apples did Jenny paint?" (three) Later, when the students are into the stage of speech emergence and beyond, they can tell about their own pictures and those of their friends or they can make up an oral group story incorporating each picture in some way.

Open-Ended Sentences   Extend the streams of comprehensible input to include utterances which the student completes.

On Saturdays you _____.
Your family likes to _____.
Ho likes to eat _____.

Or students can bring in family photos to share. Using open-ended sentences, they can talk about their relatives pictured in the photos: My sister likes _____. My brother is _____. My cousins are _____.

Matrices   Open-ended sentences that are used in certain combinations for specific situations are called *matrices*. Here are a few situations in which they might be used:

First Meeting
Hi there, my name is _____.
Nice to meet you. I'm _____.
Are you a new student too?
Yes, I came from _____.

On the Telephone
Hola.
Hola. Soy _____. ¿Con quién hablo? _____.
Con _____.

At an Office
May I help you?
My name is _____. I have an appointment with _____.

The matrices should not be drilled in audiolingual style. Instead they should be used in role-playing situations in which a variety of responses can be given. Students simply use the matrices as aids and "starters" for as long as they need them. The matrices can be placed on cue cards, which can serve as transitions into reading, or they can be incorporated into jazz chants or lyrics.

Asking for the Facts   Students can be shown simple sale advertisements from local newspaper (in second language classes) or foreign language newspapers (in foreign language classes). An alternative might be to show the students documents that have been filled out (a hospital record, an application for welfare, a passport). Pertinent questions can be asked about each:

> Questions on the sale advertisement:
> 1. What is being sold?
> 2. How much was it?
> 3. How much is it now?
> 4. How much will you be saving?

> Questions on the job application:
> 1. What is the person's last name?
> 2. What job does the person want?
> 3. Where does the person live?
> 4. What is the person's telephone number?
> 5. When was the person born?

Getting into Reading and Writing

Even though speaking is their major thrust, most of the above activities can be used as transitions into reading and writing. Key words written on the chalkboard, TPR commands which students may have listed in their notebooks, cue cards with matrices written on them, words on charts, and other visuals all lead to reading and writing in the target language. Of course, non-literate learners of all ages and students whose L1 writing system is vastly different from that of the target language will need special attention. However, the teaching should always be done through meaning rather than through a stringing together of isolated elements such as phonemes, orthographic symbols, and the like. The Natural Approach, as first described by Krashen and Terrell, is concerned mainly with oral communication skills. However, they believed for the most part that skills—listening, speaking, reading, writing—should be integrated rather than taught as separate entities.

 ## THE SPEECH EMERGENCE STAGE AND BEYOND

Because speech has been emerging all along, to distinguish *speech emergence* as a separate stage seems artificial. Perhaps this is the reason Krashen and Terrell replaced it with the term *extending production* in their book *The Natural Approach*. During this third stage, the utterances become longer and more complex. Many errors will still be made but, if enough comprehensible input has been internalized, they should gradually begin to decrease as the students move beyond this level toward full production. If undue attention has been paid to developmental errors, the process of acquiring correct grammatical forms in the new language could be impeded.

At this stage a large number of activities can be used that are somewhat more demanding and challenging but still within reach cognitively: music and poetry, role playing and drama, affective activities, and problem solving or debates at higher levels. Many of the activities already recommended in this chapter for earlier stages can be extended to provide additional opportunities for development. For example, instead of simply answering questions about an application form, the students can now fill one out; instead of just following directions, they can begin to write their own sets of simple directions to see if others can follow them. Here is a sample of other activities that might be typical at this stage and beyond:

The People Hunt (a transitional activity)   Give the students the following list and ask them to find a person who

> has shoelaces
> wears glasses
> is laughing
> is wearing black socks
> has on a plaid blouse or shirt
> has five letters in his or her last name
> has a 6 in his or her phone number

They must get the signature of a person in each category. As the students become more advanced, they can find a person who

> has been to Hong Kong within the last five years
> has a sister who likes to skate on shopping-center rinks
> hopes to be an actress after completing high school

Draw This!   Divide the students into groups of four or five. Give one student per group a picture with simple lines and geometric shapes on it. Have each student give directions to his or her group so that they can reproduce the picture without seeing it. The student who comes closest to the original picture gives directions for the next picture. You may want to brief the group on the kinds of directions that will help by giving some words that may be key: horizontal, vertical, diagonal, perpendicular, parallel, a right angle, upper-left corner, lower right, and so forth. Pictures should become progressively more difficult as the students become more proficient.

Shopping Spree[4]   Set up one corner of the room as a grocery store. Stock the shelves with empty Jell-O boxes, egg cartons, milk bottles, cereal boxes, cleaning supplies, magazines, and so forth. Mark prices on the items. Have the students make out a shopping list and go shopping; play money can be used. Students can take turn being shoppers, salespersons, and cashier. Various situations can be set up to add variety to the shopping expeditions: A shopper may have to ask where a particular item is on the shelves, may need to exchange an item, may have been given wrong change, and so forth. Similar public places can be simulated: a doctor's office, a bank, the post office, a drugstore, a clothing store, a garage. Various lists can be compiled, depending on each task. The situations can be an extension of matrices.

Whose Name Is It?   Write the name of a student in large letters on paper. Tape it on the back of a student volunteer. The volunteer needs to guess whose name is on his or her back by asking yes/no questions of the class (they are in on the secret). "Is the person a male or female?" (female) "Is she in the first desk? (no) "Does she like to sing?" (yes) "Is it _____?" (no) And on it goes until several volunteers get a chance. A variation of this activity is "Guess What's in the Box" described earlier in this chapter. One student could be given the box which would have only one object in it. The rest of the class would ask yes/no questions until the object is named.

Following Written Directions   Give students sets of simple directions to follow. The directions can be on many topics of interest: how to make a model car, how to make paper flowers, how to decoupage. See if the students can read the directions and follow them. Have students work in pairs on some projects and in larger groups on others.

Map Reading   This activity could be an extension of "Getting Around," described earlier in this chapter. Helpful phrases could be written on the chalkboard: turn right (left), go south (north, east west), go around the corner (straight), on the right (left, north, south, east, west) side of the street, in the (middle, far corner) of the block , down (up) the street, until you see a mailbox (fire hydrant, bus stop), between the drugstore and the bank, across from the hardware store, and so on. Give the students maps and have them follow directions as you give them by tracing the route with a pencil. First do a demonstration with the class. Place the map on the overhead projector and trace a route while reading a set of directions out loud—for example, "Start at the bank, go north on Second Street until you get to Central Avenue, turn left, walk straight ahead to the gas station. It's between the grocery store and the bakery." Then divide the students into pairs and have them give each other directions while they trace the routes on their own maps.

An alternative might be to combine storytelling with the activities.[5] For example, create a story about a fugitive who moves from place to place in different ways; he walks, runs, darts, crawls, skips, and drives. The students trace the route on their individual maps as you read. Instead of drawing only straight lines, the students can draw broken lines for "walks," zigzag lines for "runs," sideways carets for "darts," wavy lines for "crawls," arches for "skips," and a series of plus signs for "drives." Follow-ups could include having the students draw maps of sections of their own communities and write sets of directions to the various places within them. They may even want to write ministories to go with the directions. Eventually the students can participate in similar activities using real street maps of cities or highway maps of whole states or countries.

Sharing Books: The Classroom Library   Place several bean bag chairs in the corner of the classroom along with several bookcases set up at right angles to form a little library. Give students time to spend in this area where they can read individually, read to each other, and/or discuss books. Books might even be checked out through a system similar to that used in a public school or university library.[6] Students may even want to contribute their own books to the collection.

Writing Memos   Set up situations in which students can write memos. Some suggestions are the following:

> Your mother is at work. You are leaving for a baseball game. You and some of your friends want to go out after the game for pizza. Write a memo to your mother to tape to the refrigerator door. Tell her you will be home a little late.

> You are at home. Someone has called for your brother. He is still at school. Write a memo asking him to return the call.

> You have a job as a receptionist. A salesman has come to sell paper products to your boss. Your boss is not in. The salesman asks you to leave a message. It should say that the salesman will be back later.

> You have an appointment with your professor. You must cancel it because your mother is coming to visit that day. Write a message to give to the secretary. Explain the situation.

Using Local or Foreign Language Newspapers[7]   Here are some activities with easily obtained sources.

1. Ask the students to find, cut out, and paste on butcher paper a sample of each of the following. Students can work in groups or individually. This kind of activity could begin at much earlier stages if the items are simple enough.

    > the price of a pound of meat
    > the low temperature in a major city
    > a number greater than a thousand
    > a face with glasses
    > the picture or name of an animal
    > a sports headline
    > a letter to the editor
    > the price of a used Ford Mustang
    > a city within 50 miles of your own
    > a movie that starts between 1:00 and 4:00 P.M.
    > an angry word
    > the picture of a happy person
    > a ten-letter word
    > the picture of a bride

2. Have the students go through the ads in a recent paper. Ask them to find three things that were produced in other countries. Ask them to find three things that were produced in the state or city in which they live now.

3. Students can look for suitable jobs, apartments, and other items of interest in the want ads. They can discuss what they have found and tell why the ones they have chosen fit their needs.

4. They can also look in the want ads to find items for sale. Have them play the roles of potential sellers to gather more information about the content of the ads. A fist held to the ear makes a good pretend phone. They can then write ads advertising things they want to sell. They can even bring these items to class. Have them consider the following questions before writing: What do you want to sell? Who do you think will buy it? Why would someone want to buy it? Once they have written their ads (restrict number of words and dollar value), collect them, duplicate them, and distribute them among the class. Let them buy, sell, or trade at will.

5. Finding articles about interesting people in the news can be exciting. Students can plan a "celebrity" party and make a list of those they would like to invite. Have them tell why they would like to meet the ones they have selected.

6. Ask students to choose a headline and write an alternative story to go with it.

Pen Pals   Mainstream English classes or organizations within or outside of the school can write personal letters to ESL students. After several exchanges of letters have taken place, the groups might get together to meet for a party or outing. In foreign language classes students can write to each other on a regular basis in the target language, they can write to students studying the same language in another school, or they can obtain pen pals in the countries where the target language is spoken. You might want to establish a mailbox center in a quiet area of the classroom. Directions and information about the area can be displayed. A table with three or four chairs can be provided along with several types of paper, envelopes, and writing tools. To encourage letter writing, the teacher, teacher assistants, and advanced students can first write letters so that each student receives one. Then time can be scheduled regularly to receive, read, and respond to the letters as students become involved in writing to each other as well. If students have access to computers, they might correspond through e-mail.

 ## OTHER EXPANSIONS OF THE NATURAL APPROACH

Although the Natural Approach as originally proposed had many strengths and gained many advocates, particularly in the United States, it did appear to have some limitations. One of these was that the method itself was oriented primarily to oral skills development with beginning to low-intermediate students. While this was not a fault in and of itself, teachers needed to be aware that literacy skills required more emphasis than the Approach provided. In addition, advanced students needed to be challenged through an increased focus on higher thinking skills and on tasks that were likely to promote proficiency at higher levels.[8]

Another limitation was that it did not adequately address the formal teaching of grammar. Originally the Natural Approach assumed that grammar develops naturally by student exposure to sufficient amounts of comprehensible input. Although it was acknowledged that formal grammar should have some role, the precise nature of that role was not made clear. Terrell himself was constantly thinking about this issue and, in the late 1980s, began to address the grammar issue in talks and papers (see, for example, Terrell 1987). In an article entitled "The Role of Grammar Instruction in a Communicative Approach," he acknowledged that explicit grammar instruction "is beneficial to learners at a particular point in their acquisition of the target language" (Terrell 1991:55). Instruction can, he claimed, give students structures to use as advance organizers to aid in the comprehension of input and can help students focus on less noticeable features of language such as word endings. And it can serve as a basis for conscious monitoring and the creation of utterances using structures not yet acquired. However, he did not advocate a return to the use of a grammatical syllabus. The focus of classroom instruction must remain on communication, as emphasized in the original formulation of the Natural Approach.

A third limitation lies in the area of content and tasks. With the original Natural Approach, the content and tasks in the early stages of acquisition were mainly related to everyday survival skills. While these might be fine for students desiring such a focus, they are inadequate for those who wish to reach academic proficiency in the target language. In practice, many Natural Approach teachers have introduced subject-matter content relating to math, science, social studies, literature, and other fields early on and have involved the students in tasks that will likely lead to success academically.[9]

In addition, many teachers have related the new concepts taught to meaningful larger contexts to provide a cognitive hierarchical framework for the material. Look again at the dialogue about colors at the start of section 1 above. Think about how it might differ if it were related, for example, to a science unit on flowering plants, as in the dialogue below, which again is intended for beginners.

> **Teacher:** Flowers come in many colors. Here is a red flower. (*Holds up a red flower, then holds up another red flower just like the first one.*) Is this a red flower?
>
> **Students:** Yes.
>
> **Teacher:** (*Holding up the same kind of flower, only this time it is blue*) Is this a red flower?
>
> **Students:** (*Shaking their heads*) No.
>
> **Teacher:** (*Pointing again to the red flower*) No. Good. This is a red flower.

And thus the dialogue continues in much the same way as the first one did. The language becomes more enriched (maybe within a day or two) by including other qualities of flowers and by talking about where they grow and how they grow. In the first dialogue, the focus was on colors only. In the second dialogue, although the focus is still on colors, the teaching of them is part of a larger hierarchical unit: Flowering Plants. And this might itself be part of a still larger unit: Plants. The largest unit including plants and flowering plants might be labeled "Living Things."

It should be noted that the other activities mentioned in this paper could also be parts of larger units and themes, depending upon their content and context. For example, "Guess What's in the Box!" could be used for recycling mathematics vocabulary if the box contains items such as a ruler, a compass, a pocket calculator, and the like. "Following a Process" could be part of an art lesson if it involves a process such as creating hanging mobiles. And "Charts and Other Visuals" could be used in a geography lesson comparing various countries.

It must be remembered that a hodgepodge of activities thrown together does not a curriculum make. The activities must be carefully selected and adapted, and they must logically fit into a well-planned but flexible hierarchy of units and themes. Within this hierarchy, key concepts will need to be reinforced sufficiently to be acquired. Although the original formulation of the Natural Approach included no explicit mechanism for the recycling of key concepts, the suggestions above can be adapted by instructors to achieve such a conceptually oriented course of study.

One final limitation appeared to be the Natural Approach's penchant for putting the teacher on center stage. Of course, at beginning levels the teacher's input is of utmost importance for students just beginning to develop language proficiency. However, students even at early stages need to begin communicating with one another more and with peers (or others) who are fluent speakers of the target language. An emphasis on group/pair work should not be relegated mainly to later stages.

 ## CONCLUSION

According to Krashen and Terrell, the foundation of the Natural Approach rested on the four principles mentioned in the abstract to this paper. In the years since publication of their 1983 book, the evolution of the Natural Approach has dealt with the development of literacy skills, the inclusion of academic themes, and group/peer work during the early stages; the incorporation of explicit grammar instruction; the contextualization of learned concepts into broader, hierarchical frameworks; and the recycling of key concepts. But, ultimately, it is the teacher in the classroom who draws from the Approach and makes it work in a particular situation by combining many strategies, such as those illustrated in the many activities described in this paper. The Approach will continue to evolve in different ways in different classrooms and with different teachers. Much depends too upon the students, their learning styles, the cultural situation, course expectations, and other goals. Under optimal conditions, students can move with relative ease from comprehension to early speech production and ultimately into speech emergence and beyond, as the Natural Approach predicted.

Notes

1. Many of these activities can be adapted to several age levels, provided students are cognitively able to deal with the tasks. They can also be adapted for teaching any language, second or foreign, and for most programs: English for Academic Purposes (EAP), English for Special Purposes (ESP), and others.
2. I wish to thank Teri Sandoval for the follow-up idea.
3. Thanks to Esther Heise for introducing this idea to me.
4. Thanks to Cyndee Gustke, who introduced me to a similar idea.
5. I wish to thank Braden Cancilla for this idea.
6. Cyndee Gustke suggested this idea.
7. These activities have been adapted from the pamphlet "Newspapers in Education," published by the *Albuquerque Journal/Tribune.*
8. See, in particular, Stephen Krashen's paper in this volume entitled "What Is Intermediate Natural Approach?" Here he addresses this limitation and suggests teaching academic language using the Natural Approach in sheltered-content situations and during free reading at intermediate levels.
9. Going even further, Peggy Hashemipour (also in this volume) shows how experiential education and service in real-life situations can provide out-of-classroom language activity.

Annotated Readings and References

Asher, J. 1982. *Learning Another Language through Actions: The Complete Teacher's Guidebook.* Los Gatos, Calif.: Sky Oaks.

Bassano, S., and M. Christison. 1983. *Drawing Out.* Englewood Cliffs, N.J.: Alemany/Prentice Hall. Utilizes experience in art to motivate oral and written language development. Contains examples of student work.

Byrne, D. 1967. *Progressive Picture Compositions.* New York: Longman. This series of picture books still holds its fascination for language students of all ages. The set includes very large pictures that are coordinated sequentially. Students place the pictures in the order in which they feel the actions occurred. Discussions and/or writing assignments can follow.

Christison, M., and S. Bassano. 1981. *Look Who's Talking.* Englewood Cliffs, N.J.: Alemany/ Prentice Hall. Adults and teens in the speech emergence phase and beyond can learn interaction techniques through the activities presented in this book. The suggested lessons, which include games and problem solving, begin with lower-risk kinds of activities and progress to more personal, higher-risk ones as the students become more proficient.

DLM Teaching Resources Comprehensive Catalog. Allen, Tex.: DLM Teaching Resources. Catalogs are not normally included in annotated reading lists such as this. However, because this particular catalog contains a wide variety of realia, I have included it even though not all of the materials contained are compatible with a Natural Approach classroom. The following manipulatives, pictures, games, and other activities are especially effective for language teaching: colorful photo library sets; picture cards depicting opposites and categories of different kinds; sequence and spatial relation picture cards; map games; colored cubes for teaching cognitive skills; math games; plastic clocks; play coins and bills; association cards; functional signs.

Gill, M., and P. Hartmann. 1993. *Get It? Got It!: Listening to Others, Speaking for Ourselves.* Boston, Mass.: Heinle and Heinle. A communicative book for developing listening, speaking, and pronunciation skills in low-intermediate speakers of English. Topics are oriented toward both survival and academics and are highly appropriate for young adults.

Jespersen, O. 1904. *How to Teach a Foreign Language.* London: Allen and Unwin.

Krashen, S., and T. Terrell. 1983. The Natural Approach: Language Acquisition in the Classroom. Englewood Cliffs, N.J.: Alemany/Prentice Hall. Essential reading for any one planning to use the Natural Approach. The book clearly describes the method, offers theoretical justification for its use, and presents suggested activities for making it work.

Ligon, F., and E. Tannenbaum. 1990. *Picture Stories: Language and Literacy Activities for Beginners.* White Plains, N.Y.: Longman. This book for young adults presents survival stories told in pictures. Students begin by talking about what is happening in each picture and end by writing the story. A few of the relevant topics are washing clothes, going to the doctor, following directions, and making phone calls. Students find many of the stories humorous as well as instructive.

Rowland, P. 1990. *Happily Ever After Big Book Packages.* Reading, Mass.: Addison-Wesley. Includes classics such as "Little Red Riding Hood," "La Tortuga," "The Three Bears," and "Peter and the Wolf." Intended for lower grades, each package contains one Big Book and four Little Books of the same title. A teaching guide, story script, and activity suggestions accompany each package.

Smallwood, B. 1991. *The Literature Connection: A Read-Aloud Guide for Multicultural Classrooms.* Reading, Mass.: Addison-Wesley. A helpful guide for teachers searching for read-aloud materials and guidelines (grades K-8). Of particular interest is the extensive annotated bibliography which arranges books by theme. Along with the annotations is information about grade level, proficiency level, cultural group, vocabulary, and so forth.

Terrell, T. 1982. The Natural Approach to Language Teaching: An Update. *Modern Language Journal* 66:121-131.

———. 1987. Achieving Grammatical Accuracy: Advice for ESL/EFL Students. Presentation at the 21st annual TESOL convention, April 21-25, Miami Beach, Florida.

———. 1991. The Role of Grammar Instruction in a Communicative Approach. *Modern Language Journal* 75:52-63.

What Is Intermediate Natural Approach?

Stephen D. Krashen
University of Southern California

Terrell's Natural Approach solves the problem of beginning second language teaching. It does not address, however, the intermediate level, because Natural Approach promotes the acquisition of conversational language, not "academic" language. Two ways of applying the principles underlying Natural Approach to the intermediate level are presented here: Sheltered Subject Matter Teaching and Free Voluntary Reading. In Sheltered Subject Matter Teaching, students learn subject matter through a second language. Studies show that in tests of second language competence, students in Sheltered Subject Matter classes do about as well as comparison students in regular language classes. Sheltered students also learn a considerable amount of subject matter at the same time. Also, Free Voluntary Reading has been shown to be a powerful means of stimulating development of literacy-related aspects of language. Using Sheltered Subject Matter Teaching and Free Voluntary Reading, individually and together, will, it is predicted, better prepare students for the serious study of literature in the second language as well as for other demanding purposes.

THE LIMITS OF BEGINNING LANGUAGE TEACHING

The results of empirical studies, as well as the experience of many teachers and students, have shown that Terrell's Natural Approach is an excellent beginning language teaching method. Natural Approach students outperform traditionally taught first year foreign language students on tests involving communication (Voge 1981) and do as well or better on discrete-point grammar tests (Voge 1981; Hammond 1988). They also are more confident of their future success in foreign language study, and report that they are less worried about being called on in class (Voge 1981). Students who complete two or three semesters of Natural Approach are typically able to do things with their second language that traditional students are not able to do: they can converse comfortably with a native speaker of the second language on a variety of everyday topics, provided the native speaker modifies his speech to some extent.

But for all its virtues, Natural Approach has its limits. Natural Approach and other beginning methods based on comprehensible input such as Asher's Total Physical Response method (Asher 1988) develop conversational language. Natural Approach students are not able to use their second language for more demanding purposes: they are not able, for example, to read the classics, engage in the serious study of literature, or use the language for international business or advanced scholarship. While Natural Approach has been very successful, it does not help students acquire the advanced vocabulary, grammar, and discourse structures necessary for truly sophisticated language use. Students who complete two or three semesters of Natural Approach Spanish will not be able to study at the University of Mexico or discuss the latest political crises.

Traditional language teaching has not solved the problem. Graman (1987) has shown that students who take advanced foreign language literature courses at the university level do not typically "come up through the ranks." Most advanced foreign language students, Graman reported, get much (or all) of their second language competence elsewhere—at home, or in sojourns in the country where the second language is spoken. Elementary language instruction is not enough.

I would like to propose two ways of solving this "transition problem," two ways of extending Natural Approach (or, rather, the principles underlying Natural Approach) to the intermediate level: Sheltered Subject Matter Teaching (SSMT) and Free Voluntary Reading (FVR).

 ## SHELTERED SUBJECT MATTER TEACHING

Sheltered Subject Matter Teaching is content teaching made comprehensible for second language acquirers. Inspired by the success of Canadian immersion programs (see, e.g., Lambert and Tucker 1972), SSMT derives from one important concept: subject matter teaching in a second language, when it is comprehensible, is language teaching, because it is comprehensible input. A well-taught history class given to second language acquirers is also a language class.

SSMT has several crucial characteristics:
1. Only second language acquirers are allowed in the class. When all students are second language acquirers, that is, when all students are in the same linguistic boat, it is easier for the teacher to make the input comprehensible.
2. The focus of the class is on subject matter, not language. This encourages a focus on meaning, not form, and results in more comprehensible input, and thus more language acquisition.
3. Teachers attempt to make input comprehensible. This is done in several ways, including frequent comprehension checking (through discussion, short tests, etc.) and the use of extralinguistic information (pictures, charts, realia, and occasional readings in the students' first language).[1]

Research in Sheltered Subject Matter Teaching

SSMT studies can be divided into two types. In *Second-Language Medium* studies, second language acquirers are tested on and given course credit for subject matter. These include Buch and de Bagheera (1978), Edwards et al. (1984), Hauptman et al.

Research on Sheltered Subject Matter Teaching

STUDY	L2 Development: L2 Classes	Comparison to L2 Students Not in Class	No L2 Comparison Group	Subject-Matter Learning
Edwards et al. (French) 1984	equivalent			equivalent
Edwards et al. (English) 1984				equivalent
Hauptman et al. (French) 1988	equivalent			
Ho 1982a		superior[a]		equivalent
Ho 1982b				equivalent
Ho 1985		equivalent[b]		equivalent
Lafayette and Buscaglia 1985	equivalent[c]			
Sternfeld 1989	equivalent			
Buch and de Bagheera 1978			significant gains	
Schleppegrell 1984			significant gains	
Peck 1987			significant gains	

a: Experimental subjects had eight years of EFL, including three years of SSMT. Comparison subjects had eight years of EFL without SSMT. Experimental subjects were far superior in English before study began, reflecting previous SSMT and greater previous exposure to English.

b: See text for discussion.

c: Comparison subjects were superior on a writing test (see text for discussion).

(1988), Ho (1982a), Ho (1982b), and Ho (1985). In *Content-Based Second Language* studies, subject matter is emphasized and may be tested, but students are not given course credit for subject matter learning. Some content-based classes do not include explicit grammar study (Lafayette and Buscaglia 1985; Sternfeld 1989), but some have a grammar component, which is considered to be a peripheral part of the course (Peck 1987; Schleppegrell 1984).

As indicated in the accompanying table, studies have used several different measures for second language acquisition:

1. SSMT students have been compared to students in regular second-language classes. In this case, both experimental (SSMT) and comparison students have equivalent "time on task" (Edwards et al. 1984; Lafayette and Buscaglia 1985; Hauptman et al. 1988; Sternfeld 1989).

2. SSMT students have been compared to subjects who were not taking any second language classes ("L2 Students Not in Class") but who had had previous second language instruction for the same length of time as the experimental group. For the former, SSMT amounts to extra exposure to the second language (Ho 1982a, 1982b, 1985).

3. In some studies, there was no comparison group (Peck 1987; Schleppegrell 1984).

While researchers using measure 1 compared SSMT to regular L2 instruction, researchers using measures 2 and 3 simply asked whether SSMT has any effect at all. Some of the Second-Language Medium studies tested subject matter learning by comparing SSMT students to students in similar subject matter classes in their first language (Edwards et al. 1984; Hauptman et al. 1988; Ho 1982a, 1982b, 1985).

The table gives an overview of studies in Sheltered Subject Matter Teaching. In reviewing this research, a formal meta-analysis would certainly have been desirable. This was, however, not possible due to the difficulty, in many cases, of calculating effect sizes from the available data. Nevertheless, the results of these studies are clear: students in Second-Language Medium classes learn the same amount of subject matter as students in first language medium comparison classes. In second language development, most students in Second-Language Medium and Content-Based Second Language classes acquire just as much of the second language as comparison students in regular second language classes. Where no comparison group was used, all students in sheltered subject matter classes showed significant gains in second language acquisition. Thus, SSMT students got both language and subject matter for the same price, a substantial increase in educational efficiency.[2] In addition, SSMT goes beyond conversation, exposing students to more complex uses of language.

There is reason to suspect that second language acquisition through subject matter teaching is even more effective than the studies in the table suggest. In some cases, the comparison language classes were very well taught. I believe this to be true of the comparison classes at the University of Ottawa studied by Edwards et al. (1984) and by Hauptman et al. (1988), where I was a visiting professor in 1981. Second language classes there are taught in the target language, with the focus on communication.

In the study by Sternfeld (1989), subject matter (Latin American history, geography, and current events) was taught to *beginning* foreign language students, not intermediates. It is a tremendous challenge to teach complex material to students at this level, and it is remarkable that experimental students did as well as comparisons in second language acquisition.

In the study by Lafayette and Buscaglia (1985), comparison students outperformed experimental students on a test that was labeled "writing" (but not on other measures). Lafayette and Buscaglia (1985:333) present the following explanation for this result: "This finding is not at all surprising since the writing test consists primarily of discrete grammar points including a somewhat large segment (more than 20% of the test) on the use of the subjunctive. The control group spent a major portion of the semester studying grammar, including two chapters devoted to the subjunctive mood."

Ho (1985) reported that SSMT students did not make additional gains in English compared to students who did similar subject matter in their first language (Chinese). Both experimental and comparison subjects in his study, however, did all subject matter reading in English, which reduced the treatment differences. Also, the written English test used was actually a subject matter test, and it may have been a test of content as well as language. On an oral test of English (a five-minute interview), experimental subjects performed better, but the difference was not significant.

Swain (1988:68) has argued that "not all content teaching is necessarily good language teaching." One reason for this, she points out, is that students in content classes may receive restricted input (input that does not exploit the full formal and functional range of the language). Swain suggests that a solution is to provide language "in its full functional range" (p. 76). In my view, a simple and powerful way of doing this is by encouraging Free Voluntary Reading. We turn now to a review of research in this area. Following this review, we will consider some applications, including ways of combining Sheltered Subject Matter Teaching and Free Voluntary Reading.

 ## THE IMPACT OF FREE VOLUNTARY READING

The research literature on the impact of reading on literacy development is very consistent. Numerous studies confirm that free voluntary reading helps reading comprehension (reviewed in Krashen 1985a, 1988; see also Smart 1978; Langer et al., 1990; Hafiz and Tudor 1989; Gradman and Hanania 1991), writing style (Krashen 1984, 1985a; Salyer 1987; Janopoulos 1986; Kaplan and Palhinda 1981), vocabulary (Krashen 1989), spelling (Krashen 1989), and grammatical competence (Krashen 1985a).

Several kinds of evidence support these conclusions:

1. Studies showing that more free voluntary reading results in greater literacy development; those who say they read more, for example, do better on tests of literacy-related abilities. Several studies using students of English as a Second Language have confirmed that more reading results in increased second language literacy. Gradman and Hanania (1991) reported that "outside reading" in English was the sin-

gle most important predictor of TOEFL scores among international students enrolled in an intensive English course at Indiana University.

Salyer (1987) studied adult students of English as a Second Language studying at Andrews University (Minnesota) and found that those whose writing improved most during an academic quarter said they spent more time doing pleasure reading in English. Janopoulos (1986) reported similar results for international students at Ohio State University: incoming students who wrote better essays reported that they did more pleasure reading in English. Much the same findings were reported by Kaplan and Palhinda (1981) at Georgetown University: international students who felt they had better writing ability reported that they did more reading in English.

Smart (1978) reported that when an English-language newspaper was introduced in certain areas of Ghana, eighth and ninth graders in Ghana who had access to the paper made better gains in English reading after two years than those who did not.

2. Studies showing that children who live in more "print-rich" environments do better on tests of literacy-related abilities.

A second-language study showing the relationship of print environment to language development was conducted by Williams (1981), who found a significant correlation (r = .51) between scores on a *cloze* test and the availability of books in English (other than textbooks), either at school or at home, among young students (ages eight to thirteen) of English as a Second Language in Nigeria.

3. Controlled experiments showing that students who do more free voluntary reading in school (in, for example, sustained silent reading programs) do as well or better than comparison students in traditional language arts classes, especially when these studies last for at least seven months.

Elley and Mangubhai (1983), for example, studied third and fourth graders in the Fiji islands who participated in three different English-as-a-foreign-language programs for thirty minutes per day for two years: (a) a traditional audiolingual program, emphasizing drills and exercises and grammatical accuracy; (b) a sustained silent reading program in which children simply read what they wanted to read, without book reports or comprehension testing; (c) a "shared book experience" program, in which books of interest were discussed and read to the children. Testing done at the end of two years showed that the children in the second and third groups were far superior to the traditionally taught children in the first group in a variety of measures, including reading comprehension, grammar, and writing.

4. Studies showing that readers are able to acquire a small but significant amount of vocabulary and spelling knowledge after reading unfamiliar words in meaningful texts, even after very few exposures, and even when the readers are not focused on improving vocabulary and spelling. Most of these "read and test" studies have been done using first-language acquirers, but recent studies by Pitts, White, and Krashen (1989) and Day, Omura, and Hiramatsu (1991) confirm that second language acquirers can also increase their vocabulary knowledge after relatively few encounters with new words in texts.

The results of these four types of studies show not only that reading results in considerable literacy development but that reading is more powerful than traditional instruction. First, free reading has done very well in face-to-face confrontation with traditional language arts instruction, as noted in (3) above. Second, the results of the "read and test" studies in vocabulary acquisition described in (4) suggest that reading is more time-efficient than traditional instruction. In fact, Nagy, Herman, and Anderson (1985) concluded that reading is ten times faster, in terms of words acquired per minute, than intensive direct vocabulary instruction.

Even if traditional instruction were more effective, it is nowhere near as pleasant as free reading. Most people simply won't do drills and exercises on their own over a long period, but they will read on their own. One of the most perceptive comments I have ever read in the language acquisition professional literature was made by Nagy and Herman (1987). Noting that children differ enormously in vocabulary size, Nagy and Herman pointed out that children with larger vocabularies are not doing more drills and exercises—they are reading more.

Does Reading Make You Smarter?

There is also good reason to believe that free reading helps cognitive development, although there are surprisingly few studies in this area. Schaefer and Anastasi (1968) reported that high school students considered to be creative read more than their peers, averaging over fifty books per year. Goertzel et al. (1978) examined biographies of three hundred "eminent" people and found that as a group they read a great deal.

Ravitch and Finn (1987) in their study *What Do Our 17-Year-Olds Know?* found that those who read more also knew more: seventeen-year-olds who did better on a test of general knowledge of literature and history were those who grew up in a more "print-rich" environment, and those who did better on the literature portion of the test reported doing more free reading.

I suspect that pleasure reading is an important source of general knowledge, and for some people it is the major source. Much of what many people know about history, geography, politics, and other subjects comes from free reading. Certainly, pleasure reading in a foreign language will add considerably to a reader's knowledge of the history and customs of the speakers of that language.

 APPLICATIONS

There are, to be sure, gaps in the research. Sheltered subject matter research needs to be done with a wider range of measures and with a wider range of subjects. While I have emphasized second language studies in my discussion of free voluntary reading in this paper, second language studies make up only a small proportion of the research literature on free reading; in addition, nearly all of the second language studies have used English as the target language. Nevertheless, it is not premature to discuss application, since the research so far is consistent and compelling.

My discussion of applications here is limited to foreign language teaching in the traditional university context, where the goal of instruction is the development of the ability to read, appreciate, and discuss literature in the original language. I have discussed other possible applications of Sheltered Subject Matter Teaching elsewhere (e.g., Krashen 1985b).

After a year of Natural Approach instruction, university students should be able to begin to learn at least some academic subject matter through a second language in a sheltered class (recall, however, Sternfeld's successful experiment using first year foreign language students; see Sternfeld 1989).

Possible topics for sheltered courses, or modules, that will prepare foreign language students for the serious study of literature include the following:

1. Political and intellectual history of countries that speak the target language. At the moment, there are few texts that could be used in a course such as this. I have run across some that might be helpful. *Easy Spanish Reader* (Tardy 1988) contains a succinct history of Mexico that is certainly comprehensible to even second semester college Spanish students. *Breve histoire du Quebec* (Hamelin and Provencher 1981) is probably comprehensible to second-year college French students. It is quite possible that junior high school–level texts designed for native speakers will also be appropriate for these courses.

2. Current events in the countries of interest. Here, the best text is probably the daily newspaper. As Sternfeld (1989) has argued, the newspaper, even though it is designed for native speakers, can be quite comprehensible to second language students. As Sternfeld notes, students are already familiar with the writing style in newspapers; there are usually extralinguistic clues to meaning (e.g., photographs); students typically already have some background knowledge regarding the stories; and news stories continue over several weeks or even months, allowing students to become familiar with the topic and the language used.

   In teaching both history and current events, sheltered subject matter teachers may find it helpful to assign or recommend some readings in the students' first language, in order to fill in background knowledge rapidly. This background knowledge will help make readings and presentations in the second language more comprehensible, which will contribute to second language acquisition. The idea of using the first language to help second language acquisition in this way comes from bilingual education (for discussion and supporting research, see Krashen 1985a; Krashen and Biber 1988).

   Suggestions (3) and (4) are intended to combine the advantages of free voluntary reading and sheltered subject matter teaching:

3. Popular literature. Popular literature should be more comprehensible to second year students than the classics, and will give students linguistic competence as well as some feeling for the specific writing style used in the target language. A major goal of this course is to expose students to a variety of genres, so that they can find their own reading interests.

4. Individualized reading. This course, which could follow the sheltered popular literature course, gives students a chance to read deeply in an area of

their own interest. Appleby and Conner (1965) provide an excellent description of an elective individualized reading course for high school students in their first language, and many of their suggestions can easily be used in a sheltered foreign language class.

Students in Appleby and Conner's course spent nearly all of the class time reading. When they finished a book, a student-teacher conference was held during class time, in which the student and teacher discussed the book. Students were not required to do "book reports"; rather, the teacher tried to find out how much the student enjoyed the book and then made recommendations for additional reading. Instructors attempted to "go with" students' interests, gradually widening and deepening them. One student described by Appleby and Conner, for example, was interested only in reading war stories. Gradually, the teacher moved this student into "serious" war-related novels, such as *Battle Cry* and, eventually, *All Quiet on the Western Front*.

The grading scheme for the course was developed by students and was based on three factors: (a) the amount read, (b) the quality of the student-teacher conferences, and (c) the difficulty of the books read.

Since free voluntary reading makes such a powerful contribution to language development, it would be helpful if students could take this course for credit more than one time.

5. Linguistics. Courses or modules in linguistics could deal with the structure of the target language, its history and dialects, and the structure of closely related languages. In addition, if we are interested in students' continuing to improve on their own, we should consider sharing information with them about language acquisition, and the relevance of this information to language pedagogy and their own progress in acquiring a second language.

Not all students will be interested in the five topics mentioned here. It would thus be ideal to offer a variety of sheltered courses and allow students to choose.

B. Elbaum (personal communication) has suggested that the university foreign language requirement be fulfilled simply by passing a sheltered subject matter course. This is a very sensible idea, in that it will demonstrate that the student can use the second language to learn new information and will, as Sternfeld (1989) has noted, entail gaining a great deal of cultural knowledge.

Unlike many exotic second-language teaching methods, these suggestions are fairly easy to implement in a university or high school foreign language program. Sheltered subject matter teachers must be subject matter experts; since, however, many foreign language teachers have extensive backgrounds in the humanities as well as in language, this should not be a problem. Also, the methodology of Sheltered Subject Matter Teaching should not be difficult to acquire, since foreign language teachers are experienced at making input comprehensible to less competent speakers of the language they teach (see Wesche and Ready 1985, discussed in note 1 of this paper, for an empirical study of teacher adjustments in SSMT).

Sheltered Subject Matter Teaching and Free Voluntary Reading can be introduced gradually. Foreign language programs can build libraries of lighter reading a few books and magazines at a time. Sheltered Subject Matter Teaching can begin with Content-Based Second Language classes and gradually move toward Second-Language Medium classes as materials are gathered and as teachers get used to sheltered teaching.

 ## CONCLUSION

As currently taught, advanced foreign language literature courses at the university are not "sheltered" courses; they utilize difficult, challenging texts and demand sophisticated analyses of these texts. This is the way it should be. In addition, advanced literature courses do not encourage light reading. This is also the way it should be. But an important part of university foreign language study is to prepare students for these courses, and current language-teaching methods are not doing the job (Graman 1987). Even Natural Approach is not enough. My suggestion is that we try a combination of Sheltered Subject Matter Teaching and Free Voluntary Reading. In the short run, sheltered modules and courses can supplement our current offerings. In the long run, this kind of intermediate program could replace what we now do in the second year in college or the third and fourth year in high school.

Notes

1. There may be a considerable amount of variation in the adjustments teachers make in SSMT. Wesche and Ready (1985) compared two university teachers, one teaching in French and one in English, each presenting similar material to a regular class and to a sheltered psychology class.

   Wesche and Ready reported that there were some changes both professors made when teaching the sheltered class; for example, they both spent more time at the blackboard and labeled their board drawings more fully. There were, however, differences. The English-speaking professor made several adjustments when speaking to the sheltered class; he spoke more slowly and used fewer complex tenses, shorter clauses, and more imperatives and questions. The French-speaking professor, on the other hand, made fewer adjustments; the language she used with her regular and sheltered classes was not significantly different in many respects.

   Wesche and Ready attributed the differences between the two professors to their individual styles of presentation. The French-speaking professor presented "highly planned, relatively formal" lectures that "closely paralleled the sequence of content in the textbook and outline" (p. 108). The English-speaking professor, on the other hand, was "more spontaneous, less formal" and was "prone to asides and deviations from the central theme" (p. 108). Wesche and Ready suggest that the English-speaking professor's adjustments "were a compensatory attempt to facilitate student understanding where they were less prepared to anticipate succeeding ideas" (p. 108). This was much less necessary for the French-speaking professor, since her presentations were more predictable.

   Wesche and Ready conclude that sheltered subject matter teachers, and native speakers in general, are able to make adjustments according to what they think their listeners will understand. It remains an empirical question just what adjustments can be taught and what adjustments are a natural result of attempting to communicate.

2. Canadian immersion programs can be classified as Second-Language Medium instruction. I have not reviewed studies of Canadian immersion here, since this has been done very thoroughly by Lambert and Tucker (1972) and by Swain and Lapkin (1982).

I have also not included Prabhu's task-based teaching project (Prabhu 1987) in Table 1, since there was no well-defined subject matter that his students were learning. Including his approach would certainly strengthen the case for Sheltered Subject Matter Teaching; Beretta and Davies (1985) reported that students acquiring English using Prabhu's method did very well compared to traditional students.

Several studies supporting the efficacy of sheltered subject matter teaching did not fit into the table. Using a test of aural grammar developed by Bialystok and Frohlich (1978), Mbazogo-Engama (1984) reported that sheltered subject matter students at the University of Ottawa made gains in both acquired and learned aspects of grammar, while students in regular French-as-a-second-language classes made significant gains only in learned grammar.

Saegert, Scott, Perkins, and Tucker (1974) found that years of content instruction through a foreign language was a better predictor of EFL proficiency than years of formal study of English. Interestingly, Saegert et al.'s results held for English as a foreign language even when the medium of instruction was French. Similarly, Gradman and Hanania (1991) found significant correlations between TOEFL test performance and years of second-language medium instruction in English among international students in the United States.

d'Anglejan, Renaud, Arsenault, and Lortie (1981) reported on the progress of immigrants to Quebec in a thirty-week French-as-a-second-language program that emphasized solving problems of everyday life in Quebec. Students in the program appeared to outperform comparison students in tests of French, but statistical analysis was not possible due to the small sample size and extreme variation of test scores in both groups.

Leaver and Stryker (1989) described Content-Based Russian and Spanish courses given by the Foreign Service Institute, and concluded that Content-Based instruction "appears to enhance the speed of foreign language acquisition" (p. 273). Freeman, Freeman, and Gonzales (1987) compiled an informal report on sheltered high school biology and history classes for ESL students in Arizona. According to Freeman et al., sheltered students made substantial gains in reading comprehension. Rydell (1987; reported in Watson, Northcutt, and Rydell 1989) found that sheltered ESL students in public schools outperformed controls in reading and language arts.

Lindholm and Padilla (1990) studied students in a "partial immersion" high school Spanish program that included both regular L2 instruction and Second-Language Medium instruction in which second language acquirers were mixed with native speakers. While partial-immersion students significantly outperformed students taking only regular Spanish classes, partial-immersion students had more exposure to Spanish both inside and outside school.

References

Appleby, B., and J. Conner. 1965. Well, What Did You Think of It? *English Journal* 54:606-612.

Asher, J. 1988. *Learning Another Language through Actions: The Complete Teacher's Guidebook*. Los Gatos, California: Sky Oaks Productions.

d'Anglejan, A., C. Renaud, R. Arsenault, and A. Lortie. 1981. *Difficultes d'apprentissage de la langue seconde chez l'immigrant adulte en situation scolaire.* Quebec: International Center for Research on Bilingualism.

Beretta, A., and A. Davies. 1985. Evaluation of the Bangladone Project. *ELT Journal* 39/2. Reprinted in Prabhu 1987.

Bialystok, M., and M. Frohlich. 1978. The Aural Grammar Test: Description and Implications. *Working Papers on Bilingualism* 15:15-35.

Buch, G., and I. de Bagheera. 1978. An Immersion Program for the Professional Improvement of Non-native Teachers of ESL. In *On TESOL '78*, ed. by C. Blatchford and J. Schachter, 106-17. Washington: TESOL.

Day, R., C. Omura, and M. Hiramatsu. 1991. Incidental vocabulary learning and reading. *Reading in a Foreign Language*. 7. 541-551.

Edwards, H., M. Wesche, S. Krashen, R. Clement, and B. Kruidenier. 1984. Second-Language Acquisition through Subject-Matter Learning: A Study of Sheltered Psychology Classes at the University of Ottawa. *The Canadian Modern Language Review* 41:268-282.

Elley, W., and F. Mangubhai. 1983. The Impact of Reading on Second Language Learning. *Reading Research Quarterly* 19: 53-67.

Ferris, D. 1988. Reading and Second Language Vocabulary Acquisition. Unpublished paper, Department of Linguistics, University of Southern California.

Freeman, D., Y. Freeman, and R. Gonzales. 1987. Success for LEP Students: The Sunnyside Sheltered English Program. *TESOL Quarterly*. 21. 361-367.

Goertzel, M., V. Goertzel, and T. Goertzel. 1978. *Three Hundred Eminent Personalities*. San Francisco: Jossey-Bass.

Gradman, H., and E. Hanania. 1991. Language Learning Background Factors and ESL Proficiency. *Modern Language Journal* 75:39-51.

Graman, T. 1987. The Gap between Lower- and Upper-Division Spanish Courses: A Barrier to Coming Up Through the Ranks. *Hispania* 70:929-35.

Hafiz, F., and I. Tudor. 1989. Extensive Reading and the Development of Language Skills. *English Language Teaching Journal* 43:4-13.

Hamelin, J., and J. Provencher. 1981. Breve histoire du Quebec. Montreal: Boreal.

Hammond, R. 1988. Accuracy versus Communicative Competency: The Acquisition of Grammar in the Second Language Classroom. *Hispania* 71:408-417.

Hauptman, P., M. Wesche, and D. Ready. 1988. Second-Language Acquisition through Subject Matter Learning: A Follow-up Study at the University of Ottawa. *Language Learning* 38:433-471.

Ho, K. 1982a. Effect of Language of Instruction on Physics Achievement. *Journal of Research in Science Teaching* 19:761-67.

Ho, 1982b. Teaching Physics through English. *Language Learning and Communication* 1:283-88.

Ho, K. 1985. The Paradox of Immersion in a Second Language. *NABE Journal* 10:51-64.

Janopoulos, M. 1986. The Relationship of Pleasure Reading and Second Language Writing Proficiency. *TESOL Quarterly* 20:763-68.

Kaplan, J., and E. Palhinda. 1981. Non-Native Speakers of English and Their Composition Abilities: A Review and Analysis. In *Linguistics and Literacy*, ed. by W. Frawley, 425-57. New York: Plenum Press.

Kiyochi, E. 1988. Second Language Vocabulary Acquisition in Japanese through Reading for Meaning: A Pilot Study. Unpublished paper, Department of Linguistics, University of Southern California.

Krashen, S. 1984. *Writing: Research, Theory and Applications.* Torrance, California: Laredo Publishing Co.

———. 1985a. *Inquiries and Insights.* Menlo Park, California: Alemany Press.

———. 1985b. *The Input Hypothesis.* Torrance, California: Laredo Publishing Co.

———. 1988. Do We Learn to Read by Reading? The Relationship between Free Reading and Reading Ability. *Linguistics in Context: Connecting Observation and Understanding,* ed. by D. Tannen, 269-98. Norwood, New Jersey: Ablex.

———. 1989. We Acquire Vocabulary and Spelling by Reading: Additional Evidence for the Input Hypothesis. *Modern Language Journal* 73:440-64.

Krashen, S., and D. Biber. 1988. *On Course: Bilingual Education's Success in California.* Sacramento: California Association for Bilingual Education.

Lafayette, R., and M. Buscaglia, M. 1985. Students Learn Language Via a Civilization Course—A Comparison of Second Language Classroom Environments. *Studies in Second Language Acquisition.* 7.323-42.

Lambert, W., and G. R. Tucker. 1972. *The Bilingual Education of Children.* New York: Newbury House.

Langer, J., A. Applebee, I. Mullis, and M. Foertsch. 1990. *Learning to Read in Our Nation's Schools: Instruction and Achievement in 1988 in Grades 4, 8, and 12.* Princeton, New Jersey: National Assessment of Educational Progress, Educational Testing Service.

Leaver, B., and S. Stryker. 1989. Content-based Instruction for Foreign Language Classrooms. *Foreign Language Annals* 22:269-275.

Lindholm, K. and A. Padilla. 1990. A High School Partial Immersion Program. In *Foreign Language Education: Issues and Strategies,* ed. by A. Padilla, H. Fairchild, and C. Valadez, 140-53. Newbury Park, California: Sage Publications.

Mbazogo-Engama, M. 1984. L'apprentissage des langues secondes dans une situation naturelle et formelle: Une etude de la grammaticalite auditive. M.A. Thesis, Department of Linguistics, University of Ottawa.

Nagy, W., and P. Herman. 1987. Breadth and Depth of Vocabulary Knowledge: Implications for Acquisition and Instruction. In *The Nature of Vocabulary Acquisition,* ed. by M. McKeown and M. Curtis, 19-35. Hillsdale, New Jersey: Erlbaum.

Nagy, W., P. Herman, and R. Anderson. 1985. Learning Words From Context. *Reading Research Quarterly* 20:233-253.

Peck, B. 1987. Spanish for Social Workers: An Intermediate-Level Communicative Course with Content Lectures. *Modern Language Journal* 71:402-9.

Pitts, M., H. White, S. Krashen. 1989. Acquiring Second Language Vocabulary through Reading: A Replication of the Clockwork Orange Study Using Second Language Acquirers. *Reading in a Foreign Language* 5:271-75.

Prabhu, N. S. 1987. *Second Language Pedagogy.* Oxford: Oxford University Press.

Ravitch, D., and C. Finn. 1987. *What Do Our 17-Year-Olds Know?* New York: Harper and Row.

Saegert, J., M. Scott, J. Perkins, and G. R. Tucker. 1974. A Note on the Relationship Between English Proficiency, Years of Language Study and Medium of Instruction. *Language Learning* 24:99-104.

Salyer, M. 1987. A Comparison of the Learning Characteristics of Good and Poor ESL Writers. *Applied Linguistics Interest Section Newsletter, TESOL* 8:2-3.

Schaefer, C., and A. Anastasi. 1968. A Biographical Inventory for Identifying Creativity in Adolescent Boys. *Journal of Applied Psychology* 58:42-48.

Schleppegrell, M. 1984. Using Input Methods to Improve Writing Skills. *System* 12:287-92.

Smart, M. 1978. A School/Community Newspaper's Effect on Literacy Development in Ghana. *Journalism Quarterly* 55:119-124.

Sternfeld, S. 1989. The University of Utah's Immersion Multiliteracy Program: An Example of an Area Studies Approach to the Design of First-Year College Foreign Language Instruction. *Foreign Language Annals* 22:341-53.

Swain, M. 1988. Manipulating and Complementing Content Teaching to Maximize Second Language Learning. *TESL Canada* 6:68-83.

Swain, M., and S. Lapkin. 1982. *Evaluating Bilingual Education: A Canadian Case Study*. Clevedon, Avon, England: Multilingual Matters.

Tardy, W. 1988. *Easy Spanish Reader*. Chicago: National Textbook Company.

Voge, W. 1981. Testing the Validity of Krashen's Input Hypothesis. Paper presented at the International Congress of Applied Linguistics, Lund, Sweden.

Watson, D., L. Northcutt, and L. Rydell. 1989. Teaching Bilingual Students Successfully. *Educational Leadership* 46:59-61.

Wesche, M., and D. Ready. 1985. Foreigner Talk in the University Classroom. In *Input in Second Language Acquisition*, ed. by S. Gass and C. Madden, 89-114. New York: Newbury House.

Williams, D. 1981. Factors Relating to Performance in Reading English as a Second Language. *Language Learning* 31:31-50.

Perspectives on Language Anxiety: An Interview with Tracy Terrell

Dolly J. Young
University of Tennessee

Tracy Terrell presented his perspectives regarding language anxiety in interview format with the author. He was one of the first linguists to acknowledge the significant role of affect in second-language acquisition and to develop a pedagogical approach that took affect into account. In the interview presented here Terrell responds to four questions: (1) Can we attribute a positive aspect to anxiety? (2) Do language learners experience an equal amount of anxiety in all four skill areas? (3) How do you see anxiety manifested in your language learners? (4) What do you perceive as effective anxiety management strategies? His responses are contrasted with existing research in the growing field of language anxiety and are also used to gain further insights into this phenomenon particular to language learning.

One can dissect a human body and find a heart, a brain, but one cannot locate objects that are properly called anxiety.

—Eugene Levitt

Language anxiety is a phenomenon requiring investigation from a variety of perspectives and approaches. It refers to a psychological phenomenon particular to language learning whereby the learner experiences intrusive negative self-related thoughts and emotions as a response to aspects of the language learning process. The student perspective on language anxiety has been well documented (in Bailey 1983; Koch and Terrell 1991; Price 1991; and Young 1991) and has provided much needed information about anxiety in language learning and performance. Other points of view, such as those of linguists and language teachers, have added to our understanding of this complex issue.

Anthropologists, journalists, and novelists have long relied on interviews to provide the kind of in-depth information that allegedly more "objective" techniques cannot.[1] I chose to use this qualitative data-gathering format to gain insights on language anxiety from the perspective of an established scholar, involved teacher and teacher trainer, and well-known researcher in second-language acquisition—Tracy Terrell.[2]

Terrell was the first linguist to recognize the important role of affect in second-language acquisition and to translate the concept of the *affective filter* into practical and pedagogical terms. The affective filter hypothesis was initially proposed by Dulay and Burt (1977) to explain how affective factors influence the process of L2 acquisition. In their book, Dulay, Burt, and Krashen defined the affective filter as follows:

> The filter is that part of the internal processing system that subconsciously screens incoming language based on what psychologists call 'affect': the learner's motives, needs, attitudes, and emotional states. (1982:46)

Krashen incorporated the affective filter into his Monitor Model theory of L2 acquisition. Terrell then transformed many of Krashen's hypotheses into practical and pedagogical terms in the Natural Approach. Six general premises from the Natural Approach framed the beginning language textbooks *Dos mundos*, *Deux mondes*, and *Kontakte* co-authored by Terrrell; these premises are listed in the preface to each text:

1. Comprehension precedes production.
2. Speech emerges in stages.
3. Speech emergence is characterized by grammatical errors.
4. Group work encourages speech.
5. Students acquire language only in a low-anxiety environment.
6. The goal of the Natural Approach is proficiency in communication skills.

The Natural Approach, through these textbooks, helped to popularize the notion that we must create a low-anxiety atmosphere in our L2 classes for effective and successful L2 acquisition.

Terrell's interest in converting theoretical concepts into pedagogical applications and his recognition of the importance of affective variables in L2 acquisition are further illustrated in the co-authored article "Affective Reactions of Foreign Language Students to Natural Approach Activities and Teaching Techniques." In this study, Koch and Terrell attempted to determine which aspects of the Natural Approach result in positive attitudes and whether there are any that actually increase anxiety. They found that most of the Natural Approach techniques produced comfort rather than anxiety, and they concluded that, "should students begin language study feeling anxious about studying a foreign language, the approach will help assuage their fears" (1991: 123).

Because of Terrell's theoretical and empirical research and his experience and expertise as a language learner and teacher, he was keenly aware of the importance and complex nature of language anxiety. Few people were more qualified to address theoretical and practical aspects of anxiety, including the problem of the conceptualization of anxiety and the role it plays in language learning, manifestations of anxiety, and suggestions for reducing anxiety.

 ## INTERVIEW FORMAT AND QUESTIONS

I sent Tracy Terrell a list of general questions prior to our telephone interview, which was approximately thirty- to forty-five-minutes long. Although I asked a variety of questions, only four of the most important are included here:

1. Can we attribute a positive aspect to anxiety?
2. Do language learners experience an equal amount of anxiety in all four skill areas?
3. How do you see anxiety manifested in your language learners?
4. What do you perceive as effective anxiety management strategies?

Since research on these issues is relatively scant, the questions are important because they lead to theoretical and practical insights about language anxiety that merit recognition and further investigation. To help the reader interpret Terrell's responses, I shall now summarize the relevant research.

 ## RESEARCH RELATED TO INTERVIEW QUESTIONS

In response to the first question, Terrell discussed whether anxiety makes any contribution to the language-learning context. Although much of the general research on anxiety suggests negative effects of anxiety on learning and performance (Beier Gunter 1951; Deffenbacher 1980; Gynther 1957; Sarason and Ganzer 1962; Spielberger 1966; Verma and Nijhawan 1976; Wine 1980), some anxiety may actually enhance performance. Alpert and Haber (1960) were the first to propose a positive aspect to anxiety. Based on their theory, they developed two separate scales—the Facilitating Anxiety Scale and the Debilitating Anxiety Scale—to measure anxiety. Kleinmann's study (1977) is the only one to follow Alpert and Haber's anxiety theory. He examined the notion of avoidance in the context of second-language learning. Spanish speakers and Arabic speakers were (on the basis of contrastive analysis) expected to avoid difficult structures, but some structures that were predicted to be avoided were actually produced, depending on the affective state of the learner. Learners who scored high on facilitating anxiety tended not to avoid the predicted structure.

In the second question, I asked whether language learners experience an equal amount of anxiety in all four skill areas. Research on language anxiety has consistently indicated that students experience anxiety in speaking a foreign language

(Bailey 1983; Horwitz et al. 1986; Phillips 1990; Price 1991; Steinberg and Horwitz 1986; Young 1991a, 1991b). Conversely, reading in French was found to have a significant negative correlation with anxiety in a study by Swain and Burnaby (1976), who were interested in the effect of various personality characteristics on second-language learning. Results of a personality test were correlated with French language competency scores. Anxiety was significantly related to reading skills but did not have a significant correlation, either positive or negative, to French listening comprehension, production, or achievement.

Other language-anxiety research suggests that students may experience less anxiety in reading and writing (Young 1991a) and in achievement tests (Tucker et al. 1976). Krashen (in this volume) contends that "free reading" is by its nature a low-anxiety skill, especially if students are allowed to select their reading materials. Although some research examines the relationship between anxiety and language learning or performance, little empirical research is available that investigates language anxiety as it relates specifically to listening, reading, or writing.

In the third question, I asked Terrell to identify ways learners might express their anxiety in the classroom. In the language-anxiety research, Bailey (1983) and Horwitz et al. (1986) identify a variety of anxiety-related behaviors unique to the foreign language classroom. Horwitz and her colleagues suggest that students are anxious when they avoid conveying difficult or personal messages in the foreign language; "freeze up" in role-play activities; report they "know" a certain grammar point but "forget" it in a test or an oral exercise when many grammar points must be remembered; complain of difficulties discriminating among the sounds and structures of a foreign language message; confess they know the correct answer on a test but put down the wrong one due to nervousness or carelessness; and overstudy without any improvement in grades (1986:126-127).

Bailey also identifies competitive behavior that leads to increased states of anxiety, such as obvious self-comparison to other classmates and personal expectations; hostile reactions toward other students based on comparisons; a desire to out-perform other classmates; an emphasis on tests and grades with reference to other student performances; and a mental (or physical), temporary (or permanent) withdrawal from the language-learning experience (Bailey 1983).

With the final question, Terrell gave his perspective on anxiety-management strategies. Most of the recent research on language anxiety has offered, directly and indirectly, suggestions for reducing anxiety in the classroom. These suggestions include having students work in small groups or pairs (Koch and Terrell 1991; Price 1991; Young 1991a); using self-talk and participating in supplemental instruction and support groups (Cope-Powell 1991); dispelling student beliefs about language learning (Horwitz 1988); playing language games in class (Saunders and Crookall 1985); sensitizing students to their fears and anxieties associated with language learning (Crookall and Oxford 1991; Foss and Reitzel 1988); using relaxation techniques, deep breathing, meditation, and music, discussing feelings with someone else, and keeping a journal (Oxford 1990b).

INTERVIEW

Young: Can we attribute a positive aspect to anxiety?

Terrell: Yes, except I wouldn't call the state "anxiety." What I call it is "attention," and specifically the verb I like to use is *to attend to* the input. If the teacher is too good at reducing anxiety and getting the students really relaxed into the Natural Approach and so forth, what happens with some of the students some of the time (and probably much more than I would like) is that they don't attend to the input very carefully. That is, they learn to attend to the input just enough to understand what the question is, or what the comment is, and they ignore everything else. This essentially means they ignore almost all of the grammatical markers.

I'm not so sure that Krashen's filter hypothesis is all that accurate. His hypothesis, the way I see it, is that if you raise a filter, it will filter out some of the input, and the input won't get to the acquisition device and so you won't acquire certain kinds of things. I do think that there is something to that. But I have a different view of why people acquire grammatical morphemes. Krashen's hypothesis is based on the implicit hypothesis that if you get input and if you understand it, you will acquire—that the acquisition is automatic.

My hypothesis is that the acquisition isn't automatic. I propose that acquisition follows two underlying principles. One I call "communicative need" (that's very common and everyone accepts that): if they need it to communicate, then they'll acquire it. And unfortunately, in the classroom communicative needs are not particularly high.

The second principle is what I call "target language group identification." I believe children acquire their first language and a second language in order to identify and be a member of the group that speaks that language. And so what happens is that this strong motivation for identification, or assimilation, forces them to attend to the input very carefully, so that their output will match the input.

So in a sense, I'm positing a kind of positive drive that says a student has to search out in the input those details and reproduce them in the output. The acquirer actually has to make a positive effort to attend to the input. Krashen's position is that acquisition is an automatic process that happens unless blocked. My feeling is that automaticity is possible, and that the learner can have blocks. But acquisition needs more than that: it needs a positive drive to go after something.

Now if you look at the classroom situation, you have two problems. Number one is the students don't have that drive to go after the details, to assimilate. Number two, they also don't have any reason to attend to the input very carefully because they don't need all those details to comprehend. For example, the only reason you need to acquire gender agreement in Spanish is so you'll sound like a native speaker, because gender agreement isn't necessarily communicative. So there's no reason for our students in the Spanish classroom to attend to gender agreement, because there are no consequences to not attending to it and not acquiring it. There are no communicative-need consequences; they don't have any drive to identify with Spanish-speakers and to assimilate. And there's certainly no need to attend to it from an information point of view. You can make a case that there's a subset of gender markings, like *amigo/amiga* that they do attend to, but the things like *mesa*, *bonita/bonito*, they don't attend to. So my hypothesis is that it's not the filter that's blocking that out, but rather that there's no motivation to attend to it.

So one might say that if the affective filter is too high it won't let in the input, and Krashen is right: if there's no input, you can't acquire it. If it is too low, then there's no motivation to attend to the input, and you won't acquire either. So that what one might want to say is that you need an optimal level of attention to the input of the classroom. The big question is, How do you get that? You want an optimal level of arousal that motivates the students to pay more careful attention to what you're saying. If you look back at L1 acquisition and ask, Do little kids have high levels of anxiety about learning language? I think you would have to say, No. But I also don't think that you could say that they are just relaxed, not really paying that much attention and going about their merry way. They have heightened levels of attention. And I think little kids, when they're getting into it and interacting with language, they really do pay attention to what people are saying. There is a positive force that causes little kids to take language acquisition seriously, and they work at it. They listen to what you say, they watch the context, and they're actively working at making connections between meaning and form. When they try to pronounce things and they try to produce things, it's a great effort. And so it's not that it's anxiety per se but rather a heightened level of attention.

And this is not necessarily negative. You know, in the Natural Approach, when I walk into the class I want the students to say, You've got to put effort out and pay attention and work at this thing. It's not like you just sit there and smile, enjoy yourself, and say any old thing that pops into your head.

Young: Do language learners experience an equal amount of anxiety in all four skill areas?

Terrell: Oh, speaking, absolutely. I had a student who did a lot of work on anxiety, enumerating the techniques that we use in the Natural Approach, and asking students, "What makes you more anxious and less anxious?" She included interest and all sorts of what she called "affective factors." The students rated them. Some of the activities came out higher and lower than we expected. But I remember that, in spite of the fact that in the Natural Approach we don't correct and we encourage students to say what they want and so forth, they still reported relatively high anxiety levels for *speaking in front of the class*. That category had higher anxiety levels, but I recall that we decided that even though those were the highest anxiety levels, they still did not reach levels to worry about. You certainly could not conclude that, therefore, Natural Approach students, in general, are anxious about speaking. In fact, you would conclude the opposite: that students in general are not anxious about speaking in the Natural Approach, and they speak without high levels of anxiety. However, it is true that of all the activities that is the highest.

Young: How do you see anxiety manifested in your language learners?

Terrell: There are a lot of individual reactions: some people have nervous laughter, some people look the other way, some people make jokes, they try to turn into clowns. Some students try to get away with the shortest answer possible.

Young: What do you perceive as effective anxiety-management strategies?

Terrell: In early stages of Natural Approach the first thing we did was to simply stop error correction in free conversation. And that is, we never interrupted the student to correct. And that was a pretty strong thing, from two points of view, first from the perspective of anxiety and the other from research in this area. Research demonstrated that interrupting students to correct them didn't help anyway. So the big change was error correction. Next we tried to focus on topics the student was interested in and knew something about. Presumably he wouldn't have to think so much and would become interested in what he was talking about; consequently, the anxiety level would go down. It turns out that that is not necessarily the case. It is a mistaken idea that talking about what the student is interested in and the student's own experiences will lower his anxiety level. I suspect it's the other way around: if you do rote drills, in which the student has no emotional investment at all, then there's no anxiety in getting the answer right.

When the topics become more personal, when they're putting themselves on the line, then it isn't as easy. We have the hypothesis that the more personal, the more interested, the more involved the student, the more they'll want to say something and the less anxious they'll be, but that's not necessarily the case.

The teacher doesn't always know what topics are best for the student. The teacher might be asking things like, "How many brothers and sisters do you have?" and "What kind of work does your mother do?" or "What would you like to do this weekend?" And we all think, "Oh, those are all the kinds of personalized questions designed to lower filters." But these questions don't necessarily lower filters. Some students would much rather talk about the Middle East than talk about their mother.

DISCUSSION AND IMPLICATIONS

Tracy Terrrell's perspectives, coupled with existing research, offer clear directions for the kind of research needed to understand language anxiety more fully and completely. Although some of his insights stemmed from his own scholarship and theoretical expertise, other insights clearly came from his experience as a language teacher, suggesting that teachers may have qualitatively refined perceptions on language anxiety.

Question 1: Can We Attribute a Positive Aspect to Anxiety?

Past language-anxiety research has attempted to define anxiety using existing psychological constructs such as test anxiety, communication apprehension, and fear of negative evaluation (see Horwitz et al. 1986). Terrell's response sensitizes us to other aspects of language anxiety that need to be included in any theoretical model.

Terrell believed that there may be a positive aspect to anxiety, if by anxiety we mean a state of "attentiveness." Terrell argued that learners need input, but they also need to be attentive to that input for successful language learning. Educational psychologists have identified a psychological phenomenon similar to the idea of "attentiveness" in the Yerkes-Dodson law which claims that level of arousal is related to performance. As arousal increases so does performance. Too much arousal, however, can lead to a decrease in performance. This relationship between arousal and performance depends on the complexity of the task.

There is evidence to suggest, however, that students experience a considerable amount of foreign language anxiety in their classes (Horwitz et al. 1986) and that anxiety levels may be higher in foreign language classes than in other classes. Krashen believes there is no positive aspect to anxiety in language acquisition (but there may be for language learning) and that the traditional language learning environment is already inherently anxiety-evoking at levels beyond the beneficial (Young 1991a). In a study by MacIntyre and Gardner, for example, French-class anxiety was rated significantly higher as compared to math- and English-class anxieties (1989:13). MacIntyre and Gardner subsequently wrote:

> During the first few experiences in the foreign language, anxiety plays a negligible role in proficiency since, even if anxiety is present, it is not . . . specific to the language learning situation. Anxiety aroused in this context, as a result of early language experience, would best be called state anxiety. After several experiences with the second language context, the student forms attitudes that are specific to the situation—emotions and attitudes about learning a new language. If these experiences are negative, foreign language anxiety may begin to develop. As negative experiences persist, foreign language anxiety may become a regular occurrence and the student begins to expect to be nervous and perform poorly. (MacIntyre and Gardner 1991a:110)

Terrell also posits that anxiety in the language-learning context is "wrapped up" in what he calls "target-language group identification." He holds a view of language anxiety close to that of existential anxiety as explained by Rardin (Young 1991a).[3] For Rardin, existential anxiety is a more profound type of anxiety inherently built into the language-learning process, particularly for adolescents and adults, that "touches the core of one's self-identity, one's self-image. . . ." According to her, the learner's train of thought is somewhat as follows: "If I learn another language, I will somehow lose myself; I, as I know myself to be, will cease to exist" (p. 35). These psychological phenomena are particular to the language-learning context in much the same way as are Schumann's concept of "social distance" (1978), Guiora's idea of "language ego" (1972), and Clarke's theory of "clash of consciousness" or cultural assimilation (1976), and merit consideration in any theoretical model of language anxiety.

For Terrell, target-language group identification is not sufficient for successful language learning. He suggests that a certain amount of attention to the input is also necessary. The idea that learners need some kind of positive drive—making them attentive to the details in language for later reproduction in the output—provides a basis for the growing interest in task-based instruction and grammar activities that actually require students to attend specifically to grammatical details (see VanPatten 1993 and VanPatten et al. 1992).

Terrell's emphasis on input in L2 acquisition has also led to research on input processing. VanPatten (in progress) posits that too much anxiety might inhibit the processing and, perhaps, cause the processing system to go into overload. His hypothesis is borne out in recent research by MacIntyre and Gardner, who examined the effects of language anxiety on input. They point out that "during the initial processing of incoming information, attention and concentration are critical to the accurate representation of stimuli items in memory" (1991b:516). MacIntyre and Gardner measured anxiety through a variety of anxiety-related tests, and in this study it was only language anxiety that had a significant negative correlation with performance on a vocabulary and digit-span test in the L2 versus the native language. Their results suggest language anxiety negatively affects the processing of language input.

Regarding the relative effects of language anxiety on language learning, Terrell's remarks raise a number of issues requiring further research. Do we want to create an environment in language classes that is so anxiety-free that students do not take anything in? Terrell discussed a necessary state of attentiveness for effective language learning, but can these states be considered facilitative anxiety or a cognitive/emotional phenomenon separate from language anxiety and linked to model language-learning behavior?

Question 2: Do Language Learners Experience an Equal Amount of Anxiety in All Four Skill Areas?

Terrell believed that speaking in the foreign language probably produces the greatest amount of anxiety in language learners. Again, his insights are noteworthy and have inspired research on language anxiety as it relates to language skills. Speaking in front of the class appears to be the most anxiety-provoking situation for language learners, according to their own admission (Bailey 1983; Horwitz et al. 1986; Price 1991; Young 1991a, 1991b). Researchers have recently begun to investigate why this is so. What is it about speaking that evokes anxiety in learners, and do they experience the same negative effects of anxiety with L1 in the same contexts?

One group (Ganschow, Sparks, Anderson, Javorsky, and Skinner) found that highly anxious language learners exhibited poorer native-language skills and foreign language aptitude (particularly in expressive skills like understanding and applying the phonological code) than did learners with low levels of anxiety. Their results (to be published) suggest that phonological difficulty negatively affects learners' speaking ability and may be the root of their high levels of language anxiety. Other research demonstrates that one reason why students tend to react favorably to the Natural Approach is that this methodology recognizes the negative effects of speaking before students have had sufficient language input (Young and Oxford 1993).

Question 3: How Do You See Anxiety Manifested in Your Language Learners?

Recognizing manifestations of anxiety is an important step in reducing language anxiety. The manifestations of anxiety identified by Terrell are similar to what has been reported in language-anxiety research. Perhaps language teachers have accurate perceptions of anxiety behavior in students. Often we tend not to trust those perceptions. The first challenge for language teachers, then, is to (a) be sensitive to the signals students provide, (b) recognize the behaviors for what they are, (c) trust your perceptions, and (d) work to reduce language anxiety.

Question 4: What Do You Perceive as Effective Anxiety-Management Strategies?

Terrell's remarks sensitize us to two issues long associated with creating a comfortable atmosphere in the L2 class. Terrell believed that by being aware of individual differences in learners, or being sensitive to personalized statements that may evoke anxiety in some students, we can reduce language anxiety. In other words, he suggested that teachers get to know each class of students well and be sensitive to their needs and their emotional baggage. His insights were very much on target given that there is increasing interest in, and research on, individual differences in learners. In addition to language anxiety, there is a wealth of recent research on the differences in student learning styles (Oxford 1990a) and learning strategies (Oxford 1990b; Wenden and Rubin 1987).

 CONCLUSION

In this interview, Tracy Terrell offered insight on language anxiety from several points of view. In most instances, his perspective either corroborated empirical findings based on the student's perspective or offered insights for a growing field of research in language anxiety. Terrell's responses are particularly significant in light of MacIntyre and Gardner's recent hypothesis on foreign language anxiety (1989; 1991b) in which they suggested that language anxiety is probably a product of students' negative foreign language classroom experiences. If MacIntyre and Gardner's hypothesis is correct, then most of the problem lies not with the student but with the methodology. Student anxiety could be an indication that we might be doing something fundamentally unnatural in our pedagogy.[4] As potential solutions to this dilemma, Terrell's Natural Approach and his theoretical and empirical research focus attention on affect in L2 pedagogy and will remain an essential part of future inquiry and pedagogical growth.

Notes

1. The interview technique has a long history of use in the social sciences. Refer to Anne Fenlason, *Essentials in Interviewing* (New York: Harper and Row, 1952) and Howard Schwartz, *Qualitative Sociology* (New York: The Free Press, 1979).

2. Terrell, as well as other individuals I interviewed (Stephen Krashen, Alice Omaggio Hadley, and Jennybell Rardin), consented to be interviewed and permitted the remarks to be published.

3. The thoughts on existential anxiety expressed by Rardin are in my original interview and are not cited in the responses that comprise the report in *Foreign Language Annals*.

4. Although a classroom setting (including grades for language performance) *is* an unnatural setting, the methodologies within this setting can emphasize a more authentic approach to language learning. When they do not (as in cases where there is a harsh manner of error correction, a constant spotlighting of students in front of the class, or an emphasis on grammar versus meaning), then the method has become even more unnatural than necessary.

References

Alpert, R., and R. N. Haber. 1960. Anxiety in Academic Achievement Situations. *Journal of Abnormal and Social Psychology* 61:207-215.

Bailey, Kathleen M. 1983. Competitiveness and Anxiety in Adult Second Language Learning: Looking at and through the Diary Studies. In *Classroom Oriented Research in Second Language Acquisition*, ed. H. W. Seliger and M. H. Long, 67-102. Rowley, Mass.: Newbury House.

Beier Gunter, E. 1951. The Effect of Induced Anxiety on Flexibility of Intellectual Functioning. In *Psychological Monographs: General and Applied*, ed. Herbert S. Conrad, 1-26. Washington, D.C.: American Psychological Association.

Chastain, Kenneth. 1975. Affective and Ability Factors in Second Language Learning. *Language Learning* 25:153-161.

Clarke, Mark A. 1976. Second Language Acquisition as a Clash of Consciousness. *Language Learning* 26:377-389.

Cope-Powell, Jo Ann. 1991. Foreign Language Classroom Anxiety: Institutional Responses. In Horwitz and Young 1991, 169-176.

Crookall, David, and Rebecca Oxford. 1991. Dealing with Anxiety: Some Practical Activities for Language Learners and Teacher Trainees. In Horwitz and Young 1991, 140-150.

Deffenbacher, J. L. 1980. Worry and Emotionality in Test Anxiety. In *Test Anxiety: Theory, Research and Application*, ed. Irwin G. Sarason, 111-129. Hillsdale, N.J.: Erlbaum.

Dulay, Heidi C., and Marina K. Burt. 1977. Remarks on Creativity in Language Acquisition. In *Viewpoints on English as a Second Language*, ed. M. Burt, H. Dulay, and M. Finocciaro. New York: Regents.

Dulay, Heidi C., Marina K. Burt, and Stephen Krashen. 1982. *Language Two*. New York: Oxford University Press.

Foss, Karen A., and A. C. Reitzel. 1988. A Relational Model for Managing Second Language Anxiety. *TESOL Quarterly* 22:437-454.

Ganschow, Leonore, Richard Sparks, Reed Anderson, James Javorsky, and Sue Skinner. 1994, in press. Differences in Language Performance among High, Average, and Low Anxious College Foreign Language Learners. *Modern Language Journal*.

Gardner, R. C., P. C. Smythe, R. Clement, and L. Gliksman. 1976. Second Language Learning: A Social-psychological Perspective. *Canadian Modern Language Review* 32:198-213.

Guiora, Alexander Z. 1972. Construct Validity and Transpositional Research: Toward an Empirical Study of Psychoanalytic Concepts. *Comprehension Psychiatry* 13:139-150.

Gynther, R. A. 1957. The Effects of Anxiety and of Situational Stress on Communicative Efficiency. *Journal of Abnormal and Social Psychology* 54:274-276.

Horwitz, Elaine K. 1988. The Beliefs about Language Learning of Beginning University Foreign Language Students. *Modern Language Journal* 72:283-294.

Horwitz, Elaine K., Michael B. Horwitz, and Jo Ann Cope. 1986. Foreign Language Classroom Anxiety. *Modern Language Journal* 70:125-132.

Horwitz, Elaine K., and Dolly J. Young, eds. 1991. *Language Anxiety: From Theory and Research to Classroom Implications.* Englewood Cliffs, N.J.: Prentice-Hall.

Kleinmann, Howard. 1977. Avoidance Behavior in Adult Second Language Acquisition. *Language Learning* 27:93-107.

Koch, April, and Tracy David Terrell. 1991. Affective Reactions of Foreign Language Students to Natural Approach Activities and Teaching Techniques In Horwitz and Young 1991, 109-126.

Levitt, Eugene E. 1980. The Experimental Measurement of Anxiety. In *The Psychology of Anxiety*, ed. , 47-71. Hillsdale, N.J.: Erlbaum.

MacIntyre, Peter D., and Robert C. Gardner. 1988. The Measurement of Anxiety and Applications to Second Language Learning: An Annotated Bibliography (*Research Bulletin No. 672*). London, Ontario: University of Western Ontario.

———. 1989. Anxiety and Second Language Learning: Toward a Theoretical Clarification. *Language Learning* 39:251-275.

———. 1991a. Language Anxiety: Its Relationship to Other Anxieties and to Processing in Native and Second Languages. *Language Learning* 41:513-534.

———. 1991b. Methods and Results in the Study of Anxiety and Language Learning: A Review of the Literature. *Language Learning* 41:85-117.

Madsen, Harold S., Bruce B. Brown, and Randall L. Jones. 1991. Evaluating Student Attitudes toward Second Language Tests. In Horwitz and Young 1991, 165-185.

Oxford, Rebecca. 1990a. Language Learning Strategies and Beyond: A Look at Strategies in the Context of Styles. In *Shifting the Instructional Focus to the Learner*, ed. S. S. Magnan, 35-55. Middlebury, Vt.: Northeast Conference on the Teaching of Foreign Languages.

———. 1990b. *Language Learning Strategies: What Every Teacher Should Know.* New York: Newbury House.

Phillips, Elaine M. 1990. The Effects of Anxiety on Performance and Achievement in an Oral Test of French. Ph.D. dissertation, University of Texas, Austin.

Price, Mary Lou. 1991. The Subjective Experience of Foreign Language Anxiety: Interviews with Anxious Students. In Horwitz and Young 1991, 101-108.

Sarason, Irwin G., and V. J. Ganzer. 1962. Anxiety, Reinforcement and Experimental Instructions in a Free Verbalization Situation. *Journal of Abnormal and Social Psychology* 67:513-519.

Saunders, Danny, and David Crookall. 1985. Playing with a Second Language. *Simulation/Games for Learning* 15:166-172.

Schumann, J. H. 1978. The Acculturation Model for Second Language Acquisition. In *Second Language Acquisition and Foreign Language Teaching*, ed. R. C. Gingras. Arlington, Va.: Center for Applied Linguistics.

Spielberger, Charles. 1966. *Anxiety and Behavior.* New York: Academic Press.

Steinberg, Faith. S., and Elaine K. Horwitz. 1986. The Effect of Induced Anxiety on the Denotative and Interpretive Content of Second Language Speech. *TESOL Quarterly* 20:131-136.

Swain, Merrill, and Barbara Burnaby. 1976. Personality Characteristics and Second Language Learning in Young Children: A Pilot Study. *Working Papers in Bilingualism* 2:115-28.

Terrell, Tracy D., Magdalena Andrade, Jeanne Egasse, and Elías Miguel Muñoz. 1994. *Dos mundos.* 3rd edition. New York: McGraw-Hill.

Terrell, Tracy D., Mary B. Rogers, Betsy K. Barnes, and Marguerite Wolff-Hessini. 1993. *Deux mondes: A Communicative Approach.* 2nd edition. New York: McGraw-Hill.

Terrell, Tracy D., Erwin Tschirner, Brigitte Nikolai, and Herbert Genzmer. 1992. *Kontakte: A Communicative Approach*. 2nd edition. New York: McGraw-Hill.

Tucker, Richard, Else Hamayan, and Fred H. Genesse. 1976. Affective, Cognitive, and Social Factors in Second Language Acquisition. *Canadian Modern Language Review* 32:214-26.

VanPatten, Bill. 1993. Input Processing and Second Language Acquisition: A Role for Instruction. *Modern Language Journal* 77:45-57.

VanPatten, Bill. Forthcoming. Tailoring Grammar to Acknowledge Affect in L2 Grammar Instruction. In *Affect in L2 Learning: A Practical Guide to Dealing with Learner Anxieties*, ed. Dolly J. Young.

VanPatten, Bill, James F. Lee, Terry L. Ballman, and Trisha Dvorak. 1992. *¿Sabías qué?* New York: McGraw-Hill.

Verna, P., and H. Nijhawan. 1976. The Effect of Anxiety Reinforcement and Intelligence on the Learning of a Difficult Task. *Journal of Experimental Child Psychology* 22:302-308.

Wenden, Anita, and Joan Rubin. 1987. *Learner Strategies in Language Learning*. Englewood Cliffs, N.J.: Prentice-Hall.

Wine, Jeri Dawn. 1980. Cognitive-Attentional Theory of Test Anxiety. In *Test Anxiety: Theory, Research and Application*, ed. Irwin G. Sarason, 349-385. Hillsdale, N.J.: Erlbaum.

Wittenborn, J. R., R. P. Larsen, and R. L. Mogil. 1945. An Empirical Evaluation of Study Habits for College Courses in French and Spanish. *Journal of Educational Psychology* 36:449-474.

Young, Dolly J. 1991a. An Investigation of Students' Perspectives on Anxiety and Speaking. *Foreign Language Annals* 23:539-553.

———. 1991b. Creating a Low-Anxiety Classroom Environment: What Does the Language Anxiety Research Suggest? *Modern Language Journal* 75:426-437.

Young, Dolly J., and Rebecca Oxford. 1993. Attending to Learner Reactions to Introductory Spanish Textbooks. *Hispania*. 76: 593-605.

Attitudes, Variables, and the Affective Filter in the Acquisition of Second-Language Sound Systems

Robert M. Hammond
Purdue University

Although the Natural Approach has contributed much to current classroom methodologies for language teaching, it has not been widely applied to the teaching of pronunciation. The research reported in this paper provides empirical data on the acquisition of pronunciation in the context of certain affective variables. The data come from a group of native speakers of Spanish studying English, who were queried about attitudes and stereotypes toward foreign accents as well as their own pronunciation proficiency. In addition, their ESL teachers provided evaluations of the students' English pronunciation. Several conclusions can be drawn from the data and, it is hoped, will lead to further research on the application of Natural Approach theory to the teaching of pronunciation.

 INTRODUCTION

As a major contributor to both the theoretical development and the classroom application of the Natural Approach to language teaching, Tracy D. Terrell probably had a greater impact on present-day teaching of second and foreign languages in the United States than has any other individual. In developing his theory of second-language acquisition (Terrell 1977, 1982, 1986a, 1986b, 1989, 1990, and 1991), Terrell relied heavily on Krashen's monitor model (Krashen 1981, 1982, and 1985). Later, together with Krashen, Terrell published *The Natural Approach: Language Acquisition in the Classroom* (Krashen and Terrell 1983), in which this previously developed theoretical framework was presented so that classroom language teachers could understand it and apply its important features to their own work. To complete the cycle from abstract theory to hands-on classroom language teaching, Terrell was the major author of three highly successful textbooks (Terrell, Andrade, et al. 1994; Terrell, Rogers, et al. 1993; and Terrell, Tschirner, et al. 1992) that brought the Natural Approach into the classroom.

The Natural Approach framework successfully incorporates the well-known acquisition-learning hypothesis, monitor hypothesis, natural order hypothesis, input hypothesis, and affective filter hypothesis. The first three of these hypotheses are central to the organization of a language program using the Natural Approach (Krashen and Terrell 1983); that is, they form the underlying bases for a program to develop in beginning students as much communicative competency as possible in a beginning language course or series of beginning language courses. The input and affective filter hypotheses, however, determine on a day-to-day basis what actually takes place in the second-language classroom. In very general terms, the *input hypothesis* states that we must provide as much comprehensible input as possible for a student in the second-language classroom, since within the Natural Approach theoretical framework it is claimed that language is acquired (not learned) through comprehensible input becoming comprehended input. The notion of the *affective filter* is much less controversial and is valid for almost all language teaching methodologies. Originally presented by Dulay and Burt (1977), it states that the affective variables of motivation, self-confidence, and anxiety (Krashen 1982) have a profound influence on language acquisition (not learning). The claim of the Natural Approach, then, is that students will acquire second languages best when they are in an environment providing a maximally low (weak) affective filter and a maximally high amount of comprehensible input.[1]

After presenting their theoretical framework, Krashen and Terrell devote the remainder of their 1983 book (Chapters 4–7) to practical methods that will facilitate the classroom teacher's implementation of the Natural Approach. The authors show how curriculum organization, testing, reading, writing, vocabulary, and homework fit into the communicative teaching framework. They also discuss specific classroom topics such as teacher intervention, error correction, the order of grammar rules, modification for age differences, and additional sources of comprehensible input. Furthermore, they suggest many types of activities that can be utilized in the Natural Approach classroom.

However, neither Krashen and Terrell nor any other proponents of communicatively-based teaching methodologies make any genuine effort to deal with the teaching of pronunciation in the second-language classroom. It is particularly surprising that proponents of the so-called proficiency movement, while placing a great deal of emphasis on linguistic accuracy in the nascent stages of second-language acquisition (to avoid what they term *fossilization*), include no provision for the teaching of pronunciation in the classroom (see, for example, Omaggio 1986). After surveying different communicative methodologies, Terrell likewise arrives at the same conclusion, stating that "communicative approaches likewise have not known what to do with pronunciation" (Terrell 1989:197).

Given the fact that the teaching of pronunciation in communicative models has an undefined status, the present research was undertaken to explore some of the roles of the affective variables of linguistic stereotyping and language-learner attitudes in the pronunciation acquisition process, as these factors may have an important influence on student progress in the acquisition of a second language. The vast majority of adults who study second languages fail to acquire what could be described as a native or even nativelike pronunciation in these languages. Likewise, these same adult language learners seem initially to make remarkable progress in acquiring the sound system of these target languages, only to experience a dramatic drop-off in the pronunciation acquisition process after little more than the minimally essential elements of the second-language sound system have been internalized (acquired). That is, adult learners seem to achieve a certain level of pronunciation proficiency in a second language, but they then fail to improve their pronunciation significantly.

It is hypothesized in this paper that adult-learner attitudes toward second languages and language acquisition may be important factors underlying problems in acquiring a nativelike pronunciation. Several affective variables will be explored, with data relative to the following second-language acquisition attitudinal variables presented and analyzed: (1) the ability of subjects to evaluate their own level of pronunciation proficiency accurately; (2) subjects' attitudes toward foreign accent; (3) the correlation of second-language acquirers' degree of pronunciation proficiency with their attitudes toward foreign accent; and (4) subject reactions to three common linguistic stereotypes concerning accent in a second language.

 ## METHODOLOGY

The data under analysis in the present study come from two sources: the responses given on a questionnaire administered to 412 subjects who are all native speakers of Spanish and who have studied English as a second language for at least two years, and a pronunciation-evaluation questionnaire completed by the English instructors of these same 412 subjects. Seventy-eight percent of the subjects are natives of Cuba, while the remaining 22% come from Mexico, Puerto Rico, Spain, El Salvador, Honduras, Nicaragua, Chile, and Colombia. Fifty-seven percent of the subjects are female, and the 412 subjects ranged in age from 18 to 66 years, their median age being 27.6 years. Seventy-three percent of these subjects were between 20 and 49 years of age (mean age: 30.1 years; standard deviation: 13.7). Among the subjects, 69% had resided in the United States for fewer than five years, and all were permanent residents of the Little Havana area of Miami, Florida. A thirty-three–item questionnaire (written in Spanish) was administered to each of the subjects; the responses to six of these items will be analyzed here. The instructors who evaluated the pronunciation of the 412 subjects were all native speakers of American English. The subjects represented 412 of the total enrollment of 421 students in English-as-a-second-language classes taught by native speakers of American English in Miami over a four-year period. Nine subjects were eliminated because they were not native speakers of Spanish.

 ## SUBJECTS' SELF-EVALUATION

On the questionnaire, subjects were asked to evaluate their own pronunciation of American English according to a five-category scale. Responses to this questionnaire item are shown in the first column of Table 1.

Table 1. Overall Evaluation of Pronunciation

	Self-Evaluation %	Instructor Evaluation %
Excellent	9	6
Good	23	23
Average	51	37
Poor	16	20
Very Poor	1	4

An overall comparison of the student self-evaluations and the instructor evaluations shows basic agreement. Generally speaking, those subjects with better English pronunciation tended to underestimate slightly the quality of their pronunciation, while those individuals evaluated as having the greatest overall pronunciation deficiency tended to overestimate their pronunciation achievement in English.

The results of a one-to-one correlation of each of the 412 subjects' self-evaluation of their English pronunciation with the evaluation of their instructors are shown in Table 2.

Table 2. Correlation: Self-Evaluation and Instructor Evaluation

Type of Correlation	Levels of Difference	Correlation Percentage
Subject Overestimate	3	1
Subject Overestimate	2	3
Subject Overestimate	1	22
Perfect Correlation	0	49
Subject Underestimate	1	22
Subject Underestimate	2	2
Subject Underestimate	3	1

In 49% of the cases, there is a perfect correlation between subject self-evaluation and instructor evaluation, and there is a close correlation (only one level of difference) in an additional 44% of the cases. That is, in only seven percent of the cases were the subject self-evaluation and the corresponding instructor evaluation extremely different (by two or more levels). It is clear from these data that the 412 subjects made highly accurate evaluations of their own level of pronunciation achievement in American English.

 ## ATTITUDES TOWARD ACCENTED SPEECH

Another item on the questionnaire used in the data-collection process asked the subjects to give their opinion of foreign accents in general. They were specifically asked to give their impression of foreign accents according to one of five categories. Six

percent of the subjects indicated that second language accents sound very nice, 23% evaluated them as nice, 33% as bad, and 8% as very bad; the remaining 30% felt they were not important. In other words, only 41% of these subjects felt that, generally speaking, foreign accents should be considered as a negative factor in second-language acquisition.

A more specific item on the questionnaire tested subject reaction to a Spanish accent in their own English pronunciation. The questionnaire statement "It is very important to try to eliminate Spanish accent in your English pronunciation" drew strong agreement from 49% of the subjects, agreement in 36% of the cases, disagreement from 13% of the subjects, and a strong disagreement in only 2% of the cases. Thus, with respect specifically to Spanish accent in the English of these 412 subjects, 85% found accent to be a negative factor. This difference of 44 percentage points between the 41% of the subjects who reported that in general they considered second accents as negative and the 85% reporting that they considered a Spanish accent in their *own* English as negative factor is striking.

However, it is not immediately obvious to what exactly such a difference is to be attributed. The difference may indicate that subjects were more tolerant of another's accent but far more demanding of themselves. Another possible interpretation of this wide difference (44 percentage points) is that theoretical or hypothetical situations (second accents in general) versus specific, real personal situations elicit very different reactions on the part of adult second-language acquirers. There are, of course, other possible interpretations. The unique source of the data utilized herein, to be discussed in the conclusions of this study, may also have had a strong effect on some of the results presented.

 ## CORRELATION OF ATTITUDE AND ACHIEVEMENT

Based on data from the questionnaire, the study then constructed a correlation of the attitudes expressed by the subjects toward Spanish accent in their own English pronunciation with the actual quality of English pronunciation they had achieved, as evaluated by their instructors. The results are displayed in Table 3.

Table 3. Correlation between Subjects' Attitude Toward Pronunciation and Actual Pronunciation Achievement

Subject Attitude	Subject Pronunciation Achievement				
	Excellent	Good	Average	Poor	Very Poor
"Elimination of Spanish accent is important."					
Strongly Agree	41%	59%	44%	59%	30%
Agree	48%	27%	40%	18%	45%
Disagree	11%	9%	14%	23%	25%
Strongly Disagree	0%	5%	2%	0%	0%
TOTALS	100%	100%	100%	100%	100%

One might hypothesize a high positive correlation between the subjects' desire to eliminate foreign accent and the actual achievement of high-quality pronunciation in their own English. Therefore, we might expect Table 3 to show that the subjects evaluated as having an excellent English pronunciation would be the most intolerant of foreign accent, and that those with the poorest English pronunciation would conversely be the most tolerant of foreign accent. The data shown in Table 3, however, show inconsistent results.

Eighty-nine percent of the subjects who were evaluated as having excellent English pronunciation expressed disapproval of a Spanish accent in their English, and 86% of the subjects whose English pronunciation was evaluated as good also expressed disapproval of a Spanish accent in their English. An analysis of the data for only these two subgroups of subjects yields an expected high positive correlation between Spanish accent disapproval and the quality of English pronunciation achieved by the subjects. Up to this point, a hypothesis predicting high pronunciation achievement and lack of foreign accent tolerance appears to be tenable.

Unfortunately, the data from the three subgroups of subjects with the lowest levels of English pronunciation achievement do not support such a hypothesis. The data in Table 3 indicate that all five subgroups favor the elimination of Spanish accents in English. In particular, 84% of the subjects with an average English pronunciation, 77% with a poor pronunciation, and 75% with very poor pronunciation expressed disapproval of Spanish-accented English. Based on an analysis of these data, there seems to be no obvious correlation between tolerance of foreign accent and quality of second-language pronunciation. There does seem to be some movement toward a positive correlation in these data, in that the percentages of subjects demonstrating excellent English pronunciation to very poor pronunciation do move generally through the five subgroups from higher to lower percentages of disapproval of foreign accent (89% - 86% - 84% - 77% - 75%, respectively). These observed differences in percentages, however, are not statistically significant, at least not based on a data sample of this size.

EFFORT, INTELLIGENCE, AND FOREIGN ACCENT

The questionnaire also included an item which sought subject opinion concerning the supposed relationship between language-learner effort and intelligence and the ability to eliminate foreign accent. Subjects reacted as follows to the statement "Hard-working and intelligent people can always succeed in eliminating foreign accent": 20% of the subjects indicated strong agreement, 31% agreement, 35% disagreement, and 9% strong disagreement; the remaining 5% of the subjects didn't know if the statement was true of false. That is, 51% of these subjects believed the stereotype that if you are intelligent and make an effort you can always rid yourself of a foreign accent. Forty-four percent of the subjects expressed disagreement with the supposed relationship expressed in this questionnaire statement.

JOB SUCCESS AND FOREIGN ACCENT

The 412 subjects in the present study were also asked how they felt about the relationship between employment success and foreign accent. The questionnaire statement read, "A foreign accent decreases an individual's probability of job success." Fourteen percent of the subjects strongly agreed with this statement, 30% agreed, 38% disagreed, 14% strongly disagreed, and 4% did not know. Therefore, a majority of these subjects (52%) did not believe the stereotype that a foreign accent had a negative effect on probability of job success. It is interesting to note that although 85% of these same subjects believed that a Spanish accent in their own English was a negative factor, only 44% of them believed that a foreign accent in general was detrimental to job success. Although these two findings seem to contradict one another, there is an explanation for this seeming discrepancy due to the nature of the data source.

SECOND-LANGUAGE COMMUNICATION AND FOREIGN ACCENT

In the final questionnaire item to be included in the study, subjects were asked to agree or disagree with the statement, "If an individual can express himself in a second language, the fact that he speaks with a foreign accent is of little importance." Thirty-six percent of the subjects strongly agreed with this statement, 43% agreed, 14% disagreed, 6% strongly disagreed, and 1% did not know. Once again, although 85% of these individuals believed that a Spanish accent in their English was a negative factor, only 20% of these same subjects felt that the presence of a foreign accent in general was detrimental if an individual could otherwise express himself or herself in a second language.

 CONCLUSIONS

Before presenting any conclusions based on the information presented in this study, it should be stated that the data analyzed must be considered tentative due to both the limited size of the corpus under analysis (412 subjects) and the interim nature of the study. In the future, data that has been gathered from a more diversified group of subjects will be analyzed. Furthermore, the remaining 27 items from the subjects' questionnaire will be analyzed and correlated with the data just presented.

With these limitations in mind, these data seem to support the following conclusions:

1. A majority of the second-language learners queried believe that if one is intelligent and makes an effort at it, one can always rid oneself of a foreign accent. They also felt that a foreign accent was not a detriment to job success.

2. Only 20% of these same subjects felt that the presence of a foreign accent was a negative factor even though the speaker could otherwise communicate in a second language.

3. Second-language learners appear to be highly capable of accurately evaluating the quality of their own pronunciation in a second language.

4. The majority of the subjects surveyed (59%) did not object to foreign accents in general, but a greater majority of them (85%) did object specifically to the presence of a Spanish accent in their English pronunciation.

5. There appears to be no apparent correlation between a second-language learner's disapproval of foreign accent and his or her actual acquisition of a high-quality pronunciation in a second language.

Some of the apparent contradictions present in the data may be explainable in terms of the unique sociolinguistic nature of the bilingual community in which all 412 subjects resided. The so-called Cuban section of Miami, *La Sagüesera*, is generally understood by area residents to include most of the southwest quadrant of the city of Miami, a large portion of Miami's northwest quadrant nearest Flagler Street, a large area of the city of Coral Gables, and the cities of Westchester and Sweetwater. In this area reside more than 400,000 persons of Cuban origin (United States Bureau of the Census 1982:134) and a total of more than 750,000 Hispanics (MacDonald 1985:45). In this loosely defined area, it is extremely easy to acquire any goods, services, or other needs in Spanish. There are Spanish-speaking hospitals, police stations, grocery stores, restaurants, dentists, florists, schools, funeral homes, and any other possible business or service institution one could ever need from cradle to grave. Therefore, the actual need to speak English is only minimal for residents of "Little Havana." This fact may have had a direct influence on the opinions expressed by the 412 subjects.

Another important factor bearing on the data in this study is the ready availability of jobs to monolingual Spanish speakers in Little Havana. Because of the widespread existence of Hispanic businesses, jobs of almost every nature are available in this area. The need to speak English well is of little consequence to job success. While speaking English well can provide Hispanics in Miami with more potential jobs and potentially greater opportunities for upward social and employment mobility, speaking English well is not a requirement for either survival or job success.

Also, many Americans in the Miami/South Florida region are either bilingual in English and Spanish, functional (in varying degrees) in Spanish, or at least skillful in understanding Spanish-accented English. Unlike the case in most immigrant situations in which the immigrant has had to learn to cope linguistically and culturally with a new environment, in Miami many Americans have had to learn at least some Spanish to survive, due largely to the economic impact presented by the large Hispanic community. This situation may have strongly influenced the subjects' feelings concerning the relative importance of accent if communication is achieved.

To test the validity of the above hypothesis concerning the uniqueness of the Miami/South Florida linguistic community, several interesting follow-ups to the present study could be made. For example, the questionnaire used in the present study could be given to Hispanics in the United States who live in areas other than Miami. A comparison of these two bodies of data would prove interesting. Also, the same questionnaire given to Hispanics who live in other United States communities with large Hispanic centers (e.g., Los Angeles, New York City, San Antonio) would provide further data. One further interesting possibility would be to administer an English version of the questionnaire used in the present study to English speakers who have daily contact with Hispanics in areas such as Miami.

The present study has provided some useful data concerning attitudes and stereotypes about second-language learning in a particular community. It is clear, however, that this is an area in the field of second-language acquisition that needs to be investigated in much greater detail before any reliable conclusions can be drawn concerning affective variables and their effect on pronunciation in language learning.

Note

1. For the reader unfamiliar with the Natural Approach distinction between *acquisition* and *learning*, most introductory texts that deal with second-language acquisition provide definitions and/or discussions of these terms. See, for example, Brown (1987:188-189), Krashen (1982:10-11), Krashen and Terrell (1983:26-27), Omaggio (1986:29), Richards and Rodgers (1986:131), and Savignon (1983:64-65).

References

Brown, H. Douglas. 1987. *Principles of Language Learning and Language Teaching*, Second Edition. Englewood Cliffs, NJ: Prentice Hall.

Dulay, H., and M. Burt. 1977. Remarks on Creativity in Language Acquisition. In *Viewpoints on English as a Second Language*, ed. by M. Burt, H. Dulay, and M. Finochiaro, 95-126. New York: Regents Press.

Krashen, Stephen. 1981. *Second Language Acquisition and Second Language Learning*. Oxford: Pergamon Press.

————. 1982. *Principles and Practice in Second Language Acquisition.* New York: Pergamon Press.

————. 1985. *The Input Hypothesis: Issues and Implications.* New York: Longman, Inc.

Krashen, Stephen, and Tracy D. Terrell. 1983. *The Natural Approach: Language Acquisition in the Classroom.* Hayward, Calif.: Alemany Press.

MacDonald, Marguerite. 1985. *Cuban American English: The Second Generation in Miami.* Ph.D. diss., University of Florida, Gainesville.

Omaggio, Alice. 1986. *Teaching Language in Context.* Boston: Heinle and Heinle.

Richards, Jack C., and Theodore S. Rodgers. 1986. *Approaches and Methods in Language Teaching.* New York: Cambridge University Press.

Savignon, Sandra J. 1983. *Classroom Competence: Theory and Classroom Practice.* Reading, Mass.: Addison-Wesley Publishing Company.

Terrell, Tracy D. 1977. A Natural Approach to Second Language Acquisition and Learning. *Modern Language Journal* 61:325-337.

————. 1982. The Natural Approach to Language Teaching: An Update. *Modern Language Journal* 66:121-32.

————. 1986a. Acquisition in the Natural Approach: The Binding/Access Framework. *Modern Language Journal* 70:213-225.

————. 1986b. Recent Trends in Research and Practice: Teaching Spanish. *Hispania* 69:193-202.

————. 1989. Teaching Spanish Pronunciation in a Communicative Approach. In *American Spanish Pronunciation: Theoretical and Applied Perspectives*, ed. by Peter C. Bjarkman and Robert M. Hammond, 196-214. Washington, DC: Georgetown University Press.

————. 1990. Trends in the Teaching of Grammar in Spanish Language Textbooks. *Hispania* 73:201-209.

————. 1991. The Role of Grammar Instruction in a Communicative Approach. *Modern Language Journal* 75:52-63.

Terrell, Tracy D., Magdalena Andrade, Jeanne Egasse, and Elías M. Muñoz. 1994. *Dos mundos*, Third Edition. New York: McGraw-Hill.

Terrell, Tracy D., Mary B. Rogers, Betsy K. Barnes, and Marguerite Wolff-Hessini. 1993. *Deux mondes: A Communicative Approach*, Second Edition. New York: McGraw-Hill.

Terrell, Tracy D., Erwin Tschirner, Brigitte Nikolai, and Herbert Genzmer. 1992. *Kontakte: A Communicative Approach*, Second Edition. New York: McGraw-Hill.

United States Bureau of the Census. 1982. *General Population Characteristics, Florida.* Washington, D.C.: United States Government Printing Office.

On Achieving Competence in Two Languages: The Role of Necessity for the Cuban Mariel Entrant

Diane Ringer Uber
The College of Wooster

Schumann has shown that the primary considerations in second-language learning are (1) the degree of social distance between the second-language learning group and the target-language group and (2) the degree of psychological distance between the individual and the target-language group. This study will show that attitudes, motivation, age, family and work situation, and community of residence (as indicators of psychological distance) as well as occupation and educational level (as indicators of social distance) are the primary determining factors in the acquisition of conversational competence in English for a group of twenty-two Cuban-Americans.

INTRODUCTION

With the large number of immigrants who come to the United States every year, an issue of great importance is their adaptation and acculturation—social, psychological, and linguistic. *Social adaptation* deals with the acceptance or non-acceptance of the target culture by the immigrant group as well as with the acceptance or non-acceptance of the immigrant group by the target culture. *Psychological adaptation* refers to the individual's attitude and motivation to become acculturated.

According to Schumann (1978), social, psychological, and linguistic adaptation are often interrelated. In his study of Alberto, a thirty-three-year-old lower-class worker from Costa Rica, Schumann discusses Alberto's poor performance, with respect to other Spanish-speaking immigrant subjects, on tests of syntactic and morphological development. Since it was determined that Alberto had normal ability for language learning, factors considered were social distance, psychological distance, and age. In this paper, I hope to support Schumann's proposals that social and psychological distance are the primary considerations in second-language learning, rather than merely age, except where age also implies social and/or psychological distance. Indicators of social distance may include occupation and educational level. Indicators of psychological distance may include attitudes, motivation, age, family situation, work situation, and community of residence.

First-generation Latin American worker immigrants to the United States often experience considerable *social distance* from the target culture. This second-language learning group often considers itself subordinate and is also considered subordinate by the target-language group. This subordination is felt in many ways: politically, economically, technically, and culturally. Due to its subordination, this group often experiences a high degree of enclosure and cohesiveness (Schumann 1978:81). Latin American professional immigrants, on the other hand, are generally at considerably less social distance from the target-language group and, hence, are solidly acculturative (Schumann 1978:86). Certainly, the more social distance between the second-language learning group and the target-language group, the less likely it will be for the former to learn or acquire the target language. A goal of the present study is to show that occupation (as worker or as professional) is an important factor for the Cuban subjects participating in this investigation.

If the second-language learning group shows moderate acculturation and moderate preservation of its native culture, that group is at a midpoint between a good and bad learning situation, and success becomes a matter of the individual's attitude and motivation to become acculturated and to learn the target language. This individual attitude is referred to as *psychological distance* (Schumann 1978:86). There will be great psychological distance between a second-language learner and the target culture if the individual makes little effort to get to know target-language speakers, works day and night with no time for language classes, does not watch television or read in the target language, and maintains interest mainly in his or her native culture. Such was the case with Alberto, and this will be seen to be the case with many of the Cuban immigrants who are the subjects of the present study.

Age alone was found not to be a primary consideration in second-language learning in Schumann's study, except where age also implies social and/or psychological distance. For example, adult second-language learners tend not to participate in real communication as much as children do. In addition, adult attitudes, motivation, and/or empathic capacity brought about by psychological development or language and culture shock can prevent adults from participating in communication (Schumann 1978:107). Such situations produce greater psychological distance between the second-language learner and the target culture. Krashen, Scarcella, and Long (1982:159) point out that studies have shown that adults proceed through early stages of syntactic and morphological development faster than children do, but that children as a group will catch up to, and surpass, most adults. In addition, the child's superiority in ultimate attainment is hypothesized to be due to affective factors, because the affective filter is strengthened at about puberty, thus preventing most adults from reaching native-like levels of proficiency (Krashen et al. 1982:174). These affective factors would correspond to a greater psychological distance between the learner and target culture. In the present study, it will be shown that age does indeed intersect with psychological distance for many of the Cuban immigrants.

Gardner and Lambert (1972:14-16) identify two types of motivation in second language learning: an *instrumental motive* and an *integrative motive*. The instrumental orientation is characterized by a desire to gain social recognition or economic advantages through knowledge of a foreign language; it is therefore self-oriented toward benefits of a noninterpersonal sort. The integratively oriented learner, on the other hand, reflects a willingness or desire to be like representative members of the other language community and to become associated with that other community; it is therefore more oriented toward others. Based on results from their studies of learners of French in French Canada, Louisiana, Maine, and Connecticut and learners of English in the Philippines, Gardner and Lambert conclude that for members of ethnic minority groups in North America, learning a second language is of vital importance, and both instrumental and integrative approaches to the learning task must be developed (Gardner and Lambert 1972:130). This is the situation of Hispanics in the United States. For Cubans in northern Hudson County, New Jersey, the instrumental and integrative desires of the immigrants conflict with the desire to maintain cultural and linguistic identity while learning the second language and becoming integrated into the target culture.

In a later paper, Gardner, Lalonde, and Moorcroft (1985:217) find that degree of instrumentality (improving occupational opportunities) and attitudes toward the learning situation (type of courses and teachers) are not significant values in second-language learning. However, other attitudinal/motivational measures were significant: attitudes toward speakers of the second language, interest in foreign languages, degree of integrativeness, desire to learn the language, attitudes toward learning the language, and anxiety level while speaking the language. The authors find that attitudes, motivation, and language aptitude are important because they influence the rate at which second-language material is learned (Gardner et al. 1985:225-226). High-aptitude subjects and those with positive attitudinal/motivational characteristics perform significantly better over time than do their counterparts with low aptitude and/or low attitudinal/motivational attributes, although there are no differences during the initial stages of learning.

Hence, it is believed that people will not be motivated to acquire skills in a second language unless they have an instrumental or integrative need to use those skills. In the New York metropolitan area, many Spanish-speaking immigrants have a need to be bilingual in Spanish and English, for a variety of reasons. However, not all Spanish-speaking immigrants have acquired a high level of competence in English. In fact, some have acquired little competence at all. One group in particular—the Cuban Mariel entrants from the 1980 wave of immigration—is often cited as including a large number of monolingual Spanish speakers who have not learned English.

 ## METHODOLOGY AND COMMUNITY PROFILE

This paper presents the results of sixteen hours of interviews with twenty-two Cubans who arrived in the United States in 1980 and who now reside in northern Hudson County, New Jersey, mostly in the communities of Union City and West New York.[1] This area has the second-largest Cuban population in the United States, after Dade County, Florida. Each interview lasted approximately forty-five minutes and was conducted in a free conversational style. Twenty of the interviews were tape-recorded. Interviews were conducted in 1985.

Ten of the informants are from the Havana metropolitan area, eight are from Las Villas province in the center of the island, three are from Oriente province, and one was born in Matanzas province but lived most of her life in Camagüey, the province of origin of her parents. Of the informants, 70% are male and 75% are white, thus resembling closely the figures for the entire 1980 immigration group, which was 70.2% male and estimated to be 60%–80% white. The informants range in age from 25 to 74 years. Their educational levels range from fourth-grade completion to a doctorate in pedagogy.

In contrast to Schumann's study, tests for correct usage of morphological and syntactic features are not used in the present investigation. Rather, *conversational competence*, determined by the interviewer and based on the interviewer's impressions of the informant's ability to converse and comprehend conversational English, is the basis for grouping the subjects with regard to ability in English. Although the interviews themselves were conducted in Spanish, those who were able to speak English did so with me before and after the interview situation.

Among other topics, the informants discussed their feelings regarding the learning of English since their arrival in the United States. The pattern which emerges does show a correlation between the level of competence in English and the informant's need to use that language. We can thus support the hypothesis that a need must be created in order for there to be sufficient motivation for a first-generation immigrant to learn English. However, need depends on various factors, which include age, occupation, family situation, community of residence, and the language(s) used by friends and co-workers. In addition, as Schumann has shown, the primary considerations in second-language learning are (1) the degree of social distance between the second-language learning group and the target language group and (2) the degree of psychological distance between the individual and the target language group.

 ## RESULTS

Based on my interactions with them, I was able to divide the twenty-two informants into two groups: those who have achieved conversational competence in English, and those who have not. I have determined that the following group has learned English well enough to understand most of what they hear and to carry on a conversation. The informant number is followed by age at the time of the interview (1985), province of origin, educational level, occupation in Cuba, and gender. Only the former occupation in Cuba is shown because most have not achieved the same occupational level in the United States, since they did not know English upon arrival.

Group I (Informants who have achieved conversational competence in English):
- #21: 20 yrs., Las Villas, some high school, high-school student (M)
- #22: 20 yrs., Havana, some high school, high-school student (M)
- #1: 36 yrs., Havana, college and some graduate work, Spanish-German translator (M)
- #17: 25 yrs., Oriente, some college, philology student (M)
- #2: 30 yrs., Havana, some college, student of French and secondary school teacher of biology (M)

#7:   55 yrs., Las Villas, doctorate in pedagogy, elementary school teacher of physical geography (F)

#14:   39 yrs., Las Villas, college, accountant (M)

The members of this group have a high motivation to learn English for various reasons. One important factor appears to be age, which, of course, as Schumann (1978) has shown, often intersects with psychological distance; younger speakers often show less psychological distance between themselves and the target culture in terms of attitude and motivation. Those who came to this country at the age of twenty-one or younger (#21, #22, and #17) not only find it less difficult to learn a foreign language, due to a lower affective filter, but also have a greater motivation to learn English because it is the language used by their friends and the language they will probably have to use for the rest of their lives. In fact, the two twenty-year-olds now have a difficult time speaking Spanish. One was unable to converse with me in Spanish, even though I asked him questions in Spanish for five minutes. He rejects being associated with the group of Mariel entrants and often tells people he is Venezuelan. The twenty-five-year-old started out answering me in English but after a minute switched to fluent Spanish, although he used English words here and there throughout the interview. He recognizes that age and need were the primary factors in his success in learning English. The older members of his family, who arrived five years earlier than he, have not learned English. He states that he learned it out of necessity:

> Miran diferente a la persona cuando sabe inglés a cuando no sabe inglés.

> 'They look differently at a person when he knows English than when he doesn't know English.'[2]

However, he still has had trouble finding work here, even knowing English well. He also recognizes that Spanish has a great importance in the metropolitan New York area. He believes that everyone (including Anglos) will have to be bilingual to get work in that area soon:

> Porque como va la sociedad americana ahora, dentro de poco nadie va a poder conseguir un trabajo si no sabe por lo menos dos idiomas. Por lo menos por esta parte de aquí. Por lo menos dos idiomas. En Nueva York casi es la misma cosa. Están pidiendo muchos bilingües. Y, bueno, el inglés tiene que ser uno. El otro puede ser el español o francés, el que sea, pero están pidiendo dos idiomas. Y como van las cosas, no creo que nadie con un solo idioma pueda conseguir trabajo dentro de poco. Yo conozco muchos americanos que me han dicho, —Yo iba a aplicar para un trabajo y me han rechazado porque nada más sé inglés. Me han dicho que tengo que ser bilingüe. Ahora, después que vivo en este país, que nací en este país, tengo que aprender español.— Y me lo han dicho molestos. ¡Molestos me lo han dicho! Como que le echan la culpa al hispano, que han dejado entrar muchos hispanos, y que la culpa de eso lo tienen los hispanos.

> 'Because as American society is going now, soon no one will be able to get a job without knowing at least two languages. At least in this area here. At least two languages. In New York it's almost the same. They're asking for a lot of

bilinguals. And, well, English has to be one. The other can be Spanish or French, whatever, but they're asking for two languages. And with the way things are going, I don't think that anyone with only one language will be able to get work pretty soon. I know a lot of Americans who have told me, "I was going to apply for a job, and they've rejected me because I know only English. They've told me that I have to be bilingual. Now, after I've lived in this country, and I was born in this country, I have to learn Spanish." And they've said it to me, very upset. Offended, they've said it to me! It seems like they blame the Hispanic, because they've let a lot of Hispanics enter [the country], and like the Hispanics are to blame for that.'

The other members of the group who have learned English are older but have a high instrumental motivation to learn because they want to be successful here; they thus show less psychological distance between themselves and the target culture. They also have a comparatively high educational level, all having at least attended college, which would indicate less social distance between themselves and U.S. culture. All are frustrated at not having achieved an occupational level equivalent to what they had in Cuba due to lack of fluency in English. Says one,

Sin inglés acá, no hay progreso.

'Without English here, there is no progress.'

One might wonder how those who have been relatively successful went about learning English. Most took classes as at least part of their preparation. One is now studying to be a bilingual secretary. Another does some reading and watches television in English. A third carried a bilingual dictionary with him everywhere and cultivated friendships with people who were bilingual. All of these traits again indicate lack of psychological distance as manifested by positive attitudes, motivation, and empathic capacity toward the language and people of the U.S. Thus, it would appear that Gardner and Lambert (1972:130) are correct in stating that both instrumental and integrative motivation are needed in the case of minority groups learning English in North America, because both types of motivation are manifested by those informants who have been successful in achieving a degree of conversational competence in English.

Three members of this Group I (#1, #2, and #7) work at a social service agency whose clients include other Mariel entrants, most of whom do not speak any English and are forced to work in factories or gas stations. Many of these clients think English is not necessary, or they don't want to study, saying that it is difficult to work all day in a factory and go to school at night. Some appear to be unwilling to make the effort to help themselves, as evidenced by this statement from one of the social service agency employees:

En muchos casos... no han tratado de superarse, de mejorar en el idioma, que es lo fundamental.

'In many cases... they haven't tried to excel, to get better in the language, which is the fundamental thing.'

Furthermore, northern Hudson County is not a conducive environment in which to learn English because more that half of the population is Cuban. Therefore, many are able to conduct their daily affairs without speaking English. Even Asians who own businesses on Bergenline Avenue (the main commercial street) generally speak Spanish in order to deal with their clientele. This situation is clearly one in which the second-language learning group shows a high degree of enclosure and cohesiveness, contributing to a greater social distance between themselves and the target-language group. Therefore, such a community does not encourage either instrumental motivation (for occupational self-improvement) or integrative motivation (for development of personal ties with members of the Anglo-American cultural group).

Indeed, lack of motivation to learn English emerges as an important factor for those who were found, based on my interactions with them, to have little or no conversational competence in that language.

Group II (Informants who have not achieved conversational competence in English):
- #3:   30 yrs., Havana, some high school, student and working (M)
- #8:   30 yrs., Havana, 8th grade, working (M)
- #10: 25 yrs., Las Villas, 6th grade, textile worker (M)
- #12: 56 yrs., Camagüey, some law school, physical education teacher (F)
- #15: 42 yrs., Las Villas, high school, manager of grocery store (F)
- #16: 34 yrs., Havana, college, elementary and secondary school teacher of Spanish (M)
- #18: 73 yrs., Havana, high school and some college, elementary teacher of reading (F)
- #4:   41 yrs., Oriente, 4th grade, construction worker/political prisoner (M)
- #5:   37 yrs., Oriente, some college, elected representative (M)
- #9:   60 yrs., Las Villas, 10th grade, shoe repairman/political prisoner (M)
- #20: 31 yrs., Havana, 10th grade, stevedore (M)
- #6:   37 yrs., Havana, 6th grade, mechanic/political prisoner (M)
- #11: 45 yrs., Las Villas, some college, elementary school teacher (F)
- #13: 61 yrs., Las Villas, college, elementary school teacher of mathematics (F)
- #19: 74 yrs., Havana, 6th grade, upholsterer (M)

We can see that this group includes older speakers and/or those who had a somewhat lower educational or occupational level in Cuba, which may be an indicator of greater social distance between themselves and U.S. culture. Some have experienced severe depression in the United States; others have a lack of motivation to learn English and hence are at a greater psychological distance from the target-language group. Many have tried to take classes but claim that they are unable to learn the language. Says one,

> Yo no he logrado aquí por el idioma porque no he podido aprenderlo.
> 'I haven't achieved much here because of the language, because I haven't been able to learn it.'

All claim to feel the instrumental need to learn English to advance in the job market, having been refused work because they did not know the language. However, for many of these informants, there is not *sufficient* motivation to learn English, given the absence of integrative orientation toward the target culture. One says that he lives with friends on whom he depends financially. Therefore, he feels that he should look for work rather than take a class and ask his friends to buy his pencils and notebooks. Another states that he cannot study because of mental depression:

> Sí, he tratado, pero es que yo prácticamente, como yo dejé toda esa familia mía en Cuba, mis hijos, mi esposa y todo, y voy a la escuela, y me comienza un dolor de cabeza, y no es fácil tampoco, uno con tantos problemas arriba, ir a una escuela y aprenderse así el idioma. No es fácil.

> 'Yes, I've tried, but I, practically, since I left all my family in Cuba, my children, my wife and everything, and I go to school, and I start to get a headache, and it's not easy either, when you have so many problems, to go to a school and learn the language like that. It's not easy.'

An example of the lack of instrumental motivation to learn English is a man who claims to know hardly any English because he has not taken the time to learn. He says he needs it, but since he is a creative, artistic person who doesn't like day-to-day jobs, he prefers to manage without it. Indeed, he traveled alone in a trailer from San Francisco to Miami through rural areas of the South, supporting himself by setting up a shop to make signs in his trailer. Since he does not concern himself with future financial security, he has not felt the instrumental need to learn the language.

Another informant says that he does not worry about tomorrow either, believing that everything will work out for the best. He states,

> Mi cuñado no habla ni una palabra de inglés, y tiene dos trabajos en este momento, los dos de electricista. En uno gana once pesos, once dólares la hora, y en otro nueve. Y que están bien.

> 'My brother-in-law doesn't speak even a word of English, and he has two jobs right now, both as an electrician. In one he makes eleven dollars an hour, and in the other nine. And they're fine.'

Perhaps the most convincing argument for remaining monolingual comes from an informant who says that he works mostly with Cubans, again indicating high enclosure and cohesiveness within his group (social distance) and low integrative and instrumental motivation. If an American comes into his workplace, he gets someone who knows English to interpret. He tells of having bought a tape recorder to learn English:

> Yo tengo en mi casa una máquina. La compré, ¿me entiendes? Me costó cuatrocientos y pico pesos con todos sus cassettes completos, lecciones todas las tengo, ¿no? Pero el problema es lo siguiente, que como trabajo tanto. Quiero trabajar primero, ¿tú sabes?, y tener dinero. Pues, entonces, poderme sentar un rato a oír inglés y aprender, porque si yo me pongo ahora, yo digo, —No, voy a terminar a las cuatro de la tarde para ir a mi casa a oír, a aprender inglés.— Si yo tengo el dinero ahora que, ¿sabe?, el dinero que ganarme, puedo ganarme el dinero ahora, sin aprender inglés, yo me lo gano. Entonces, mañana cuando me sea difícil de ganar dinero porque no hay trabajo, porque la cosa está floja, ¿tú me entiendes?, pues, entonces, me siento en mi casa y pongo la máquina y aprendo inglés. ¿Tú me entiendes lo que te digo? Tú sí me

entiendes, ¿no? Sí. Me es mejor, porque, vaya, mañana, entonces yo me pongo a aprender inglés hoy, mañana sé inglés, y entonces sé inglés, sé trabajar, pero no tengo trabajo. ¿Tú me entiendes? ¿Tú sabes lo que te digo? Sí, es así. Hay que pensar.

'I have a recorder at home. I bought it, you understand me? It cost me four hundred and some dollars with all the cassettes. I have all the lessons, right? But the problem is this, that I work so much. I want to work first, you know? And have money. So then to be able to sit down for a while to listen to English and learn . . . Because if I say to myself now, "No, I'm going to finish at four in the afternoon to go home and listen, to learn English." If I have the money now, you know? The money to earn—if I can earn the money now, without learning English, I'll earn it. Then tomorrow when it's difficult for me to earn money because there is no work, because work is slow, you understand me? Well, then, I'll sit down in my house and turn on the recorder and learn English. You understand what I'm telling you? You do understand me, don't you? Yes. It's better for me, because, look, tomorrow, if I start to learn English today, tomorrow, I'll know English, and then I'll know English, I'll know how to work, but I won't have work. You understand me? You know what I'm saying? Yes, that's the way it is. You have to think about it.'

Thus, we can see that success within a given occupation does not necessarily require knowledge of English. Certainly, if one is content to work in a factory or gas station (low instrumental motivation), and if one lives with Spanish-speaking friends or family in an enclosed and cohesive Spanish-speaking community like northern Hudson County, New Jersey (low integrative motivation), one will not feel a strong need to learn English.

 ## DISCUSSION

Eleanor Rogg has shown that one crucial factor in the assimilation of refugees is the strength of the community. Her research shows that the strong Cuban ethnic community in northern Hudson County favorably influences the adjustment of its members by "providing a comparison referent which does not demean the refugees' sense of self-worth as well as by providing psycho-social strength and satisfaction to its members" (Rogg 1971:481). Although Rogg's research dealt with Cubans from earlier waves of immigration, the strength of the cohesive Cuban community in that area is still a great factor. Indeed, like more recent immigrants, most of the earlier Cuban immigrants have not achieved as high an occupational level as they had in Cuba. In fact, Queralt (1984:115) states that "contrary to popular belief, Cuban émigrés do not compare favorably to the rest of immigrants entering the United States." Her study includes Cubans from all three waves of immigration. She claims that this popular belief has arisen due to the fact that

> because of their higher average age, Cubans have proportionately more persons participating in the labor force, fewer unemployed individuals, and more workers at the peak of their earning power than have the Mexicans, Puerto

Ricans, or the total U.S. population. . . . But if the Cuban population in the United States were similar in age to the Mexican or Puerto Rican groups, their average income might be as low or even lower than that of Mexican Americans or Puerto Ricans. The inaccurate stereotype of Cuban exiles as economically successful has caused problems, particularly in their relations with other minority group members. (Queralt 1984:115-116)

This stereotype has also caused problems with the Cuban Mariel entrants, who often feel that the opinion is that they have given Cubans a "bad name" in this country. However, we have seen that many of the earlier Cuban immigrants are still at a considerable social distance from the target culture, not having achieved the occupational level, or the economic level, that they had in Cuba. Furthermore, many of the earlier Cuban immigrants have also remained monolingual, especially those living in the cohesive Spanish-speaking areas such as Dade County, Florida, and northern Hudson County, New Jersey. Queralt (1984:118) states that "few Cubans in this country are highly articulate in both Spanish and English."

Indeed, my study has shown that, except for those who arrived in the United States in their early twenties or younger (showing less psychological distance from the target culture due to a low affective filter) and those who were well-educated professionals in Cuba (showing less social distance from the target culture), few of the Cuban Mariel entrants have felt a strong need or motivation to learn English. This should probably not be viewed as a deficiency on their part, considering the fact that there are strong Cuban communities in southern Florida, and northern New Jersey in which it is possible to live, work, and play almost entirely in Spanish. Certainly, second-generation Cubans and their descendants will acquire English in these communities, as their social and psychological distance from U.S. culture decreases. But Spanish is alive and well in these areas, and the strong refugee community provides a welcome haven for the first-generation monolingual immigrant.

The results of the present study can therefore support the statement of Gardner and Lambert (1972:130) that both instrumental and integrative motivation are necessary for successful learning and acquisition of English by Hispanic immigrants to the United States. As Schumann (1978:86) has shown, when a group is between a good and bad learning situation, success becomes a matter of the individual (psychological distance). The data for the Cuban-Americans examined here confirms Schumann's proposals that social and psychological distance are the primary considerations in second-language learning, rather than age, except where age also implies social and/or psychological distance. In addition, my results extend Schumann's proposals to include educational differences as a factor contributing to success in second-language learning. Informants with a higher educational level show greater instrumental and integrative motivation to learn English as well as less social and psychological distance from the target culture. Those with a lower educational level are lacking in one or more of the factors which contribute to success in acculturation.

Notes

1. I would like to express my gratitude to Marta San Martin and her entire staff at the Lutheran-Catholic Resource Center in Union City, New Jersey, for their wonderful help in contracting informants. Special thanks also go to Maria Arcos, Keith Mason, Dayci Chivukula, and Sally Jo Weber. In addition, I would like to thank the editors and publisher of this volume for their excellent suggestions toward improving this manuscript. Remaining inconsistencies are, of course, my own. Finally, my deepest thanks to my informants, who remain anonymous, for allowing me to interview them and for sharing their fascinating experiences with me.
2. Given that the interviews produced colloquial speech in most cases, colloquial English translations have been provided as a means preserving style.

References

Gardner, Robert C., and Wallace E. Lambert. 1972. *Attitudes and Motivation in Second-Language Learning.* Rowley, Mass.: Newbury House.

Gardner, R. C., R. N. Lalonde, and R. Moorcroft. 1985. The Role of Attitudes and Motivation in Second Language Learning: Correlational and Experimental Considerations. *Language Learning* 35:207-227.

Haskins, James. 1982. *The New Americans: Cuban Boat People.* Hillside, N.J.: Enslow.

Krashen, Stephen D., Robin C. Scarcella, and Michael H. Long, eds. 1982. *Child-Adult Differences in Second Language Acquisition.* Rowley, Mass.: Newbury House.

Llanes, José. 1982. *Cuban Americans: Masters of Survival.* Cambridge, Mass.: Abt.

Queralt, Magaly. 1984. Understanding Cuban Immigrants: A Cultural Perspective. *Social Work* March-April: 115-122.

Rogg, Eleanor. 1971. The Influence of a Strong Refugee Community on the Economic Adjustment of Its Members. *International Migration Review* 5 (4):474-481.

Schumann, John H. 1978. *The Pidginization Process: A Model for Second Language Acquisition.* Rowley, Mass.: Newbury House.

French Immersion and Its Offshoots: Getting Two for One

Merrill Swain
The Ontario Institute for Studies in Education

This paper describes the outcomes of late immersion programs at the secondary school and university levels. The outcomes are discussed in terms of whether one can have "two for one": enhanced second language learning and high academic achievement in the content taught via the second language. Additionally, based on observations made in immersion classrooms, a suggestion for a less transmission-oriented model of instruction in favour of a more interactive pedagogical model is made in order to facilitate the integration of second language and content learning.

 INTRODUCTION

In the mid 1960's, one lone class in a school outside of Montreal embarked on an innovative second language teaching experiment. The purpose of the experiment was to improve the students' level of proficiency in French as a second language (FSL) relative to other students who were taught FSL in short daily periods of grammar-based lessons. The experimental class was referred to as the French 'immersion' group because, throughout the school day, the teacher used only French. In other words, all classroom management and all instruction of content material took place in the second language.

That class happened to be a kindergarten class. The students in it continued in later grades to study at least part of their academic subjects in French. Over the years, offshoots from the original French immersion program have been started. They vary with respect to the age the students start the program, and the proportion of the school day devoted to instruction in French. What all these immersion programs have in common, though, is that substantive academic content is taught using the medium of the students' second language. Today in Canada, over 250,000 students are currently enrolled in some form of a French immersion program. And in both Canada and the United States, immersion now exists in a number of languages: Ukrainian, German, Spanish, Cree, Hebrew and Japanese, to name just a few.

The French immersion programs in Canada have been extensively evaluated, and the purpose of this paper is to consider some of the research findings associated with the programs. The findings which will be discussed relate to the issue of whether one

Reprinted from *Foreign Language Acquisition Research and the Classroom*, edited by Barbara Freed (Lexington, Mass.: D. C. Heath and Company, 1991), by permission of the editor and publisher.

can have "two for one"; that is, whether one can enhance second language learning without sacrificing content knowledge. In this context, two basic questions have been addressed:

1. How proficient do students become in their second language?
2. How knowledgeable are students about the content taught to them in their second language?

In order to understand the results obtained, particularly with respect to second language learning, recent research has begun to examine the nature of the teaching in immersion classrooms. Thus, an important third question is:

3. What teaching and learning processes account for the outcomes identified in question 1?

TWO IMMERSION OFFSHOOTS

The discussion in this paper will concentrate on two offshoots of the original primary level French immersion program: one which begins with 12–14 year-old adolescents, and one which is taught at the university level. The first has come to be known as 'late' immersion, in contrast to the 'early' immersion program which begins in kindergarten or grade one. The second has come to be known as a 'sheltered' program, in contrast to one intended for native speakers of the target language.

1. Late Immersion

Late immersion begins at grade six, seven or eight. Instruction in French may be for as much of the day as 100% or as little as 50%. During that time students take, for example, history, geography, mathematics and/or science in French. Prior to entering the late immersion program, students will have had short (20–40 minutes) daily periods of what, in Canada, is referred to as 'core' FSL classes for at least a year. Following the late immersion program, which may last for one or more years, students are usually able to take several subjects per year in secondary school in French if they so choose. (For more detailed descriptions of these programs, see Swain and Lapkin 1982; Genesee 1987).

French skills   In addressing the question of how proficient late immersion students become in French, there are several possible benchmarks. One can ask how well they do relative to students taking core FSL classes who, although they get much less exposure to French, nevertheless get more focussed instruction ABOUT the language. Or one can ask how well late immersion students perform relative to immersion students who begin their program at a much earlier age. Or one can ask how well late immersion students perform relative to native-speakers of French. Let us consider each of these comparisons in turn, at appropriate points in time.

The most appropriate time to compare late immersion students with core FSL students is immediately after the first year of the program when both groups have had similar FSL backgrounds, and what differs is the FSL program they have followed during the school year in question. The findings have been consistent across a number of studies (e.g., Barik and Swain 1976; Genesee, Polich and Stanley 1977): late immersion students do significantly better than core French students on all tests of French administered.

For example, Genesee, Polich and Stanley (1977) evaluated a late immersion program that began at grade 7. They report that at the end of grade 7, based on a standardized test of French achievement and on interviews with students where their comprehension, grammar, enunciation, rhythm and intonation, vocabulary use and fluency were assessed, late immersion students were significantly better than core French students. Similarly, Barik and Swain (1976) evaluated a late immersion program that began at grade 8. Assessment of the students' French involved their reading, listening comprehension and speaking skills. The late immersion students' scores were, again, significantly better than those of core French students.

Comparisons of late immersion students with immersion students who began at an earlier age—usually in kindergarten or grade 1—are probably most appropriate to make as the students graduate from secondary school, when the time spent studying in French is as equivalent as possible given the nature of the two programs. Such comparisons suggest that there are surprisingly few differences between early and late immersion students in their French skills as they graduate from secondary school. Early immersion students do tend to show superior speaking skills, and less consistently, superior listening comprehension skills relative to late immersion students. However, in their ability to read and write in French, early and late immersion students appear to be similar. (Hart and Lapkin 1989a, 1989b; Wesche 1989). These findings are consistent with other recent research which suggests that 'older may be better', in the sense of 'being more efficient', in acquiring at least some aspects of a second language (see Swain and Lapkin 1989).

To get some indication of these students' functional ability in French, it is useful to look at their results on the Canadian Public Service Commission Test. This is a test used by the Canadian Federal Government to assess the ability of its employees to function in designated bilingual positions. This test has three levels, A, 13 and C, with C representing the highest level of proficiency. Each level of the test has a reading, writing, speaking and listening part. Grade 12 immersion students in the Ottawa region were given levels A and B of the test (Morrison 1981). The majority of students obtained level a. Many might have been able to function in French at level C, but, unfortunately, they were not given that level of the test. The description of levels is specific to the work environment. For example, for speaking, functioning at level a involves:

> Oral expression: This level implies the capacity to take part in a variety of verbal exchanges using a variety of sentence types (simple, compound and complex). The individual at this level would function optimally in a one-to-one interview, but should also be able to contribute to meetings and discussion groups. One would be able to convey the essentials of his/her line of reasoning. There would likely be difficulty in expressing nuances or in using specific vocabulary, idioms, and regional variants in their appropriate contexts.

Grammar and pronunciation will often show mother tongue interference but will only occasionally result in misunderstanding. Hesitations of moderate length may be relatively frequent on general or work-related topics and would increase as one attempts to speak in detail on any specific subject matter.

Comparisons with native speakers of French have been made throughout the students' immersion schooling. Generally, the results have revealed a pattern whereby the scores of similar-aged francophones and late immersion students on listening comprehension and reading tests are close or similar; whereas on tests assessing speaking and writing skills, late immersion students' performance is significantly poorer than that of their francophone peers (Genesee 1987; Hart and Lapkin 1989a). For example, in a study recently conducted, Hart and Lapkin (1989a) found that graduating late immersion students performed similarly to Quebec francophones on a listening comprehension and reading test, but not on a cloze test. The listening comprehension test consisted of three excerpts from radio broadcasts, similar to that which a student might hear in academic situations. The reading test involved three reading passages dealing with the exploration of space, bilingualism in the United States, and the French language. The cloze test was based on an extract from a journalistic essay on the proliferation of opinion polls. Students perceive their most serious weaknesses to be in the areas of grammar ('not being able to get things like verb tenses and prepositions right') and vocabulary knowledge ('not having the right words to write what you want to communicate'), which corresponds to test results (e.g. Harley and Swain 1984; Harley and King, in press).

The opinions and plans of a sample of immersion students as they graduate from secondary school have been polled (Hart and Lapkin 1989a). Asked about the ease with which they could accomplish selected real life activities in French compared to English on a four-point scale ranging from 'just as easily' to 'probably couldn't do it', late immersion students tended to respond with 'a little more difficult'. There were interesting differences noted though:

> In general, students evidence, on average, less confidence in coping with activities removed from academic settings—telephoning a travel agent, having a job interview, writing a letter of complaint—than activities which are, at most, extensions of their school experience. The strongest indication of this pattern is the sharp contrast in ratings regarding two speaking activities—participating in a history class discussion and having a job interview....The class discussion item...attracts the most positive ratings, the job interview item, the least positive. (Hart and Lapkin 1989a:9).

An overwhelming overwhelming proportion of late immersion students questioned planned to attend university after graduating from secondary school. Of those planning to attend university, about 80% of them said they wanted to take from a quarter to three quarters of their courses in French. A significant proportion (approximately 40 to 60%) of the late immersion students would 'definitely' or 'most likely' seek a job where they would use French, would accept a job which involved working totally in French, and would take an interesting job in an area where they would need French for everyday activities outside of work.

Thus, the late immersion experience appears to have achieved for its students significant second language learning in the four skill areas, particularly in listening comprehension and reading. The students, naturally enough, feel more confident about their ability to function in their second language in domains that are similar to, or extensions of, their academic environment. Furthermore, in general, the students wish to continue to learn and use French in future education and work settings.

Academic achievement   But what about the immersion students' mastery of the content taught to them using French as the language of instruction? Generally speaking, this question has been broached through the use of standardized tests of achievement given to the immersion students and to a comparison group of English-speaking students who have studied the subject in English, in which case the language of the test has been English; or to a comparison group of French-speaking students who have studied the subject in French, in which case the language of the test has been French.

The results associated with the mastery of content appear to be related to the subject and to the amount of prior core FSL instruction that the immersion students have had. Where late immersion students have had—as in Montreal and Ottawa—core FSL instruction each year through to the immersion year(s), the level of mastery of content taught in French by the late immersion students is similar to that attained by regular English-instructed students (Genesee, Polich and Stanley 1977; Stern et al. 1976). If the amount of prior core FSL instruction is limited to only one year, however, short-term gaps in knowledge in some subjects, for example in science, have been noted (Barik and Swain 1976).

In the province of Quebec, the Ministry of Education administers Secondary School Leaving Examinations in a number of subjects at the end of grade 11. Late immersion students in Montreal who continued to take several course options in French after a one year late immersion program, obtained higher scores than those obtained by students attending French-medium schools throughout the province. These examinations include histoire, geographie, mathematiques and dactylo. The interpretation of these results should be made cautiously owing to possible differences in the characteristics of students who comprise the two populations (Genesee 1987). However, in another study, Genesee (1976, 1977) compared a one year late immersion group at grade 11 with a group of English-speaking students, controlling for IQ. Both groups of students took Leaving Examinations in physics, chemistry and history. The immersion group took the exams in French and the English group took the exams in English. Results of the comparisons showed the immersion group to be doing as well as the English group on all three exams.

Overall, then, the results suggest that late immersion students with several years of core FSL 'back-up' are able to master the content taught to them using French as the language of instruction.

2. The University of Ottawa Sheltered Program

On the surface, the main differences between the late immersion program and the sheltered program offered at the University of Ottawa is that the latter starts at an even later age, and it is less intensive. Both programs use the teaching of content subjects as the means for second language learning. This section will focus particularly on the sheltered course in which "Introduction a la psychologie" was taught because that is the course which has been most extensively researched from a content learning and language learning perspective. In principle, however, any university subject holds the potential for similar adaptation (see, for example, Sternfeld 1988).

In order to enter the sheltered psychology course, students must demonstrate an intermediate level of receptive proficiency in French (Brinton, Snow and Wesche 1989). These learners typically come from a school background of enriched—by, for example, student exchanges—core FSL. (A large portion of immersion graduates are beyond the proficiency range considered appropriate for being in the sheltered class (Wesche 1985).) For these learners, the course is seen as an alternative to advanced second language courses and as a transition to being able to take courses intended for native speakers. To take the course, the students sign a contract. The contract requires them to do all the assigned reading in French and to attend at least 80% of all class sessions.

The course is taught twice weekly for 1 1/2 hours per class. The first 15 to 20 minutes is taught by a second language instructor, while the rest of each class is taught by the psychology professor. The FSL instruction is intended to help students understand the readings and to prepare them for upcoming topics through, for example, the introduction of key vocabulary and concepts. Strategies for 'polite interruption' or requesting restatement are taught. Specific language problems that students inquire about are dealt with, but there is no explicit teaching of grammar (Brinton, Snow and Wesche 1989).

Whether consciously or not, the psychology professor makes adjustments in his/her language use as compared to when native speakers of French are taught. Wesche and Ready (1985) have documented a number of these adjustments which include slower pace, more careful enunciation, more frequent and longer pauses, more explicitness and more redundancy of both form and content. (For a more complete description of the University of Ottawa program, see Brinton, Snow and Wesche, 1989.)

French skills   The second language and content learning of three successive groups of students who have been enrolled in the sheltered psychology course have been studied (Edwards et al. 1984; Hauptman, Wesche and Ready 1988). The examination of French language skills has not been as extensive as for late immersion students. Nevertheless, the results are interesting.

The progress made in French was examined in two ways. First, pre-test French scores were compared with post-test scores to determine if significant gains had been made in the students' proficiency as a result of attending the sheltered psychology course. Second, post-test scores of the sheltered group were compared with those of students who had taken a regular four hour per week advanced FSL class for a total of 45 hours. The students in the advanced FSL classes came from within the same proficiency band as the students enrolled in the sheltered classes. (Nevertheless, comparisons of the two groups at the end of their respective courses took into account pre-test differences through analysis of co-variance.) The FSL advanced course emphasized receptive skills. Authentic text materials in both reading and listening are used. The written texts are taken from introductory university textbooks in the students' area of concentration. The listening materials represent tasks that students would probably encounter in the university context (Hauptman, Wesche and Read 1988).

French proficiency measures that were used measured the receptive skills and included a listening comprehension test in which students listened to a tape-recorded radio interview and answered questions about it, a dictation test (scored to reflect listening comprehension), a translation test which involved translating a short passage from the psychology text from French to English, and a cloze test based on a passage about world records.

Overall, the results show that the sheltered psychology students made significant gains in their receptive French skills as a result of attending the course. Thus, even though the exposure to French in the subject matter course was relatively brief—39 hours—these adult students were able to make significant progress in their understanding of French. Additionally, the gains in French proficiency of these students were comparable to those of students studying French in regular second language classes.

Academic achievement   How well did the students in the sheltered psychology course master the content they were taught? As it turns out, the same course was taught to native speakers of English using the same course outline and the same textbook, only in English. The end of semester multiple-choice exam was the same for both groups, and was bilingually presented. Comparisons were made between the grades obtained on the final psychology examination by the sheltered group and by the students who took the course in their native language. The comparisons showed that their grades were similar, providing evidence that students in the sheltered classes learn the subject matter as well as students taking the course in their first language (Edwards et al. 1984; Hauptman, Wesche and Ready 1988). The students in the sheltered psychology course received both an FSL credit and a psychology credit. It appears that they deserved this 'two for one' reward.

 ## CLASSROOM-BASED OBSERVATIONS

The goal of immersion programs has been to develop a functional level of proficiency in French that will permit students to continue their education in French or to fill jobs requiring bilingual skills. Sheltered courses are intended "to provide a transition between the second language classroom and the 'real world'" (Brinton, Snow and Wesche 1989). In the case of immersion programs, the development of all four skills is seen as important. In the sheltered program, emphasis has been placed on the development of receptive skills, on the assumption that the development of productive skills will follow suit (Krashen 1985). In the case of immersion programs, however, we have seen that although the students attain levels of comprehension skills comparable to native speakers, their productive skills remain far from native-like, particularly with respect to grammatical competence. In the case of students' improvement of speaking or writing skills as a result of the sheltered program, we simply do not know whether or not they improve: it is an issue which has not been investigated.

There are several hypotheses which have been put forward to suggest why the productive skills of the immersion students lag considerably behind their comprehension skills. One hypothesis is that once students have developed a level of proficiency which allows them to be understood by each other and their teacher, there is no social motivation to go beyond (Swain 1978). Given that language is learned for communication, this hypothesis is likely to find some support. However, other hypotheses, based on the teaching methodology itself have been proposed. For example, Harley and Swain (1984) hypothesized that in order to promote greater accuracy in the production of French by immersion students, there is a twofold need:

1. for the provision of more focused L2 input which provides the learners with ample opportunity to observe the formal and semantic contrasts involved in the relevant target subsystem.
2. for the increased opportunity for students to be involved in activities requiring the productive use of such forms in meaningful situations. (p. 310)

Swain (1985) argues that there are at least two roles in second language acquisition that might be attributed to production (output), independent of input. One, as Schachter (1984) has suggested, is the opportunity it provides to test out hypotheses—to try out means of expression and see if they work. A second function is that using the language, as opposed to simply comprehending the language, may force the learner to move from semantic processing to morphosyntactic processing. As Krashen (1982) himself has said: "In many cases, we do not utilize syntax in understanding—we often get the message with a combination of vocabulary, or lexical information plus extra-linguistic information" (p. 66). Thus, it is possible to comprehend input—to get the message without a syntactic or morphological analysis of that input. The claim, then, is that producing the target language may be the trigger that forces the learner to pay attention to the means of expression needed in order to successfully convey his or her own intended meaning. Of course, if the student is given inconsistent or no feedback as to the extent to which his or her message has successfully (accurately, appropriately and coherently) been conveyed, output may not serve these roles.

It was with these ideas in mind that we decided to observe in immersion classrooms to determine the degree to which these hypothesized needs were found. Our observations were made in early immersion programs rather than late immersion programs. From informal observations and discussions with teachers we know that, generally speaking, as grade level increases, there is more teacher talk and less student talk. This culminates, as Wesche and Ready (1985) observed, in the university level sheltered psychology class, with little interaction between students and the professor, who mostly lectured to the students. Thus, if the hypothesized needs are not present in the early immersion program, they are unlikely to be found at later grade levels.

The observations from early immersion classes were made in nine grade three and ten grade six classes in Ontario school boards (Swain and Carroll 1987). These classes were each observed and tape-recorded for a full day, and the tapes were subsequently transcribed and analyzed from a number of different perspectives. Let me summarize some of our findings.

We found that teachers created few opportunities for systematically using contrasting forms and functions in their content teaching. Rather, teacher talk was spontaneously used in service of the content being taught. Consequently, for example, the use of different verb forms was extraordinarily skewed. Over 75% of the verbs used were in the present or imperative. Only about 15% of verbs used by the teachers were in the past tense, 6% in the future tense and 3% in the conditional. Of the 15% used in the past tense, about two-thirds were in the past indefinite and one-third in the imperfect. The use of the imperfect was almost completely limited to the verbs *avoir*, *etre*, *faire* and *vouloir*. Its use with action verbs was virtually non-existent (Swain 1988). Sorting out form and function on this basis would be difficult, and indeed, it is an enduring problem of the immersion students.

Another enduring problem is the students' use of *tu* and *vous*, which among early immersion students tends to be restricted to *tu* (Swain and Carroll 1987). We counted the frequency with which *tu* and *vous* were used by the teachers and the functions they served. That is, we noted whether *tu* and *vous* were being used to signal grammatical information (singular or plural) or sociolinguistic information (familiar or formal/polite). As it turned out, *vous* and *tu* as forms were used about equally often. On average, each was used approximately once a minute by teachers. However, when we looked at the use of *tu* and *vous* functionally, the picture changed dramatically. There was on average less than one instance per day of the use of *vous* as a marker of politeness or deference (Swain 1988).

These examples illustrate the absence of planned input focussing on problematic areas. Perhaps planned focussed input is best accomplished in the French language arts part of the immersion curriculum—as an 'adjunct' to content teaching. Such an adjunct model has been described at the university level by Brinton, Snow and Wesche (1989), where "students are enrolled concurrently in two linked courses—a language course and a content course—with the idea being that the two courses share the content base and complement each other in terms of mutually coordinated assignments" (p 16). In the immersion context, the adjunct course could supplant the type of grammar activities that we observed occurring, which mainly emphasized the learning of formal paradigms and categories (e.g., conjugating verbs, parsing sentences, identifying object complements) and rules of written grammar (e.g., verb agreement), rather than relating the forms to meaning in context (Harley 1985).

Other observations illustrate the limited output of the students and the inconsistent feedback students receive based on that output. In our analysis of the data, we categorized each time students spoke without interruption according to the length of their utterance(s). The utterances were categorized as minimal (one or two words), phrase (adverbial, nominal or verb), clause or sustained (more than one clause in length). We found that, excluding students' reading aloud, less than 15% of student utterances were sustained, that is, greater than a clause in length. Furthermore, a substantial portion of their utterances—40%—consisted of minimal one- or two-word responses to teacher initiations (Swain and Carroll 1987). In reaction to their utterances, teachers, on average, corrected only 19% of the grammatical errors students made.

Teachers were not consistent about the corrections they made. For example in the same lesson, the teacher corrected the use of the auxiliary as shown in the first example, but ignored its incorrect use as shown in the second and the third examples.

(1) S: J'ai venu te prendre.
     T: Pardon?
     S: Je suis venu.
(2) S: J'étais très froid dehors, alors j'ai revenu dans la maison.
(3) S: J'ai allé en haut.

There seems to be little sense in which students are 'pushed' towards a more coherent and accurate production (comprehensible output) of French (Swain 1985). When they are corrected, that frequently suffices and there is no further follow-up. In relatively long student turns, teachers rarely made corrections at all. For example, in one class, students were asked to summarize or read aloud what they had written about their favourite TV program. Over 65 grammatical errors were noted in this portion of the transcript. However, not one error was corrected.

The issue of error correction—or negative feedback—is an important one both theoretically and pedagogically. Pedagogically, the question is where error correction fits into communicative language teaching as it can severely disrupt the flow of communication. Theoretically, issues such as whether error correction can influence the path of language learning at all, and if so, is its impact restricted to specific kinds of linguistic knowledge, are at stake. Furthermore, are certain ways of correcting errors more effective than others? For example, does it take 'explicit hypothesis rejection' to effect change, or are indirect means such as clarification requests and comprehension checks equally as effective? (See, for example, Birdsong 1988; Pica et al. 1988; Carroll et al. 1989). These are issues that future research will have to resolve.

In the meantime, it is clear that the immersion students are getting limited opportunities to speak in class, and when they do, the feedback they get is more likely to be content focussed rather than language focussed. This situation is due, in large part, to the implementation in our schools and universities of the typical transmission model of content teaching, where the teacher is seen as the provider of information and the students, the recipients (Goodlad 1984). Other pedagogical models, such as cooperative learning (Kagan 1986), are more learner-centered and interactive in nature, thus maximizing students' productive use of the second language. Experimentation with such models must be extended and carefully evaluated in our search to improve ways of 'getting two for one', that is of integrating content and second language learning.

References

Barik, H. C., and M. Swain. 1976. A Canadian Experiment in Bilingual Education: The Peel Study. *Foreign Language Annals* 9: 465-479.

Birdsong, D. 1988. *Metalinguistic Performance and Interlinguistic Competence*. New York: Springer-Verlag.

Brinton, D. M., U. A. Snow, and U. Wesche. 1989. *Content-Based Second Language Instruction*. New York: Newbury House.

Carroll, S., Y. Roberge, M. Swain, H. Brasche, and M. Shechter. 1989. The Effectiveness of Error Correction in Promoting Adult FSL Learning. Toronto: OISE/Modern Language Centre, mimeo.

Edwards, H., M. Wesche, S. Krashen, R. Clément, and B. Krudenier. 1984. Second Language Acquisition Through Subject-Matter Learning: A Study of Sheltered Psychology Classes at the University of Ottawa. *Canadian Modern Language Review* 41: 268-282.

Genesee, F. 1976. Evaluation of the 1975-76 Grade 11 French Immersion Class: Addendum. Montreal: Protestant School Board of Greater Montreal.

———. 1977. Departmental Leaving Examination Results: June 1977. Montreal: Protestant School Board of Greater Montreal.

———. 1987. *Learning Through Two Languages: Studies of Immersion and Bilingual Education*. New York: Newbury House.

Genesee, F., E. Polich, and M. Stanley. 1977. An Experimental French Immersion Program at the Secondary School Level. *Canadian Modern Language Review* 33: 318-332.

Harley, B. 1985. Second Language Proficiency and Classroom Treatment in Early French Immersion. Paper presented at the FIPLV/Eurocentres Symposium on Error in Foreign Language Learning: Analysis and Treatment, Goldsmiths' College, University of London.

Harley, B., and M. L. King. (in press) Verb Lexis in the Written Compositions of Young L2 Learners. *Studies in Second Language Acquisition*.

Harley, B., and M. Swain. 1984. The Interlanguage of Immersion Students and Its Implications for Second Language Teaching. In A. Davies, C. Criper and A.P.R. Howatt (eds.) *Interlanguage*. Edinburgh: Edinburgh University Press, 291-311.

Hart, D. J., and S. Lapkin. 1989a. French Immersion at the Secondary/Postsecondary Interface: Final Report on Phase 1. Toronto: OISE/Modern Language Centre, mimeo.

———. 1989b. French Immersion at the Secondary/Postsecondary Interface: Final Report on Phase 2. Toronto: OISE/Modern Language Centre, mimeo.

Hauptman, P., M. Wesche, and D. Ready. 1988. Second Language Acquisition through Subject-Matter Learning: A Follow-up Study at the University of Ottawa. *Language Learning* 38, 433–475.

Kagan, S. 1986. Cooperative Learning and Sociocultural Factors in Schooling. In *Beyond Language: Social and Cultural Factors in Schooling Language Minority Students*. Los Angeles: Evaluation, Dissemination and Assessment Center, California State University, 231-98.

Krashen, S. D. 1982. *Principles and Practice in Second Language Acquisition*. Oxford: Pergamon.

———. 1985. *The Input Hypothesis: Issues and Implications*. New York: Longman.

Morrison, F. 1981. Longitudinal and Cross-Sectional Studies of French Proficiency in Ottawa and Carleton Schools. Ottawa: Research Centre, Ottawa Board of Education, Ontario.

Pica, T., L. Holliday, N. Lewis, and L. Morgenthaler. 1988. Comprehensible Output as an Outcome of Linguistic Demands on the Learner. *Studies in Second Language Acquisition* 11, 63-90.

Schachter, J. 1984. A Universal Input Condition. In W. Rutherford (ed.) *Universals and Second Language Acquisition*. Amsterdam: John Benjamins, 167-183.

Stern, H. H., M. Swain, L. D. McLean, R. J. Freidman, B. Harley, and S. Lapkin. 1976. *Three Approaches to Teaching French*. Toronto: Ontario Ministry of Education.

Sternfeld, S. 1988. The Applicability of the Immersion Approach to College Foreign Language Instruction. *Foreign Language Annals* 21, 221-226.

Swain, M. 1978. Home-School Language Switching. In J. Richards (ed.) *Understanding Second Language Learning: Issues and Approaches*. Rowley, Mass.: Newbury House, 238-251.

———. 1985. Communicative Competence: Some Roles of Comprehensible Input and Comprehensible Output in Its Development. In S. M. Gass and C. G. Madden (eds.) *Input in Second Language Acquisition*. Rowley, Mass.: Newbury House, 235-253.

———. 1988. Manipulating and Complementing Content Teaching to Maximize Second Language Learning. *TESL Canada Journal* 6, 68-83.

Swain, M., and S. Carroll. 1987. The Immersion Observation Study. In B. Harley, P. Allen, J. Cummins and M. Swain (eds.) *The Development of Bilingual Proficiency Final Report Volume II—Classroom Treatment*. Toronto: OISE/Modern Language Centre, 190-341.

Swain, M., and S. Lapkin. 1982. *Evaluating Bilingual Education: A Canadian Case Study*. Clevedon, Avon: Multilingual Matters.

———. 1989. Canadian Immersion and Adult Second Language Teaching: What's the Connection? *Modern Language Journal* 75, 150-159.

Wesche, M. 1985. Immersion and the Universities. *Canadian Modern Language Review* 41, 931-935.

———. 1989. Long-term Outcomes of French Immersion Education. Paper presented at Second Language Research Forum, Los Angeles.

Wesche, M., and D. Ready. 1985. Foreigner Talk in the University Classroom. In S. M. Gass and C. G. Madden (eds.) *Input in Second Language Acquisition*. New York: Newbury House, 89-114.

Intermediate Natural Approach Beyond the Classroom: Experiential Education in Language Learning

Peggy Hashemipour
California State University, San Marcos

The Natural Approach developed by Tracy Terrell was largely intended for beginning language study. Teachers, however, have long desired to continue this type of language learning at the intermediate level. This paper presents recommendations on how the Natural Approach may be extended based on the educational goals of beginning-level studies: (a) attainment of a certain level of linguistic proficiency in the target language; (b) development of a good affective and self-motivated attitude toward second language learning; and (c) an increase in the knowledge of the target culture. On the basis of these outcomes, instructors of intermediate courses can concentrate on the teaching of socially interactive language in addition to Krashen's suggested content-based instruction and Free Voluntary Reading. It is also proposed that socially interactive language draw upon the fields of ethnomethodology, experiential education, and service-learning to place language learners in real-life settings in the target language and culture.

 INTRODUCTION

Educators in the United States today are becoming sensitive to the need to provide for the intellectual, social, and personal development of all students. Many are thus actively participating in a national movement of multicultural education which "seeks to foster [an understanding of] cultural pluralism within culturally diverse societies and an interdependent world" (Bennett 1990). Although this movement at the post-secondary level initially focused on the liberal arts and teaching fields, its effect is now being felt throughout the curriculum.[1] These curricular changes have called attention to the teaching of foreign languages, which had previously served as a principal source of culture instruction. Furthermore, despite the increased presence of multicultural perspectives outside of the foreign language classroom, there is nevertheless no apparent change in the national patterns which show that Americans are less inclined to study foreign languages than are other societies (Fishman 1989). Therefore, my intent in this paper is to discuss the place of foreign language study in multicultural education and to offer strategies for improving its position in light of increased national interest in experiential education and service-learning. My suggestions are based on research on language used within a social context and on bridging cultural diversity within service settings. It will be clear that such proposals are consistent with the principles and structure of the Natural Approach.

In general, instructors are delighted with teaching beginning Natural Approach classes. They see immediate results from their efforts: students communicate and are pleased. Yet at the end of the year they frequently ask, What next? Krashen (in this volume) has proposed content-based instruction for intermediate study, for which many techniques and methods have been suggested. While I concur with his proposals, other factors must also be considered in light of the movement toward multicultural education and the need for bilingual citizens. To address these issues, we must first recognize our starting point for continued language study. That is, we must ask: What are the educational *outcomes* of one year of language study under the Natural Approach? Generally, beginning NA courses hope to accomplish the following:

    a. the attainment of a certain level of linguistic proficiency in the target language;

    b. the enablement of a good affective and self-motivated attitude toward second language learning; and

    c. an increase in the knowledge of the target culture.

An understanding of what has been achieved in the above three areas at the beginning level is critical toward the development of an intermediate curriculum. In the next section, I examine each of these outcomes in the context of the NA methods and techniques used to achieve them. From these observations, I argue that an additional focus for continued NA learning at the intermediate and advanced level is socially interactive language, complementing Krashen's content-based instruction and voluntary reading. Section three addresses the content and topics for teaching socially interactive language. In section four, I discuss ways of experientially teaching socially interactive speech through the use of ethnographic observation techniques and by exposing second language learners to real-life situations in community service. Through service-learning (where students apply knowledge in the language classroom to real-life situations and benefit the community in need), they learn to deal with cultural diversity and thus transcend their own (often ethnocentric) cultural values, thereby enhancing acquisition of both language and culture.

2 NATURAL APPROACH GOALS

Proficiency

It is generally assumed (and hoped) that, after one year of second language study, a student will have a higher level of proficiency than when she started. With Terrell's approach, the development of linguistic competence means that the student will gradually progress from initial comprehension to making one-word responses, to forming lists, then phrases, then larger and larger sentences.[2] This transition from one stage to another in the Natural Approach is carried out through communicative exercises which promote two-way communication and facilitate language acquisition through actual use.

Moreover, the target language in the NA classroom is not used in isolation but instead is *contextualized*, with the teacher using verbal, nonverbal, prosodic, and paralinguistic cues by which the learner can ascertain meaning. For example, the teacher may employ visual nonverbal cues such as pictures and realia to bind the meaning of vocabulary with objects. In addition, hand gestures, facial expressions, and a slower speaking speed are strategically used to enable the student to focus on key items to be learned. Moreover, mnemonic devices are taught, so that learners associate new linguistic material with particular classmates. Collectively, such features of instructor input are known as *teacher talk*.

Terrell's recommendations are based on the idea that these superimposed prosodic paralinguistic cues are important for comprehension, which in turn is vital in language acquisition. This belief is supported by studies indicating patterns of increasing ability of linguistic accuracy and the gains of redundancy produced in language classrooms (Long and Porter 1985; Bejarano 1987; Ellis 1990; McGroarty 1991). A widespread audience has accepted these recommendations for modifications of speech.[3] Nevertheless, one might argue that adapted teacher talk is an impediment to natural second language acquisition, since the intermediate-level learner must eventually learn to communicate with native speakers who are not always likely to modify their speech.

Two facts suggest that adapted teacher talk is pedagogically and linguistically sound and that the lack of transition into higher studies is not the result of adapted teacher talk. First, although the phonological structure of teacher talk is different from nonadapted language (it contains pauses before and after key words, and phrasal stress reaches higher pitch levels), such modification is temporary. As a student progresses in her acquisition, the instructor incrementally decreases his use of these devices according to the three stages of beginning-level Natural Approach.

Second, in addition to being beneficial to the learner's linguistic comprehension and acquisition process, the use of adapted speech may also increase the learner's awareness of verbal and nonverbal social markers and strategies employed in socially and culturally interactive language (Jordon 1990). These benefits are accessible mainly to classroom learners (Ellis 1990). Terrell's 1990 study (re-printed in this volume) of non-class interactions of a learner with non-native speakers further demonstrated that many of the adaptations found in good teacher talk are not found in foreigner talk. Terrell showed that foreigner talk does not always contain the reduced code that is helpful to second language learners. Yet this classroom-acquired sensitivity has an essential function for the second language learner's development of social interpretation of language and is critical for improving communicative proficiency in terms of both discourse competence and strategic competence.

In summary, the outcome of effective beginning NA teaching is the students' incremental increases in language competence as based on comprehension and communication activities. A subsidiary outcome is an increased sensitivity and analytical ability of linguistic and paralinguistic cues that, as discussed below, are essential in the acquisition of socially interactive language.

Affective Attitude toward Language Learning

A second assumption of NA classroom language acquisition is that "attitudinal variables relating to success in second language acquisition generally relate directly to
language acquisition" (Krashen and Terrell 1983:37). Based upon the work of
Gardner and Lambert (1972) and Burt and Dulay (1981), Krashen and Terrell recommended that the NA classroom provide students with comfortable, supportive settings
and positive affective situations in which there is a good student-instructor relationship with lowered anxiety. They proposed that these are conducive to risk taking.
Such an environment bolsters the student's self-esteem and results in a good educational experience. With a positive initial experience, a subsidiary outcome naturally
follows: the student may be more inclined to continue her study and thereby further
her second language acquisition.

Nevertheless, this does not appear to figure as one of the principal motivators for
continued language study. As noted by Krashen (in this volume), "students who complete two or three semesters of Natural Approach Spanish will not be able to study at
the University of Mexico or discuss the latest political crises." This fact requires further analysis since breakdown in transference of study to further situations is also evidenced in transfer students from high school. These language learners frequently
experience placement difficulties at the post-secondary intermediate level due to limited survival language proficiency (Morris 1984). Instead of risking placement at a
higher level, students frequently opt to enter courses at a level lower than their ability.

While it appears that these students have not advanced from a limited survival
language taught within a contextualized environment to a higher-level, de-contextual-
ized academic language, there are other variables contributing to failure to advance.
One discussed by Wesche and Ready (1985) and Nocon (1991) involves the forced
participation found in required language study. In many cases, students' motivation
for beginning level study is a foreign language requirement which does not hold for
intermediate and advanced study. This in part explains the difference in value placed
on second language study of ESL and FSL students at the University of Ottawa, where
French-speaking students admitted to a bilingual occupational therapy program had
more negative responses to a required sheltered-English course in physiology
(Wesche and Ready 1985). Their English-speaking counterparts had more positive
evaluations of sheltered-French classes taken voluntarily. Furthermore, Nocon
argues, negative language attitudes found in students who were required to study language inhibited their language acquisition.

Another consideration affecting attitudes toward outcome of language study is the
proficiency demand placed upon low-intermediate students. In many cases the
demands are high and do not concur with independently documented patterns of second language acquisition patterns of adults. Krashen, Scarcella, and Long (1982)
demonstrate that although the extent of acquisition is quite rapid in the initial acquisition period, the rate of acquisition tapers off notably later: acquisition becomes
slower and more difficult. In light of these studies, the results of Sudermann and
Cisar's critical assessment of two National Endowment for the Humanities grants to

integrate Foreign Languages Across the Curriculum (FLAC) at Earlham College and St. Olaf College is not surprising (1992). Both of these post-secondary projects stemmed from efforts to develop and/or modify liberal arts and general education courses by appending an adjunct or "trailer" course where the class content is discussed and read about in a foreign language. In an analysis of the enrollment patterns at both institutions, Sudermann and Cisar show that students with two years of foreign language study lacked the reading competency to participate in advanced FLAC study in which authentic foreign language texts were used.

In addition to the externally motivated factors of required participation in and high demands of language study, internally and personally driven elements affect transition into intermediate and advanced language study. In a survey of learner fears at George Mason University, Goldin (1987) proposes that two social-suggestive norms involving personal affect and attitude may influence continued language studies: *negative images of self* (insecurity, anxiety about risk-taking), and *negative expectations of classroom experience* (students felt that language classes should only focus on grammar and that speaking is possible only with a solid basis in grammar).[4]

While this discussion has presented the external and personal factors as separate entities, the dichotomy is not so clear. In fact, these elements are interdependent: there is a significant correlation between personal affect and the fluency and negotiation skills in second language learners. Cummins and colleagues (1984) studied the interdependence between L1 and L2 reading skills in Japanese immigrants and tourists and Vietnamese refugee children in grades 2, 3, 5, and 6. They noted an interactional-style factor related to the amount of elaboration and detail volunteered by students in an interview and personality-attribute variables of the student (parents rated student personality traits of extroversion and introversion).

In summary, a second outcome of beginning NA is a positive learning experience which has the potential of transference to intermediate studies. Nevertheless, demands placed on the learner may impede advanced work. Feelings of uncertainty, forced participation, and high teacher expectations are externally driven forces. Students may also have internally driven factors such as personality type or negative self images of themselves as L2 learners.

Knowledge of Target Culture

A third common expected outcome of Natural Approach teaching is that the student will have an increased understanding of the culture of the target language group. The third edition of *Dos mundos* has amplified the significance of cultural knowledge for the second language learner through increasing the number of photographs, cultural readings, and discussions of characteristics of Hispanic cultures in the communicative activities. Cultural knowledge is further enhanced through the use of video, music, and realia such as food. Analysis of the cultural content within the chapters of the second and third editions of this text reveals an overall increase in the number of exercises, especially in latter sections of the texts.

In many respects, the communicative activities—the principal mode of Natural Approach study—may also induce a positive language and culture learning experience. Insofar as they are completed in a low-anxiety environment, students learn to negotiate their own communication needs with other language learners. However, another factor important to the lowering of anxiety results from the fact that the students in a foreign language class are comparatively homogeneous in their values and social membership. In contrast, teachers of English as a Second Language have observed that in culturally and linguistically diverse classes it is often more difficult to lower the affective filter given the disparity of beliefs regarding classroom and learning behavior and the differences in cultural values (Enright 1990; McGroarty 1990; Peck 1990; Snow 1990). Thus, even though foreign language and ESL students acquire a second language through the same communicative exercises, foreign language students do so in an environment of less resistance where they do not have to cross the limits of their own beliefs and attitudes.

These basic facts are reminiscent of underlying distinctions between foreign language programs (where the target language is not indigenous) and second language programs (where the target language is commonly used outside the classroom). Differences in acquisition outcomes of the two learner types have been attributed to extent of exposure to the language and to the educational and economic motivations of the two types of learners. What is perhaps more surprising about these acquisition rates is that in the United States, particularly California, there are high numbers of speakers of languages other than English. In southern California alone, Spanish speakers make up some 70% of the population of Limited English Proficient students in K-12 schools, and 56% of the total California school population is of non-Anglo origin (California Census 1990). These census results indicate that in the case of some foreign languages (Spanish in particular), exposure to the language outside of the classroom is available.

However, the proportion of student-centered activities to culturally distinct activities, the need for understanding, and the availability of cultural diversity outside of the classroom do not lead necessarily to a student's examination of his own ethnocentric values in order to expand his world view. In addition, the complexity of linguistic interaction as it reflects social and group membership is an aspect of culture which is minimally taught and yet is a critical developmental marker for the intermediate student.

The outcomes of beginning Natural Approach language study in terms of proficiency, affective attitudes, and cultural understanding and the factors which contribute to smaller enrollments in more advanced language study are the bases for the proposals presented in section three. The principal tenet of these proposals is that in addition to content-based instruction and voluntary reading, intermediate language studies should develop both linguistic proficiency and cultural proficiency as taught within the realm of socially interactive language.

3 TEACHING SOCIALLY INTERACTIVE LANGUAGE

The idea that language learners should also acquire knowledge of social aspects of language usage is not new. Canale and Swain (1980) in their definition of communicative competence propose that in addition to grammatical competence, the language acquirer should of necessity also acquire discourse competence, strategic competence, and sociolinguistic competence.

Indeed, the initial development of sociolinguistic competence is addressed in *Dos mundos,* as the authors encourage a gradual development of cultural understanding in the Natural Approach learner by balancing activities "relating directly to [American] students and their lives, and those relating to the Hispanic world." However, culturally specific activities do not necessarily lead to the examination of and dispersion of a student's xenophobia. Nevertheless, it is this self-analytical skill that optimizes sociolinguistic and cultural proficiency. That is, this skill that guides the student toward a more flexible world view also enhances her understanding of how linguistic interaction reflects social and group membership.

Furthermore, the development of this self-analytical skill is critical for the students' comprehension of decontextualized language (Cummins 1991), which is the basis of content-based instruction. Insofar as comprehension is essential in second language acquisition, it follows then that a *productive* ability in language use is contingent on the availability of comprehensible input. However, the ability to produce socially interactive language involves socially and situationally appropriate use of language forms and the knowledge of how to communicate effectively within the cultural domains of a language.

Brown and Levinson (1979) contend that communicators in one culture or across several cultures must also possess the cognitive structures by which they can *interpret* interaction. They further argue that interpretation of meaning entails not only understanding the content of an utterance by its syntactic and semantic structure, but also involves interpreting (a) *interactional structure* (conventions of conversation and discourse) and (b) *social markers* that demonstrate correlations between linguistic and social variables.[5] Thus, in order to develop socially interactive language, a student must have comprehensible input that is rich in these two items, which we now discuss further.

Interactional Structure

Through the use of structured cooperative learning in groups and pairs, beginning Natural Approach students learn by interacting and holding conversations with their classroom peers (McGroarty 1990). In foreign language classes, participants are typically homogeneous in their proficiency levels, culture, and social class. While the manipulation of interactional structure in these environments may advance discourse competence at the beginning level of language study, this parallel relationship between illocutors hardly represents real-life experience for learners. Outside the classroom learners will face a dynamic where the interactional relationships will be unequal due to their own level of proficiency. Furthermore, due to age and time constraints, most adult learners are unlikely to reach maximum native proficiency in their second language. As a result, successful L2 communicators of necessity develop strategies in order to compensate for deficits in linguistic competence. The non-native speaker must learn how to deal with affluency and the break-down of communication. However, studies of the development of strategic competence in second language learners indicate that this type of proficiency results from interactions with either native speakers or learners from different cultural and linguistic backgrounds (Jordon 1990). We conclude then that the homogeneous classroom is unlikely to present opportunities such as these and thus this fact strongly argues for experience outside of the classroom.

Social Markers

According to Laver and Trudgill (1979), social markers indicate social characteristics such as regional affiliation, social status, educational status, occupation, and social role. Laver and Trudgill also propose two additional categories, *psychological* and *physical markers*, which reveal important information about the physical characteristics, personality, and affective state of the illocutor.[6] Brown and Levinson (1978, 1979) demonstrate how social structure, group membership, and social relationships are displayed via social markers. Using well-accepted categories, they discuss four types of speech varieties displayed via social marking: *dialect, language choice, registers*, and *social deixis*. I now describe each of these in turn; they will serve as the areas of sociolinguistic content for study in intermediate classes.

1. Dialect   One way that social markers are identified is through the phonological, syntactic, lexical, and prosodic features that are a subset of the distinctive features of a language and reflect membership in regional and/or social groups (corresponding to class, age, gender, and ethnicity). Although typically used to refer to regional variation, a dialect can be a marker of social group membership in at least two known cases: (1) whenever the regional boundaries of a group are coincide with social boundaries; and (2) whenever a regional group migrates into another area, and the former regional dialect becomes a social dialect. Dependent upon the status of this latter group of émigrés, the use of the dialect serves as either a positive or negative marker of social group membership. The negative case is more common and is of special importance given the immigration patterns of communities which speak different dialects of Spanish.

Because emigration is one of the central sources of speakers of languages other than English in the United States, and because dialect can function as a socio-cultural marker, an intermediate curriculum for second language learners could include materials to develop learners' understanding of phonological, lexical, syntactic, and morphological features of the dialect so that they can interact and function more fully in native-speaker groups. While Krashen (1994) has argued that such explicit knowledge is difficult and therefore unsuccessfully acquired, attainment of such knowledge will further the development of both productive and interpretative social skills for the L2 speaker. Furthermore, the difficulty of the task does not result from the level of knowledge required by this content but rather by the methods used to teach the material. Instead, the teaching of these social facts about dialect are especially necessary in order for learners to live in the global culture of the next century.

Second language learners especially need to be aware that native speakers with distinct regional accents may espouse different cultural beliefs and values. This is especially critical for Spanish students, who should know that although Spanish speakers from Latin America may share a geographical region, there is no single Latin American culture; rather, there are many Latin American cultures. This is also important for Spanish L2 speakers who hope to use the target language in the United States, where dialect can identify distinct cultural patterns in regions with large immigration population.

2. Language Choice   In multilingual societies, the choice of language can often function as a social marker of group identity. Grosjean (1989) and Romaine (1989) present an analysis of language choice involving psychological and sociological dimensions such as topical domain, emotion, age of addresser and addressee, and the perceived language competence of the illocutors. They conclude that language choice corresponds to physical variables (age), relationship variables (degree of intimacy, solidarity, and power), and psychological variables (emotive and affective states).

Studies of language choice indicate a high correspondence between negative language attitudes and negative social perceptions of alienated groups. That is, sociological perceptions of non-group members may be negative when a language is chosen to exclude potential conversational participants. From this it follows, then, that language choice is a social-psychological marker of communication. This is important knowledge for the L2 speaker, who, outside of class, may face resistance from native speakers to speak in their native language with him. Such insight can aid the learner in developing cultural understanding and negotiation strategies, which are essential to developing higher levels of cultural competence and to being able to learn from native speakers as opposed to learning about them.

3. Registers   Speech varieties which are contextually and situationally based are known as *registers*. The same person may employ different registers to express more or less the same meaning on different occasions. Thus, register use projects clues about the speakers' referential relationships and about the range of the speakers' identities and group membership. Brown and Gilman (1960) use the notion of register to explain the power and solidarity relationship determining pronouns of address. Since the employment of a register may signal social power or deference, it follows that it is a marker of the speaker's social and educational identity. In fact, the use of registers is stratified according to group loyalty and group alienation. The second language speaker will be greatly handicapped in terms of what she/he hopes to accomplish communicatively without this knowledge.

4. Social Deixis   Brown and Levinson extend the traditional use of linguistic deixis to include socially relational properties involving "speaker-addressee or speaker-referent relationships" (1978:311). The use of social deitic markers in Spanish is quite distinctive, and certainly at least one form, the *tú/usted* alternation, is addressed in most Spanish texts; in *Dos mundos* the teaching of the alternation comes early in *Paso* B.[7] While this presentation is certainly clear enough for the student who is in the third week of study and will suffice for conversations with classmates and instructor, and will minimally provide access to conversations outside of class, additional presentations are needed on the complex structure of the *tú/usted* alternation involving the demarcation of interpersonal relationships of power and solidarity (Brown and Gilman 1960). Language students may thus come to understand the "interpersonal" reality in Mexican culture as compared to the U.S. "objective" reality (Condon 1986).

In summary, we have proposed four types of socially interactive language which could form the content of intermediate studies. Knowledge of these areas of language use will enable the second language learner to interact more fully with native speakers and subsequently increase the quantity of comprehensible input available. However, although acquisition of this knowledge may be consistent with Krashen's input hypothesis, the instructional mechanisms by which the student may move from contextualized to decontextualized language, as evidenced in the transition from beginning to intermediate studies, require serious consideration.

4   METHOD OF STUDY OF SOCIALLY INTERACTIVE LANGUAGE

The issues discussed above have been researched in the fields of sociolinguistics, dialectology, sociology, anthropology, and intercultural communication. While research materials are accessible to classroom teachers and learners for study and learning, an explicit learning methodology must be developed. Krashen (1994) and others have argued that explicit instruction on this type of sociolinguistic information is both tedious and cumbersome. However, such knowledge for the learner is vital toward effective social communication. Furthermore, in their 1984 article, Kirschner and Stephens show (in a qualitative study of students enrolled in a course which discussed bilingualism and code-switching) that L2 learners achieved academic, attitudinal, and linguistic gains as a result of study of these aspects of language. For this type of language learning to be optimal, the method of study must promote internalization. Based on the hypotheses of the Natural Approach, acquisition of this type of sociolinguistic competence for the second language may be congruent with patterns used in acquiring the first language.

Within the field of experiential education and service-learning, Kolb (1984) comments that "education is not only a function of books, but a function of experience and connecting what one reads with ongoing observations and experiences." Accordingly, Kolb proposed four constructions of knowledge through practical and real-life experience: *concrete experience, reflective observation, abstract conceptual-*

ization, active experimentation. Kolb proposed these as steps in the process of experiential learning.

> Concrete Experience: direct, current experiences; actualization of feelings and senses, including a consciousness of holistic experience within one's environment (e.g., someone who readily senses the mood of a group or responds kinesthetically to music)
>
> Reflective Observation: paying close attention to what one observes and experiences, and thoughtfully considering these according to meanings assigned by the group observed; comparisons of meanings; examination of one's world view and oneself in light of others' perceptions; uncovering the misknown world of others (e.g., someone who absorbs experiences and begins to make sense of them from his own self-perspective and the perspectives of others)
>
> Abstract Conceptualization: creation of ideas and concepts that organize experience, action, and observations; holistic explanation of reality based on self-perception and perception of others without placing value on one interpretation over another (e.g., someone who constructs knowledge based on concepts and models used to explain things; someone who enjoys learning about others' theories)
>
> Active Experimentation: acting out one's ideas and theories, or at least using them as guides for experimenting in the real world (e.g., someone who gets involved with people or tries out new and even risky ideas)

Kolb's proposals are in large part the foundation of attainment of knowledge within the field of service-learning. Although education and research in this area have been conducted for some time, today it is regarded as a national initiative (see the U.S. Federal National Service Acts of 1990 and 1993). There are many definitions of service-learning in the field: Kendall notes over 147 (1990). For the purposes of this paper, we will assume that *service-learning* is a process in which students assume responsibility for their learning and are involved in a reciprocal relationship with the community; students apply knowledge obtained in the classroom to real-life, practical situations and benefit—and receive benefit from—the community.

Although Kolb's proposals are not frequently discussed in foreign language pedagogy, the concepts are not new to the field or to studies of language acquisition and acculturation. For example, Krashen's input hypothesis of the Monitor Theory proposes that comprehensible input is integral to language acquisition, and Terrell's Natural Approach provides techniques and methods by which the instructor can make input comprehensible via concrete experiences within the classroom (role-play, simulations, and other types of communicative exercises). In addition, instructors who structure their lesson plans around review, re-entry of material, presentation of new material, and a final summary provide a holistic and integrated presentation of material. In turn, English as a Second Language teachers have effectively used learning outside of the classroom to promote language learning via field trips, social events, and other types of co-curricular activities.

These types of ESL activities, which increase the exposure to the target language, are in fact founded in experiential learning and are also available to foreign language learners within language-rich communities. Beginning language learners frequently may benefit from the concrete experience of a language classroom where the instructor sets up situations requiring use of interactive language. Moreover, the student may readily respond to and be successful in her language acquisition because the classroom environment is congruent with her cultural patterns. From these in-class activities, it is natural to develop subsequent concrete experiences involving real-life situations. For the language teacher these can be field trips (e.g., across the U.S.-Mexican border, or to local neighborhoods of the target culture group) or social events (e.g., *El cinco de mayo*) where students may observe and directly experience. However, these types of activities are only the initiation of effective experiential learning.

An additional factor which must considered in the curricular planning is that the three latter steps of experiential knowledge proposed by Kolb (reflective observation, abstract conceptualization, active experimentation) are not readily accessible to the intermediate foreign language learner within the classroom. For example, in order for reflective observation to be possible and effective, the learner needs additional exposure that is not naturally found within classroom experience. Abstract conceptualization and subsequent active experimentation are dependent upon reflective observation and therefore may present difficulty for the learner. That is, the proficiency of intermediate language learners may not be at the level where they are able to reflect fully on experiences in the target language. Therefore, for the experiential learning of socially interactive language to be effective, the language instructor must develop techniques to activate the learning process and to promote a *safe place* where the language learner may express his ideas without anxiety resulting from fear of repercussions.

To actualize abstract conceptualization and active experimentation, the student who hopes to advance linguistic and cultural proficiency must have the opportunity to connect experientially based knowledge with passive knowledge of history, economics, sociology, and language. From a linguistic point of view that means an understanding of how a group constructs social meaning. Inherent to this construction lies the Sapir-Whorf hypothesis, which proposes that "language functions not simply as a device for reporting experience, but also, and more significantly, as a way of defining experience for its speakers" (Hoijer 1954).

One of the most effective ways of understanding how others construct meaning is through the use of the qualitative methodology of ethnography developed and used by anthropologists, sociologists, and linguists. The educational outcomes of ethnographic studies include sensitivity to and understanding of different world perspectives, meanings attached to events and to actions and behaviors including social markers. Many regard ethnographic studies as a means by which an individual can construct a theory of culture (Spradley 1979:5). Elements of ethnographic study include:

1. development of the observational skills necessary to examine the proposed cultural features

2. interview skills that allow for the interviewee to express maximally her point of view without judgment from the interviewer, with the goal being not studying a human subject but, rather, learning from someone else

3. description of what was observed and the information collected in the form of field notes

4. presentation of native concepts and meanings in an ethnographic report portraying a sense of being "on the inside" of another way of life, including a description of the culture in its own terms; the report is presented without evaluation on the basis of superiority or inferiority

Although the practice of ethnography is a skill that must be learned, there is a certain parallel with the cognitive and analytical skills used in first language acquisition discussed by Wong Fillmore:

> The primary linguistic data which learners have available to them as input for their analyses consist of speech samples produced by speakers of the target language during social contacts in which the learners are themselves participants . . . Hence what the learners have to work with are *observations of the social situations* in which the language was produced, and streams of vocal sounds produced by speakers according to complex and abstract systems of grammatical and social rules that systematically and symbolically link up sounds, meaning representations, and communicative intentions. . . . The cognitive tasks involve figuring out the principles by which the speakers of the language use it to achieve their communicative goals and intentions: what do the speakers of the language talk about, and what can they do with the language they speak? Learners apply a host of cognitive strategies and skills to deal with the task at hand: they have to make use of associative skills, memory, social knowledge, and inferential skills in trying to figure out what people are talking about. They use whatever analytical skills they have to figure out relationships between forms, functions, and meaning. (1991:56-7)

That is, the child acquires linguistic and cultural knowledge via observation, association, and inference. In this fashion, she/he comes to develop a world view. These are in large part skills similar to those of the ethnographer. Ethnographic strategies and skills guide learners through systematically analyzing their own world view in order to enable them to see the *mis*known view of another culture. Although it is a difficult and disconcerting task, this kind of self-examination can empower and enhance learning (Robinson 1991; Richlin-Klonsky and Strenski 1994:101). In fact, most students who successfully complete ethnographic studies are those who have a good self image but are willing to risk expanding their world view. It is important for the ethnographic instructor to emphasize the validity and integrity of differing viewpoints. These are difficult tasks for anyone, let alone the second language learner.

On the basis of the ethnographic methods as well as standards established within the field of service-learning, the language teacher should consider each of the steps outlined below in the development of a service-learning curriculum for intermediate language studies (see the Principles of Good Practice in Kendall 1990). The suggested steps are *pre-placement*, *pre-observation*, *participant observation*, and *reflection*.

In any type of new curriculum development, planning for the event is critical. This is especially true for service-learning and even more so for community learning involving second language speakers with limited proficiency. At the *pre-placement* stage of the development, the instructor must carefully consider several factors. First, the community setting and the community need must be identified. The types of community service activities available are largely dependent upon the size of the target language community, their length of stay, and their social and economic status. The instructor must identify any community or governmental agency that addresses the needs of the target culture. From there the instructor (or community coordinator) must contact the group to establish a working relationship and to understand the expectations of the agency and the community. Following the standards of the service-learning field, it is neither the instructor nor the student who determines what the community wants, but rather the community members themselves. This step is all too often not fully observed. Yet it is essential in working with diverse populations where cultural misconceptions may exist. Cruz (1990) warns that "even carefully crafted guidelines for practice can do damage if they are not placed in the context of social realities, namely different and competing interests as well as outright conflict, based on, for example, class, race, gender, and even nationality." The nationally established guidelines were intended to integrate the effective use of experience with education, empowerment of learners, and promotion of the common good. Cruz goes on to argue that "it is possible to empower learners (through service-learning) and *not* promote the common good by reinforcing a sense of inferiority among those 'served' or a false sense of power among those who 'serve.'" That is, it is possible to experience a piece of social and political reality as an integral part of education and "simply duplicate the realities we wish to change" (Cruz 1990:322-3).

With the community identification of its need, the instructor (possibly the community or service-learning coordinator if available) must work carefully to match the student with a service setting. This requires, in addition to an understanding of the community setting and the help requested, a knowledge of the level of second language proficiency of the learner, as well as second-culture proficiency. Placement planning should also consider the student participant's abilities. The instructor must also be aware of the student's attitudes toward the target community. The result of this process should be the student's development of learning goals which are formally stated in a service contract. Such contracts are recognized as important instruments by which all students understand their responsibility for their own actions and learning.

The second step in the development of service-learning for intermediate language students involves *pre-observation* instruction in the skills of ethnographic observation and interview discussed above. It is useful to introduce ethnographic study in the classroom by using videos (professional and amateur), movies, and tapes of actual native-speaker language. The intent of this stage is not necessarily to instruct students about the cultural or social differences between themselves and the target group but, rather, to raise their awareness of inbred observational skills described by Wong Fillmore (1991) and to heighten those learned at the beginning level NA. Activities in this stage may involve contextualized communicative exercises such as paired students viewing five-minute scene of a video with no audio. During the video observation, each student writes as many details of the scene as possible. Then both students compare notes using the target language. Together they assemble and interpret their observations of the video narrative. Finally, the students view the scene with the audio to determine the actual intended meaning. From this they examine their interpretation and determine the basis of their conclusions. Suggested films for this exercise are *Like Water for Chocolate* and *The Scent of Green Papaya*.

Once students are aware of their observational abilities, learners may begin their community experience outside of the classroom where they will receive concrete exposure to language and its social and cultural use. During this stage, students will *participate* in community events while they are *observing*. In southern California, examples of service opportunities based on the social needs of the Latino culture might include: working with Spanish-speaking children in English classrooms; assisting in the planning and implementation of Parent Institutes where non-English speaking parents learn how schools in the U.S. operate; assisting an organization where non-English speaking people learn about diabetes at a health fair; or working in a homeless shelter with Spanish-speaking clientele. In any of these service activities, the party who is responsible for the training and supervision of the students must be previously and clearly defined in order to guarantee the safety of both the service recipients and the student participants.

The benefits resulting from participant observation are several. While students are involved in a community activity at this stage, they will be working with and for native speakers of the target language. Establishing a relationship where native speaker and learner are working hand-in-hand frequently dispels stereotypes and misunderstandings and establishes rapport between student participant and community member.

During this stage, contact between the student and community may be largely tactile and conversation or language use may be minimal. While both students and teacher may question the validity of this step, Cruz (personal communication) argues that this is in fact beneficial for a student's service-learning experience. In her terms, the absence of language and the corresponding use of the senses and other modes of communication (e.g., visual and emotive) are important in cross-cultural community settings. In this way, all participants are able to recognize pre-linguistically these similarities which allow them to bond. This type of cultural silent period is similar to that featured in the Natural Approach, during which students are allowed to develop a comprehension of language without being compelled to produce language. In addition, the use of tactile and physical experience is parallel to Asher's *total physical response* used in the silent period of the NA, in which students physically respond to language (Asher 1982).

The final step of *reflection* is essential in order for the community service experience to advance the student's intellectual development. Some regard this as the stage where learning actually occurs (Hutchings and Wutzdorff 1988; Zimmerman et al. 1990). A service experience in and of itself does not guarantee that learning or effective service will occur. Instead, students must have structured opportunities in which to think about and to express what they have experienced and what they have learned about their own world view and that of others. For intermediate second language students, reflection might involve oral discussion of critical incidents and of daily observations. Morton (1993) suggests informal settings for student reflections. This recommendation matches Krashen and Terrell's original 1983 proposal that language acquisition is best facilitated in low-anxiety situations. Another common type of reflection involves journal writing. At the initial stages of intermediate study, this assignment may be more problematic for students who are developing writing skills and have less well-developed skills in conveying observation and meaning in written form. The dilemma of this stage is well justified by the richness of exchanges between student and instructor based on the service-learning experience.

From the viewpoint of ethnographic study, the student's written fieldnotes may be used as a precursor to reflection. Recall that fieldnotes are the student's written record of what she has noticed about the surroundings and the setting, the actions and events she has observed, and what she learned about the meaning assigned to these elements by the community members. Reflection, on the other hand, is the student's opportunity to relate how the field experience has affected her. Furthermore, written reflection is optimal when completed as a dialog journal rather than as a diary.

Finally, it is this stage which leads to abstract conceptualization and subsequently active experimentation. Students advance holistically both in their second language skills and their ability to understand different world views. Nevertheless, there is no predetermined point of time at which the student will reach abstract conceptualization or active experimentation. However, these are the ultimate goals of the service-learning instructor.

5 CONCLUSION

Several proposals for intermediate second language study have been offered. These proposals are based on the outcomes of beginning language study within a Natural Approach classroom and on the need to advance cultural understanding and to deal with enrollment decreases. On these bases, I propose that in addition to content-based instruction, intermediate language study include an examination of socially interactive language including interactional structure and such social markers as dialect, language choice, register, and social deixis. The use of ethnographic techniques (observation, interview, fieldnotes, and report) is appropriate for study of socially interactive language. They allow for the student to learn experientially, to reflect, to conceptualize abstractly, and to experiment. Ethnography within the intermediate course may be used in a service setting where the student applies her knowledge both to give benefit and to receive benefit from the community. Finally, the careful combination of ethnography, service-learning, and intermediate language study will advance students' ability to use a second language and to understand, respect, and appreciate other cultures. It will thereby strengthen our communities.

Notes

1. A survey of college campuses in the state of California reveals an array of types for institutionalizing multicultural perspectives ranging from the distribution of individual classes across the curriculum, to modification of required general education courses (Stanford University, San Francisco State University), to graduation requirements of global awareness (California State University, San Marcos).
2. The Natural Approach proposes three stages of acquisition: comprehension, early speech, and speech emergence. For a fuller discussion of these stages, the reader is referred to the essays by Richard-Amato and Baltra in this volume.
3. See the State of California Department of Education regulations and standardized examinations for credential programs, which are offering Culture and Language Academic Development training for teachers of Limited English Proficient students.
4. A third norm proposed by Goldin suggests a *negative understanding of the target language and culture* (even though the participating students were encouraged to participate in outside language experiences such as foreign films, Spanish television, and interactions with native speakers).
5. Brown and Levinson (1978) also discuss *social strategies* which encode social information into speech. For the purposes of this paper I discuss the use of only interactional structure and social markers with second language instruction.
6. The study of psychological and physical markers is also important to the extent that they are culturally determined. For example, studies of multicultural communication indicate two types of culturally determined eye-gaze: high gaze and low gaze. In high eye-gaze cultures, interactors maintain eye contact in some form during conversation. In contrast, in low eye-gaze cultures, eye contact is avoided. Differences of this type frequently lead to affective misunderstanding in cross-cultural communication between individuals from cultures of differing eye gaze. Another example of cultural differences in psychological marking is seen in the expression of emotive states. For some cultures (Japanese), smiling is common to a non-descriptive emotive state, whereas in other cultures (United States), non-smiling is a common expression of non-descriptive emotive state.
7. Other types of socially deitic markers include the use of titles and honorifics as found in English and Japanese, respectively.

References

Asher, J. 1982. *Learning Another Language through Actions: The Complete Teacher's Guide*, 2nd ed. Los Gatos, CA: Sky Oaks Productions.

Bejarano, Y. 1987. A Cooperative Small-Group Methodology in the Language Classroom. *TESOL Quarterly* 21:483-504.

Bennett, C. 1990. *Comprehensive Multicultural Education: Theory and Practice*, 2nd ed. New York: Allyn and Bacon.

Brown, R., and A. Gilman. 1960. The Pronouns of Power and Solidarity. *American Anthropologist* 4:24-9.

Brown, P., and S. Levinson. 1978. Universals in Language Use: Politeness Phenomena. In *Questions and Politeness*, ed. E. Goody, 56-311. Cambridge: Cambridge University Press.

Brown, P., and S. Levinson. 1979. Social Structure, Groups and Interaction. In *Social Markers in Speech*, ed. K. R. Scherer and H. Giles. Cambridge: Cambridge University Press.

Burt, M., and H. Dulay. 1981. Optimal Language Learning Environments. In *The Second Language Classroom*, ed. J. Alatis, H. Altman, and P. Alatis, 177-192. New York: Oxford University Press.

Census of 1990 of the State of California.

Canale, M., and M. Swain. 1980. Theoretical Bases of Communicative Approaches to Second Language Teaching and Testing. *Applied Linguistics* 1:1-47.

Condon, J. 1986. . . . So Near the United States: Notes on Communication between Mexicans and North Americans. In *Intercultural Communication: A Reader*, 6th ed., ed. L. A. Samovar and R.E. Porter, 106-114. Belmont, CA: Wadsworth.

Cruz, N. 1990. A Challenge to the Notion of Service. In *Combining Service and Learning: A Resource Book for Community and Public Service*, Vol. I., ed. J. Kendall, 321-323. Raleigh, NC: National Society for Experiential Education.

Cummins, J. 1991. Interdependence of First- and Second-Language Proficiency in Bilingual Children. In *Language Processing in Bilingual Children*, ed. E. Bialystok, 70-89. Cambridge: Cambridge University Press.

Cummins, J., M. Swain, K. Nakajima, J. Handscombe, D. Green, and C. Tran. 1984. Linguistic Interdependence among Japanese and Vietnamese Immigrant Students. In *Communicative Competence Approaches to Language Proficiency Assessment: Research and Application*, ed. C. Rivera. Clevedon, Avon, England: Multilingual Matters.

Ellis, R. 1990. *Instructed Second Language Acquisition: Learning in the Classroom*. Oxford: Basil Blackwell.

Enright, D. S. 1990. Supporting Children's English Language Development in Grade-Level and Language Classrooms. In *Teaching English as a Second or Foreign Language*, 2nd ed., ed. M. Celce-Murcia, 386-401. Boston: Heinle and Heinle.

Fishman, J. A. 1989. *Language and Ethnicity in Minority Sociolinguistic Perspective*. Philadelphia: Multilingual Matters.

Gardner, R. C., and W. E. Lambert. 1972. *Attitudes and Motivation in Second Language Learning*. Rowley, MA: Newbury House.

Goldin, M. G. 1987. Why Johnny Can't Learn Spanish. *Hispania* 70:650-654.

Grosjean, F. 1989. *Life with Two Languages*, 2nd ed. Cambridge, MA: Harvard University Press.

Hoijer, H. 1954. The Sapir-Whorf Hypothesis. In *Language in Culture*, ed. H. Hoijer. Chicago: University of Chicago Press.

Hutchings, P., and A. Wutzdorff. 1988. *Knowing and Doing: Learning through Experience*. San Francisco: Jossey-Bass.

Jordon, I. J. 1990. Self-Selection in Turn-Taking: An Approach to Teaching Spanish. *Hispania* 73:1154-1157.

Kendall, J. 1990. Combining Service and Learning: An Introduction. In *Combining Service and Learning: A Resource Book for Community and Public Service*, Vol. I., ed. J. Kendall, 1-33. Raleigh, NC: National Society for Experiential Education.

Kirschner, C., and T. M. Stephens. 1984. Bilingual Theory and Attitudinal Change: The Spanish-English Bilingual and the English-Speaking L2 Student of Spanish. In *Research in Second Language Learning: Focus on the Classroom*, ed. J. P. Lantolf and A. Labarca.

Kolb, D. A. 1984. *Experiential Learning: Experience as a Source of Learning and Development*. New York: Prentice-Hall.

Krashen, S. 1994. A Teleconference on the Natural Approach. February 23, 1994.

Krashen, S. D., R. Scarcella, and M. H. Long. 1982. *Child-Adult Difference in Second Language Acquisition*. Rowley, Mass.: Newbury House.

Krashen, S. D., and T. D. Terrell. 1983. *The Natural Approach: Language Acquisition in the Classroom*. Oxford: Pergamon Press.

Laver, J., and P. Trudgill. 1979. Phonetic and Linguistic Markers in Speech. In *Social Markers in Speech*, ed. K.R. Scherer and H. Giles. Cambridge: Cambridge University Press.

Long, M. H., and P. Porter. 1985. Group Work, Inter-Language Talk, and Second Language Acquisition. *TESOL Quarterly* 19:207-228.

McGroarty, M. 1990. English Instruction for Linguistic Minority Groups: Different Structures, Different Styles. In *Teaching English as a Second or Foreign Language*, 2nd ed., ed. M. Celce-Murcia, 372-385. Boston: Heinle and Heinle.

McGroarty, M. 1991. What Can Peers Provide. In *Georgetown University Round Table on Languages and Linguistics 1991*, 40-55.

Morris, M.R. 1984. Foreign Language Teaching: Bridging the Gap between High School and College. *ERIC Clearinghouse on Languages and Linguistics*.

Morton, K. 1993. Reflection in the Classroom. In *Re-Thinking Tradition*, ed. T. Y. Kupiec, 89-100. Providence, RI: Campus Compact.

Nocon, H. 1991. Attitudes and Motivation of Beginning Students of Spanish at a Border University. Manuscript, San Diego State University.

Peck, S. 1990. Recognizing and Meeting the Needs of ESL Students. In *Teaching English as a Second or Foreign Language*, 2nd ed., ed. M. Celce-Murcia, 363-371. Boston: Heinle and Heinle.

Richlin-Klonsky, J., and E. Strenski. 1994. *A Guide to Writing Sociology Papers*, 3rd ed. New York: St. Martin's Press.

Robinson, G. L. 1991. Second Culture Acquisition. In *Georgetown University Round Table on Languages and Linguistics 1991*, 114-122.

Romaine, S. 1989. *Bilingualism*. Oxford: Basil Blackwell.

Snow, M. A. 1990. Teaching Language through Content. In *Teaching English as a Second or Foreign Language*, 2nd ed., ed. M. Celce-Murcia, 315-327. Boston: Heinle and Heinle.

Spradley, J. P. 1979. *The Ethnographic Interview*. Fort Worth, TX: Harcourt Brace Jovanovich College Publishers.

Sudermann, D. P., and M.A. Cisar 1992. Foreign Language Across the Curriculum: A Critical Appraisal. *Modern Language Journal* 76:295-308

Terrell, T. D. 1990. Foreigner Talk as Comprehensible Input. *Georgetown University Round Table on Languages and Linguistics*, 193-206.

Terrell, T. D., M. Andrade, J. Egasse, and E.M. Muñoz. 1994. *Dos mundos, Instructor's Edition*, 3rd ed. New York: McGraw-Hill Publishing Company.

Wesche, M., and D. Ready. 1985. Foreigner Talk in the University Classroom. In *Input in Second Language Acquisition*, ed. S. Gass and C. Madden. Rowley, MA: Newbury House Press.

Wong Fillmore, L. 1991. Second-Language Learning in Children: A Model of Language Learning in Social Context. In *Language Processing in Bilingual Children*, ed. E. Bialystok, 49-69. Cambridge: Cambridge University Press.

Zimmerman, J., V. Zawacki, J. Bird, and V. Peterson. 1990. Tools for Journals and Debriefing. In *Combining Service and Learning: A Resource Book for Community and Public Service*, Vol. II., ed. J. Kendall, 69-70. Raleigh, NC: National Society for Experiential Education.

Cognitive Aspects of Input Processing in Second-Language Acquisition

Bill VanPatten
University of Illinois at Urbana-Champaign

In this paper, I situate input processing within a model of second-language acquisition and use. I then argue that certain principles of cognitive psychology, in particular those dealing with attention and attentional capacity, interact with what I call "communicative value" to determine which features of language a learner attends to in the input. I suggest that these aspects of input processing are not only important for developing a coherent theory of acquisition but are also useful for generating important pedagogical research.

 ## INTRODUCTION

Current thinking about second-language acquisition (including foreign language learning) acknowledges the role of comprehensible input in the acquisition of a non-primary language (Krashen 1982; Ellis 1990; Larsen-Freeman and Long 1991).[1] Perhaps the strongest position on the role of comprehensible input can be found in Krashen's Monitor Theory (Krashen 1982), in which comprehensible input is said to cause acquisition. Krashen's theory has received substantial criticism, ranging from the vagueness of some of his theoretical constructs to the difficulty in testing his hypotheses (e.g., Pienemann 1985, White 1987, McLaughlin 1987). However, rather than undermine the role of comprehensible input as an important variable in acquisition, this criticism has served to underscore the need for second-language researchers to examine what learners do *with* and *to* input as part of the acquisition process. In other words, the criticism has pointed to the need for investigation into input processing and its relationship to the acquisition of a non-native language.

In this paper, I will examine certain cognitive aspects of input processing from the perspective of how learners attend to form and meaning in second-language input. First, I will outline a model of second-language acquisition and use based upon current research and theory in order to situate input processing in second-language acquisition. I will then list and describe two sets of principles that guide learner attention during input processing and will summarize the empirical evidence that supports these principles. I will then discuss how a theory of input processing might inform second language instruction, including suggestions for future research.

SECOND-LANGUAGE ACQUISITION AND USE

While second-language acquisition and use are complex and involve cognitive, linguistic, and socio-cultural aspects of learning, a principle concern of the field is how learners build an internal representation of the language they are learning. As a general scheme, acquisition can be viewed as consisting of three distinct sets of processes, as depicted in Figure 1. The first set of processes (I) involves those that the

---

input $\xrightarrow{\text{I}}$ intake $\xrightarrow{\text{II}}$ developing system $\xrightarrow{\text{III}}$ output

I : input processing
II : accomodation of intake, restructuring
III : access, monitoring

Figure 1. A model of language acquisition and use

learner's internal system uses to attend to input data. (Since this set of processes is the subject of more detailed discussion later in the paper, I shall not discuss it here.) From intake the learner must still develop an acquired system; that is, there is no a priori reason to assume that all intake data are automatically fed into the acquired system. It is believed that the internal system restructures over time (McLaughlin 1990), and, based on theories of the role of Universal Grammar, there is reason to believe that some intake data trigger changes in parts of the system that are superficially irrelevant to the specific intake data (White 1989). Thus, a second set of processes (II) can account for how intake is incorporated into the developing linguistic system. In short, input processing provides the developing system with intake data, but there are independent processes that work on the incorporation of these data into the system. Finally, it is clear from output studies that learner language is not a direct reflection of acquired competence. It is often the case that learners "know" more than they can produce and that second-language use can vary according to context, task, and other factors. Thus, a third set of processes (III) is posited in order to account for certain aspects of language production (e.g., monitoring, accessing, and so forth).

The focus of this paper is the first set of processes in acquisition, namely, input processing. What do learners attend to in the input, and why? In the next section, I will list and describe a set of hypotheses about learner attention during input processing.

 ## ATTENTION DURING INPUT PROCESSING

Based on certain aspects of general cognitive principles, there are two major hypotheses concerning input processing that are important for the present discussion. In addition, the first hypothesis is followed by a set of sub-hypotheses. These hypotheses and sub-hypotheses are listed below.

H1. Learners process input for meaning before they process it for form.

H1(a). Learners process content words in the input before anything else.

H1(b). Learners prefer processing lexical items to grammatical items (e.g., morphological markings) for semantic information.

H1(c). Learners prefer processing "more meaningful" morphology before "less or non-meaningful morphology."

H2. For learners to process form that is not meaningful, they must be able to process informational or communicative content at no (or little) cost to attention.

The first hypothesis, H1, addresses the relationship between form and meaning and is consistent with the observations of other researchers in both first-language acquisition and second-language acquisition (e.g., Sharwood Smith 1986; Peters 1985; Klein 1986; Faerch and Kasper 1986; Swain and Lapkin 1989). Simply put, it states that learners are driven to look for the message in the input ("What is this person saying to me?") before looking for how that message is encoded. While meaning and form are not necessarily mutually exclusive (see discussion of H1[b] and [c] below), this hypothesis suggests that form and meaning very often compete for processing time, with meaning generally winning out—especially during the early and intermediate stages of acquisition. Form here is defined as surface features of language: verb endings, noun endings, particles, functors, and so forth. No claims are made about abstract syntax, rules of movement, or constraints on movement rules. It should also be pointed out that H1 is context dependent: the input is communicative in nature and encodes information to which the learner must attend.

In order to understand H1 more fully, it is appropriate to backtrack and examine the concept of attention and attentional capacity in cognitive psychology. It is widely accepted in current cognitive theory that learning takes place almost exclusively when stimuli are attended to by the learner. Attention brings stimuli (in this case, language data) into focal awareness rather than allowing them to be merely perceived (Lachman, Lachman, and Butterfield 1979). In addition, attention is effortful, and cognitive psychologists generally agree that attention involves a limited capacity to deal with stimuli: only so much incoming data can be attended to at a given time (Wickens 1984). Those in cognition also generally believe that learning takes place via attention. In first-language acquisition, for instance, Slobin has argued that the degree to which linguistic information is acquired is determined by whether or not the information is attended to:

> . . . the only linguistic material that can figure in language-making are stretches of speech that *attract the child's attention to a sufficient degree to be noticed and held in memory.* (Slobin 1985:1164, emphasis added)

The belief that children learn their mother tongue as well as second languages effortlessly is folklore at best: children must attend to incoming data if they are eventually to incorporate them into a linguistic system (see Peters 1985 for further discussion of the effortful nature of L1 acquisition).

From the perspective of second-language acquisition, Schmidt has provided the profession with an excellent synthesis and analysis of the literature on attention, consciousness, and learning. Arguing against any kind of subconscious or subliminal learning, Schmidt concludes that as far as input processing in second-language acquisition is concerned, adult language learning requires attention to form in the input in order to convert input to intake:

> The existing data are compatible with a very strong hypothesis: *you can't learn a foreign language (or anything else, for that matter) through subliminal perception.* (Schmidt 1990:142, emphasis added)

In short, the language learner's limited-capacity processor must make decisions about how to allocate attention when processing input. When the learner's purpose is to process input for meaning, then the processor will encourage the storage and analysis of data that are most directly relevant to deriving meaning from the input. This leads us to a set of secondary hypotheses:

H1(a). Learners process content words in the input before anything else.

H1(b). Learners prefer processing lexical items to grammatical items (e.g., morphology) for semantic information.

H1(c). Learners prefer processing "more meaningful" morphology before "less or non-meaningful" morphology.

Secondary hypothesis H1(a) is borne out in both first-language and second-language research by the fact that learners in input-rich environments tend to pick out and start using single words and/or whole unanalyzed chunks of language in the early stages and then combine these to form utterances (e.g., first language: "doggie," "no soap," "Where train?"; second language: "Why test?", "no drink beer," "megusta las clases"). Learners are assisted, of course, by adjustments in input made by mature and/or native(-like) speakers of the language as well as certain phonological and intonational features of language (e.g., strong stress as opposed to weak stress, melodic contours). In one experiment with second-language learners, Klein (1986: Chapter 5) demonstrated that subjects tended to pick out and repeat content words when presented with a repetition task. Hulstijn (1989) also demonstrated the tendency for second-language learners to attend to content words as opposed to function words and particles when focal attention was on meaning.

Of more interest in terms of the acquisition of grammar are the secondary hypotheses H1(b) and (c). The baseline evidence for suggesting these hypotheses is (1) research on acquisition and processing of past tense and (2) research on acquisition of certain other verb-related morphemes. The latter point will be discussed first.

In both first-language and second-language literature, a fairly consistent picture has developed regarding the acquisition of verb morphemes (see VanPatten 1984a for more detail). In English, *-ing* (progressive) is always acquired before *-s* (third person present), and *-ed* (past tense) is acquired somewhere in between. While one could argue that *-ing* is syllabic and therefore perceptually more salient in the input, we are left with the question of why *-ed* is acquired before *-s*. Both are non-syllabic, consonantal, and verb-final morphemes realized as [t] (and its allomorphs) and [s] (and its allomorphs), respectively. Clearly, something other than structural features is at work here. If one looks at the acquisition of Spanish, one finds that person-number inflections (*-o, -n, -mos, -s, -is, -∅*) are generally acquired before markings of adjective concordance (-*o*, -*a*, -*s*, -∅). Given the overall lack of structural differences between these two sets of morphemes (all are word final morphemes, both sets contain syllabic and non-syllabic forms, and so forth), something other than structural features is at work in acquisition. As I shall argue later, it is the relative *communicative value* of a linguistic item that plays a major role in determining the learner's attention to it during input processing and the likelihood of its becoming part of intake.

Regarding the acquisition and processing of past tense, there are two different kinds of evidence in the second-language literature to support H1(b). The first are those data that report how tense is first encoded in learner output. Typically, learners mark time early in the acquisition of verb morphology through lexical items ("yesterday," "last week") and subsequently begin to add past-tense verb markings to their linguistic repertoire. If one assumes that output is partially (if not mostly) shaped by the intake derived from input, then these data are consistent with the hypothesis that lexical items are more likely to be attended to than verb morphology if both mark the same semantic feature.

More direct evidence comes from a recent series of investigations with classroom learners of Spanish. VanPatten (1989a, 1990) placed learners under four different experimental conditions involving specific attentional tasks while listening to a short passage:

· focal attention on content only;
· focal attention on content and a specific lexical item;
· focal attention on content and a functor (definite article);
· focal attention on content and a present tense verb form.

After listening, the subjects performed a free written recall of the content of the passage in their native language, English. An analysis of variance revealed that there was a large significant difference in the recall scores of the content only and the content + lexical item groups vs. the content + functor and content + verb ending groups. Furthermore, there were no significant differences between the content only group and the content + lexical item group when compared with each other. Similarly there was no significant difference between the content + functor group and the content + verb ending group when these were compared with each other. Figure 2 summarizes these findings.

The results of the 1989a, 1990 studies revealed that learners experience a notable drop in comprehension when faced with the simultaneous task of processing for both meaning and form. However, the simultaneous task of processing for both meaning and a specific lexical item does not reveal such a drop. These data thus provide supporting evidence for the primacy of lexical items during input processing over such things as morphology and functors.

Recent research has tested H1(b) by specifically focusing on tense. Glass, Cadierno, VanPatten, and Lee (ms.) report on the effect of providing learners with two different kinds of discourse-level input: one in which temporal adverbials are present and one in which they are absent. On a post-exposure test, subjects in the "adverbial group" were better able to determine whether a given event mentioned in the input occurred, is occurring, or will occur than were those who were in the non-adverbial

Figure 2. Results of analysis of variance performed on recall scores for simultaneous attention tasks (adapted from VanPatten 1989a and 1990)

	content	content + lexical item	content + functor	content + verb ending
content		n.s.	**	**
content + lexical item n.s.	n.s.		**	**
content + functor n.s.	**	**		n.s.
content + verb ending	**	**	n.s.	

n.s. non-significant difference in recall scores
** significant difference in recall scores p ≤ .01.

verb morphology–only group. (It is worth noting here that unlike English, the Spanish past-tense morphemes are syllabic and receive strong stress, thus placing them in the category of "perceptually salient.") We subsequently identified several good and poor learners who were subjects in the group and conducted an introspective probe with each. The probe revealed that the subjects were relying on the lexical information (adverbials) and not on verb inflections to assign tense.

Musumeci (1989) has conducted similar research at the sentence level and used learners of both Italian and French in addition to learners of Spanish. Musumeci asked her subjects to assign tense to input sentences delivered under one of four conditions:
- · verb morphology accompanied by adverbials of time;
- · verb morphology accompanied by typical teacher physical gestures (e.g., thumb over the shoulder to indicate past) but no adverbial marker of temporal reference;
- · verb morphology accompanied by both an adverbial and a physical gesture;
- · verb morphology as the sole source of information about the tense of the sentence.

Subjects in the morphology + adverb group and those in the morphology + gestures + adverb group consistently outperformed the subjects in the other two groups, in which adverbs were absent. Her results clearly demonstrate that the presence or absence of a temporal adverbial was the significant factor determining correct tense assignment. This finding supports H1(b) on the primacy of lexical items over grammatical markers during input processing.

In short, there is supporting experimental evidence as well as field data on both L1 and L2 learners for hypotheses H1, H1(a) and H1(b). These results indicate that learners' focal attention during input processing is on meaning, and precedence is given to lexical items for the conveyance of that meaning. When lexical items and morphology containing the same information compete for processing time, lexical items again have precedence.

H1(c)—that learners are inclined to process more meaningful morphology before non-meaningful morphology—was originally posited to account for the differential acquisition of -ing, -ed, and -s (see VanPatten 1984a, 1985). As already noted, formal or acoustical features alone cannot account for this differential acquisition. However, again assuming that output is at least partially a result of the attention during input processing, the relative communicative value of a form can explain the differential acquisition of morphemes. Before proceeding, a brief discussion of communicative value is in order.

Communicative value refers to the relative contribution a form makes to the referential meaning of an utterance and is based on the presence or absence of two features: inherent semantic value and redundancy. A form that can be classified as having inherent semantic value and is not a redundant feature of language will tend to have high communicative value. For example, in English verbal morphology, -ing tends to have high communicative value for the following two reasons: first, it has inherent semantic value because it encodes progressive aspect; second, it tends not to be redundant since, more often than not, no lexical information in the utterance co-occurs to provide cues to aspect (e.g., "Where are you going?"). To put this another way, it is the verbal inflection -ing that must be processed in the input for the learner to grasp progressive aspect.

Other features of language will tend to have lower communicative value if they lack inherent semantic value and/or are redundant. Third person -s, for example, has inherent semantic value since it encodes person-number, but it is also redundant because a subject noun-phrase is almost always obligatory. Its communicative value is thus lower than that of progressive -ing. Given H1(a) and H1(b), the learner is likely to process the subject noun-phrase for person-number and not the verb form.

Past-tense -ed falls somewhere between. It clearly has inherent semantic value since it encodes an important temporal distinction. However, unlike third person -s, the past-tense marker is not consistently redundant, and, unlike progressive -ing, it is not consistently non-redundant. Sometimes it co-occurs with lexical markers of time, and sometimes it does not.

A scale of meaningfulness might be difficult to apply to all features of language, but in a recent study H1(c) was tested directly. Bransdorfer (1989) tested subjects' ability to process meaning and form simultaneously in Spanish when the form was either the preposition de or the definite article la. Bransdorfer argued that these two forms are structurally similar (both are syllabic and occur in roughly the same environments, that is, before nouns), but he also argued that the preposition would carry greater communicative value than would the article. According to Bransdorfer, the preposition de signaled possession and, if absent, could pose problems of misinterpretation (El libro es Juan 'The book is John' vs. El libro es de Juan 'The book is John's') He thus classified de as having inherent semantic value. On the other hand, the absence of the article *la* would *not* pose interpretation problems (*La pluma es verde* 'The pen is green' vs. *Pluma es verde* 'Pen is green') He thus classified *la* as lacking inherent semantic value.

The results of Bransdorfer's experimentation revealed that there indeed seemed to be some differentiation in how simultaneous attention to meaning and to different forms affected comprehension of content. Attending to *de* affected comprehension much less than attending to *la*, suggesting that as learners processed input for meaning, *de* was more likely to be included in the processing than *la*. In his 1991 dissertation, Bransdorfer later replicated his study using elements that carried stress: the lexical item *exámenes* 'exams' which he classified as having inherent semantic value but not redundant, and the copular verb *está* which he classified as lacking inherent semantic value. His results revealed that attending to *exámenes* while listening to meaning posed no problem for comprehension but attending to *está* did result in a drop in comprehension.

The hypotheses and evidence presented so far suggest that attention is allocated during on-line processing according to relative communicative value. Processing capacity limits what a learner can attend to when engaged in the ongoing process of deriving meaning from input. The internal processor seeks to carry out efficiently the task of getting information, and, in the early and intermediate stages of acquisition, the result is a tendency not to process or hold in memory those items that do not contribute to meaning. However, L1 learners eventually do acquire most if not all features of adult language, and *some* L2 learners in input-rich environments do acquire many of the features of language that do not contribute to meaning (although in pidgins and fossilized speech, it is precisely those non-meaningful features that tend to be absent). Putting aside the socio-affective motivation for increased proficiency and focusing strictly on psycholinguistic aspects of learning, a second hypothesis helps to account for language development beyond the early stages:

H2. For learners to process form that is not meaningful, they must be able to process informational or communicative content at no or little cost to attention.

The results of VanPatten (1989a, 1990) as well as Glass and his colleagues (m s.) provide evidence of the difficulty of attending to form in the early and intermediate stages of acquisition when the primary intent of attention is to derive informational content. In a test of H2, Berne (1989) replicated VanPatten's attention task but she altered the input to make it more comprehensible to the subjects. She hypothesized that simplified input would result in a decreased cognitive load and thus release processing time for more attention to form. Her results, nonetheless, matched those of VanPatten: attending to form and meaning at the same time is difficult if the form does not contribute to meaning. Berne's data suggest that for learners to process form in the input that is not related to meaning, the input must be comprehended with ease. In other words, input must be fairly simple in the early and intermediate stages if learners are to attend to the various linguistic features that exist in the second language.

In another study, Leow (1993) found that simplified written input resulted in increased attention to formal features of language, but this effect was washed out by problems in random sampling. Like Berne, he hypothesized that simplified input allows the learner's internal processor to reallocate processing capacity so that increased attention can be placed on form. Using gain-score measures from a test on the present perfect and the present subjunctive in Spanish, he found that subjects improved in recognizing the two verb forms after having read a structurally simplified passage. However, the improvement cannot be considered statistically significant due to existing differences in abilities between the experimental group and a control group that received an unsimplified passage.

While these studies lend some support to H2 (informational content must be processed at little or no cost to attention if non-meaningful formal elements are to be attended to), it should be noted that they are still preliminary studies and that the connection between simplified input and processing ease has yet to be fully investigated. While it is reasonable to conclude that simplification decreases demands on attentional capacity, attentional capacity does not interact solely with communicative value to determine what is attended to in the input; attentional capacity is also affected by task demands of which processing time is a significant variable. Research needs to include studies in which pressure to perform the task is varied by amount of time available to do the task. While we await such studies, it is worth stating that even if processing time proves to be an important variable in determining attentional load for L2 input processing, processing time alone does not ensure attention to formal features of the input. In other words, processing time might be a necessary but not sufficient ingredient for attention to form in the input.

In terms of developing a model/theory of input processing in second-language acquisition, it is important to remember that H1 (learners process meaning before they process it for form) and H2 and the three secondary hypotheses H1(a-c) (preference for processing content words, preference for processing lexical as opposed to grammatical items for semantic information, preference for processing more meaningful morphology before less meaningful morphology) cannot account for all of input processing. In VanPatten (1989b), seven hypotheses regarding L2 input processing were posited. These hypotheses include processes that co-exist with those contained in H1 and H2. For example, at the same time that a learner is processing for meaning by searching for lexical items, he/she may also be processing utterances using particular word-order strategies such as the well-known first-noun strategy: interpret the first noun in a string as the agent of the action or the subject of the verb (Bever 1970). In other words, input processing involves more than searching out the meaningful elements in an utterance in an attempt not to tax attentional capacity; the input processor must also assign some sort of syntactic representation to the input string. A series of studies (Nam 1975; Ervin-Tripp 1974; VanPatten 1984b; LoCoco 1987) have shown that L2 learners do indeed use the first-noun strategy as a means of assigning argument structure to input strings. And as has been shown in the research on comprehension, listeners have access to syntactic, semantic, and pragmatic knowledge in processing (see Tanenhaus 1988 and Flores d'Arcais 1988 for discussion). Although L2 learners process input for meaning, and although we can argue that attention is guided by the interaction of communicative value and attentional capacity, processing is actually multidimensional: learners use knowledge from various sources to assign meaning to input strings.

In short, it is not my intent to reduce input processing to essentially one phenomenon. Instead, my purpose has been to discuss particular cognitive aspects of input processing and to focus on two hypotheses in particular. I will now take up the issue of what implications a theory or model of input processing might have for language teaching.

PEDAGOGICAL ISSUES

Those working in second-language acquisition research and theory are often asked if the research offers suggestions for specific classroom practices. Lightbown (1985) has referred to inquiry as "great expectations." Because second-language researchers work with second-language learners, it is often assumed that the research should automatically translate into pedagogy or that researchers have some special insight into what should happen in the classroom. As Lightbown points out, this is just not the case. Second-language acquisition research can help instructors understand why their students often perform the way they do, and certain *general* principles for the language-teaching enterprise can be gleaned from the research (see, for example, VanPatten 1986 as well as VanPatten and Lee 1990), but second-language acquisition research per se is not about language teaching.

For those looking for insights into classroom practice based on research in input processing, any suggestions about instruction based on the discussion in this paper would be purely speculative. Rather, the hypotheses discussed in this paper can be used to suggest pedagogical *research*. Swain and Lapkin (1989), for example, advocate that immersion programs need to provide learners with more opportunities to create output. Typically, immersion students process great quantities of input but are required to produce far less language. While not specifically referring to H1 and H1(a-c), Swain and Lapkin suggest that immersion learners process input for meaning and do not attend to many syntactic and morphological aspects of language (see also Swain 1985). Swain and Lapkin suggest that producing the target language may be the trigger that forces learners to pay attention to syntactic and morphological features in the input. One could approach the same issue another way. If we assume H1 and H1(a-c), would it not be beneficial to teach explicitly those items that learners might otherwise not attend to in the input? This is precisely the kind of pedagogical research inspired by the hypotheses presented in the present paper.

Another interesting question for pedagogical research is the following: Is it possible to alter the way that learners process input so that they get more grammatically rich intake? In a series of recent studies we have shown that this is indeed possible (VanPatten and Cadierno 1993). As noted above, learners tend to process the first noun in input strings as the agent or subject. Since Spanish has flexible word order and allows clitic object pronouns to precede verbs, our experimental instruction involved teaching learners not to rely on this processing strategy. *The instruction involved a focus on input only and no practice in production or manipulation of form.*

The results were striking: teaching learners not to rely on the first noun strategy had a significant impact on how they process input strings. Just as important, however, is that even though these subjects did not practice object pronouns during the instructional phase, they were able to use them in creating sentences during the testing phase. We compared these results with those of traditional output manipulation in instruction and found that while traditional approaches may help bring about changes in output, they do not have an effect on how learners process input. We have found, then, that in the case of the first-noun strategy, directly altering learners' input processing strategies is superior to traditional approaches that manipulate learners' output.

In another study, Cadierno (1992) replicated the VanPatten and Cadierno study using past tense in Spanish as the linguistic item. Recall that H1(b) suggests that lexical items—and not inflectional morphology—are more likely to be processed in the input. In her experiment, Cadierno taught learners to rely on verbal inflections and not adverbials for assigning tense and created "structured input" activities (see VanPatten 1993) that encouraged learners to attend to verb endings. Her results were as striking as those of VanPatten and Cadierno: learners who received instruction in processing input both comprehended and produced the targeted item better than did those who received traditional output instruction.

 ## CONCLUSION

In this paper, I have outlined several hypotheses concerning how second-language learners process input, that is, how they derive intake from input. In addition, I have cited some already existing evidence for these hypotheses. I have also suggested how the hypotheses might be used as the bases for pedagogical research.

What I have not discussed here is input processing and the acquisition of syntax. It is not entirely clear to me at this point how the two are related. Since syntax is the expression of purely formal and often abstractly formal relationships among elements in a sentence, the hypotheses in this paper might have little to do with the acquisition of syntax. However, the intake derived from input is the stuff upon which the acquisition of syntax depends. In other words, if there are triggers to parameters and principles that are responsible for the syntax of a language, it is probably true that the triggers themselves must also be attended to in the input.[2] In any event, Universal Grammar and the setting of parameters are more likely linked to the second set of processes (II) of Figure 1, where the grammar restructures itself according to new data (cf. White 1987, 1989). That is, as intake is accommodated by the developing system, those mechanisms responsible for the acquisition of syntax are instantiated to promote restructuring. A discussion of this is far beyond the limits of the present paper. What I hope to have made clear, nonetheless, is that the cognitive aspects of input processing are certainly worthy of investigation; that a theory of second-language acquisition cannot be achieved until input processing is examined in its own right; and that insights into input processing might prove to have important suggestions for language pedagogy.

Notes

1. I would like to thank the volume editors for their helpful comments on earlier versions of this paper. In addition, I would like to thank my students who, over the years and with many questions, have helped me to clarify the ideas contained in this paper. In particular, I would like to thank Rodney Bransdorfer, Teresa Cadierno, Diane Musumeci, and Cristina Sanz.
2. As an example, learners of English might have to attend to lexical material in AUX before it is possible for their internal grammars to (re)set the null-subject parameter from + to - (Hyams 1986).

References

Berne, Jane. 1989. Effects of Increased Comprehensiblity on Learners' Ability to Attend to Content and Form During Input Processing. Paper presented at the annual meeting of the American Association of Teachers of Spanish and Portuguese, San Antonio, Texas.

Bever, Thomas G. 1970. The Cognitive Basis for Linguistic Structure. In *Cognition and the Development of Language*, ed. J. R. Hayes, 279-362. New York: Wiley.

Bransdorfer, Rodney. 1989. Processing Function Words in the Input: Does Meaning Make a Difference? Paper presented at the annual meeting of the American Association of Teachers of Spanish and Portuguese, San Antonio, Texas.

Bransdorfer, Rodney. 1991. Linguistic Knowledge and Communicative Value in Second Language Oral Input Processing. Ph.D. dissertation, University of Illinois at Urbana-Champaign.

Cadierno, Teresa. 1992. Explicit Instruction in Grammar: A Comparison of Input Based and Output Based Instruction in Second-language acquisition. Ph.D. dissertation, University of Illinois at Urbana-Champaign.

Chaudron, Craig. 1985. Intake: On Models and Methods for Discovering Learners' Processing of Input. *Studies in Second Language Acquisition* 7:1-14.

Ellis, Rod. 1985. *Understanding Second Language Acquisition*. Oxford: Oxford University Press.

Ellis, Rod. 1990. *Instructed Second Language Acquisition*. Oxford: Blackwell.

Ervin-Tripp, Susan. 1974. Is Second-language Learning Like the First? *TESOL Quarterly* 8:11-127.

Faerch, Claus, and Garbriele Kasper. 1986. The Role of Comprehension in Second Language Learning. *Applied Linguistics* 7:257-274.

Flores d'Arcais, Giovanni. 1988. Language Perception. In *Language: Psychological and Biological Aspects*, ed. Frederick Newmeyer, 97-123. Cambridge: Cambridge University Press.

Gass, Susan. 1988. Integrating Research Areas: A Framework for Second Language Studies. *Applied Linguistics* 9:198-217.

Glass, William R., Teresa Cadierno, Bill VanPatten, and James F. Lee. ms. Processing Input for Tense: Lexical Items vs. Morphological Inflections. University of Illinois.

Hulstijn, Jan. 1989. Implicit and Incidental Second Language Learning: Experiments in the Processing of Natural and Partly Artificial Input. In *Interlingual Processes*, ed. H. W. Dechert and M. Raupach, 49-73. Tübingen: Gunter Narr Verlag.

Hyams, Nina. 1986. *Language Acquisition and the Theory of Parameters*. Dordrecht, Netherlands: Reidel.

Klein, Wolfgang. 1986. "The Problem of Analysis." Chapter 5 in *Second Language Acquisition*. Cambridge: Cambridge University Press.

Krashen, Stephen. 1982. *Principles and Practice in Second Language Acquisition.* Oxford: Pergamon Press.

Lachman, Roy, Janet L. Lachman, and Earl C. Butterfield. 1979. "Consciousness and Attention." Chapter 6 in *Cognitive Psychology and Information Processing: An Introduction.* Hillsdale, N.J.: Earlbaum.

Larsen-Freeman, Diane, and Michael H. Long. 1991. *An Introduction to Second Language Acquisition Research.* London: Longman.

Leow, Ronald P. 1993. To Simplify or Not to Simplify: A Look at Intake. *Studies in Second Language Acquisition* 15 :333-355.

Lightbown, Patsy. 1985. Great Expectations: Second Language Acquisition Research and Classroom Teaching. *Applied Linguistics* 6:173-189.

LoCoco, Veronica. 1987. Learner Comprehension of Oral and Written Sentences in German and Spanish: The Importance of Word Order. In *Foreign Language Learning: A Research Perspective,* ed. Bill VanPatten, Trisha R. Dvorak, and James F. Lee, 119-129. Cambridge, Mass.: Newbury House.

McLaughlin, Barry. 1987. *Theories of Second Language Learning.* London: Edward Arnold.

———. 1990. Restructuring. *Applied Linguistics* 11:113-128.

Musumeci, Diane. 1989. The Ability of Second Language Learners to Assign Tense at the Sentence Level. Ph.D. dissertation, University of Illinois at Urbana-Champaign.

Nam, Eileen. 1975. Child and Adult Perceptual Strategies in Second Language Acquisition. Paper presented at the annual TESOL Convention, Los Angeles.

Peters, Ann. 1985. Language Segmentation: Operating Principles for the Perception and Analysis of Language. In *The Crosslinguistic Study of Language Acquisition, Volume 2: Theoretical Issues,* ed. Dan Slobin, 1029-1067. Hillsdale, N.J.: Erlbaum.

Pienemann, Manfred. 1985. Learnability and Syllabus Construction. In *Modelling and Assessing Second Language Acquisition,* eds. Kenneth Hyltenstam and Manfred Pienemann, 23-75. Clevedon, U.K.: Multilingual Matters.

Schmidt, Richard. 1990. The Role of Consciousness in Second Language Learning. *Applied Linguistics* 11:127-158.

Sharwood Smith, Michael. 1986. Comprehension vs. Acquisition: Two Ways of Processing Input. *Applied Linguistics* 7:239-255.

Slobin, Dan. 1985. Crosslinguistic Evidence for the Language Making Capacity. In *The Crosslinguistic Study of Language Acquisition, Volume 2: Theoretical Issues,* ed. Dan Slobin, 1157-1256. Hillsdale, N.J.: Earlbaum.

Swain, Merrill. 1985. Communicative Competence: Some Roles of Comprehensible Input and Comprehensible Output in its Development. In *Input in Second Language Acquisition,* eds. Susan Gass and Carolyn Madden, 235-253. Rowley, Mass.: Newbury House.

Swain, Merrill, and Susan Lapkin. 1989. Canadian Immersion and Adult Second Language Teaching: What's the Connection? *The Modern Language Journal* 73:150-159.

Tanenhaus, Michael K. 1988. Psycholinguistics: An Overview. In *Language: Psychological and Biological Aspects,* ed. Frederick Newmeyer, 1-37. Cambridge: Cambridge University Press.

VanPatten, Bill. 1984a. Processing Strategies and Morpheme Acquisition. In *Universals in Second Language Acquisition,* ed Fred Eckman, Lawrence Bell, and Diane Nelson, 88-98. Rowley, Mass.: Newbury House.

———. 1984b. Learners' Comprehension of Clitic Pronouns: More Evidence for a Word Order Strategy. *Hispanic Linguistics* 1:57-67.

———. 1985. Communicative Value and Information Processing in SLA. In *On TESOL '84: A Brave New World for TESOL,* eds. Penny Larson, Elliott Judd, and Diane Messerschmitt, 89-100. Washington, D.C.: TESOL.

————. 1986. Second Language Acquisition Research and the Learning/Teaching of Spanish: Some Research Findings and Implications. *Hispania*, 69:202-216.

————. 1987. On Babies and Bathwater: Input in Foreign Language Learning. *The Modern Language Journal* 71:156-164.

————. 1989a. Can Learners Attend to Form and Content While Processing Input? *Hispania* 72:409-417.

————. 1989b. Towards a Model of Input Processing in SLA. Paper presented at the annual meeting of the American Association of Teachers of Spanish and Portuguese, San Antonio, Texas.

————. 1990. Attending to Form and Content in the Input: An Experiment in Consciousness. *Studies in Second Language Acquisition* 12:287-301.

————. 1993. Grammar Teaching for the Acquisition-Rich Classroom. *Foreign Language Annals* 26:435-50.

VanPatten, Bill, and Teresa Cadierno. 1993. Explicit Instruction and Input Processing. *Studies in Second Language Acquisition* 15, 225-241.

VanPatten, Bill, and James F. Lee. 1990. *Second Language Acquisition and Foreign Language Learning.* Clevedon, U.K.: Multilingual Matters.

White, Lydia. 1987. Against Comprehensible Input: The Input Hypothesis and the Development of L2 Competence. *Applied Linguistics* 8:95-110.

————. 1989. *Universal Grammar and Second Language Acquisition.* Philadelphia: John Benjamins.

Wickens, Charles. 1984. Processing Resources in Attention. In *Varieties of Attention*, eds. R. Parasuraman and D. Davies. Orlando, Fla.: Academic Press.

The Reading/Writing Relationship: Implications for ESL Teaching

Ann M. Johns
San Diego State University

In this paper, I review selected literature on the issues of comprehension (reading) and production (writing) of academic texts. First, I discuss psycholinguistic/cognitive theories, since they have had considerable recent influence upon ESL/EFL and foreign language practice. Particular attention is paid in this discussion to issues of interactivity and the influences of one skill upon the other. Second, I review some of the sociocultural literature, with particular emphasis upon theories of audience and discourse community. Third, I make some suggestions for classroom teaching by exploring possibilities for exploiting current research literature and for making texts accessible. Finally, I present a lesson that draws from the literature reviewed as well as from Natural Approach and Whole Language theory.

In his wide-ranging discussion of methodology, Robert Blair (1991) suggests that language-teaching approaches can be classified as either *comprehension based* or *production based*. After spending years with production-based approaches, particularly the Audio-Lingual Method, many ESL and bilingual-education teachers and students have welcomed the Natural Approach (NA), a coherent, comprehension-based program. Like other approaches of this type, NA "focus[es] on establishing receptive skills first...and do[es] not specifically train production, fluency being expected to emerge naturally and gradually out of the database established through ample comprehension experience of the right kind" (Blair 1991:25). In NA, spoken and written fluencies are thus predicted to emerge when the acquirer has received sufficient and appropriate oral or written *comprehensible input.*

It is my purpose in this paper to examine issues of comprehension (reading) and production (writing) of written texts, with specific emphasis upon second language students in academic environments. Initially, it might be supposed that NA has little to offer teachers or students when approaching written texts, for it "is designed primarily to enable a beginning student to reach acceptable levels of *oral* communication ability in the language classroom" (Krashen and Terrell 1983:131; emphasis added). However, in the 1983 description of the approach and in Krashen's many subsequent articles, the development of reading skills has been advocated as contributing "to a general language competence that underlies both spoken and written language" (1983:131). Krashen's argument seems to be that students who read widely have a much greater chance of acquiring both reading and writing proficiency, "a 'feel' for the look and texture of reader-based prose" (1984:20). And, although in NA "output is theoretically secondary with regard to the acquisition process" (1983:149), writing—and the reading/writing relationship—has also been discussed by Krashen (1984) and by Terrell (1988) in his work as director of teaching assistants at University of California, San Diego.

Though NA originates with comprehension and thus focuses upon input, there is considerable support in the literature for the argument that the literacy skills of reading (input) and writing (output) are inseparable, for they are complementary sides of the same coin. Research on native-speaking students indicates correlations between reading achievement and writing ability, writing quality and reading experiences, and reading ability and the comprehension of syntactically complex texts (Stotsky 1983; Belanger 1987). Therefore, the comprehension/production dichotomy discussed by Blair might not be applicable to the teaching and learning[1] of reading and writing.

In this paper, I will support the argument for the reading/writing connection by providing an overview of current literature and discussing some of the key issues in theory and research. Throughout, and especially in my final section (on classroom approaches), I will suggest how the literature cited might influence ESL classroom practice.

ISSUES IN READING/WRITING THEORY AND RESEARCH

It is important to note that the research on reading and writing is not integrated in much of the literature. One important indication of this artificial separation between the two skills, and their researchers and practitioners, appears in the recent 25th-anniversary issue of *TESOL Quarterly* (Vol. 25, 1991).[2] In one article, William Grabe discusses current reading research and theory; in another, Ann Raimes discusses writing from different, though overlapping, perspectives. This separation is not universally advocated (see, for example, Carson and Leki 1993), but in many research projects and in many ESL classrooms, the separation nevertheless continues.

Ironically, though these skills continue to be separated in the bulk of the literature and in much of classroom practice, there is considerable evidence that researchers and practitioners in both skill camps draw from the same theoretical sources. For these reasons, then, I will organize my discussion according to the major shared theoretical perspectives: the *psycholinguistic/cognitive* (PC) and the *sociocultural* (SC). As much as possible, I will examine issues in reading and writing simultaneously.

1. Psycholinguistic/Cognitive Views

The psycholinguistic/cognitive viewpoint has dominated theory, research, and classroom practice in reading and writing for the past fifteen years or so. PC experts have been concerned with two basic issues I will discuss here, among others: the processes involved in reading and writing, and the "interactivity" between *top-down* (conceptual) and *bottom-up* (linguistic) factors in this processing.

Processes   Considerable agreement exists in the literature that reading and writing processes are, for the most part, parallel (Flower et al. 1990; *Proceedings* 1986; Bishop and David 1986; Clifford 1987). Tierney, for example, notes that "[reading/writing processes] are similar acts of construction and response" (1985:110; see also Lewis 1985). Raphael and Englert (1988) describe reading and writing as comparable complex cognitive operations requiring similar stages: planning (pre-writing or pre-reading), drafting (writing or guided reading), and revising (modifying, extending, and postreading).[3] These experts recommend that teachers recognize the similarities between reading and writing operations and, accordingly, structure their classroom activities to reflect these similarities.

However, issues of process are highly complex, and this might not be acknowledged in classroom contexts. For example, even though reading and writing processes have similar stages, individual processes successful in approaching a variety of tasks may differ considerably. These differences—as well as the similarities—must be taken into account in classrooms (Bulakowski 1981; Huot 1988).

So far, there is not much evidence of a pedagogical interest in process complexity. Researchers are particularly concerned about the tendency in classrooms to reduce "process" to a linear, lock-step set of identical activities followed in the teaching of both skills. They have found that in many ESL reading and writing classes, "The Process" has been codified into the following stages, with resulting classroom activities: pre-reading/pre-writing, drafting, revising/editing, and post-reading/post-writing. This codification is highly reductionist, for reading and writing are in reality recursive rather than linear processes (Flower and Hays 1981; Raimes 1987). In addition, individual strategies and approaches to texts will undoubtedly differ depending upon reader/writer proficiency and background and the tasks required.

Thus, what students *do* with input or how they produce output in written texts (in other words, their *processes)* may vary considerably depending upon factors internal to the processors, found in the texts, or characteristic of the contexts. Encouraging students to be flexible in their approaches to tasks—to use different strategies and processes in reading and writing—is demanding for teachers, both intellectually and practically. Perhaps this is the reason that encouragement does not appear to be a common practice in "process" classrooms.

Interactivity   As can be seen in the literature, characterizing the nature of complex psycholinguistic/cognitive reading and writing processes has been a major concern in theory and research in native-speaker contexts (*Proceedings* 1986) and in work with ESL/EFL students (see Casanave 1988, Grabe 1991, and Raimes 1991 for overviews). One term that has become very important in discussions of processing is *interactivity*. In early use of this term, it referred to the instantiation of schemata (or background knowledge) of readers and writers when planning or conceptualizing a text (Carrell 1983; Collins et al. 1980; Flower and Hays 1981; Meyer 1982; Rubin and Hansen 1984). This was, in effect, the interactivity between reader and text that results in appropriate comprehension or text production. Most of the schema-theoretical studies of interactivity have focused on reading; we now have more than ten years of reading research indicating that text comprehension is enhanced if the reader shares schemata with the text writer and therefore "interacts" with the text predictably, resulting in comprehension (Bernhardt 1991). As a result of this work, many textbooks include exercises to encourage top-down or schema-driven processing: pre-reading questions to stimulate knowledge of content; semantic maps to assist students in developing appropriate vocabulary for the text (Carrell et al. 1989); and, less frequently, "problem/solution" exercises to assist students in predicting text macrostructure (Johns 1988).

Though schema-instantiation concerns appear less frequently in the writing literature, some promising work has appeared in *writing-task representation*, a complex process in which schemata are activated before and during student writing (Carey et al. 1989; Flower 1987). My own case study of a Vietnamese ESL student's task representation of a writing competency examination may provide insights into how ESL students activate schemata to process assigned texts and to prepare for important writing tasks (Johns 1991). What I discovered was that certain types of prompts for writing examinations (e.g., persuasive) and certain content in readings (in this case, an article entitled "The Crisis in American Education") assume the values, prior knowledge, and assumptions foreign to many ESL authors.[4] For the ESL student whom I interviewed, whose values were considerably different from the teacher's, activating text-appropriate schemata for reading and writing about the crisis in American education was a daunting task. But he was highly motivated to complete this task, for his failing scores on the writing competency examination prevented him from continuing his education.[5]

In recent years, the focus upon schema-theoretical issues has been criticized by second-language theorists who contend that having a general understanding (or *schema*) of text form and content—and thus being able to process from the top down—does not guarantee efficient or effective text processing for ESL/EFL students. Weber, for example, notes that the top-down perspective

> fails to accomodate important empirical evidence adequately. The [new] interactive models, attempting to be more comprehensive, rigorous, and coherent, give emphasis to the interrelations between the graphic display in the text, various levels of linguistic knowledge and processes, and various cognitive activities. (1984:113)

Grabe, supporting this argument, notes that for ESL/EFL readers, particularly readers who are less proficient in English, linguistic (or bottom-up) factors may inhibit text processing and comprehension fully as much as top-down factors. As a result, Grabe proposes a revised interactive model, in which bottom-up features (letters, words, phrases, sentences, local cohesion, and paragraph structuring) join the more global top-down features in a text-processing theory (1988:59). He thus agrees that reading and writing are interactive but argues that the complexity of this interactivity is much greater than schema-theorists have indicated.

The implications of this revised model of interactivity are significant. As ESL/EFL teachers, we need to consider in a new light the local, sentence-level factors that inhibit text processing and production when selecting texts for reading or assigning writing tasks. This does not mean that we should return to sentence-level activities in the classroom, for it is discourse that our students must process and produce. However, the new definition of *interactive* may justify dictation to understand better student difficulties with comprehending input, particularly as it relates to spelling, punctuation, and syntax. It also suggests our use of *cloze* (that is, discourse-based fill-in-the-blank exercises; see Rathmell 1984:51) in order to understand student vocabulary and cohesion problems. We should not, however, replace more natural reading and writing assignments with these controlled exercises. Instead, the bottom-up activities should augment the more natural ones (Scardamalia et al. 1981).

Skills influences   We need now to consider the relationship between reading (input) and writing (output), since the influences between them are of particular theoretical and practical interest in the Natural Approach. In comprehension-based approaches such as NA, a significant amount of linguistic input must be provided before production is required of the learner. In this section, therefore, I begin by reviewing studies of the influences of reading upon writing. I then explore briefly the writing-on-reading influences, the first- and second-language effects, and, finally, some implications for teaching.

Shanahan (1981) asked whether developmental reading level among English-speaking students influenced transfer from reading to writing. He found, not surprisingly, that for students reading below the third-grade level, the relationship between reading and writing could be found only in the area of vocabulary: students recognized a word in their reading and attempted to use it in their writing. However, for more proficient readers the relationship between reading and writing was at the comprehension and prose-production levels. Thus, advanced students were able to perceive the structures and essential content of their readings and transfer their perceptions to their writing.

Bereiter and Scardamalia, two of the most insightful researchers in this area, noted that teachers and textbooks often use a single reading model as a stimulus for writing.[6] They selected three genres (a suspense story, a restaurant review, and concrete fiction) to ask the question, What transfers from a single-text model to the writing of students at various academic levels? The results of their study support some—but not all—of Shanahan's findings:

> Students at all levels demonstrate some ability to acquire rhetorical knowledge from single examples (these abilities differed considerably from student to student). The rhetorical knowledge students are able to derive is biased at all ages toward discrete elements of language and content rather than toward more global aspects of form and rhetorical strategy. (Bereiter and Scardamalia 1984:177)

Thus, although Shanahan found that more proficient students were able to process and transfer some of the top-down rhetorical and content elements, Bereiter and Scardamalia found that students at all levels were more likely to transfer small, discrete elements (such as vocabulary) than more global elements of texts.

Crowhurst (1987) selected one distinctly difficult academic discourse mode—persuasion—to investigate the effect of reading in this mode upon writing.[7] She discovered that among English-speaking sixth graders who were given reading instruction in persuasion schema, writing quality improved in two areas: the number of conclusions and the variety of text markers (e.g., conjunctions). Undoubtedly, the students understood that when they read, they were processing complex discourse, and that when they wrote, they had a responsibility to lead the readers through their texts. Fielden (1990) conducted a similar study of ESL students enrolled in their first college writing course. He found that teaching them to read and identify the major features of a causation text improved their ability to write texts of this type. Improvement was found at the discourse and metalinguistic as well as the word levels.

Teachers and researchers who study writing processes know that students must become critical readers of their own writing in order to revise effectively. My 1986 paper, "The ESL Student and the Revision Process," outlines a technique in which students employ a problem/solution schema to evaluate their own texts. Like Fielden, I found that students' writing reflected text structure if they had been instructed to read for the elements of that structure.

Other researchers have refused to take a "chicken-egg" approach of investigating the influence of one skill on the other. Instead, they have taught the two skills together and then measured the results. The subjects of Dobson's 1988 study were inner-city kindergarten and first-grade students working in a classroom where reading and writing often interacted. She found that her students considered the mechanics of written language when reading story books and that the books assisted them in developing strategies for writing. Therefore, writing and reading supported each other with a transfer of strategies occurring in both directions.[8]

Perhaps of most interest to ESL teachers are studies (of which there are still very few) of bilingual students. In one case, Carson and her colleagues asked a number of questions about the reading/writing relationship in their students' first language and its influence on second-language production (1990). The researchers found that among groups of adult Chinese- and Japanese-speaking students, there was a strong first language reading-to-writing transfer; but in the second language (English), the transfer between reading and writing among the Chinese students was considerable, whereas among the Japanese it was not.

Additional studies of the influences of one skill upon another need to be conducted, especially among ESL/EFL and bilingual students, to develop testable hypotheses. Several hypotheses could be drawn from the conclusions discussed here: that reading can enhance vocabulary and sentence-level sophistication in writing; that with schema-based reading instruction we can enhance writing skills at higher discourse levels; and that first-language reading/writing transfer may not be replicated in second-language writing. There is also some evidence for the complex influence of one skill upon the other when the two are carefully integrated.

A question related to this discussion is, How should we integrate or sequence the two skills in the classroom? In comprehension-based approaches such as the Natural Approach, reading precedes writing in the teaching of language. Much current theory and practice supports this view; it is, incidentally, the one I tend to use more frequently.

Examples of reading-into-writing are plentiful in the literature. An entire volume, for example, is devoted to studies of students' reading of writing prompts in order to produce text and their efforts to integrate what they have read into their academic research papers (Flower et al. 1990). This volume underscores the centrality of reading-to-write for academic tasks at all levels of instruction and the necessity for research and practice to recognize the difficulties that some reading-to-write tasks pose. The 1992 book by Carson and Leki also has an excellent collection of chapters on the reading-into-writing relationships and the uses of reading in writing contexts, especially for second-language students.

However, there are alternative pedagogies that suggest writing-to-read possibilities. Marino and colleagues (1985) employ a specific, generative writing task as a pre-reading activity with fourth graders; their results support a technique for using writing as a pre-reading task. Bode (1988) advocates the use of journals for writing experiences as students become academically literate. Dyson (1984) argues that writing-to-read may have some developmental basis: she has discovered that young children often attempt to write before they can read.

Whatever the decision about priorities, Carson maintains that no academic classroom can separate the two skills; thus, though sequencing may be an issue in some situations, *literacy* requires integration:

> Reading and writing together allow students to develop critical literacy—the ability to transform information for their own purposes in reading and to syn-

thesize their prior knowledge with another texts in writing...The claim that some combination of reading and writing enhances thinking and learning argues for the value of using reading and writing collaboratively in composition as well as in reading classrooms. (1993:100)

2. Sociocultural Views

So far, I have discussed psycholinguistic/cognitive (PC) approaches to reading and writing, including the mutual influences between them and the implications of selected research for the classroom. Undoubtedly, the PC views are central to what occurs in many ESL/EFL classrooms, especially in the United States (see Leki 1992; Raimes 1991; Reid 1993). Nonetheless, theoretical stances with a more sociocultural perspective (SC) are being taken in native-speaker contexts in the United States and in ESL/EFL research in other parts of the world (notably in Australia and Great Britain). Because the literature in SC is almost as comprehensive as the PC literature, I have again selected two core issues for exploration: *audience* and *community*.

Audience   To understand issues relating to audience, we can turn to the theory and research on the native-speaking community in the United States and, especially, on its production of written texts.[9] In the literature, researchers ask questions such as, Is audience awareness the key factor in explaining writing ability?

The work of Rubin and Hansen explores this issue in detail (1984). Other researchers are studying how writers create a text that is

> considerate,....that produces an appropriate reference scenario in the mind of the reader at the right time. [The writer's] objective is then to produce written discourses such that the message is interpreted by the reader in terms of a model resembling the writer's source model. (Sanford and Garrod 1981:191)

In a study of English-speaking seventh graders who wrote first for a grade assigned by the teacher and then for their peers, researchers found that the peer audience elicited better essays in terms of content, organization, vocabulary, grammar, and mechanics (Cohen and Riel 1989). Work in native-speaking contexts is beginning to influence ESL/EFL contexts. I found, for example, that it is useful to provide ESL/EFL students with real audiences to address outside of the classroom in the production of well-structured and edited texts (Johns 1993).

Community identity   The idea of *community* is more controversial in the literature.[10] Many experts say that in order to understand the concept of audience, students must think not only of individuals but of the particular values, conventions, and categories of the group with which these individuals identify (Fish 1980; de Beaugrande 1984; Jolliffe and Brier 1988; Swales 1990). These groups, or communities, may be very large and heterogeneous (such as readers of a newspaper), or they may be more specific and academic (astrophysicists). Whatever the community, SC theorists and researchers are interested in the relationship between its genres and values and its readers and writers. For SC theorists, an understanding of text is not complete without an understanding of community. Purves tells us, for example, that a good writer's schemata reflect not only form and content in the text but shared community knowledge:

> A great part of becoming literate is learning not only the textual conventions but also the conventional acts of a particular community and thus becoming a part of that community as it engages in the activity of literacy . . . [Schemata] include semantic knowledge, or content, as well as rhetorical structure . . . [However] this view is too limited . . . Schemata should be broadened to include models of the structure and style of various types of discourse in certain situations . . . [They] should also include the functions of certain texts within a culture. (1991:62)

Of particular interest to ESL/EFL teachers should be the work in genres and critical literacy that is taking place in classrooms at all levels of instruction in Australia, influenced by the theories of Halliday (1989) and Martin (1992), among others.[11] In many Australian textbooks, activities focus upon the use of authentic texts and the contexts in which these texts are written. Students work together to discover writers' and readers' purposes, the type of text (e.g., factual account), and the organization and style of the text that in turn reflect the values of communities of readers and writers. The classroom focus, then, is not only upon writer/reader processes but also upon "understanding how texts achieve their purposes most effectively" (Derewianka 1990:1). In one textbook series for Australian elementary school children, teachers are told the following: "The genres as they are defined and introduced in this program can be thought of as prototypes—clear instances of generic types found and used frequently in our culture" (Christie et al. 1990:5).

 ## SOME TEACHING SUGGESTIONS

1. Exploiting the Literature

The disadvantage of much of the literature discussed here is that it is based upon research with monolingual, English-speaking subjects rather than with students who are attempting to acquire a new language, a new culture, and new (or modified) literacy skills. Monolingual readers and writers have distinct advantages over second-language students: they are generally members of a "colingual community," in which groups share not only a language but also cultural experiences (Swales 1990). For ESL/EFL students, understanding the values and knowledge presupposed in a text (Benson 1991) and producing a text that is appropriate for a foreign target community are very difficult second-language tasks. Thus, in an ESL/EFL classroom, we must consider students' first-language background, educational history, prior knowledge, and cultural values, in addition to the traditional language issues.

Despite the limitations of the literature, there are several insights that ESL/EFL and foreign-language teachers can exploit. One is that the conscious integration of reading and writing is necessary to academic literacy (Carson 1993). For example, research indicates that students who write about what they read can more deeply process and retain what they have read (van Dijk 1977; Smith 1988). Any writing helps; however, writing that assists students to manage information and to integrate what they have read—in summaries, paraphrase, and research reports—leads to improved processing and understanding (Carson 1993; Newall 1984; Stein 1990). Another research insight relates to the developmental nature of reading and writing skills. Shanahan (1988) recommends that we assist students to integrate reading and writing at every level while varying the focus of teaching and learning. However, for younger children or less proficient ESL students, we should begin integrating the two skills at a word-and-sentence level, asking students to recognize and use words from reading texts in their writing. We can move quickly into text macrostructures (e.g., argumentation and problem/solution) so that students will be able to process a variety of texts when they are sufficiently proficient and mature. For ESL/EFL students, the reading texts must be accessible in order to be transferable to writing. Thus, NA's comprehensible input principle should apply (Krashen and Terrell 1983:33).

2. Making Reading Texts Accessible

If reading and writing are to be integrated (or even if they're not), reading texts must be accessible to our second-language students. There are several approaches to achieving text accessibility. One method that is popular but does not always achieve its ends for ESL/EFL students is to control difficulty by rewriting a text to fit a read-ability scale (Fry 1964; Gilliland 1972). This type of simplification is problematic, since readability for ESL students involves much more than the sentence-length and word-length features that standard readability scales measure (Coxey 1992). It involves culturally determined schemata of the writer that are often at odds with the schemata of the linguistically diverse reader; also at odds are the previous experiences with the genre (e.g., an American story) that might not reflect the student's first-language genres. The ESL/EFL reader might not share an understanding of the author's purposes and responsibilities or of the variety of stylistic factors employed for metaphor, irony, or humor.

Another way to achieve accessibility is simplification of natural texts, still a common practice among international publishers (*Longman Structural Readers Handbook* 1980; Hindmarch 1990). Simplification "can be regarded as a special kind of translation, a reiteration of written text material, or the special writing of that material for a particular audience" (Mountford 1975:145). Accomplishing this task is much more complex than the handbooks imply, for simplification requires the retention of the original style, the author's purpose, the major ideas and details, and the coherence features (Tickoo 1993). According to Lautamatti, who analyzed several simplified texts (1978), textual cohesion and coherence can be adversely affected if simplification is poorly done. In short, simplifying or even shortening text should not be attempted by someone who has not studied the issue carefully. Even when carried out by experts, decisions about simplification must be based upon a model of text and text processing and a knowledge of the text's purpose within the discourse community—not just upon word lists or grammatical hierarchies (Johns 1985).

Another possibility for attaining text accessibility, one that is supported by the sociocultural literature, is the use of carefully selected, naturally occurring texts. There are a number of natural texts that are accessible, especially to the intermediate and advanced student. Some popular writing may be chosen because "it contains shorter sentences and greater use of accompanying illustration and typographical features which aid comprehension" (Dubin 1986:137) In other cases, however, academic or technical writing related to the students' majors or the classes in which they are enrolled is more accessible than newspaper or magazine materials (Johns 1991).

Summarizing the uses of texts in the teaching of reading, Tim Johns and Florence Davies argue that almost any text can be accessible if appropriately presented by the teacher:

> We wish as early as possible to introduce authentic, unmodified texts. It is important to note, we believe, that with authentic texts the teacher's responsibility for grading does not disappear; it is, however, transferred from control of linguistic features of the text to control of the difficulty of the tasks a student is expected to carry out and the amount of assistance he is offered. (1983:8)

3. Classroom Approaches

Once we have identified the texts we plan to use, how do we assist students to read and write about them? Moustafa (1987) suggests that we must make use of the tenets of the Natural Approach by devoting considerable time to preparing students to read, thereby activating prior knowledge or filling in the knowledge and values gaps. In a carefully delineated set of steps, she presents an approach for less-proficient students in which they ease into reading—and writing—after a number of visually based activities in which the language of the text to be processed is slowly presented. This is an excellent example of the use of comprehensible input in making reading accessible and writing possible.

My classroom preference is for Whole Language approaches (Freeman and Freeman 1989, 1992; Loucks-Horsley 1988; Moore 1990) that are specifically designed for developing academic literacy skills. These approaches have many features in common with the Natural Approach (e.g., acquisition, comprehensible input, monitor theory), but since literacy development is the principal goal, they focus upon the issues central to the discussion here.

The most iimportant element in Whole Language is its "wholeness." Thus, lessons proceed

> from whole to part. Students need the big picture (e.g., the whole text) first. They develop concepts by beginning with the general ideas and then filling in the specific details. (Freeman and Freeman 1992:7)

Thus, students begin with the entire reading (or writing) and its context; they start with meaning rather than form. In addition, writing, reading, and critical thinking are always linked. When accomplishing literacy goals, students use both sides of the brain, through visuals and other activities, a component suggested by the Natural Approach as well.[12] Students are aware that writing is generally a social activity;

therefore, they write collaboratively, often in front of a computer. They combine responses to reading and writing in ways that do not require constant correction, thus developing an optimal monitor.

One activity that I have used effectively with young students and in teacher-training sessions combines the best of Natural Approach and Whole Language methods. Here it is:

1. Students look at a picture presenting some type of conflict or problem and write down every word they can generate relating to it.[13] In this way, they are combining the visual and written as well as drawing from their prior knowledge.

2. In small groups, students compose a single word list consisting of all the words they have generated. Then they classify the words using any categories that they can imagine: colors, emotions, parts of speech, things you can buy, actions. This step encourages cooperation among students.[14] It also requires an essential higher-level thinking skill, namely classification.

3. Students make a semantic map from the words they have classified (see Miccinati 1988; Carrell et al. 1989) The technique of mapping words into categories is appropriate for preparing to read or write. The activity allows students to learn this method in a nonthreatening manner.

4. The students save their maps and return to the picture for an exercise that develops their understanding of text macrostructures. With the teacher or in groups, they discuss the problem presented in the picture. Generally, students come up with a variety of problem possibilities. They select one of the possibilities before going on.

5. They then explore together what the causes of the problem might be. These are listed by each group of students.

6. Finally, each group comes up with possible solutions for the problem. These are also listed.

7. When the students have complete lists of the problem, its causes, and possible solutions, they are ready to write their own texts.

8. The teacher begins the writing activity by supplying the first sentences: *Carmelita has a problem. She doesn't like to go to school. This is because...* Students are reminded to include the causes of the problem and some of the solutions in their papers. They are also asked to look at their semantic maps in order to build their productive vocabularies.

9. When the students have finished the first drafts of their papers, they read them to themselves, thus following a step in the writing-to-read sequence (McCleary 1991). Then, they revise their papers and read their revisions to the other members of the group.

10. The groups can evaluate the papers in a number of ways, depending upon the purposes of the lesson. One possibility is to ask whether the paper included all of the problem/solution *slots* (Johns 1988). Another is to ask whether students included words from the semantic maps.

CONCLUSION

From this discussion of the literature and teaching implications, it can be concluded that for reading and writing, the strict dichotomy between comprehension-based and production-based approaches cannot always be maintained effectively. There seems to be considerable evidence for integrating the teaching of these skills at every proficiency level, and some evidence that either skill can precede the other. The Natural Approach and the Whole Language methods can—and do—provide ample evidence for the necessity for significant input, both verbal and visual, in an ESL/EFL classroom as students acquire knowledge and learn to process and produce texts.

Despite what seems obvious from the literature, many ESL, bilingual, and foreign-language practitioners continue to teach reading and writing as if they were separate skills—or do not teach them at all. In my university, as in many others, there is a writing requirement for all students. But there is no requirement that students read at a specific level, although reading and listening have been identified by the faculty as most important for academic survival (Johns 1981). Much more research needs to be done on the reading/writing relationship in order to support the argument for integration. In the meantime, current research and methods can be exploited to establish a more viable reading/writing connection in second-language classrooms at every level.

Notes

1. If one wants to perpetuate the Krashen distinction, then *acquisition* must also be mentioned.
2. The essays in this anniversary edition have just been republished in a single volume, edited by Sandra Silberstein and entitled *State of the Art TESOL Essays: Celebrating 25 Years of the Discipline* (TESOL 1993).
3. However, they do not claim that these stages are all required in processing—nor do they say that these stages are linear.
4. Benson (1991) provides an excellent discussion of the features of reading texts that inhibit the comprehension of the second-language reader.
5. He did succeed in passing the examination—on the fifth attempt. The story ends happily: because he was an outstanding biochemistry student, he is now studying dentistry in graduate school.
6. This is particularly true in so-called current/traditional classrooms, in which the classical rhetorical modes (e.g., description, cause and effect) are taught (see Johns 1990 and Silva 1990).
7. See Johns 1993 for a discussion of the features of persuasion (argumentation) that make it difficult for students to produce.
8. For pedagogical implications of classroom reading and writing integration at this level, see the 1987 article by Scott and Piazza (1987).
9. See my 1993 article for a more complete discussion of audience theory.
10. For a much more complete discussion of why this is a controversial term, see my forthcoming volume entitled *Academic Purposes: A Literacy Reference for EAP Practitioners*.

11. We must also acknowledge the work of others, such as the 1981 book by Scardamalia, Bereiter, and Fillion. Unfortunately, they have so far had little effect on ESL classrooms in this country.
12. In his several Natural Approach presentations to students and teachers at San Diego State University, Tracy Terrell always recommended keeping a supply of "at least a hundred really good pictures."
13. I have used pictures from "big books" (for example, McDaniel 1983).
14. It is not my purpose here to discuss cooperative learning; however, those readers unfamiliar with its principles and practices should consult a reference such as Holt 1993.

References

deBeaugrande, Robert. 1984. *Text Production*. Vol. 11. Norwood, N.J.: Ablex.

Belanger, J. 1987. Theory and Research into Reading and Writing Connections: A Critical Review. *Reading-Canada-Lecture* 5:10-18.

Benson, Malcolm J. 1991. University ESL Reading: A Content Analysis. *English for Specific Purposes* 10:75-88.

Bereiter, Carl, and Marlene Scardamalia. 1984. Learning about Writing from Reading. *Written Communication* 1:163-188.

Bernhardt, Elizabeth. 1991. The Psycholinguistic Perspective on Second Language Literacy. In *ALIA Review 8*, ed. Jan H. Hulstijn and Johan F. Matter, 31-44. Amsterdam: Free University.

Bishop, Wendy, and Kevin David. 1986. *The Reading/Writing Relationship: A Selected Bibliography*. ERIC: ED 272-848.

Blair, Robert W. 1991. Innovative Approaches. In *Teaching English as a Second/Foreign Language*, ed. M. Celce-Murcia, 23-45. 2nd ed. Rowley, Mass.: Newbury House.

Bode, Barbara A. 1988. Dialogue Journal Writing as an Approach to Beginning Literacy Instruction. Paper presented at the annual meeting of the Florida Reading Conference, Orlando.

Bulakowski, Carole. 1981. Reading Strategies to Improve Writing Instruction. Paper presented at the annual meeting of the International Reading Association, New Orleans.

Carey, Linda, Linda Flower, J. R. Hays, Karen A. Schriver, and Christine Haas. 1989. *Differences in Writer's Initial Task Representations*. Technical Report 35. Berkeley, Calif.: Center for the Study of Writing.

Carrell, Patricia L. 1983. Some Issues in Studying the Role of Schemata, or Background Knowledge, in Second Language Comprehension. *Reading in a Foreign Language* 1:81-92.

Carrell, Patricia L., Becky G. Pharis, and Joseph C. Liberto. Metacognitive Strategy Training for ESL Reading. *TESOL Quarterly* 23:647-678.

Carson, J.G. 1992. Reading for Writing: Cognitive Perspectives. In *Reading in the Composition Classroom*, ed. J. G. Carson and Ilona Leki, 85-104. Rowley, Mass.: Newbury House.

Carson, Joan G. 1993. Academic Literacy Demands of the Undergraduate Curriculum: Literacy Activities Integrating Skills. Paper presented at the International TESOL Conference, Atlanta.

Carson, Joan, and Ilona Leki, eds. 1993. *Reading in the Composition Classroom*. Rowley, Mass.: Newbury House.

Carson, Joan G., Patricia L. Carrell, Sandra Silberstein, Barbara Kroll, and Phyllis A. Kuehn. 1990. Reading-Writing Relationships in First and Second Language. *TESOL Quarterly* 24:245-66.

Casanave, Christine P. 1988. The Process Approach to Writing Instruction: An Examination of Issues. *CATESOL Journal* November:29-39.

Christie, Frances, Pam Gray, Jim Martin, Mary Macken, Brian Gray, and Joan Rothery. 1990. *Exploring Explanations.* Sydney, Australia: Harcourt Brace Jovanovich.

Clifford, Geraldine J. 1987. *Sisyphean Task: Historical Perspectives on the Relationship Between Writing and Reading Instruction.* Technical Report 35. Berkeley, Calif.: Center for the Study of Writing.

Cohen, M., and M. Riel. 1989. The Effect of Distant Audiences on Students' Writing. *American Educational Research Journal* Summer:143-59.

Collins, A., J. S. Brown, and K. M. Larkin. 1980. Inference in Text Understanding. In *Issues in Reading Comprehension,* ed. R. J. Spiro, B. C. Bruce, and W. F. Brewer, 144-161. Hillsdale, N.J.: Erlbaum.

Coxey, C. 1992. An ESL Readability Measure for Business Case Studies. Master's thesis, San Diego State University.

Crowhurst, Marion. 1987. The Effect of Reading Instruction and Writing Instruction on Reading and Writing Persuasion. Paper presented at the annual meeting of the American Educational Research Association, Washington, D.C., April.

Derewianka, Beverly. 1990. *Exploring How Texts Work.* Maryborough, Victoria, Australia: Australian Primary English Teaching Association. (Distributed in the United States by Dormac)

Dubin, Fraida. 1986. Dealing with Texts. In *Teaching Second Language Reading for Academic Purposes,* ed. F. Dubin, D. E. Eskey, and W. Grabe, 127-59. Reading, Mass.: Addison-Wesley.

Dyson, Anne. H. 1984. Learning to Write/Learning to Do School. *Research in the Teaching of English* 18:233-264.

Fielden, C. J. 1991. *An Investigation of the Effects of Two Methods of Overt Text Structure Instruction on Students' Production of Causation Text.* Master's thesis, San Diego State University.

Fish, Stanley. 1980. *Is There a Text in This Class?* Cambridge, Mass.: Harvard University Press.

Flower, Linda. 1987. *The Role of Task Representation in Reading-to-Write.* Technical Report 34. Berkeley, Calif.: Center for the Study of Writing.

Flower, Linda, and John R. Hays. 1981. Cognitive Process Theory of Writing. *College Composition and Communication* 32:365-87.

Flower, Linda, Victoria Stein, John Ackerman, Margaret Kintz, Kathleen McCormick, and Wayne C. Peck. 1990. *Reading-to-Write: Exploring a Cognitive and Social Process.* New York: Oxford University Press.

Freeman, Yvonne S., and David E. Freeman. 1989. Whole Language Approaches to Writing with Secondary Students of English as a Second Language. In *Richness in Writing: Empowering ESL Students,* ed. Donna M. Johnson and Duane H. Roen, 177-92. White Plains, N.Y.: Longman.

————. 1992. *Whole Language for Second Language Learners.* Portsmouth, N.H.: Heinemann.

Fry, E. 1964. Judging Readability of Books. *Teacher Education* 5:34-9.

Gilliland, J. 1972. *Readability.* London: University of London Press.

Grabe, William. 1988. Reassessing the Term "Interactive." In *Interactive Approaches to Second Language Reading,* ed. P. C. Carrell, J. Devine, and D. Eskey, 56-72. New York: Cambridge University Press.

————. 1991. Current Developments in Second Language Reading Research. *TESOL Quarterly* 25:375-406.

Halliday, M.A.K. 1989. *Spoken and Written Language.* London: Oxford University Press.

Hindmarch, R. 1990. *Cambridge English Lexicon*. Cambridge, U.K.: Cambridge University Press.

Holt, Daniel D. 1993. *Cooperative Learning: A Response to Linguistic and Cultural Diversity*. Alexandria, Va.: ERIC/CAL.

Huot, Brian. 1988. Reading/Writing Connections on the College Level. *Teaching English in the Two-Year College* 15:90-98.

Johns, Ann M. 1981. Necessary English: A Faculty Survey. *TESOL Quarterly* 15:51-58.

———. 1985. The New Authenticity and the Preparation of Commercial Reading Texts for Lower-Level ESL Students. *CATESOL Occasional Papers* 11:103-107.

———. 1986. The ESL Student and the Revision Process: Some Insights from Schema Theory. *Journal of Basic Writing* 5:70-80.

———. 1991 Interpreting an English Competency Examination: The Frustrations of an ESL Science Student. *Written Communication* 8:379-401.

———. 1993. Written Argumentation for Real Audiences: Suggestions for Teacher Research and Classroom Practice. *TESOL Quarterly* 27:75-90.

Johns, Tim, and Florence Davies. 1983. Text as a Vehicle for Information: The Classroom Use of Written Texts in Teaching Reading as a Foreign Language. *Reading in a Foreign Language* 1:1-19.

Jolliffe, David A., and Ellen M. Brier. 1988. Studying Writers' Knowledge in Academic Disciplines. In *Advances in Writing Research, Vol. II: Writing in Academic Disciplines*, ed. David A. Jolliffe, 35-88. Norwood, N.J.:Ablex.

Krashen, Stephen D. 1984. *Writing: Research, Theory, and Applications*. Oxford, U.K.: Pergamon Institute of English.

Krashen, Stephen D., and Tracy D. Terrell. 1983. *The Natural Approach: Language Acquisition in the Classroom*. Englewood Cliffs, N.J.: Alemany/Prentice-Hall.

Lautamatti, Lisa. 1978. Some Observations on Cohesion and Coherence in Simplified Texts. In *Cohesion and Semantics: Reports on Text Linguistics*, ed. Jan-Ola Ostman, 3-23. ERIC: ED 275 191.

Leki, Ilona. 1992. *Understanding ESL Writers*. Portsmouth, N.H.: Heinemann/Boynton-Cook.

Lewis, Janice. 1985. Support for Reading and Writing as Shared Developmental Processes. Presented at the annual meeting of the Western College Reading and Learning Association, Denver.

Longman Structural Readers Handbook. 1980. Hong Kong: Sheck Wah Tong Printing Press.

Loucks-Horsley, Susan, ed. 1988. The Reading-Writing Connection: A Whole Language Approach. An Annotated Resource List. In *Linking Research and Development to Practice*, No. 9603. Washington, D.C.: Office of Educational Research and Improvement.

Marino, Jacqueline L., Sandra M. Gould, and Lester W. Haas. 1985. The Effects of Writing as a Prereading Activity on Delayed Recall of Narrative Text. *Elementary School Journal* 86:199-205.

Martin, James. 1992. Genre and Literacy: Modeling Context in Educational Linguistics. *Annual Review of Applied Linguistics* 13:141-74.

McCleary, Bill. 1991. IBM Begins Selling "Writing to Write" for Second Graders as Sequel to "Writing to Read." *Composition Chronicle* 4(4):1-2.

McDaniel, Becky B. 1983. *Fue Carmelita (Mis primeros libros series)*. Chicago: Children's Press.

Meyer, B.J.F. 1982. Reading Research and the Composition Teacher. *College Composition and Communication* 33:34-49.

Miccinati, Jeannette L. 1988. Mapping the Terrain: Connecting Reading with Academic Writing. *Journal of Reading* 2:543-52.

Moore, Alex. 1990. *The Whole Language Approach to the Teaching of Bilingual Learners.* Occasional Paper 15. Berkeley, Calif.: Center for the Study of Writing.

Mountford, Alan. 1975. The Notion of Simplification and Its Relevance to Materials Preparation for English for Science and Technology. In *Teaching English for Science and Technology,* ed. Jack Richards, 142-61. Singapore: Singapore University Press (SEAMEO Regional Language Centre).

Moustafa, Margaret. 1987. Comprehensible Input PLUS the Language Experience Approach: A Long-term Perspective. *Reading Teacher* 41:276-86.

Newell, George E. 1984. Learning from Writing in Two Content Areas: A Case Study Protocol Analysis. *Research in the Teaching of English* 18:265-87.

Proceedings of the Conference on Reading and Writing Connections. 1986. Urbana, Ill.:Center for the Study of Reading.

Purves, Alan. 1991. The Textual Contract: Literacy as Common Knowledge and Conventional Wisdom. In *Literate Systems and Individual Lives: Perspectives on Literacy and Schooling,* ed. Edward M. Jennings and Alan C. Purves, 51-72. Albany, N.Y.: State University of New York Press.

Raimes, Ann. 1987. Language Proficiency, Writing Ability, and Composing Strategies: A Study of ESL College Student Writers. *Language Learning* 37(3):439-468.

―――. 1991. Out of the Woods: Emerging Traditions in the Teaching of Writing. *TESOL Quarterly* 25:407-430.

Raphael, Taffy E., and Carol Sue Englert. 1988. *Integrating Writing and Reading Instruction.* Occasional Paper 118. East Lansing, Mich.: Institute for Research on Teaching.

Rathmell, George. 1984. *Benchmarks in Reading: A Guide to Instruction in the Second Language Classroom.* Hayward, Calif.: Alemany Press.

Reid, Joy. 1993. *The Teaching of ESL Writing.* Englewood Cliffs, N.J.: Regents-Prentice Hall.

Rubin, Andree, and Jane Hansen. 1984. *Reading and Writing: How Are the First Two Rs Related?* Reading Education Report 51. Washington, D.C.: National Institute of Education.

Sanford, A.J., and S.C. Garrod. 1981. *Understanding Written Language.* Chichester, N.Y.: Wiley.

Scardamalia, Marlene, Carl Bereiter, and Bryant Fillion. 1981. *Writing for Results: A Sourcebook of Consequential Composing Activities.* La Salle, Ill.: Open Court Publishers.

Scott, Diana, and Carolyn L. Piazza. 1987. Integrating Reading and Writing Lessons. *Reading Horizons* Fall:57-63.

Shanahan, Timothy. 1981. A Canonical Correlational Analysis of Learning to Read and Learning to Write: An Exploratory Analysis. Paper presented at the annual meeting of the International Reading Association, New Orleans.

Smith, Carl. 1988. Does It Help to Write about Your Reading? *Journal of Reading* 32:276-77.

Stein, V. 1990. Exploring the Cognition of Reading-to-Write. In Flower et al., eds. 1990.

Stotsky, S. 1983. Research on Reading/Writing Relationships: A Synthesis and Suggested Directions. *Language Arts* 60:627-642.

Swales, John. 1990. *Genre Analysis: English in Academic and Research Settings.* Oxford: Oxford University Press.

Terrell, Tracy. 1988. Conversation with author.

Tickoo, M. L., ed. 1993. *Simplification: Theory and Application.* Singapore: Singapore University Press (SEAMEO Regional Language Centre).

Tierney, Robert J. 1985. The Reading-Writing Relationship: A Glimpse of Some Facets. *Reading-Canada-Lecture* 3:109-116.

van Dijk, Teun A. 1977. Semantic Macrostructures and Knowledge Frames in Discourse Comprehension. In *Cognitive Processes in Comprehension,* ed. Marcel Just and Patricia Carpenter, 3-32. New York: Erlbaum.

Weber, E. 1984. Reading: United States. *Annual Review of Applied Linguistics* 4:111-23.

On the Need for Discourse Analysis in Curriculum Development

Marianne Celce-Murcia
University of California, Los Angeles

It is commonly acknowledged in the area of Language for Specific Purposes (LSP) that discourse analysis should be an integral part of needs assessment. Occasionally, this is also the case with materials development. In the more general domain of second or foreign language teaching, however, much less attention has been given to the potential role of discourse analysis in developing language curricula and materials. This paper proposes, and illustrates with three example courses, that there appears to be a need to apply discourse analysis to all language curriculum development but that this need is of greater or lesser importance depending on learner characteristics and needs as well as the type of language course under consideration. The paper also suggests that discourse analysis may provide the language curriculum with a more appropriate form-based component than does decontextualized, sentence-level grammatical analysis for eventual integration with communicative approaches to language teaching such as Terrell's Natural Approach.

1 INTRODUCTION

With the exception of some models typical of the "Language for Specific Purposes" (LSP) movement, current thinking in language methodology does not give adequate emphasis to the need for discourse analysis in developing optimal curricula and materials. And even when discourse analysis is acknowledged to be important in language teaching (in, for example, needs assessment), there is often lack of specification on the precise role that discourse analysis should assume. It is furthermore unclear how the information gained from doing such a discourse analysis should be applied in the development of language-teaching curricula or materials.

In this paper I will argue that discourse analysis, the study of language in context, should be an important part of curriculum development, not only for LSP settings but for all second and foreign language courses where there are definable discourse-level tasks. Furthermore, I propose that the objectives of a given language course will determine both the extent and type of discourse analysis to be done as well as the extent to which findings from discourse analysis should ultimately shape the content and materials of the course. In other words, the question to ask is whether discourse analysis will play a peripheral and supplementary role in the design of a course, or whether it will be a crucial central element in the course's design. In order to argue my case for discourse analysis in as concrete a manner as possible, I shall invite the reader to consider three very different language-teaching contexts:

1. an English-for-Science-and-Technology reading course (a supplementary role for discourse analysis);
2. a university-level ESL course for academic purposes (a shared role for discourse analysis, one among several important sources of input);
3. an in-service EFL teacher upgrading program (a central role for discourse analysis, one of the most important elements).

Finally, on a more general level I will conclude by suggesting that discourse analysis provides teachers and learners an appropriate form-based component to integrate into communicative language-teaching approaches such as the Natural Approach (Terrell 1977, 1983), in all cases where some focus on form is warranted. In such situations, use of discourse analysis instead of decontextualized sentence-level grammatical analysis or vocabulary instruction may well avoid many of the problems previously associated with focus on form (i.e., grammar and vocabulary) in the language classroom.[1]

2 A DISCOURSE-BASED APPROACH TO COURSE DESIGN

Preliminaries

Before proceeding further, a more complete definition of discourse analysis is in order. Discourse analysis, a very broad area of inquiry in linguistics, deals primarily with the ways in which language users produce and interpret oral and/or written language in context. Discourse analysts carry out research on the linguistic structure of phenomena as diverse as speech acts, conversational structures, written and oral narratives, and published research articles in specific fields, among many other spoken or written language activities. They seek to relate such oral and written constructions to social and cultural norms, preferences, and expectations. Going well beyond the sentence level, discourse analysis shows how lexico-grammatical options and discourse structures systematically vary across social situations and, at the same time, help to define those situations.[2] Analysis is conducted primarily through data-based or corpus-based research supplemented by other forms of research as appropriate. Analysts attend to the form, meaning, and function of language whether they begin with discourse-level segments and work down to forms or begin with forms and work up to the discourse level.

I will now explore the role of discourse analysis in the three language-teaching contexts listed above. I have chosen these three instances since I have had some first-hand experience with all of them. As a result of these experiences, I have come to realize that discourse analysis, in varying degrees, has had an important contribution to make in each context. From these three examples I believe the reader will be able to gain a clearer appreciation regarding the need for discourse analysis in the development of language curricula.

Needs Analysis

The *needs analysis* is the stage where tasks should first be identified in relation to a given learner group. Among the most important learner characteristics and tasks for the three different populations mentioned above are the following:

Context 1: The EFL learners, who are native speakers of Spanish and who have minimal proficiency in English, will learn to read chemical engineering articles and textbooks in English as part of their undergraduate university preparation as chemical engineers.

Context 2: The ESL students, among other assignments, are to write a comparison/contrast essay on a topic such as "Compare public transportation in Los Angeles with modes of transportation in a major city in your country," or "Compare a Holiday such as Christmas or Easter in the United States with an important holiday in your country." These students, both graduate and undergraduate, are at the high-intermediate level and are taking a required ESL course as part of their course work at a major American university.

Context 3: Nonspecialist Egyptian EFL teachers (that is, teachers of subjects such as history or mathematics), who lack both language methodology and English proficiency, will be retrained to conduct a beginning-level preparatory (middle) school EFL class using a newly adopted textbook and using English as the medium of instruction. This must be a short, intensive course.

Databases

Once the learner population and specific tasks and objectives have been established (as in the above descriptions), a set of typical or acceptable discourse samples reflecting the form and content of these tasks should be collected or, if necessary, elicited. Here are some examples.

Context 1: A corpus of articles in English dealing with relevant topics in chemical engineering that the students should be able to read are identified with the help and input of professors in the chemical engineering faculty and used as the database for the discourse analysis.

Context 2: Using the same topics on which the ESL students write, comparison/contrast essays are elicited from native English speakers. The compositions of both the native and non-native writers are available for the discourse analysis.

Context 3: The following two sources can serve as databases for the discourse analysis that will shape the in-service course: (1) the text of the beginning-level EFL textbook and (2) transcriptions of videotapes showing both native and non-native EFL teachers successfully using the textbook in classes conducted almost exclusively in English.

The texts and corpora thus assembled can, of course, be used for many purposes, one of which is to serve as the database for a careful discourse analysis. Such an analysis can reveal how the language associated with the text or the tasks is organized globally and also what structures, words or lexical chunks, and cohesive devices (as described in Halliday and Hasan 1976) are most typical and prevalent.

3 ILLUSTRATIVE COURSES

Of the three example courses I discuss, the first two have actually been implemented and the third remains a recommendation which (to my knowledge) has received only partial implementation. Each reflects a different way of using discourse analysis to enhance curriculum design and language instruction. Let us now examine each of the three different courses in more detail to see how discourse analysis was used, or could be used, to expedite the process of curriculum development and materials development.

A Course in Reading English for Science and Technology (EST)

Eight sample authentic texts were assembled at the Faculty of Chemical Engineering at the University of Guadalajara, Mexico, and sent to the University of Calfornia, Los Angeles (UCLA), where Jan Frodesen carried out rhetorical and lexico-grammatical analyses of the texts (Frodesen 1987a) and then developed exercises (Frodesen 1987b) that would encourage recognition of the most frequent rhetorical and lexico-grammatical patterns identified in the corpus. In this database of more than 17,000 words, the rhetorical genres used were: problem/solution (four texts), description of a mechanism (two texts), description of a process (one text), and definition plus description of a process (one text).

In addition to identifying the rhetorical patterns, Frodesen (1987a) found that several lexico-grammatical and discourse-level structures were highly frequent in this type of written scientific discourse: two cohesive devices, reference and conjunction (Halliday and Hasan 1976); active/passive voice,[3] modal verbs, noun modifiers (including prepositional phrases, adjectival participles,[4] and relative clauses), subordinating conjunctions and/or adjuncts, infinitives,[5] and gerunds. The pedagogical materials subsequently prepared by Frodesen (1987b) make use of insights from the discourse analysis and also make further use of the texts themselves by developing exercises featuring both sentence-level and multi-sentence excerpts that allow the students to become aware, for example, of the frequent use of *this* and *such* as cohesive referential markers, the use of the modals to signal probability, the use of the passive voice to focus on a process or a mechanism rather than the agent (the inventor or user), and so on.

The primary objectives of this course are to teach reading skills such as skimming, scanning, and intensive reading, and reading strategies such as cognate recognition and activation of prior knowledge of a topic to ensure comprehension of chemical engineering texts written in English.[6] Much of class discussion is conducted in Spanish. Whenever discourse or lexico-grammar is the source of a comprehension problem, the descriptions and exercises developed by Frodesen are available for the teacher to make use of as needed. Grammar and discourse have not normally been taught as separate components. They are occasionally dealt with as problems arise with a given text or are presented to enhance comprehension when the teachers know that a particular structure is very frequent and important in a given text.

However, during the 1990–91 academic year at the University of Guadalajara, Joyce Slaughter offered a modified version of the established curriculum to an experimental group of students, adding a text-based grammar and discourse component based on Frodesen's earlier research. What did this discourse-based grammar component look like? For a unit on "statements of purpose" Slaughter gave the students explicit instruction and a handout with examples showing them how the following structures are used to express purpose in their chemical engineering texts (Slaughter 1992:16):

1. *in order to/ for/ that* + Verb + Noun phrase
   Ex: In order to provide the most efficient nebulizer for varying sample solution systems, the nebulizer should be adjusted.
2. *so as to* + Verb + Noun phrase; *so that* + Clause
   Ex: A sample gas is passed over the cell so that the oxygen molecules can diffuse.
3. *to* + Verb
   Ex: Burner heads are constructed of titanium to provide extreme resistance to heat and corrosion.
4. *for* and *in* + Gerund
   Ex: Absorbance is the most convenient term for characterizing light absorption.
5. logical connectors of purpose: *for this reason, for this purpose*

Then the students did some follow-up sentence-level exercises. For example:

Underline purpose statements and circle the part of the sentence that states what has been done for the purpose mentioned. Put an "X" if the sentence does not express purpose.

1. Hollow cathode lamps are designed to emit the atomic spectrum of a particular element.
2. The assembly is mounted in an acrylic block so that only the lower edge of the screen is under the surface of the electrolyte.
3. One of the most important contributions of the microcomputer is the ability to calibrate and compute concentrations from absorbance data. (Slaughter 1992:17)

After that the students were given a paragraph of text and asked to read and answer the two comprehension questions using phrases from the text:

A flow spoiler is placed inside the mixing chamber directly in front of the nebulizer. Larger sample droplets, which are not carried around the spoiler by the gas flow, impinge on the spoiler and fall to the bottom of the chamber, where they are removed from the system through the drain. The drain utilizes a liquid trap to prevent combustion gases from escaping through the drain line. The inside of the burner chamber is either constructed of, or coated with, a wettable inert plastic material to provide free drainage of excess samples and prevent burner chamber "memory."

1. What keeps combustion gases from escaping through the drain line?
2. What two purposes are served by the wettable inert plastic material inside the burner chamber?

The experimental group did several units of this type over a ten-week period (Slaughter 1992:18).

Comparing scores for the experimental and control groups from different forms of the same placement and achievement examination, Slaughter concludes that there were no significant differences in reading comprehension scores between the two groups. However, the experimental group was extremely positive about the explicit instruction and practice they had received in the discourse and grammar of their reading texts: all felt that their discourse-based grammar work had been "necessary" or "very necessary." Some of the open-ended written comments from the experimental group cited by Slaughter (1992:27) are:

-Without grammar phrases don't mean anything.
-Grammar facilitates global understanding.
-If you want to understand 100%, grammar is the tool.

According to Slaughter, the most positive aspect of the discourse-based grammar instruction was that it increased the motivation and confidence of the experimental group. In contrast to the control group, which focused only on reading strategies, the experimental group had better class attendance and participation, borrowed each others' notes, made use of the instructor's office hours, and were always eager to see the results of their assigments and quizzes.

Thus we can conclude that discourse analysis plays a useful supplementary role in this EST reading course, which spans two years (the third and fourth of a five-year degree program) with five thematically-based units covered per year.[7] Discourse analysis appears to be especially useful in the case where the findings were exploited pedagogically in a rather explicit manner, as reported by Slaughter.

An Intermediate-Level University ESL Course

Although all four skills are covered, reading and writing receive particular emphasis because the course is intended to prepare students for academic work at the University of California, Los Angeles. Furthermore, the undergraduates in the class must ultimately satisfy the university's composition requirement. One of the rhetorical genres which the students practice in this class in both speech and writing, receptively as well as productively, is "comparison/contrast."

Here I will focus on the written task for this genre, in which the ESL student either compared and contrasted the public transportation system in Los Angeles with that of a major city in his or her country, or compared the Christmas or Easter holiday in the United States with a major holiday in the home country. The database for the discourse analysis consisted of the essays written by the ESL students as well as essays produced by native speakers on equivalent topics. I should mention that the essays written by the native speakers were elicited for purposes of comparison and analysis after the ESL essays had been written. As I explain below, the process should be reversed if one starts with a pedagogical focus rather than a *post hoc* research focus.

The ESL students, using *Paragraph Development*, a composition textbook by Arnaudet and Barrett (1981), had been exposed to a review of sentence-level use of comparative adjectives and adverbs, examples of comparative writing, and lists of coordinators, subordinators, and other words and phrases that can be used to form contrastive or comparative connections between the two elements being compared. An organizational strategy was also suggested: Arnaudet and Barrett (1981) encourage students to write an introductory paragraph and two additional paragraphs, one in which all the similarities of the two elements being discussed are compared and a second in which all the differences between the elements are contrasted.

Despite this additional organizational guidance, the essays written by the ESL students fell short rhetorically. The instructors reported dissatisfaction with the formulaic organizational structure the students followed when they studied comparison/contrast in this way, since it resulted in unnatural, awkward writing which seemed non-native, as illustrated in the following example, reproduced just as it was written by one of the better non-native writers:

The Chinese New Year is the biggest holiday that Chinese people celebrate over their societies. Since Hong Kong is also a Chinese society, the Chinese New Year is the most important holiday in Hong Kong. Although the Chinese New Year and Christmas are the major holiday in Hong Kong and the U.S., there are some differences and similarities between these two holidays in the different places.

The first similarity is that both holidays are the most important holiday in the two different countries respectively. The people from both of the countries can enjoy a week holiday. For instance, the people in Hong Kong have a week off during the Chinese New Year. Secondly, the people from both countries celebrate these holidays seriously. In the U.S. we have Christmas trees, Christmas shopping, Christmas dinners, etc. Similarly, in Hong Kong, we have several kinds of plants which are especially for the Chinese New Year. We have shoppings before the New Year Day and usually we buy new clothes and wear them at the New Year Day. We also have our New Year dinner which every family member will meet together and have dinners.

The major difference is the way we celebrate the holidays. Obviously, the Americans celebrate Christmas in their western culture. On the other hand, the Chinese celebrate their New Year in their Chinese culture. For examples, the plants that we have in Chinese New Year are typically Chinese plants and we will not buy a Christmas tree in our New Year holiday. We have our dinners with all Chinese foods compare to the Christmas dinners that have all the western foods.

Even though we celebrate these two holidays in a similar way, but if we go into details then we will find some different ways that people celebrate these two holidays.

Although comparison and contrast are certainly accomplished in this essay, the organization which the textbook encourages the students to use, and which this student obviously tries to follow, makes the writing seem unnatural and very non-native.

If we compare this essay with a parallel product written by a relatively skilled native writer, who simply received a topic and was asked to write without receiving any explicit rhetorical instruction, we can see that writing effective comparison/contrast compositions on the topics assigned requires something other than the use of comparative adjectives and adverbs or the formulaic organization suggested in the Arnaudet and Barrett textbook.

Most Americans recognize Christmas and Easter as major holidays but the ways in which each are celebrated vary significantly. Christmas enjoys the most status as a holiday in America. We begin to celebrate it right after Thanksgiving and continue through the month of December. Although the basis for Christmas is of religious significance, the celebration of Christmas is characterized by commericalism. Advertisements attempt to sell toys, Santa Claus is on every corner, and shoppers search frantically for the right gifts, or any gift, up until Christmas Eve.

For Americans Christmas centers around the giving of gifts which is usually done on either Christmas Eve or Christmas morning. Stockings are customarily hung on fireplaces, supposedly filled with treats by Santa Claus during the night. The gifts are colorfully wrapped and placed under a decorated plastic or live tree. These gifts are then presented to relatives and close friends around Christmas time. Christmas, then, draws families together, not only to give gifts but to enjoy a large meal together, a meal of turkey, stuffing, and cranberry salad.

Like Christmas, Easter is celebrated for religious purposes. Easter comes and goes much more quietly than Christmas, though. Commercialism, in the form of the Easter Bunny, chocolate eggs, and Easter baskets, is central to Easter but is much less pervasive than the commercialism found at Christmas time.

Celebrating Easter also involves families getting together to go to church and then to share a large meal. The meal usually consists of ham rather than turkey, but it serves to bring relatives and friends together, though not to the same extent that Christmas does.

Christmas in America has become a multi-million dollar business and it has a great deal of custom and ritual associated with it. The same phenomena has not occurred with Easter, although in many ways the celebration involving gift giving and increased family relations is the same.

Jean Turner, who in her 1987 paper analyzed both the native and non-native datasets for this comparison/contrast essay assignment, discovered that most of the native speakers and some of the non-natives were able to complete the writing task without using even one sentence-level comparative structure. Nor was the organizational strategy suggested by Arnaudet and Barrett followed by the native speakers. Seven of the eight native writers managed to perform the comparison task by following a procedure something like this: (1) in the first paragraph introduce the two things you are comparing; (2) describe the salient features of the first element in the comparison in one or two paragraphs; (3) describe the salient features of the second element in one or two paragraphs, bringing out contrasts with the first element, if useful; and (4) tie everything together in a brief concluding paragraph. This is exactly what the native writer of the above essay did, and it reflects a more appropriate organizational strategy for the topic than does the formula given in Arnaudet and Barrett (1981).[8]

In order to express comparison, the native speakers did not use *more, less,* or *-er* but preferred instead to write "X is like Y" or "both X and Y..." when bringing out similarities and to write "X is not the case," "X is not the same," or use logical connectors such as "on the other hand" or "in contrast" to bring out a difference or a contrast. Much of the actual comparing or contrasting, however, is left to the reader since the native writer tends to describe in separate paragraphs the salient features of the two things being compared or contrasted. It is assumed that if the descriptions are adequate, the reader will be able to infer the relevant similarities and differences.

The pedagogical implications of this discourse analysis are fairly obvious. Whether the non-native speakers are writing as they do because of first language rhetorical transfer or faulty instruction (due, perhaps, to the inadequate models and inappropriate grammatical constructions presented in their textbooks), the results are awkward and non-native-like. For pedagogical purposes, it would be better for the ESL teacher to use several adequate sample compositions written by native speakers in the target rhetorical genre instead of using misleading textbook materials. The sample compositions from native speakers could be used initially for reading comprehension and then could be analyzed by the ESL students to identify the overall organization and the preferred structures. With such fully contextualized information in mind, the ESL students should be better able to write a more satisfactory comparison/contrast essay.[9]

Finally, we need to point out the faulty logic that too many of us might be tempted to follow when moving from syntax to discourse. The fact that certain structures express comparison/contrast at the sentence level does not mean that these structures will be necessary or useful when comparison/contrast is being expressed at the discourse level. Doing a proper discourse analysis ensures that we will avoid pitfalls of this sort—pitfalls that apparently exist in a number of currently-used composition textbooks.

In this type of academic ESL course, discourse analysis plays an important role. Whenever a rhetorically motivated genre such as description, argumentation, or comparison/contrast is being covered in class, authentic samples written by native speakers that parallel the kinds of essays the ESL students are expected to produce should be part of the instructional materials. The teacher and students can then carry out a discourse analysis of the native-speaker texts as part of the preparation for writing.

The students do, of course, have other objectives to meet in this type of intermediate-level academic ESL course: improving reading and listening skills, grammar editing, vocabulary development, and oral fluency, among others. Thus it would be fair to conclude that discourse analysis has a moderately important role to play in such a setting, and that the role of discourse analysis is especially important with regard to the composition component of this academic ESL course.

An In-Service EFL Teacher Upgrading Program

The third example is more hypothetical than the first two since it represents a solution I proposed (but did not implement) in the spring of 1988 while on an academic-specialist trip to Egypt sponsored by the United States Information Service. There I was asked by university professors and administrators from the Ministry of Education to make specific proposals for short-term in-service training that would upgrade the linguistic and pedagogical skills of Egyptian EFL teachers. This was critical especially at the preparatory (middle school) level, where about sixty percent of the English teachers are nonspecialists: they have been prepared to teach subjects such as math or history, but not English, and typically have very low levels of English proficiency. The following discussion summarizes the recommendations I made after consultation with local teachers and experts (Celce-Murcia 1989).

To improve EFL instruction in Egypt, an intensive program in English proficiency upgrading and methodological training must be implemented for the large number of nonspecialist classroom teachers. To guarantee optimal efficiency, such a short-term in-service program should emphasize the teachers' speaking and listening skills because what they most lack is the ability to speak English or conduct English classes in English. The English taught to the teachers should focus on the English of the newly adopted textbook, which is a very elementary oral communication text. It should also relate to the English needed in the classroom to teach the *content* and activities of the text *through* English (rather than through Arabic). The short-term training program definitely should not consist of oral English for general communicative purposes-time is too limited for such a vague objective.

In practical terms, the content and discourse of the new textbook should be analyzed, and the typical classroom language of several competent Egyptian and native English teachers should be transcribed and analyzed (this is possible, since many videotapes of English classes have been made and are available in Cairo at the Centre for Developing English Language Teaching). The findings can then be used to develop a very practical and focused in-service course, to be conducted largely in English, for retraining nonspecialist EFL teachers to do the following:

1. comprehend and analyze the content of the new English textbook the preparatory schools are using;
2. discuss the possible ways of teaching the content of the textbook effectively, with focus on using English as the medium of instruction;
3. engage in workshop sessions to prepare lessons;
4. teach the lessons to peers or actual students;
5. evaluate and discuss each lesson as well as the teaching of it.

Another goal of the in-service course would is to view videotaped lessons of preparatory school EFL classes taught by competent specialist Egyptian teachers of English to observe the methodology and the level of English language proficiency needed for classroom management. A relatively small repertoire of terms and expressions is needed for a teacher to be able to conduct a beginning-level middle school class in English. These terms and expressions can be extracted from the videotaped lessons via transcripts, and can then be explicitly taught to the in-service trainees, who will then use this repertoire of classroom English in their practice teaching during the training course. After getting such in-service training, the teachers will be better prepared and motivated to continue using English as the medium of instruction when they return to their classrooms since they will be familiar with the English needed for classroom management. This is an important outcome since it is well known that, other things being equal, pupils in "direct method" (or rich input) classes acquire more of the target language and can do more with it than students who have "grammar translation" (or poor input) classes, where all instruction in the foreign language is carried out via their first language (in this case, Arabic).

In the type of in-service course that I have recommended for Egypt, discourse analysis plays a central role in the development of the curriculum and in the content and materials of the course. It is an absolutely crucial prerequisite if an effective, intensive short-term in-service program is to be developed and executed in such a setting. Thus, this type of teacher upgrading course is perhaps my strongest (albeit only partially implemented) example of the need for discourse analysis in the development of language curricula and materials.[10]

4   Discussion and Conclusions

We have now considered three examples of language teaching programs in which discourse analysis can have a positive impact. In the first example, an EST reading course, we saw that discourse analysis is available to guide and assist teachers as problems arise and that it can play either a peripheral, supportive role or a more important supplementary role. In the second example, a university-level ESL course, discourse analysis is one important element among many, and it is employed specifically to improve the writing component of such a multi-skills ESL course for academic purposes. In the third example, a short-term in-service teacher retraining course, the role of discourse analysis is central and crucial in developing the recommended curriculum and retraining materials.

It is my belief that most second or foreign language courses are like one of my three illustrative courses and can benefit from discourse analysis to a greater or lesser degree depending on the learner population and its needs and objectives. We are just beginning to define the potential roles that discourse analysis can play in the development of optimal language curricula and materials. I hope that descriptions of many other courses that apply (or could apply) discourse analysis to the development of better and sounder language curricula will be available to us in the near future. This would allow us to develop an even clearer understanding of the need for—and the roles of—discourse analysis in curriculum development.[11] On a more general level, I conclude this paper by suggesting that discourse analysis is important not only to the development of appropriate language curricula and materials but also to the development of a comprehensive teaching methodology. By *comprehensive* I mean a methodology that emphasizes concern for comprehension and communicative fluency without sacrificing linguistic accuracy, which is, after all, one component of communicative competence (Canale and Swain 1980; Canale 1983); the other components being (minimally) sociolinguistic competence, discourse competence, and strategic competence. Instead of presenting language forms or correcting errors at the level of the word or sentence, the perspective provided by discourse analysis suggests that language should always be presented, practiced, and (if necessary) corrected in a context and activity that involves natural language use at the level of discourse. The natural language input might be a conversation, a comic strip, a written essay, a videotaped speech event, or another similarly useful piece of discourse. If this input is analyzed by the teacher for salient discourse features at all levels (rhetorical/organizational, lexico-grammatical, phonological), then a discourse-sensitive and context-sensitive awareness of form can be encouraged in the learner.[12]

The same perspective can apply to correction. Correction should be carried out not during attempts at communication (Terrell 1983) but during periods of reflection on chunks of discourse (that is, reflection on something more than isolated words and sentences). Parallel discourse samples produced by the learner, the teacher, native speakers, and other learners should be available for comparison and informal analysis and, on occasion, for correction. (For oral discourse samples the videotape or audiotape plus a written transcription should be available.)

Using oral or written discourse rather than words or sentences as the point of departure for any learning activity that focuses on form, when this is deemed necessary, prevents the learner from viewing language form as something abstract and decontextualized. Most of us would agree that context-free accounts of language are not pedagogically useful in communicative language teaching. The discourse perspective gives us a view of language form that reflects language use. It also gives us a description of language form that is part of communicative competence and is thus ultimately compatible with communicative approaches to language teaching like the Natural Approach.

Notes

1. This is a revised and expanded version of a paper with a similar title that the author presented at the TESOL Convention in San Antonio, Texas, March 8–11, 1989.
2. I would like to acknowledge the influence that Elinor Ochs has had (through personal communication) in my formulation of this definition of discourse.
3. In this corpus, forty percent of the tensed clauses were passive voice, and, of these, over ninety percent were agentless.
4. Frodesen discusses both pre-posed and post-posed adjectival participles in her paper.
5. Both infinitives of purpose and normal infinitives were discussed. In the data under consideration infinitives of purpose occurred frequently.
6. For a more detailed description of this EST Reading Project, see Lynch and Hudson (1991).
7. Adina Levine (personal communication) of Bar-Ilan University in Israel disagrees with the University of California, Los Angeles-University of Guadalajara approach to EST reading as I have described it in this paper. She feels that much more work on language (i.e., grammar and vocabulary as well as discourse) is needed for a university student to become an effective reader of technical English. Our different perspectives, I believe, stem from the fact that Professor Levine teaches native speakers of Hebrew to read in English whereas the EST project I have described involves native speakers of Spanish as students. The degree of linguistic similarity or difference between the L1 and the L2 is thus an additional factor to consider when judging to what extent discourse analysis with related work on grammar and lexis in context will be crucial to effective development of reading instruction.
8. To be fair to Arnaudet and Barrett, I should mention that Jean Turner found in subsequent research that two types of comparison-contrast organization are used in writing by native English speakers (personal communication). Writers use the block organization like the one the native speaker used in his comparison/contrast essay on Christmas and Easter for fairly general expository comparisons, but they use the point-by-point organization advocated by Arnaudet and Barrett for very specific detailed comparisons, often of a scientific nature. A satisfactory unit on the comparison/contrast essay would have to give the novice writer a clear sense of topics and contexts appropriate to each rhetorical pattern, for the two are clearly not interchangeable.
9. Christine Holten, in the winter of 1990 at UCLA, did in fact use a version of the approach I have suggested here to teach the "comparison-contrast" essay to advanced non-native speakers of English. Available data (pre- and post-essays and student feedback and evaluation) indicate that the approach was successful both academically and affectively. The classroom experiment is reported in Holten's 1991 paper.
10. Although the teaching context is very real, this teacher in-service course is hypothetical since I do not know to what extent my recommendations were carried out, although Bill Martin informed me after I had presented a version of this paper at the TESOL conference in San Antonio that computer-based text analysis of the newly adopted textbook was in progress at the Centre for Developing English Language Teaching. In the meantime, teacher in-service training was being conducted somewhat intuitively without all the information that would be available from a thorough discourse analysis of the transcripts of videotaped middle-school English classes. I have not received any more recent feedback on this project.
11. I could also have discussed here the numerous advantages inherent in teaching language learners how to do basic discourse analysis as an effective strategy to encourage continued, and independent, language learning. This, however, is a topic for another paper.
12. When the data are oral, they must be transcribed before any careful analysis can be carried out.

References

Arnaudet, Martin L., and Mary Ellen Barrett. 1981. *Paragraph Development: A Guide for Students of ESL*. Englewood Cliffs, N.J.: Prentice-Hall.

Canale, Michael. 1983. From Communicative Competence to Communicative Language Pedagogy. In *Language and Communication*, eds. J. C. Richards and R. W. Schmidt. London: Longman.

Canale, Michael, and Merrill Swain. 1980. Theoretical Bases of Communicative Approaches to Second Language Teaching and Testing. *Applied Linguistics* 1:1-47.

Celce-Murcia, Marianne. 1989. A Life-long Perspective on Teacher Training: Linguistic and Pedagogical Considerations. In *Professional Development: Education and Training* (Proceedings of the 8th National Symposium on English Language Teaching in Egypt, 1988), ed. M. Abousenna, 14-22. Cairo: Center for Developing English Language Teaching.

Frodesen, Jan. 1987a. Rhetorical and Grammatical Structures in Chemical Engineering Texts. Ph.D. qualifying paper, Department of TESL & Applied Linguistics, University of California, Los Angeles.

Frodesen, Jan. 1987b. Grammatical Structures in Chemical Engineering Texts: Reading Exercises for Non-native Speakers of English. Ph.D. qualifying paper, Department of TESL & Applied Linguistics, University of California, Los Angeles.

Halliday, Michael and Ruqaiya Hasan. 1976. *Cohesion in English*. London: Longman.

Holten, Christine. 1991. Discourse Analysis: A Tool for Students Writing Comparison/Contrast Essays. Paper presented at TESOL annual meeting as part of the colloquium titled "Discourse Analysis and the Teaching of Writing," organized by Cynthia Holliday. March 26, 1991, New York.

Lynch, Brian, and Thom Hudson. 1991. EST Reading. In *Teaching English as a Second or Foreign Language*, ed. M. Celce-Murcia, 216-232. Boston: Heinle and Heinle.

Slaughter, Joyce. 1992. The Role of Content-Based Grammar Instruction in Reading Comprehension. M.A. thesis, Department of TESL & Applied Linguistics, University of California, Los Angeles.

Terrell, Tracy. 1977. A Natural Approach to the Acquisition and Learning of a Language. *Modern Language Journal* 61: 325-336.

Terrell, Tracy. 1983. The Natural Approach to Language Teaching: An Update. In *Methods that Work*, eds. J. Oller and P. Richard-Amato, 267-283. New York: Newbury House.

Turner, Jean. 1987. An Analysis of Comparison in Native and Non-native Writing. Unpublished English 252K paper, Department of TESL & Applied Linguistics, University of California, Los Angeles.

Foreigner Talk, Baby Talk, Native Talk

Barbara F. Freed
Carnegie Mellon University

This article, published in 1981, was one of the first detailed empirical studies of Foreigner Talk. Unlike many studies which followed, it was not classroom based, and related in no way to Teacher Talk. The study, which focuses on "Foreigner Talk," "Baby Talk," and what I called "Native Talk," analyzes these registers from both a syntactic and functional perspective. In this way, I was able to demonstrate differences in the adjustments made by native speakers to a variety of perceived attributes of their interlocutors. It is precisely this notion of native speaker adjustments to a variety of listener attributes that Tracy Terrell identified in one of his last papers. My position, that speech modifications are made in response to "an aggregate of facts, including variables such as age, purpose of communication, cognitive ability, relative status, linguistic sufficiency, relationship between speakers, and topic," seemed to be the source of Tracy's research focus and the aspect of my work that led him to "look at foreigner talk as far removed from 'mainstream ESL' research as possible" (Terrell 1990, in this volume, pp. 233–245).

To investigate this question, the language of 11 native speakers of English in naturally-occurring conversation with 11 non-native speakers of English was compared to the language of these same 11 Americans in conversation with another native speaker of English. The results of these comparisons were then compared to those of a similarly designed and coded study of the language of a group of mothers in conversation with their young children. The Baby Talk (now more frequently called Caretaker Speech), Foreigner Talk and Native Talk (casual conversation between native speakers) speech samples were then compared on dimensions of well-formedness, syntactic complexity, surface sentence type and functional meaning in context. The findings which emerged from this study demonstrate that syntactically speech to both groups of insufficient listeners (young children and non-native speakers) is similar, but that functionally speech to non-native speakers is more similar to speech to other native speakers. Foreigner Talk therefore is seen to be comparable to Baby Talk inasmuch as it is based on the linguistic limitations of the foreign listener; but, it differs from Baby Talk in that native speakers also respond to

Reprinted, with changes, from *International Journal of the Sociology of Language*, Vol. 28 (1981):19–39, by permission of Mouton de Gruyter, Inc. Research was supported by the Wm. T. Carter Foundation. Appreciation is extended to Lila Gleitman, Henry Gleitman, and Dell Hymes; their insights and suggestions contributed to all aspects of this study.

the relative status and cognitive abilities of their foreign listeners. The conclusions drawn from these findings support the hypothesis that speech adjustments are made through a complex set of factors and in response to perceived attributes of the listener including status, cognitive ability and conversational meaning as well as the linguistic sophistication of the listener.

Foreigner talk (FT) denotes only one of several circumstances in which adult speakers of a language may feel the need to modify their 'normal' language to make themselves understood to certain types of listeners. Such listeners include, among others, the mentally retarded, the blind, the deaf, the elderly and the very young as well as foreigners.

In the case of two of these special registers, FT and baby talk, it has sometimes been suggested that the features of both are almost identical. Both are characterized by frequent pauses, often at constituent boundaries, limited vocabulary and brevity. Repetition is a frequent discourse feature, and imitations of different types (restatements, repairs, expansions) may appear in either of these corpora.

Some differences also have been isolated. Foreigner talk is usually spoken with increased volume: baby talk is often whispered (Garnica 1975). Phonological distinctions are made in FT which do not exist in baby talk (e.g., adding a vowel to a final consonant: talkee-talkee). On the other hand, diminutives are used in baby talk which do not appear in FT (Ferguson 1977b). A special lexicon exists in FT which does not appear in baby talk (e.g., savvy, wampum and foreign words). In addition to special lexical items, grammatical replacements exist in FT which do not occur in baby talk; for example, the insertion of the subject 'you' in imperatives and replacement of nominative pronouns by accusative ('me go') and the use of analytic paraphrase (always = all time). On a gross functional level, some preliminary differences have been identified. Conversation between adults tends to include references to the past, present and future while child-directed conversation is more limited to the here and now (Hatch, Shapira, and Gough 1978).

It has been hypothesized that the basis for both these registers is the linguistic insufficiency of the two listener groups: young children and foreign adults. While surely linguistic limitations are characteristic of both categories of listeners, linguistic limitations are only one of the attributes to which speakers respond and are perhaps the only attribute shared by both young children and foreign adults. Young children, in addition to being linguistically insufficient, are socially immature and cognitively limited as well. In relationship to the adult caretaker, they are also of reduced status. By contrast, foreign adults are not by definition of inferior status to a native speaker, and their cognitive capacity is presumably equal to that of the native adult speaker. It should therefore be assumed that the communicative intent of conversational interaction between native adults and either young children or foreign adults would be considerably different.

To date, most studies of FT have looked at various morpho-syntactic features and/or phonological features of the register. While there has been some inconsistency in the findings, these differences can be attributed to a wide range of sociolinguistic variables. To account for some of the conflicting findings in FT and others in baby talk, interactionist interpretations have been proposed (Blount 1972; Gelman and Shatz 1975; Newport 1976). Such positions imply that speech is shaped by an aggregate of facts including variables such as age, purpose of communication, cognitive ability, relative status, linguistic sufficiency, relationship between speakers, topic, etc. This interpretation suggests that speakers respond to a variety of perceived attributes in their listeners. Such an interactionist interpretation suggests further, as argued by Gelman and Shatz, that modifications in speech style are more communicatively than syntactically based. That is, speakers elect to use certain utterance types as opposed to others based on conversational need. To accept such an interactionist interpretation requires identification of speaker adjustments made in response to different listener attributes. However, within both child and foreign listeners, many variables are confounded. Even with the most penetrating analyses it is difficult to establish with certainty which adjustments are made to perceived reasoning problems, which to linguistic limitations, status differences or conversational constraints. If at least one of these variables is controlled, the differentiation will become more distinct. By looking at the language addressed to both the child listener, limited linguistically and cognitively, and the foreign adult, presumably limited only linguistically, it should be possible to specifically isolate those attributes of a listener to which speakers respond in their differential use of language. While some similarities and differences between FT and baby talk have been identified, no systematic study exists which compares the properties of speech to foreigners and young children as contrasted with speech to fully competent listeners.

The aims of this study are dual: to systematically compare the syntactic and functional features of FT and baby talk to those of native talk (my term for casual conversation between native speakers) and to determine which perceived listener attributes are responsible for the adjustments characteristically made in both. In so doing, I hope to demonstrate that speech adjustments emerge from a set of interacting responses made to various perceived attributes of the listener.

In order to complete the goals of this study, it was necessary to establish independently the respective properties of FT, baby talk, and native talk. The characteristic features of both have been described in two companion studies, similarly designed and coded. The first is Newport's (1976) study of 'motherese' (Newport's term for baby talk); the second my own study of FT (Freed 1978a). For purposes of this study, the independent analyses of both will be compared.

 PROCEDURE

Subjects

Baby talk In Newport's study, the native speakers were 15 white, middle-class mothers in conversation with their daughters who ranged in age from 12 to 27 months. Newport visited the mothers and their children in their homes and recorded conversations between the mothers and their children and between the mothers and herself. The analysis to be discussed here is based on a 100 utterance sample of the mothers' speech to their children and to Newport during the first of two visits.

Foreigner talk   The group selected for the FT study was a naturally occurring population of American native speakers of English in conversation with adult speakers of several different languages. All were roughly of the same socioeconomic class and shared equal status as students. This group of English and foreign speakers was brought into contact through a Conversational Partners Program (CPP), a university program which related in no way to this study. In this program, volunteer American and foreign students were paired for purposes of weekly conversation and culture exchange. Each of the American/foreign pairs was formed by the English Program for Foreign Students (EPFS) office. They were based on a commonality of academic and avocational interests and/or desires to speak each other's language.

Eleven conversational pairs from this larger group volunteered to participate in the study. At the outset they agreed to having their private meetings tape-recorded for what they believed was a study of communication patterns between small groups of people who had just met.

The Americans were all from the northeastern United States. Among their academic majors were psychology, education, urban studies, marketing and international relations. All had studied at least one foreign language; six were currently taking language courses. Only three had taken a linguistics course, but all had taken at least one psychology course. All had traveled outside of the United States, but only three had traveled to their partner's country or to a country in which their partner's language was spoken. These Americans for the most part had had previous contacts with foreigners, either through part-time work or leisure activities. With the exception of two of the students who had tutored on a brief, part-time basis, none had ever been involved in teaching English as a second language.

The American students thus represented a special sample of university students in that they had a broad range of interests in travel, language and in other cultural and linguistic communities. Presumably these special interests explain why they volunteered for the CPP. The foreign students were all students in the EPFS at the time the study began. Some were engaged in other academic study as well. Their ability to speak English ranged from almost fluent to absolute beginners. They came from Nicaragua, Venezuela, Denmark, Iran, Algeria, Vietnam and Japan.

Experimental Situation

The meetings of the conversational partners took place, in a variety of informal settings of their own choosing. The standard procedure for collecting the speech sample was for me to bring a tape recorder with a condensor microphone to the pair's meeting place, turn it on and leave. I would return at a previously arranged time, usually an hour later, to collect the tape. I was never present during the conversation between the two. Each of the 11 pairs was taped at least 2 times within a period of no more than 10 days.

Control Situation

Since our interest was in comparing the adjustments made by native speakers in conversation with foreigners to their language when in conversation with another native speaker, it was necessary to establish a control situation. To do so, I met individually with each of the 11 American partners. Prior to the control meeting, I listened to all of the taped conversations between the Americans and their foreign partners and was able to engage the Americans in a discussion of several topics which they had previously discussed with their foreign partners. Except for these three or four preselected topics, the conversation was spontaneous and related primarily to university life, travel, personal experiences or any subject initiated by the American subject. As the conversation drew to a close, all of the Americans were told the real purpose of the study and consent was obtained to use their tapes for purposes of this study.

Transcription and Segmentation into Utterances

A total of 150 utterances spoken by the Americans to their foreign partners in the course of their first and second conversations was transcribed using standard punctuation based on normal intonation patterns. An additional 100 running utterances of the Americans' speech to me were also transcribed. Segmentation of speech into analyzable units was done at the utterance level and utilized these criteria:
    1. Speech by one person, though sometimes spanning two 'turns'.
    2. Intonation contour which would indicate completion of a unit.
    3. Pause, but allowance for pause within an utterance was made.
These criteria, however, were subjectively applied. For example, though an utterance was generally understood to incorporate not more than one turn, it sometimes happened that an abrupt interruption by the foreigner obliged cessation of talk where an utterance was clearly incomplete. Such cases were treated in two ways. If, following the interruption, the first speaker continued, without beginning again so that it was a clear continuation, then the speech before and after the interruption was considered part of the same utterance. If, however, the speaker recapitulated after the interruption, then the speech before the interruption was considered one utterance (though usually a fragment of some sort) and the speech after the interruption as at least one more utterance.

Secondly, while intonation contour was a major indication of utterance boundary, the total lack of pause while a speaker continued on the topic sometimes required a determination that the utterance was not complete. There are thus instances where an utterance consists of several sentential units and/or fragments thereof.

Finally, pauses were considered indicative of potential utterance boundaries, but allowance was made both for pauses within an utterance and/or after a false start. For purposes of reliability, all utterances were tested by a second judge.

RESULTS

In accordance with the purposes of this study, the respective adjustments made when speaking to a child or to a foreigner and to another adult native speaker were then compared syntactically and functionally. For obvious reasons, no statistical comparisons were made between speech to foreigners and to children. However, statistical data is presented for speech to two types of foreign listeners (beginner and advanced) and the difference between speech to foreigners and to natives.[1] What emerges from this comparison is, in part, what was suspected all along. Syntactically, speech to young children and foreign adults shares the same gross properties. Functionally, however, speech to both groups of limited listeners is essentially non-overlapping. This distinction will be made clear in the following discussion.

Syntactic Analyses

As shown in Table 1, speech to young children, foreign adults and native speakers is characteristically well formed. The most striking finding is that there are no ungrammatical utterances and almost none so slurred or garbled that they are unanalyzable. Within the tolerance granted to colloquial speech, over one-half of all utterances are well-formed, grammatically acceptable utterances. That is, they consist of at least one, and sometimes more than one, complete English sentence. However, significantly more utterances of this type are addressed to fully competent adult listeners than to the other listener types. On the average, 58% of all FT utterances and 60% of all baby talk utterances are well-formed, grammatically acceptable utterances as compared to 70% of all native talk utterances. Viewed another way, significantly more stereotyped stock expressions ('mmm', 'uhuh', 'really?') and fragments (isolated sentence constituents such as 'the what?', 'for three days', 'red') are used in conversation with linguistically limited listeners than with native adult listeners. Somewhat more stock expressions are directed to young listeners and more fragments to the foreign listener.[2] Despite these small differences, from the point of view of well-formedness both FT and baby talk are strikingly similar and reliably different from the native talk corpus.

Each well-formed, grammatically acceptable sentence was then analyzed for syntactic complexity. As shown in Table 2, native speakers reduce the sheer linguistic complexity of utterances directed to both groups of limited listeners when compared to their speech to the native adult. Moreover, not only are there significant differences between speech to native listeners and to foreigner listeners, but there are also significant differences between a native speaker's speech to beginner and advanced foreigners.

The average sentence addressed to young children and both groups of foreign listeners is shorter lexically and propositionally than that addressed to a native listener. For example, there is an average of one main verb (labeled S-node) per sentence in all sentences directed to young children and roughly 1.5 S-nodes in the average FT sentence, compared to somewhat more than 2 S-nodes in the average native-talk sentence. There are roughly four words in the average sentence intended for the young listener, eight words in the average FT sentence and approximately twelve in the

Table 1. Analysis of well-formedness

Utterance	Mother to child†	Native speaker to beginner foreigner	Native speaker to advanced foreigner	Native speaker to native speaker
		Mean percent	*Mean percent*	*Mean percent*
Unanalyzable	0.04	0.01	0.01	0.01
Ungrammatical	0.00	0.00	0.00	0.00
Grammatically acceptable utterances	0.60	0.60	0.57	0.70**
Stock expressions	0.19	0.16	0.18	0.12*
Fragments	0.17	0.24	0.25	0.17**

†All mother-to-child data in this and succeeding tables is based on Newport (1976).

*	$p < 0.05$	Statistical comparisons between speech to foreign listeners and
**	$p < 0.01$	native listeners.
***	$p < 0.001$	
†	$p < 0.05$	Statistical comparisons of the difference between natives'
††	$p < 0.01$	speech to beginner foreigners and advanced foreigners.
†††	$p < 0.001$	

The above is the key for all tables.

Table 2. Analysis of syntactic complexity

Sentence Complexity	Mother to child+	Native speaker to beginner foreigner	Native speaker to advanced foreigner	Native speaker to native speaker
		Mean percent	*Mean percent*	*Mean percent*
No. of S-nodes/ average sentence	1.16	1.38	1.81††	2.24***
MLSW (mean length of sentence in words)	4.24	6.74	9.66††	12.13***
% of sentences with one S-node	0.82	0.71	0.55†	0.41***
MLSW of one S-node sentences	4.54	5.34	6.10	6.90*

average sentence directed to native listeners. Not only are baby talk and FT sentences shorter and propositionally less complex, but more simple sentences (those with only one main verb) are addressed to both groups of linguistically limited listeners than to native listeners: 82% of sentences intended for the child listener contained only one main verb compared with 66% directed to the average (beginner and advanced) foreign listener and only 41% for the native listener.

As the table shows, the less proficient the foreign listener the greater the syntactic reductions. As the foreigners' proficiency in English increases, there is, on every measure, a consistent increase in syntactic complexity. These findings suggest that linguistic adjustments are not solely attributable to a foreigner's 'foreignness', but, rather, that they are related to perceived linguistic sophistication.[3] Syntactically, then, differences between FT and baby talk are very slight as has been suspected all along. However, as different types of analyses are considered, a new picture emerges.

In addition to analyses of well-formedness and syntactic complexity, each well-formed sentence in all corpora was analyzed for surface sentence type as displayed in Table 3.

Table 3. Analysis of surface sentence type

Sentence type	Mother to child†	Native speaker to all foreign speakers (1st & 2nd meeting)††	Native speaker to beginner foreigner (2nd meeting)	Native speaker to advanced foreigner (2nd meeting)	Native to native speaker
		Mean percent	*Mean percent*	*Mean percent*	*Mean percent*
Declarative	0.30	0.68	0.71	0.73	0.97***
Wh-question	0.15	0.11	0.07	0.07	0.01*
Yes/No question	0.23	0.14	0.11	0.15	0.01**
Imperative	0.18	0.03	0.03	0.01	0.01
Deixis	0.16	0.02	0.03	0 01	0.00
Wh deixis	0.06	0.01	0.01	0.00	0.00

††Since data for speech to beginner and advanced foreign speakers are from the second meeting of the pair, they will not necessarily equal the means for both meetings grouped together as presented in Column 2.

Young children were exposed to the widest distribution of representative samples of English sentences: 30% declarative sentences, 44% questions (yes/no, wh and wh deixis), 18% imperative, and 16% deixis. Speech to both groups of foreign listeners was far less varied, with the greatest proportion of sentences being declarative followed by questions. Speech addressed to native speakers was the least varied consisting almost entirely of declarative sentences with just a scattering of imperative and deictic forms.

While questions were the most common surface type in the baby talk corpus, the declarative sentence was the most frequently used sentence form in FT and native talk. There was, however, a significant difference in the relative proportions of each. Column 2 of the table represents the means of the first and second meeting of the conversational pairs. When considered together, 68% of all FT sentences were declarative, compared to an overwhelming 97% of native talk sentences. By contrast, interrogatives occurred with greater frequency in FT than in native talk. Again in column 2, 26% of all FT sentences but only 2% of all native talk sentences were questions.[4] The proportion of FT interrogatives is seemingly more similar to the proportion of interrogatives used in child-directed speech. However, when these forms are compared functionally, these differences diminish.

By contrast to declaratives and questions, the relative proportion of imperative and deictic sentences used in conversation with all groups of adult listeners is almost identical and vastly different from the proportion of such statements addressed to young listeners (imperative: 3% FT, 1% native talk, 18% baby talk; deixis: 2% FT, 0% native talk, 16% baby talk). Interestingly, unlike indices of syntactic complexity, measures of surface sentence type do not vary as a function of the foreign listener's proficiency in English.

These data demonstrate that distinction of surface sentence type is enormously different for different categories of limited listeners. At the level of surface sentence type, the native speaker distinguishes between the attributes of the young child, the non-native adult and the fully competent adult listener. The type of sentence characteristically used in conversation with foreign adults is different from that characteristically and appropriately used in conversation with young children.

Discussion of registers used with different categories of limited listeners inevitably raises the question of simplicity. Therefore, an effort was made to compare the transformational complexity of several surface sentence types in each corpus. The distribution of surface sentence forms accounts for the major differences in transformational complexity of the speech samples. As just described, the vast majority of all sentences in both FT and native talk were declarative in form and retained in their surface structure a relatively close representation of base structure form with standard subject, verb, object order.[5] By comparison, slightly more than a quarter of all baby talk sentences were canonical in shape. The mere presence of a more diverse range of surface sentence types accounts for more deformation of the sentences addressed to young children.

Deformations from canonical shape appeared in all corpora in the imperative formation where the subject 'you' and the auxiliary 'will' were obligatorily deleted. Note though, there were a few instances in FT where the subject 'you' was retained before the imperative: 'You' call me tonight! This phenomenon did not appear in native talk or baby talk.

Other deformations occurred as a result of obligatory subject-auxiliary inversion and wh-replacement and preposing in question formation as shown in Table 4.

Table 4. Analysis of transformational complexity of yes/no and wh-questions

Question type	Mother to child	Native speaker to foreign speaker (1st & 2nd meetings)	Native speaker to native speaker
		Mean percent	*Mean percent*
Wh-question	0.15	0.11	0.01**
wh-questions with no fronting of wh-particle	0.00	0.01	0.002
Yes/no questions	0.23	0.14	0.01 **
% of yes/no questions with no subject-aux. inversion and 'do' and/or 'you' deletion	0.06	0.05	0.01 **

The 2% of native talk questions almost always exhibited subject-auxiliary inversion as well as wh-replacement and preposing ('Were you in France for a long time?' or 'Where can I buy a tape recorder?'). By contrast, a significant portion of the yes/no questions and a non-significant but noticeable portion of wh-questions in FT and baby talk did not exhibit standard question formation. Five percent of the yes/no questions in FT and 6% in baby talk (but only 1% in native talk) preserved canonical shape and signalled the question by a final rising intonation ('You're not afraid of that?'; 'It's too loud to sleep?').[6] Furthermore, for some of these, in addition to failing to observe obligatory subject-auxiliary inversion, there was no insertion of the dummy auxiliary 'do' when the sentence had no auxiliary and the subject 'you' was sometimes deleted ('You feel like you are understanding English better now?').

For wh-questions in baby talk, the wh-particle was always preposed to the front of the sentence ('Where's Daddy?'). This was not always the case in FT. A noticeable number of wh-questions were formed by keeping the wh-particle at the end of the sentence and thus retaining canonical form ('You're studying what?'; 'You will return to your country when?').

As the table shows, 1% of FT wh-questions compared to a mere .002 of the native talk questions did not prepose the wh-particle. While the percentage of such cases in foreigner talk is not significantly different from native talk, the tendency deserves comment. It is possible that native speakers unconsciously notice the deformation caused by moving the wh-particle to the front of the sentence and monitor this by sometimes avoiding preposing the wh-particle. This claim is reinforced by the fact that native speakers occasionally monitor their use of wh-questions by following them immediately with yes/no questions: 'How is the food there? Is the food very good?' Sometimes this change takes place mid-utterance. 'How much. . . . Did you pay a lot?'

While this tendency to change from wh to yes/no questions was also not reliably different in the two corpora, the slight inclination to do so supports the above hypotheses that native speakers do notice the complexity of wh questions and monitor it by failing to prepose the wh-particle. Another explanation for this tendency has been offered by Hatch (1976) who suggests that the change is a function of the native speaker's effort to limit the demand placed on the foreigner's response. That is, it is easier to answer a yes/no question than a wh-question. As a result of more yes/no questions with subject-auxiliary inversion in baby talk and more wh-questions which retained canonical form in FT, the surface structure of FT is somewhat less deformed than that of baby talk.

To summarize, it has thus far been shown that insofar as young children and foreign listeners are considered linguistically deficient, native speakers reduce the linguistic complexity of utterances directed to them. On many of these measures speech to a fully competent native speaker is radically different from that to the other listener types. When surface sentence type is analyzed, similarity between native speaker adjustments to young children and foreign adults begins to diminish. While there are still some significant differences between speaker selection of surface forms in speech to foreign and native listeners it will be shown that speech to foreign adults is related in reasonable ways to normal speech to native adults. When analyzed functionally, these distinctions take on another light and are clarified on the basis of conversational constraints.

FUNCTIONAL ANALYSIS

In addition to the preceding analyses, a gross functional analysis of the conversational meaning in context of various utterance and sentence types was also carried out. Since syntactic descriptions cannot detect relationships between utterances within the communicative context, we decided to look, as far as possible, for the functional intent of an utterance as distinguished from its surface form. This analysis, based on audio recordings alone, comprised an inferential interpretation of the underlying intent of spoken utterances. No quantitative analysis was computed. Factors affecting the assignment of functional role included preceding utterance, succeeding utterance and tone of voice. There emerged from this method of analysis 10 functional categories to which an utterance could potentially be assigned (Appendix). The functional analyses of baby talk were, with few exceptions, those previously reported by Newport.

When we looked for functional meaning in context, *information exchange* was inferentially identified as the primary communicative intent in conversations between both groups of adults, native and foreign alike. In this regard, no distinction is made between beginner and advanced foreign listeners. The means by which native speakers share information with the foreign listener are somewhat different than those selected for information sharing with the native listener. For both groups, the declarative and interrogative forms account for over 90% of all sentences. As Table 4 showed, speech to natives consisted almost entirely of declaratives while speech to foreign listeners consisted of somewhat fewer declaratives and significantly more questions. Analysis of functional meaning in context revealed, however, that both questions and declaratives contributed to the exchange of information. Declaratives provided for the direct transmission of information and questions, elicited information and nominated topics. The few imperatives in both corpora were, when analyzed functionally, also contributors of information. Statements such as 'Let the bread rise for three hours' or 'Walk down Spruce Street. Turn right and look for the big white house' were not directives in the usual sense but rather supplied information as to procedures to follow.

In all instances, topics pertained to a wide variety of subjects to which both participants could contribute equally. Despite the foreign listener's limitations in English, conversations were not characterized by 'here and nowness' as is partially evidenced by the vanishingly small proportions of deictic utterances. The few explicitly referential forms (such as, 'There's the bathroom'; or 'That's a picture of my mom') when analyzed for meaning in context made situationally appropriate contributions to the exchange of ill formulation.

Analysis of surface sentence type in baby talk showed a wide distribution of surface sentence forms. Analyzed for functional meaning in context it was inferred that 62% of all child-directed utterances served the communicative function of directing the child's behavior. Of the declarative sentences addressed to young children, many were not functionally providers of information at all, but rather were indirect imperatives: 'Your juice is on the table'. Questions, interpreted as 'information elicitors' in FT, infrequently served the same function in baby talk. Some questions were, of course, expressions of interest in the child's well-being but more often they were indirect requests for verbalization of behavior: 'Can you show me your nose?'; 'Where are your eyes?' These action-directives realized as declaratives and questions were in addition to the 18% of direct imperatives. In FT and native talk, however, there were essentially no action-directives, either direct commands or indirect requests in the form of questions or declaratives. Furthermore, constraints on commonality of interest limited topics which might be discussed with the child listener, as did limitations in processing ability and attention span.

In principle, the responsibility for maintaining a conversation is shared equally by both participants in that conversation. In FT, however, it appears that many of the native speakers' utterances were motivated by the need to keep the conversation going. Stock expressions, more common in FT than native talk, were interpreted as serving this function. These *conversation continuers* conveyed attention and interest as the foreign speaker attempted to construct a phrase. Questions, too, conveyed interest at the same time that they helped to keep conversation alive. They served to elicit a new bit of information that might not otherwise be forthcoming.

Conversation continuers were frequent in baby talk but their surface form varied. While questions and stock expressions were the most obvious conversation continuers in FT, maternal self-repetitions were the major conversation continuers in baby talk. Subsequent analyses of these repetitions (Newport and Gleitman 1977) concluded that repetitions are motivated by an effort to captivate an inattentive child.

By contrast, the self repetition in FT were found to be motivated by an expression of misunderstanding on the part of the foreigner. A considerable portion of a native speaker's efforts in conversation with the foreign listener was directed at clarifying speech to aid the exchange of information. Most often this was achieved by isolating a portion of an utterance which had not been understood. Unlike native talk *clarifications* which were often expansions, FT clarifications were commonly in the form of a partial repetition of a misunderstood utterance. In other instances clarifications were realized as synonyms or analytic paraphrases.

Imitation, also in the form of fragments, assumed a functional role in FT. In some instances it was the native speaker who did not understand the foreign speaker's utterance. The need for clarification was frequently signalled by the native speaker's imitating, with a rising intonation, some portion of the foreigner's utterance. In a conversation concerning American television cartoons the following occurred:

Foreign speaker (FS): 'I like White Snow and Shop men.'

Native speaker (NS): 'White Snow and Shop men?'

FS: 'Yes, Seven Shop Men.'

NS: 'Shop Men?' 'Shop Men?'

FS: 'White Snow and Seven Shop Men.'

NS: 'Oh, White Snow, I mean, Snow White and the Seven Short, and the Seven Dwarfs!'

A foreigner's need for an unknown lexical item or correct syntactic form was also met through the use of fragments which served functionally as *contributors*. Sometimes a native speaker anticipated this need and provided the item in question. On other occasions the word was supplied in response to a direct question, an obvious pause or a sentence constituent followed by a rising intonation which signalled uncertainty about a word or a form:

FS: 'Return Iran this summer. . . go, go back this Autumn?'

NS: 'Will come back.'

FS: 'Ah yes, will come back here in Autumn.'

A *contribution* such as this is distinguished from a *correction* to the extent that the foreign speaker communicated uncertainty about its use. Mothers, too, supplied words for their children most frequently in an effort to make sense of the child's attempts at verbalization.

Similarity in function, then, does exist for *contributors*. The major difference in their role is the inference that speakers must make about what the partner wishes to communicate.

Some small portion of native speakers' utterances were *corrections*. These corrections, far more common in FT, usually appeared as fragments and tended to be of syntactic form, not substance:

FS: 'I have bathroom and chicken.'

NS: 'No, bathroom and kitchen.'

FS: 'My room is more bigger.'

NS: 'Your room is bigger.'

By contrast, correction of child language as reported by Brown and his colleagues (1969) tends to be minimal and is more likely to be correction of truth value than of incorrect grammatical form. To this extent, correction in native talk is similar to that in baby talk.

A small proportion of native speakers' utterances have been inferred to be *conversational supports*. Such utterances communicated the native speakers' understanding of the foreign speakers' difficulties in expressing themselves ('Go on, try again.' 'I know it's hard to speak English'). Mothers' speech to their children is commonly affective, but the functional role of the affective response tends to be of warmth and affection for the child, not necessarily support for their linguistic limitations.

Claims and counterclaims as to the utility of baby talk and FT as *language instruction* corpora per se will not be examined here. However, acknowledgement is made of the fact that explicitly referential (deictic) forms function in baby talk to provide conventional labels for the referents of English words. Such naming devices serve an instructive function (Newport 1976).

Similarly, no determination of the role of language instruction in FT is made as there is no correlational analysis of input and the foreign subjects' improvement in English. A small number of deictic forms did exist, but, as previously stated, their function was informational. Indirectly, corrections and contributions serve an instructional function but this has not been interpreted as their primary intent when analyzed within the conversational context.

To review, a major functional intent of child-directed speech has been interpreted as the directing of the child's behavior. A wide variety of surface forms served to carry out this function. By contrast, the primary functional intent of both FT and native talk is here characterized as the exchange of information. This is so regardless of the foreigner's proficiency in English. The unifying intent of information exchange is accomplished primarily through the declarative commentary form. Beyond information exchange, native speakers in conversations with foreign speakers have two other concerns: comprehension and the continued flow of conversation. There are thus many questions which function to express interest and to elicit information. Conversation with foreigners is also punctuated by the frequent use of fragments and stock expressions which are less common in native talk. These forms complement the exchange of information by expressing interest and attention and by clarifying misunderstood speech. Declaratives, questions and many isolated sentence constituents are thus closely related when analyzed for functional meaning in context. All contribute to the exchange of information; the motive is identical in speech to all adult listeners; only the means are different.

 SUMMARY

This investigation was motivated by two questions: What would we find if we systematically compared the properties of speech used with two categories of limited listeners who share the attribute of linguistic limitation but who differ on all other dimensions and, secondly, to what does the native speaker respond in making characteristic adjustments to each listener type? Based on method of data collection and analyses, the following summary and conclusions seem warranted.

Speech to all listener types is clearly articulated and well-formed. The proportions of utterances classified as sentence fragments, stock expressions and well-formed, grammatically acceptable utterances varied according to listener type. Higher proportions of fragments were directed to the foreign and child-listeners than to native adults. Despite relative and sometimes significant differences between proportions of utterance type to particular listener groups, somewhat more than half of all utterances to all listeners were complete, grammatically acceptable utterances.

The syntactic complexity of these well-formed utterances varied enormously depending on listener type. Limitations in linguistic proficiency and/or processing capacities apparently dictated speakers' adjustments of syntactic complexity. There was a consistent increase in complexity corresponding to increased listener ability in English.

Speaker selection of surface sentence types varied considerably in response to different listeners. Distribution of representative samples of English sentence forms was most varied to young children, far less varied to both groups of foreign listeners and least varied to the native speaker.

Native speakers as a rule were exposed to more undeformed sentences than the other two groups. As a consequence of the higher proportion of questions to the non-native and non-adult and of imperatives to the non-adult, more canonical sentences were addressed to the native listener. However, more embeddings and transformations within the declarative mode (dative movement, passivization, etc.) occurred to natives than to the other two listener groups.

If comparisons were limited to analyses of syntactic complexity, it might justifiably be concluded that FT and baby talk are very similar indeed. In fact, FT is like baby talk in just the places where it should be. Insofar as foreign speakers and young children are considered to be linguistically insufficient, formal characteristics of the selection of English forms are the same in these two speech samples. Moreover, although native speakers' adjustments diminish with increased proficiency on the foreigners' part, language addressed to the advanced foreigner is still significantly different on many measures than language to native speakers.

Syntactic analysis does not, however, totally account for the properties of FT, for it does not consider the relationship of the foreigner talk utterance to the total communicative situation. Analysis of functional meaning provides another dimension which alters this conclusion.

While baby talk and FT appear more similar on the basis of syntactic analyses, FT and native talk are much more alike with respect to functional meaning in context. The adjustments native speakers made in response to foreigners' linguistic limitations dissipate on the conversational level.

A functional description of foreigner talk and native talk suggests that regardless of reduced syntactic complexity, native speakers relate to foreign speakers much as they do to other adults. The foreign speaker is treated as a conversational peer with whom one engages in conversation for the purpose of exchanging ideas. To achieve the goal of information exchange, native speakers will, when conversing with foreigners, resort to clarification and continuation devices not needed in talk with most native speakers. Functionally, though, these devices are directed to the major goal of the conversational interchange. On a conversational level, native speakers interact with the foreign listener as an adult with cognitive and social presence.

Conversely, the underlying intent of mothers' speech to children is to direct their behavior. Analyses of utterances in conversational context as they relate to preceding and succeeding utterances has revealed that the same functional meaning can be expressed by different sentence types.

Analysis of conversation roles has helped support the claim that adjustments are made in response to various listener attributes. Consequently, foreign adults are seen and treated as conversational peers despite their linguistic limitations. Young children who share the foreigners' linguistic limitations are treated conversationally as inferiors. Such inferential analysis of the speakers' intent suggests that conversational intent might be as responsible for the features of foreigner talk as are the listener's linguistic deficiencies. By comparing syntactic and functional analyses, it is possible to see that native speakers' adjustments are motivated by an interacting set of evaluations of their listeners. Unconscious judgements appear to be made, and speech is adjusted in different ways to different characteristics of the listener. While listener fluency determines to some extent the nature of linguistic adjustments, other attributes influence the communicative devices selected in speaking with different categories of listeners. An interacting set of perceptions vis-à-vis perceived cognitive ability, linguistic ability and status appear to account for these sensitive differences.

APPENDIX: Functional categories

1. *Information exchange* — utterances which serve to communicate information in the broadest sense: facts, opinions, ideas. This category incorporates a wide range of potential statements that have been defined elsewhere as assertions, modulations, expressions of mental state and descriptions.

2. *Conversation continuers* — utterances utilized to signify attention and interest or to maintain the flow of conversation.

3. *Clarification* — utterances used to elaborate or explain the meaning of a previous utterance. Clarifications appear in the form of repetitions, imitations, synonyms and analytic paraphrases. They are frequently prompted by a verbal or nonverbal lack-of-comprehension clue.

4. *Correction* — utterances which repair another's incorrect fact or form. They often, but not always, occur in 'correction-invitation formats' (Schegloff, Jefferson, and Sacks 1977). They are distinguished from clarifications to the extent that clarifications were contextually analyzed to be motivated by a need to isolate or establish meaning; correction was then a secondary result. Corrections are also distinguished from word-search responses.

5. Contribution — utterances which supply an unknown lexical item or grammatical form. Contributions are usually provided in response to direct or indirect requests (obvious word searches) but sometimes they are predictions or foreshadowings prompted by a pause or hesitation.

6. *Conversation support* — empathetic utterances which convey understanding or support for the partner's state or situation.

7. *Action-directive* — utterances which serve as direct or indirect requests for behavior or verbalization.

8. *Reported speech* — utterances which convey a third party's speech. Such utterances are always in the indirect discourse.

9. *Self-directed speech* — utterances which are self-directed and which call for no response from the conversational partner.

10. *Language instruction* — utterances which serve an explicitly instructive function. That is, where it is clear that the speaker is trying to 'teach'. Indirectly corrections, clarifications and contributions serve an instructional function, but their primary intent is interpreted otherwise.

Notes

1. We were anxious to determine if native speakers distinguish between the type of adjustments made when speaking to foreigners with little proficiency in English as compared to those with greater ability. For this purpose the foreigners were divided into groups of beginner and advanced speakers. The distinction between the two groups is based on an analysis of the mean length of utterance in words (MLUW) of 25 of their utterances from the second meeting of the conversational pair. The MLUW was based only on those utterances which were at least one complete sentence in length and excluded all imitations and repetitions. The beginner group consisted of five foreign speakers: MLU of 4.70 words (range 2.64–6.48), the advanced group of six foreign speakers, MLU of 8.23 words (range 7.28–9.44). While the MLUW overlooks considerations of grammaticality and/or pronunciation, as a gross measure it indicated fluency and verbosity. The MLUW analysis also corresponded to the subjective ratings provided by the American partners of their foreign partners' speech.

2. Fragments are the only category which appear to be considerably different in the foreigner talk and baby talk speech corpora. This difference results in part from a slight difference in coding. Broken-off or incomplete sentences were coded as fragments in the foreigner talk study but as unanalyzable utterances in the Newport study. In addition, fragments assumed an important functional role in foreigner talk which dictated the appearance of a great number of isolated sentence constituents which did not appear in baby talk.

3. Much previous work on FT has been done on adjustments made to foreigners who are represented as having minimal knowledge of the target language, or who in fact have very little (Ferguson 1975). In this study even the very lowest foreigner has an average sentence length of 2.64 words and is capable of (at least sometimes) forming a complete, if short, sentence of English. It is entirely possible that previous descriptions will differ from those made here at least in part because even the very lowest foreigners in this study have a rudimentary competence in English.

4. When the first and second meetings are considered together, the relative proportion of wh and yes/no questions are roughly equivalent. Note, however, when data for the second

meeting alone are considered, as in columns 3 and 4, the relative proportion of wh-questions diminishes. Independent comparisons of the first and second meetings has shown that for wh-questions alone there is a significant difference between the first and second meeting. On all other measures there was no reliable difference in any of the properties of foreigner talk between the first and second meeting (Freed 1978a).

5. The Declarative sentences exchanged between native speakers did display more dative and particle movement. There was also more passivization in native talk, and as previously stated, native talk sentences were more commonly multi-clausal.

6. It may be the case as Zobl (1977) points out that yes/no questions which exhibit no subject-auxiliary inversion and are signalled by rising intonation might be, when addressed to native speakers, sociolinguistically marked. That is, the informality of a situation (as between mother and child or between native speakers) may elicit such terms. Such is probably not the case in conversation between natives and foreigners, even in this study where the conversations were not chance encounters on the street. Thus, it is possible that the yes/no questions which display no subject-auxiliary inversion and deletion of 'do' and/or 'you' cannot be compared at all because the motivation for their use is different: reduced complexity in one case and informality in the other.

References

In the years since the publication of this article, numerous studies of various aspects of Foreigner Talk have appeared. Many of these have addressed the use of what is sometimes called the "foreigner register" in the classroom. Some have analyzed the contribution of foreigner talk to comprehension and ultimately to acquisition, while others have focused on interactional adjustments in foreigner talk in response to proficiency levels of the foreign speaker. The bibliography of this article, as originally published, has been updated to include several of the major works that have appeared since that time. Since it is not possible, in this context, to provide an exhaustive review of all foreigner talk research, the reader is referred to the ERIC bibliography for the most complete source of published and unpublished work in this area.

Arthur, B., Weiner, R., Culver, M., Lee, Y., and Thomas, D. 1980. The Register of Impersonal Discourses to Foreigners: Verbal Adjustments to Foreign Accent. In *Discourse Analysis in Second Language Research*, D. Larsen-Freeman (ed.) Rowley, Mass.: Newbury House.

Blount, B. G. 1972. Parental Speech and Language Acquisition: Some Luo and Samoan Examples. *Anthropological Linguistics* 14:119-130.

Brown, R., Cazden, D., and Bellugi, U. 1969. The Child's Grammar from I to III. In *Minnesota Symposium on Child Psychology*, J. P. Hill (ed.). Minneapolis: University of Minnesota.

Brulhart, Marilyn 1986. Foreigner Talk in the ESL Classroom: International Adjustments to Adult Students at Two Language Proficiency Levels. *TESL Canada Journal*, Special issue 1:29-42.

Campbell, C., Gaskill, W,. and Brook, S. V. 1977. Some Aspects of Foreigner Talk. In *Proceedings of the Los Angeles L2 Forum*, C. A. Henning (ed.).

Chaudron, Craig 1979. Complexity of ESL Teachers' Speech and Vocabulary Explanation/Elaboration. Paper presented at the TESOL Conference, Boston, Mass.

Ferguson, C. A. 1975. Toward a Characterization of English Foreigner Talk. *Anthropological Linguistics* 17:1-14.

———. 1977a. Simplified Register, Broken Language and Gastarbeiterdeutsch. In *German in Contact with other Languages*, C. Molony et al. (eds.), 25-39. Kronberg/Ts: Scriptor Verlag.

———. 1977b. Baby Talk as a Simplified Register. In *Talking to Children*, C. E. Snow and C. A. Ferguson (eds.). Cambridge: Cambridge University.

———. 1981. 'Foreigner talk' as the Name of a Simplified Register. *International Journal of the Sociology of Language* 28, 9-18.

Freed, B. 1978a. Foreigner Talk: A Study of Speech Adjustments Made by Native Speakers of English in Conversation with Non-native Speakers. Unpublished Ph.D. thesis, University of Pennsylvania.

———. 1978b. Functional Language and the Second Language Classroom. Paper presented at the meeting of the American Association of Applied Linguistics, Boston, Mass.

———. 1978c. Speech Adjustments to Perceived Listener Attributes . Paper presented at the winter meeting of the Linguistic Society of America, Boston, Mass.

———. 1979. Foreigner Talk and Conversational Interaction. Paper presented at the TESOL Conference, Boston, Mass.

———. 1981. Talking to Foreigners Versus Talking to Children: Similarities and Differences. In *Research in Second Language Acquisition*, R. Scarcella and S. Krashen (eds.). Rowley, Mass.: Newbury House.

Garnica, O. K. 1975. Some Characteristics of Prosodic Input to Young Children. Unpublished Ph.D. thesis, Stanford University.

Gaskill, W. 1978. Correction in Adult Native Speaker, Non-native Speaker Conversation. Paper presented at the TESOL Conference, Mexico City.

Gass, Susan M., and Varonis, Evangeline Marlos 1985. Variation in Native Speaker Speech Modification to Non-Native Speakers. In *Studies in Second Language Acquisition*, 7,1:37-57.

Gelman, R., and Shatz, M. 1975. Rule-Governed Variation in Children's Conversations. Unpublished manuscript, University of Pennsylvania.

Gough, J., and Hatch, E. 1975. The Importance of Input Data in Second Language Acquisition Studies. *Language Learning* 25:297-338.

Hatch, E. 1976. Discourse Analysis and Second Language Acquisition. Paper presented at NAFSA Conference, San Diego, California.

———. Shapira, R., and Gough, J. 1978. Foreigner Talk Discourse. *ITL Review of Applied Linguistics*, 39-60.

———. 1983. *Psycholinguistics: A Second Language Perspective*. Rowley, Mass.: Newbury House.

Hymes, Dell 1972. Models of the Interaction of Language and Social Life. In *Directions in Sociolinguistics: The Ethnography of Communication*, J. J. Gumperz and D. Hymes, (eds.). New York: Holt, Rinehart and Winston.

Long, M. 1981. Input, Interaction and Second Language Acquisition. In *Native Language and Foreign Language Acquisition*, H. Winitz (ed.), 379. New York: Annals of the New York Academy of Science.

———. 1985. Input and Second Language Acquisition Theory. In *Input in Second Language Acquisition*, S. Gass and C. Madden, (eds.). Rowley, Mass.: Newbury House.

Molony, D., Zobl, H., and Stolting, W. (Hrsg) 1977. *Deutsch in Kontakt mit anderen Sprachen*. Kronberg/Ts.: Scriptor Verlag.

Newport, E. 1976. Motherese: The Speech of Mothers to Young Children. Unpublished Ph.D. thesis, University of Pennsylvania.

Newport, E., and Gleitman, H. 1977. Maternal Self-Repetitions and the Child's Acquisition of Language. *Papers and Reports on Child Language Development* 13.

Sacks, H., Schegloff, E., and Jefferson, G.A. 1974. Simplest Systematics for the Organization of Turn-Taking for Conversation. *Language* 50:696-735.

Schegloff, E., Jefferson, G.A., and Sacks, H. 1977. The Preference for Self-Correction in the Organization of Repair in Conversation. *Language* 53:361-382.

Snow, C.E. and Ferguson, C.A. (eds.) 1977. *Talking to Children: Language Input and Acquisition.* Cambridge: Cambridge University.

Snow, C.E., van Eeden, R., and Muysken, P. 1981. The Interactional Origins of Foreigner Talk: Municipal Employees and Foreign Workers. *International Journal of the Sociology of Language* 28:83-93.

Wesche, M., and Ready, D. 1985. Foreigner Talk in the University Classroom. In *Input in Second Language Acquisition,* S. Gass and C. Madden, (eds.). Rowley, Mass.: Newbury House.

Zobl, H. 1977. The Forms of Interference: Some Evidence for a Complexity Metric in Foreign Language Learning. In *German in Contact with Other Languages,* C. Molony et al. (eds.), 307-317. Kronberg/Ts.: Scriptor Verlag.

Foreigner Talk As Comprehensible Input

Tracy D. Terrell

 ## INTRODUCTION

There is some research evidence that native speakers (NS) modify their speech to make it more comprehensible to language learners. Apparently, they accomplish this by slowing down, focusing on key words, using shorter sentences, using visuals, gestures, and other nonlinguistic resources, and so forth. Such input can be referred to as modified or simplified speech. On the other hand, it is rare for a learner in natural interactions to have access to direct grammar explanations (or grammar exercises) since native speakers do not normally possess nor are they able to provide such information to the learner. Hatch (1983:153) reviews the research literature on such modified speech, which she defines as "language addressed to those who are learners or relearners." She attempts to provide evidence for the following assertions:

1. Certain modifications occur in speech when the language is addressed to those who are learners or relearners.

2. These modifications facilitate communication.

3. There are strong similarities in speech modifications regardless of whether the addressee is a first or second language learner or relearner.

4. The modifications are a natural outcome of the negotiation of communication.

Reprinted from *Linguistics, Language Teaching, and Language Acquisition: The Interdependence of Theory, Practice, and Research,* ed. J. E. Alatis, The Georgetown University Round Table on Languages and Linguistics (1990), pp. 193–206, by permission of Georgetown University Press.

This sort of interest in the characteristics of input in natural second language acquisition originated in child L1 acquisition research. One of the tactics was to study input to children to see what effect characteristics of the input had on the acquisition process (for example, Snow 1986). The study of the input to child L1 acquisition known first as 'motherese' and later as *caretaker (or caregiver) speech*, had an important impact on research in the field of second language acquisition.[1] The following example of input to a child was hastily written down while 'eavesdropping' on a mother talking to her child on a flight backing out from the gate at the Dallas-Fort Worth airport.

> M: Look, they're loading luggage. See the airplane? Those men are unloading luggage. They're taking off luggage. See the suitcase? See the door? See the man in the orange suit? See the man with the suitcase? He's putting it on the cart.
>
> C: Where's _____?
>
> M: She's at home.

The example illustrates clearly some of the characteristics of caretaker speech that are thought to aid comprehension: repetition, reference to the 'here and now,' emphasis on key words, and so forth. In the next example, taken from the same conversation, the mother is willing to repeat the instructions until the child finally understands.

> M: Pull it up (referring to the tray table). Do it again. Pull hard. Pull hard. Pull hard. Pull harder. There you did it!

Ferguson (1971) introduced the term *foreigner talk* to refer to the modified code used by native speakers to talk to foreigners (or nonnative speakers (NNS)).[2] Freed (1980) contains a comparison of foreigner talk and caretaker speech. From her analysis of syntactic complexity she found that the two reduced codes are very similar. However, a more detailed functional analysis revealed differences. For example, information exchange was identified as the primary communication intent of the foreigner talk, while the caretaker speech was "replete with direct and indirect imperatives" (23). The conversations between native and nonnative speakers ranged over a variety of topics not restricted to the here and now, while topics of conversations with children were much more limited.

In addition to caretaker speech and foreigner talk, many researchers have used a third term, *teacher talk*, to describe the input a language instructor provides in the classroom. Teacher talk has been grouped with caretaker speech and foreigner talk as examples of modified codes, input with special characteristics for easier comprehension by a language learner.

While everyone agrees that modified speech serves to make the input more comprehensible to learners, many researchers have suggested that these same modifications may aid language acquisition. An even stronger position would be that input in the form of modified speech is both necessary and sufficient to guarantee acquisition.

The L2 research on modified codes has been concentrated in two areas. Early studies described the characteristics of modified speech. According to Gass and Madden (1985:4), "some of the salient characteristics of foreigner talk, for example, are: slower rate of speech, louder speech, longer pauses, common vocabulary, few idioms, greater use of gestures, more repetition, more summaries of preceding utterances, shorter utterances and more deliberate articulation."[3] Later studies, such as Long (1985), looked at the effects of reduced codes (and modified interactional patterns) on second language acquisition. As Long has frequently pointed out, it is one thing to show that speakers use reduced codes with learners and quite another to show that this practice usually influences the acquisition process.

Here I am not going to address either of these two issues. I assume that we know the characteristics of modified speech and further, that the use of this type of input facilitates language acquisition. My purpose here is to present new data that support the notion that foreigner talk is frequently not easily comprehended by the learner it is directed to and that it does not always exhibit the characteristics we believe to be useful for language acquisition.

One of the problems in evaluating research on foreigner talk is that in much of the L2 research, foreigner talk and teacher talk have been assumed to be the same, or at least, highly similar. The most comprehensive review of the topic (Hatch 1983:155-58) does not separate the two. Wesche and Ready (1985), a recent representative example, study *Foreigner talk in the university classroom*. Ellis (1985) lists several studies describing (in his words) 'foreigner talk' or 'teacher talk.' Interestingly, all of the papers he cites (Arthur et al. 1980; Long 1981; Gaies 1977; Henzl 1979) look at input in the classroom, not at foreigner talk. This was not always the case. Most of the early studies of foreigner talk cited by Ferguson (1981), for example, indeed are of native speakers talking to foreigners outside a classroom setting, such as the Heidelberger Forschungsprojekt (1975).

Several recent research projects do look at input that is not teacher generated, but most of these studies use NNS language students (usually ESL students) as the subjects and use other students NS providers of input. Furthermore, the source of the input and interaction is talk between a NS and a NNS during some sort of artificial task used by the researcher to bring the two subjects together and assure a reason for input and communication. Information from such tasks is certainly interesting, but it may be the case that we cannot generalize from these contexts to more natural interactional contexts. Native speakers (NSS) who regularly associate with foreign students, or even fellow students, might modify their speech more readily than other NSS without this contact. In addition, when subjects are asked to complete a task, it is to be expected that modified input and interaction would occur in an effort to complete the task set by the researcher.

Freed (in this volume) suggests that modified speech is shaped by "an aggregate of facts including variables such as age, purpose of communication, cognitive ability, relative status, linguistic sufficiency, relationship between speakers, topic, etc." This position seems to me to be intuitively correct, especially for adult-adult speech. For this reason, I have chosen here to look at foreigner talk as far removed from the "mainstream ESL" research as possible. My data came from working-class native speakers of Spanish who have had little or no experience with language instruction or with non-native speakers (NNSS) of Spanish.[4] The native speakers did not know the learner personally and in most cases had just met him on the day of the recording.[5] Most of these interactions occurred in relaxed environments—in the kitchen fixing lunch, at the pool before and after a swim, and so forth. However, in no case were the NSS and the NNS in an artificial task set up by the investigator. The recorder was turned on for several hours, picking up not only the conversations with the learner but among NSS and with other fluent speakers of Spanish. Some of the data is based on recorded telephone conversations. Thus, none of the characteristics that we might suppose as being supportive to better input and interaction are present in these conversations: the background and cultural experiences are very different, the social status is different, the educational levels are different, the participants have nothing in common, there is no particular topic focus, nor any particular task to complete that would ensure motivation for cooperation. In addition, all of the NNS are males, since some of the researchers have suggested that females tend to give better input than males.

The learner, R, is not a student and has never had any formal training in Spanish and has not studied or looked at Spanish learning materials.[6] All the Spanish he knows has been picked up through interactions with the NSS described above.

2 THE DATA

The most striking feature of the recordings of R interacting with native speakers is the very poor quality, from the point of view of R's acquisition, of both input and interaction.[7]

Poor Quality of Input

With few exceptions, most of the foreigner talk provided by the native speakers to R exhibits few of the characteristics imputed to modified speech that are supposed to be helpful to the learner in the acquisition process. In this particular data set there are eleven clearly identifiable problems for the learner.[8]

Little or no adjustment for Krashen's 'i+1' criterion   In spite of the fact that R's Spanish is very rudimentary, these NSS have difficulty in simplifying their speech for him. Although they do not speak to him as they would to another native speaker, in most cases the input does even approach R's i+1. In the following example recorded from a telephone conversation with N, whom R had known for several weeks, there is no possibility that R could have understood N's reply.

    R: ¿Alvaro dice what? ¿secreto?   Alvaro says what? secret?
    N: No, Alvaro no ha dicho.   No, Alvaro hasn't said.
       Usted es el que dice.   You are the one who says (it.)

No highlighting of key words without learner request   These NSS do not routinely emphasize and clarify key words in the input. This forces R to attempt to identify the key words and then specifically ask for an explanation. In the following example, R has segmented incorrectly and asks for an explanation. N ignores the request.

N: ¿y algo más?	And something else?
R: ¿Yalgo más?	"Yalgo más"?
N: Sí.	Yes.
R: ¿Cómo dice "yalgo más"?	What does "yalgo más" mean?

Few repetitions   Native speakers do not volunteer repetitions unless R specifically requests them to do so. Unfortunately as often as not, when the NSS do repeat, they give exact repetitions without additional help or expansion. And even when the NSS do restate what the learner has not understood, the restatement is frequently more complex than the original version, or not helpful to R at all. In the following example, N repeats the word *tenía* slowly, but he still does not make any attempt to help R understand its meaning.

N: Porque no tenía que trabajar ahora.	Because I didn't have to work now.
R: No teniejos. ¿Cómo dice teniejos?	No "teniejos"? What does "teniejos" mean?
N: (slowly) Tenía.	Had.
R: Oh, tenía. OK. (but does not understand)	Oh, had. OK.

Difficulty in slowing down/poor articulation   NSS sporadically slow down in response to R's obviously low level input; however, in these conversations the slow rate is quickly abandoned and rapid speech is resumed within a couple of turns. The fast speech frequently results in incorrect parsing.

R: No, tu cara es similar de caras de hombres Indonesia.	No, your face is similar to an Indonesian face.
A: Por mi forma de ser o . . .	Because of my way of being or . . .?
R: ¿Formasero? What is formasero?	"Formasero"? What is "formasero"?

No awareness of linguistic difficulty   The NSS in my data exhibit absolutely no awareness of linguistic difficulty. They do not restrict themselves to simple vocabulary and they do not avoid idioms and slang. They constantly use vocabulary and structures with R that a language teacher immediately recognizes as too complex for his level proficiency. In the following example, R has talked to A for two hours or so giving him ample time to judge his level of proficiency.

R: ¿Ya? OK. (finishing a haircut)	
A: Me quedó bien. Así lo quería yo. Me quedó a todo dar. Sin decirte nada tú lo hiciste solo. El trabajo me quedó a todo dar. Me quedó bien.	It turned out nice. That's the way I wanted it. It turned out great. Without telling you anything you did by yourself. The job turned out great. It turned out fine.

No awareness of 'localisms' and slang   These NS use local expressions and slang that R cannot possibly know. In the following turns, D uses *órale*, a Mexican slang expression meaning 'OK'. R ignores it and concentrates on understanding D's question.

R: Yo durmiendo con mis lentes.	I sleep with my glasses.
D: Orale. ¿No te lastima?	I see. Doesn't it hurt you?
R: Delastima? What's delastima?	"Delastima? What's "delastima"?
D: Un huh. Lastima.	Un huh. Hurt.

Few expansions   Unlike caretakers and teachers, NSS do not pay attention to the form of the learner's responses. Consequently, 'expansions' in which the learner's output is corrected are very rare. Usually, NSS simply respond to R's question without much elaboration.

R: ¿Cuándo días de Sinaloa de Tijuana?	How many days from Sinaloa to Tijuana?
J: Tres.	Three.
R: ¿Con bus o con what? Burro? ¿Con tren? ¿Avión?	With a bus or with what? A donkey? With the train? Plane?
J: Bus.	

Deletions, shortened versions, pronominaliazations are operative in NS input   In the following example, R asks for clarification, but the response is a reduced version of the original and even more difficult for R to understand.

N: Lo que puede hacer es que... ¿usted va a invitar a Alvaro a salir hoy?	And what you can do is . . . Are you going to invite Alvaro to go out today.
R: ¿Huh?	
N: ¿Lo va a invitar a salir?	Are you going to invite him to go out?

Comprehension checks infrequent and not helpful   Most of the comprehension checks in this data consist of words like *¿comprende?* with little or no attempt made to see if comprehension is really taking place.

N: Roan va la casa donde Alvaro. (baby talk)	Roan goes to the house where Alvaro is.
R: Un huh.	
N: ¿Comprende?	Do you understand?

No empathy with learner   NSS are frequently impatient (in spite of the fact they are in the United States and do not speak English) and not willing to put out much effort to make themselves comprehensible. In the following example, R is talking to G, who speaks very quickly and is very difficult to understand. G doesn't really want to continue the effort and tells me as an aside that R is a *burro*.

R: No, el hablar mucho rápido.   No, he talks very fast.
G: Es muy burro.   He's real dumb (a donkey).
R: ¿Burro? Who? ¿Yo? Cállate.   Donkey? Who? Me? Shut up.
    (laughs, but is somewhat
    offended.)

Does not rephrase to help learner   NSS frequently ignore R's indication
of noncomprehension of requests for help. In the following example, R clearly doesn't
understand what N has said, but N's only response is *sí*. R makes a guess (wrong) and
the conversation proceeds.

N: ¿Cómo le va? ¿Bien?   How are things? Fine?
R: ¿Cómo le va bien? (in a
    question intonation)
    Oh, did I get up good?
    Sí, yo durmiendo, bien.   Yes, I sleep good.
    ¿Y tú?   And you?

Poor Quality of Interaction

Not only is the output of poor quality for language learning, but most of the interactions do not meet the criteria that we suppose are useful for language acquisition.
This is true even though many of the conversations are relaxed and superficially
pleasant, with lots of laughter and enjoyment by the native speakers and R.

No interest in learner's question/response   Frequently, the NSS display
little interest in R's responses. The resulting topic switches make comprehension
more difficult for R. Both the learner and native speaker often seem to have their
own "agenda" and one pays only enough attention to the other's response to keep the
conversation going. I suspect that this low level of attention to each other may be a
characteristic of adult-adult speech in general. In the following example, R asks a
specific question, which apparently is uninteresting to the native speaker, who
ignores the question and asks one of his own.

R: ¿Cuántas horas tú trabajar   How many hours do you work
    arriba? ¿Dos?   upstairs?
E: ¿No vas al parque manaña?   Aren't you going to the
                                                    park tomorrow?

Few expansions of incorrect output   In the following example, R's
response is so ungrammatical it is amazing that N understood anything at all, but he
makes no attempt to confirm his interpretation of what R has said. Expansions and
comprehension confirmations provide the learner with an opportunity to comprehend
an utterance whose meaning is predictable from context. Their absence severely
hampers R in improving his ability to understand the input.

N: ¿Comprende?
R: Sí, el, un... el voy   Yes, he, a . . . he I'm going to
   de tu casa a uno momento.   your house in a moment.
N: Sí.

Severely reduced NS responses   Native speakers do not seem to make any
adjustment in their responses in order to give good feedback to the learner; rather
they respond as they would to another NS using drastic ellipsis and deletions.

R: ¿Cuánto tiempo tú eres aquí?   How much time are you here?
E: Dos meses.   Two months.

Little negative feedback   Direct or indirect correction is extremely rare.

R: ¿Cuántos años tú estudiante   How many years are you
   escuela?   a student in school?
J: Hasta la secundaria.   Up to secondary.

Confusing feedback/corrections   When negative feedback does occur, it
is more often than not incorrect or very confusing to the learner. In the following
example, the feedback was relatively clear, but R still never managed to understand
the meaning of *tampoco*.

R: Ahora yo no trabajar.   Now I'm not working.
E: ¿Mañana?   Tomorrow?
R: No, yo también.   No, me too.
E: Tampoco (correcting).   Neither.
R: Huh?
E: Mañana tampoco.   Tomorrow neither.
R: ¿Mañana nada trabajar?   Tomorrow nothing work?
E: Ahora no.   Not now.
R: Hum...?
E: Mañana tampoco.   Tomorrow neither.

Baby-talk   Most native speakers do not severely reduce their speech, but a few
resort to a sort of pidgin. It is not clear to me whether this helps R's comprehension of
the input or not.

R: Oh, ¿yo con Alvaro?   Oh, me with Alvaro?
N: No antes. Usted llama (self   No before. You call,
   corrects), Felipe llama   Phillip calls Nelson,
   Nelson (speaker), dice Ron   Ron to his house so that
   (listener) a su casa para   I leave. Do you understand?
   yo salir. ¿Comprende?

Does not help the learner reformulate questions/comments   In
cases in which R's output is so bad that the native speaker does not understand, the

NS indicates noncomprehension minimally without giving R any help in reformulating the question or statement.

R: ¿Cuándo tiempo tú regresa de México?

How much time you go back from Mexico?

G: ¿Eh?

Difficult transition from one turn to another This makes it more difficult for R to follow the conversation.

R: ¿Dónde es tu familia?

Where is your family?

A: Sinaloa, México.

R: Sinaloa. Ah muchas personas es de Sinaloa. Es estado de popular.

Sinaloa. Oh, a lot of people are from Sinaloa. It's a popular state.

A: Un huh.

R: ¿Estado grande?

Is it a big state?

A: Mucha mota pa'llá.

Lots of pot over there.

R: ¿Mucha mota?

Lots of pot?

No help with output In the following example, R questions a verb form and is given an incorrect answer. This was a crucial sequence since it was the first time that R had noticed that verbs can take different forms according to the subject. His hypothesis that *tú* 'you' goes with *eres* 'are' was correct, but it was disconfirmed by the native speaker. Later the native speaker corrects himself since in reality a different verb *tener* 'to have' is more appropriate in this context.

R: ¿Cuándo tiempo tú es aquí?

How much time are you here?

M: Dos meses.

Two months.

R: Dos meses.

Two months.

M: Tres, tres meses. Mayo, junio, julio, agosto.

Three months. Three months. May, June, July, August.

R: ¿Agosto? OK, julio, agosto, junio, tres meses. Mayo, ¿sí? Junio, julio, agosto, cerca de septiembre, cerca de cuatro meses tú es aquí. ¿Es it tú es aquí or tú eres aquí?

August? OK, July, August, June, three months, May, yes? June, July, August, almost September, almost four months here. Is it 'tú es aquí' or 'tú eres aquí?

M: ¿Huh?

R: Is it tú es aquí or tú eres aquí? ¿De qué es correctamente?

What is it correctly?

M: Es.

R: Tú es aquí.

M: O sea lo correcto es cuánto tiempo tienes aquí.

That is, the correct way is How much time do you have here?

R: ¿Tienes? Oh. Tiempo.	Have? Oh, time.
M: (slowly) ¿Cuánto tiempo tienes aquí?	
R: ¿Cuándo tiempo tienes aquí?	
M: Aquí.	

 ## CONCLUSION

The research to date has shown that some native speakers in some circumstances do give input that is presumably at least an aid in the acquisition process. However, Hatch (1983:175), in her review of the literature, comments that "in contrast to these successful ways of negotiating conversations among children, negotiation for the adolescent and adult can be very difficult . . . . These negotiations can be very protracted and often end in frustration if not total communication breakdown." The data in this paper suggest that the reduced speech used by some native speakers is often not easily comprehended by the learner and in addition does not contain many examples of the characteristics of caretaker speech that we believe to be useful to the acquisition process. Admittedly, the data are sketchy and incomplete, and in addition, I did not provide examples of the few conversational turns that do illustrate characteristics of foreigner talk that make the input more comprehensible. On the other hand, it is entirely possible that the data presented here are more representative of normal NS-NNS interactions than has been supposed.

At the time of these recordings, R had had approximately 100-150 hours of input-interaction with NSS, spread over one and one-half years.[9] This is equivalent in hours to one year or so of formal study at the university level. It is also quite an impressive figure when we take into consideration that the input has almost always been in a one-on-one situation with at least as many opportunities for output as for input. Clearly, R has spoken more Spanish than an average foreign language student after one year of formal study; and yet neither his comprehension nor his speech is even close to that of a normal first year student of Spanish. On the other hand, there are some positive sides to R's Spanish. His confidence and ability to maintain conversation are impressive. (Indeed, so impressive that fossilization appears to be setting in!) In addition, what he does know is accessible without conscious monitoring.

I believe that R's slow progress is a consequence of the poor quality input and interaction that he is forced to deal with. First, R has to struggle to maintain the conversations and to get input. NSS rarely initiate any conversational turns with R and do not usually ask him questions. In most cases the NSS are quite willing to address fluent speakers of Spanish present in the environment and to ignore R altogether. Some NSS clearly consider talking to R somewhat of a burden, and they are willing to let the conversation with him terminate at the end of most conversational turns. My impression is that only his wit and laughter, his positive attitude toward Spanish and easy-going personality, keep the conversations going.

There are several possible explanations for why the NSS in this study do not give useful input. One I mentioned at the beginning of the paper: these NSS have not had extended experience with nonnative speakers trying to learn Spanish. In addition, the fact that none of the NSS has learned English himself means that they have a very low awareness of linguistic difficulties of Spanish and in learning a second language. Another important factor is that the NSS did not know R well, and in reality had no strong external motivation to communicate with him. Several colleagues have suggested that male-to-male working-class speech may be characterized by the absence of facilitative characteristics and that the perceived social differences between the NSS and R may only increase these tendencies.

Much of the input itself is very difficult to understand. R struggles to comprehend most turns and is forced to rely more on guessing and context than on language for meaning. He rarely hears more from the native speakers than just a short comment, a response, or a reply. Key words are lost in the utterance, and in order to understand anything at all, he is forced to 'negotiate meaning' constantly. While it is clear that these negotiations are the primary source for comprehended utterances and for learning new words and phrases, the negotiations are frequently not successful since the NSS tend to give very confusing and often incorrect responses.

Given the consistently poor quality of the input R receives, it is surprising that he has acquired anything at all. I attribute his level of success to his affectively positive attitude toward Spanish and his desire to join in the activities and conversations with the rest of the group. I suspect that he has not yet become discouraged for two reasons: (1) his ability to speak continues to improve,[10] and (2) this is the only input in Spanish he has ever received. He is not aware that other NSS, or a teacher, might provide more helpful input.

In conclusion, the foreigner talk provided by the NSS of this study did not contain many examples of the characteristics of reduced codes that we believe to be helpful to learners. Indeed, the input from NSS in these data can be characterized as difficult to process and of limited use in language acquisition.

These data show that we cannot assume that foreigner talk automatically provides good input. Some NSS in certain contexts may be very good at providing comprehensible input to other adults, but my suspicion is that most are not. One possible line of further research would be to compare in some detail foreigner talk with caretaker speech. It may well turn out that the fact that L1 acquisition is 'perfect' and L2 adult acquisition is usually 'faulty' may be explained by the differences between the input children and adults receive and the interactions they engage in. Another possibility that suggests itself to me from these data is that the fossilization common in L2 acquisition is caused by the very poor quality of the input and interactions in adult-to-adult speech.

Second, these data suggest that as classroom instructors we can learn from adult natural second language acquisition in two ways: what works and what does not. There are two other successful models to follow. We should be willing to look more carefully at child L1 acquisition insofar as the results can be applied to adult language learning. In addition, we can look at successful classroom models: experienced teachers know what 'works' for students. The fact that these techniques are different from what occurs in natural L2 may be just what makes classroom learning so much more successful than natural L2 acquisition.

Notes

1. Snow, herself, uses the term *child directed speech* (CDS).
2. See also his review of the research literature in Ferguson (1981).
3. See also Hatch (1983: chap. 9).
4. Some of the informants in the project have had experience speaking Spanish and here in the United States, particular in the work situations, but these sorts of experiences could not have been extensive since most of the NSS used in this study were recent arrivals to the United States.
5. The native speakers were told that the recordings were being made to enable R to get his Spanish output corrected by a teacher afterwards. To date we have done no such correction or analysis and all tapes have been erased after transcription. As far as I could tell, the NSS paid no attention to the recorder at all since they were rightly convinced that the focus was on R.
6. R was born in Indonesia and attended Dutch-medium schools there and later in Holland. He came to the United States at the age of 14 and is now English dominant although still fluent in Dutch. R studied French for two years in high school over 20 years ago. The French seems to have aided with the acquisition of certain similar words, but surprisingly I have not noticed any positive carryover with the grammar.
7. I am using a loose version of Krashen's criteria for good input and Long's criteria for good interaction.
8. R's output has not been corrected in these examples.
9. The figure may be actually be higher, but the first 50 hours or so were mostly spent over-hearing conversations he was not much interested in, and I have not included them in this figure.
10. While his fluency has improved, he has acquired very little grammar to date. He has some elementary notions of gender, but he has not yet acquired either plural agreement or person-number agreement for verbs.

References

Arthur, B., R. Weiner, M. Culver, Y. Lee, and D. Thomas. 1980. The Register of Impersonal Discourses to Foreigners: Verbal Adjustments to Foreign Accent. In: D. Larsen-Freeman, ed. *Discourse Analysis in Second Language Research.* Rowley, Mass.: Newbury House.

Ellis, Rod. 1985. *Understanding Second Language Acquisition.* Oxford: Oxford University Press.

Ferguson, Charles. 1971. Toward a Characterization of English Foreigner Talk. *Anthropological Linguistics* 17:1-14.

———. 1981. "Foreigner talk" as the Name of a Simplified Register. *International Journal of the Sociology of Language* 28:9-18.

Freed, Barbara. 1980. Talking to Foreigners Versus Talking to Children: Similarities and Differences. In: R. Scarcella and S. Krashen, eds. *Research in Second Language Acquisition.* Rowley, Mass.: Newbury House.

———. 1981. Foreigner Talk, Baby Talk, Native Talk. *International Journal of the Sociology of Language* 28:19-39 (reprinted in this volume).

Gaies, S. 1977. The Nature of Linguistic Input in Formal Second Language Learning: Linguistics and Communicative Strategies in ESL Teachers' Classroom Languages. In: H. D. Brown, C. Yorio, and R. Crymes, eds. *On TESOL '77*. Washington, D.C.: TESOL.

Gass, S. and C. Madden, eds. 1985. *Input in Second Language Acquisition*. Rowley, Mass.: Newbury House.

Hatch, E. 1983. *Psycholinguistics: A Second Language Perspective*. Rowley, Mass.: Newbury House.

Heidelberger Forschungsprojekt 'Pidgin Deutsch'. 1975. Sprache and Kommunikation ausländischer Arbeiter. Kronberg/Ts: Scriptor Verlag.

Henzl, V. 1979. Foreign Talk in the Classroom. *International Review of Applied Linguistics* 17:159-67.

Krashen, S. 1985. *The Input Hypothesis: Issues and Implications*. London and New York: Longman.

Krashen, S., and T. Terrell. 1983. *The Natural Approach: Language Aquisition in the Classroom*. Hayward, Calif.: The Albany Press.

Long, M. 1981. Input, Interaction and Second Language Acquisition. In: H. Winitz, ed. *Native Language and Foreign Language Acquisition* 379. New York: Annuals of the New York Academy of Science.

Long, M. 1985. Input and Second Language Acquisition Theory. In: Gass and Madden, eds. (1985).

Snow, C. 1986. Conversations with Children. In: P. Fletcher and M. Garman, eds. *Language Acquisition*, 2nd. ed. Cambridge: Cambridge University Press.

Terrell, T. 1977. A Natural Approach to the Acquisition and Learning of a Language. *Modern Language Journal* 61:325-37.

———. 1982. The Natural Approach to Language Teaching: An Update. *Modern Language Journal* 66:121-32 (reprinted in this volume).

———. 1986. Acquisition in the Natural Approach: The Binding/Access Framework. *Modern Language Journal* 70:213-27.

Wesche, M., and D. Ready. 1985. Foreigner Talk in the University Classroom. In: Gass and Madden, eds. (1985).

Recognition, Retention, Retrieval: The Three Rs of Vocabulary Use

Wilga M. Rivers
Harvard University Emerita

Meaning comprehended is a creation of the receiver—personal, individual, and covert—so communication of meanings is never simple, even in a common language. Concepts, which are elusive and elastic, find realization in the words of a language, but are understood only in a context, which may be linguistic, physical, or psychological. Consequently vocabulary use is even more complicated in a second language, where the context-related and interverbal associations may be quite different. There is, at present, much research in cognitive psychology on the dynamic nature of memory processes, particularly in parallel distributed processing theory, which throws light on how speakers of a language may develop a rich personal vocabulary for expression and recognition. Such approaches help us identify the many potential routes by which what has been encountered enters into semantic networks or becomes accessible, sometimes in quite unexpected ways; they make clear that acquisition and use of vocabulary will be very personal and individual, with a strong affective element. With some understanding of these processes, teachers will be better equipped to guide students in the use of associative techniques and mnemonic devices to "bind" (in Terrell's terminology) new vocabulary of interest to them and facilitate its retrieval.

Author's note:
Tracy Terrell, in developing the Natural Approach, was always very conscious of the need for a wide vocabulary, readily accessible, for comprehension and communication of meanings in a second language. Tracy loved language and used language well, exploiting its potentialities in his writing. We were friends for many years, and we shared many ideas and insights. I have written this article for Tracy as a special offering and tribute, focusing it on a subject that was of primary interest to him. I have also indulged in a certain playfulness in the use of words and metaphor that I know he would have enjoyed. Also in line with Tracy's own emphasis, I have not neglected what teachers need to know about cognitive processes and classroom research if they are to facilitate their students' personal acquisition of a wide-ranging, retrievable vocabulary.

"What's in a name?" asks Shakespeare's Juliet. "That which we call a rose by any other name would smell as sweet."[1] This is undoubtedly true, and roses worldwide are called by many names. We are all familiar with the concept of the arbitrary relationship between sound-form and meaning. Even so-called onomatopeic words are specific to particular languages. An English-speaking child will wave a piece of wood and cry "Bang! Bang!" while a French-speaking child will cry "Crac! Crac!" An English sheep will "baa," while a Spanish speaker will hear "meee." *Crac/Bang, Baa/Meee*—knowing the meaning of the action and the sound represented by these expressions, we may declare some similarity, but objectively we must admit that in phonological shape and graphic representation, they have little in common. To learners of a new language, even onomatopeic words are a new experience and not necessarily transparent in meaning, although context helps. This is the simplest of our problems.

Unfortunately, meanings in first and second languages rarely occur as one-to-one equivalents, in substitutable words, even for simple concrete objects; such common items as *bread* and *lemon* have different meanings for persons of different languages and cultures. "Bread" to the French represents the warmth of family togetherness over a meal; "lemon" to an American may represent something disappointing—an object that fails to be what it is vaunted to be and leaves a "sour taste in the mouth." Beyond these culturally rich connotations, meaning is personal and covert, sometimes deliberately concealed in euphemisms or prevarications, especially in subgroup jargons (among children or sports fans, among doctors or prisoners); at other times, it is partially and tentatively revealed through the selection of words but frequently requires illustration or gesture to make it clear.

Meaning comprehended is a creation of the receiver: again personal, individual, and covert. Communication of meanings even in a common language is not simple. How often do we hear such exclamations as: "He never understands what I tell him!" "She seems almost deliberately to misinterpret everything I say!" "They react in the strangest ways! Don't they understand plain English!" Winston Churchill once observed that England and the United States were two countries divided by a common language. Different world views can lead to quite different semantic content for outwardly identical words. We may speak, then, of the chameleon-like quality of words, whose meanings (and often forms) change and blend to create new meanings. Even borrowings from other languages cease to be reliable, as they interact with existing words of the language.

In this article I will use the term *words* to cover not only individual words, but also phrases and short sentences that serve many purposes—set expressions or lexical phrases, as we sometimes call them (Nattinger 1988). Words in this sense are building blocks that combine to form the structure of meaningful messages.

Words express concepts. What, then, is a *concept?* For Saussure, "initially the concept is nothing [it is] only a value, determined by its relations with other similar values and ... without [relations among values] the signification would not exist" (1959:117). What is the meaning, for instance, of *warm* or *cool?* For a language that has only *hot* or *cold* in its vocabulary, these are difficult concepts to pin down. Even for us, what is hot in one situation may be cold in another. We may find the room hot at a temperature at which we would consider the tea or coffee cold. In the Saussurean sense, *warm* and *cool* have a signification only in relation to *hot* and *cold*, to each other, and to such terms as *piping hot*, *tepid*, *lukewarm*, *warmish* , or *coolish*. Without a culturally accepted relationship among these terms, they have no definable meanings in and of themselves. Their meanings derive essentially from their relationships and associations.

Cognitive psychologists share this linguistic viewpoint. In the structure of memory, say Collins and Quillian, "a concept [is] a set of relationships among other concepts, not a primitive absolute....Everything is defined in terms of everything else" (1972:313-4). Darkness is absence of light; without the existence of light, there would be no concept of darkness. What is twilight, for instance? Is it between light and the absence of light, or "between the swallow and the bat," as one language puts it. Since concepts have no primitive term, no one absolute meaning, when may we call an object a cup and not a mug, a beaker, or a tumbler? When is a stone a stone and not a piece of grit, a pebble, a rock, or a boulder. Without the concepts of "pebble" and "rock" we would not be able to define *stone*. Concepts are elusive and elastic, while words are definite and delimited, so the fit is difficult. Yet it is through words that concepts find expression in language use. Concepts straddle words; words straddle concepts and develop new meanings as they enter into different combinations and relationships. It is by using cups and beakers and mugs, by emptying our shoes of small pebbles, throwing stones, tripping over rocks, and climbing over boulders that we learn these concepts and understand their meanings in context. It is through such experiences that we learn to use words appropriately in our first language. If this is a lengthy process in our own language, how much more is it compounded by the shifting concepts behind the words of another language! Then, to muddy the waters further, idiom and metaphor enter the picture. (This may not be your cup of tea, and you may consider that I am making mountains out of molehills.) No wonder learning to use a language is a lengthy and effortful process.

Concepts find realizations in the words of a language (in this extended sense), and concepts, combining to form complex meanings, direct the behavior of words. Concepts enter into the skins of words and push, shove, and pull them into combinations and associations to meet their purposes in the expression of meaning. It is through concepts similar to those intended, aroused in our minds, that we as listeners extract meaning from the combinations and permutations that we hear. Even then we can never be sure that the meaning we are creating is a perfect match. Nevertheless, this process makes communication of meaning sound at least possible, until context steps in.

Context is the broadest term of all. It can be linguistic, physical, or perceptual (including the individual perception of the physical or the linguistic); it can be social or psychological. The psychological context brings with it the effects of expectations, emotions, and attention focus or distraction related to personal intentions, wants, needs, fears, and even ego involvement, often resulting in the extraction of a message the listener wanted to hear, rather than the one the speaker wished to convey.

Concepts can find expression in words, but without context they are trapped, as it were, in sealed units or black boxes.

Hymes has pointed out that language users are not abstract isolated individuals, almost unmotivated cognitive mechanisms, as some linguists, teachers, and materials writers seem to see them, but they are persons in a social world who need to be able to communicate (1979:8). To be able to communicate in a social world the student, quite obviously, must learn to communicate in a social world, not in a sterile test tube. So all learning of languages, second as well as first languages, must take place in a meaningful context.

Terrell in his Natural Approach always recognized the importance of vocabulary and of learning vocabulary in a comprehensible context. In "A Natural Approach to Second Language Acquisition and Learning," he says: "The learning of vocabulary is the key to comprehension and speech production. With a large enough vocabulary the student(s) can comprehend and speak a great deal of L2 even if (their) knowledge of structure is for all practical purposes non-existent" (1977:333). He quotes Bolinger as saying that anyone who has mastered a foreign language knows well that a great deal of the time is spent mastering the lexicon of that language—"the most important thing is to get the words in" (1970:78). According to Terrell, the students' first task is to learn a large number of common words, so that they can understand what the teacher is saying to them. This view is also that of Lozanov, who has found that students can learn 2,000 words during a 24-day period in an intensive learning situation (1978: 321-2); in an American college setting, Terrell found the recognition of 25 words a day (500 in a four-week period) a realistic goal that students could realize without undue difficulty (1977:333), these words being learned always in comprehensible contexts.

Words apart from situations (physical or psychological), then, are mere formulas, and language becomes more like algebra, of a kind that is the delight of the abstract linguist. For the general run of humanity, language is fleshed out with meaningful words: rich words, trite words, cliches, metaphorical expressions, or idioms. Language teachers have long known this fact and have tried in many ways to help students learn vocabulary. This process has never been easy, because vocabulary cannot be inculcated. It can only be learned by individuals, who absorb it into their cognitive systems (their semantic networks), because it seems to have some use or because it has a certain beauty or whimsicality that appeals to the learner.

Halliday's concept of *meaning potential* encapsulates this view of concepts and words. Halliday speaks of "sets of options, or alternatives in meaning [that is, choices] available to the speaker-hearer" in the context of a situation that is culturally determined (1973:72). He emphasizes the dependence of the meaning of each word for the individual upon practical experience, and of the structure of each utterance upon the momentary situation in which it is spoken. For Halliday, context refers to the inner as well as the outer context—the outer context being the observable features of the situation, while the inner context, linguistic and emotional, is strongly influenced by the attitudes and values that the speaker-hearer has derived from the cultural environment.

In a new language, then, we need practice in making choices if we are to develop an extensive vocabulary that will enable us to express our meaning to the fullest. We need to acquire words for concepts through practical experience in culturally appropriate situations in which we feel involved. In this sense each student's vocabulary is an individual achievement and a personal possession, which can be neither used by another nor taken away from its possessor. It can be lost temporarily, only to be retrieved inexplicably through very personal associations, as with material that disappears from the computer screen only to turn up again at the most unexpected moment. Or it can become irretrievable in some more permanent fashion in ways we do not yet understand.

Let us examine for a moment the psychological mechanisms that account for the extraordinary ability we possess to expand our means of expression daily, hourly, minute by minute.

The *first R* of vocabulary use is *recognition*. Learners of another language must perceive a particular group of sounds (or graphic symbols) as representing a specific meaning or set of meanings for the speakers of that language. Having perceived this fact, they must recognize a further occurrence of this form, in slightly varying pronunciation or graphic shape, as a recurrence of the same meaning token—a process of pattern matching. They must then store or *retain* this form (the *second R*), indexed in a way that will make it *retrievable* (the *third R*) for comprehension of spoken and written output and, in most cases, for later use in conveying their own meanings—a process of pattern completion (Kintsch 1972).

◼ RECOGNITION

Recognition of the meanings carried by phonological (or graphic) segments of another language is not automatic or obvious. When a word is just a vague sound or a shape, like many other shapes, to be remembered mechanically, there are very few features that can be stored as triggers for future recognition or recall. Language learners need something more than this to latch on to, to help them with organization of words for storage along with other compatible associations in memory, and to facilitate access when the word is re-encountered or needed for production. Ullman (1962) speaks of three forms of transparency that help students to organize new words for later recognition:

   a. *Morphological transparency*, or use of what one knows of word-forms in order to associate new words with old (e.g., *head/ache, finger painting; un/deni/able*). Students need to be taught to build up meanings from what they can recognize in the segments. This may be misleading out of context, but a context soon reveals weaknesses in the hypotheses the students are proposing, while making the real meaning, when it is discovered, more transparent.

b. *Phonological transparency* (the *toot* of the horn, the *yapping* of the dogs), onomatopeias which, as stated earlier, may not always be transparent across languages.

c. *Semantic transparency,* which helps with metaphorical expressions (e.g., *coat* of paint, flower *bed, glass ceiling*).

To these may be added the *translation transparency* of cognate words and the modern industrial and cultural international vocabulary that is sweeping the world, as with *jet, jazz, jeans, stress, information, pollution* (see also Chapter 9 in Rivers 1983). Each of these forms of transparency helps students to infer meanings of many unfamiliar words.

Laufer (1989) reminds us of the need to warn students of the dangers of *deceptive transparency:* misleading morphological structure (e.g., *shortcomings* interpreted as "short visits"); idioms whose meaning is not made transparent by the elements of which they are constructed (e.g., *you can't bank on it*); false friends, that is, cognates that look or sound familiar but actually diverge in meaning (French/English: *occasion*); words with multiple meanings of which the students are aware of only one (English *bow* or *figure*); and synforms, or words that are coincidentally similar in lexical form, sound, or morphology (*crack; sew/sow; undiluted/undulate*). Students must be aware of the degree of their ignorance, so that they can maintain a cautious approach to apparent transparencies, checking their insights first against context and the development of the discourse, having recourse to a dictionary only when the degree of frustration warrants it. The effort of figuring out meaning circulates the word through the cognitive system, thus increasing the probability of its being retained.

Awareness of the mechanisms of word formation in a new language provides the student with a vast area of what Palmberg (1989) calls *potential vocabulary,* and with growing confidence students can draw on this reservoir, while watching out for possible traps and pitfalls (the word *pitfall* being itself a semantically transparent word). In Haastrup's investigations in Denmark, the low English proficiency group (L) tended to draw inferences about the whole word from the context, while the high English proficiency group (H) looked for linguistic cues within the word to fill out the meaning that inference from context left imprecise. For example, in working out the meaning of "*insatiable* political ambitions," the L group decided *insatiable* meant "great," while the H group, delving into the form of the word, came up with "not to be satisfied" (Haastrup 1989:38).

Students can be encouraged to use such procedures as *topping and tailing* (cutting off prefixes and suffixes to find the nucleus of the word, so that each unfamiliar-looking word is not considered to be an impenetrable new experience); *dissolving compounds* (seeking meaning from the combined meanings of the segments, thus making expressions like *fail-safe* and *child-proof* more transparent); *penetrating disguises* (applying regular phonological or orthographic transformations to words in the new language in order to detect hidden cognates, as in such words in Spanish as *seguridad* 'se<u>curity</u>'; *fisica* '<u>ph</u>ysics', *fotografia* '<u>photograph</u>'). Techniques like these reduce the information load for storage in memory. In reverse, students can be challenged to make up *possible words* of the language applying these transformations; this may occasionally produce non-existent words, but ones that sound perfectly English, Spanish, German, or French. For example, *glass shatterer* may not exist as an occupational term in English dictionaries, but it is a possible one (conforming to the rules of word formation) for a demonstrator who takes out his or her frustrations on public buildings. In these ways, we exploit potential vocabulary and make it actual, while giving the students a "feel" for the language that will certainly help them when caught in a communicative situation where they need a word they have not so far encountered.

Essential to all autonomous language learning for use is the inductive process of *inferencing*. According to cognitive psychologists, we possess a semantic memory in the form of complex networks in which conceptual nodes (not verbal nodes) are linked by inferential relations that draw on redundancies within concepts. Thus there are innumerable directions in which these networks can take off. Perhaps *gatepost* does not link in your mind with *pouring rain* and *money in the pocket,* but it does for me, because one very dark night in pouring rain I forgot that my drive gate was closed, ran into a gatepost, and collected accident insurance. Our personal networks are as distinctly individual as this.

Note that the nodes in semantic networks are conceptual, not language-specific. In 1985, when I was learning Spanish in Chile, I one day found myself, while traveling with a Spanish-speaking group, producing for a straightforward concept of opposition the conglomeration *mais aber sed pero.* I had reached the conceptual node for *but* and retrieved several associated words in different languages—French (in which I am very fluent), German (of which I have elementary knowledge), and Latin (which I thought I had forgotten)—before connecting with the sought-after Spanish word *pero* (Rivers 1981:510).

Words of a new language become linked in all kinds of ways with the interconnections of the conceptual networks and proceed to draw on the redundancies within established concepts and on the inferential relations among these; in other words, we draw on our knowledge of the world, which is expanded and enriched by the cultural notions of the new language. As words and expressions are absorbed into the organizational structure, they become usable. For effective use, however, the forms of the new language must be linked up with their own culture-specific inferences, which are created through experiences with the language within the culture, either in actuality or vicariously through authentic print and video materials or contacts with native speakers in the area. We must come to know the limitations, expansions, and cross-associations of meanings in the new language in relation to apparently similar meanings of words and expressions in our first language. For this we need to experience the new expressions in a culturally and linguistically rich context. Language learning must be through purposeful use in culturally probable ways. According to Jenkins, "The mind remembers what the mind *does,* not what the world does" (1973:170). Vocabulary acquisition, like all aspects of language acquisition, is a dynamic process within a constantly active mind.

■ RETENTION

Time was when memory was regarded as a locatable storage space, a series of bins (short-term and intermediate stores, now more likely to be called "working memory"), through which selected items passed on their way to long-term storage. More recent models of memory are notably dynamic and process oriented. Memory is now viewed as a process, whereby knowledge (factual and experience-derived) enters into networks with a multiplicity of interconnected nodes (like the neurons in the nervous system). The nodes are conceptual and the interconnecting networks are relational, as noted above. Entering information activates nodes, which activate nodes on nodes, so that processing of the information is effected by many processes occurring at the same time, that is, in parallel. Anything one encounters, and selectively or peripherally perceives, enters the networks and is immediately bounced around, compared, discriminated, matched, linked up in the networks with information related to it in a multiplicity of obvious and unexpected ways, to serve some purpose eventually along with all the other elements operating in parallel for a more detailed description, see Hinton and Anderson 1989). Consequently, memories come to us in many unexpected ways and through a variety of sensory stimuli. As Rumelhart and Norman have expressed it, "Information is better thought of as 'evoked' than 'found' (1869:12).

Memory retention is facilitated by *chunking* information, that is, by grouping items according to some common feature or semantic link. Alliteration, for instance, links words beginning with a particular sound, so that "stinking, smoking stack" is easier to retain in memory than "malodorous, black-belching factory chimney." Vocabulary, it has been found, is learned more easily when there is some collocational link among items: for example, "castles, manors, and cottages" links different types of dwellings. Similarly, the mind *organizes* material for storage: "the beautiful roses in the garden" is easier to remember than six disparate, unconnected words. Where words have no obvious relationship, we inevitably create a mental organization or semantic link to draw them together. Consequently, words learned in a short context are much more memorable. Visual images also organize material for recall: Roman orators, it seems, remembered the order of points in their speeches by picturing their passage through different rooms in a house and associating various points they wished to make with the sequence of rooms. (Many interesting examples of visual memory are recounted in Luria 1968.) The more we know about the way memory works, the more we can help students improve their learning strategies.

In recent years interest has revived in long-practiced techniques of *mnemonics* to help students remember unfamiliar words by developing all kinds of links in their memory networks. Some learners are visually oriented and will create visual images that they associate with the new word—images that in some way relate to the meaning of the word; the author, like many others, has found this useful for remembering Chinese and Japanese characters, for instance. Others prefer to associate sound images, sometimes associating the new word with a sound image from the native language and a visual image that recalls the meaning of the new word (the Spanish *jefe*,

for instance, might be associated with *heavy* and a visual image of a physically imposing leader, and *falda* might be associated with the *folds* in a skirt). This has been
called the *keyword technique* and is discussed in more detail by Nation (1990:166-8).
Other techniques are humorous or gestural associations; association with a word in a
third language; learning the unfamiliar word in association with a familiar word of the
new language (*una falda negra*); or associating the word with a musical intonation
pattern, sometimes grouping several semantically related words (we all remember
words we learned in songs, particularly refrains, or in rhythmic chants). Terrell
describes a number of associational techniques that lead to binding of vocabulary.
"Binding," he says, "is complete when the form evokes the meaning without delay
and the form finally 'sounds like what it means'" (1986:214).

Because our associational networks in memory are very personal and individual,
students, with encouragement and a few examples, will soon develop their own techniques, which will work much better for them just because they are their own. For
amusement, they may share these with their fellow students in the early stages.
However they go about it, students need to develop ways of relieving the load on memory of great numbers of unfamiliar and confusing items. Through trying out approaches like these, they will soon realize that simple rote memorization is ineffectual.

There is a strong affective element in what we will select and retain in memory.
Learners will seek the meaning of words that are important to them in texts that interest them, and this involvement and attention focus facilitate retention. Since learners
show a marked predilection for their own personally selected vocabularies, they
should be encouraged to gather their own treasures from their reading and communicative activities. This they will do if given some real choice in areas about which
they are to read or converse. They should also be given many opportunities to introduce into their learning activities in speech and writing these personally culled vocabularies. Since rehearsal or recirculation in different contexts of material stored in
memory helps strengthen associational links, games, word puzzles, and other activities
that evoke these associations and encourage students to use vocabulary previously
encountered are valuable. Here, students can shine by demonstrating aspects of their
personal vocabularies, and this is motivationally stimulating. Some provision should
be made in tests for students to display vocabulary they have personally collected.

 ## RETRIEVAL

According to recent theorists, because of the interrelationships of the semantic networks, items of knowledge and memory traces of events are not localized but *distributed throughout the system*. Rather than our being able to retrieve them from one node
or spot in long-term storage, through a few cues or triggers, memory traces can be
accessed anywhere in the system through the multitude of different connections firing
simultaneously; for this reason this approach to memory is called *parallel distributed
processing*, or PDP[2]. It is the many relationships that make this possible.
Consequently, memories come to us in many unexpected ways and through a variety
of sensory stimuli. This approach tallies with common experience, where we are fre-

quently bombarded with activated memories, perhaps on encountering a particular scent or taste (as with Proust's famous *madeleine*), or in searching for a word or the name of a person or place.

With this approach to memory, accessibility becomes the keyword as basic to retrieval. Schouten-van Parreren observes that often "when the memory of a word is 'forgotten', it has not disappeared from memory, but it simply cannot be retrieved" (1989:77–78). She reports on an experiment on retention of unfamiliar vocabulary acquired from reading of different types of material in different languages at various levels of difficulty. Through think-aloud protocols, she discovered that students used many different access roads to retrieve word meanings. She mentions the following strategies: (1) drawing on recollections of the situation in which a word had occurred in the text; (2) recalling images that formed in the student's mind during the reading process; (3) recalling the literal word group or sentence in which the word occurred or the position of the word in the text, (4) recollection of the fact that the word had occurred more than once in the text or (5) that a word with the same root had also appeared; (6) thinking back to the emotions or experiences that the word or text had evoked while they were reading, such as experiencing the word as "funny" or "strange," or feeling proud about a correct guess or stupid when having to look the same word up twice. These reactions are very illustrative of the many ways in which the mind absorbs cues or triggers for retrieval, and they support the use in classroom learning of as many different approaches through different modalities as possible, thus allowing for the great diversity of learning styles and personal strategies gathered together in any one class. In this way, we ensure more accessibility for retrieval for more students than by imposing one way of learning on all.

Parallel distributed processing theory throws light also on the observed fact that speakers of several languages acquire a new vocabulary more easily than monolinguals and frequently produce in communication a word or expression from another language they know that seems to convey more appropriately a semantic nuance or a relationship—hence the mixing of languages that occurs when two or three speakers are equally bilingual. It also explains the word blocks speakers sometimes experience in their native language after a period of immersion in a second language, when the only word or expression that comes to mind is the way the second language encodes the concept. Syntactic structures also convey meanings: having learned to operate within the syntactic systems of several languages seems to facilitate operation within yet another system for expressing propositional relations, time, aspect, comparison, actual and hypothetical occurrences, and so on. Parallel distributed processing further illuminates the "tip of the tongue phenomenon" (Brown 1970:274-301), when we seek for a name or a word in another language and come up with candidate words that are related phonologically, in what seem like extraordinary nonsequiturs (e.g., *hula hoop, hooligan, Mulligan, Goolagong*); or when we replace words when reading aloud with synonyms of quite a different perceptual shape (reading, for instance, "storm" when the word in the text is *tempest*). It also provides a psychological explanation of how it is possible to translate from one language to another and to recognize the untranslatable (Rheingold 1988). It illustrates the way we find approximations in the second language to the meanings conveyed by the first when parallel terms do not exist; this process of paraphrasing and circumlocuting is a very useful one, for which the second-language learner should have much practice. Finally, it provides a plausible explanation for the speed with which simultaneous interpreters can perform their task.

In brief, then, vocabulary cannot be taught; it is learned by motivated individuals, in individual ways, to satisfy individual interests and needs. Imaginative teaching arouses this motivation. Even in the native language many people become fascinated with words, word puzzles, the use of fancy words. Learners will commit words and expressions to memory and retrieve them in very individual and idiosyncratic ways. The important thing is not how they are recalled, but their actual retrieval for active use in expressing personal meanings. For this, language learners need many opportunities to use their own resources in innovative ways. An interactive, participatory class encourages and rewards such creativity.

Notes

1. W. Shakespeare, *Romeo and Juliet* II.ii.43.
2. For further discussion of parallel distributed processing (PDP), see Rivers 1990.

References

Bolinger, D. 1970. Getting the Words In. *American Speech* 45:78-84.

Brown, R. 1970. *Psycholinguistics* . New York: Free Press/Macmillan.

Collins, A. M., and M. R. Quillian. 1972. How to Make a Language User. In *Organization of Memory*, ed. E. Tulving and W. Donaldson. New York: Academic Press.

Haastrup, K. 1989. The Learner as Word Processor. *AILA Review* 6:34-46.

Halliday, M.A.K. 1973. *Explorations in the Functions of Language*. London: Edward Arnold.

Hinton, G. E., and J. A. Anderson, eds. 1989. *Parallel Models of Associative Memory*. Updated ed. Hillsdale, N.J.: LEA.

Hymes, D. H. 1979. On Communicative Competence. In *The Communicative Approach to Language Teaching*, ed. C. J. Brumfit and K. Johnson. Oxford University Press.

Jenkins, J. A. 1973. Language and Memory. In *Communication, Language, and Meaning*, ed. G. A. Miller. New York: Basic Books.

Kintsch, W. 1972. Notes on the Structure of Semantic Memory. In *Organization of Memory*, ed. E. Tulving and W. Donaldson. New York: Academic Press.

Laufer, B. 1989. A Factor of Difficulty in Vocabulary Learning: Deceptive Transparency. *AILA Review* 6: 10-20.

Lozanov, G. 1978. *Suggestology and Outlines of Suggestopedy*. New York: Gordon and Breach.

Luria, A. 1968. *The Mind of a Mnemonist: A Little Book about a Vast Memory*. New York: Basic Books.

Nation, I.S.P. 1990. *Teaching and Learning Vocabulary*. New York: Newbury House/ Harper and Row.

Nattinger, J. 1988. Some Current Trends in Vocabulary Teaching. In *Vocabulary and Language Teaching*, ed. R. Carter and M. McCarthy, 62–82. New York: Longman.

Palmberg, R. 1989. What Makes a Word English? Swedish Speaking Learners' Feeling of "Englishness." *AILA Review* 6: 47-55.

Rheingold, H. 1988. *They Have a Word for It: A Lighthearted Lexicon of Untranslatable Words and Phrases*. Los Angeles: J. P. Tarcher.

Rivers, W. M. 1981. *Teaching Foreign-Language Skills*. 2d ed. Chicago: University of Chicago Press.

———. 1983. *Communicating Naturally in a Second Language: Theory and Practice in Language Teaching*. Cambridge: Cambridge University Press.

———. 1990. Mental Representations and Language in Action. In *Linguistics, Language Teaching, and Language Acquisition: The Interdependence of Theory, Practice, and Research*, ed. J. A. Alatis, 48–63. Washington, D.C.: Georgetown University Roundtable. Reprinted in *Canadian Modern Language Review* 47 (1991):1-16.

Rumelhart, D. E., and D. A. Norman, 1989. Introduction. In Hinton and Anderson, eds. (1989), 15-21.

Saussure, F. de. 1959. *Course in General Linguistics*. Ed. C. Bally and A. Sechehaye, trans. W. Baskin. New York: Philosophical Library.

Schouten-van Parreren, C. 1989. Vocabulary Learning through Reading: Which Conditions Should Be Met When Presenting Words in Texts? *AILA Review* 6: 75-85.

Terrell, T. D . 1977. A Natural Approach to Second Language Acquisition and Learning. *Modern Language Journal* 61: 325-37.

———. 1986. Acquisition in the Natural Approach: The Binding/Access Framework. *Modern Language Journal* 70:213-27.

Ullman, S. 1962. *Semantics: An Introduction to the Science of Meaning*. New York: Barnes and Noble.

SPANISH LANGUAGE STUDIES

Language study was at the very center of Tracy Terrell's life. Starting with Latin, he went on to learn Spanish, French, German, Italian, Dutch, and many others. But Spanish was always the second language closest to his heart, and he spoke it, taught it, and researched it all his life. The papers in Part 3 represent the two areas on which Terrell's research was focused: (a) the sociolinguistics of Spanish pronunciation and (b) topics in Spanish grammar.

SOCIOLINGUISTICS

racy Terrell's work in the area of Spanish sociolinguistics was a milestone in research devoted to Spanish language variation. He was strongly influenced by Labov's analyses of American English dialects, in which specific language groups were identified through a precise characterization of phonemic variables. Specific features of vowels, for example, were linked by Labov to particular groups of speakers in New York and other cities. In a similar way, Terrell identified the degree of aspiration of /s/ as crucial to social differentiation in Caribbean Spanish, with his main goal being the definition of those variables determining social stratification in Cuban and Puerto Rican Spanish. He found that three significant variables (preservation of /s/, aspiration /h/, and deletion /Ø/) were directly associated with particular speech groups, and these findings subsequently enabled him to extend his analysis to Argentinean and Dominican Spanish.

It is not surprising that Terrell's work was well accepted by Hispanic linguists: the long tradition of Spanish dialectical studies made the Hispanist a natural reader of his reports and articles. Furthermore, the precision of his research and analysis had a strong influence in the development of Spanish linguistics. One of Terrell's seminal studies of Caribbean Spanish (1977) appears as the first paper in this section. It reflects two aspects of his work that were to remain significant throughout his career: illuminating findings coupled with a rigorous methodology in delimiting norms of language varieties. The remaining papers in this section represent the areas in which Terrell's research in sociolinguistics has been highly influential: language variation, historical linguistics, and social stratification.

Two of the papers reflect Terrell's own interest in studying the phoneme /s/. In their study of the youth of Madrid, Mark Turnham and Barbara Lafford address a problem of social stratification based on phonemic variation, in this case the velarization of /s/ before a velar phoneme /k/. They offer systematic confirmation of general sociolinguistic correlations between the use of a phonemic variable and social class, sex, and level of formality. Giorgio Perissinotto's paper is a study of the sibilant system of sixteenth-century Spanish. Based on orthographic contrast between the stability of most graphic forms and the variation of *s, ss, z, and ç* as found in a text from Mexico, the author concludes that by the end of the century the sibilant system in New Spain was clearly becoming a *seseoso* system very similar to that found in contemporary Spanish.

Joseph Matluck's contribution addresses another classical problem of Spanish language variation, namely the resolution of hiatus (two contiguous vowels in separate syllables) in current Spanish. The author finds a strong tendency to resolve hiatus into diphthongs, even in contexts where a hiatus should be preserved. ➤

Because such resolution is performed in different ways in distinct socioeconomic groups, it becomes critical evidence for social stratification. We note here that, as Tracy Terrell's graduate school mentor, Matluck provided a model of rigor in analysis and argumentation, as demonstrated so clearly in this paper.

The final paper, by Carmen Silva-Corvalán and Manuel Gutiérrez, presents a sociolinguistic problem in a syntax/morphology environment. Based on recordings of twenty Mexican-American speakers from three generations, their study shows that verbal clitics are rather impermeable to interlinguistic influence in a bilingual situation. The low frequency of clitic omissions and other features supports the authors' claims.

Constraints on the Aspiration and Deletion of Final /s/ in Cuban and Puerto Rican Spanish

Tracy D. Terrell

There are three major dialects of Spanish spoken and learned natively by American citizens. We may refer to them conveniently by the names of the countries of origin of the speakers of their ancestors: Mexican, Puerto Rican, and Cuban. These are the Spanish "accents" most often heard in the United States and the varieties of Spanish our students—native speakers or Anglos—will most often encounter. Although there has been a substantial amount of research and study of the varieties of "Chicano" Spanish, very little has been done on Puerto Rican and Cuban varieties.[1] In addition the "standard" Latin-American pronunciation taught in most schools in the United States, although almost identical to "Chicano" or Mexican Spanish, is quite different from Puerto Rican and Cuban styles.

Problems arise principally in two situations. Anglo students, mostly in the Eastern areas of the United States, who have learned standard Latin American pronunciation, often have difficulties comprehending Cubans and Puerto Ricans. Frequently their reaction, often unspoken, is that Puerto Rican or Cuban pronunciation is somehow sub-standard or inferior and therefore the lack of comprehension is the fault of the native speakers themselves and not the students or the school system. In addition, native speakers of these dialects often encounter teachers of Spanish who, perhaps unintentionally, imply that Puerto Rican or Cuban pronunciation is not as acceptable as the standard. In both cases, these sorts of problems can arise because teachers do not understand the phonological system of Cubans and Puerto Ricans. This is not surprising since native speakers themselves are normally unaware of their phonological systems. Even linguists have been in part unaware of the phono-

Reprinted from *The Bilingual Review/La Revista Bilingüe*, Vol. 4(1,2):35–51, by permission of Bilingual Press/Editorial Bilingüe (Arizona State University, Tempe, Arizona).

logical systems of Cuban and Puerto Rican speech; thus one cannot really blame the teacher for his or her ignorance in this matter.[2]

The phenomenon known to linguists as aspiration of /s/ and in common language as *comerse la ese*, is one of the most complicated, and unfortunately, least understood, of the phonological features of any variety of Spanish. The facts are simple from a phonemic point of view: syllable final (*este*) and word final (*niños*) /s/ may be rendered as a simple sibilant [s], as a weak or strong aspiration [h], or simply deleted, Ø. I will use the following classification of the possible phonetic realizations of syllable- and word-final /s/.

Phoneme	Symbol	Phonetic Realization		
	S	s	z	s^z
/s/	h	h	ĥ	h^s -CC-
	Ø	Ø		

Examples: *costo* [koh^s to], [kotto], [kohto], [koto]
　　　　　　mismo [mis^z mo], [mizmo], [mihmo], [mim mo], [mihmo], [mi mo]
　　　　　　los tres [loh tre]

The distribution of these phonetic variants is determined by context. The voiced or partially voiced phones [s^z], [z], [ĥ], are present only if /s/ precedes a voiced segment as in *mismo, desde, los niños*, and so forth. The assibilated aspiration, [h^s], is common before dental obstruents, as in *este, costo, los dos*, and so forth. Gemination occurs frequently in syllable final position, *desde* [ded-de], *español* [ep-pañol], as does glottal stop, *esconder* [ekonder].[3]

These phonetic variants are difficult to distinguish systematically. More important is the fact that their use is relatively unimportant with respect to the phonological system itself. By positing [s], [h], and Ø as the principal allophones, I claim that there are two major phonological processes which operate in Cuban and Puerto Rican Spanish: aspiration and deletion. If neither rule applies, the sibilant will be retained: *niño*[s]. If aspiration applies the result will be some phonetic manifestation of /s/ : *niño*[h]. If deletion applies the /s/ is completely absent: *niño*Ø. In this latter case there is the possibility of the creation of homonyms:[4]

los - lo	[lo]
niños - niño	[niño]
tienes - tiene	[tjene]
nos - no	[no]
les - le	[le]

The greatest problem presented by the Cuban and Puerto Rican systems is this inherent variability of certain phonemes, the /s/ being perhaps the most noticeable.[5] Recent advances in linguistic theory, primarily stemming from the studies of William Labov on phonological variability, permit us to systemize what in structural phonemic theory was called "free" variation. (See Labov 1972, and Cedergren 1973.) Thus, with Cuban/Puerto Rican word-final /s/, it has often been said that for a word like *niños*, the forms *niño*[s], *niño*[h], or *niño* were interchangeable. Labov's contribution was to show that this variation, or interchangeability, is restricted systematically by factors which he termed "constraints," that is, factors which influence the speaker's choice between possible forms in any specific context. These constraints may be linguistic, i.e., phonological context such as prevocalic position, preconsonantal position, etc., or extralinguistic, i.e., age, sex, socioeconomic level of speaker, style, and speed of speech. These factors may interact in very complicated patterns to produce the resulting forms of a given speech situation. In this paper we will examine the system of constraints which influence the speaker's use of [s], [h], or Ø for a word- and syllable-final /s/ in Puerto Rican and Cuban Spanish, in the hope that this information will be of use to teachers of Spanish in areas in which these varieties of Spanish are spoken.[6]

 ## GENERAL CONSIDERATIONS

We may formalize the process of aspiration as s → h and deletion such as h → Ø. In this way we may speak of separate and possibly different constraints on aspiration and deletion. If we encounter a form such as *libro[h]*, we will say that "aspiration" has applied. If the form is *lo[h] libro*, we will say that "deletion" has applied to the final /s/.[7]

Extralinguistic Constraints

There are no detailed studies of either Cuban or Puerto Rican Spanish in which extralinguistic constraints are systematically investigated. However, there is information from several sources that, contrary to popular beliefs, the aspiration and deletion of /s/ are affected very little by most extralinguistic considerations.[8] There is some evidence that the use of aspiration and especially deletion is favored more by males, the younger generations, and lower socio-economic classes.[9] However, the differences do not appear to be great and certainly not of such a magnitude to be of great importance to us as teachers or students. In fact, it is more important to realize that neither process appears to be stigmatized and both are used by all social classes and on almost all occasions. Thus, these processes are a part of the "standard" cultured speech of educated Cubans and Puerto Ricans as well as those of other socioeconomic levels; aspiration and deletion are regular features of educated Cuban and Puerto Rican Spanish and are not a matter of "sloppy" pronunciation.[10]

 ## PHONOLOGICAL, GRAMMATICAL, AND LEXICAL CONSTRAINTS

1. Word Internal (*desde*)

The total distribution of major phone types for word internal position appears in Table I.

Table I
Word Internal Position

	P.R.	Cuban
S	6%	3%
	(176)	(52)
h	89%	97%
	(2512)	(1658)
Ø	5%	0%
	(127)	(4)
N =	2817	1714

The /s/ in word internal position is almost categorically aspirated, but not deleted, by Puerto Ricans and Cubans alike. Thus, only in the most formal styles—reading, speeches, special emphasis, affected speech—will the /s/ be rendered anything other than [h] in words such as espero, esto, isla, desde, mismo.

2. Word Final (*niños*)

It is in word final position that the intricate interplay of phonological, grammatical, and lexical constraints is evident. The total distribution of phone types for word final position is given in Table II.

Table II
Total Phone Distribution

	P.R.	Cuban
S	20%	22%
h	51%	52%
Ø	29%	26%
N =	6677	6364

In words such as colores, sus actividades, la luz, además, lápiz, tienes, fuimos, ellos, etc., the /s/ is aspirated approximately one-half of the time. In one-fourth of the cases the sibilant is retained, and in another fourth the /s/ is completed deleted. The retention of [s], its aspiration, or its deletion is systematic for all Cuban and Puerto Rican speakers.[11]

These data are almost identical for Cubans and Puerto Ricans. In fact, considering that the two sets of interviews were carried out under diverse circumstances, were of varying lengths, and included different numbers of informants, the results indicate that, in general, the operation of the two phonological rules in Cuban and Puerto Rican varieties is identical and that both dialects are at the same stage of development with respect to the adoption and spread of these rules.

There appear to be four relevant phonological environments: (1) 90 before consonants, (2) before unstressed vowels, (3) before stressed vowels, (4) before a pause. The following examples will illustrate these contexts:

(1) before consonants

Los libros que les di son interesantes.

(2) before unstressed vowel

Las intenciones parecen difíciles de juzgar.

(3) before stressed vowels

Sus hijos eran los únicos.

(4) before pauses

Estarán listos...pero antes...tengo que lavarlos.

The overall data are displayed in Table III and Figure I.

Table III
Total Phone Distribution by Phonological Environment

	[S] P.R.	[S] CU	[h] P.R.	[h] CU	Ø P.R.	Ø CU	N P.R.	N CU
$\underline{\quad}$ C Pre-Consonant	4	2	69	75	27	23	3238	3276
$\underline{\quad}$ V̆ Pre-Unstressed Vowel	16	10	53	53	30	37	1320	1026
$\underline{\quad}$ V́ Pre-Stressed Vowel	45	48	32	28	23	25	326	278
$\underline{\quad}$ // Pre-Pause	46	61	22	13	32	26	1793	1784
TOTAL	20	22	51	52	29	26	6677	6364

The strongest constraint favoring retention of [s], rather than its aspiration or deletion

...en aquello[s]/lugare[s]/poblacionale[s]/ (P.R. #21 p. 1)

...a una serie de dama[s]/ (P.R. #13 p. 2)

...pasarán mucho[s] y mucho[s] año[s]/ (P.R. #13 p. 6)

...cuando se ha actuado sobre unos supe[h] to[s]/de una... (P.R. #19 p. 8)

...porque lo llevé a la inspección e[h]te me[s]/ (Cu. #13 p. 23)

...yo digo en pueblo[s]/ (Cu. #6 p. 1)

...cuando ya se sirve una/algo mas sustancioso algo ma[s]/ (Cu. #7 p. 18)

Figure I

Word-final by Phonological Environment

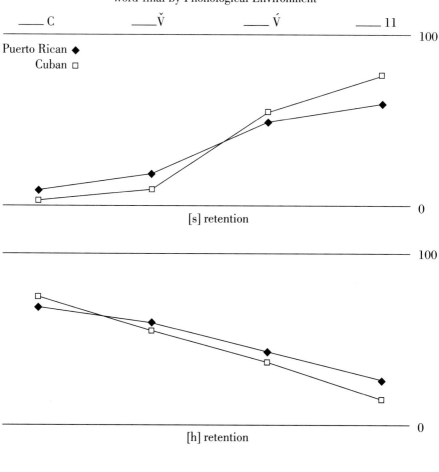

Puerto Rican ◆
Cuban □

[s] retention

[h] retention

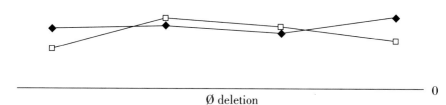

Ø deletion

Both aspiration, [h], and deletion are, of course, possible:

...de una serie de circunstancia [h]/ (P.R. #42 p. 1)

...lo[h] modalo[h] lo[h] patrone[s]/ (Cu. #2 p. 26)

On the other hand, preconsonantal position is very unfavorable for [s]. It only appeared in less than 5% of all occurrences for both Puerto Ricans and Cubans. Aspiration is clearly the norm, although complete deletion may occur, following rules to be discussed shortly. The following are examples:

...persona[h] como Dino Bussatti... (P.R. #22 p. 1)

...e[h] cue[h]tión de veinte añoØ / (P.R. #22 p. 1)

...por la[h] floreØ o de rayaØ depende en/ (Cu. #2 p. 26)

Prevocalic position favors retention of [s] only slightly, from about 10% to 20% of the time, if the following vowel is unstressed.

...de antiguo[h] techoØ y muroØ y... (P.R. #1 p. 1)

...a la [h] idea[h] pra[h]tica[h] de... (P.R. #24 p. 1)

...en lo[h] E[h]tado[s] UnidoØ/ (P.R. #23 p. 4)

...por la[h] mucha[h] lucha[h] internaØ insi[h]tenta[h] en Inglaterra/ (Cu. #3 p. 16)

In the case of a stressed vowel, the rate of [s] retention is quite high, almost one-half of the possible occurrences in both Cuban and Puerto Rican speech. However, we shall see that these totals are misleading because of a special interaction of grammatical and phonological constraints in this context.

...do[s] año[h] de france[h]. (P.R. #6 p. 4)

...todo[h] lo[s] años se enfermaba... (P.R. #5B p. 3)

...en varia[s] horaØ/ (Cu. #12 p. 3)

...do[h] eran... (P.R. #23 p. 2)

...mucho[h] dijeron...que se leØ hizo difícil... (P.R. #5 p. 3)

Deletion is somewhat more complex than aspiration (or [s] retention) and varies more between individuals, different social groups, and even between Cuban and Puerto Rican speech. However, these differences are not so great and we need not be overly concerned since in any case we are interested in general tendencies, not specific figures. The overall rate for both Cubans and Puerto Ricans is about one-fourth. Deletion does not appear to be especially affected by phonological environment. The deletion rate *is* affected greatly, however, by grammatical and lexical constraints which we will discuss in some detail.

Word-final /s/ in Spanish may function in several ways. It may be simply a part of a lexical item with no morpheme function, as in vez, más, entonces, pues, luz, lápiz, and so forth. This function will be termed lexical /s/. The /s/ phoneme also functions as a morpheme or a part of a morpheme in nouns, pronouns, adjectives, and verbs. In nouns, pronouns, and adjectives, the /s/ is normally the plural marker, niños, buenos, interesantes, les, ellos; in verbs it may be the second person singular, tienes, haces, estudias, a part of the first person plural morpheme -mos, hablamos, vinimos, hacíamos or an integral part of the form es, third person singular of ser.

It was shown in previous studies that the deletion of /s/ was governed primarily by functionalist considerations, such as the preservation of certain grammatical morphemes (Terrell 1975 i, j). We will examine each grammatical category in some detail to show how the constraints on aspiration and deletion interact to prevent the loss of information important to normal communication in Spanish.

The most important grammatical morpheme in Spanish for the normal continuation of the exchange of information which is represented by /s/ is the plural morpheme of the noun phrase. We will examine the data for adjective modifiers, nouns, and pronouns in that order. The retention rates of [s], i.e., non applications of aspiration or deletion, are given for noun modifiers in Table IV.

Examples of each of the categories are: 1. Los (e.g., los niños), 2. Las (e.g., las chicas), 3. Other First Modifiers (e.g., mis amigos), 4. First Modifiers (a summary of 1., 2., and 3., all essentially determiners), 5. Number Modifiers (e.g., dos, instituciones). This /s/ is not really a plural marker, but the data indicate that it is treated a determiner by Cuban and Puerto Rican speakers with regard to aspiration and deletion of the /s/ of these words (dos, tres, seis, diez). 6. Second Position Prenominal Modifier (e.g., los primeros hijos). Included are any other prenominal modifiers which are not in first position. 7. Post-nominal (e.g., Las escuelas primarias). Any adjective that follows the noun. 8. Predicate adjective (e.g., son interesantes), 9. Redundant plural marker (a composite of categories 6, 7, and 8). 10. Todos (e.g., the word todos in phrases such as todos los años in which los was still counted as a first modifier. Speakers tend to disregard the fact that todos is really in first position and treat the /s/ as a redundant plural marker). 11. The total for all types of adjectives. 12. The averages for the entire corpus.

The data indicate that [s] retention in preconsonantal, pre-unstressed vowel, and prepausal position is normal in all grammatical categories and does not deviate greatly from the phonological norm for the entire corpus. This is not the case if the modifier precedes a word beginning with a stressed vowel. In this latter case, the retention of [s] is practically obligatory for "first" position modifiers, and somewhat high for "second" position modifiers. In modifiers that follow the noun and in the term todos, there is for all practical purposes no [s] retention at all.

The data indicate that with regard to [s] retention before stressed vowels, modifiers are divided into two groups by native speakers unconsciously.

los	libros
Mis primeras	lecciones
(son)	interesantes
Todos aquellos	cuadros
Muchos otros	tipos sútiles

The corresponding data for pronouns is given in Table V.

The figures are highly variable in all contexts, due, perhaps, to the smaller number of cases. Some interesting trends do appear, however. The [s] of nosotros is retained as a sibilant only in prepausal position and even in this position the retention rate is much below normal. It can be no accident that it is precisely this /s/ which is completely redundant, since nosotro can only mean nosotros whereas in all the other forms there is a semantic contrast: nos-no, les-le, los-lo, ellos-ello, etc. In these cases the [s] retention follows normal phonological constraints except in pre-stressed

Table IV
Retention of [s] in Modifiers

		1 LOS	2 LAS	3 OTHER FIRST MOD	4 FIRST MOD	5 NUMB. MOD	6 SEC POS PRE	7 POST NOM	8 PRED ADJ	9 RE-DUND	10 TODOS	11 ADJ.	12 TOTAL CORPUS
TOTAL	Cu	13	13	16	14	28	13	31	33	30	4	19	22
	P.R.	15	12	16	14	19	10	21	33	22	7	17	20
—C	Cu	3	2	1	2	4	0	1	0	1	0	2	2
	P.R.	3	0	4	3	4	2	2	7	3	3	3	4
—V̌	Cu	18	35	16	20	5	14	9	6	7	50	17	10
	P.R.	21	8	8	12	4	5	8	8	7	0	10	16
—V́	Cu	88	86	90	88	96	40	0	0	17	0	76	48
	P.R.	83	83	81	83	95	80	0	0	40	7	73	45
—11	Cu	54	67	86	74	77	50	50	57	52	100	57	61
	P.R.	48	67	70	63	38	43	32	60	37	100	43	46

Table V. [s] Retention in Pronouns

		Nosotros	Nos	Ellos-as	Los-las-les	Total Corpus
Total	Cu	7	15	15	14	22
	P.R.	8	14	22	14	20
___ C	Cu	0	6	0	3	2
	P.R.	0	4	6	7	4
___ V̌	Cu	0	6	14	9	10
	P.R.	0	9	22	6	16
___ V́	Cu	0	40	25	80	48
	P.R.	0	22	0	0	45
___ 11	Cu	32	50	55	57	61
	P.R.	31	82	46	57	46
N =	Cu	121	66	60	122	
	P.R.	52	122	79	96	

vowel position. In this context there is more variability than in any other. The number of cases is limited: thirty-one for Puerto Rican and thirteen for Cuban. Even so it appears that Cubans treat the object pronouns: *los-las-les* as first position adjectives, i.e., determiners, in retaining the [s] almost categorically (8/10); on the other hand, the Puerto Ricans of this study did not (0/9 cases).

Table VI. [s] Retention in Pre-Vocalic Position

	Cu ___ V́	P.R. ___ V́	Cu ___ V̌	P.R. ___ V̌
Preceding Modifier	88%	84%	18%	11%
	(105/120)	(97/115)	(32/173)	(34/307)
Noun	7%	22%	9%	18%
	(3/43)	(9/41)	(23/265)	(61/334)
Verb	8%	33%	10%	20%
	(7/26)	(21/64)	(26/270)	(69/346)
Pro (los-las-les)	80%	0%	8%	6%
	(8/10)	(0/9)	(2/23)	(1/16)
Pro—Others	28%	9%	5%	14%
	(5/18)	(2/22)	(3/56)	(7/51)

At this point it is apparent that we must determine the limits of this complex interaction of stress, vowels, and grammatical categories. To this end, we compare in Table VI the [s] retention rates in pre-stressed vowel positions and pre-unstressed vowel positions.

Prevocalic position weakly conditions the retentions of [s]. However, it is clear that to conclude from the overall tabulation of the data in Table III that a stressed vowel in itself conditions the non-application of the rules of aspiration and deletion, would be incorrect. Stress plays a role only if the /s/ is final in a determiner or other prenominal modifier, or, in the case of Cubans, if it is the final /s/ of the object pronouns, *les, los, las*. In all other cases, the position of stress seems to play little or no role as a phonological constraint.

Let us now turn to an account of the constraints on deletion. The operation of deletion is extremely crucial from the standpoint of communication, since, as was pointed out, if this process operated freely, the result would be the obliteration of the plural morpheme in nouns, adjectives, and pronouns. For this reason we will examine first the grammatical constraints on the deletion of plural /s/ in some detail.

The rates of deletion for modified are displayed in Table VII.

The phonological environment appears to have little effect on the operation of deletion. The function of /s/ within the noun phrase, on the other hand, determines the rate of deletion. Deletion in categories 1–5, (i.e., modifiers in the first position) is very low in all phonological contexts. In categories 6–10, (i.e., categories in which the /s/ is a redundant plural morpheme) deletion is at least equal to and usually higher than the average rate for the entire corpus. In fact, if the category of "First position modifiers" is discounted, deletion rates rise to about 33% for the entire corpus in both Cuban and Puerto Rican Spanish. However, the redundant /s/ of adjectives is deleted at an even higher rate: 37% for Cubans and 46% for Puerto Ricans.

The following are typical examples of the output of these constants:

...lo[h] díaØ fe[h]tivoØ /(P.R. #23 p. 1)

...yo he tenido caso[h]/interesanteØ/ y difícile[h]/ (P.R. #42 p. 4)

...tampoco en toda[h] la[h] carreraØ profesionaleØ el inglé[h]... (P.R. #21 p.1)

...sí, la[h] carosaØ/ (Cu., #6 p. 26)

...o esa[h] boberíaØ de juventud... (Cu., #11 p. 15)

...mucha[h] personaØ que han sido invitadaØ aquí/ (Cu., #14 p. 6)

The data for nouns is found in Table VIII.

If the noun is unmodified, as in for example "un juego para niño*s*," deletion is suppressed (only 19% deletion vs. 39% for modified nouns). For Puerto Ricans this constraint operates but only weakly (35% vs. 44%). Some examples follow:

...fuera de hora[h] de clase... (P.R., #6 p. 14)

...para tirar bola[h] al cana[h]to... (P.R., #23 p. 1)

...el material educativo como cartelone[h]... (P.R., #33 p. 9)

...no dan resultado[s]/ (Cu., #4 p. 12)

...o cuando se hace autopsia[h]/ al tomar mue[h]tra[h]... (Cu., #4 p. 6)

Table VII
Rates of Deletion for Modifiers

		1 LOS	2 LAS	3 OTHER MODI-FIERS	4 FIRST MOD	5 NUMB. MOD	6 SEC POS PRE	7 POST NOM	8 PRED ADJ	9 RE-DUND	10 TODOS	11 ADJ	12 TOTAL CORPUS
TOTAL	Cu	1	1	5	3	9	18	40	36	37	7	12	26
	P.R.	8	11	15	11	13	28	51	44	46	37	23	29
—C	Cu	1	1	5	2	11	18	39	35	35	5	7	23
	P.R.	7	9	18	11	14	33	56	58	50	37	20	27
—V̌	Cu	0	0	9	3	16	14	64	56	55	50	18	37
	P.R.	9	23	13	13	16	15	53	54	45	67	22	30
—V́	Cu	0	0	0	0	0	0	60	50	33	9	4	25
	P.R.	6	4	7	5	0	0	75	0	30	33	11	23
—ll	Cu	31	8	10	15	6	50	36	32	35	0	30	26
	P.R.	12	7	5	7	14	43	49	31	45	0	36	32

Even cases of deletion, the plurality is usually available from context or special forms:

...la[s] hija[h] de mi esposo, que él tiene hijoØ de otro matrimonio/ (Cu., #11, p. 15)

...no hay dietaØ e[h]pecialeØ/(Cu., #2, p. 21)

...son llaveØ de cerradura... (Cu., #5 p. 22)

The data on deletions in pronouns is displayed in Table IX.

Deletion of the /s/ in *nosotros* is very high in all phonological contexts for both Cubans and Puerto Ricans, whereas deletion in other pronouns is in general lower. These differences, as in nouns and adjectives, correspond directly to the function of the /s/. In *nosotros* the final /s/ is completely redundant; in the other forms the loss of /s/ could create in certain contexts misunderstandings.

Table VIII. Deletion in Nouns

		Unmodified	Modified	Nouns	Total Corpus
Total	Cu	19	39	34	26
	P.R.	35	44	42	29
___ C	Cu	21	38	34	23
	P.R.	42	47	46	27
___ V̆	Cu	20	58	49	37
	P.R.	38	42	41	30
___ V́	Cu	67	43	47	25
	P.R.	30	42	39	23
___ 11	Cu	17	34	29	26
	P.R.	29	42	39	32
N =	Cu	486	1450	1936	6364
	P.R.	381	1559	1940	6678

...cuando nosotroØ tratamoØ de compar... (P. R., #33 p. 1)

...y naturalmente nosotroØ quisiéramoØ... (P. R., #21B p. 7)

...empezaron elloØ como empezamoØ nosotroØ/ (P. R., #24 p. 9)

...lo que nosotroØ allá llamamoØ comida es/ (Cu., #7 p. 18)

Table IX. Deletion in Pronouns

		Nosotros	Nos	Ellos-as	Los-las-les	Total Corpus
Total	Cu	85	18	8	27	26
	P.R.	56	16	23	30	29
___ C	Cu	96	15	0	32	23
	P.R.	58	9	13	28	27
___ V̆	Cu	91	24	29	26	37
	P.R.	80	30	39	44	30
___ V́	Cu	100	20	0	0	25
	P.R.	50	33	40	44	23
___ 11	Cu	54	17	9	14	32
	P.R.	46	9	21	14	32
N =	Cu	121	66	60	122	6364
	P.R.	52	122	79	96	6678

The /s/ of the pronoun *nos* is on the other hand infrequently deleted (Cuban 18%; Puerto Rican 16%):

    ...no[h] gu[h]ta ver... (P. R., #33 p. 3)
    ...no[h] han explicado, verdad... (P. R., #33 p. 9)
    ...nunca no[h] tuvo que decir... (P. R., #16 p. 6)

Even in cases of deletion the meaning is normally clear from context.

    ...do[h]de e[h]ta[s] obraØ / que noØ han llegado/ (P. R., #20 p. 17)

(The larger context of discourse makes it clear that the speaker could not have meant a negative sentence.)

Deletion in *ellos, los, las, les* is somewhat below one-third, but still rather frequent considering the possibility of morphological confusion: *ellos-ello; los-lo; las-la; les-le.* In context, however, the meaning even with deleted forms is normally clear.

    ...el otro, ello[h] no conciben por que... (P. R., #6 p. 8)
    ...comenzar a dirigirle[s] / (P. R., #6 p. 8)

Although the system of deletion is most important in the noun phrase, there are other fairly strong tendencies which should be noted. The data for verb forms are displayed in Table X. In verb forms both Cubans and Puerto Ricans differentiate between the /s/ of the first person plural morpheme /mos/ and the /s/ of the third person singular present indicative of *ser* (es). Speakers of both varieties avoid complete deletion of the /s/ of *es*; Cubans more so (only 4%) than Puerto Ricans (19%). The /s/ in /mos/ is freely deleted, however; Cubans more (66%) than Puerto Ricans (31%).

Table X. Deletion in Verb Forms

		es	tú -s	nosotros -mos	Total Verb	Total Corpus
Total	Cu	4	43	66	29	26
	P.R.	19	30	31	23	29
___ C	Cu	2	47	73	27	23
	P.R.	17	44	35	23	27
___ V̌	Cu	6	13	78	36	37
	P.R.	29	50	33	30	30
___ V́	Cu	0	0	75	46	25
	P.R.	13	0	39	20	23
___ 11	Cu	8	71	30	23	26
	P.R.	9	0	18	14	32
N =	Cu	542	30	367	939	
	P.R.	700	34	390	1124	

The /s/ of *tú* forms, such as *tú tienes*, does not appear to be treated in any special way, regardless of the fact that there is a theoretical possibility for confusion with the third person singular forms if the /s/ is totally deleted. I say "theoretical" because in actuality the confusion is rarely realized because of the context of discourse. The following are typical examples:

...vamoØ a suponer una campaña educativa... (P. R., #39 p. 9)
...donde vivíamoØ/ (P. R., #10 p. 1)
...Bien/pue[h] vamo[h] a/ decirte... (P. R., #10 p. 13)
...que nosotroØ le decíamØ sólo que... (Cu., #14 p. 22)
...mi vida e[s] ante[h] de... (P. R., #16 p. 6)
...me parece que e[h] una enorme pena que... (P. R., #37 p. 1)
...e[s] el má[h] grande pintor... (P. R., #13 p. 1)
...creo que e[h] la única... (Cu., #3 p. 16)
...e[s] una cigüeña/ (Cu., #5 p. 9)

In words in which the /s/ is not a morpheme but an integral part of the word, *luz, entonces, antes, después, lunes, análisis,* deletion as applied to the entire group is fairly normal (Cuban 30%; Puerto Rican 23%). However, there are some minor tendencies worth noting. The data are displayed in Table XI.

Table XI. Deletion of Lexical /s/

		MÁS	PROPER NAMES	PUES	OTHER LEXICAL	ENTON-CES	TOTAL LEXICAL /s/
Total	Cu	2	11	24	21	80	30
	P.R.	1	32	37	19	55	22
___ C	Cu	1	0	26	22	91	33
	P.R.	6	34	28	22	58	19
___ V̆	Cu	6	–	58	41	90	43
	P.R.	0	38	55	17	70	18
___ V́	Cu	0	–	57	47	92	60
	P.R.	0	17	53	44	33	30
___ 11	Cu	2	15	11	11	42	16
	P.R.	0	30	30	13	50	56
N =	Cu	239	18	112	482	244	1095
	P.R.	197	148	180	412	69	1006

The /s/ of *entonces* is usually deleted (Cuban 80%, Puerto Rican 55%). Cubans avoid deleting the /s/ of proper names (11%); Puerto Ricans do not (32%). Both groups avoid deleting the /s/ of *más* (Cuban 2%; Puerto Rican 1%). Other items are deleted following normal rates (about one-third).

> ...el género que má[s]/eh...que má[s]/ se pre[h]ta... (P. R., #22 p. 4)
> ...pue[h] e[h]tá pendiente de... (P. R., #5 p. 6)
> ...anteØ era un siglo... (P. R., #22 p. 1)
> ...era don Pablo Ruſ[s]/ (P. R., #13 p. 2)
> ...entonceØ e[s] una literatura... (P. R., #37 p. 3)
> ...y entonceØ de allí/ (Cu., #11 p. 1)
> ...la e[h]case[h] de hombre[h]... (Cu., #3 p. 20)

As we have seen the rule of /s/ deletion is governed primarily by complex grammatical and lexical constraints of a functional nature. Deletion applies at three rates: low (0–15%); medium (16–30%); high (30–90%). Word-final /s/ is classified in this way in Table XII.

Deletion is suppressed in (1) the essential plural marker of the noun phrase usually the first constituent and in (2) monosyllabic grammatical morphemes /nos/, /mas/ (comparative) and /es/. Deletion is high if the /s/ is completely redundant as in (1) redundantly plural nouns or adjectives and in (2) the pronoun *nosotros* and its corresponding verb form and in (3) polysyllabic *entonces*.

Table XII. Deletion of Word-Final /s/

	Cu	P.R.	
MÁS	1%	3%	
FIRST MOD	3%	11%	
#'s MOD	9%	13%	LOW DELETION
ES	4%	19%	
NOS	18%	6%	
ELLOS-AS	8%	23%	
LEXICAL	21%	19%	
PROPER NAMES	11%	32%	
UNMOD NOUNS	19%	35%	MODERATE DELETION
OBJ PRO —LOS-LAS-LES	27%	30%	
PUES	24%	37%	
VERB FORM TÚ	43%	30%	
MOD NOUNS	39%	44%	
RED ADJ	37%	46%	
VERB FORM NOSOTROS	66%	31%	HIGH DELETION
ENTONCES	80%	55%	
PRONOUN NOSOTROS	85%	56%	

CONCLUSIONS

(1) The variability of word-final /s/ in Cuban and Puerto Rican speech is systematic.

(2) The basic system followed by both Puerto Ricans and Cubans is in all essential respects the same.

(3) [s] retention is controlled, for the most part phonologically: it is retained most before a pause, less between a vowel and at least before a consonant.

(4) The [s] of phenominal modifiers is retained almost categorically before a stressed vowel.

(5) Deletion is governed mainly by grammatical categories.

(6) The /s/ is rarely deleted in first position nouns modifiers; it is frequently deleted in nouns, especially if they are modified, and in adjectives whose number indicator would be redundant.

(7) Deletion is rare with *es, más* and *nos.*

(8) The /s/ is often deleted in *nosotros,* the /mos/ forms, and the word *entonces.*

One would not of course advocate that such a complex system be taught to students; such a task may well be impossible in any case. Students who interact with speakers who use this system will normally learn it unconsciously, if they so desire.

The importance of this information for teachers and students lies in the development of a positive attitude toward different varieties of Spanish. However, the information in this article is only background; the teacher will decide, as always, on its usefulness in particular situations.

Notes

1. For Chicano Spanish see Bowen and Ornstein (1975) among many others. The only important works previous to the research of this author are Ibasescu's Cuban study (1968), Vallejo-Claros study of social and geographical variation for certain Cuban phonological phenomena (1970), Navarro Tomás famous study of the speech of illiterate Puerto Ricans published in 1948, but with data collected in 1928, and Ma and Herasimchuk's (1971) excellent study of stylistic variation in the speech of Puerto Rican immigrants in New York.

2. For example, even an eminent authority on Puerto Rican Spanish such as Rubén del Rosario (1970) thought that the [s] was restored "ocasionalmente, sin regla fija" (p. 82).

3. It is important for those comparing data to note that this classification of phonetic variants is different from Cedergren's classification for Panamanian Spanish (1973:41). Cedergren classifies germination and glottal stop with phonetic zero, i.e., as a possible output of the application of the Deletion rule. In the Cuban and Puerto Rican studies only the complete absence of any phonetic residue of /s/ was considered the result of deletion.

4. It is a widely held view that if the /s/ is totally deleted the preceding vowel is opened to preserve the singular-plural contrast. Thus, *niño* and *niños* would contrast as [niño] vs. [niño]. There is evidence that this is not the case for Cuban Spanish (Clegg 1968, and Hammond 1973) and there is no reason to believe that it is valid for Puerto Rican Spanish. See Terrell (1975a, 1975b, 1975c) and Hooper (1973) for discussion. It will be made apparent in later sections of this paper why no such vocalic contrast is necessary to preserve the singular-plural distinction.

5. Other important variables include word final /n/, which is velarized before vowels or pause in both Cuban and Puerto Rican varieties (Terrell 1975f) and word- and syllable-final /r/, to which a number of processes apply including lateralization (r ► l), see Terrell (1975h, 1975g).

6. The data for the following sections are taken from the Cuban and Puerto Rican dialect projects which form part of the "Proyecto coordinado de la norma culta de las principales ciudades de América Latina y de España." The directors of the Cuban and Puerto Rican dialect projects are Dr. Joseph Matluck and Dr. Humberto López-Moreles to whom I owe my sincerest gratitude for the extensive help they have given in these long months of investigation. The informants from which the data are taken are all members of the middle or upper socio-economic classes, most with advanced degrees. Therefore, the results cannot be considered anything less than representative of the "cultured norm" of these countries. The Cubans are of necessity refugees who were interviewed in Miami shortly after their arrival. The interviews are mostly semiformal but not forced. The Puerto Ricans were interviewed mostly in San Juan, Puerto Rico.

7. There are important theoretical considerations involved in the formalization of these rules which are discussed in (Terrell 1975i, 1975j), which will be ignored in this paper in order to simplify the presentation of the data and the conclusions.

8. Principally Vallejos-Claro (1970), Ma and Herasimchuk (1971), and Cedergren (1973).

9. At least this is the pattern reported by Cedergren (1973) for Panamanian Spanish.

10. For stylistic variation in Puerto Rican see Ma y Herasimchuk (1971).

11. The individual studies are at this point incomplete. However, preliminary results tend to show that only deletion varies to any extent, and even in this case, the general constraints hold for all speakers although the specific rates may vary.

12. This interaction is a special case discussed in some detail for Panamanian Spanish by Cedergren (1973).

References

Bowen, J.C. and J. Ornstein, eds., 1975, *Studies in Southwest Spanish*, Newbury House Publishers.

Cedergren, Henrietta C.J., 1973, *The Interplay of Social and Linguistic Factors in Panama*, Ph.D. Dissertation, Cornell University.

Clegg, Hal, 1968, *An Acoustic Study of Cuban Vowels*, Masters thesis, University of Texas, Austin, Texas.

Hammond, R.M., 1973, *An Experimental Verification of the Phonemic Status of Open and Closed Vowels in Spanish*, Master's Thesis, Florida Atlantic University, Boca Raton, Florida.

Hooper, Joan B., 1973, *Aspects of Natural Generative Phonology*, Ph.D. dissertation, University of California, Los Angeles, California.

Ibasescu, Cristina, 1968, *El español en Cuba*, Sociedad Rumana de Lingüística Románica, Bucarest.

Labov, William, 1971, "Methodology" in William Dingwall, ed., *A Survey of Linguistic Science*.

———. 1972, *Sociolinguistic Patterns*, University of Pennsylvania Press, Philadelphia, Pennsylvania.

Ma, R. and E. Herasimchuk, 1971, *The Linguistic Dimensions of a Bilingual Neighborhood in L.A. Fishman*, R.L. Cooper and R. Ma, eds., *Bilingualism in the Barrio*, Indiana University Press, Bloomington, Indiana.

Navarro Tomás, Tomás, 1948, *El español en Puerto Rico*, Editorial de la Universidad de Puerto Rico, Río Piedras, Puerto Rico.

Rosario del, Rubén, 1970, *El español de América*, Troutman Press, Sharon, Connecticut.

Terrell, Tracy D., 1975a, "La aspiración, y elisión en el español cubano—implicaciones para una teoría dialectal," Ponencia ante el IV Congreso Internacional de la Asociación de Lingüística y Filología de la América Latina, Lima, Perú.

———. 1975b, "Functional Constraints on Deletion of Word Final /s/ in Cuban Spanish", *Berkeley Linguistics Society*, Vol. 1, Berkeley, California.

———. 1975c, "Natural Generative Phonology: Evidence from Spanish", *Proceedings of the Northwest Conference on Foreign Languages*, Vol. II, Vancouver, Canada.

———. 1975d, "La aspiración en el español de Cuba—observaciones teóricas", manuscript, University of California, Irvine, California.

———. 1975e, "Dialectologia', in J. Guitart and J. Roy, eds., *El español y la gramática generativa transformacional*, Ediciones 62A, Barcelona, Spain.

———. 1975f, "La nasal implosiva y final en el español de Cuba", to appear in the *Anuario de Letras*, Universidad Autónoma Nacional de México, México, D.F.

———. 1975g, "Lateralization and Velarization in Puerto Rican /r/ and /rr/", manuscript, University of California, Irvine, California.

———. 1975h, "La distribución de las variantes de /r/ y /rr/ en el español de Cuba", manuscript, University of California, Irvine, California.

———. 1975i, "The Interaction of Phonological and Grammatical Constraints on Aspiration and Deletion in Cuban Spanish", manuscript, University of California, Irvine, California.

———. 1975j, "La interacción de la aspiración y la elisión sobre la /s/ implosiva y final en el
    español de Puerto Rico", to appear in *Nueva Revista de Filología Hispánica*.
Vallejos-Claro, Bernardo, 1970, *La distribución y estratificación de /r/ /r̄/y/s/ en el español
    cubano*, Ph.D. dissertation, University of Texas, Austin, Texas.

Hiato, sinéresis, y sinalefa:
A Sociolinguistic Updating

Joseph H. Matluck
The University of Texas at Austin

Linguists have for various reasons done surprisingly little recent research on
the Spanish morphophonemic system. The study reported herein is part of an
ongoing project employing recorded spoken materials from Spanish-speaking
cities of the Western Hemisphere. The specific focus in this paper is the set of
phenomena known as *hiato, sinéresis,* and *sinalefa.* We investigate the attitudes of the speakers themselves toward the social acceptability of eliminating the hiatus (*hiato*) in vowels across word boundaries. The results
demonstrate a wider acceptance of this practice than linguists have generally
suspected, despite the reported negative reaction to it among the speakers
themselves.

For centuries, and especially since the first appearance early in the 1900s of the
works of Tomás Navarro Tomás, students and scholars interested in Spanish have
heard or read of *hiato, sinéresis,* and *sinalefa* and have usually dismissed the terms
from their consciousness with some vague remembrance that they had something to
do with syllabication, diphthongs, or versification. And most scholars of Spanish
without an extensive background in linguistics have rarely even gotten to read either
the long chapter in Navarro's *Manual de pronunciación española* (1957) on *sonidos
agrupados* or the references to glide formation, glide strengthening, and classification
of semiconsonants and semivowels, "buried" deep within "unfathomable" phonological studies by structuralists,[1] generativists,[2] and lexical phonologists,[3] as well as in
works on the theoretical role of the syllable[4] and on metrical phonology.[5]

    In recent years relatively little has been written specifically and uniquely on the
Spanish morphophonemic system, so that since Navarro the interesting, even exciting, sociolinguistic phenomena surrounding this critical aspect of Spanish phonotac-
tics have seldom received more than a passing mention. Some exceptions are the
rules posited by the above linguists along with a host of other phonological and morphological rules of the language. This study examines those phonotactic phenomena
with specific regard to phonetic and phonemic detail and, especially, to some of the

patterns of use across socioeconomic lines. More specifically, our present research demonstrates that: (1) usage of *sinalefa* and *sinéresis* is more widespread than phonologists generally have reported or supposed; and (2) there is a growing tendency in Spanish to eliminate the hiatus across word boundaries by *sinalefa* among individual speakers in higher socioeconomnic classes despite their negative reaction to such usage.

1 INTRODUCTION AND BACKGROUND

In section 1 of this paper we shall (a) define our terms, (b) deal with the processes underlying *hiato, sinéresis,* and *sinalefa,* and (c) summarize our observations on social dialects and related attitudes and usage. In section 2 we shall describe a relevant study by this author of *"Norma Culta"* recordings. Finally, in section 3 we shall present some implications of the study.

Hiato, sinéresis, and *sinalefa:* Definitions

Let us first review and clarify our terms. *Hiato* (or *hiatus*) is, literally, the break in sound between two vowels, used in Spanish (and in Romance languages in general) to indicate that two contiguous vowels are pronounced as separate syllables, either within the confines of a word (e.g., *caos, peor*) or across word boundaries (e.g., *se hará, la envió, la ordenó*). *Hiato* is also used more loosely, in Spanish morphophonemics, to indicate the vowel cluster itself, where two or more contiguous vowels might be pronounced with two or more separate syllables. Hence even the vowel clusters of *siesta, suave, peine,* and Europa, normally diphthongized and pronounced in one syllable under the phenomenon of *sinéresis,* could be uttered as two syllables (i.e., the *hiato* maintained) when the occasion calls for it—as, for example, in the counting of syllables in versification (*si-es-ta, su-a-ve, pe-i-ne, E-u-ro-pa*). *Sinéresis* and *sinalefa,* therefore, are both indications of the same phenomenon: the breaking up of the *hiato,* that is, the uttering of two contiguous vowels as one syllable, either within a word (*sinéresis: sjes-ta, Eu-ro-pa*) or across word boundaries (*sinalefa: la u-nión, me in-vi-tó, sj ur-ge, sw am-pa-ro*).

Processes Underlying *hiato, sinéresis,* and *sinalefa*

1. Vowel reduction   The reduction of two or more contiguous vowels to one syllable may be realized in various ways:
  (a) Like vowels. In the case of like vowels (two /a/, two /e/, etc.) the reduction may be realized
      (1) through fusion of the two vowels: *leen > len, lo ordenó > l'ordenó*
      (2) through vowel raising plus diphthongization: *lein, lw'ordenó*
  (b) Unlike vowels. In the case of unlike vowels the reduction may be realized
      (1) through diphthongization, without vowel raising: *sjesta, Europa, la imagen, la union*);

(2) through vowel raising plus diphthongization: (*pjor, herwe, la uración, lo involvió, nw es, mj ha*);

(3) through deletion of one of the vowels: (*ora > ahora, l'envolvió, l'esposa, l'oración*).

2. Diphthongization in Spanish (glide formation)   Let us look more closely at the process of glide formation, with or without vowel raising, in the case of two or more contiguous unlike vowels, that is, vowel clusters of two or more unlike vowels.

(a) Diphthongization without vowel raising. This is the most frequent type of diphthongization, representing the normal "standard" Spanish glide formation in which one of the vowels must be a high, weak-stressed vowel /i/ or /u/ (the so-called "weak vowels"). When such vowel phonemes glide in this phonological environment, their phonetic shape changes from vowel to semi (semiconsonant [j, w] or semivowel [i, u]) and they therefore lose their nuclearity, producing sinéresis such as *pjenso, cwatro, oigo, pausa* and *sinalefas* such as *sj hay, mj olfato, la imagen, lo usé.*

(b) Diphthongization resulting from vowel raising. This type could be called "nonstandard" Spanish glide formation; it occurs in vowel clusters in which the weak-stressed vowel element is a mid vowel, either /e/ or /o/, which—academically speaking—must *not* glide, since they are *not* high vowels (i. e., /i, u/). Most phonologists agree, however, that the phonetic data across all dialect areas point overwhelmingly to the fact that glide formation rules operate on high vowels and *also on underlying mid vowels* through rules such as vowel raising (see Harris 1977; Cressey 1978; Morgan 1984), so that /e/ and /o/ also produce *sinéresis* such as *pjor, herwe* and *sinalefas* such as *la uración, lo involvió.*

Summary of Observations on Attitudes and Usage

1. Attitude groupings   Thus, if we attempt to group speakers according to both dialect and speech style criteria, and add the question of attitude, we can make some interesting observations.

(a) Social dialects: high socioeconomic ranges. Most of the members of this group speak "standard" academicians' Spanish, which accepts both *sinéresis* and *sinalefa* but only with high vowels /i/ and /u/ (*sjesta, la invité, swerte, la unión*). We are using the term *accepts* advisedly, in full cognizance of the fact that the acceptance is tacit, since allophones of the same phoneme (in this case the vowels [i] and [u] and the front and back glides [j], [w], [i], [u]) are perceived by native speakers as the same "sound," although most native speakers accept the *hiatos* within word boundaries as "okay, but strange sounding." Native speakers might accept the forms *[si-és-ta]* and *[su-ér-te]* much as they would accept any positional allophone used in the wrong phonetic environment—with comprehension, of course, but with raised eyebrows. Such a "standard" dialect would be taught orthoepically as not permitting glide formation from *any* non-high vowels (/a/, /e/, /o/) in *any* environment (forms such as *pjor, herwe, lw es, lo involvió*). At this point we are not concerning ourselves with actual *usage* by this group, but only with their attitudes toward what constitutes and what should be taught as "correct" usage.

(b) Social dialects: low socioeconomic ranges. This group characteristically has minimal metalinguistic awareness and therefore usually reflects minimal attitudinal behavior in this particular area.

2. Usage Groupings   If we add the actual usage patterns by the above groups to their attitudes about those patterns, we find that in most regional dialects the following configurations seem to appear (granting, of course, the everpresent possibility that a particular regional dialect or subdialect might conceivably show some variation).

(a) Social dialects: low socioeconomic ranges. This group tends to glide all non-low vowels (i. e., all but /a/) thereby diphthongizing the cluster: *pjor, herwe, lw es, lo involvió.* As just mentioned, members of this group usually reflect little metalinguistic awareness at this level of phonological behavior, with some exceptions at the upper ranges of the group.

(b) Social dialects: high socioeconomic ranges. Members of this group tend to use *sinalefa* but not *sinéresis* with vowel clusters formed by any combination of non-high vowels /e/, /o/, and /a/, but usually admits to neither. That is, they tend not to use (and usually react very negatively to its use by others) *sinéresis* in which the glide results from the raising of the mid vowels /e/ and /o/ (e.g., *pjor, herwe, cai, ríu*). At the same time they tend to use automatically and unconsciously *sinalefas* such as *lw es, lj hablaré, lo invió, se ufreció,* while usually denying, very positively and sometimes rather emotionally, the use of such forms in their own speech, and condemning their use by others as "incorrect" and as evidence of the worst kind of "*barbarismo*" and of Spanish at the very lowest level of "*lenguaje vulgar.*"

3. Deletion of /a/   Both the usage and attitude patterns in the case of /aé/, /aó/, /aí/, and /aú / as well as /ae/ and /ao/ seem to follow the same tendencies as those just described for diphthongization. Weak-stressed /a/ as the first vowel of a cluster in which the second is any other vowel under strong stress (or /e/ or /o/ under weak stress) tends to be deleted in some regional dialects (e.g., *ora <ahora, l'otra, l'envió, l'hembra, l'esposa, l'hijita*). In rare cases the second vowel will be the one deleted: for example, *ara <ahora,* the norm in all of Puerto Rico when *ahora* serves as the crutch word at the beginning of the sentence. Sometimes the deleted first vowel is either /e/ or /o/ (*l'onrado, l'uno <lo uno*), but this pattern occurs less frequently.

2 STUDY OF "*NORMA CULTA*" TAPE RECORDINGS

I examined the recorded speech of ten *culto* speakers from our database at the University of Texas of the Hispanic Cities Language Project, known throughout the Hispanic linguistic world as the *Norma urbana culta* (more specifically *Estudio coordinado de la norma lingüística culta de las principales ciudades de Iberoamérica y de la Península Ibérica*). These speech samples, taken from five reels of tape in our archive, came from five of the Project's capital cities: Buenos Aires, Argentina; La

Paz, Bolivia; Havana, Cuba; Mexico City, Mexico; and Caracas, Venezuela. They were selected by my research assistant from among some sixty hours of recordings recently transcribed into Spanish and entered into our Database and Retrieval Network. No criteria were specified except that I wanted samples in a dialogue format from five different countries in the Project. For example, I did not request a specific level of formality, that is, a more formal or less formal register within the dialogue format.

Procedure

I analyzed about fifteen minutes from each tape using the following procedure:

1. Every *hiato* (i.e., vowel cluster, contiguous vowels) across word boundaries was located and marked on the triple-spaced hard copy of the transcription with the particular vowel phonemes involved and their stress pattern. For example, if we were dealing with /-a/ as the first vowel of the sequence and /o-/ as the second vowel, then there were four possible phonemic combinations: /-a/ and /o-/ with both vowels weak-stressed (*la organización*); /-á/ and / o-/ with V^1 strong-stressed and V^2 weak-stressed (*tendrá obligaciones*); /-a/ and /ó-/ with V^1 weak-stressed and V^2 strong-stressed (*la otra*); or /-á/ and /ó-/ with both vowels strong-stressed (*da otro*). See the figure below listing all such combinations.

2. After many, many audio repetitions of the context in which each of the clusters appeared, the phonetic resolution of each cluster was marked in red on the second line above the cluster: for example, [ó] if the realization were, let us say, *l'otra* , or [áu] if it were [láutra], and so forth.

3. The phonetic results were then entered on one of five charts, each chart focusing on one of the five vowel phonemes as V^1 and the twenty possible phonemic combinations of the V^1V^2 sequence, as illustrated in step (1) above by /-a/ as V^1 and any one of the four other vowel phonemes as V^2. Thus, all five charts would, together, include the 100 possible phonemic combinations of V^1V^2 accounting for the variables of vowel phonemes and their stress patterns. In addition, a fairly large number of the 300 to 400 possible phonetic shapes would also be represented—depending, of course, on the individual phonetic realizations of each informant.

4. The results were then classified and tabulated as either *sinalefa* or *hiato* according to (1) the syllabication of the phonetic realization of the vowel cluster: *sinalefa* if it was reduced to one syllable, maintenance of the hiatus if two syllables; and (2) the exact phonetic realization (diphthongization, fusion, or deletion).

Phonemic environments of contiguous vowels across word boundaries in Spanish:

V^1 = /i/	V^1 = /e/
V^2 = /i/: /ii íi ií íí/	V^2 = /i/: /ei éi eí éí/
= /e/: /ie íe ié íé/	= /e/: /ee ée eé éé/
= /a/: /ia ía iá íá/	= /a/: /ea éa eá éá/
= /o/: /io ío ió íó/	= /o/: /eo éo eó éó/
= /u/: /iu íu iú íú/	= /u/: /eu éu eú éú/

$$V^1 = /a/$$
$$V^2 = /i/: /ai \text{ } ái \text{ } aí \text{ } áí/$$
$$= /e/: /ae \text{ } áe \text{ } aé \text{ } áé/$$
$$= /a/: /aa \text{ } áa \text{ } aá \text{ } áá/$$
$$= /o/: /ao \text{ } áo \text{ } aó \text{ } áó/$$
$$= /u/: /au \text{ } áu \text{ } aú \text{ } áú/$$

$$V^1 = /o/$$
$$V^2 = /i/: /oi \text{ } ói \text{ } oí \text{ } óí/$$
$$= /e/: /oe \text{ } óe \text{ } oé \text{ } óé/$$
$$= /a/: /oa \text{ } óa \text{ } oá \text{ } óá/$$
$$= /o/: /oo \text{ } óo \text{ } oó \text{ } óó/$$
$$= /u/: /ou \text{ } óu \text{ } oú \text{ } óú/$$

$$V^1 = /u/$$
$$V^2 = /i/: /ui \text{ } úi \text{ } uí \text{ } úí/$$
$$= /e/: /ue \text{ } úe \text{ } ué \text{ } úé/$$
$$= /a/: /ua \text{ } úa \text{ } uá \text{ } úá/$$
$$= /o/: /uo \text{ } úo \text{ } uó \text{ } úó/$$
$$= /u/: /uu \text{ } úu \text{ } uú \text{ } úú/$$

Summary of Tabulations

As shown in the table below, there were a grand total of 1,235 incidences of contiguous vowels across word boundaries. (There were actually almost 300 more in which the hiatus was maintained by a pause of one kind or another between the vowels, which made them unusable in this study, since the pause precludes the possibility of *sinalefa*).

1. Of these 1,235 clusters, the *hiatos* were eliminated by *sinalefas* in 669 (or approximately 54% of the cases), whereas the *hiatos* were maintained 566 times (or 46%).

2. A total of 291 of these clusters were cases of like vowels (two /a/'s, two /e/'s, etc.). This represented about 24% of the total number of incidences. Of this group, 243 (or 84%) were reduced to one syllable (i.e., *sinalefa*) by fusion of the two vowels into one (e.g., *l'amistad, l'envió*); in only 48 cases (16%) was the *hiato* maintained (e.g., *la amistad, le envió*).

3. A total of 231 of these clusters (19% of the total number of incidences) were those in which at least one of the vowels was a weak-stressed high vowel (either /i/ or /u/). Of these, 139 (or 61%) were reduced to one syllable (i.e., *sinalefa*) by diphthongization (i.e., the weak-stressed /i/ or /u/ became a glide—either semiconsonants [j] and [w] or semivowels [i] and [u])—whereas 92 (or 39%) maintained the hiatus by not gliding the weak-stressed vowel, thereby allowing it to maintain its nuclear status and maintain the two-syllable configuration.

4. And, finally, a total of 713 of these clusters (58% of the total number of incidences) were those in which *neither* of the vowels was weak-stressed /i/ or /u/. Of these, 287 (or 40%) reduced the cluster to one syllable (*sinalefa*) by either vowel-raising + diphthongization, or deletion of one of the vowels (e.g., *lj habló, l'esposa*). In 426 (or 60%) of these clusters, the *hiato* was maintained (e.g., *le habló, la esposa*).

Vowel Reduction in Spanish
Resolutions using *hiato* and *sinalefa*

Total # of Instances of -V⌣V-	Total Resolutions		Resolution by Phonological Structure of the Vowel Cluster								
			Like Vowels			Unlike Vowels					
			V¹ = V²			One "Weak" Vowel**			Both "Strong" Vowels***		
	Hiato Maintained	*Sinalefa*	#	*Hiato* Maintained	*Sinalefa*	#	*Hiato* Maintained	*Sinalefa*	#	*Hiato* Maintained	*Sinalefa*
1,235	566	699	291	48	243	231	92	139	713	426	287
	46%	54%		16%	84%		39%	61%		60%	40%
			(24%)*			(19%)			(58%)		

*Figures in parentheses = % of total # of instances

**"Weak" vowels = weak-stressed high vowels: /i/ and /u/

***"Strong" vowels = non-high vowels: /e/, /o/, and /a/

Some Observations and Conclusions

These pilot-study figures would seem to speak for themselves as an indication that the overwhelmingly strong tendency of Spanish speakers is to eliminate the hiatus across word boundaries by *sinalefa*, even in the speech of individuals in the high socioeconomic ranges. To be sure, the tendency is attenuated to one degree or another as we go higher up on the educational ladder and as the level of formality increases. The figures I have cited represent the total number of *sinalefas* and *hiatos* in a sampling of ten speakers from five different countries. What they do not show is (1) the tremendous rise in *sinalefa* as we examine speech samples of this group in less formal speech environments, such as discourse involving interpersonal relationships; and, conversely, (2) the greater incidence of *hiato* maintenance in the speech of individuals speaking in more formal registers, along with the presence of a whole series of indicators of those formal registers: the increase in the number of false pauses and the correspondingly shorter phonic groups, the increase in the number of glottal stops in hiatus, a certain degree of pontification on the part of the speaker, a greater number of all kinds of phonetic and allophonic detail that represent clear cases of hypercorrection, and so forth.

Moreover, what is most revealing about these figures and, I believe, highly supportive of the principal thesis of this paper, is that the percentage of *sinalefa* was as high as it was, given the fact that the level of formality in the speech of these ten subjects was, by pure chance, for the most part extremely high. Especially revealing—in fact, to many even startling—is the last set of figures, the 40% (!!) of *sinalefa* in the hiatuses where *no* weak-stressed high vowel was present in the vowel cluster. This is noteworthy since, although most academicians do not find particular fault with the notion of fusion of like vowels (*l'americana*) or of diphthongization of unlike vowels when one of them is a weak-stressed high vowel (*sw amigo*), they usually deny most heatedly (1) the diphthongization by educated speakers of *hiatos* formed by the vowel raising and glide formation of /e/ or /o/ (*nw hay, la intrada*), and (2) the deletion of one of the vowels by this same group of speakers (e.g., *m'iba, m'imagino, l'otra, l'estrella*).

3 | SOME IMPLICATIONS

We found an incidence of *sinalefa* totalling 40% in a phonetic environment in which academicians say, and truly believe, that the incidence in "*el habla culta*" is closer to 0. We feel certain that our larger study—now in progress—will bear out these pilot results. If so, then we must ask ourselves what these results mean. I would once again remind you that we don't talk the way we think we do, especially those of us who have had a good bit of formal education. It would also mean that perhaps Menéndez Pidal was right when he said, about fifty years ago, that the past participle affix -*ado* was on the way out and that a hundred years later it would be reduced to [au], spelled as in the word *hablau*. He wasn't too far wrong, although his timetable may have been off a hundred years or so, and I don't think the spelling will change in that period of time.

But the preliminary results of the present study could also mean that even we Hispanic academicians should finally realize that English speakers don't have a corner on the [dziytzet] and "Mairzie Doates" market; that Spanish, too, has a morphophonemic system that must be reckoned with; and that we should begin to lose some of our long-standing and built-in prejudices against the real, live, everyday spoken language. Perhaps an analogy with old Rome is apropos at this point. Just as Cicero and Virgil, along with everyone else in Rome, spoke not classical (written) Latin but vulgar (spoken) Latin, because it was the only Latin that people spoke, so it is with modern Spanish. Perhaps it is now time to talk about *el español clásico*, the written language, and *el español vulgar*, the spoken language, spoken by everyone—even college professors of Spanish.

Notes

1. See, for example, Alarcos (1968), Trager (1942), Bowen and Stockwell (1955), Chavarría Aguilar (1951), King (1952), López-Morales, Matluck, and Quilis (1973), Foster (1967), Baena (1967).
2. Harris (1969, 1977), Cressey (1978), Hooper and Terrell (1976).
3. Clements and Keyser (1983), Kiparsky (1982), Mohanan (1982), Morgan (1984).
4. Bell and Hooper (1978), Safir (1979), Harris (1983), Clements and Keyser (1983).
5. Liberman and Prince (1977), Halle and Vergnaud (1978), Kiparsky (1979), McCarthy (1979), Hayes (1980).

References

Alarcos Llorach, E. 1968. *Fonología española*. Madrid: Editorial Gredos.

Baena-Zapata, L. 1967. *Fonología española de Antioquía*. Ph.D. dissertation, University of Texas, Austin.

Bell, A., and J. Hooper (eds.). 1978. *Syllables and Segments*. Amsterdam: North Holland.

Bowen, J.D., and R. Stockwell. 1955. The Phonemic Interpretation of Semivowels in Spanish. *Language* 31:236-40.

Chavarría Aguilar, O.L. 1951. The Phonemes of Costa Rican Spanish. *Language* 27:248-53.

Clements, G.N., and S.J. Keyser. 1983 *CV Phonology*. Cambridge, Mass.: MIT Press.

Cressey, W.W. 1978. *Spanish Phonology and Morphology*: A Generative View. Washington, D.C.: Georgetown University Press.

Foster, D.W. 1967. A note on the /y/ Phoneme of *Porteño* Spanish. *Hispania* 50:119-21.

Halle, M., and J.R. Vergnaud. 1978. Metrical Structure in Phonology. Manuscript, MIT, Cambridge, Mass.

Harris, J.W. 1969. *Spanish Phonology*. Cambridge, Mass.: MIT Press.

Harris, J.W. 1977. Remarks on Diphthongization. *Lingua* 41:261-305.

Harris, J.W. 1983. *Syllable Structure and Stress in Spanish: A Nonlinear Analysis*. Cambridge, Mass.: MIT Press.

Hayes, B.P. 1980. A Metrical Theory of Stress Rules. Ph.D. dissertation, MIT, Cambridge, Mass.

Hooper, J., and T. Terrell. 1976. Stress Assignment in Spanish: A Natural Generative Analysis. *Glossa* 10:64-110.

King, H.V. 1952. Outline of Mexican Spanish Phonology. *Studies in Linguistics* 10:3.

Kiparsky, P. 1979. Metrical Structure Assignment Is Cyclic. *Linguistic Inquiry* 10:421-41.

Kiparsky, P. 1982. Lexical Morphology and Phonology. *Linguistics in the Morning Calm*, 3-92. Seoul: Hanshin Publishing Co.

Liberman, M., and A. Prince. 1977. On Stress and Linguistic Rhythm. *Linguistic Inquiry* 8:249-336.

López Morales, H., J.H. Matluck, and A. Quilis. 1973. *Cuestionario para el estudio coordinado de la norma lingüística culta de las principales ciudades de Iberoamérica y de la Península Ibérica, 1: Fonética y fonología.* Madrid: Programa Interamericano de Lingüística y Enseñanza de Idiomas (PILEI) and Consejo Superior de Investigaciones Científicas (CSIC).

McCarthy, J.J. 1979. Stress and Syllabification. *Linguistic Inquiry* 10:443-66.

Mohanan, K.P. 1982. Lexical Phonology. Ph.D. dissertation, MIT, Cambridge, Mass.

Morgan, T. 1984. Consonant-Glide-Vowel Alterations in Spanish: A Case Study in Syllabic and Lexical Phonology. Ph.D. dissertation, University of Texas, Austin.

Navarro, T. 1957. *Manual de pronunciación española.* Hafner Publishing Co.

Safir, K. 1979. Syllable Structure, Metrical Structure, and Harmony Processes. *MIT Working Papers in Linguistics*, 1. Saporta, S. 1956. A Note on Spanish Semivowels. *Language* 32:287-90.

Trager, G.L. 1942. The Phonemic Treatment of Semivowels. *Language* 18:220-23.

The Spanish Sibilant Shift Revisited: The State of 'seseo' in Sixteenth-Century Mexico

Giorgio Perissinotto
University of California, Santa Barbara

The scarcity of extant texts by *criollos* (native–born Americans of European stock) has made it difficult to document the state of the phonological system of American Spanish at the close of the sixteenth century. It is here argued that by the end of the century the sibilant system of Spanish as spoken in New Spain (Mexico), though far from resolved, was rapidly acquiring the pattern it possesses today. The documentary evidence is drawn from a close scrutiny of a recently edited manuscript by Juan Suárez de Peralta (born circa 1537), a native of Mexico City who wrote around 1590. In contrast with the regularity of most of his orthography, the representation of the sibilants shows an abundance of variations that point to a yet unresolved—but clearly *seseoso*—system of sibilants.

THE STATE OF THE QUESTION

The marked difference between the sound systems of the Peninsular Spanish dialects and the Latin American varieties is, on the one hand, the result of different settlement patterns and, on the other, the consequence of linguistic evolution. While it may be beyond the reach of scholars to state with precision how the different factors shaped the national languages of the Latin American republics, it will be argued here that,in at least one case, it is possible to point to a particular historical juncture. Specifically, I will affirm that the Spanish spoken in Mexico in the sixteenth century was well on its way to acquiring those traits that separate it from the linguistic system(s) that generated it. In this case, I will use the sibilant system of Mexican Spanish to illustrate the process of linguistic change and separation. The corpus comprises the writings of a Mexico City–born (1537) chronicler; the methodology is an analysis of orthographic patterns that reveal an underlying phonological system, which is in turn compared with those of his Spanish born contemporaries.

 ## THE MEDIEVAL SPANISH SIBILANTS: ORIGINS AND DEVELOPMENT

The process of realignment of the Spanish sibilants began, as is well known, in the Middle Ages, with the gradual loss of the voiced/voiceless opposition in favor of the voiceless solution. The related phenomenon of the weakening and loss of the stop element in the affricates resulted in a crowded system of sibilants with a low functional yield. While the northern provinces of Spain followed the solution of the prestigious Toledan dialect, the southernmost lands adjusted their systems to the Sevillan model. The sound system that reached America was therefore one of unresolved flux. Scholars have long debated whether the similarity between the Andalusian and American phonologies is causal or simply a case of plurigenesis.

The consonant system of Latin was fairly simple, especially if compared with those of the modern Romance languages. The stops were aligned in two series, one voiced and one voiceless. There were two nasals, two liquids, a labial fricative, and, in all likelihood, only one sibilant: a voiceless /s/ that, if not generally apicoalveolar in all of Romania, was most likely so in Hispania (Galmés de Fuentes 1962; Torreblanca 1982:447). As with the vowels, the Latin consonant system relied heavily on the long/short opposition, though only in the intervocalic position.

In its simplicity, the Latin sibilant system contrasted significantly with those that evolved from it in the neo-Latin languages. All the Romance languages, in the medieval stage, had a crowded system of opposition among the sibilants. Modern Italian still maintains a substantial inventory of them: *pazzo* /ŝ/, *azzurro* /ẑ/, *giorno* /ǧ/, *bacio* /ĉ/, *uscio* /š/, and many other varieties present in the historical dialects of the peninsula.

Medieval Spanish was particularly rich in oppositions among sibilants. Its substantial inventory is as follows:[1]

Voiceless apicoalveolar fricative /ś/ (*s–*, *–ss–*) as in *osso* 'bear', *passar* 'to pass'

Voiced apicoalveolar fricative /z̧/ (–s–) as in *oso* 'I dare', *rosa* 'rose'
Voiceless predorsal affricate /ŝ/ (ç) as in *façes* 'bundles'
Voiced predorsal affricate /ẑ/ (z) as in *fazes* 'you do'
Voiceless palatal fricative /š/ (x–, –x–) as in *quexa* 'lament'
Voiced palatal fricative (or possibly affricate) /ž/ (j, g+e, i) as in *hijo* 'son', *gente* 'people'.

The oppositions are thought to have had a higher functional yield in medial position that at the initial or final, where the sibilants tended to neutralize. On the other hand, /š/ and /ž/ did contrast phonemically in word initial position (Lloyd 1987:267).

The Medieval Spanish sibilant shift has long attracted the attention of historical linguists. It would be of little interest to our purpose to explain how such a complex system evolved from one with a single /s/, but it would not be totally idle to summarize the salient features of the shift from the medieval to the modern system and the views of the scholars who have studied it.

It has been widely maintained—but not universally accepted—that by the end of the sixteenth century the voiced series was quickly disappearing in favor of the voiceless articula tions. This shift, it has been suggested, can be regarded as part of the general trend towards the devoicing of consonants, but this view is untenable if one considers that voiced/voiceless oppositions were and are fully functional in other areas of Spanish phonology. Substratum influence has been adduced by others as a possible explanation for this phenomenon. André Martinet (1951:149), for example, pointed out that the sibilant system of Medieval Spanish was remarkably similar to that of modern Basque, thus suggesting the possibility of Basque influence. But, as Lloyd has remarked (1987:269), it may be difficult to promote a theory of Basque influence on Castilian in the sixteenth century, when the prestige factor would work in favor of Castilian and not of Basque, which, as a language, was in territorial retreat. It seems more plausible to suggest that if such influence did take place, it did so in the formative period of Spanish, when bilingualism was common and the notion of national language was not yet developed.

The merger of voiced and voiceless sibilants did occur, but not simultaneously across the system and not in all strata of society. The separate regions have markedly different timetables for the change. A widely held opinion is that the fusion took place first in the popular speech of the Burgos region and then spread to the south; the prestigious dialect of Toledo, on the other hand, is considered to have been conservative and to have acted as a constraint to the leveling of the sibilants.

 ## ORTHOGRAPHIC INCONSISTENCIES AS INDICATORS OF PHONOLOGICAL CHANGE

Orthographic inconsistencies pointing to the dephonemization of /s/=/z/, /ŝ/=/ẑ/, and /š/=/ž/ are legion, even at the earlier stages of the language. Devoicing was quickly becoming the norm, "but was still resisted in the usage of the court and of those influenced by it" (Lloyd 1987:329). The migration from the northern provinces to the south and the establishment of Madrid as the capital in the middle of the sixteenth century finally led to the general spread and acceptance of the merger by the close of the century.

The merger of /ś/ and /ź/ in favor of /ś/ (with the voiced sibilant remaining only as an optional positional variant before voiced consonant) is a general development that occurred in all regions of the Spanish–speaking world. As to the point of articulation, it has remained apicoalveolar in central and northern Spain, while the predorsoalveolar variants are to be found in southern Spain and in America.

Deaffrication and loss of voice as the distinctive trait in the /ś/ and /ź/ opposition resulted in the interdental voiceless fricative /Ø/ in central and northern Spain and in a predorsoalveolar /s/ in much of America. The dating of the fricativi zation and interdentalization is still a matter that requires clarification. While there is ample evidence that the affricate articulation could still be heard in the sixteenth century, it is also possible to document spellings pointing to a deaffrication as early as the thirteenth.[2] The interdental articulation is first documented in the second half of the sixteenth century in grammars intended for the use of foreigners, but seems to be firmly established in the first quarter of the seventeenth when Juan Pablo Bonet, in a treatise to teach the deaf and mute wrote (as quoted in Alatorre 1989:251):

> *Para que pronuncie esta letra [sound], ha de poner el mudo la punta de la lengua entre los dientes y expeler la respiración, que salga sin que la lengua se aparte de aquel lugar.*

> In order to pronounce this letter [sound], the mute must place the tip of his tongue between his teeth and expel his breath in such a way that it can be expelled without moving the tongue from that position.

Again, northern Spain and the lower classes seem to have been the spreading agents of this articulation, which, it may be necessary to point out, is not found in America. While there are many descriptions of the interdental /Ø/ for sixteenth–century Spain, there are no bona fide records that it ever reached the New World. That these radical changes and mergers should have occurred at the time of settling the Americas raises the issue of which phenomena reached across the ocean, which took hold, and which never reached the shores of this hemisphere.

THE SIBILANT SYSTEM IN THE AMERICAS: DETERMINING REGIONAL SOURCES/ORIGINS IN SPAIN

Much, if not all, of the literature on American Spanish touches, even if tangentially, on the linguistic similarity between Andalusian Spanish and the American dialects. While many linguists would agree that both regions share a considerable number of phonetic traits, the issue of Andalusian Spanish as the Ur–dialect for American Spanish has divided the field into *andalucistas* and *antiandalucistas*.[3]

If one were to divide General Spanish (GS) into General European Spanish (GES) and General American Spanish (GAS), the phonological differences between the two would practically be limited to their sibilant systems. While GES, with the exclusion of parts of Andalusia, opposes the apicoalveolar voiceless fricative /ś/ to the interdental counterpart /Ø/ in words like *casa* 'house' and *caza* 'hunt', GAS treats them as homophones, articulated with some type of dorsal [s]; /Ø/ is not in the phonological inventory of GAS.

Historical linguists have long since determined that the complex medieval system of sibilants resulted in two solutions. The Andalusian regions maintained the voiced/voiceless opposition but confused the point of articulation of the predorsoalveolars with that of the apicoalveolars. The voiced articulations were further reduced and coalesced with the single voiceless phoneme /s/ of GAS. The northern castillian dialects, on the other hand, eliminated the opposition based on voice and thus reduced the six sibilants to three: an apicoalveolar /ś/, a predorsodental /ŝ/, and a palatal /š/. The /š/, in turn, became /x/ or /h/ on both sides of the Atlantic.

It is generally accepted that the phonological system of GAS owes its similarity to the Andalusian modality to the large number of Spanish settlers that came from the southern regions of Spain at the onset of the colonial period. Though the regional percentages shifted from Andalusia to the central and northern provinces as the sixteenth century progressed, it has been proposed that the initial preponderance of southerners—especially from Seville—was sufficient to render American Spanish permanently as an Andalusian variety (Boyd–Bowman 1956; Parodi 1976). It is furthermore assumed that the speech of Seville, rather than that of Madrid or Toledo, served as the linguistic norm for the nascent American–Spanish dialects.

Many scholars agree that by the beginning of the fifteenth century the affricates ç /ŝ/ and z /ẑ/ had generally become fricatives, distinguished from –s– /ẓ/, –ss– /ṣ/, and x, j, g /š/ by the point of articulation: predorsoalveolar [s] versus apicoalveolar [ṣ] for ç, z versus –s–, –ss–, palatal for j– g, x. Assuming that the medieval affricates ç and z had indeed become fricatives by the beginning of the fifteenth century, the affricate pronunciation could not have reached the American shores. Words in the native American Nahua language containing the affricate /ŝ/ were represented by sixteenth century grammarians with a ç or z preceded by the letter t to mark the stop element of the sound, which would not have been necessary if the ç and z had represented an affricate (Parodi 1976:118). As to the apicoalveolar –ss–, and –s–, it is said that they maintained their point of articulation in America. Nahua words containing the sound /š/ were often transcribed with the Spanish letters s or x. This articulation eventually fused with that of the predorsoalveolars ç and z, though the chronology of the fusion and the circumstances are far from clear.[4]

The coexistence of both the apicoalveolar and dorsoalveolar sibilants in America would not have lasted very long, especially if we assume that they were all fricatives. The phonetic space shared by the two articulations made the opposition very unstable. On the other hand, it is reasonable to assume that throughout the sixteenth century one could hear all kinds of pronunciations in the New World. The fleet bound for the New World left from southern ports, around Seville and the Casa de Contratación, where there gathered a multitude of people with the expectation of finding a position on one of the ships. The stay in the south lasted many months—often years—with the layover in the Canary Islands and the Caribbean ports adding even more time. It is not unreasonable to assume that Andalusian traits colored the speech of population strata so removed from the courtly norms of Toledo and Madrid.

It is therefore not surprising to note that much of what has been said about the Spanish spoken in America in the sixteenth century is actually a statement about the phonological conditions at that time in southern Spain and, mainly, in Seville. It has simply been assumed that if a genetic relationship could be established between Andalusian and American Spanish, the language of Seville could be considered the language of the New World. The documentation that is adduced to support this idea is almost invariably the writings of native Spaniards who migrated to America or scribal documents that are nearly impossible to connect with regional varieties. Yet one might argue that the dialectalization of Latin America must have had its beginnings in the diverse regional origins of the immigrants as well as in the indigenous languages. Five hundred years after the encounter, Spanish–speaking America is divided—or united, one might say—by many national and regional language varieties.

 ## THE LATIN AMERICAN SPANISH DIALECTS: THREE SIXTEENTH-CENTURY CHRONICLERS

The dialectal richness of Spanish–speaking America has produced a massive literature dealing with regional variation. Though Mexico in particular has been the subject of many studies, one is struck by the paucity of works dealing with language in Mexico during the formative sixteenth century. At this time, normative models were few and the regional and social composition of the new society was an amalgam not found anywhere else, except in Seville, the gathering point for all who wanted to gain passage to the Indies.[5]

The spelling systems used by educated chroniclers and simple scribes writing at the time were no less diverse than their personalities and backgrounds. Yet it is this very variability that allows us to reconstruct—however imperfectly—the phonological system of the period.

1. Fernández González de Eslava: A Remarkably Consistent Spelling System

The writings of Fernández González de Eslava have long come to represent a phonological system that, though Peninsular in origin, had adjusted to that of New Spain.[6] Amado Alonso (1940:213– 319), noting González de Eslava's extensive use of indigenous words and a considerable adherence to an older system of opposition of sibilants, is nevertheless at a loss to attribute a specific regional origin to a writer who is usually considered simply as being from of New Spain. Unsatisfied with the fuzzy state of affairs regarding González de Eslava's regional origin, Margit Frenk (1989a) undertakes the reconstruction of the sibilant system in a study that examines the rhyme patterns in his works, which, Frenk underscores, were written almost exclusively to be recited and heard, not to be read in print. Had González de Eslava adopted the pronunciation of his audience, his rhyme scheme would, for example, have allowed *moça* to rhyme with *rosa*. Frenk posits that the orthographic pairings in the rhyme schemes correspond to the author's pronunciation, which, she states, was typical of neither New Spain, Andalusia, nor northern Spain but was more in tune with the normative speech of Toledo. Eslava pairs *pieça* with *cabeça*, *abraça* with *traça*, and *promessa* with *confiessa*, *hiziesse* with *viniesse*. The pair *–s–* and *–ss–*, which most scholars agree had long come together into a single voiceless /s/, was carefully distinguished by the prescriptive González de Eslava. And there is every indication that the confusion between the voiced *–z–* and the voiceless *ç* (affricate or fricative) was not in his phonological system: *pobreza* rhymes with *fortaleza* and *holgança* with *alcança*. He also distinguished between the voiceless *x* and the voiced *j*, *g* in his rhymes, though he also wrote *dijo* and *trujo*.

This rather anachronistic system maintains all of the oppositions of the medieval pattern, including the aspiration of *h* < Latin *f* and a careful distinction between *b* and *v*. To the suggestion that González de Eslava might have maintained in writing differences that he did not make in his speech, Frenk responds:

> *Esto es impensable: implicaría demasiada vigilancia, vigilancia inútil además, puesto que, como veremos, Eslava escribía básicamente para el canto y la recitación, realizados por gentes que no respetarían tan sutiles diferencias fonéticas y destinados a quienes no practicaban ya esas diferencias.* (Frenk 1989b:258)

> This is unthinkable: it would imply excessive monitoring, useless monitoring as we will see, since Eslava wrote basically for songs and recitations to be performed by persons who would not make such subtle phonetic differences and directed at those who no longer maintained those differences.

Margit Frenk's conclusions remove as a corpus of data one of the few references to what might have been considered a phonological system operating in New Spain in the sixteenth century. While it is true that the underlying system reflects a Toledan norm by either birth or literary adherence, it raises the issue of linguistic adaptation to a medium that in all likelihood had moved away from that norm (which means, of course, that it is not operative). But perhaps one should not be so hasty in accepting the rhyme scheme as proof of an operating phonological system; in spite of Frenk's conviction that González de Eslava's writing mirrored his pronunciation, one is taken aback by his readiness to accept and use, as has been pointed out, themes, words, and expressions that were typical of New Spain. It is the inconsistencies and departures from norms that are usually indicators of a sound system; an orderly adherence to an orthographic system speaks more of the learned background of the author than of his actual pronunciation.

2. Diego de Ordaz: A Mexican or Spanish Phonological System?

In his study of the language of Diego de Ordaz (born circa 1480), Juan Lope Blanch (1985) examines the writings of a Spaniard from Castile who migrated to America in his twenties and possibly reached Mexico at age forty. The seven letters that make up the data (written around 1530 in Spain by de Ordaz to his nephew in Mexico City) show that the devoicing of the // was complete: de Ordaz consistently wrote *s* to represent the old /ś/ and /ź/, orthographically *–ss–* and *–s–*. This apicoalveolar voiceless fricative does contrast, however, with the dorsoalveolars /ŝ/ and /ẑ/, which he regularly rendered as ç or z: *negoçiar, pedaço, hazer, doze,* and so forth. The Lope Blanch reports, however, that this careful orthographic distinction contrasts with the rather chaotic spelling of sibilants in two other letters dictated by Ordaz to a scribe, in which the apicoalveolar versus dorsoalveolar opposition did not seem to obtain: *haser, hazer, desir, dezir, favorescan, perjuisio,* and so forth. The voiced/voiceless opposition, Lope Blanch claims, was nevertheless still maintained with the pair /ŝ/ and /ẑ/, as evidenced by the spellings *caça, moços, vezinos, razón.* On the thorny question of affricate versus fricative, Lope Blanch (1985:45) suggests that /ẑ/ might still be affricate, thus maintaining its opposition with /ẑ/ even if the latter was being devoiced.[7]

De Ordaz also distinguishes regularly between /š/ and /ž/: he wrote *dexar, baxas,* but *mujer, espejos.* These sounds would eventually become a voiceless velar fricative /x/ in both Spain and America; in the Caribbean region the /x/ developed further into a glottal aspiration /h/.

If one were to extract the sibilant system of New Spain during the first half of the sixteenth century from the evidence of de Ordaz, one would state that voice and the apical and the predorsal points of articulation were still operating as distinctive traits, as follows:

An apicoalveolar voiceless fricative /ś/ resulting from the devoicing of the pair /ś/, /ź/

A dorsodental voiceless affricate /ŝ/

A dorsodental voiced fricative /ẑ/

A palatal voiceless fricative /š/

A palatal voiced fricative /ž/

These findings suggest that parts of the sibilant system were still operating on the fricative/affricate and voice/voiceless oppositions, which seems to contradict the notion that the affricates had become fricatives in the fifteenth century and therefore would not have reached America. It is more plausible to posit, as Lope Blanch himself does, that the system of de Ordaz is not typical or representative of New Spain but, rather, closer to that of Castile and of educated Seville. Again, we may be forced to withdraw the de Ordaz writings as a corpus from which to construct the phonological system of New Spain and, ultimately, Mexico.

3. Scribal Evidence of Linguistic Variations: Spaniards Writing in Mexico

In her 1976 study, Claudia Parodi examines fourteen brief documents written in Mexico in 1523 by scribes.[8] Her findings, supported by data regarding the transcription of Spanish texts into Indian languages (Canfield 1934), suggest that the affricate articulation did not reach Mexico but that /ś/ was definitely apicoalveolar. To support that assertion, she reports that the dental voiceless affricate /ŝ/ of Nahua was invariably transcribed as ç or z preceded by *t,* which would have been unnecessary if Spanish ç and z represented an affricate sound. But the ç and z were used in rendering the dorsodental voiceless fricative /s/ of the indigenous languages, which strong-

ly suggests that they corresponded to a dorsoalveolar and possibly voiceless articulation. She also finds evidence of the fusion/confusion of the apicoalveolar and predorsoalveolar articulation: *hasiendas, haser, perescan,* but both *Caçerez* and *Cázeres*
(Parodi 1976: 121). As to the timing of the devoicing of the pair, Parodi reaffirms that
–s– and –ss–, formerly /z/ and /s/, had fused into one voiceless articulation, with only
token orthographic attempts to maintain the old distinction. Since it has generally
been accepted that this devoicing is a phenomenon of the second half of the sixteenth
century, one would have to adjust this dating in view of the Mexican documents
adduced by Parodi. However, evidence of devoicing of the dorsoalveolar frica-
tive/affricate /z/ is not conclusive: one finds only sporadic examples of orthography
with *ç* where *z* would be expected, but the distinction between the two is still the
norm, bringing the Parodi data, as far as devoicing is concerned, in line with the system proposed by Lope Blanch for de Ordaz.

One must not forget, however, that the speech of Toledo was still felt as normative
by a considerable number of Spaniards and Creoles who, though perhaps following
the Andalusian pattern in their speech, felt compelled to use an orthography that
would reflect the Toledan modality. This suggests that de Ordaz was perhaps conservative only in his orthography and that the state of the phonological system of the language of his time is better represented by the "confusion" found in the letters he
dictated (but obviously did not proofread) to the scribes, who, one suspects, would
have written in accordance with the norm in use.

The orthographies of González de Eslava and de Ordaz, in their systematic distinctions among –s– and –ss– (in González de Eslava, but not in de Ordaz), *ç* and *z, j*
and *x,* contrast significantly with the overall system outlined by Parodi, which seems
to have moved rapidly towards the fusing of all sibilants into a dorsoalveolar voiceless
/s/ and a voiceless /š/ > /x/. It must be noted that the authors of the texts analyzed by
Lope Blanch, Parodi, and Frenk were all from Spain. Even though one might argue
that these writings reflect the state of the language in New Spain in the sixteenth century, it is also true that they probably reflect the speech of the regions of origin of the
authors—as modified, perhaps, by their stay in America. It is worth noting that if we
compare the three systems outlined above, the one that emerges from scribal writings
is more in tune with the historical development of the sibilants, exhibiting vacillations
and confusions; in contrast, the writings of González de Eslava, and to a lesser extent
those of de Ordaz, reveal the internal consistency of the systems of men of letters.

4. Juan Suárez de Peralta

The language of the *criollos* (American–born offspring of European–born parents) has
hardly attracted the attention of scholars. This is doubtless due to the paucity of
extant texts and, to no lesser extent, to the difficulty of establishing authorship and
birthplace. Even when it is known that a particular person was born in America, it is
often the case that he was sent to Spain for schooling, thus making linguistic affiliation a difficult issue to resolve. Texts whose authors' biographies are known, however
imperfectly, are thus important and relevant. Such is the case of Juan Suárez de

Peralta, a *criollo* born (circa 1537) in Mexico City of Spanish parents who had settled in the Caribbean during the first years following the encounter of the two worlds.

Suárez de Peralta wrote *Tratado del descubrimiento de las Yndias y su conquista* in 1589.[9] Although a major part of the book deals with the history of America from Columbus to Cortés, the most interesting sections are accounts of events that the author witnessed or that took place during his lifetime. His often casual and spontaneous style betrays a profound attachment to his birthplace, to his fellow *criollos*, and, not infrequently, even to the Indian natives. His perspective is always that of the native son relating incidents about his own country, thus making this manuscript an almost ideal corpus for the study of the Spanish used in New Spain in the sixteenth century.[10]

Nothing is known of his education, although his style leads one to believe that he was not learned. He writes spontaneously and often in very long and convoluted sentences; his vocabulary, though not particularly rich, is nevertheless descriptively precise and abundant in Nahua terms. His readings did not go much beyond a few classics and the most notable chroniclers of his time (Sahagún, Motolinía, Durán, las Casas). Of his own culture he confesses that he

> ...*no tenía sino una poca de gramática, aunque muncha afiçión de leer historias y de tratar con personas doctas.* (Peralta 1990:71)
>
> ... had but little study of grammar, though much craving for reading histories and dealing with learned persons.

Toward linguistic separation: devoicing   There is very little trace in Suárez de Peralta of the old voiced/voiceless opposition between the sounds represented in medieval Spanish by –*s*– and –*ss*–, *s*–, –*s*. The spelling –*s*– is generally used to represent the by now coalesced phonemes /ś/ and /ź/: *fertilísima, cosas, dexasen, metiesen, munchísimos,* and so forth. He uses –*ss*– in only two cases and, as it turns out, once antietymologically: he writes *opressos,* but also both *ossó* and *osó.* In this respect Suárez de Peralta's system coincides with that of de Ordaz and the writers, with one exception, studied by Parodi.

The devoicing of *z,* on the other hand, is evidenced in Suárez de Peralta's writing by only one occurrence of *deçir* and one of *diçen,* and by the troublesome numerals, always spelled – *çientos* to reflect the spelling revision from the medieval –*zientos.*

The voiced/voiceless opposition between /ž/ and /š/, represented in the spelling by *j, g,* and *x,* is not found in Suárez de Peralta. In marked contrast with the systems of de Ordaz and González de Eslava, he wrote *aconsexaron* and *consejo, xamás, lixítimamente (legítimamente), xuezes (jueces), exiçios (egipcios),* while he also registered *baje* (from *bajar), truje, pájaros, aguxerillos, deuaxo (debajo), texuelo.* Most interestingly, he writes *esecución* and *esecutase,* but also *ejecuçión* and *ejecutar.*[11] The spelling *j* often alternates with *g* in words like *gente/jente* and *gentiles/jentiles,* though the *g* is more common.

The language of the *Tratado* suggests a sibilant system strikingly divergent from those of González de Eslava and de Ordaz, again raising the issue of chronology. Amado Alonso (1976:92) states that the devoicing took place circa 1500 or before. Other scholars move the change to the middle of the sixteenth century (Canfield

1952:27; Catalán 1957:287). The data presented here suggest that by 1589 the devoicing of the sibilants was in a very advanced stage, with only token representation of the previous oppositions between /ś/ and /ź/ and between /š/ and /ž/.

The situation for /ŝ/ and /ẑ/, however, is not entirely clear. The scant and isolated examples of the spelling –ç– where –z– is expected (deçir and diçen) are not sufficient to posit systematic devoicing and are overshadowed by the methodical use of the etymological –z–: dezir and fazer (in all its morphological representations), azia (hacia), rayzes, juizio, narizes, naturaleza, razón, reduzen. Yet it might be safe to assume that, if not entirely gone, the voiced/voiceless opposition was close to being the general pronunciation. One can again recur to the often quoted passage of Juan de Córdoba, a Spanish friar in Mexico who wrote Arte en lengua zapoteca in 1578:

> Entre nosotros y en nuestra España es lo mesmo: que los de Castilla la Vieja dizen açer, y en Toledo hazer; y dizen xugar, y en Toledo jugar; y dizen yerro, y en Toledo hierro; y dizen alagar, y en Toledo halagar.

> Among us and in our Spain it is the same: those from Old Castile say açer and in Toledo hazer; and they say xugar and in Toledo jugar; and they say yerro, and in Toledo hierro; and they say alagar, and in Toledo halagar.

The categorical statement about devoicing of /ẑ/ and /ž/ in New Castile begs the question as to why no mention is made by de Córdoba of the –s– versus –ss– opposition. Amado Alonso (1976:23) suggests that they must have followed the pattern of the other two pairs and maintained the distinction,[12] while Parodi (1976:123) is inclined to interpret the testimony of de Córdoba literally: it is not mentioned because not even Toledo distinguished –s– from –ss–. We have, then, an apicoalveolar /ś/ contrasting with a predorsoalveolar /s/ and, possibly, a lingering voiced /z/.

Further linguistic separation: deaffrication   While Lope Blanch finds that de Ordaz maintained the affricate pronunciation, Parodi contends that the affricate articulation did not reach the American shores. The criollo Suárez de Peralta, who most likely did not feel the pressure of a peninsular norm, exhibited a rather chaotic mixture of spellings pointing to a system of fricative rather than affricate sibilants. He wrote desendençia, Ynquisisión, posisión (posición), suseçión, and seçaba (cesaba), though he generally kept the z spelling for what was already a fricative, but perhaps still occasionally voiced, pronunciation: juizio, juezes, bezes, dize, and razón.[13] The very numerous spellings with s where ç would be expected, while speaking clearly to the fricative articulation,[14] make us reconsider the notion that the dephonemization of /ś/ and /ź/ resulted in an apicoalveolar articulation that would then contrast with the dorsoalveolar modality coming from the deaffrication of /ŝ/ and, eventually, of /ẑ/.

There is no evidence that Suárez de Peralta made any distinction between the s coming from the older /ś/ and /ź/ and the s derived from the deaffrication of /ŝ/: spellings such as seçaba ("Oy dezir que tampoco seçaba [cesaba] la tormenta"), Medinaçidonia, Ynquisisión, sierra, and çierra ("...y auiendo pasado la sierra neuada del bolcán. Estas dos son çierras que pareçen, según su altura, se comunican con el çielo"), çuçedió ("...aunque no le çuçedió en la bentura como en el estado y en la *hazienda*"), *françeces* (once) and *françeses* (three times), and *çuzios*, betray an advanced stage of leveling of sibilants to one dorsodental voiceless fricative /s/ with remnants of a voiced articulation for the likely fricative –z–.

 CONCLUSIONS

The evidence from the language of Juan Suárez de Peralta, a native Mexican writing in the last quarter of the sixteenth century, is rather conclusive. Not only had the process of coalescence of /s/ and /z/ into a single voiceless /s/ been completed, but the apicoalveolar articulation (if it ever existed) was absorbed by the dorsodental variety resulting from the dorsoalveolar affricates. While he may have had lingering voiced pronunciations of the old /ẑ/ z, we can confidently assert that by 1579, when he left Mexico City, his *seseo* was firmly established.

Notes

1. We follow the established convention of slashes // to mark phonemic rendering, brackets [ ] for phonetic representation,and parentheses ( ) for spelling, modern or archaic.
2. The evidence on this matter is rather conflicting. Sixteenth–century grammarians are fond of comparing ç and z to Italian z and zz, but there are also indications that the lower economic strata were using the fricative pronunciation by the same period. The Hebrew letter *samekh* was the preferred transcription for ç and not the letter *sadhe*. The grammarians were likely reporting on the preferred and prestigious articulation (Lloyd 1987:333).
3. There are, of course, scholars who take no side and some who change position as recent scholarship adduces more data. The literature on this subject is voluminous; a recent summary of the discussions is found in Moreno de Alba 1988.
4. There is still considerable discussion on the point of articulation for z and ç. Amado Alonso (1940:93), relying heavily on the testimony of Antonio de Nebrija, maintained that they were apicodental, even when they shifted from affricates to fricatives. Galmés de Fuentes (1962:53), reading the same sources, suspects that Nebrija,in his insistence on describing the position of the tip of the tongue in the articulation of the sounds, may in fact have neglected the real point of articulation, which, in Galmés's view, would be the predorsum, with the tip of the tongue resting interdentally or on the lower incisors.
5. To a lesser extent, the Canary Islands and Hispaniola, as obligatory layovers for the journey, also reflected the configuration of New World society.
6. He was born in Spain in 1534 and reached America in 1558.
7. De Ordaz wrote ç to represent the dorsodentoalveolar voiceless affricate /ŝ/ of Náhuatl, while he employed –z or –s to represent the voiceless fricative /s/ of the same language.
8. Parodi treats the regional origins of the scribes only briefly. It is clear, however, that they were almost invariably born in Spain.
9. The manuscript was not published in the author's lifetime. It was first edited in 1878 by Justo Zaragoza with the title *Noticias Históricas de la Nueva España* and reedited in 1949 by F. Gómez de Orozco (Mexico City: Secretaría de Educación Pública). Both editions are difficult to obtain and contain errors of transcription (the 1949 edition is a reprinting of the 1878 edition). A study and new edition based on the original manuscript of the Biblioteca Pública de Toledo, Spain, has been edited and published by Giorgio Perissinotto (1990).
10. I say "almost ideal" because Suárez de Peralta traveled to Spain in 1579 and, presumably, wrote the *Tratado* there. There are indications in the text, however, that parts of it were written in New Spain. It is not known whether he ever returned to his homeland.

11. Though one could argue that since both *s* and *j* spellings for *ejecu-* are documented since the Middle Ages, the phenomenon is phonetically insignificant, a simple case of free variation.

12. He says:

> *Nada se dice aquí [in Juan de Córdoba] de –s– y –ss–, pero la historia de las parejas s–ss, z–ç y j–x está coordenada casi en todas partes, la de s–ss y z–ç en todas, de modo que, por lo menos como guía provisional, es lícito extender a la pareja s–ss lo que el P. Córdoba decía de las otras dos: Toledo (y el Sur) conservaba la correlación de sonoridad en una época en que Castilla (y el Norte en general) la había perdido.*

13. He also rendered the Nahua words *cocoloztli* and *teponaztle* invariably with the *z*, which before a *t* was most likely voiceless, though possibly still affricate. *tiza* 'chalk' corresponds to a Nahua voiceless affricate.

14. *Medinaçidonia, minsión (mención), desendençia (descendencia), çuzios (sucios), Ynquisisión, sierra and çierra (sierra), blanquisco, persuaçión, çolícita (solícita), çuçedió (sucedió), françeces (franceses), Baltasar, seçaba, Falses (Marqués de Falçes).*

References

Alatorre, Antonio. 1989. *Los 1001 años de la lengua española.* Mexico City: Fondo de Cultura Económica and El Colegio de México.

Alonso, Amado. 1940. Biografía de Fernán González de Eslava. *Nueva Revista de Filología Hispánica* 2:213–319.

———. 1976. De la pronunciación medieval a la moderna en español. 2 vols. Madrid: Gredos.

Boyd–Bowman, Peter. 1956. The Regional Origins of the Earliest Spanish Colonists of America. *Publications of the Modern Language Association* 71:1152–1172.

Canfield, D. Lincoln. 1934. *Spanish Literature in Mexican Languages As a Source for the Study of Spanish Pronunciation.* New York: Instituto de las Españas.

———. 1952. Spanish American Data for the Chronology of Sibilant Changes. *Hispania* 35:25–30.

Catalán, Diego. 1957. The End of the Phoneme /z/ in Spanish. *Word* 13:287.

Frenk, Margit. 1989a. *Villancicos, romances, ensaladas y otras canciones devotas.* Mexico City: El Colegio de México.

———. 1989b. Fernán González de Eslava y las sibilantes. *Anuario de Letras* 27.255–262.

Galmés de Fuentes, Álvaro. 1962. *Las sibilantes en la Romania.* Madrid: Gredos.

Lloyd, Paul M. 1987. *From Latin to Spanish.* Philadelphia: The American Philosophical Society.

Lope Blanch, Juan. 1985. *El habla de Diego de Ordaz. Contribución a la historia del español americano.* Mexico City: Universidad Nacional Autónoma de México.

Martinet, André. 1951. The Unvoicing of Old Spanish Sibilants. *Romance Philology* 5:133–56.

Moreno de Alba, José. 1988. *El español en América.* Mexico City: Fondo de Cultura Económica.

Parodi, Claudia. 1976. Para el conocimiento de la fonética castellana en la Nueva España: 1523. Las sibilantes. *Actas del III Congreso de ALFAL.* Puerto Rico: Publicaciones del Instituto de Lingüística. 115–25.

Suárez de Peralta, Juan. 1990. *Tratado del descubrimiento de las Yndias y su conquista (1589).* Ed. Giorgio Perissinotto. Madrid: Alianza Editorial.

Torreblanca, Máximo. 1982. La *s* hispano–latina: El testimonio árabe. *Romance Philology* 35:447–63.

On Transfer and Simplification: Verbal Clitics in Mexican-American Spanish

Carmen Silva-Corvalán   Manuel J. Gutiérrez
University of Southern California   University of Houston

In this paper we examine verbal clitic pronouns (CLs), an area of Spanish grammar that lends itself to the investigation of the processes characteristic of language contact, namely, simplification, transfer, and overgeneralization. The study is based on data obtained from recordings of conversations between one of the authors and twenty Mexican-American speakers from three cross-generational groups, all residing in the eastern section of Los Angeles. The analysis of the data allows us to conclude that some aspects of the morphosyntax of a language (e.g., verbal CLs) are rather impermeable to interlinguistic influence in a context of societal bilingualism.

INTRODUCTION

This paper is part of a larger ongoing project to investigate the linguistic effect that intensive bilingualism has on Spanish as a subordinate language across different generations of Spanish-English bilinguals in Los Angeles, California.[1] Our ultimate goal is to determine whether different types of grammatical phenomena (lexical, morphological, and syntactic) in the speech of bilinguals are affected by language contact in the same ways. We also seek to determine whether any changes identified may be more appropriately accounted for by any of the processes hypothesized to be characteristic of language contact, namely simplification (both structural and stylistic-pragmatic), transfer, and overgeneralization. In addition, we are investigating the question of the acceleration of changes already in progress in languages involved in bilingual communities, as compared with the same changes in one of the feeder communities in Mexico.[2] Thus, we expect to contribute both to a general theory of language change and, more specifically, to language contact theory.

With these goals in mind, we discuss here verbal clitic pronouns (CLs), underlined in Examples 1 and 2, elements of Spanish grammar that are conducive to the investigation of the processes of simplification, transfer, and overgeneralization.

(1) *La vi ayer*
   her saw-1sg yesterday
   'I saw her yesterday'

(2) *Se cortó*
   himself cut-3sg
   'He cut himself'

Researchers in the fields of language contact, language shift, second-language acquisition, and language change have not yet agreed on the meaning of the term simplification. Nor can they stipulate what constitutes unarguable evidence in support of the existence of this phenomenon in relevant sociolinguistic situations. For our purposes, however, we adopt Silva-Corvalán's (1990) definition of simplification as a complex process that implies rule generalization in the sense that a given form is expanded to a larger number of contexts. *Simplification*, then, involves the higher frequency in the use of a form X in context Y (i.e., generalization) at the expense of a form Z, usually in competition with and semantically closely related to X, where both X and Z existed in the language prior to the start of simplification. Thus, X is an *expanding form* while Z is a *shrinking/contracting form*. The final outcome of simplification is loss of forms, (i.e., a *simplified system* with fewer forms and possibly, though not necessarily, loss of meanings). An example of simplification in non-bilingual Spanish is provided by the competition between morphological and periphrastic future. As Silva-Corvalán and Terrell (1989) show, the morphological future in spoken Latin American Spanish is being simplified (i. e., used less and less frequently with its tense meaning) while the periphrastic future is expanding in its frequency of use.

This definition of simplification appears to correspond to the notion of *overgeneralization* (see Preston 1982) as the more extensive use of a form than would be expected in ordinary practice. The only difference is that simplification explicitly refers to contraction, that is, the less frequent use of a competing form. Overgeneralization, on the other hand, may affect contexts where no corresponding competing form exists—where XY may extend to XØ or vice versa:

$Ø + V_i \rightarrow se + V_i$: *Mi hermana recuerda eso muy bien* →
Mi hermana se recuerda eso muy bien
'My sister (se) remembers that very well.'

Transfer is undoubtedly a controversial notion as well. It might be defined simply as the incorporation of language features from one language into another. The problem is, however, as Meisel (1983) has clearly argued, that nonlexical transfer is difficult to prove. Still, we consider that transfer might have occurred whenever one or more of the following phenomena is present in the data (Silva-Corvalán 1990):

a. the replacement of a form in language S with a form from language F, or the incorporation from language F into language S of a form (with or without its associated meaning) previously absent in S (this is usually referred to in the literature as 'borrowing');

b. the incorporation of the meaning of a form R from language F, which may be part of the meaning of a form P in S, into another form, structurally similar to R, in system S (cf. Weinreich's 'extension or reduction of function' [1974:30]);

c. the higher frequency of use of a form in language S, determined on the basis of a comparison with more conservative internal community norms (Klein-Andreu 1986; Mougeon et al. 1985; Silva-Corvalán 1986), in contexts where a partially corresponding form in language F is used either categorically or preferentially;

d. the loss of a form in language S that does not exist in the system of F (cf. Weinreich's 'neglect' or 'elimination' of obligatory categories).

Transfer leads to, but is not the single cause of, *convergence*, defined as the achievement of structural similarity in a given aspect of the grammar of two or more languages that are assumed to be different at the onset of contact. Indeed, convergence may result as well from internally motivated changes in one of the languages, most likely accelerated by contact, rather than as a consequence of direct interlingual influence (Silva-Corvalán 1986).

The results of this study will show that the clitic category in the Spanish of bilinguals is affected by a general process of simplification but not necessarily by transfer.

 ## THE DATA

We collected data from recordings of conversations between Silva-Corvalán and twenty Mexican-American speakers from three groups, all residing in the eastern section of Los Angeles. Group 1 consisted of speakers born in Mexico who immigrated to the U.S. after the age of eleven. Group 2 encompassed speakers who were born in the U.S. or who immigrated to the U.S. before the age of six. Group 3 comprised speakers born in the U.S. who had at least one parent corresponding to the definition of those in Group 2. The speakers were recorded twice, with an interval of about six months between the two recordings, for periods ranging from 75 to 100 minutes on each occasion. This paper incorporates analyses of approximately 40 hours of taped conversations.

Contact between Spanish and English in the bilingual community of Los Angeles has been long and intensive and has involved large numbers of individuals. This fact plus the demographic complexity of the community account for the existence of a *bilingual continuum*, similar to a creole continuum in that one may identify a series of lects ranging from full-fledged to emblematic Spanish. The twenty speakers included here, fifteen of whom belong to four different families, reflect the different degrees of bilingual proficiency characteristic of the continuum.

 ## VERBAL CLITICS ALONG THE CONTINUUM

Even though it is not entirely clear to us how comparable Spanish CLs may be to oblique pronouns in English, we assume cross-linguistic equivalence when, in a given English sentence, an oblique pronoun translates the Spanish verbal clitic.[3] Accordingly, *lo* is considered to be equivalent to 'him,' unstressed, in Examples 3 and 4:

(3) *Lo conocí en la fiesta de Pepe*
   him met-1sg in the party of Pepe
   'I met him at Pepe's party'

(4) *Quería verlo temprano*
   wanted-1sg see him early
   'I wanted to see him early'

Overgeneralization, simplification, and transfer allow us to advance certain hypotheses with respect to the behavior of CLs along the continuum. Simplification accounts for the extension of one of two or more structures that have the same or similar meaning. This justifies the expectation of a trend toward the categorical occurrence of one of the two possible alternative positions for CLs in constructions with verbal periphrases: either preverbal (Example 5a) or postverbal (Example 5b). Overgeneralization, on the other hand, might result in the extension of so-called obligatory reflexive constructions, as in Example 6b, a trend which appears to characterize the diachronic development of Spanish.

(5) a. *Lo puedo hacer mañana*   b. *Puedo hacerlo mañana*

       it can-1sg do tomorrow   can-1sg do it tomorrow

                     'I can do it tomorrow'

(6) a. *¡Mi hermano no creció hasta cuando tenía cuarenta!* (Group 1: standard nonreflexive form)

     b. *¡Mi hermano no se creció hasta cuando tenía cuarenta!* (Gr. 3: nonstandard reflexive form)

       'My brother didn't (*se*) mature until he reached forty!'

Furthermore, if transfer from English affects this area of the Spanish grammar, the bilingual's propensity to make both languages structurally more similar should result in omission of the CL when the corresponding English construction does not require an oblique pronoun (Example 7).

(7) ... *y me dieron en la cara, y Ø quebraron mi, mi 'jaw'* (Gr. 3)

     and me hit-3pl in the face, and Ø broke-3pl my, my jaw

     ... *y me dieron en la cara, y me quebraron la, la mandíbula* (Gr. 1)

                       to me broke-3pl the, the jaw

     '... and they hit me in the face, and broke my, my jaw'

Transfer should also result in the preference for postverbal placement of the CL (5b). This type of transfer, which at first evidences itself not in ungrammaticality but in an increased frequency of use of parallel structures, is proposed by Klein-Andreu to be the most likely to occur, as well as the most likely to become part of community language norms.[4] Furthermore, though previous research has shown that, as compared to free morphemes, bound morphology is more resistant to change (Meisel 1983; Pfaff and Portz 1979; Poplack's 1978 'free morpheme constraint'; Weinreich 1974),[5] the presence or absence of inflectional markings in one language is also cited as one of the possible features to be affected by the presence or absence of corresponding inflections in the contact language (Meisel, Weinreich). Thus, as inflections, CLs may be a plausible site for transfer from English, which may affect both their position and actual occurrence.

1. Omission of Clitics

For the examination of CL omission, in every sentence where a CL occurred or should have occurred, the CL was classified according to its functional relation to the verb. We established nine categories, listed as Examples 8 to 16:

(8) Accusative: *lo va a grabar*

     'She's going to record him'

(9) Dative: *le mostré el libro*

     'I showed him the book'

(10)   Obligatory reflexive: _se salió del juego_
       'He (_se_) left the game'
(11)   True reflexive: _se cortó_
       'He cut <u>himself</u>'
(12)   Indirect reflexive: _se cortó el dedo_
       'He (_se_) cut his finger'
(13)   Inanimate subject reflexive: _se quemó el pan_
       'The bread (_se_) got burnt'
(14)   Reciprocal: _nos peleábamos a menudo_
       'We (_nos_) often argued'
(15)   Impersonal _se_ : _ahí se come bien_
       'One (_se_) eats well there'
(16)   Affective: _yo te corro tres millas todos los días_
       'I run (<u>you</u>) three miles every day'

Regarding the possible omission of CLs, it is interesting to note that in a subset sample of thirteen speakers in Groups 2 (speakers born in or immigrated to the U.S. before the age of six) and 3 (speakers born in the U.S. with at least one parent belonging to group 2), of a total of over two thousand possible contexts for the occurrence of an obligatory clitic (Examples 8 to 15), only sixty-nine are missing. Seven speakers in Group 1 were also examined. Only one of these failed to provide an obligatory clitic, three times in 298 cases. Table 1 displays the results by speaker, and Table 2 displays them by group according to type of CL; Examples 17 and 18 illustrate omissions:

(17)   — _tenemos una_ i _y nosotros_ Øi _llevamos_ [_la moto_ i] [_la_ i]
       — have-1pl onei and we Øi take-1pl [the bikei]
       '— we have onei and we take iti' (Son,f19,3)[6]
(18)   — _muy amarradas las tenían_ — _y ellas_ i Øi _rebelaron,_ Øi _rebelaron_ [_se_ i]
       — very controlled them had-3pl — and they Ø rebelled, Ø rebelled
       '— they had them very controlled — and they rebelled, they rebelled'
       (Dan,m45,3)

Table 1. Clitics omitted in required contexts.

		Group 1				Group 2				Group 3	
Sil	f24	0/308	0%	Rita	f21	2/277	0.7%	Son	f19	1/184	0.5%
Ali	f62	0/317	0%	Virgi	f18	6/148	4.1%	Dol	f28	3/295	1.0%
Rose	f42	0/296	0%	Hra	m21	0/320	0.0%	Aal	f31	0/77	0.0%
Eva	f44	0/296	0%	Rra	m20	0/207	0.0%	Rod	m15	24/45	53.0%
Moi	m17	3/298	1%	Alb	m60	2/263	0.8%	Joe	m17	7/257	2.7%
Ion	m41	0/247	0%					Heny	m39	0/131	0.0%
Phil	m54	0/298	0%					Dan	m45	23/255	9.0%
								Rro	m46	3/292	1.0%
TOTALS		3/2063	0.1%			10/1225	0.8%			61/1597	3.8%

Table 2. Clitics omitted in required contexts, by clitic type and by group.

Clitic type	Group 1 (1 spkr: Moi,m17)		Group 2 (5 spkrs)			Group 3 (8 spkrs)		
Accusative		0%	2/262	0.8%	0.7%	15/433	3.4%	2.7%
Dative	2/119	1.6%	4/487	0.8%		11/521	2.1%	
Oblig. refl.	1/100	1%	2/278	0.7%		13/355	3.6%	
True reflex.		0%	2/39	5%		6/54	11%	
Indir. refl.		0%		0%	1.2%	10/77	13%	6.0%
Inan. subj. refl.		0%		0%		4/26	15.4%	
Reciprocal		0%		0%		2/15	13.3%	
Impersonal (Affective)		0%		0%			0%	

In Table 1, observe that in Group 3 omission is somewhat more noticeable and that Rod has the highest frequency of omission (53%); Dan has the second highest percentage of omission (9%). In Group 2, Virgi has the highest (4.1%). Observe, furthermore, that in Groups 2 and 3 omission occurs more frequently when it concerns a reflexive or reciprocal clitic (see table 2). Indeed, the total percentage of reflexive and reciprocal clitics omitted in Groups 2 and 3 is 1.2% and 6%, respectively, while fewer than 1% of dative and accusative clitics are omitted in Group 2 and only 2.7% of these CLs are omitted in Group 3. If we eliminate Rod from Group 3, we have the results given in Table 3, but these results still show higher omission with reflexives and reciprocals:

Table 3. Quantification of clitic omission for seven speakers in Group 3.

Clitic type		
Accusative	6/408	1.5%
Dative	9/518	1.7%
Oblig. reflex.	9/349	2.6%
True reflex.	6/54	11.1%
Indir. reflex.	0/66	0.0%
Inan. subj. reflex.	4/26	15.4%
Reciprocal	2/15	13.3%

Separating Rod from the rest of the speakers in Group 3 is justified. This speaker represents an interesting case: he did not develop productive competence in Spanish as a child but was nevertheless exposed to this language from birth both at home and in the community. At the time of the data collection, he had completed three semesters of Spanish in high school. He was able to converse during the interview with a fair degree of fluency and showed a high level of oral comprehension. If he had not had at least a fairly well-developed receptive proficiency in Spanish, he would not have reached the degree of productive proficiency he now demonstrates. However, his Spanish does appear to show the effect of schooling, and this sets him apart from other youngsters who have acquired this language in natural settings. Thus, even though another young man in Group 3, Joe, appeared to have an overall level of proficiency in Spanish similar to Rod's, a closer examination of their speech shows that Rod's use of CLs is further removed from the norms of Group 1 despite the fact that he, and not Joe, received formal instruction in Spanish in high school. This difference is also apparent in regard to CL position, as we show later.

With respect to the omission of dative and accusative clitics, we conclude that transfer from English does not play any role: if it did, we should have obtained a higher percentage of omission of datives and accusatives when the coreferential element was expressed, but this was not the case. As for reflexives, note that in most cases the factors that determine which verbs have a reflexive form in Spanish are opaque. Here, then, we may have a case of lexical transfer with apparently syntactic consequences, as in Example 7.

2. Clitic Position in Verbal Periphrases

The position of CLs in contemporary spoken Spanish may be either categorically or variably preverbal or postverbal depending on the type of verbal phrase, as explained below in Examples 19 to 21:

A. CLs are *categorically preverbal* with finite verbal forms:

(19) *Lo compró / lo ha comprado ya*
      'She bought it / She has bought it already'

B. CLs are *categorically postverbal* with infinitives, present participles, and gerunds in complement clauses:

(20) *Vine para verte*
      came-1sg for see-you
      'I came to see you'

(21) *Viéndola te acordarás de ella*
      seeing-her you-refl remember-fut-2sg of her
      'Seeing her, you'll remember her'

C. When CLs refer to an argument of an infinitive or a present participle in a verbal periphrasis with a finite 'semi-auxiliary' verb, they may *variably* occur *before the finite verb*. The appearance of the CL in front of the finite verb has been proposed to be the consequence of clause union by Aissen and Perlmutter (1976), and as the consequence of restructuring by Rizzi (1978). This, then, is the only *variable context* for CL placement in Spanish (cf. Myhill 1988, 1989). Example 22 illustrates:

(22) *Viene a verte / Te viene a ver*
      comes-3sg to see-you / you comes-3sg to see
      'He's coming to see you'

None of the twenty speakers studied violates the categorical preverbal or postverbal placement constraints illustrated in Examples 19 to 21. However, in regard to those utterances which allow one of two positions for CLs (Example 22), our study indicates that, contrary to what a naive view of transfer might predict, postverbal placement is less frequent in the speech of bilinguals. Furthermore, the variables that simply *favor* preverbal placement in Spanish dominant bilinguals — and in monolinguals, as shown by Myhill 1988 — appear as *almost* categorical contexts for this order; that is, the Spanish of bilinguals moves in the direction of strengthening Spanish internal trends rather than English patterns.[7]

In his study of CL placement in written Spanish, Myhill (1988) shows quantitatively that this phenomenon is constrained by at least two factors: the semantic properties of the finite verb and the relative topicality of the subject and the CL. The former factor favors restructuring more strongly than the latter. Furthermore, Myhill shows that of the three semantic classes of verbs that allow restructuring (modals, aspectuals, and motion verbs), those that are more likely to be represented with more grammaticalized morphemes in natural languages (progressives, epistemic modals, and future reference verbs; see Bybee 1985) occur with pre-finite verb CLs most frequently.

These findings are confirmed by our study of CL placement in bilingual Spanish, as Table 4 shows. This table displays the quantification of preverbal versus postverbal placement of CLs in verbal periphrases with those verbs that occurred at least ten times in the samples of speech from the twenty speakers. We have included a comparison with some of the results obtained by Myhill (1989:5) for written Spanish.

Table 4. Preverbal clitic placement in verbal periphrases.

Finite verb	Group 1 (7 spkrs)		Group 2 (5 spkrs)		Group 3 (8 spkrs)		Written Spanish (Myhill 1989)	
ir (a) 'go'	85/92	92%	35/36	97%	61/66	92%	136/181	75%
estar 'be'	30/33	91%	19/20	95%	31/35	89%	75/84	89%
poder 'may'/'can'	23/38	60%	18/19	95%	36/47	83%	33/178	19%
tener que 'have to'	17/30	57%	12/16	75%	8/13	65%	7/46	15%
querer 'want to'	6/19	32%	6/11	55%	12/23	52%	12/90	13%
empezar 'begin'	8/11	73%	0/1	0%	2/2	100%	3/32	9%
deber 'must'	1/6	17%	3/5	60%	1/2	50%	7/62	11%

As our data in Table 4 indicate, future (*ir a* 'going to'), progressive (*estar* 'be'), and epistemic (*poder* 'may') meanings clearly favor preverbal position, even more strongly than in written Spanish in every semantic class. This preference for preverbal position applies as well to the less-favoring root modality (*deber* 'must', *tener que* 'have to', *querer* 'want') and inceptive (*empezar* 'begin') classes. This tendency increases among second-generation bilinguals. Speakers in Group 3, on the other hand, though still reflecting this general trend, have slightly lower percentages of preverbal CLs than do those in Group 2. This general result needs to be examined in more detail. However, based on a comparison of other features of Group 3 Spanish with those of Group 2 (namely, verb morphology and the extension of *estar* 'to be'), we note that third-generation immigrants do not seem to continue a "natural" historical development of their ancestors' language. The language of this group moves much further away from the norms of Group 1 speakers and shows signs of stronger convergence with the dominant contact language.

Although we have seen a certain amount of individual variation within each group, the only speaker who clearly departs from the strong general tendency to place the CL preverbally is Rod (Gr. 3). In only one of ten possible contexts was the CL preverbal in his data: in other words, Rod strongly favored postverbal position (90%) when this was a grammatical alternative in Spanish. We would like to suggest, then, that this is a further consequence, in addition to CL omission, of his formal learning of Spanish, an experience that sets him apart from other members of his community and appears to have made him more vulnerable to transfer from English. Assuming that formal learning increases the speaker's awareness of form, this result would support Meisel's (1983) observation that speakers who focus on form are more likely to use transfer strategies than are those who focus on the messages they wish to convey.

 ## CONCLUSION

The present study gives evidence that some aspects of the morphosyntax of a language (e.g., verbal CLs) are rather impermeable to interlinguistic influence in a context of societal bilingualism.[8] The preverbal slot for verbal CLs appears to be firmly imprinted in speakers' minds, and so-called reflexive clitics are tightly associated with their verbal lexemes in the case of obligatory reflexive verbs. This accounts for the extremely low percentage of omission of CLs in the data. Further evidence of the "reality" of CL morphemes is offered by utterances in which the CL appears in Spanish and the verb in English, as in Examples 23 to 25:

(23)   *Mi mom quiere que los* keep ... my grades up
       my mom wants that them keep ... my grades up
       'My mom wants me to keep my grades up' (Joe,m17,3)

(24)   *y lo que* i *queda ... lo* i invest in stock *o algo así*
       and whati remains ... iti-acc. invest in stock or something like that
       'And whatever remains you invest it in stock or something like that'
       (Joe,m17,3)

(25)   *No, uno ... no se quieren* tie down
       no, some ... not se want tie down
       'No, some don't want to get tied down'
       [get tied down = *amarrarse*]   (Joe,m17,3)

In the case of naturally developed bilingualism, our study also offers evidence against transfer when the parallel structure in the dominant language is not characterized by analyticity. In regard to Klein-Andreu's hypothesis, then, our study suggests that it should be modified to incorporate a constraint on the type of parallel structure likely to be transferred or preferred. Further, we suggest that a theory of simplification—motivated by interactional, cognitive, and intralinguistic factors, and predicting the loss of certain morphosyntactic variables in subordinate contact languages—accounts more appropriately than transfer for the tightly constrained postverbal placement of CLs. This theory also explains, we suggest, the preference for progressive over simple forms observed by Klein-Andreu in the Spanish of Puerto Ricans in New York, as well as the preference for the prepositional phrase *à la maison (de)* over the "simple" prepositions *chez, sur,* and *à* verified by Mougeon, Beniak, and Valois in Canadian French.

Notes

1. Our investigations for this paper were supported by the U.S. National Science Foundation under Grant BNS-8721453. This larger ongoing project obtained its first funding from the NSF as well (grant BNS-8214733, awarded to C. Silva-Corvalán).
2. Gutiérrez has collected data in Michoacán, México, to study these comparisons. We have compared a change in the opposition *ser/estar* going on in Michoacán with the same phenomenon taking place in Los Angeles.
3. We note, however, that stressed oblique pronouns in English must be translated with nonverbal clitic pronouns in Spanish, as in the example below. See García et al. (1987) for an illuminating analysis of the question of inter-translatability and cross-linguistic equivalence.
   I saw <u>him</u> at the store   (not <u>her</u>)
   <u>Lo</u> i vi <u>a él</u> i en la tienda   (*no <u>a ella</u>*)
4. Klein-Andreu (1986:7) demonstrates that Puerto Rican bilinguals in New York use the present progressive in Spanish much more frequently than do Puerto Rican Spanish monolinguals.
5. In agreement with a number of researchers (Givon 1976; Meisel 1983; Silva-Corvalán 1981), we view CLs as verbal inflections, that is, as bound morphology.
6. The information given in parentheses gives the speaker's identification, sex, age, and group (1, 2, or 3). A series of dashes in some of the examples stands for language material omitted because it is not relevant to the discussion; dots represent pauses.
7. The direction of the change in the *ser/estar* opposition in Los Angeles (Silva-Corvalán 1986) follows Spanish internal trends, evident throughout the history of the language. This is further demonstrated by Gutiérrez (1992) with data from Michoacán. The difference between the two communities is found in the speed of the change process: while in the monolingual community the percentage of the innovative form is 16%, in the bilingual community it is 34%.
8. Silva-Corvalán (1991) arrives at the same conclusion in regard to the simplification and loss of tense-mood-aspect morphology.

References

Aissen, Judith, and D. Perlmutter. 1976. Clause Reduction in Spanish. *Proceedings of the Second Annual Meeting of the Berkeley Linguistics Society*, 1-30. Berkeley, Calif.: Berkeley Linguistics Society.

Bybee, Joan. 1985. *Morphology: A Study of the Relation between Meaning and Form.* Amsterdam: John Benjamins.

García, Erica, Florimon van Putte, and Yishai Tobin. 1987. Cross-linguistic Equivalence, Translatability, and Contrastive Analysis. *Folia Linguistica* 21:373-405.

Givon, Talmy. 1976. Topic, Pronoun and Grammatical Agreement. In *Subject and Topic*, ed. by C.N. Li, 149-88. New York: Academic Press.

Gutiérrez, Manuel. 1992. The extension of *estar*: A linguistic change in progress in the Spanish of Morelia, Mexico. *Hispanic Linguistics* Vol. 5 (1-2):109-141.

Klein-Andreu, Flora. 1986. La cuestión del anglicismo: apriorismos y métodos. *Thesaurus*, Tomo XL, 1-16. Boletín del Instituto Caro y Cuervo.

Meisel, Jürgen M. 1983. Transfer as a Second Language Strategy. *Language & Communication* 3:11-46.

Mougeon, Raymond, E. Beniak, and D. Valois. 1985. A Sociolinguistic Study of Language Contact, Shift, and Change. *Linguistics* 23:455-87.

Myhill, John. 1988. The Grammaticalization of Auxiliaries: Spanish Clitic Climbing. *Proceedings of the Fourteenth Annual Meeting of the Berkeley Linguistics Society*. Berkeley, Calif.: Berkeley Linguistics Society.

Myhill, John. 1989. Variation in Spanish Clitic Climbing. In *Synchronic and Diachronic Approaches to Linguistic Variation and Change*, ed. by Thomas J. Walsh, 227-250. Washington D.C.: Georgetown University Press.

Pfaff, Carol, and R. Portz. 1979. Foreign Children's Acquisition of German: Universals vs. Interference. Paper presented at the annual meeting of the Linguistic Society of America, Los Angeles.

Poplack, Shana. 1978. *Quantitative Analysis of Constraints on Code-switching*. [Center for Puerto Rican Studies Working Paper No. 2] New York: Center for Puerto Rican Studies.

Preston, Dennis R. 1982. How to Lose a Language. *Interlanguage Studies Bulletin* 6:64-87.

Rizzi, Luigi. 1978. A Restructuring Rule in Italian Syntax. In *Recent Transformational Studies in European Languages*, ed. by Samuel J. Keyser, 113-58. Cambridge, Mass.: MIT Press.

Silva-Corvalán, Carmen. 1981. The Diffusion of Object-Verb Agreement in Spanish. *Papers in Romance* 3:163-76.

———. Carmen. 1986. Bilingualism and Language Change: The Extension of *estar* in Los Angeles Spanish. *Language* 62:587-608.

———. 1990. Current Issues in Studies of Language Contact. *Hispania* 73:162-76.

———. 1991. Cross-Generational Bilingualism: Theoretical Implications of Language Attrition. In *Cross-Currents in Second Language Acquisition and Linguistic Theories*, ed. by Thom Huebner and Charles A. Ferguson, 325-345. Amsterdam/Philadelphia: John Benjamins.

Silva-Corvalán, Carmen, and Tracy Terrell. 1989. Notas sobre la expresión de futuridad en el español del Caribe. *Hispanic Linguistics* 2:191-208.

Weinreich, U. 1974. *Languages in Contact*, 8th printing. The Hague: Mouton.

Sex, Class, and Velarization: Sociolinguistic Variation in the Youth of Madrid

Mark S. Turnham and Barbara A. Lafford
Arizona State University

In a sociolinguistic study of the youth of Madrid, statistically significant correlations between the dependent variable /s/ followed by a velar stop (/k/) and several independent variables including socioeconomic class, sex, and style were discovered. The results supported general trends established in other sociolinguistic studies: A high percentage of the prestige variant [s] and low occurrences of the stigmatized variants [x] and [0] were found in upper classes, in women's speech, and in the speech of all informants in formal styles. Additional observations included the high realization of [s] in the filler expression *es que* and types of stylistic sensitivity found among female, male, and lower-class informants.

1 INTRODUCTION[1]

The velarization of /s/ to [x] before /k/ (*asco* [áxko], *los campos* [loxkámpos])[2] in Madrid has been attested by the Spanish linguists Antonio Quilis (1965:22) and Diego Catalán (1955:46). Manuel Alvar and Antonio Quilis (personal communication[3]) have noted the similarity between this velarization of the phoneme /s/ in implosive final position and the widespread Andalusian, Caribbean, and Southern Cone aspiration of /s/—[h] in the same linguistic context. Alvar (personal communication) has suggested that since in its inventory of phonemes the Spanish of Madrid contains a very pronounced velar fricative /x/ (*Jorge* [xórxe]), this [x] sound would be the one naturally produced by a "backing of /s/" phenomenon rather than the aspirate sound [h] that normally realizes the pharyngeal phoneme /h/ in the geographic areas mentioned above.

Although various sociolinguistic studies have analyzed the aspiration [h] and deletion [0] of implosive /s/ in various dialects of Spanish in Andalusia and lowland parts of Latin America over the past two decades (Cedergren 1973; Fontanella de Weinberg 1974; Hammond 1977; Terrell 1978, 1979, 1986; Poplack 1979; Carbonero 1985; Lamíquiz 1976, 1985; Lafford 1982, 1980 [1985], 1989), no systematic sociolinguistic study has been carried out to date of the velarization and deletion of implosive /s/ in the dialect of Madrid.

Due to the lack of existing sociolinguistic research on the speech of Madrid and because scholars believe the velarization of /s/ to be a fruitful topic for sociolinguistic analysis (Moreno, Alvar, and Quilis [personal communication]), the present study was undertaken.

2 SOCIAL AND STYLISTIC VARIABLES AND HYPOTHESES TO BE TESTED

The purpose of this study was to investigate the strength of correlations between the dependent variable (syllable and word final /s/ realized as [s], [x], or [0] before /k/) and several independent variables (class, sex, and style) with a margin of error of 5% ($p < .05$).

2.1 Social Variables

The social variables chosen for this study were socioeconomic class and the sex of the informant. Traditional sociolinguistic studies generally include age as another important factor. However, a lack of time prevented our interviewing informants older than high school age for this sample.

Socioeconomic class of the informants   Studies correlating the realization of /s/ with socioeconomic class or education level have been carried out by Cedergren (1973), Fontanella de Weinberg (1974), Lafford (1982), Poplack (1979), López Morales (1983) and Terrell (1982). All of these studies positively correlated higher socioeconomic class/education levels with the realization of the prestigious variant [s]. Therefore, we hypothesized the same for the Madrid data:

> H1: *There will be a significant positive correlation between an increase in the socioeconomic class and an increased production of the prestige variant [s]. Conversely, the lower classes will produce more of the stigmatized variants [x] and [0] before /k/.*

Sex of the informants   An interesting hypothesis we considered that differed somewhat from the findings of most of the other sociolinguistic studies was that young women in Madrid generally would not use more prestigious speech than the men. Previous sociolinguistic studies to date have found that adult women use less stigmatized patterns than men in casual as well as in careful/guarded speech (Fischer 1958; Shuy, Wolfram and Riley 1967; Wolfram 1969; Trudgill 1971). Specifically, Cedergren (1973), Fontanella de Weinberg (1974), Poplack (1979), Alba (1982), and Terrell (1982) all found more deletion of final Spanish /s/ among adult men than women.

However, with the fall of Franco and the consequent liberalization of Spain, we postulated that young adolescent women may take on certain linguistic constructs normally used by males in order to demonstrate their newfound freedom. Other studies have attested linguistic ramifications of rapid social or political change, such as the consolidation of kinship terms in post-revolutionary and post-war Russia (Friedrich 1972), the shift from a power to a solidarity semantic in the use of Indonesian terms of address after post-war independence (Wittermans 1967), and a shift in the use of the terms *compañero/a, señor/a* and *don/doña* in Nicaragua under the Sandinista popularist government (Patterson 1986).

Although these studies basically deal with semantic change, we postulated that perhaps the new freedoms afforded to women in post-Franco Spain may actually cause them to relax their adherence to conservative linguistic norms of pronunciation in an effort to assert their new independence from many aspects of oppression that they suffered during the Franco regime. For instance, since Franco's death in 1975, divorce has become legalized and women's role in the political process has become more visible (the spokesperson for the Socialist government in 1989 was a woman, Rosa Conde).

In addition, over the last twenty years the authors have noted that *younger* Spanish women seem to be making more prevalent use of *tacos* (blue language) and other stigmatized forms now than they did a generation ago. Moreover, we postulated that even if adult Spanish women still speak more normatively than men, young adolescent (high school age) women may not yet have taken on the traditional, more conservative speech patterns of older women in the society and, thus, may use more stigmatized forms as a form of youthful rebellion, like their male counterparts.

Consequently, we hypothesized the following for this study:

> H2: *There will be no significant difference in the realizations of /s/ before /k/ between men and women among the youth of Madrid.*

2.2 Stylistic Variables

Traditional sociolinguistic studies following Labov's (1972) methodology (e.g., Cedergren 1973; Fontanella de Weinberg 1974; Lafford 1982, 1980/[1985]; Poplack 1979; Terrell 1982) have all shown more use of the prestige variant [s] in more formal styles. We have no reason to believe that the results of this Madrid study will in any way differ from these previous analyses: when the situation lends itself to more self-observation (reading a passage or reciting a word list), more monitoring of one's own speech patterns takes place and, consequently, a more formal style is used. Therefore, we hypothesized the following:

> H3: *Significantly more production of the prestige variant [s] and less use of the stigmatized variants [x] and [0] before /k/ will occur in more formal styles used by all speakers.*

If the results of this study show that the realization of /s/ as [x] or [0] differentiate the population socially and stylistically, then this phenomenon will be considered a social *marker* in Labov's (1966) definition of the term.

3 METHODOLOGY

The 47 informants were selected at random from two high schools in Madrid and one from a suburb of Madrid. The 25 women and 22 men varied in age from 14 to 23, with an average age of 18 years. The distribution of the informants in terms of socioeconomic class and sex is shown in Chart 1:

Chart 1. Distribution of informants with respect to socioeconomic class and sex

	upper class	middle class	lower class	total
male	2	11	9	22
female	6	10	9	25
total	8	21	18	47

All of the informants were born in Madrid of Castilian parentage. The original requirement of having both parents born and raised in Madrid was soon dropped because few informants had parents who met this standard.

3.1 The Determination of Socioeconomic Class of the Informants

All of the factors that entered into the determination of the socioeconomic class of the informants concerned their home environment; none of these young people would have normally separated themselves from their family's socioeconomic situation since most people in this society live at home until they marry. Therefore, our criteria for determining the socioeconomic class of the informant were based almost exclusively on only two factors: parents' educational level and parents' profession.

In most cases, the profession of the parents was congruent with the educational level attained: those with a university education held professional jobs (e.g., doctors, lawyers, engineers—our upper class), those with a high school education held non-professional positions (e.g., government workers and owners of small businesses—our middle class) and those who had little or no formal education held service or manual labor positions (e.g., construction workers and market vendors—our lower class).

3.2 Place and Format of Interview

The interviews were carried out in Madrid during the spring of 1989 in three public high schools in different socioeconomic districts within the urban area. Since the goal of the interview was to produce a relaxed atmosphere conducive to spontaneous speech, the interviewer (Turnham) would usually interview three students at a time who were acquainted with each other. The interviews lasted approximately thirty minutes and included open-ended questions, a short reading passage, and a list of words[4] to be read by each of the informants. The interviews were transcribed, the tokens coded, and the data were analyzed for chi-square significance with a program written by Turnham in ICON (Griswold and Griswold 1983).

3.3 The Diaphasic Component

One of the major difficulties encountered by Labov and others in conducting a stylistic study was the elicitation of truly casual, spontaneous speech in the artificial setting of an interview (the Observer's Paradox). Like many researchers, we found the task of deciding which fragments are spontaneous and which are guarded to be somewhat arbitrary. Therefore we decided not to distinguish between formal spoken and spontaneous speech, opting instead to observe the correlation between spoken (conversational) and reading (passage vs. word list) styles in order to gain a general idea of what speech patterns are followed in different social situations among the youth of Madrid.

3.4 The Effect of *es que* on the Data

The effects that the use of the common filler expression *es que* had on the realization of our targeted phenomenon /s/ was surprising. We decided to include it as an independent variable because of our rather late discovery that it occurred with such frequency that it might very well have skewed the results had it not been extracted from the data. For instance, the conversation portion of the interviews consisted of 1,348 tokens of /s/ before /k/, over one-third (459) of which were cases of *es que*. If we observe the effects this expression had on the overall realization of the variable /s/ before /k/ in conversational style, we find a significant difference in the realizations of the variants (chi-square = 28.89).

Chart 2. Realization according to presence of *es que* in conversation[5]

	[s]	[x]	[0]	total
es que	70.5 (324)	23.5 (108)	5.9 (27)	459
not *es que*	58.0 (516)	27.4 (244)	14.5 (129)	889

chi-square = 28.89

Chart 2 shows that the filler *es que* tends to favor the retention of /s/ in the form of its prestige variant [s]. Perhaps, because *es que* is a filler expression logically used by native speakers (as well as non-native speakers) when they are searching for the right word, speech is slowed down when it is used. This "slowing effect" would simulate a more formal style in which more attention is paid to speech, thus producing high retention of the prestige variant [s].

As the analysis progresses through the study of the effect of sex, class, and style on the variable /s/ before /k/, we will include (in Notes 5, 6, and 7) information regarding the significance of the effect of *es que* on the data in the various charts.

4 THE DIASTRATIC AND DIAPHASIC DIMENSIONS OF THE REALIZATION OF /S/ BEFORE /K/

4.1 The Diastratic Dimension: Socioeconomic Variation in the Realization of /s/ before /k/

As predicted by hypothesis H1, the results of this study reflect a higher degree of the use of the prestige variant [s] as social status increases, and more use of the stigmatized variants [x] and [0] in the two lower classes.

Although the chi-square is quite high (74.91) when taking all three social classes into account (Chart 3), less of a difference exists between the lower-class and the

Chart 3. Realization according to SOCIOECONOMIC CLASS: all styles[6]

	[s]	[x]	[0]	total
upper class	89.9	8.9	1.2	575
	(517)	(51)	(7)	
middle class	74.6	18.1	7.2	1305
	(974)	(237)	(94)	
lower class	75.0	15.2	9.7	1041
	(781)	(159)	(101)	

chi-square = 74.91
chi-square of middle and lower classes = 7.20

middle-class realizations of the dependent variable /s/ than between these two classes and the upper class. However, Chart 3 also shows that the difference between the middle and lower classes is still significant (chi-square = 7.20) even when we omit the upper-class tokens from the chart. Moreover, when these data are analyzed by style of speech, various conclusions can be drawn.

If we observe the overall effect of style on the realization of /s/ (Chart 4), we see that a significant difference indeed exists in terms of the distribution of variants among the various styles when the group is not constrained for class differences. As predicted by hypothesis H3, the more formal reading styles elicit higher percentages of the prestige variant [s], while the stigmatized variants [x] and [0] occur more frequently in spoken style.

Chart 4. Realization according to STYLE: all social classes[7]

	[s]	[x]	[0]	total
conversation	62.3 (840)	26.1 (352)	11.5 (156)	1348
reading	87.6 (972)	8.2 (91)	4.1 (46)	1109
word list	99.1 (460)	0.9 (4)	0.0 (0)	464

chi-square = 371.86

When looking at the interaction of style and social class, however, more insights into the realization of /s/ by these different social groups may be gleaned. For instance, Chart 5 demonstrates a significant difference between the realization of /s/ in conversation style by all social classes, even when the upper class tokens are eliminated from the chart. However, if we confine the data to reading style (Chart 6) we see that despite the overall significance (chi-square=24.01) of the correlation between class and reading style, the lower class brings the level of attention paid to pronunciation of /s/ up to that of the middle class when reading and the difference in realization of /s/ is, therefore, no longer significant between these two lower classes (chi-square = 0.65). In the word-list style (Chart 7) there is no longer any significant difference in the realization of /s/ among the various social groups.

Chart 5. Realization according to SOCIOECONOMIC CLASS: conversation

	[s]	[x]	[0]	total
upper class	82.1 (248)	15.5 (47)	2.3 (7)	302
middle class	58.3 (362)	30.0 (186)	11.6 (72)	620
lower class	53.9 (230)	27.9 (119)	18.0 (77)	426

chi-square = 80.20
chi-square of middle and lower classes = 8.63

Chart 6. Realization according to SOCIOECONOMIC CLASS: reading

	[s]	[x]	[0]	total
upper class	97.9 (189)	2.1 (4)	0.0 (0)	193
middle class	85.5 (415)	9.9 (48)	4.5 (22)	485
lower class	85.3 (368)	9.0 (39)	5.6 (24)	431

chi-square = 24.01
chi-square of middle and lower classes = 0.65*

Chart 7. Realization according to SOCIOECONOMIC CLASS: word list

	[s]	[x]	[0]	total
upper class	100.0 (78)	0.0 (0)	0.0 (0)	78
middle class	98.5 (197)	1.5 (3)	0.0 (0)	200
lower class	98.9 (183)	0.5 (1)	0.0 (0)	184

chi-square = 3.35*[8]
chi-square of middle and lower classes = 1.93*

Chart 8 illustrates the data from Charts 5, 6, and 7 in a different format to show that within each class the stylistic changes are also statistically significant, and become more so (higher chi-square) as the social status of the informants decreases. In other words, the differences in percentage of the variants [s], [x], and [0] used in the three styles are greater in the two lower classes than in the highest class. In Figure 1, this is reflected in the steeper slopes in the lines representing the use of [s] by the lower social classes compared to the upper class as the formality of the level of speech increases.

Chart 8. Realization according to STYLE: by socioeconomic class

		[s]	[x]	[0]	total
upper class	conversation	82.1 (248)	15.5 (47)	2.3 (7)	302
	reading	97.9 (189)	2.1 (4)	0.0 (0)	193
	word list	100.0 (80)	0.0 (0)	0.0 (0)	80

chi-square = 43.00

		[s]	[x]	[0]	total
middle class	conversation	58.3 (362)	30.0 (186)	11.6 (72)	620
	reading	85.5 (415)	9.9 (48)	4.5 (22)	485
	word list	98.5 (197)	1.5 (3)	0.0 (0)	200

chi-square = 177.50

		[s]	[x]	[0]	total
lower class	conversation	53.9 (230)	27.9 (119)	18.0 (77)	426
	reading	85.3 (368)	9.0 (39)	5.6 (24)	431
	word list	99.4 (183)	0.5 (1)	0.0 (0)	184

chi-square = 183.90

In Figure 1 we observe an excellent example of a phenomenon observed in this study that is similar to the hypercorrection found in other sociolinguistic studies (Labov 1966; Lafford 1982), which usually involves a crossover pattern (Figures 2a and 2b), whereby the prestige variant becomes more prevalent in upwardly mobile middle- or lower middle-class informants than in the highest strata of society in more formal styles (reading passages and word lists—styles C, D, and D').

Madrid, Spain

Stylistic variation in the use of [s] by various social classes

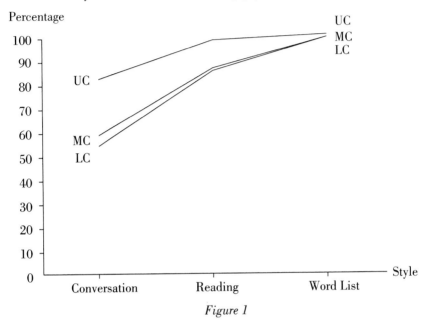

Figure 1

New York

Stylistic variation in the use of [r] by various social classes

(from Labov 1972:114)

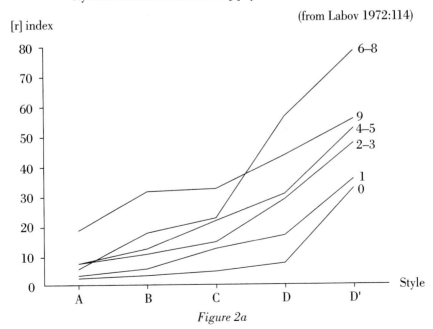

Figure 2a

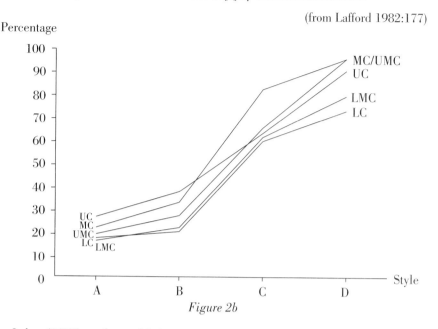

Cartagena, Colombia

Stylistic variation in the use of [s] by various social classes

(from Lafford 1982:177)

Figure 2b

Labov (1972) attributes this hypercorrective pattern to linguistic insecurity on the part of socioeconomic classes who strive to emulate the most successful strata of society in their quest for upward mobility. In both Labov (1972) and Lafford (1982) the informants who hypercorrected most strongly were members of the middle or lower-middle classes. However, in the present Madrid study we note the tendency of hypercorrection (or quasi-hypercorrection, since there is no real crossover pattern in more formal styles) by the lowest socioeconomic class, one that has not traditionally lent itself to that tendency. This may be due in part to the fact that the data were all collected from informants attending high schools in Madrid, and, therefore, the lower-class informants in our study would probably be more accurately classified as lower middle-class, rather than being true representatives of the lowest socioeconomic strata in the city. The young people belonging to the actual lower class probably do not attend high school because of their entrance into the work force at a young age out of economic necessity.

Future researchers would need to collect data from other young informants who truly represent the lowest socioeconomic strata of Madrid in order to get a more accurate picture of the diastratic realization of /s/ before /k/ by informants from all levels of urban Madrid society.

4.2 The Diastratic Dimension: Gender-based Differences in the Realization of /s/

Our original hypothesis H2 maintained that the new political outlook adopted since the fall of Franco would have an effect on young women's speech. It was posited that the greater political and social freedom experienced by Spanish society in the last fourteen years would manifest itself in young adolescent women by an increased usage of linguistic constructs traditionally associated with male speech, such as the use of the more stigmatized speech elements. Therefore no significant difference in the use of /s/ before /k/ by young adolescent men and women was expected to be found in this study.

However, Chart 9 shows that the young adolescent women's use of language in Madrid parallels that of older women in other sociolinguistic studies of urban societies (see section 2.1); thus, females tend to be more conservative than men in their speech patterns from a very young age. The data show that in Madrid, young adolescent women's overall use (85%) of the prestige variant [s] was significantly higher than that of the adolescent males (71%; chi-square = 87.08).

Chart 9. Realization according to SEX: all classes, all styles

	[s]	[x]	[0]	total
male	70.5 (993)	21.1 (298)	8.3 (117)	1408
female	84.5 (1279)	9.8 (149)	5.6 (85)	1513

chi-square = 87.08

The effect of sex and style on the realization of /s/   Charts 10 and 11 and Figure 3 provide information on the interaction of style and sex in the realization of /s/ before /k/ in Madrid.

Chart 10. Realization according to SEX: by style

		[s]	[x]	[0]	total
conversation	male	54.1 (366)	32.8 (222)	13.0 (88)	676
	female	70.5 (474)	19.3 (130)	10.1 (68)	672

chi-square = 40.48 > 5.99

reading	male	80.4 (420)	13.9 (73)	5.6 (29)	522
	female	94.0 (552)	3.1 (18)	2.9 (17)	587

chi-square = 50.66 > 5.99

word list	male	98.0 (205)	1.4 (3)	0.0 (0)	208
	female	99.6 (253)	0.4 (1)	0.0 (0)	254

chi-square = 2.68 < 3.84*[8]

Chart 11. Realization according to STYLE: by sex

		[s]	[x]	[0]	total
	conversation	54.1 (366)	32.8 (222)	13.0 (88)	676
male	reading	80.4 (420)	13.9 (73)	5.6 (29)	522
	word list	98.5 (207)	1.4 (3)	0.0 (0)	210

chi-square = 191.60
chi-square of reading/word list = 40.14

	conversation	70.5 (474)	19.3 (130)	10.1 (68)	672
female	reading	94.0 (552)	3.1 (18)	2.9 (17)	587
	word list	99.6 (253)	0.4 (1)	0.0 (0)	254

chi-square = 186.93
chi-square of reading/word list = 13.54

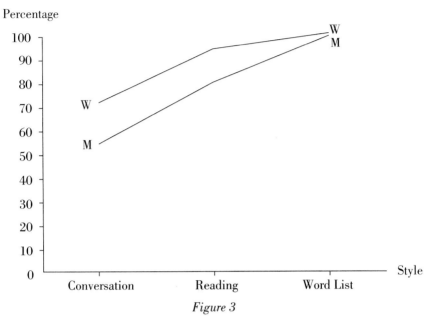

Madrid, Spain

Stylistic variation in the use of [s] by young men and women

Figure 3

These data show that both young adolescent men and women are stylistically sensitive to the use of the prestige variant [s]: both groups tend to use more [s] in more formal reading styles, and more [x] and [0] in conversational style, although the absolute percentages differ. Similar to the findings of Fontanella de Weinberg (1974) for the speech of men and women in Bahia Blanca and Terrell (1982) for both sexes in Santo Domingo, the young men in this Madrid study are much more liberal in their use of stigmatized variants [x] and [0] in conversational styles. However, the young males in this study echo the behavior of those in Terrell (1982)[9] (Figure 4) by more sharply "correcting" their speech in reading styles and word lists to attain the level of the females: almost 100% use of the prestige variant in word lists in the Madrid sample.

The relatively sharp slope between reading and word-list styles that forms the patterns of correction for males in Figures 3 and 4 has most often characterized informants from "insecure" middle- or lower middle-class backgrounds who perceive themselves as upwardly mobile. Therefore, this seemingly anomalous behavior in the young males from a traditional Spanish male-dominated society, in which a self-confident *machismo* attitude is prized, may indicate at least two different phenomena at work.

First, the report on the youth of Spain carried out by the Ministry of Culture (de Zárraga 1985) attests that the maturing process for adolescents is different for males and females in Spanish society. This official study indicates that in a traditional society the passage from infancy to youth is less socially problematic for girls than for

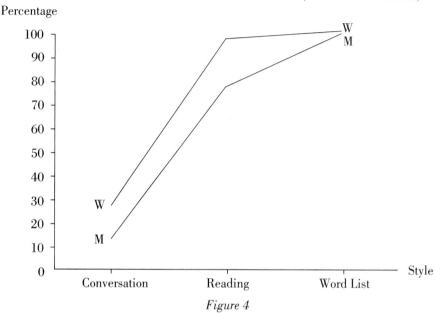

Santo Domingo, Dominican Republic

Stylistic variation in the use of [s] by young men and women

(from Terrell 1982:305)

Figure 4

boys, since the latter experience more of a drastic change in their expected roles as they mature. Moreover, in the process of social maturation, two seemingly paradoxical (although linked) phenomena are at work. On one hand, girls are expected to take on caretaker roles at an early age, which helps to produce early social maturation (adoption of societal norms) in females. On the other hand, young women are also subjected to a prolonged dependent period, more rigid than that of the males, that reduces the girls' personal autonomy. For example, adolescent girls do not have the same kind of freedom that boys possess in dating practices. Also, as they mature, the girls usually trade one type of dependence for another: they go from financial and emotional dependence on their parents to economic and social dependence on their husbands.

The Ministry of Culture report summarizes this situation as follows (de Zárraga 1985:29):

> *Mientras para el joven el ideal tradicional era "que se haga un hombre", para la mujer el ideal era que traspasase la juventud sin mutaciones importantes y que llega al matrimonio entrenada para la tarea doméstica...* [While for the young man the traditional ideal was to "become a man," for the woman, the ideal was to go through adolescence without drastically changing, and enter matrimony trained for domestic work...].

In conclusion, the report states that despite the advances that have been made by the feminist movement, the asymmetry between male and female role expectations still continues to exist in Spanish society; that is, women are still seen in a caretaker (social-behavioral role model) position in the family but have yet to gain economic or social parity with their male counterparts.

Thus, the greater amount of liberty regarding social norms on the part of young males may, in part, account for their greater use of the stigmatized variants [x] and [0] in conversational (less formal) styles. On the other hand, the sharp shift toward the use of the prestige variant [s] on their part in more formal styles may be due to their awareness of the need to conform to societal norms for language use when the situation warrants.

This awareness of the need to speak more "correctly" in more formal contexts may be due to the fact that none of these male informants is probably very representative of Madrid's lowest social classes; all of these young men can not only read but also seem to be aware of the appropriateness of the use of the prestige variant [s] in reading styles. We might not expect this linguistic sensitivity from young people who were not attending school, were illiterate, or who had no social aspirations.

Thus, the data show that all the young men and women in this study are aware of socially acceptable linguistic norms and have learned to style shift to a more conservative use of the prestige variant [s] when the situation calls for it. However, a closer look at the influence of social class, sex, and style on speech patterns brings up even more interesting issues.

The influence of sex, class, and style on the realization of /s/   An interesting phenomenon can be observed when we look at the breakdown of men's and women's speech by class as well as style. If we look at the women represented in Charts 12, 13, and 14, we see no significant difference in pronunciation between the middle and lower classes in either conversation, reading, or word-list styles, which is confirmed by the low chi-square values (0.62, 0.03, and 2.00, respectively).

Chart 12. Realization according to SOCIOECONOMIC CLASS: conversation by sex

		[s]	[x]	[0]	total
	upper class	73.7 (129)	24.0 (42)	2.3 (4)	175
male	middle class	51.0 (163)	36.6 (117)	12.2 (39)	319
	lower class	40.6 (74)	34.6 (63)	24.7 (45)	182

chi-square = 59.61
chi-square of middle and lower class = 13.60

		93.7	3.9	2.4	
	upper class	(119)	(5)	(3)	127
		66.1	22.9	10.9	
female	middle class	(199)	(69)	(33)	301
		63.9	22.9	13.1	
	lower class	(156)	(56)	(32)	244

chi-square = 41.15
chi-square of middle and lower class = 0.62*

Chart 13. Realization according to SOCIOECONOMIC CLASS: reading, by sex

		[s]	[x]	[0]	total
		93.7	6.3	0.0	
	upper class	(45)	(3)	(0)	48
		79.7	15.1	5.1	
male	middle class	(205)	(39)	(13)	257
		78.3	14.2	7.4	
	lower class	(170)	(31)	(16)	217

chi-square = 7.59*
chi-square of middle and lower class = 1.12*

		99.3	0.7	0.0	
	upper class	(144)	(1)	(0)	145
		92.1	3.9	3.9	
female	middle class	(210)	(9)	(9)	228
		92.5	3.7	3.7	
	lower class	(198)	(8)	(8)	214

chi-square = 9.73
chi-square of middle and lower class = 0.03*

Chart 14. Realization according to SOCIOECONOMIC CLASS: word list, by sex

		[s]	[x]	[0]	total
		100.0	0.0	0.0	
	upper class	(18)	(0)	(0)	18
		98.0	2.0	0.0	
male	middle class	(98)	(2)	(0)	100
		98.1	1.1	0.0	
	lower class	(89)	(1)	(0)	90

chi-square = 1.86*[8]
chi-square of middle and lower class = 1.34*

		[s]	[x]	[0]	total
		100.0	0.0	0.0	
	upper class	(60)	(0)	(0)	60
		99.0	1.0	0.0	
female	middle class	(99)	(1)	(0)	100
		100.0	0.0	0.0	
	lower class	(94)	(0)	(0)	94

chi-square = 3.24*
chi-square of middle and lower class = 2.00*

However, a significant speech difference (chi-square = 13.60) does occur between men of the middle and lower classes in conversational style (Chart 12). But, as Charts 13 and 14 show, informants of the lower class do correct their pronunciation in the most formal reading (chi-square = 1.12) and in the word lists (chi-square = 1.34). There is thus no significant difference in the male realization of /s/ between these two social classes in the conversation style.

We must now ask: To what do we owe the apparent lack of significant difference in the speech of middle- and lower-class women (and not men of the same two social classes) in conversational style? One possible explanation is revealed when we examine on an individual basis the realizations elicited. For instance, Informant 29, a middle-class female, uses the stigmatized variant [x] with such frequency that it gives us reason to consider what the results would be if she were not included in Chart 12. Chart 15 gives us these data, and Informant 29 was indeed atypical enough to skew the results so that middle-class women appeared to use the stigmatized variant with roughly the same frequency as did lower-class women in the conversational style.

Chart 15 shows that without Informant 29 the difference between middle- and lower-class women *is* significant in conversational style (chi-square = 8.76). In the reading and word-list styles, however, the difference in the realization of /s/ between lower- and middle-class women continues to be non-significant when Informant 29 is discounted (chi-square = 3.47 for reading style and 1.05 for word-list style).

Chart 15. Realization according to SOCIOECONOMIC CLASS: female, different styles, without Informant 29

		[s]	[x]	[0]	total
	upper class	93.7 (119)	3.9 (5)	2.4 (3)	127
conversation	middle class	75.0 (199)	13.5 (36)	11.3 (30)	265
	lower class	63.9 (156)	22.9 (56)	13.1 (32)	244

chi-square = 40.56
chi-square of middle and lower class = 8.76

		[s]	[x]	[0]	total
	upper class	99.3 (144)	0.7 (1)	0.0 (0)	145
reading	middle class	96.6 (199)	1.5 (3)	1.9 (4)	206
	lower class	92.5 (198)	3.7 (8)	3.7 (8)	214

chi-square = 10.62
chi-square of middle and lower class = 3.47*

		[s]	[x]	[0]	total
	upper class	100.0 (60)	0.0 (0)	0.0 (0)	60
word list	middle class	99.0 (89)	1.0 (1)	0.0 (0)	100
	lower class	100.0 (94)	0.0 (0)	0.0 (0)	94

chi-square = 1.71*
chi-square of middle and lower class = 1.05*

Chart 16 demonstrates a clear preference by this informant for the velar [x] realization of /s/ before /k/ in conversational style (91.7%) and fairly elevated use of [x] (27.3%) and [0] (22.7%) in the reading passage. However, the 100% use of the prestige variant [s] by Informant 29 in the word-list style clearly demonstrates her stylistic sensitivity to this social marker.

Chart 16. Realization according to STYLE: Informant 29

	[s]	[x]	[0]	total
male	0.0 (0)	91.7 (33)	8.3 (3)	36
female	50.0 (11)	27.3 (6)	22.7 (5)	22
word list	100.0 (10)	0.0 (0)	0.0 (0)	10

chi-square = 48.88

Several explanations may be posited for this individual's anomalous behavior vis-à-vis the rest of the members of her social class and sex. The most compelling one appears to be that Informant 29 is a member of the national volleyball team. Because of environmental conditioning, she is the type of individual who might tend to counter-hypercorrect with the intention of sounding more masculine or aggressive. Whether she displayed these characteristics before her athletic training and consequently had them in common with other members of her athletic environment, or whether she acquired them during the course of her sports career, it seems likely that masculine speech habits may be a byproduct of women in fields (such as sports) normally associated with a masculine domain.

Sex, class, style and 'es que'   We make a final observation about the interaction of sex, class, and style in the realization of /s/ vis-à-vis the use of *es que*. In section 3.5 we postulated that frequent use of this filler expression might skew the data in the conversational style. However, the notes accompanying the charts in sections 4.1 and 4.2 prove otherwise; for the most part, exclusion of cases of *es que* does not affect the overall significance of the correlations of the independent and dependent variables. Nevertheless, a closer look at the realization of /s/ in this expression by certain segments of Madrid society may give us some interesting insights into the stylistic behavior of the men and women of certain social classes.

If we examine the data on *es que* with regard to sex and class, we get a greater indication of who is making a greater effort to distinguish realizations of /s/ in this filler expression. Consider the data in Chart 17.

Chart 17. Realization according to *es que* or not *es que:* female conversation, by class

		[s]	[x]	[0]	total
upper class	*es que*	92.3 (48)	3.8 (2)	3.8 (2)	52
	not *es que*	94.6 (71)	4.0 (3)	1.3 (1)	75

chi-square = 0.84*

		[s]	[x]	[0]	total
middle class	*es que*	75.0 (63)	19.0 (16)	6.0 (5)	84
	not *es que*	62.6 (136)	24.4 (53)	12.9 (28)	217

chi-square = 4.82*

		[s]	[x]	[0]	total
lower class	*es que*	82.1 (78)	10.5 (10)	7.4 (7)	95
	not *es que*	52.3 (78)	30.8 (46)	16.7 (25)	149

chi-square = 22.41

Here again we see an interesting conservative trend that occurs only in the lowest class: the lower-class women guard their speech significantly more (30 percentage points with a chi-square value of 22.41) in cases of *es que* than in cases other than *es que*. On the other hand, Chart 18 shows that the men of both the middle and lower class significantly differentiated their realization of /s/ in the use of *es que* compared to other expressions.

Thus, Charts 17 and 18 confirm the more conservative trend among women found in Charts 9 and 10. The "normative" women of the upper and middle classes use a high percentage of the prestige variant [s] in their speech as a whole, and therefore do not differentiate greatly between their realization of /s/ in their general speech and in the filler expression *es que* that normally signals a slow-down or monitoring of one's speech. The stylistically sensitive (upwardly mobile) lower-class women, however, show a greater disparity between their realization of /s/ in normal conversation and their monitored use of [s] in the filler expression *es que*.

Chart 18. Realization according to *es que* or not *es que:* male conversation, by class

		[s]	[x]	[0]	total
upper class	*es que*	71.8 (46)	26.5 (17)	1.6 (1)	64
	not *es que*	74.7 (83)	22.5 (25)	2.7 (3)	111

chi-square = 0.55*

		[s]	[x]	[0]	total
middle class	*es que*	62.6 (57)	35.1 (32)	2.2 (2)	91
	not *es que*	46.4 (106)	37.2 (85)	16.2 (37)	228

chi-square = 13.87

		[s]	[x]	[0]	total
lower class	*es que*	43.8 (32)	42.4 (31)	13.6 (10)	73
	not *es que*	38.5 (42)	29.3 (32)	32.1 (35)	109

chi-square = 8.46

This type of "style shifting" within the conversational mode is characteristic not only of lower-class male speech, but of middle-class male speech as well. As stated earlier, the young men in this study deviate more from the accepted norm than do their female counterparts in their realization of /s/, especially in conversational style. In fact, as a whole, the young men really approximate the standard quality of female speech in only the most formal reading styles (Figure 3).

The same quasi-hypercorrection on the part of some male informants as they shift into a more formal style may be seen in the behavior of middle- and lower-class men. They augment their use of the prestige variant [s] while they "shift" from normal speech to the monitored filler expression *es que* in spoken style. The difference in the realization of /s/ in these two categories is statistically significant in male speech of the two lower social strata: chi-square = 13.87 for middle-class men and 8.46 for lower-class men. However, the difference between these two types of speech is not significant in the upper-class men: chi-square= 0.55.

Thus, the greater differentiation of male speech from the norm in this Madrid sample stems mostly from the behavior of the middle- and lower-class male informants, since the upper-class young males monitor all of their speech more to conform to the societal norm the way the females in the upper and middle classes do. These findings support the hypothesis that "deviant" linguistic behavior on the part of males is more widely accepted in society, even among the upwardly mobile middle and lower classes. Thus, it is only in the highest levels of society that male speech is expected to conform to the societal norm, whose principal proponents are females.

5 CONCLUSIONS

The results of this study of the realization of /s/ as [s], [x], or [0] by the youth of Madrid confirmed two out of our three hypotheses about the realization of /s/ as a social and stylistic marker: (1) the higher the social class and the more formal the style (through switching from spoken to reading styles or using a stylistic filler such as *es que* in spoken style), the greater is the probability of the realization of /s/ as the prestige variant [s]; and, conversely, (2) as the social class of the informant diminishes or the style becomes more informal, the percentage of realizations of /s/ as the stigmatized variants [x] and [0] increases.

The hypothesis that was not confirmed by our study concerned the use of the /s/ variants by the male and female informants in our study. Informal observations and a superficial knowledge of the social changes that had taken place in Spain over the last fifteen years led us to posit that Madrid's young adolescent women were striving to imitate male speech patterns in order to gain social parity. Indeed, in isolated cases such as that of Informant 29, this may occur. However, it was our initial lack of understanding of male vs. female adolescent speech patterns and the true nature of the changes that have taken place in Spanish society that led to our original hypothesis.

Almost a year after undertaking this study we had the opportunity to interview Professor José Cazorla Pérez, the new dean of the College of Sociology at the University of Granada and a widely renowned expert on Spanish society. During this interview he expressed the same view that permeated his recent book, *Sobre los andaluces* (1990): *"España es un país que se ha modernizado sin desarrollarse"* [Spain is a country that has modernized itself without developing.](personal communication). According to Cazorla Pérez many of the changes that one may notice in Spanish society are often examples of what he calls *"desarrollo cosmético... modernización sin desarrollo"* [cosmetic development... modernization without development] (1990:151). In both instances, Cazorla states that Spain is a country that has taken on a superficial modern look without really developing the infrastructure of its society. In other words, whatever changes the outsider sees are really cosmetic and the essential values and the economic and societal infrastructure have not really evolved.

Thus, despite the higher visibility of women in the workforce and in politics, feminist ideology has not deeply penetrated the thought processes of the country's female population. Indeed, Matsell implies that the main factor keeping women from fully entering male-dominated professional and political arenas is a *machista* view held by Spanish women as well as men: A woman's first priority should be home and family, and any career aspirations should not interfere with these responsibilities. Matsell also notes that Spanish women holding university degrees are more likely to give up work upon marriage. She attributes this trend to the heritage of the Franco regime:

> One of the greatest inhibitors to the advance of women was the continued emphasis by the Franco regime on their traditional role within the home and it

is this factor which is most reflected in the number of women who seek education beyond the elementary stages and the number of women who continue to work after marriage. (Matsell 1981:142)

In our 1990 interview, Cazorla Pérez stated that although the percentage of women in the university population has continued to increase during the 1980s, in reality very few of today's women graduates continue to hold full-time careers in a male-dominated workforce long after marriage.

Echoing Cazorla Pérez, Matsell also refers to the cosmetic use of women in visible positions in the country's political parties and to the fact that women still have a long road ahead of them to challenge the *macho* infrastructure of the society and achieve more parity for women. However, she ends on a positive note referring to the more open nature of Spanish society since Franco's death:

> The experience of having to mobilize and organise themselves and of being able to do so for the first time in many years without fear of censorship may mean that improvements, although harder-won, will be more permanent. (Matsell 1981:149)

Thus, while it may be true that young women are slowly gaining ground in the normally male-dominated political and social arena and may be beginning to compete with men in the workforce, the results of this study indicate that young adolescent (high-school age) women have already adopted the more normative speech patterns of older females in Spanish society and are not attempting to take on male speech patterns in an effort to emulate the more powerful male social model. Nor do these young women simply deviate from the linguistic norm as a sign of adolescent rebellion, like their male counterparts. Thus, despite the example of Informant 29, whose involvement with a male-dominated sport may explain her elevated use of the stigmatized variant [x] more associated with males, every indication points to the conclusion that Spanish women as a whole will continue to serve as normative linguistic models in all social strata, at least in terms of pronunciation, for the foreseeable future.[10]

Notes

1. This paper is dedicated to Tracy Terrell, an outstanding scholar, mentor, and friend. The authors wish to express their appreciation to the College of Liberal Arts and Sciences at Arizona State University for the Summer Research Grant awarded to them in 1989 that made this research possible. The authors thank Professors Manuel Alvar, Antonio Quilis, Francisco Moreno, and José Cazorla Pérez for their willingness to be interviewed on this topic. We also wish to thank David W. Foster, an esteemed colleague, who helped to inspire the idea for this research on the interrelatedness of sexual roles and speech patterns. Appreciation is also owed to Peter Lafford, whose computer expertise and comments on the conclusions of this paper were invaluable to the completion of this project.
2. As opposed to the s > h > 0 change before any consonant in syllable final position, the velarization of /s/ to [x] occurs only before a velar consonant, specifically /k/, since /g/ never occurs after the phoneme /s/ in Spanish.
3. All of the references to personal communications with Manuel Alvar, Antonio Quilis, and Francisco Moreno are to interviews with them held in Madrid in June 1989 during the duration of the CLAS Summer Research Grant.

4. The reading of the list of words is the most formal of all the styles. Since the informant does not have to read ahead and can concentrate on every word, the tendency to use the most prestigious variants increases tremendously in this style. In order to test for any difference between word-internal and word-final realizations of /s/ before /k/, the authors included a short sentence fragment: *yo he querido...tú has querido*. Although not purely an element of a word list, this phrase falls short of being considered a reading passage. The results show that there is no significant difference in the realization of /s/ before /k/ in word-internal and word-final position in word lists or any other style. Furthermore, it is only in this word-final position in the word-list phrase *tú has querido* that the variant [x] occurs; that is, only [s] occurs for /s/ in internal position in other items of the word list.

5. It is important here to note that the reading passage used in the interview contained only one instance of *es que*, while the word list did not include this two-word filler. Therefore, data concerning this expression will be analyzed only in conversational style, where its occurrence depends on speaker choice.

Throughout this paper chi-square values accompany the charts. The threshold of significance for 3X3 charts (4 d.f.) is 9.49; for 2X3 charts (2 d.f.) it is 5.99; for 2X2 charts (1 d.f.) it is 3.84. Those charts which demonstrate non-significant correlations among the independent and dependent variables carry an asterisk (*) next to the chi-square value.

6. When *es que* is eliminated from the data, the differences between the middle and lower classes are no longer significant (chi-square = 5.67). However, discounting cases of *es que* does not change the fact that the overall differences among all three classes are still significant (chi-square = 68.75). When Informant 29 is eliminated from the database, the same results occur: The differences between the lower and middle classes lose their significance (chi-square = 5.70), but the overall results are not altered (chi-square = 65.72).

7. Although the absolute chi-square values changed without the inclusion of *es que* and Informant 29's data in the analyses that follow, neither the elimination of *es que* nor the discounting of Informant 29's data altered the overall statistical significance of the correlation between the independent variables and the realization of /s/ (the chi-square values are still compared to the figures 3.84, 5.99, or 9.49, depending on the degrees of freedom) in any of the charts that follow, unless otherwise indicated.

8. In Charts 7, 10, and 14 dealing with word lists, if the column representing the [0] realization has no tokens in it, the chi-square value must be computed based on one degree of freedom less than would otherwise be required. Therefore, in Chart 7, the degrees of freedom are two (for all classes, minimum chi-square = 5.99) and one (for middle and lower classes, minimum chi-square = 3.84). In Chart 10, the word-list style has one degree of freedom (minimum chi-square = 3.84), and in Chart 14, the minimum chi-square values must be 5.99 (two degrees of freedom) and 3.84 (one degree of freedom).

9. Terrell's (1982) informants were all from a lower-class background but had varying degrees of education. The only educational level for which he separated men's and women's speech was the university level, a population a few years older than the high school population for this study. Figure 4 was created by the authors using data from Terrell (1982:305). The sharp difference in the use of the prestige variant [s] between conversational and reading styles may be attributed to the fact that Terrell attested that in low-class Dominican speech, the [s] variant is very rarely used (less than 10%). Thus, the sharply increased use of the [s] variant in more formal styles indicates a high degree of linguistic sensitivity to style shifts on the part of university students from low socioeconomic backgrounds.

10. An interesting line of research for future studies would be the sound-symbolic use of back consonants such as [x]. For example, Fonagy (1979) has proposed a direct correlation between velar consonants and ideas of "force" (emphasis), "aggressiveness," "hardness,"

"ugliness," and "masculinity." In support of his argument, we have found in our study a strong correlation between the use of [x] for /s/ on the part of males.

In addition, many speakers told us that the difference between the pronunciations of the expression ¡Qué asco! as [ke ásko] and as [ke áxko] was one of stronger emphasis on the part of speakers using the latter pronunciation. In other words, the use of velar [x] reinforces the lexically implied negativity in the word asco. Thus, further research may indeed demonstrate an emotive as well as physiognomic function of the use of [x] for /s/. Use of the velar realization of /s/ would give information about the mood or attitude of the speaker (emotive) as well as his/her sex, age, or social class (physiognomic).

References

Alba, Orlando. 1982. Estratificación social del español de Santiago de los Caballeros: la /s/ implosiva. (Tesina inédita, Universidad de Puerto Rico, Río Piedras.

Carbonero, Pedro. 1985. Norma estandar y actitud sociolingüística. In *Sociolingüística Andaluza 1*, ed. by Pedro Carbonero, 137-146. Seville: Secretariado de Publicaciones de la Universidad de Sevilla.

Catalán, Diego. 1955. *La escuela lingüística española y su concepción del lenguage*. Madrid: Gredos.

Cazorla Pérez, José. 1990. *Sobre los andaluces*. Málaga: Editorial Librería Agora, S.A.

Cedergren, Henrietta. 1973. The Interplay of Social and Linguistic Factors in Panama. Ph.D. dissertation, Cornell University.

Fischer, John L. 1958. Social Influences in the Choice of a Linguistic Variant. *Word* 14:47-56.

Fonagy, Ivan. 1979. *La métaphore en phonétique*. Ottawa: Didier.

Fontanella de Weinberg, B. 1974. Un aspecto sociolingüístico del español bonaerense: la -s en Bahía Blanca. *Cuadernos de Lingüística*. Bahía Blanca: Universidad Nacional de Bahía Blanca.

Friedrich, P. 1972. Social Context and Semantic Feature: The Russian Pronouns and Usage. In *Directions in Sociolinguistics: The Ethnography of Communication*, ed. by J. Gumperz and D. Hymes. New York: Holt, Rinehart and Winston, Inc.

Griswold, Ralph E., and Madge T. Griswold. 1983. *The Icon Programming Language*. Englewood Cliffs, New Jersey: Prentice-Hall.

Hammond, R. 1977. Restricciones sintácticas y/o semánticas en la elisión de /s/ en el español cubano. *Boletín de la Academia Puertorriqueña de la Lengua Española* VII:14-27.

Labov, William. 1966. The Linguistic Variable as a Structural Unit. *Washington Linguistics Review* 3:4-22.

———. 1972. *Sociolinguistic Patterns*. Philadelphia: University of Pennsylvania Press.

Lafford, B.A. 1980 [1985]. El nuevo conservadurismo en el caribe hispánico: el habla de Cartagena, Colombia. *Boletín de la Academia Puertorriqueña de la Lengua Española* VIII-2: 72-90.

———. 1982. Dynamic Synchrony in the Spanish of Cartagena, Colombia. Ph.D. dissertation, Cornell University.

———. 1989. Is Functionalism a Fact? Data from the Caribbean. *Hispanic Linguistics* 3/1:49-74.

Lamíquiz, Vidal. 1976. Fronteras sociolingüísticas de Sevilla. In *Sociolingüística Andaluza 1*, ed. by Pedro Carbonero, 47-56. Seville: Secretariado de Publicaciones de la Universidad de Sevilla.

———. 1985. Sociolingüística en un habla urbana: Sevilla. *Revista Española de Lingüística* 6/2:345-62.

López Morales, Humberto. 1983. *Estratificación social del español de San Juan de Puerto Rico.* México, D.F.: Universidad Nacional Autónoma de México.

Matsell, Catherine. 1981. Spain. In *The Politics of the Second Electorate: Women and Public Participation,* ed. by Joni Lovenduski and Jill Hills. Boston: Routledge and Kegan Paul.

Patterson, Margaret Ann. 1986. Conflicts in Title and Address in Revolutionary Nicaragua. M.A. thesis, Arizona State University.

Poplack, Shana. 1979. Function and Process in a Variable Phonology. Ph.D. dissertation, University of Pennsylvania.

Quilis, Antonio. 1965. Description phonétique du parler madriléne actuel. *Phonetica* 12:19-24.

Samper Padilla, José Antonio. 1990. *Estudio sociolingüístico del español de Las Palmas de Gran Canaria.* Las Palmas: Imprenta Pérez Galdós.

Shuy, Roger, Walter A. Wolfram, and William K. Riley. 1967. *Linguistic Correlates of Social Stratification in Detroit Speech.* Washington, D.C.: Office of Education.

Terrell, Tracy. 1978. Sobre la aspiración y elisión de la /s/ implosive y final en el español de Puerto Rico. *Nueva revista de filología hispánica* 27:24-38.

———. 1979. Final /s/ in Cuban Spanish. *Hispania* 62:599-612.

———. 1982. Relexificación en el español dominicano: Implicaciones para la educación. In *El español del Caribe,* ed. by Orlando Alba, 303-318. Santiago, Rep. Dominicana: Univ. Católica Madre y Maestra.

———. 1986. La aspiración y elisión de /s/ en el español de Caracas. In *Actas del V Congreso Internacional de la ALFAL.* Caracas, Venezuela: Univ. Central de Venezuela.

Trudgill, P.J. 1971. The Social Differentiation of English in Norwich. Ph.D. dissertation, Edinburgh University, Scotland, U.K.

Wittermans, E. 1967. Indonesian Terms of Address in Situations of Rapid Social Change. *Social Force* 46/47:48-51.

Wolfram, W. 1969. *A Sociolinguistic Description of Detroit Negro Speech.* Washington, D.C.: Center for Applied Linguistics.

de Zárraga, José Luis. 1985. *Informe juventud en España.* Madrid: Ministerio de Cultura.

SPANISH GRAMMAR

The broad range of Tracy Terrell's research interests covered several areas of Spanish grammar, and his grammar analyses have had lasting impact on further developments in the field. As a reflection of his work in syntax and semantics, the papers in this section represent the main areas of his expertise. Several papers deal with teaching techniques for particular grammatical elements or with theoretical problems such as transitivity and tense/aspect marking. Most papers, however, focus on the area in which Terrell's work was particularly influential: Spanish mood choice.

The indicative/subjunctive contrast is a problem that has long resisted a clear explanation in grammar studies. Among the wide variety of proposals from both semantic and syntactic perspectives, the 1974 paper by Terrell and Joan Hooper (-Bybee) entitled "A Semantically Based Analysis of Mood in Spanish" shed light on the systematization of mood choice. Basing their analysis on Keenan's notion of *presupposition*, they were able to postulate that the indicative/subjunctive contrast directly correlates with the speaker's desire to convey certain information about the truth of a proposition included in a sentence. Instead of using convoluted transformations (then common during the heyday of generative grammar), Terrell and Hooper proposed *assertion* as the determining factor for indicative sentential complements.

In 1976 Terrell published "Assertion and Presupposition in Spanish Complements," a refinement of that 1974 paper. He showed that the system of complementation was determined by the relationship between assertion and presupposition: the indicative was to be used in cases of assertion and weak presupposition, while the subjunctive corresponded to cases of non-assertion, including strong presupposition. Both papers have been influential for subsequent mood-choice research. Not only did the results establish new criteria for analysis; they also showed that the semantic characterization of mood choice rendered systematic results. That 1976 work—the most detailed analysis of the problem—is reprinted as the lead paper in this section, so that readers can see how later developments stem from that seminal work.

The five papers that follow reflect Terrell's interest in the theoretical issues related to mood choice. Some address the specific notion of presupposition. Sanford Schane proposes an analysis of commissive verbs, such as *prometer* 'promise', which constituted a problematic area in Terrell's work. Schane adapts Searle's classification of speech acts to account for Spanish indicative/subjunctive alternation, and he introduces the concept of *subject responsibility* as complementary to Terrell's notion of presupposition. In Errapel Mejías-Bikandi's paper, the notion of presupposition is further developed as a problem of *presupposition inheritance*, with indicative/subjunctive choice accounted for within Fauconnier's framework of mental spaces.

While taking into consideration the theoretical problem of presupposition, Flora Klein-Andreu concentrates on the pedagogical problem of teaching Spanish mood selection to English-speaking students. Basing her argument on a set of semantic notions regarding the relative assertiveness of the verb, she suggests specific techniques for classroom instruction.

Two papers offer mood analyses not directly related to the presupposition approach. Jorge Guitart's work focuses on the indicative/subjunctive contrast in the use of relative clauses. His proposal underlines the need to consider the whole noun phrase as the antecedent of the relative clause: the degree of individuation of the referred nominal and its inclusion in a "location" determine mood choice. Ricardo Maldonado attempts a general characterization of mood choice from the perspective of cognitive grammar. Based on Langacker's notion of *dominion*, he investigates the interaction between the reflexive/middle marker *se* and the semantic contrast imposed by the use of indicative/subjunctive.

Three papers address Spanish grammar issues not directly related to mood choice. While one examines a transitivity issue, the others are related to the problem of grammatical marking of future events in Spanish. Ronald Langacker offers a cognitive-grammar analysis of the preposition *a*, which marks direct human objects; he sees the grammatical value of *a* as a semantic/syntactic derivation from the locative meaning of that preposition. Based on information from a wide variety of languages, Joan Bybee presents two problems in the development of grammatical morphemes over time: (a) the prominence of aspect over tense, and (b) the semantic differences between the synthetic future *cantaré* and the analytic *voy a cantar*, corresponding to a general evolutionary pattern of future markers found across the languages of the world. Finally, as a historical issue in Spanish grammar, Margaret van Naerssen points out the decreasing usage of the synthetic future and relates her findings to the fact that, in most current second-language textbooks, the synthetic form has been replaced by *voy a cantar*.

Assertion and Presupposition in Spanish Complements

Tracy D. Terrell

1 INTRODUCTION

Much of the recent work in theoretical linguistics has been directed to developing an understanding of the relationship between semantics and syntactic processes. The work of the Kiparskys (1970) established the importance of the semantic notion of PRESUPPOSITION for explaining certain syntactic phenomena in English. Hooper and Terrell (1974) postulated a correlation between the semantic notion of ASSERTION and the use of mood in Spanish sentences containing sentential complements.[1] In particular, we tried to show that in sentences with several complements, the relation of both the mood of the verb in the complement and the matrix in which the complement is embedded is dependent upon this factor of assertion, and that the choice of mood is meaningful and not transformationally derived.

In this paper we analyze the Spanish system of complementation in order to examine in semantic terms the relationship between ASSERTION and PRESUPPOSITION and their correlation with certain syntactic processes and their associated classes of matrix predicates. We make no attempt to formalize our theories; we consider such formalizations inappropriate because (a) there is no global theory which would further elucidate the data to be presented here, and (b) we doubt that a syntactic-semantic theory can be developed until the relationships between syntax and semantics have been better defined.

2 DEFINITIONS

The term PRESUPPOSITION has been widely used by both philosophers and linguists. In this paper we are concerned with the notion of presupposition as defined by Keenan (1971), which we take to be essentially the same as the notion used by the Kiparskys.[2] Keenan gives two criteria for the recognition of presupposition in complements. First, the truth of the complement is presupposed by the entire sentence.

    (1) Le sorprendió que María se enojara.
        'It surprised him that Mary got mad.'

If the proposition, que María se enojara is, in fact, untrue, then the entire sentence (1) is neither true nor false; it simply has no truth value. In addition, the truth value of a

Reprinted, by permission, from *Current Studies in Romance Linguistics*, ed. by Marta Luján and Fritz Hensey, Georgetown University Press, 1976.

presupposed proposition will remain constant under the normal processes of sentence negation or questioning.

(2) No le sorprendió que María se enojara.
     'It didn't surprise him that Mary got angry.'
(3) ¿Le sorprendió que María se enojara?
     'Did it surprise him that Mary got angry.'

The Kiparskys showed that presupposition in English is associated regularly with a variety of syntactic processes.[3] Presupposition was said to occur in English with matrices which group themselves into two semantic types: matrices which describe some subjective or emotional reaction to a proposition (to be significant, odd, tragic, exciting, relevant, to regret, deplore, etc.),[4] or those which describe cognitive or other mental acts with regard to a proposition (be aware of, grasp, comprehend, take into account, forget, ignore, etc.).

In the case of sentences with matrices from the former class, Spanish normally requires the subjunctive:[5] see (1), (2), and (3). With matrices of mental acts the verb forms are normally indicative:

(4) Se dio cuenta de que no iban a poder llegar antes de las seis.
     'He realized that they weren't going to be able to arrive before six.'

Consequently, it was thought that presupposition, although semantically operative in Spanish as well as in English, had very few syntactic consequences and certainly played no role in the use of moods. In Hooper and Terrell (1974), the matrices of mental acts were considered to be exceptions to the rule that the indicative forms are used in assertive propositions and subjunctive forms in all others, including presupposed ones, since we knew of no independent evidence to show that these propositions were also assertive. We showed that the presupposition in these propositions differs from that found in the sentence of subjective comment and that these sentences are indeed assertive in many fundamental ways.

Karttunen (1971) first suggested that there may be two kinds of presupposition with differing semantic and syntactic correlates for English. These differences were further investigated in Hooper (19774), where strong presupposition was distinguished from weak presupposition. In sentences with strong presupposition, the complement is accepted as true under any conditions. With complements only weakly presupposed, it is possible to construct sentences in which the truth of the complement cannot be inferred. Consider the following sentences:

(5) No me sorprende el hecho de que hayan podido hacer el viaje sino que hayan podido quedarse allí por tanto tiempo.
     'It doesn't surprise me that they were able to take the trip, but rather that they were able to stay so long.'

Even in a contrastive situation the complement in (5) remains presupposed.

(6) No supe que se había cancelado el vuelo sino que todavía no había llegado.
     'I didn't find out that the flight had been canceled, only that it hadn't arrived.'

In (6), however, the proposition may or may not be presupposed.

Kartunnen points out questions in English which are ambiguous between a presupposed and a nonpresupposed reading. Let us examine such questions in Spanish.

(7)   ¿Sentiste que no dijeras la verdad?
       'Were you sorry that you didn't tell the truth?'

(8)   ¿Supiste que no habías dicho la verdad?
       'Did you learn that you hadn't told the truth?'

In (7) the speaker assumes that the addressee had not told the truth. In (8), however, there are two possibilities of interpretation: one in which the matrix is questioned (¿Lo supiste?) and the complement presupposed, and the other in which the speaker actually wishes to question the complement, i.e., 'Did or did you not tell the truth?'

We assume that it has been demonstrated that in strictly following our definition there are two types of presupposition which we label strong and weak. What remains to be shown is that the notion of weak presupposition is compatible with the notion of assertion.

Assertion

In this paper we use the term ASSERTION loosely to mean a proposition expressed in a declarative sentence. More specifically, the speaker claims the proposition which he has announced to be true to the best of his knowledge.[6] An assertion is a claim to truth which, on at least one reading, may be taken as the semantically dominant proposition in the discourse context. Suppose the speaker wishes to assert that he believes a certain proposition to be a true statement. This may be done syntactically in a number of different ways, depending on whether or not he wishes to qualify the assertion. If there is no qualification, he states the proposition directly.

(9)   María irá a la playa con nosotros.
       'Mary will go to beach with us.'

He may, of course, qualify in various degrees his belief in the validity of the proposition, with the use of an appropriate matrix.

(10)   Me parece (creo, es seguro, etc.) que María irá a la playa con nosotros.
        'It seems to me (I believe, it's sure, etc.) that Mary will go to the beach with us.'

Assertions may also be indirect; that is, we may report the assertions of others and describe the way in which the assertion was reported to us.

(11)   Juan me dijo (confesó, comunicó, explicó, etc.) que María iría a la playa con nosotros.
        'John said to me (confessed, communicated, explained, etc.) that Mary would go to the beach with us.'

This in no way commits the speaker to the truth of the reported assertion.

We shall also try to show that an assertion may be embedded in a matrix which describes the way in which knowledge was obtained or perceived.

(12)   Sabía (me enteré, reconocí, vi, noté, etc.) que María iba a la playa con nosotros.

'I knew (learned, recognized, saw, noted, etc.) that Mary was going to the beach with us.'

In all the foregoing cases, the verbs are indicative in form. In fact, all simple declarative sentences (both positive and negative) are assertions and are expressed with indicative verb forms. Questions simply request an affirmation as a reply. There are only two types of nonembedded sentences in which indicative verb forms are not used: imperatives and sentences of doubt.

Imperatives are clearly not assertions and subjunctive verb forms are used in all cases except one.[7]

(13)   ¡No hables con ella!
       'Don't talk to her!'
(14)   ¡Vuelva mañana, señor!
       'Come back tomorrow, sir!'

The assertion in (14), if there is one, is something close to 'I want something', not 'You come back tomorrow.' Commands may also be reported or qualified just as in the case of assertions. Matrices of the latter type are referred to variously as matrices of volition, persuasion, or influence.

Reported commands:

(15)   Carlos nos dijo (escribió, insistió en, gritó) que pasáramos las vacaciones con él en el campo.
       'Carlos told (wrote, insisted, shouted) (for) us to spend our vacation with him in the country.

Volition:

(16)   Marta quería (prefería, propuso, permitió) que nos fuéramos inmediatamente.
       'Marta wanted (preferred, proposed, permitted) us to leave immediately.'

The verb forms of the matrices are indicative since the matrix predicate is always asserted. Commands, direct or qualified, embedded or nonembedded, are never assertions; the verb forms of the command are subjective.

Since both assertions and commands may be reported, there is a minimal formal contrast between the indicative and subjective verb forms.[8]

(17)   Le dijo que regresara.
       'She told him to return.'
(18)   Le dijo que regresaba.
       'She told him that he was returning.'

There are simple nonembedded sentences which express degrees of doubt in the mind of the speaker as to the validity of the proposition.

(19)   Acaso (tal vez, quizás) {viene/venga} mañana.
       'Perhaps (maybe, possibly) he's coming tomorrow.'

If the proposition is felt to be essentially an assertion with qualification, then the indicative forms are used. If, in the speaker's mind, there is sufficient doubt so that he wishes to avoid making a clear assertion, then the subjunctive forms are used.

Usually, doubted propositions are embedded so that the matrices express varying degrees of doubt.

(20)   Es dudoso (no es seguro, es posible, es probable, etc.) que llegue temprano.
'It's doubtful (it's not certain, it's possible, it's probable, etc.) that I'll
arrive early.'

Negation of matrices of belief often results in matrices of doubt. In this case the subjective forms will be used in the complement.

(21)   No creo (no es cierto, no es evidente, no parece, etc.) que hayan podido
terminar.
'I don't believe (it isn't certain, it isn't evident, it doesn't seem, etc.) that
they have been able to finish.'

In summary, the correlation of mood with assertion and presupposition appears to
be clear. The indicative is used in cases of assertion and weak presupposition, the
subjunctive in cases of nonassertion, including strong presupposition. We will now
examine other syntactic correlates of assertion and presupposition other than mood
with two purposes in mind: we wish to show that (1) weak presupposition is treated
syntactically and semantically as a type of assertion and that (2) the syntactic
processes involved may be explained by the semantic properties of the class of matrices to which they are restricted.

Classifying Propositions

The following classification is given for ease of reference in the discussion. Many
matrices are semantically ambivalent and may be used in more than one sense. We
will return to this problem. For the present we have listed those which, with rare
exceptions, are used as members of a single class. The subclassifications are according to syntactic structure: (1) contains matrices which take object complements; (2)
contains matrices consisting of the copula plus an adjective or noun which take subject complements; (3) contains other matrices which take subject complements, mostly intransitive verbs.

(a) Factives (strong presupposition)
(1) deplorar, sentir, resentir, lamentar, alegrarse de, entristecerse de,
estar contento (alegre, triste, avergonzado, furioso, enojado) de.
(2) ser ridículo, triste, significativo, raro, trágico, emocionante, divertido,
natural, extraordinario, una tragedia, una cosa de risa.
(3) dar náusea, dar asco, dar vergüenza, sorprender, alegrar, molestar,
tener sentido, gustar, divertir, emocionar, extrañar, encantar, indignar,
fascinar, enojar.

(b) Semifactives (weak presupposition)
(1) poner en claro, revelar, clarificar, descubrir, ver, darse cuenta de,
fijarse en, olvidarse (de), aprender, tomar en consideración, percibir,
ver, reconocer, reflexionar sobre, acordarse de, contar con.

(c) Opinion (announcing assertion)

(1) saber, sostener, opinar, asegurar, jurar, concluir, mantener, juzgar, creer, pensar, suponer, imaginarse, no dudar, tomar por dado, estar seguro, cierto.

(2) ser verdad, cierto, seguro, claro, indiscutible, obvio.

(3) parecer, pasar, ser, resultar.

(d) Reporting (indirect assertion)

(1) contar, explicar, relatar, predecir, confesar, reportar, afirmar, intimar, declarar, prometer, proclamar.

(e) Doubt (lack of assertion)

(1) dudar, no creer, no estar seguro de.

(2) ser inseguro, probable, dudoso, no ser seguro, verdad, obvio, evidente, ser una mentira.

(f) Volition (command)

(1) anhelar, querer, preferir, desear, oponerse a, exigir, pedir, sugerir, proponer, rogar, mandar, dejar, permitir, aconsejar, impedir, ordenar, suplicar, recomendar, evitar, implorar.

(2) ser necesario, recomendable, inevitable, perferible, deseable.

Let us now turn to supporting our claim that weakly presupposed matrices are also cases of assertion. To see this, we will examine the effects of negation and questioning on sentences with a matrix from each of the six classes.

Effects of Negation

Simple sentence negation does not, of course, affect the strong presupposed of sentences with factive matrices (subjective comment).

(22) Estoy contento (de) que hayan podido hacer el viaje.
'I'm glad that they were able to make the trip.'

(23) No estoy contento (de) que hayan podido hacer el viaje.
'I'm not happy that they were able to make the trip.'

In either case, the presupposed preposition remains constant; only the comment is varied.

The negation of matrices of volition only changes the assertion, that is, the matrix itself; the complement remains a nonassertion.

(24) Quiero que vayan con nosotros.
'I want them to go with us.'

(25) No quiero que vayan con nosotros.
'I don't want them to go with us.'

In sentences with matrices of doubt, if the effect of negation does not change the semantic class of the matrix, the proposition remains a nonassertion.

(26) Es probable que lo compren.
'It's probable that they'll buy it.'

(27) No es probable que lo compren.
'It isn't probable that they'll buy it.'

If, however, the negated matrix turns out to be equivalent to a positive opinion matrix, it will naturally be treated as assertive.

(28) Dudo que lo leyeran.
       'I doubt that they were reading it.'

(29) No dudo que lo leían.
       'I don't doubt that they were reading it.'

Thus, in general, negation of a nonassertive matrix does not affect its complement.

The negation of sentences with assertive matrices, on the other hand, is quite complex. The negation of an opinion matrix may cause the meaning to be equivalent to that of a doubt matrix. In this case, the proposition is not affirmed and the subjunctive must be used.[9]

(30) Es seguro que irán.
       'It's sure that they'll go.'

(31) No es seguro que vayan.
       'It's not sure that they'll go.'

This is the case when the opinion is personal, that is, the speaker's own. However, if the opinion is someone else's and is being reported by the speaker, there may be complications. The speaker may choose simply to report the opinion as given.

(32) Juan no cree que irán.
       'John thinks they'll go.'

(33) Juan no cree que vayan.
       'John doesn't think they'll go.'

However, if the speaker wishes to affirm as true a proposition another speaker has doubted, he may do so by using the indicative.[10]

(34) Juan no cree que Uds. fueron al cine.
       'John doesn't believe that you went to the movies.'

The negation of matrices of reporting is also quite complex.

(35) Juan no dijo que Uds. querían ir.
       'John didn't say that you wanted to go.'

(36) No predijeron que el temblor ocurriría tan pronto.
       'They didn't predict that the earthquake would occur so soon.'

(37) Tu no dijiste que mis padres estaban en casa.
       'You didn't say that my parents were at home.'

Out of context and without any indication of emphasis, it is difficult to interpret the negation. In (35), without any special emphasis, the interpretation seems to be that 'You wanted to go' is a possible assertion (neither presupposed nor rejected), but that in this case it just simply is not the assertion which Juan uttered. That is, it is not the complement which is negated, but its relation to the matrix.

If emphasis is added, one can negate various parts of the sentence.

(38) Juan no <u>dijo</u> que Uds. querían irse sino que lo <u>gritó</u>.
       'John didn't <u>say</u> you wanted to go, he <u>yelled</u> it.'

(39) Juan no dijo que <u>Uds.</u> querían irse sino que <u>ellos</u> querían irse.
       'John didn't say that <u>you</u> wanted to go, but that <u>they</u> wanted to go.'

(40) Juan no dijo que Uds. <u>querían</u> irse sino que <u>tenían</u> que irse.

'John didn't say that you <u>wanted</u> to go, but that you <u>had</u> to go.'

(41)   Juan no dijo que Uds. querían <u>irse</u> sino que <u>querían</u> <u>quedarse</u>.

'John didn't say that you wanted <u>to go</u>, but that you wanted <u>to stay</u>.'

In (38), the complement is not affected. However, in (39) to (41), although the proposition is still a possible affirmation, various parts are negated. The mere fact that with negation of the matrix different parts of the complement may be negated shows that these complements contain an assertion. Now let us examine sentences with semifactive matrices of perception or knowledge.

(42)   No vio que Uds. habían salido.

'He didn't see that you had left.'

(43)   No supieron que se había cancelado el vuelo.

'They didn't find out that the flight had been cancelled.'

(44)   No tomó en consideración que hacía calor.

'He didn't take into consideration that it was hot.'

The preferred reading for most speakers is that the complement is presupposed to be true. However, if contrastive stress is added, these sentences behave similarly to sentences of reporting.

(45)   No vio que Uds. habían salido, solamente que ya no estaban allí.

'He didn't see that you had left, only that you were no longer there.'

(46)   No supieron que se había cancelado el vuelo, sino que no había llegado todavía.

'They didn't learn that the flight had been cancelled, only that it hadn't arrived yet.'

(47)   No tomó en consideración que hacía calor, solamente que no llovía.

'He didn't take into consideration that it was hot, only that it wasn't raining.'

If used personally, the semifactives may be similar to matrices of opinion; if so, the negated form may be used to express doubt and the subjunctive is used.

(48)   No era obvio que fuera tan importante.

'It wasn't obvious that it was so important '

(49)   No vi que hiciera tanto trabajo.

'I didn't see that she did so much work.'

(50)   Yo no me acordé de que fuera tan lejos.

'I didn't remember that it was so far.'

If the speaker, however, wishes to assert the proposition but negate its relationship to the matrix, the indicative is used.

(51)   No era obvio que era tan importante.

'It was important, but it wasn't obvious that it was.'

(52)   No vi que hacía tanto.

'She did a lot; I just didn't see it.'

(53)   Yo no me acordé de que era tan lejos.

'It was far, but I didn't remember it.'

The negation of a semifactive used in the present tense first person singular is anomalous if the combination of the meaning of the matrix and assertion is contradictory.

(54)   *No me doy cuenta de que ella está adelantada.
       *'I don't realize she's ahead.'
Sometimes contrastive stress can make the sentence acceptable.

(55)   No veo que empieza a llover.
       'I don't see that it's starting to rain.'
In general, then, it seen that the semifactives are similar to both matrices of reporting and opinion with regard to sentence negation and have little in common with nonassertions.

Effects of Interrogation

Just as with sentence negation, question formation has no effect on the complements of nonassertive sentences unless the effect of interrogation is to change the semantic class of the matrix.

(56)   ¿Estás contento que tomaran tanta cerveza?
       'Are you glad that they were drinking so much beer?'

(57)   ¿Le aconsejaste que fuera al médico?'
       'Did you advise him to go to the doctor?'

(58)   ¿Era dudoso que no la pudieran alcanzar?[11]
       'Was it doubtful that they couldn't reach her?'

In assertive sentences the effects of interrogation are more complicated, as might be expected. In sentences of reporting, i.e., indirect assertion, there are two possibilities of interpretation: parenthetical and nonparenthetical.[12]

(59)   ¿Dijo Juan que iba a salir temprano?
       'Did John say that he was leaving early?'

(60)   ¿Anunciaron que el partido terminó ya?
       'Did they announce that the game is already over?'

On the nonparenthetical reading we are interested in whether John actually said something or whether something was announced. On the parenthetical reading the speaker is really interested in questioning the proposition.

(61)   ¿Iba a salir temprano Juan?
       'Was John going to leave early?'

(62)   ¿Terminó el partido ya?
       'Did the game already end?'

With matrices of belief the parenthetical reading is most common.

(63)   ¿Crees que ganará mañana?
       'Do you think she'll win tomorrow?'

(64)   ¿Es verdad que irán los dos?
       'Is it true that both of them will go?'

(65)   ¿Te parece que quieren quedarse?
       'Does it seem to you that they want to stay?'

If, however, the matrix is used nonparentetically to cast doubt on the proposition of the complement, then the subjunctive forms appear.[13]

(66) ¿Crees que gane mañana?
      'Do you really think she'll win tomorrow?'

Questions with matrices of knowledge also seem to have a parenthentical and a nonparenthetical reading in most cases.

(67) ¿Te diste cuenta que no lo hiciste?
      'Did you realize you didn't do it?'

(68) ¿Viste que no lo terminaron?
      'Did you see that it wasn't finished?'

Although by far the most common interpretation is that the question applies to the matrix, it is easy to imagine contexts in which the complement itself is being questioned.

(69) Viste que no lo terminaron, o ¿es que lo terminaron?
      'Did you see that they didn't finish it, or did they finish it?'

 ## THE EVIDENCE OF SYNTAX

Let us now turn to syntactic evidence to support our claims concerning assertion and nonassertion. In a recent paper (1973), Hooper and Thompson investigated certain syntactic processes first studied by Emonds (1969) and found a correlation between their application and the semantic notion of assertion as used in this paper. It is important to examine these notions in detail since, even though examples from Spanish seem to refute the Hooper-Thompson hypothesis, they actually support it.

Most of the syntactic processes defined by Emonds as Root Transformations are movement transformations which result, in English, in a shift of emphasis in the sentence.[14] Directional Adverb Preposing is a typical example.

(70) 'Over the trees flew the birds.'

(71) 'The birds flew over the trees.'

Hooper and Thompson demonstrate that these 'emphatic' transformations such as Directional Adverb Preposing, Negative Constituent Preposing, VP Preposing, and so forth, may occur only in assertive sentences.

(72) 'He said that over the trees flew the birds.'

(73) *'I'm happy that over the trees flew the birds.'

(74) *'It's doubtful that over the trees flew the birds.'

Their point that was that emphatic RT's apply in assertions, but not presupposed clauses or other nonassertions because it is inappropriate, in general, to emphasize backgrounded material.

Although there are differences of opinion among English speakers on the acceptability of many of these types of sentences, the main thrust of the argument seems to be valid.

Let us now turn to Spanish and examine the possibilities. If the hypothesis of Hooper and Thompson is correct, it must be also valid for Spanish. In that case, emphatic transformations should be restricted to assertive sentences, i.e., those with indicative verb forms.[15] However, consider the following sentences, all perfectly acceptable in Spanish.

(75) Dijo que sobre los árboles volaban miles de aves.
'He said that above the trees were flying thousands of birds.'
(76) ¡Qué maravilloso que sobre los árboles volaran tantas aves!'
*'How wonderful that above the trees flew so many birds!'
(77) Dudo que por las calles se viera tanto de interés.
*'I doubt that in the streets could one see so many interesting things.'

These results lead us to conclude that either the Hooper-Thompson hypothesis is incorrect, our indicative mood-assertion hypothesis is incorrect, or that something is wrong with our definition of emphasis.

Consider the following parts of sentences:

(78) Miles de aves volaban sobre los árboles.
(79) Sobre los árboles volaban miles de aves.
(80) 'Thousands of birds flew above the trees.'
(81) 'Above the trees flew thousands of birds.'

It is immediately apparent to anyone who knows Spanish and English well that the correspondences are not at all exact. Sentence (81) is definitely less common than (80) and is used only for special emphasis. In Spanish, on the other hand, (79) is as common as (78) and certainly draws no special attention to itself as does the English transformed sentence (81). In (78) the focus[16] (but not the emphasis) is on the place where the birds flew and in (79) the focus is on the fact that it was birds that were flying over the trees, instead of something else, perhaps insects. One is simply not more emphatic than the other. Therefore, since Directional Adverb Preposing is quite common in Spanish and not at all emphatic, it may freely occur in nonassertions; in English, it does not.[17]

The task now, then, is to ascertain which of these movement transformations actually result in emphasis and to test their correlation with the assertion-nonassertion distinction.

Complement Preposing

Bolinger (1968) very perceptively described in detail perhaps the most important case of an emphatic transformation, which he labeled Postponed Main Phrases and which we term Complement Preposing. Complement Preposing is an operation which fronts all or part of the complement clause. Thus, the structure underlying (82) may yield (83) or (84) when Complement Proposing is applied.

(82) Creo que la situación se ha vuelto muy complicada.
'I believe that the situation has become quite complex.'
(83) La situación, creo, se ha vuelto muy complicada.
'The situation, I believe, has become quite complex.'
(84) La situación se ha vuelto muy complicada, creo.
'The situation has become quite complex, I believe.'

Bolinger showed that this process in English and Spanish is correlated almost exactly with the use of the subjunctive in Spanish; he did not at that time try to relate the process to notions of assertion or presupposition. Emonds (1969) assumed that

Complement Preposing was restricted to nonpresupposed complements. Hooper (1974) showed that for English, at least, the distinction between matrices which allow Complement Preposing and those that do not is the assertion-nonassertion distinction; this is equally true for Spanish complements. All classes of assertive matrices allow Complement Preposing:

Reporting

(85)   No ha hecho su trabajo, me confesó (dijo, explicó, etc.).

'He hasn't done his work yet, he confessed (said, explained, etc.) to me.'

Knowledge

(86)   No lo iban a completar, (como) pronto se dieron cuenta.

'They weren't going to finish it, as they soon realized.'

Belief

(87)   Irán todos, creo (me parece, estoy seguro, etc.).

'Everyone will go, I think (it seems to me, I'm sure , etc.).'

Nonassertive matrices do not allow Complement Preposing.

Doubt

(88)   *Lo buscó en el diccionario, dudo.

*'He looked for it in the dictionary, I doubt.'

Volition

(89)   *No lo encontrarás, quiero.

*'You won't find it, I want.'

Comment

(90)   *Guillermo quería estudiar para abogado, me alegro.

*'Bill wanted to be a lawyer, I'm happy.'

In other words, nonassertive matrices may not be used parenthetically in their predicate forms.[18]

The effect of Complement Preposing is to make the complement proposition the main assertion of the sentence. The original main element, the matrix, is reduced to secondary, almost parenthetical, status. The explication for the restriction of this process to assertions is simple. All simple, declarative sentences are taken to be assertions (or commands: see further). If we utter a sentence like 'John doesn't eat much', this is equivalent to saying 'I say (believe, affirm, etc.) that John doesn't eat much.' Thus any preposed complement will be taken to be an assertion, and Complement Preposing cannot therefore be applied to nonassertions.[19]

There are two classes of sentences which are apparent exceptions to the rule of Complement Preposing. First, certain nonassertions may be preposed.

(91)   Me dijo que fuera a comprarme uno.

'He told me to go buy one.'

(92)   Vaya a comprarse uno, me dijo.

'Go buy one, he said.'

Matrices of volition may not be used in this manner, however.

(93)   *Vaya a comprarse uno, quiere.

*'Go buy yourself one, he wants.'

In fact, the only matrices which can be so used are those which can report either an assertion or a direct imperative.

(94) Venga a visitarnos, me escribió.

   'Come to see us, he wrote.'

(95) No saltes, gritó.

   'Don't jump, he shouted.'

Since independent sentences are either assertions or commands,

(96) Juan va al cine.

   'John is going to the movies.'

(97) Juan, no vayas al cine.

   'John, don't go to the movies.'

therein lies the explanation as to why, in these cases only, the complement may be preposed.[20]

The other class of exceptions consists of what appear to be assertions which cannot be preposed.

(98) Juan no me dijo que Uds. habían estudiado tanto.

   'John didn't tell me that you all had studied so much.'

(99) *Uds. habían estudiado tanto, Juan no dijo.'

   *'You all had studied a lot, John didn't say.'

In the section on negation we saw that, without emphasis, the effect of negation on matrices of reporting was to negate the relationship between the matrix and its complement. In (98) the proposition that you all had studied so much is a possible assertion, hence the indicative mood, but in this case it was not the assertion which John uttered. If we were to front the complement, it would be interpreted as a direct assertion followed by a contradiction. The sentence would make sense only if we used but.

(100) Uds. habían estudiado mucho, pero Juan no lo dijo.

   'You all have studied a lot, but John didn't say it.'

Verb Phrase Preposing

Another transformation which in Spanish results in emphasis is what Emonds termed Verb Phrase Preposing. Although highly restricted in Spanish, the transformation does apply in certain cases of auxiliary plus main verb.

(101) Juan quiere que Lola se case con él, pero ella no puede casarse con él.

   'John wants Lola to marry him, but she can't marry him.'

(102) Juan quiere que Lola se case con él; pero, casarse con él, no puede.

   'John wants Lola to marry him; but, marry him, she can't.'

Now let us compare the effects of a matrix, one assertive and one nonassertive.

(103) Juan quiere que Lola se case con él; pero, parece que casarse con él no puede.

   'John wants Lola to marry him; but it seems that marry him she can't.'

(104) *Juan quiere que Lola se case con él; pero, ella duda que casarse con él, pueda.

   *'John wants Lola to marry him; but she doubts that marry him she can.'

The other movement transformation discussed by Emonds (1969) and Hooper and Thompson (1973) do not produce emphasis in Spanish and are not restricted to sentences of assertion.

Negative Constituent Preposing.

(105) Es verdad que jamás he visto yo tanta gente.

'It's true that never have I seen so many people.'

(106) Estoy contento de que jamás tenga yo que regresar aquí.

*'I am pleased that never will I have to return here.'

Preposing around be

(107) Es obvio que más significativo sería el desarrollo de una teoría semántica.

'It's obvious that more significant would be the development of a semantic theory.'

(108) Dudo que más significativo sea el desarrollo de una teoría semántica.

*'I doubt that more significant would be the development of a semantic theory.'

(109) Me di cuenta de que este libro lo habían encontrado hace años.

*'I realized that this book they had found years ago.'

(110) Quisiera que este libro lo leyeran antes de clase mañana.

*'I want this book for you to read before class tomorrow.'

 ## Conclusion

We have tried to show that the syntactic properties discussed here, the use of mood in Spanish, and the application of the various movement transformations, are directly related to the semantic notions of assertion and presupposition. We showed that by distinguishing two types of presupposition, weak and strong, we can at least partially account for the seemingly aberrant nature of the knowledge matrices. We believe that this is more evidence against the claims of some transformationalists that the use of mood is syntactically based, and it supports the traditional view that its use is meaningful. However, we do not mean to imply that vague statements about factualness, truth, or reality so often found in grammars and in texts used to teach the subjunctive are anything other than incorrect and misleading.

Notes

1. This paper is the result of long hours of conversation and correspondence with Professor Joan B. Hooper, without whose help it would never have been completed.

2. In the other article of which I am aware dealing with presupposition and mood in a Romance language, María-Luisa Rivero (1971) discusses what she considers to be presupposition in complements with matrices such as *creer*, *parecer*, and certain others. Her notion of presupposition is never precisely defined in the paper, but is certainly different from Keenan's and from that which is adopted in this paper. In fact, as will be seen, her use of presupposition correlates closely in some respects with my notion of assertion.

3. Most of these processes which are relevant for English do not operate in Spanish. (a) Only presupposed complements may be used with the full range of gerundive constructions. *The professor's not knowing the answer was surprising.* (b) Presupposed complements do not

allow subject raising. *He is tragic to finish his paper.* (c) Vacuous extraposition from object is optional with presupposed complements. *I hate it that we have to get up so early.* (d) Presupposed complements do not allow the accusative and infinitive construction. *He supposes the president to be responsible.* (e) Only presupposed complements allow the phrase *the fact that* + S. *I am pleased about the fact that she will remain on this campus.* Only the last item (e) may be applied to Spanish since the other syntactic processes, (a)-(d), do not exist.

4. This is the same definition used by the Kiparskys for their class of emotive matrices. The emotive category for the Kiparskys cut across the lines of presupposition. However, their emotive factive (presupposition) matrices correspond roughly to our true factive matrices, and most of their emotive nonfactive matrices fall into our category of volition.

5. Actually, there are many Spanish speakers who do not use subjunctive forms in these sentences. I will return to this matter shortly.

6. That does not imply, of course, that the speaker cannot lie or deliberately mislead his listeners.

7. Only the singular familiar positive commands are not subjunctive in form. Most traditional grammarians have posited an imperative mood for Spanish but this analysis is purely semantic, since there are no forms which differ from indicative or subjunctive forms. The second person singular positive command is identical in form to the third person singular indicative form indicative form (except in a few cases which are verbal stems: *sal, ven, ten, haz,* etc.).

8. As is well known, this formal contrast exists also in English for many, although certainly not all, speakers.
   (i) I insist that he is there now.
   (ii) I insist that he be there tomorrow.

9. It must be pointed out, however, that there exists much variation in the Spanish-speaking world with regard to the use of mood with matrices of opinion or doubt. Theoretically, there could be four basic possibilities combining mood and negation:
   (i) Creo que irá. Most certainly.
   (ii) Creo que vaya. Some doubt.
   (iii) Creo que va. Some doubt.
   (iv) No creo que vaya. Most doubt.
   However, many factors weight against the full use of such a system. Most matrices of opinion or doubt are not as flexible as are perhaps *creer, parecer,* and others; most are fairly clearly clean-cut cases: *dudo, no dudo.* In addition, there is a tendency on the part of most speakers to regard any opinion, however qualified, as an assertion and sentences like (ii) are unacceptable. Also important is the fact that except for subtle differences in intensity of the doubt, the use of the subjunctive or indicative is quite redundant because the main thrust is carried by the matrix. Most speakers, therefore, use the subjunctive only when the doubt (nonassertion) is clear and indicative if they do not wish to deny completely the possibility that the assertion may be true. We also would not wish to deny that for some speakers the assertion-nonassertion contrast for mood does not operate and that any use of the subjunctive in sentences of doubt may be formulaic.

10. Such cases are discussed in detail by María-Luisa Rivero (1971), where she describes such complements as presupposed. This is clearly not the case using our definition of presupposition since (a) the truth of the proposition is not implied by the sentence as a whole, and (b) the truth of the proposition is affected by the processes of negation and questioning. It seems clear that such cases are examples of assertion; the fact that the proposition is known to the listener does not prevent the speaker from (re)affirming it. Many speakers, of course, do not make the semantic distinction and simply use subjunctive in all cases.

11. In certain cases, if the speaker wishes to affirm the complement, he may use the indicative (although many speakers do not accept the combination of affirmation and doubt and hence always use the subjunctive).

> ¿Dudaste que lo hice yo?
> 'Did you doubt that I did it?'

12. The terms 'parenthetical' and 'nonparenthetical' in this sense are taken from Hooper (1974) and Urmson (1963). I quote from Hooper (1974): 'The reading in which the main (assertive) verb itself makes the main assertion of the sentence is called the nonparenthetical reading. On the reading in which the complement proposition is the main proposition, the assertive verb is used in its parenthetical sense.'

13. I do not mean to imply that all speakers use the subjunctive forms in these sentences.

14. Two are not: Tag-Question Formation, which does not exist as such in Spanish, and Subject-Auxiliary Inversion, which is also is quite different in Spanish. I will not discuss these two transformations in this paper.

15. Joan Hooper has pointed out (personal communication) that Spanish may be a VSO language, and if this is the case, then one would not expect correspondence of items such as Root Transformations. See note 16 for another hypothesis.

16. Helas Contreras has suggested that these data be explained in terms of theme (old material) and rheme (new material). In this framework neither word is basic; rather, both derive from the native speaker's selection of different elements as the rheme of the sentence.

17. I suspect that this will also explain why some English speakers also accept certain of these transformations in nonassertive sentences.

18. There are, however, sentence adverbials which may be used in this manner.

> (i)   Estarán allí a las nueve, a lo mejor.
>   'They will be there at nine o'clock, in all likelihood.'
> (ii) El tren llegará dentro de poco, probablemente.
>   'The train will arrive soon, probably.'

One might argue that the hypothesis that the mood is directly correlated with assertion-nonassertion is falsified by these examples since one can find minimal pairs in which the difference is only syntactic.

> (iii) Es posible que vengan.
>   'It's possible that they'll come.'
> (iv) Posiblemente vendrán.
>   'Possibly they'll come.'
> (v)   Vendrán posiblemente.
>   'They'll come, possibly.'

However, I would argue that there are some semantic differences between these sentences, slight though they may be. In (iii) no assertion is made; a proposition is stated as a possibility. In (v) it is asserted that they will come and then the assertion is qualified; (iv) is intermediate between (iii) and (v), and one also finds the sentence (vi):

> (vi) Posiblemente vengan.
>   'Possibly, they'll come.'

according to how doubtful the speaker feels about the proposition. We could find no sentence adverbs of volition.

Sentence adverbials of comment are completely different, both syntactically and semantically, from their corresponding matrices.

> (vii) Es interesante que fueran a Acapulco en vez de Puerto Vallarta.
>   'It's interesting that they went to Acapulco instead of Puerta Vallarta.'
> (viii) Interesante que sea, fueron a Acapulco en vez de Puerto Vallarta.
>   'Interesting that it may be, they went to Acapulco instead of Puerto Vallarta.'

In (vii) it is presupposed that they went to Acapulco; in (viii) this same proposition is asserted.

19. For an even more detailed discussion of the details of Complement Preposing see Bolinger (1968). A syntactic process which appears to be quite similar to Complement Preposing is Extraposition. The Kiparskys (1970) gave credit to Jespersen for the introduction of this term. Ross's (1967) study of extraposition in English is perhaps the cause of recent interest in the phenomenon. The Kiparskys correlated extraposition in English to lack of presupposition; nonpresupposed complements must be extraposed.

Extraposition is the process which describes the relationship between sentences such as (i) and (ii).

(i)   Que no querían ir con Uds. es evidente.
      'That they didn't want to go with you all is evident.'
(ii) Es evidente que no querían ir con Uds.
      'It's evident that they didn't want to go with you all.'

Since sentence (ii) is far more common than (i), it appears at first glance that this is just another case of Complement Preposing. There are, however, certain syntactic and intonational differences.

(iii) Querrán ir, es seguro.
      'They will want to go, it's sure.'
(iv) Que querrán ir es seguro.
      'That they will want to go is sure.'
(v)   Es seguro que querrán ir.
      'It's sure that they will want to go.'

In (iii) the matrix is parenthetical; in (iv) the sentence follows the normal subject-predicate order. In (v), with extraposition the subject (complement) has been moved to the end of the sentence. (Emonds presents considerable evidence that sentential subjects such as these are actually generated in the 'extraposed' position and moved by a transformation he calls Subject Replacement to this position.)

The complements in sentence initial position will not be taken necessarily as assertions, since they must be preceded by *que*, and they are usually followed by the copula or another intransitive verb. Therefore, subject complements may appear in sentence initial position with all classes of matrices. This is not necessarily the most common or preferred position.

(vi) Que no compraron el carro es evidente.
      'That they didn't buy the car is evident.'
(vii) Que Juan no había sacado buenas notas no me fue explicado muy bien.
      'That John hadn't gotten good grades wasn't explained to me very well.'
(viii) Que Alfredo es un buen nadador es reconocido en todas partes.
      'That Alfred is a good swimmer is recognized everywhere.'
(ix) Que se queden conmigo es dudoso.
      'That they stay with me is doubtful.'
(x)   Que se vayan inmediatamente es preferible.
      'That they leave immediately is preferable.'
(xi) Que te lo hayan regalado es magnífico.
      'That they gave it to you is magnificent.'

In sentences in which the matrix is not the copula, if the complement is asserted, then it must preposed.

(xii) Resulta que se irán mañana.
      'It turns out that they'll leave tomorrow.'
(xiii) Que se irán mañana resulta.

*'That they'll leave tomorrow turns out.'
However, nonassertions are not so restricted.
(xiv) Que nos devuelva el dinero basta (importa, cuenta, emociona).
       'That he return the money to use is enough (is important, counts, is exciting).
It is not entirely clear why the extraposed sentences are preferred. Perhaps it is to avoid
misinterpretation of all subject-complements as (preposed) assertions.
20. Although it is clear that this is the explanation for the possibility of either assertions or
    commands in first position in the sentence with the predicate for reporting in parenthetical
    position, it is not at all clear that these commands are completely parallel to the sentences
    we have taken to be the result of Complement Preposing. However, this does not affect my
    claims and I will not pursue the matter further. Note also that it is obvious that reported
    commands differ syntactically from sentences with regular matrices of volition. In most
    work done within the transformational framework, sentences of volition were 'derived' from
    underlying commands. Consider the following sentences.
    (i)   Me dijo que viniera a las nueve.
           'He told me to come at nine.'
    (ii)   Me dijo 'Venga a las nueve.'
           'He said to me "Come at nine".'
    (iii) Venga a las nueve, me dijo.
           'Come at nine, he said to me.'
    Although (i) may be 'derived' from (ii) or even (iii), such is not the case for the following set
    of sentences in which (v) and (vi) do not even exist.
    (iv)   Quería que viniera a las nueve.
           'He wanted me to come at nine.'
    (v)   *Quería, 'Venga a las nueve.'
           *'He wanted "Come at nine".'
    (vi)   *Venga a las nueve, quería.
           *'Come at nine, he wanted.'
    However one may wish to formalize this difference, it is clear that the syntactic difference
    is a direct result of the semantic difference between matrices of reporting and volition.

References

Bolinger, D. 1968. Postponed Main Phrases: An English Rule for the Romance Subjunctive.
    Canadian Journal of Linguistics 14:3-33.
Emonds, J. 1969. Root and Structure-Preserving Transformations. Ph.D. dissertation.
    University of California, Berkeley.
Hooper, J. 1974. On Assertive Predicates. In *Syntax and Semantics,* Vol. 4. New York: Seminar
    Press.
Hooper, J., and S.A. Thompson. 1973. On the Applicability of Root Transformations. *Linguistic
    Inquiry* 4:465-98.
Hooper, J., and T. Terrell. 1974. A Semantically Based Analysis of Mood in Spanish. *Hispania*
    57:484-94.
Karttunen, L. 1971. Some Observations on Factivity. In *Papers in Linguistics* 4:55-69.
Keenan, E.L. 1971. Two Kinds of Presuppositions in Natural Language. In *Studies in Linguistic
    Semantics,* ed. C. Fillmore and T. Langendoen, 45-52. New York: Holt, Rinehart and
    Winston.
Kiparsky, P., and C. Kiparsky. 1970. Fact. In *Progress in Linguistics,* ed. M. Bierwisch and K.E.
    Heidolph, 143-73. The Hague: Mouton.
Rivero, M.L. 1971. Mood and Presupposition in Spanish. *Foundations of Language* 7:305-36.

Ross, J. 1967. Constraints on Variables in Syntax. Ph.D. dissertation, Massachusetts Institute of Technology.

Urmson, J.O. 1963. Parenthetical Verbs. In *Philosophy and Ordinary Language*, ed. C.E. Caton, 220-40. Urbana, Ill.: University of Illinois Press.

Illocutionary Verbs, Subject Responsibility, and Presupposition: The Indicative versus the Subjunctive in Spanish

Sanford Schane
University of California, San Diego

The matrix verbs of Spanish that govern complement clauses can be assigned to one of the five illocutionary categories (assertive, directive, commissive, expressive, declaration) proposed by Searle. The indicative mood will appear in the complement clause whenever the subject of the matrix illocutionary verb takes responsibility for the truth or fulfillment of the propositional content expressed in the complement clause; the illocutionary verbs that govern the subjunctive lack this feature of "subject responsibility." But where there is tension between the subject's rejection of the truth of the propositional content and a presupposition about its truth value, the force of the presupposition may prevail and the indicative will be favored.

Spanish-language teachers know all too well the difficulty frequently experienced by American students trying to master the indicative versus the subjunctive. It was natural for Tracy Terrell to turn his attention to the intricacies of this distinction. His research in this area constitutes a significant contribution to the syntax and semantics of Spanish complementation. At a time when many transformationalists attempted to treat the distinction as a purely syntactic phenomenon involving nothing more than the classification of the matrix verb, Terrell was already advocating "a semantically based analysis of mood in Spanish" (Terrell and Hooper 1974; Terrell 1976).

I shall review Terrell's treatment of Spanish complementation in nominal clauses. The semantic concepts of *assertion* and *presupposition* are central features of this analysis. Together they define six kinds of complement structures. The main deficiency of the analysis, though, is its inability to accommodate matrix verbs of the type "promise." Such verbs, called *commissives*, constitute a particular kind of speech act. Searle (1979) has proposed a classification of the various speech-act types. I shall adapt that schema to the Spanish data.

I develop an analysis of mood in nominal clauses that takes into account both the illocutionary type of the matrix verb and presuppositions concerning the truth value of the propositional content of the embedded clause. I argue for a notion of *subject responsibility:* Whenever the subject of the matrix clause takes responsibility for the truth or fulfillment of the contained propositional content, the indicative occurs in the complement clause; where there is lack of subject responsibility, one finds the subjunctive. The indicative may still occur where there is lack of subject responsibility, but in such cases there is a presupposition that someone else regards the propositional content as true.

1 THE ASSERTION/PRESUPPOSITION ANALYSIS OF TERRELL AND HOOPER

The analysis proposed by Terrell and Hooper maintains that "the choice of mood in Spanish is directly correlated with what the sentence as a whole expresses about the truth of the proposition included in the sentence" (1974:484). For evaluating the propositional truth of complement clauses they resort to the concepts of *assertion* and *presupposition.* (The latter corresponds to the idea of the *factive* as formulated by Kiparsky and Kiparsky in 1970. Terrell and Hooper establish three principal categories, each with two variants. A speaker may: (1) *assert* the truth of a proposition by (a) *asserting* directly his belief in its truth, or (b) *reporting* how the information was conveyed; (2) *presuppose* the truth of a proposition by (a) describing his *mental reaction* to (or cognitive awareness of) the proposition, or (b) *commenting* about his subjective reaction (or emotional feelings) to it; or (3) neither assert nor presuppose the truth of a proposition because (a) he *doubts* its truth, or (b) what he expresses functions as an *imperative.* The indicative will occur in a complement clause whenever the matrix verb expresses either one of the two kinds of assertion or else a mental-act presupposition, whereas the subjunctive will occur with a comment presupposition or else with either kind of nonassertion/nonpresupposition. The chart below (Terrell and Hooper 1974:488) summarizes these observations.

SEMANTIC NOTION	CLASS	MOOD
ASSERTION	(1) Assertion	Indicative
	(2) Report	Indicative
PRESUPPOSITION	(3) Mental Act	Indicative
	(4) Comment	Subjunctive
NEITHER	(5) Doubt	Subjunctive
	(6) Imperative	Subjunctive

Here are some examples, from Terrell and Hooper, of each type. (The number from each of their original examples is cited between brackets.)

1)   [4] *Creo que María estudiará mañana.*
             'I believe that Maria will study tomorrow.'
      [6] *Me parece que María estudiará mañana.*
             'It seems to me that Maria will study tomorrow.'
      [5] *Es seguro que María estudiará mañana.*
             'It's certain that Maria will study tomorrow.'

2) [19] *Le dije que María no quería jugar tenis.*
        'I told him that Maria didn't want to play tennis.'

3) [47] *Yo me doy cuenta de lo que quieren.*
        'I realize what they want.'

   [43] *Tomó en consideración el hecho de que Juan es muy joven.*
        'He took into consideration the fact the Juan is very young.'

4) [42] *Estoy contento de que María haya venido a visitarnos.*
        'I'm happy that Maria has come to visit us.'

   [27] *Es una lástima que María no haya podido terminar a tiempo.*
        'It's a shame that Maria hasn't been able to finish on time.'

5) [25] *Dudo que hayan terminado ya.*
        'I doubt that they've already finished.'

   [26] *Es posible que hayan terminado ya.*
        'It's possible that they've already finished.'

   [44] *No creo que Martín haya leído ese libro.*
        'I don't think that Martin has read that book.'

6) [22] *Quiero que nos quedemos un rato más.*
        'I want us to stay a little longer.'

   [50] *Insisto en que no retiren las tropas.*
        'I insist on their not withdrawing the troops.'

In the examples of (1) and (2) above, the speaker asserts his belief that the proposition expressed is true. The different matrix clauses of (1) serve to qualify that assertion in various ways. The assertion of (2) is reported; that is, the matrix clause establishes the way the assertion was conveyed. In the sentences of (3) and (4), the speaker does not assert the truth of the propositions but instead presupposes that they are true. The matrix clauses of (3) refer to mental acts regarding, but not caused by, the events of the propositions. On the other hand, the psychological states described by the matrix clauses of (4) are direct consequences of the events. In the sentences of (5) and (6), the propositions are neither asserted nor presupposed. In the sentences of (5) there is doubt about the validity of the propositions; hence one cannot assert or presuppose their truth. The propositional clauses of (6), because they contain implied imperatives, can be neither true nor false.

This analysis has some desirable consequences. It accounts for the ambiguity of certain matrix verbs by assigning to them two different semantic classifications. For example, the verb *insistir* has both reporting and imperative readings, and the verb *sentir* both reporting and subjective comment. The reporting readings will govern an indicative complement, whereas the imperative or comment reading will take the subjunctive.

7) [51] *Insisto en que no retiran las tropas.* (Indicative)
        'I insist that they are not withdrawing the troops.' (Reporting)

   [50] *Insisto en que no retiren las tropas.* (Subjunctive)
        'I insist that they not withdraw the troops.' (Imperative)

   [54] *Siento que se va.* (Indicative)
        'I feel that he's leaving.' (Reporting)

[55]   *Siento que se vaya.* (Subjunctive)
'I'm sorry that he's leaving.' (Comment)

The analysis accommodates also the polarity switching that takes place between the categories of assertion and doubt. A matrix verb of assertion, when negated, can govern a subjunctive in its complement, and, conversely, a matrix verb of doubt, when negated, will trigger the indicative. This switching follows from the semantics of these two classes. The negation of an assertion is equivalent to a denial of the truth of the proposition asserted, and the negation of a denial is equivalent to an acceptance of the truth of that proposition.

8) [44a]   *Creo que Martín ha leído ese libro.* (Indicative)
'I think that Martin has read that book.' (Assertion)

[44b]   *No creo que Martín haya leído ese libro.* (Subjunctive)
'I don't think that Martin has read that book.' (Doubt)

[45a]   *Dudo que Consuelo sea culpable.* (Subjunctive)
'I doubt that Consuelo is guilty.' (Doubt)

[45b]   *No dudo que Consuelo es culpable.* (Indicative)
'I don't doubt that Consuelo is guilty.' (Assertion)

Although in the analysis proposed by Terrell and Hooper the choice of mood depends on the semantic features of assertion and presupposition, the correlation between these semantic categories and their syntactic reflexes is not so clean-cut as one might wish. Whereas the analysis establishes a nice connection between assertion and the use of the indicative and, conversely, nonassertion/nonpresupposition and the use of the subjunctive, a direct correlation of this type fails to hold for the category of presupposition, where mental-act verbs govern the indicative but comment verbs take the subjunctive. Terrell and Hooper acknowledge this shortcoming. In defense they note that mental-act verbs, intuitively, seem more similar to assertions than comment verbs do, but the analysis itself has no explanation for this observation.

A more serious problem with the analysis is its inability to account for verbs like *prometer* 'promise', verbs that are categorized as *commissives* within speech-act theory. These verbs are similar to speech-act directives (which Terrell calls imperatives) in that their complements too are neither asserted nor presupposed. The propositional content of a promise, for example, is neither true nor false. Yet commissives, unlike imperatives, do not govern the subjunctive, the mood that is predicted for the category of nonassertion/nonpresupposition.

9)   *Prometo que iremos al cine esta noche.* (Indicative)
'I promise that we'll go to the movies tonight.'

Searle (1979) has proposed a taxonomy of the different kinds of illocutionary acts. I shall make use of this framework for classifying the verbs of matrix clauses and for analyzing mood in their complements.

2   THE SPEECH-ACT ANALYSIS

Searle recognizes five illocutionary types. He summarizes them at the conclusion of his article (1979:29):

If we adopt illocutionary point as the basic notion on which to classify uses of language, then there are a rather limited number of basic things we do with language:

(a) we tell people how things are [i.e., assertives];

(b) we try to get them to do things [i.e., directives];

(c) we commit ourselves to doing things [i.e., commissives];

(d) we express our feelings and attitudes [i.e., expressives];

(e) we bring about changes through our utterances [i.e., declarations].

2.1 Illocutionary Verbs

One can assign verbs to these categories on the basis of the illocutionary points they convey. Here are a few examples.

    a.   assertives: *decir* 'tell', *jurar* 'swear', *conceder* 'concede';

    b.   directives: *ordenar* 'order', *aconsejar* 'advise', *permitir* 'permit':

    c.   commissives: *prometer* 'promise', *consentir* 'consent', *garantizar*, 'guarantee';

    d.   expressives: *felicitar* 'congratulate', *protestar* 'protest', *lamentar*, 'be sorry';

    e.   declarations: *declarar* 'declare', *repudiar* 'repudiate', *nominar* 'name'.

In Spanish, matrix verbs with the illocutionary force of assertives, directives, commissives, and some declarations can govern finite complement clauses. (Many of these verbs also take infinitive clauses, but these constructions will not be of concern to us.) Verbs conveying expressives are found most often with noun phrases or infinitive clauses, and verbs of declaration usually take noun phrases. The following examples all have first-person subjects and present-tense verbs so that the utterances will express the intended illocutionary points:

10)   (a)   *Te juro que Juan estuvo aquí esta mañana.* (Indicative)
            'I swear to you that Juan was here this morning.'

       (b)   *Te aconsejo que estudies para el examen.* (Subjunctive)
            'I advise you to study for the exam.'

       (c)   *Te prometo que llegaremos allí a tiempo.* (Indicative)
            'I promise you that we'll arrive there on time.'

       (d)   *Te felicito por haberte casado.* (Infinitive)
            'I congratulate you on having gotten married.'
            Te felicito de tu matrimonio. (Noun phrase)
            'I congratulate you on your marriage.'

       (e)   *Declaro que el acusado es culpable.* (Indicative)
            'I declare that the accused is guilty.'
            Nomino a Jorge como candidato para presidente. (Noun phrase)
            'I nominate Jorge as a candidate for president.'

In the performance of an illocutionary act, the speaker expresses at the same time a particular psychological state in regard to the propositional content. The state of mind is the *sincerity condition* for that illocutionary act (Searle 1979). An assertive is associated with an underlying *belief*, a directive with a *want*, a commissive with an *intent*, and an expressive with an *emotion*. (Declarations have no accompanying psychological state.) That is, a speaker who makes a sincere assertion affirms at the same time his belief in the truth of the asserted proposition; one who requests something must sincerely desire that which has been requested; one who makes a commitment must intend to carry out the act stated in the commitment; and one who expresses a particular attitude toward an event must sincerely have experienced the emotional state that accompanies that attitude. Here are examples of verbs that express these different psychological states:

  a. belief: *creer* 'believe', *pensar* 'think', *ver* 'see', *darse cuenta* 'realize', *ser verdad* 'be true';
  b. want: *querer* 'want', *desear* 'desire', *ser necesario* 'be necessary';
  c. intent: *tener la intención*, *tener planeado* 'intend'
  d. emotion: *estar contento* 'be happy', *lamentar* 'be sorry', *ser sorprendente* 'be surprising'.

Verbs of belief, want, and emotion can occur in matrix clauses that govern finite complement clauses; verbs of intent tend to take an infinitive.

  11) (a) *Pienso que va a llover esta tarde.* (Indicative)
            'I think that it's going to rain this afternoon.'
       (b) *Quiero que te vayas ahora.* (Subjunctive)
            'I want you to leave now.'
       (c) *Tengo la intención de llevarte al cine.* (Infinitive)
            'I intend to take you to the movies.'
       (d) *Estoy contento de que nos visiten.* (Subjunctive)
            'I'm pleased that they'll visit us.'

What has evolved thus far is a classification of verbs that express either illocutionary acts or their accompanying psychological states. Because the performance of an illocutionary act takes place as the speaker is speaking, the verb forms in matrix clauses that express illocutionary acts generally occur in the first person and in the present tense and there is often an indirect object in the second person. Consider now the following examples:

  12) (a) *Te aconsejo que no hagas eso.*
            'I advise you not to do that.'
       (b) *Les aconsejé que no hicieran eso.*
            'I advised them not to do that.'
       (c) *Pedro me aconsejó que no hiciera eso.*
            'Pedro advised me not to do that.'
       (d) *Es aconsejable que no hagamos eso.*
            'It's advisable that we not do that.'

Only (12a), with its first-person present-tense verb, illustrates a true directive illocutionary act. Sentences (12b) and (12c), with other persons and tenses, constitute instead descriptions of illocutionary acts, and (12d) exemplifies an impersonal construction. Yet all the examples are syntactically similar; the subjunctive mood still occurs in the complement clauses. What this means is that our classificatory schema, although it began as a taxonomy of types of illocutionary acts, is actually, at least for its application to complements, a classification of illocutionary verbs and of verbs expressing associated psychological states. I define an *illocutionary verb* as one that has the potential of expressing a performative illocutionary act. It is this illocutionary potential that establishes the semantic categorization of a matrix verb and will determine the syntactic mood of the complement clause.

The following chart lists the different classes of verbs (both the illocutionary types and their associated psychological states). For those verb classes that govern a finite complement clause, the chart indicates whether the verb of the embedded clause will occur in the indicative or in the subjunctive. (Intent and expressive verbs take infinitival or nominal clauses.) Note that an illocutionary type and its derived psychological state take the same mood when both can occur with a finite complement clause.

ILLOCUTIONARY TYPE	PSYCHOLOGICAL STATE
1. Assertive	Belief
(Indicative)	(Indicative)
2. Directive	Want
(Subjunctive)	(Subjunctive)
3. Commissive	Intent
(Indicative)	—
4. Expressive	Emotive
—	(Subjunctive)
5. Declaration	—
(Indicative	

This classificatory schema, like that of Terrell and Hooper, accommodates those situations where a verb governs at times the indicative and at other times the subjunctive. Such verbs can play more than one illocutionary role. We noted in (7) that the verbs *insistir* and *sentir* behave in this way. When *insistir* takes the subjunctive it functions as a directive, and when it takes the indicative it functions as an assertive; *sentir* functions as an emotive verb with the subjunctive and as a belief verb with the indicative.

2.2 Subject Responsibility

The categories of "assertion" and "presupposition" (as proposed in Terrell and Hooper) cannot account adequately for the distribution of the indicative and the subjunctive in the complement clauses of the five illocutionary types and the associated psychological states. Although one might argue that declarations constitute a special type of assertion and, thus, one could account for the use of the indicative with declarations, one cannot make a similar argument for the indicative with commissives. Unlike an assertion, the propositional content of a commissive (the truth value of its embedded clause) can be neither true nor false. Presupposition as a criterion fares no better. Both emotives (e.g., *estar contento* 'be happy') and some verbs of belief (e.g., *darse cuenta* 'realize') take complements whose truth is presupposed; yet the former group governs the subjunctive, and the latter the indicative. Finally, the classification of nonassertion/nonpresupposition fails as well. Included in this group are directives and commissives; the former class of verbs takes the subjunctive, and the latter the indicative.

Why should the illocutionary and psychological categories of assertive, belief, commissive, and declaration take the indicative mood in complement clauses, whereas directive, want, and emotive take the subjunctive? To account for this dichotomy I propose the notion of *subject responsibility*. The indicative is used whenever the subject of the matrix clause takes responsibility for the truth, fulfillment, or eventuation of the propositional content expressed in the complement clause. For an assertive or a belief, one commits oneself to accepting as true that which has been stated, believed, perceived, or realized. If I tell you that Joe was here this morning, not only do I convey my belief in the truth of Joe's having been here, but I must accept any consequences resulting from that belief. If I realize that you were right about something, then I have acknowledged that your being right has been incorporated as a true proposition in my belief structure; that is, I accept responsibility for representing something as true even though its truth has been presupposed. For a commissive, one has responsibility for the fulfillment of that which has been promised or intended. If I promise that we will go to the movies later, then I am responsible for ensuring that the act expressed in the propositional content (our going to the movies) will indeed take place. For a declaration, one takes responsibility for the successful bringing about of that which has been declared. If I am a judge and I sentence you to thirty days in jail, I have effected that which I have declared and as a consequence of that speech act the propositional content of that utterance becomes true.

The illocutionary types that govern the subjunctive lack this feature of subject responsibility. There will be absence of subject responsibility whenever (a) someone other than the subject must assume the responsibility, (b) the subject is neutral in regard to expressing responsibility, or (c) the subject explicitly rejects responsibility. Directives and expressives exemplify the first two situations, respectively. For a directive, the fulfillment of that which is demanded, wanted, or desired rests on another individual and not on the subject of the matrix clause. If I request that you be here at eight o'clock, then you are the one who must take the responsibility for ensuring that my request (your arriving on time) will be fulfilled. For an expressive, the propositional content is presupposed and the subject merely relates his emotional reaction to it. If I tell you that I am sorry that you failed your exam, I am stating that I have a particular emotional feeling about a fact that is presumed true. Although I must be sincere about having experienced the emotion expressed in the matrix clause (my sorrow)—the sincerity condition for this kind of speech act—I do not take responsibility for the recognition of the presumed truth of the propositional content of the complement clause (i.e., your having failed).

This distinction should become clear with the following example. Suppose that you tell me that you have flunked your exam, but you are lying to me and I do not know that your statement is a lie. I respond by saying that I am sorry that you failed your exam. If I sincerely report having a particular emotional reaction to an event, it is because I accept as true the propositional content describing the event (otherwise I could not experience the purported emotional reaction), but I certainly take no responsibility for its truth value. Contrast this kind of presupposition with the assertive type. Recall the example in which I realize that you were right about something. With that kind of a matrix verb I assert that something presupposed has been incorporated into my belief structure and I take the responsibility for acknowledging that I hold that belief.

The third type of lack of subject responsibility occurs when the subject rejects acceptance of the truth of the propositional content of the complement clause. Verbs expressing the illocutions of denial (e.g., *negar*) and doubt (e.g., *dudar*) would fall into this category. Denial and doubt can also be conveyed through the negation of verbs of assertion and belief, respectively (e.g., *no decir*, *no creer*). All of these verbs can trigger the subjunctive in Spanish complement clauses (see also the examples of (8)).

13) (a) *Negaron que María hubiera dicho eso.*
          'They denied that Maria had said that.'

     (b) *Dudan que vaya a llover.*
          'They doubt that it's going to rain.'

     (c) *No creo que Juan lo haga.*
          'I don't think that Juan will do it.'

In Searle's taxonomy of speech acts, the illocution of denial belongs to the category of assertive because in denying that something is the case one is asserting that one does not believe that it is so; moreover, doubt is the particular mental state that accompanies a denial. The notion of subject responsibility can explain the use of the subjunctive in complement clauses whose matrix clauses express either negative assertives (denial) or negative beliefs (doubt). One who denies (or doubts) something does not take responsibility for the truth of that which has been asserted.

A similar phenomenon involving the relinquishment of subject responsibility happens with commissives. The subject of a commissive verb (e.g., *prometer*) takes responsibility for the fulfillment of the act stated in the propositional content of the complement clause (that which has been promised). With a negated commissive verb, the subject rejects any responsibility for carrying out that act. Accordingly, the verb of the complement clause will be in the subjunctive:

14) *No puedo prometer que vayamos a un restaurante más tarde.*
     (Subjunctive)
     'I can't promise that we'll go to a restaurant later.'

Although commissive verbs take the indicative when positive and the subjunctive when negative, directives and verbs of wanting take only the subjunctive. The fulfillment of whatever the subject of the matrix verb wants or does not want rests entirely with the individual addressed.

15) (a) *Quiero que te vayas.*
          'I want you to go away.'

     (b) *No quiero que te vayas.*
          'I don't want you to go away.'

2.3 Presupposition

Verbs expressing denial and doubt nonetheless do occur with complement clauses in the indicative. In such cases the use of the indicative seems to emphasize that there is a presupposition that someone other than the subject—often the speaker of the utterance—accepts the truth of the propositional content. In other words, the rejection of responsibility on the part of the subject has been overridden by the presupposition. Consider the two versions in (16):

16) (a) *Guillermo no cree que la tierra sea redonda.* (Subjunctive)
    (b) *Guillermo no cree que la tierra es redonda.* (Indicative)
    'Guillermo doesn't believe that the earth is round.'

In both versions, the speaker reports Guillermo's doubt. In (16b), one might infer that Guillermo doubts a fact presumed to be true—by the speaker, or even more likely by the entire scientific community. Note that the individual who accepts the proposition as true need not be the speaker. This must necessarily be so whenever the speaker is also the subject.

17) (a) *No es seguro que nuestro candidato haya ganado la elección.* (Subjunctive)
    (b) *No es seguro que nuestro candidato ha ganado la elección.* (Indicative)
    'It's not certain that our candidate has won the election.'

In both versions, the speaker, who is the implied subject, doubts that our candidate has been elected; in (17b), however, there is a presupposition that other people may believe our candidate to have won. Compare also the two sentences in (18):

18) (a) *No digo que seas tonto; sólo digo que debes estudiar más.* (Subjunctive)
    'I'm not saying that you're stupid; I'm only saying that you should study more.'
    (b) *No digo que eres tonto; lo dice Carlos.* (Indicative)
    'I'm not saying that you're stupid; Carlos is saying it.'

In (18a), the speaker denies asserting that the hearer is stupid; nor is there a presupposition that anyone else believes him to be stupid. In (18b), there is indeed a presupposition that someone (other than the subject of the denial verb) believes the hearer is stupid; that individual is in fact named.

The preceding judgments may not be valid for all Spanish speakers; there is much dialectal and individual variation for such sentences. Some speakers can imply a presupposition reading even with the subjunctive, but there is a stronger tendency for this particular reading with the indicative.

3   COMPARISON OF THE TWO ANALYSES

The semantic concepts of *assertion* and *presupposition* are the cornerstones of the Terrell and Hooper analysis. Although I have argued that these notions by themselves are inadequate for accommodating all of the various types of Spanish matrix verbs, they are still necessary elements of an analysis of mood in complement clauses. In the speech-act treatment, there is a classification of assertive, and the notion of presupposition is found there too. However, these two concepts play different roles in the two analyses.

3.1 Assertion versus Assertive

Terrell and Hooper's category of "assertion" is considerably less extensive in its application than the speech-act classification of "assertive." Their category of assertion encompasses verbs of reporting (e.g., *decir*, *notar*) and verbs of belief whose complements are not necessarily presupposed (e.g., *creer*, *ser verdad*), but verbs of belief whose complements are presupposed—their mental-act verbs—(e.g., *darse cuenta*, *olvidar*) belong to their presupposition category. Yet both kinds of belief verbs govern the indicative in complement clauses. This result is embarrassing for them since other presupposed complements—their comment verbs—(e.g., *lamentar*, *ser sorprendente*) take the subjunctive. Terrell and Hooper remark that mental-act verbs resemble assertions, but they are unable to incorporate this observation into their approach.

This problem does not arise with the speech-act analysis. Its classification of *assertive*, as it applies to illocutionary verbs and to associated psychological states, encompasses verbs of reporting and *both* kinds of verbs of belief. It is irrelevant whether the belief verbs have presupposed complements. Notice that this effect does not come about simply because I have chosen to define "assertive" so as to include both types of belief verbs. The classificatory schema is Searle's, not mine, and it was not designed with the Spanish data in mind. Yet the illocutionary category of assertive, when applied to these Spanish matrix verbs, sorts them out precisely in the desired fashion.

In the speech-act schema, verbs expressing denial and doubt belong also to the classification of "assertive." In the Terrell and Hooper analysis, these verbs constitute their own category, because they are able to govern the subjunctive in complement clauses. They either are lexically simple (*negar*, *dudar*) or are negated assertions (*no decir*, *no creer*). In the Terrell and Hooper analysis, as well as in most of the traditional taxonomies of Romance verbs, the same verb (*creer*) will be assigned to one class when positive (assertion) but to a different class when negative (doubt). Separate classes are necessary simply because, in those analyses, each verb class tends to govern uniquely the indicative or the subjunctive. (This is not entirely true, for verbs of denial and doubt may occur with both moods.) Such analyses leave as unexplained why the psychological states of belief and doubt enter into polarity switching. Now, in speech act theory, verbs that express denial or doubt have the illocutionary force of negated assertives. Hence, from the perspective of that theory there is nothing mysterious about polarity switching: the verbs that allow it belong to the category of assertive. Since these verbs govern the indicative when positive and can take the subjunctive when negative, the category of "assertive" cannot, by itself, be a factor that governs the choice of mood. I have advocated that the principal criterion is the pragmatic notion of subject responsibility. For matrix clauses with positive assertives, the subject always assumes responsibility for the truth of the propositional content expressed in the complement clause; for negated assertives, the subject relinquishes any such responsibility. In the case of negated assertives, the indicative may nonetheless occur when there is an overriding presupposition that someone else may hold the propositional content as true.

3.2 Presupposition

In Terrell and Hooper's analysis, presupposition is the other main criterion for classifying matrix verbs. We have seen that this trait, too, fails in the determination of a unique choice of mood. Both their mental-act verbs (e.g., *darse cuenta, olvidar*) and their comment verbs (e.g., *lamentar, estar contento*) take complements with presupposed truth values. Yet the former class governs the indicative and the latter the subjunctive. In the speech-act analysis, the so-called mental-act verbs belong to the category of assertives. When positive, these verbs exemplify subject responsibility and, accordingly, they must govern the indicative. We have also seen that in the negative, where there is no subject responsibility, those assertive verbs that do not necessarily have presupposed complements (*creer*) can take a subjunctive, resulting in polarity switching. However, mental-act verbs, although they are assertives, will never take the subjunctive when negated. A mental-act verb always takes a complement whose propositional content is presumed true. It is this presupposition that will override the rejection of subject responsibility. Compare the negations of *creer* and *darse cuenta*:

19)   (a)   *Juana no cree que Miguel esté en Europa.* (Subjunctive)
              'Juana doesn't think that Miguel is in Europe.'

       (b)   *Juana no se da cuenta de que Miguel está en Europa.* (Indicative)
              *Juana no se da cuenta de que Miguel esté en Europa. (Subjunctive)
              'Juana doesn't realize that Miguel is in Europe.'

In both (19a) and (19b), the subject of the matrix clause does not take responsibility for the truth of the propositional content of the complement clause. This fact should trigger the subjunctive, which it does in (19a). Whereas a verb like *creer* does not necessarily entail any presuppositions about the truth value of the propositional content, a verb like *darse cuenta* does. That is, in (19b) there is a presupposition that Miguel is in Europe, a presupposition that is not acknowledged by the subject. Where there exists a tension between the subject's rejection or lack of knowledge about the truth of the propositional content and the presupposition about its truth value, the force of the presupposition prevails and the indicative is favored.

Note that it is not the mere presence of a presupposition that yields the indicative in a complement clause, but rather the clash between that presupposition and the subject's rejection of responsibility vis-à-vis the propositional content. Emotive verbs always have presupposed complements. Yet, regardless of whether the verb of the matrix clause is positive or negative, the verb of the complement is always subjunctive.

20)   (a)   *Estoy contento de que estén aquí.*
              'I'm pleased that they are here.'

(b)　*No estoy contento de que estén aquí.*
　　　'I'm not pleased that they are here.'

The subject of the matrix clause acknowledges, through the expressed emotion, the truth value of the propositional content of the complement clause. Although the subject does not reject that which has been presupposed, he does not take responsibility for it either. Because there is absence of responsibility, the verb of the complement clause will be in the subjunctive. Now a negated emotive verb is also an emotive. Since it is a property of emotives that the subject never rejects that which is presupposed in the propositional content, there can be no clash between the presupposition and the subject's absence of responsibility. Hence the complement verb will remain in the subjunctive.

3.3 Subject Responsibility

I have suggested that Spanish matrix verbs can be classified according to their illocutionary potential as established in Searle's taxonomy. Some of these illocutionary types—assertives, commissives, declarations—entail subjects that assume responsibility for the truth, fulfillment, or eventuation of the propositional content that is expressed in the complement clause (provided the verbs are not negated). This property is reflected by the indicative mood in that clause. But when these illocutionary forces are negated or when the illocutions are directives or emotives, there is lack of subject responsibility. Accordingly, the subjunctive can occur. That a pragmatic condition such as subject responsibility governs the choice of mood in a complement clause is not unexpected in an analysis that looks at matrix verbs in terms of their speech-act potential. It is in the nature of an illocutionary verb for its subject to have a particular attitude or stance vis-à-vis the propositional content of the complement clause.

Subject responsibility interracts with the *sincerity condition*. The former concept involves a relationship between the subject and the propositional content of the complement clause, and the latter concept relates the subject to a particular psychological state in regard to that content. If I promise that we will go to the movies later, then I must intend to go there with you (the sincerity condition) and moreover, I am responsible (subject responsibility) for seeing that we indeed do go there. The intent accompanies the making of the promise, whereas the responsibility is subsequent to it. For this reason, it is possible for one to renege on a promise (and, thus, not fulfill one's responsibility) that one had intended to keep at the time of its making. Consider, too, how the sincerity condition and subject responsibility affect emotives. If I am sorry that you failed your exam, then I must truly feel the emotion that I have expressed (the sincerity condition), but I am not responsible for the truth value of the propositional content that is stated as the cause of that emotion. Recall that I can be emotionally moved upon hearing something that is not true. (I can also believe something that is not true, but then I must take responsibility—assuming all consequences—for holding that belief.) To elucidate further the concept of subject responsibility, I should like to compare it to two other notions: Comrie's *subject/object control* and Searle's *direction of fit*.

Within the context of speech-act theory, Comrie (1985) has discussed the notions of subject control and object control as they relate to matrix clause verbs that require co-reference between the subject or object of the matrix clause and the understood subject of a dependent infinitive. Comrie explains the difference between the following examples.

21)   (a)   Arthur persuaded Beryl to leave.
      (b)   Arthur promised Beryl to leave.

Comrie states: "...the subject of the infinitive is the participant in that action most likely to have the ability to bring about the action." In (21a), he continues, "the reported speaker [i.e., Arthur]...presupposes that the addressee [i.e., Beryl] has the ability to bring about the action required by the *directive*," whereas in (21b), "the reported speaker...presupposes that the speaker has the ability to bring about the action required by the *commissive*" (1985:57-58, emphasis added). My notion of subject responsibility is much broader than Comrie's. It includes not only his subject/object control but other attitudes toward the propositional content, such as emotion, belief, want, and so forth.

Searle's idea of *direction of fit* provides another way of looking at subject responsibility. According to Searle, assertives and declarations have "as part of their illocutionary point to get the words...to match the world..." (1979:3). If I state that it is raining outside, the propositional content of my statement is supposed to match (i.e., be a linguistic description of) the current meteorological conditions. For assertions and declarations it is the subject's responsibility to bring about this *word-to-world* direction of fit. Commissives and directives, on the other hand, are attempts "to get the world to match the words" (Searle 1979:3). If I promise to take you to dinner, then I am obligated to carry out a subsequent action (take you to dinner) that will match the propositional content of my promise. If I ask you to bring me a glass of water, I would like for you to perform a subsequent action (bringing me water) that will match the propositional content of my request. Notice that for commissives it is the subject who is responsible for effecting this *world-to-word* direction of fit, and for directives it is the addressee. For expressives, "...the speaker is neither trying to get the world to match the words nor the words to match the world..."(Searle 1979:15). If I state that I am delighted that you are here, it is not my intent that the expressed propositional content (your being here) match the world, or that I am to effect a change whereby the world will match the words. The truth of the propositional content is presupposed, and it is my purpose to comment on the proposition.

The three categories of fit—*word-to-world*, *world-to-word*, and *no fit*—by themselves are insufficient for determining mood in complement clauses. Both commissives and directives constitute world-to-word fits; yet the former class of verbs governs the indicative and the latter the subjunctive. What I call "subject responsibility" corresponds to situations in which *the subject is in charge of direction of fit*, whether word-to-world (with assertives and declarations) or world-to-word (with commissives), and it is precisely in these situations that the indicative occurs in Spanish complement clauses. There is lack of subject responsibility whenever someone other than the subject is responsible for the direction of fit (with directives), when there is no direction of fit (with emotives), or when the subject explicitly rejects a fit (with negated assertives or commissives). Of course, under these conditions the subjunctive occurs. But, then, for negated assertives the indicative can still surface, if there is a presupposition that some one else holds the contained propositional content as true.

References

Comrie, Bernard. 1985. Reflections on Subject and Object Control. *Journal of Semantics* 4:47-65.

Kiparsky, Paul, and Carol Kiparsky. 1970. Fact. In *Progress in Linguistics*, ed. by M. Bierwisch and K.E. Heidolph, 143-173. The Hague: Mouton.

Searle, John. 1979. A Taxonomy of Illocutionary Acts. In *Expression and Meaning: Studies in the Theory of Speech Acts*, ed. by John R. Searle, 1-29. Cambridge: Cambridge University Press.

Terrell, Tracy. 1976. Assertion and Presupposition in Spanish Complements. In *Current Studies in Romance Linguistics*, ed. by M. Luján and F. Hensey, 221-245. Washington, D.C.: Georgetown University Press.

Terrell, Tracy, and Joan Hooper. 1974. A Semantically Based Analysis of Mood in Spanish. *Hispania* 57:484-494.

Presupposition Inheritance and Mood in Spanish

Errapel Mejías-Bikandi
University of Nebraska—Lincoln

In this paper I examine, within the framework of Mental Spaces, cases in which either the indicative or the subjunctive mood can be used in Spanish. I claim that presuppositions associated with some expression in a sentence in which the indicative mood is used are necessarily assumed by the hearer to be presuppositions held by the speaker. On the other hand, use of the subjunctive mood does not necessarily make the hearer assume that presuppositions associated with some expression in the sentence are presuppositions held by the speaker. I also examine the interaction of mood with Grice's conversational maxims. I claim that the use of the indicative mood creates some expectation of relevance on the part of the hearer. When this expectation is not fulfilled, the use of the indicative mood is considered unnatural.

 INTRODUCTION

In this paper I investigate the interaction of mood and presupposition in Spanish within the framework of Mental Spaces (Fauconnier 1985). In particular, I will examine the phenomenon of inheritance, that is, those cases in which a presupposition associated with an expression in a particular space is also a presupposition in the parent space (the notions *space* and *parent space* are introduced in the next section). I consider sentences in Spanish in which either the indicative or the subjunctive mood can be used. The claim is that use of the indicative mood makes the hearer assume that a presupposition associated with an expression is a presupposition held by the speaker (or, in Mental Spaces terminology, a presupposition associated with an expression in a space M is inherited in M's parent space M'). On the other hand, use of the subjunctive mood does not necessarily make the hearer assume that a presupposition associated with an expression is a presupposition held by the speaker (or, again in technical terms, a presupposition associated with an expression in M may not be inherited in M's parent space M').[1]

The paper is organized as follows: In the first section I briefly introduce the framework and the phenomenon under discussion. In the second section I consider several sentences in Spanish to illustrate the central claim of this paper. In the third section I discuss some instances in which the use of the indicative generally is considered awkward. I claim that this awkwardness can be explained provided that we assume that the participants in the conversation follow Grice's cooperative principle and maxims of conversation (Grice 1975). In particular, I claim that the lack of naturalness of such sentences is due to the lack of relevant presuppositions to be inherited in the parent space.[2] Finally, I relate the phenomenon under discussion to some previous analyses of the use of the indicative or the subjunctive in Spanish.

 ## MENTAL SPACES AND PRESUPPOSITION INHERITANCE

Some linguistic expressions build *mental spaces*, where elements can be introduced or pointed to, and where relations can be defined among these elements. Linguistic expressions that establish mental spaces are *space builders* (SB).

As an example, consider (1):

(1) 'Peter believes that Mary saw John.'

The expression 'Peter believes' is a SB, which sets up a space M, the space corresponding to Peter's beliefs. The expression 'Mary saw John' establishes a relationship between Mary and John in M. A SB_M always establishes a space M relative to or included in a *parent space* M'. In the case of (1), the space M is included in the parent space R, which is the space of the speaker's reality. Notice that the relationship established between Mary and John in M, the space of Peter's beliefs, does not necessarily hold in R, the space of the speaker's reality; that is, it might be the case in (1) that Peter believes that Mary saw John but that the speaker does not believe so.[3]

The expression 'maybe' is another SB. It creates a possibility space M, where certain relations hold that might not hold in the parent space R, the space of the speaker's reality. Consider, for instance, Example 2 (taken from Fauconnier 1985):

(2) 'Maybe Max's son is giving him trouble.'

The expression 'maybe' creates the possibility space M, and a relation is established in that space between Max's son and Max, a relation that does not necessarily hold in the space of the speaker's reality, the parent space R. That is, the speaker who utters (2) may not believe that it is in fact the case that Max's son is giving Max trouble. Rather, the speaker is just speculating about that possibility.

Fauconnier (1985:88ff.) discusses the phenomenon of *presupposition inheritance*. This term refers to cases in which presuppositions introduced by expressions in a space M are also presuppositions in the parent space R. Fauconnier considers the following examples (the sentence used by Fauconnier is (2), repeated below). The speaker A and the hearer B see Max in the street.[4] Max looks glum. A knows Max and B assumes that A knows whether Max has a son. A says:

(2) 'Maybe Max's son is giving him trouble.'

As we saw above, the expression 'maybe' creates a possibility space M. Again, the parent space is R, the space of the speaker's reality. The presupposition P_2, "Max has a son," is associated with the expression 'Max's son.'[5] Then P_2 is a presupposition in the possibility space M. However, since B assumes that A knows whether Max has a son or not, P_2 is inherited in the parent space R. Consequently, the presupposition P_2, associated with the expression 'Max's son' in (2), is also a presupposition in R; that is, B assumes that A presupposes that Max has a son in the real world (as perceived by A) and not just in the possibility space created by the expression 'maybe.'[6]

Consider on the other hand the following context in which A and B see a man on the street looking glum. A says:

(3)   'Maybe that guy's son is giving him trouble.'

B does not assume that A knows anything about this man. The presupposition associated with the expression 'that guy's son' is P_3, "That guy has a son." P_3 is a presupposition in M, the possibility space built by 'maybe.' In this case, since B assumes that A does not know anything about 'that guy,' P_3 is not inherited in R. B does not assume that A presupposes P_3 (in R); in other words, B does not assume that the speaker A presupposes that 'that guy' has a son in the real world.[7]

In this section I introduced the framework of Mental Spaces and the phenomenon of presupposition inheritance. In the next section I consider this phenomenon in its interaction with mood in Spanish.

 ## PRESUPPOSITION INHERITANCE AND MOOD

In Spanish, the expression *tal vez* 'maybe' also establishes a possibility space M. When this expression is used, the verb of the clause can appear either in the indicative or in the subjunctive mood, as Example 4 illustrates.[8]

(4)   *Tal vez Pedro tiene/tenga un hijo.*
       'Maybe Peter has (IND/SUBJ) a son.'

Consider, now, the following scenario. The speaker A and the hearer B see a person, C, in the street. C looks glum, and A utters:

(5)   *Tal vez su hijo está en la cárcel.*
       'Maybe his son is (IND) in jail.'

In (5) the IND mood is used. The expression *su hijo* 'his son' carries the presupposition P_5, "He has a son." P_5 is a presupposition in the possibility space M. However, upon hearing (5), B assumes that A knows C has a son (in a situation in which B does not know prior to the utterance whether A knows C or not). Consequently, P_5 is inherited in the parent space R, the space of the speaker's (A's) reality; B assumes that A presupposes C has a son in the real world. But consider another possible scenario. A is speculating about what it might be that makes C look so glum. A says:

(6)   *Tal vez su hijo esté en la cárcel.*
       'Maybe his son is (SUBJ) in jail.'

Upon hearing (6), B does not necessarily assume that A knows whether C has a son or not (in a situation, again, in which B does not know whether A knows C or not). The presupposition P_5 is a presupposition in M. But P_5 is not necessarily inherited in R in this case. In other words, upon hearing (6), B does not necessarily assume that A presupposes that C has a son in the real world (although B could assume this, if B knew independently of this situation that A knows C).

Examples 5 and 6 show that when the IND is used, a presupposition in the possibility space M is also a presupposition in the parent space R, the space of the speaker's reality, whereas when the SUBJ is used, a presupposition in M is not necessarily a presupposition in R. In other words, the hearer B, upon hearing (5) (=IND), assumes that the speaker A knows whether the person C has a son or not. Consequently, P_5 is inherited in R, and B assumes that A presupposes that C has a son in the real world. The same is not necessarily the case when (6) (=SUBJ) is uttered; that is, it is not necessarily the case that, upon hearing (6), the hearer B assumes that the speaker A presupposes that C has a son in the real world.

I will now consider some cases in which a different SB is involved. Consider the following scenario. In a press conference, the speaker A denies the rumor that George Bush has given up smoking. A says:

(7)   *No es cierto que el presidente ha dejado de fumar.*
       'It is not true that the President has (IND) given up smoking.'

The negative *no* establishes a counterfactual space M, where the sentence 'The President has given up smoking' is satisfied. Again, the parent space is R, corresponding to the speaker's reality. The presupposition P_7, "The President used to smoke," is associated with the expression 'The President has given up smoking' in M. In hearing (7), however, the hearer B assumes that P_7 is also a presupposition in R. In other words, B assumes that the speaker A presupposes that the President used to smoke in the real world.

On the other hand, consider Example 8:

(8)   *No es cierto que el Presidente haya dejado de fumar.*
       'It is not true that the President has (SUBJ) given up smoking.'

In this case, P_7 is also a presupposition in the counterfactual space M, but the hearer B may not assume that the speaker A presupposes that George Bush used to smoke. P_7 is not necessarily inherited in R. Thus, A might expand (8) naturally as in (9):[9]

(9)   *No es cierto que el Presidente haya dejado de fumar; el Presidente no ha fumado nunca.*
       'It is not true that the President has (SUBJ) stopped smoking; the President has never smoked.'

Consider now a presupposition associated with the word 'even' in the following scenario. An epidemic in the area is making people sick. Mary is a very healthy person who is unlikely to get sick. But the speaker A is beginning to think that even Mary might be sick. A utters:

(10)   *Tal vez incluso María está enferma.*
       'Maybe even Mary is (IND) sick.'

A presupposition associated with 'Even Mary is sick' in this particular reading is P_{10}, "Somebody else is also sick." As before, P_{10} is a presupposition in the possibility space M. In this case, the hearer B assumes A presupposes that somebody else is sick in the real world. The presupposition P_{10} in M is also a presupposition in R.

Consider, on the other hand, another situation. The speaker A is speculating about people in the area who look unusually pale. A thinks that maybe everybody is sick, even Mary, the healthiest person in the area. A utters:

(11)   *Tal vez incluso María esté enferma.*
       'Maybe even Mary is (SUBJ) sick.'

Hearing (11), B may not assume that P_{10} is a presupposition in R. In other words, B does not necessarily assume A presupposes that somebody else is already sick.[10]

In all the cases presented so far, the use of the IND allows the hearer B to infer that the speaker A presupposed some presupposition P in the space of the speaker's reality R. On the other hand, the use of the SUBJ leaves open for B the possibility that P is presupposed in R. In the next section, I consider some expressions that apparently render the use of the IND awkward. Upon closer examination, it is apparent that such expressions in isolation are not likely to be associated with relevant presuppositions to be inherited in R. I claim that this lack of relevant presuppositions inherited in R accounts for the anomaly of the IND in those particular sentences.

 ## SOME PROBLEMATIC DATA

Example 12 is a sentence in which the use of the IND is generally considered unnatural.

(12) *Tal vez ni siquiera María esté/??está enferma.*
'Maybe not even Mary is (SUBJ/??IND) sick'

The presupposition P_{12}, "Somebody else is not sick," is associated with the expression 'Not even Mary is sick.' P_{12} is a presupposition in the possibility space M created by the expression *tal vez*. In this section, I account for the unnaturalness of a sentence such as (12) when the verb appears in the indicative mood. In order to do so, I first explain why a speaker A would use the IND rather than the SUBJ in a sentence, when A has a choice.

1. Presupposition Inheritance and Grice's Conversational Maxims

It was claimed above that a hearer B, upon hearing a sentence with the IND (in a context where the SUBJ is also possible), infers that a speaker A presupposes in the space of A's reality R some presupposition P associated with that sentence (or with an expression of that sentence). Thus, upon hearing a sentence such as (5), the hearer B infers that the speaker A presupposes that C has a son. Let's assume that both A and B observe Grice's cooperative principle and maxims of conversation. Now, again consider sentence (5). If the speaker A uses the IND in (5), A must intend the hearer B to infer that A knows that the person in the street, C, has a son. Similarly, the hearer B, upon hearing (5) (=IND), must know that the speaker A intends B to infer that A knows that C has a son. In other words, if A uses the IND, A must intend the hearer B to infer that A presupposes some presupposition P in R, and B must know that A intends so.

In order to see why this must be the case, consider Grice's Maxim of Quantity, which can be paraphrased as follows: make your contribution as informative as necessary, and do not make your contribution any more informative than is required.

We can imagine a context in which a speaker A has a choice between the IND and the SUBJ. A knows that the use of the IND conveys some information that the use of the SUBJ does not; namely, some presupposition in some space M is inherited in the parent space R. In this situation, and if A observes the Maxim of Quantity, A would use the IND only if (s)he wanted that information to be conveyed (to be as informative as necessary). If A did not want that information to be conveyed, (s)he would use the SUBJ; that is, (s)he would avoid being more informative than required or conveying false information.

To illustrate this, consider again Examples 5 and 6. The speaker A wants to produce an utterance that expresses the proposition that probably his son is in jail, where 'his' refers to a person in the street, C. A can use either the IND or the SUBJ. If, for whatever reason, A wants to convey to the hearer B the information that A knows that C has a son, A will use the IND in order to be as informative as necessary (since the SUBJ does not convey that information). On the other hand, if for whatever reason the speaker A does not want to convey that information (that A knows that C has a son) to the hearer B, A will use the SUBJ, not the IND. By using the SUBJ in this case, A avoids being more informative than required or conveying false information (it might be the case that A does not know whether C has a son or not).

We can further assume that, again in a sentence such as (5), if the speaker A intends the hearer B to infer that A knows that C has a son, A does so because A considers such information relevant for B. Similarly, upon hearing (5), the hearer B infers that the speaker A intends to convey the information that A knows that C has a son, and B must assume that A does so because A regards such information as relevant for B. In technical terms, if A intends B to infer that P is a presupposition in R, A does so because A considers such inference relevant for B. This follows from Grice's Maxim of Relevance: Be relevant.

In summary, assuming that both speaker and hearer follow Grice's maxims of conversation and cooperative principle, it must be the case that a speaker will use the indicative in a sentence (in a context where a choice exists between the indicative and subjunctive) to convey some information that the speaker considers relevant to the hearer. Specifically, the information that certain presuppositions are held by the speaker. Similarly, upon hearing a sentence in the indicative mood, the hearer assumes that the speaker is trying to convey some information that the speaker considers relevant for the hearer.

2. Accounting for Problematic Data

Now we can try to explain the unnaturalness of a sentence such as (12) in its IND form. Consider P_{12}, "Somebody else is not sick." In a normal, everyday situation (what I will call a default situation) the information that somebody presupposes P_{12} cannot be considered to be relevant. People are normally assumed not to be sick; consequently, P_{12} does not contribute anything new to the set of assumptions that represents the knowledge a person has about the world. In other words, if A is following the Maxim of Relevance, it would be unlikely in a default situation that A would intend B to infer that A presupposes P_{12}. After all, P_{12} would not provide B with any relevant information. From the perspective of the hearer B, upon hearing (12) with the IND, B assumes that A intends to convey some information by using the IND. In this case, the information is that A presupposes P_{12} in R. But since P_{12} seems obvious, B is puzzled. This would account for the unnaturalness of a sentence such as (12) in the IND mood. Informally, the use of the IND creates some expectation of relevance on the part of the hearer, expectation that is not fulfilled in (12). A context is needed where the fact that A presupposes P_{12} is relevant.

Now, consider the following situation. The speaker A and the hearer B are in a hospital, where generally everybody feels bad. María is the most unhealthy patient in the hospital, the most likely to feel bad. Today, however, to their surprise, A and B find that everybody is feeling quite well. A is really surprised and says:

(13)   *Tal vez ni siquiera María se siente mal hoy.*
       'Maybe not even Mary feels (IND) bad today.'

In Example 13 the IND can be naturally used. P_{13}, "Somebody does not feel bad," is a presupposition in *M*. Upon hearing (13), B assumes that P_{13} is a presupposition in *R*. In the scenario above, the information carried by P_{13} is relevant, since the expected state of affairs in that particular setting is one in which people feel bad. Consequently, the information that somebody does not feel bad adds something new to the background of assumptions held by B. Then, it is more likely that A would intend B to assume that A presupposes P_{13}.

Consider likewise the following example:

(14)   *Tal vez María está/esté todavía enferma.*
       'Maybe Mary is (IND/SUBJ) still sick.'

The presupposition P_{14}, "Mary has been sick," is associated with the expression 'Mary is still sick.' When the IND is used, P_{14} is necessarily a presupposition in *R*, the space of the speaker's reality. In this case, the hearer B assumes that the speaker A presupposes P_{14} in *R*. When the SUBJ is used, P_{14} is not necessarily a presupposition in *R*. In this case, (14) could be uttered in the following context: A is speculating that Mary might have been sick these last days and that, in fact, she might still be sick.

Consider, now, Example 15:

(15)   *Tal vez María ya esté/??está enferma.*
       'Maybe Mary is (SUBJ/??IND) already sick.'

As in the case of (13), this isolated sentence is awkward if the IND is used. The presupposition associated with 'Mary is already sick' is P_{15}, "Mary was not sick." As before, the information carried by P_{15} is information expected in an everyday, default situation.[11] People normally are assumed not to be sick. Consequently, P_{15} will normally be considered not to be relevant in a normal, default context; it does not contribute anything new or unexpected to the assumptions held by B. Consequently, A probably will not intend to make sure that B assumes that P_{15} is a presupposition in *R*, if A follows Grice's conversational maxims. Compare (15) with (16):

(16)   *Tal vez María ya está recuperada.*
       'Maybe Mary is (IND) already recovered.'

Here the presupposition is P_{16}, "Mary was sick," which is associated with the expression 'Mary is already recovered.' P_{16} carries information that is more likely to be considered relevant in an everyday situation. Consequently, it would be more natural for the speaker A to use the IND and to intend the hearer B to assume that A presupposes P_{16} in R.

To summarize, I have examined the phenomenon of presupposition inheritance. I have claimed that, when the IND is used, a presupposition P in a space M is inherited in M's parent space R. When the SUBJ is used, P may not be inherited in R. If we assume that the speaker A follows Grice's maxims of conversation, A will use the IND to cause the hearer B to assume that A presupposes P in R; presumably, A will do so whenever A assumes that P is relevant for B. In the next section I discuss other analyses that have used the notions of presupposition or relevance to explain the use of the IND or the SUBJ in Spanish.

 ## PREVIOUS ANALYSES

The use of the indicative has been associated in several previous studies with the presuppositions of the speaker. Thus, Rivero (1971), Terrell (1976), and Bergen (1978) claim that the use of the IND in a sentence such as (17) below indicates that the speaker presupposes that the complement is true or considers the complement as an established, objective fact.

(17) *Pedro no cree que el Presidente está enfermo.*
       'Peter does not believe that the president is (IND) sick.'

Notice that in a sentence such as (7) (repeated below), it cannot be the case that the speaker presupposes that the complement is true.

(7) *No es cierto que el presidente ha dejado de fumar.*
     'It is not true that the President has (IND) given up smoking.'

In (7) the speaker would be denying what (s)he ought to be presupposing.[12] The claim in this paper is slightly different. When the IND is used, it is not that the speaker A presupposes the truth of the complement, but rather that A presupposes, in the space of A's reality R, the presuppositions associated with expressions in the complement clause. Thus, upon hearing (17), the hearer B would assume that A presupposes that there is a president, but not that A necessarily believes that the President is indeed sick.

Lunn (1989) relates the use of the IND to the notion of relevance. She claims that when a speaker A assumes that some information is relevant for a hearer B, A will tend to use the IND. Lunn's analysis is related to that presented here in an obvious way, although some differences still exist. To illustrate these, consider Examples 5 and 6 again:

(5) Tal vez su hijo está en la cárcel.
     'Maybe his son is (IND) in jail.'

(6) Tal vez su hijo esté en la cárcel.
     'Maybe his son is (SUBJ) in jail.'

Lunn would claim that when A utters (5) (=IND), A regards the information conveyed as relevant for B, whereas this presumption of relevance on the part of A does not exist when A utters (6) (=SUBJ). In the analysis presented here, A utters (5) (=IND) when A intends B to assume that A presupposes that P_5, "He has a son," holds in the real world as perceived by A. Presumably, A would do so in a situation in which A assumes that P_5 conveys some information that is relevant to or unexpected by B. On the other hand, A utters (6) (=SUBJ) when A does not intend B to assume that A presupposes P_5 in R. A would do so for at least two reasons: A does not in fact presuppose P_5 in R, or A does not consider that the information conveyed by P_5 is relevant for B.[13]

 ## CONCLUSION

In this paper I present several cases in Spanish in which either the IND or the SUBJ mood can be used. I claim that when the IND is used, some presupposition P in a space M is necessarily inherited in M's parent space R. When the SUBJ is used, P may not be inherited in R (depending on the knowledge that the hearer B has prior to the utterance of the sentence). I have assumed that both the speaker A and the hearer B follow Grice's maxims of conversation. In that case, when A uses the IND mood, A intends B to assume that A presupposes P in R. This must be so by the Maxim of Quantity. Furthermore, A must intend so only if A believes that P is relevant for B. Again, this follows from the Maxim of Relevance. In cases where P is unlikely to be regarded as relevant to an everyday, default situation (Examples 12 and 15) and, thus, where the Maxim of Relevance seems to be violated, the IND is generally considered awkward.

Notes

1. Thanks are due to Kathy Carey, Aintzane Doiz-Bienzobas, Gilles Fauconnier, Ricardo Maldonado, and Maura Velázquez-Castillo. The usual disclaimers apply.
2. I will use the word *relevant* in an intuitive, pretheoretical sense. In this sense, *relevant* could be roughly equated with *informative*. Sperber and Wilson's technical notion of relevance (1986) could equally have been used in this discussion.
3. I will consistently use R to refer to the space of the speaker's reality, which is the parent space of another space M.
4. I will consistently use A to refer to the speaker and B to refer to the hearer.
5. I use single quotes to mark expressions of English that are representations of utterances and double quotes to mark presuppositions that are associated with these utterances. I refer to presuppositions by using the letter P with a subscript. The subscript indicates the example that represents the utterance with which the presupposition is associated.
6. Fauconnier (1985) gives a set of rules, definitions and strategic principles that account for the results described. Namely, if B assumes that A knows whether Max has a son or not, then P_2 will be regarded by B as a presupposition in R. This is so by the optimization strategic principle, which requires B to structure M and R as closely as possible with respect to presuppositions and background assumptions, as long as a contradiction does not arise.
7. The expression 'the real world' should always be understood as 'the real world as perceived by the speaker A.'
8. IND=indicative; SUBJ=subjunctive

9. Example 7 can also be expanded in a similar way. In that case, P_7 will not be inherited in R, in order to avoid a contradiction (which follows from Faucconnier's strategic principles). However, Example 7, in isolation, strongly implicates that A presupposes P_7 in R.

10. I am considering an existential presupposition associated with the expression 'even.' There is also a scalar presupposition associated with 'even' that is always inherited.

11. As in the case of (12), a context could be constructed in which (15) would be natural with the IND. For example, A and B have poisoned Mary's dinner. They are waiting for her to be sick. Then, A can utter (15) with the verb in the IND. Outside of a definite context, though, the IND is generally rejected in favor of the SUBJ.

12. Contrast (7) with (i)*'I don't realize that he has gone away' (Kiparsky and Kiparsky 1970). The verb 'realize' is a factive verb. As such, the proposition expressed by its complement is presupposed to be true by the speaker. The anomaly of (i) is due to the fact that the speaker is negating what (s)he presupposes.

13. Lunn's account and the account presented in this paper are not incompatible, and it is not my intention at this point to evaluate one at the expense of the other. However, it should be noted that the claims made by both accounts are different.

References

Bergen, John J. 1978. One Rule for the Spanish Subjunctive. *Hispania* 61: 218-233.

Fauconnier, Gilles. 1985. *Mental Spaces*. Cambridge, Mass.: MIT Press.

Grice, H. P. 1975. Logic and Conversation. In *Syntax and Semantics. Vol. 3, Speech Acts*, ed. P. Cole and J. L. Morgan. New York: Academic Press.

Kiparsky, Paul, and Carol Kiparsky. 1971. Fact. In *Semantics: An Interdisciplinary Reader*. Cambridge: Cambridge University Press. Reprinted from *Progress in Linguistics*, ed. M. Bierwisch and K. Heidolph. The Hague: Mouton (1970).

Lunn, Patricia V. 1989. Spanish Mood and the Prototype of Assertability. *Linguistics* 27: 687-702.

Rivero, María Luisa. 1971. Mood and Presupposition in Spanish. *Foundations of Language* 7: 197-229.

Sperber, Dan, and Deirdre Wilson. 1986. *Relevance*. Cambridge, Mass.: Harvard University Press.

Terrell, Tracy. 1976. Assertion and Presupposition in Spanish Complements. In *Current Studies in Romance Linguistics*, ed. M. Luján and F. Hensey, 221-245. Washington, D.C.: Georgetown University Press.

The NP-Based, Class/Member Analysis of Mood Choice in Spanish Relative Clauses

Jorge M. Guitart
State University of New York at Buffalo

Mood choice in Spanish relative clauses can be more accurately described by basing the analysis not on the so-called antecedent (as traditional approaches do) but on the entire noun phrase (NP) composed of antecedent plus clause, and by regarding NPR—or the entity to which such an NP refers—as a member or set of members of the class defined by the clause. The relevant features are not the traditional [±Existent], [±Unknown], or [±Experienced] but rather [±Indiv(iduated)], [±Fut(ure)], and [±Rec(urrent)]. The indicative is used when NPR is [+Indiv] (one or more specific individuals labeled 'NPR') and the subjunctive when it is [−Indiv] (one or more unspecific members of the class), except if NPR is involved in a present or past situation in which it appears or appeared recurrently ([-Fut, +Rec]), which calls for the indicative. However [±Rec] plays no part in inclusion predicates (IPs), which are sentences about inclusion or noninclusion of NPR in a location or container L (the universe or smaller). In IPs the indicative is used when asserting that L contains/does not contain one or more [+Indiv] NPRs and when verifying if L contains such members. The subjunctive is used when asserting that L contains no members of NPR (or hardly any members) and when inquiring whether it contains any.

1 INTRODUCTION

I would like to present a new analysis of mood choice in Spanish relative clauses that departs considerably from certain traditional explanations. Traditional accounts have influenced greatly the presentation of this grammar point in Spanish textbooks in the United States and are inadequate, as I will show. I believe that there should be a better foundation for pedagogical explanations in this area of Spanish grammar, and I would like to provide such a foundation here.[1]

As is well known, the verb in a Spanish relative clause may be in either the indicative or the subjunctive mood. Differences in mood transmit differences in meaning, as in the minimal pair in (1):[2]

(1)   a.   *Habla con el que está a cargo.* [IND]
         'Talk to the [specific person] who is in charge.'
     b.   *Habla con el que esté a cargo.* [SUB]
         'Talk to whoever is in charge.'

Consider also the contrast in (2):

(2) a. *Hay una sola persona que puede ayudarme.* [IND]
'There is only one person who can help me.'

b. *No hay una sola persona que pueda ayudarme.* [SUB]
'There isn't a single person who can help me.'

A popular traditional analysis of mood in Spanish relative clause, widely echoed in pedagogical treatments, describes these contrasts in terms of the so-called antecedent. Proponents of this analysis would say that the subjunctive is used in (1b) because the antecedent is indefinite or unknown or has not been experienced—it is *non-experienced,* and in (2b) because the antecedent is non-existent (and therefore also non-experienced). Conversely, they would say that the indicative is used in (1a) because the antecedent is definite, known, and has been experienced beforehand, and in (2a) because the antecedent is existent (and therefore has been experienced).

In contrast with this popular traditional account, I would like to propose here a framework that rejects both the antecedent as the basis for the analysis and the dichotomies known-unknown, existent-nonexistent, and experienced/non-experienced as the determinants of mood choice in Spanish relative clauses. I propose instead to describe mood choice in relative clauses in terms of the entire noun phrase in which the clause is embedded and of which the antecedent is an integral part. Traditionally the antecedent has been defined as the element to which the relative pronoun refers: the antecedent is *of the pronoun,* not of the whole clause. In contrast, in the present proposal, the antecedent is seen as the nominal element that the clause modifies as an adjective: the antecedent and the clause together constitute a noun phrase (henceforth NP).

The present analysis is based on the notion that any NP that contains a relative clause refers to one or more members of a class. This class is precisely that defined by the clause; that is, the members share a property or quality described by the clause. To illustrate, *Los libros que Carlos compró ayer* 'The books that Carlos bought yesterday' is an NP in which *Los libros* is the antecedent and the clause *que Carlos compró ayer,* functioning as an adjective, conveys the property or quality that the books share, namely, that Carlos bought them yesterday. In this specific example I am talking about all the members of the class 'books that Carlos bought yesterday' but if I say *un libro que Carlos compró ayer* 'a book that Carlos bought yesterday', I am only talking about one member. Crucial for my analysis is to consider whether the entity[3] to which the NP refers is regarded by the speaker (or the person(s) whose viewpoint the speaker reflects) as an individual or set of individuals, rather than merely as a non-individuated member or set of members of the class defined by the clause.

Also of crucial importance is to consider whether the relative clause is or is not part of an *inclusion predicate.* Inclusion predicates are sentences that are about whether or not an entity is included in a certain location or container, which may be the universe or smaller. This includes all existential sentences. The distinction between inclusion predicates and sentences that are not so is necessary because mood criteria are not identical in the two.

The present study is divided into six sections. Following this introductory section, section 2 critiques the traditional antecedent-based analysis and proposes NP as the unit of analysis. Section 3 uses the class/member analysis to show that individuation, futurity, and recurrence are key features in mood choice in certain sentences, but futurity and recurrence play no role when the clause is part of an inclusion predicate. Section 4 applies the class/member analysis to the description of mood choice in inclusion predicates. Section 5 summarizes the true criteria for mood choice in Spanish relative clauses, and section 6 summarizes the study.

2   THE INADEQUACY OF THE ANTECEDENT-BASED ANALYSIS

I would like to begin by showing the inadequacy of the traditional antecedent-based analysis (henceforth ABA), which formulates mood choice in Spanish relative clauses in terms of the antecedent. Consider first Gili y Gaya's description:

> En las oraciones de relativo se pone el verbo en indicativo cuando el antecedente es conocido; si es desconocido o dudoso, el verbo va en subjuntivo, p.ej.: *Haré lo que usted manda* [IND], significa que el mandato es conocido; *Haré lo que usted mande* [SUB], quiere decir que cumpliré la parte conocida y la desconocida de su mandato. (1961:136)
>
> [In relative clauses the verb is in the indicative when the antecedent is known; if it is unknown or doubtful, the verb is in the subjunctive. For example, *Haré lo que usted manda* [IND] 'I'll do what you have ordered' implies that the order is known; *Haré lo que usted mande* [SUB] 'I'll do whatever you order' implies that I will follow the known part of your order as well as the unknown part.]

Certain reference grammars used in the United States follow ABA. For instance, Solé and Solé state that the subjunctive is used when "the existence of the antecedent is negated, denied," and one example given is *No encontró nada que le gustara* [SUB] 'He did not find anything that he liked' (1977:193; all translations of their examples are theirs). According to Solé and Solé, the subjunctive is also used when "the antecedent is unknown to the speaker or doubtful" (agreeing in this with Gili y Gaya). And one of the examples they offer is *Muéstrame lo que hayas escrito* [SUB] 'Show me what you have (might have) written'. In contrast, for the same authors, if "the existence of an antecedent is affirmed" or if the antecedent is "known to the speaker or assumed to be a certainty," the indicative is used, as exemplified by *Encontró algo que le gustó* [IND], 'He found something that he likes [sic]' and *Muéstrame lo que has escrito* [IND] 'Show me what you have written'.

A recent work offered as a standard reference grammar (Butt and Benjamin 1988) also follows ABA. The subjunctive is said to be used in relative clauses "when the existence of the antecedent is denied," and one of the examples given is *No hay nadie que sepa tocar más de un violín a la vez* [SUB], 'There is no one who can play more than one violin at once'. (All translations of their examples are theirs.) For these authors, the subjunctive is also used "when the antecedent is not yet known or experienced," and two of their examples are *Prefiero un coche que tenga cuatro puertas* [SUB] 'I prefer a car with four doors (i.e., any car)' and *No leo novelas que tengan más de doscientas páginas* [SUB] 'I don't read novels which have more than two hundred pages.' (Butt and Benjamin 1988:240-241.) Though these authors do not state it explicitly, the examples they give in which the verb in the clause is in the indicative (e.g., *Prefiero ese coche que tiene cuatro puertas* [IND] 'I prefer that car with four doors'; *Tengo muchas novelas que tienen más de doscientas páginas* [IND] 'I have many novels with more than two hundred pages') imply that for them the indicative is used when the antecedent is known or has already been experienced. No examples are given of sentences in the indicative affirming or establishing existence.

The incorporation by Butt and Benjamin of *experienced/non-experienced* as a criterion for mood choice shows the influence on their treatment, and on many other current treatments of Spanish mood, of William Bull's ideas. To my knowledge, Bull was the first grammarian to explain mood choice using that criterion. According to Bull, "When the speaker has no experience or knowledge of an entity, that entity is described, in an adjectival clause, by a verb in the subjunctive mode" (1965:182). And he asks us to compare *Hay un hombre que puede hacerlo* [IND] 'There is a man who can do it' with *No hay hombre que pueda hacerlo* [SUB] 'There is no man who can do it'. Bull has substituted entity for antecedent, but still the formulation is in terms of the nominal element that the clause modifies. For Bull, in other words, if the entity is non-experienced, the verb in the clause that says something about that entity will be in the subjunctive. Bull's analysis, then, is a variant of the ABA analysis.

It is instructive to note what Bull meant by non-experience. He states:

> Non-experience may be accounted for in three ways: (1) the event is yet to take place or the entity is yet to be encountered, (2) the event cannot take place or the entity does not exist, and (3) the speaker has not experienced the event (though it may have taken place) or has not encountered the entity (though it may exist). (Bull 1965:183)[4]

I would now like to show that ABA as formulated is incorrect. Consider (3):

(3) *Todavía no existen computadoras que puedan traducir sin errores de una lengua a otra* [SUB], *pero sí hay algunas computadoras que se aproximan bastante a esa meta* [IND].

'No computers yet exist that can translate without error from one language to another but there are indeed some computers that come close to that goal.'

According to ABA, if I utter (3), the verb in the relative clause contained in the first independent sentence is in the subjunctive because for me the antecedent is non-existent; that is to say, I think that computers do not exist! This is absurd, of course. The context (provided by the second sentence) clearly indicates that for me computers do exist.

Then consider the case in which, according to ABA, the subjunctive is used because the antecedent is unknown, as in (4):

(4) *Yo conozco a mucha gente pero no conozco a nadie que hable turco.* [SUB] 'I know lots of people but I don't know anybody who speaks Turkish.'

Holding ABA strictly to its formulation, I would have to say that I use the subjunctive in the relative clause contained in (4) because I don't know anybody! Clearly this is not the case since I am declaring in the same context that I know many people. A similar argument can be constructed against the notion that the subjunctive is used because the antecedent is non-experienced. Notice for instance that in (3) the antecedent has indeed been experienced. I have encountered computers, since I am saying that there are some computers that come close to translating without error from one language to another.

Clearly, then, it cannot be simply the non-existence of the antecedent or the fact that the antecedent alone is not known or not experienced that causes the verb in the clause to be in the subjunctive. We need a unit other than the antecedent for the analysis of mood choice in Spanish relative clauses.

The Antecedent as Part of an NP: Introducing NPR

What then requires the clause to be in the indicative or the subjunctive? This is of course the question that I intend to answer in this study. But first let us consider what the unit of analysis should be in lieu of the antecedent.

It is easy to show that a Spanish sentence containing a relative clause does not predicate something exclusively about that clause's antecedent. Or, more precisely, it does not predicate something exclusively about the entity to which the antecedent refers. Rather, it predicates something about the entity represented by the NP composed of antecedent plus clause. Let $\underline{A}$ be the entity represented by the antecedent and $\underline{NPR}$ the entity to which an NP containing a relative clause refers. We can see that (3) above is not just about the non-existence of A (computers) but about the non-existence of NPR (computers that can translate without error from one language to another). Similarly (4) is not about my not knowing A (anybody) but about my not knowing NPR (anybody who speaks Turkish). I could also say that (4) is not about my not experiencing A but about my not experiencing NPR.

The Inadequacy of Existent/Non-Existent, Known/Unknown, and Experienced/Non-Experienced

Is it possible to reformulate the ABA analysis in terms of NPR, leaving the determinants of mood choice intact? In other words, would it be accurate to say that the subjunctive is used in the clause whenever NPR (rather than A) is non-existent, or unknown, or non-experienced? The answer is no, since the criteria existent/non-existent, known/unknown, and experienced/non-experienced are descriptively inadequate, as I will now demonstrate.

Consider first the sentences in (5):

(5)   a. *El bar en que nos conocimos ya no existe.* [IND]
           'The bar where we met no longer exists.'

       b. *La computadora que yo quiero no existe todavía.*[5] [IND]
           'The computer I want does not yet exist.'

c. *Hay muy pocos que entiendan esa teoría.* [SUB]
'There are very few who understand that theory.'

In (5a) and (5b) the entity NPR does not exist and yet I use the indicative, and in (5c) the entity NPR does exist and yet I use the subjunctive.[6] Obviously existent/non-existent is not an adequate criterion for mood choice.

Next consider (6):

(6)   *Todavía no conozco a la gente que se va/*se vaya a mudar al lado de Carlos.* [IND][*SUB]
'I still don't know the people who are moving next door to Carlos.'

In (6) the entity NPR is unknown and yet I use the indicative—the subjunctive would be ungrammatical. Clearly known/unknown is not an adequate criterion either.

Finally consider (7):

(7)   *Pero, amor, ¿cómo quieres que me case contigo si no sé lo que te gusta/*guste o te disgusta/*disguste?* [IND] [*SUB].
'But, darling, how do you want me to marry you if I don't know what you like or dislike?'

In (7) the entity NPR (what the listener likes or dislikes) is—to use Bull's own words—"yet to be encountered" by the speaker: it certainly has not been experienced by him or her. And yet the clause is in the indicative and it would be ungrammatical to use the subjunctive. Therefore experienced/non-experienced is also inadequate as a criterion for mood choice in Spanish.

What are then the true criteria? This is the question that I would now like to address.

3 THE CLASS/MEMBER ANALYSIS OF MOOD CHOICE

I believe that in order to formulate the true criteria for mood choice in Spanish relative clauses it is essential to regard NPR *as a member, or set of members, of a class*— precisely the class defined by the clause. At the same time, it is essential to consider whether or not the speaker (or the person(s) whose viewpoint the speaker reflects) regards NPR an an individual entity. NPR has either been *individuated* or it has not. When NPR is non-individuated, it is regarded simply as one, some, or all of the members of the class NPR, and exclusively as such rather than as individuals. On the other hand, an individuated NPR is regarded at the time of speaking as a separate individual or set of individuals labeled as NPR by the speaker. It is useful to illustrate this difference using English, where individuation or the lack thereof does not affect mood in relative clauses. Suppose NPR is *a woman who knows Vietnamese.* Consider then the contrast between (8) and (9):

(8)   I need to get in touch with a woman who knows Vietnamese; I don't remember her name but I know she works here and I need her to translate something for me.

(9)   I need to get in touch with a woman who knows Vietnamese. Any woman who knows Vietnamese will do. I need a female translator of Vietnamese.

In (8), NPR is an individual, whom the speaker is labeling 'a woman who knows Vietnamese.' However, in (9) the speaker is clearly not talking about any individual woman in particular, since any female member of the class 'who speak Vietnamese' will do. Using distinctive features, we can say that in (8) NPR is [+Indiv] (for individuated), whereas in (9) it is [−Indiv].

Consider now that when the antecedent begins with a definite article and NPR is singular, NPR is—within the universe of the speaker or person(s) whose viewpoint is represented—*the sole member* of the class defined by the clause. Still, NPR is either [+Indiv] or [−Indiv]. Suppose NPR is *the man that she married* and suppose that the man in question is named Arthur and his present wife is named Ann and they have never been married to anybody else. Consider now (10) and (11):

(10)   On that occasion, Ann, who was still single and had not met Arthur, said that the man that she married must know how to cook.

(11)   Ann told me that the man that she married turned out to be a great cook.

Notice that from (10) we can deduce that what Ann said originally was "The man that I marry must know how to cook." From her perspective that man was not an individual. The individuality of her husband lay in the future at that time. In contrast, in (11) NPR is an individual who in this instance is labeled 'the man that she married' by the speaker. In (10) NPR is [−Indiv]; in (11) it is [+Indiv].

Now, when NPR is plural and the antecedent begins with a definite article, NPR refers to every member of the class defined by the clause. Suppose NPR is *the employees who left early*. Consider (12) and (13).

(12)   No one had left and Pete said that the employees who left early would be fired.

(13)   Pete told me that the employees who left early were fired.

In (12) the speaker reports Pete saying "The employees who leave early will be fired." Therefore NPR is [−Indiv] in (12), since no one had yet become an employee who left early on that occasion. Individuation lay in the future at that time. In contrast, in (13) NPR is [+Indiv]: the people fired were the individuals labeled 'the employees who left early.'

It is important to point out that [+Indiv] and [−Indiv] are not notational variants of experienced and non-experienced, since NPR can be [+Indiv] *and* non-experienced. To individuate someone or something, it is not a requirement to have experienced NPR in any of the senses of 'experiencing' implied in Bull's formulation, for example, having encountered the entity already. In *I never learned who the employees who left early were, and I still don't know*, NPR is [+Indiv] and non-experienced. Here is another example: if NPR is *what you like*, then if I say *You want me to fix you what you like for dinner, but I don't know what you like*, NPR is both [+indiv] and non-experienced from my perspective since I don't know what you like but I know it is something specific: it is an individual entity (though in this case a specific set of items as opposed to a single item), which I am labeling 'what you like.' One more example: if NPR is *an experience that fortunately no astronaut has ever had*, then in *To run out of oxygen in outer space is an experience that fortunately no astronaut has ever had*, NPR is obviously non-experienced, and yet it is [+Indiv] because it is another label for the same individual event that 'To run out of oxygen in outer space' describes.

It is convenient to add that the antecedent of a clause that refers to a [+Indiv] NPR does not have to be modified by an article, definite or indefinite: *I have interviewed women who have been sexually harassed.* On the other hand, the same type of NP may refer to a [–Indiv] NPR, e.g., *For my research I need to interview women who have been sexually harassed, no matter who they are.*

Incidentally, these last two examples, as well as those given in (8–13), would seem to indicate that English never marks morphologically the difference between [+Indiv] and [–Indiv] NPRs, relying instead entirely on the context. However, English does mark non-individuation unambiguously by adding the morpheme -ever to the antecedent. Compare, for instance, *I'll do what you want* with *I'll do whatever you want*, and *The person who did this deserves to be punished* with *Whoever did this deserves to be punished.*

Individuation and Mood in Spanish

Moving now to Spanish, consider the pairs of sentences in (14) and (15), which translate examples already given in English in (8)–(11) above and are repeated here:

(14) a. *Necesito ponerme en contacto con una mujer que sabe vietnamita* [IND]. *No recuerdo su nombre pero sé que trabaja aquí y necesito que me traduzca algo.*
       'I need to get in touch with a woman who knows Vietnamese; I don't remember her name but I know she works here and I need her to translate something for me.' (NPR is [+Indiv].)

      b. *Necesito ponerme en contacto con una mujer que sepa vietnamita* [SUB]. *Cualquier mujer que sepa vietnamita me sirve. Necesito una traductora, mujer, de vietnamita.*
       'I need to get in touch with a woman who knows Vietnamese. Any woman who knows Vietnamese will do. I need a female translator of Vietnamese.' (NPR is [–Indiv].)

(15) a. *Ana me dijo que el hombre con quien ella se casó resultó ser un gran cocinero.* [+Indiv, IND]
       'Ann told me that the man that she married turned out to be a great cook.' (NPR is [+Indiv].)

      b. *En esa ocasión, Ana, que todavía era soltera y no había conocido a Arturo, dijo que el hombre con quien ella se casara tendría que saber cocinar* [SUB].
       'On that occasion Ann, who was still single and had not met Arthur, said that the man that she married must know how to cook.' (NPR is [–Indiv].)

The contrasts in mood in (14) and (15) suggest that the following rule, (R1), is an adequate characterization of mood choice in Spanish relative clauses:

(R1) Use the indicative when NPR is [+Indiv], but use the subjunctive when it is [−Indiv].

(R1) serves to describe accurately the use of the subjunctive in the Spanish equivalents of English clauses that contain -ever as a mark of lack of individuation. Consider the contrasts in (16) and (17):

(16) a. *Haré lo que quieres.* [IND]
'I'll do what you want.' [+Indiv]

b. *Haré lo que quieras.* [SUB]
'I'll do whatever you want. [−Indiv]

(17) a. *El que hizo esto merece ser castigado.* [IND]
'The [one] who did this deserves to be punished' [+Indiv]

b. *El que haya hecho esto merece ser castigado.* [SUB]
'Whoever did this deserves to be punished.' [−Indiv]

Unfortunately (R1) cannot account for mood choice in all Spanish relative clauses because, though it is true that reference to a [+Indiv] NPR always takes the indicative, reference to certain [−Indiv] NPRs take the indicative, too, instead of the subjunctive, as I will demonstrate shortly.

A Role for Aspect and Tense in Mood

I would now like to show that when NPR is [−Indiv], mood depends in certain cases on temporal and aspectual factors. Consider (18–20):

(18) *En los buenos colegios privados, a cualquiera que agarran copiando en un examen lo expulsan inmediatamente.* [IND]
'At the good private schools, anybody caught cheating on an exam is expelled immediately.'

(19) *A cualquiera que agarraban copiando en un examen lo expulsaban inmediatamente.* [IND]
'[Customarily] anybody caught cheating on an exam was expelled immediately.'

(20) *Seguirán expulsando a cualquiera que agarren copiando en un examen.* [SUB]
'They will continue to expel anybody they catch cheating on an exam.'

What these three sentences have in common is that the appearance of a member of the class described by the clause is recurrent. In this case a person caught cheating on an exam appeared, appears, or will appear periodically in the experience of those having to deal with it, but of course each time it is a different person. Reference is not to any person in particular. Therefore, NPR is [−Indiv] in all three cases. Let [± Rec] stand for whether or not the appearance of a [−Indiv] NPR is recurrent, and let [±Fut] represent whether or not the situation involving a [−Indiv] NPR lies in the future, so that [+Fut] is future and [−Fut] is either present or past. Using these two features it is possible to characterize partially the mood of clauses referring to non-individuated NPRs, as follows:

[+Rec, −Fut] takes IND, as in (18 and 19)

[+Rec, +Fut] takes SUB, as in (20)

Notice now that if the appearance of a [−Indiv] NPR is not recurrent, the subjunctive is used, whether the situation in which it is involved is future, as in (21), or non-future as in (22):

(21) *Mañana voy a entrevistar a la primera persona con quien me tropiece.* [SUB]

'Tomorrow I am going to interview the first person I bump into.'

(22) *Los que hayan terminado el examen pueden irse.* [SUB]

'Those who have finished the exam may leave.'

That is to say, using the same two features:

[−Rec, +Fut] takes SUB, as in (21);

[−Rec, −Fut] takes SUB, as in (22).

In short, when NPR is [−Indiv], the subjunctive is used, except when the appearance of NPR is recurrent and the situation in which it is involved is not future (present or past). But this exception overthrows (R1) as an accurate formulation of mood choice in Spanish relative clauses. A more exact formulation would be (R2):

(R2) Use the indicative when NPR is [+Indiv] and when it is [−Indiv, +Rec, −Fut]; otherwise use the subjunctive.

Unfortunately (R2) is not without exceptions itself. Consider (23):

(23) *Aquí normalmente los fines de semana no hay nadie que te pueda ayudar.* [SUB]

'Normally, there is no one here on weekends who can help you.'

In (23) NPR is certainly [−Indiv], since the description 'who can help you' is applicable to no one. Furthermore, the situation in which NPR is involved is non-future, and its appearance—or, in this case, its non-appearance—is recurrent, but the subjunctive is used.

4   MOOD IN SPANISH INCLUSION PREDICATES

The sentence in (23) is an example of an *inclusion predicate* (henceforth IP). I would like to show that the criteria for mood choice in Spanish relative clauses that are part of IPs are different from those that apply to non-IPs. IPs that contain relative clauses describe whether members of the class defined by the clause are located, contained, or (in general) included in a certain 'place' which I will call L. L can be the universe (or 'the world') or something smaller. All *existential sentences* (that is, those about the existence or non-existence of an entity) are IPs. However, not all IPs are existential. In existential IPs, L is the universe or the world, which is normally left out of the reference. For instance, if I say Todavía no existen/no hay computadoras que le ganen a Bobby Fischer en ajedrez, 'No computers yet exist/There are yet no computers that can beat Bobby Fischer at chess,' I do not have to insert *en el mundo* 'in the world' after *computadoras*.

In contrast, in *non-existential IPs* L is smaller than the world or universe, and it is frequently referred to by an adverb or adverbial phrase of place such as *aquí* 'here' or *en ese lugar,* 'in that place'. Notice that an L smaller than the world or universe does not have to be what we usually call a location or place, or what we normally think as a container, but can be instead anything in which NPR can be included: an "includer." Examples of includers are *en mi familia* 'in my family', *en esa película* 'in that movie', and *entre mis amigos* 'among my friends'.

With regard to mood choice, IPs share with non-IPs the criterion that reference to a [+Indiv] NPR takes the indicative. However, as (23) above suggests, the features [±Fut] and [±Rec] do not play any role in the determination of mood in IPs.

Furthermore, mood in IPs is best characterized in terms of what the speaker is doing with respect to the inclusion or non-inclusion in L of members of the class defined by the clause. The speaker may assert that L contains members of that class or assert the opposite: that it contains no members. The speaker may also assert that L contains hardly any members of that class. In addition the speaker may inquire whether L contains any members. Mood choice in relative clauses in Spanish IPs may be described in terms of these operations of the speaker, as follows:

> The indicative is used when it is asserted that L contains or does not contain the individual entity or entities labeled as NPR, and when it is asserted that L contains members of the class defined by the clause; the subjunctive is used when it is asserted that L contains no members of the class defined by the clause or hardly any members, and when an inquiry is made as to whether L contains members of such a class.

Examples are in (24)–(29), where in each case sentence (*a*) is an existential IP and sentence (*b*) a non-existential one:

(24) [L CONTAINS THE INDIVIDUAL(S) LABELED AS NPR: IND USED]
    a. *La Lola de quien hablo en mi novela existe realmente.*
       'The Lola I talk about in my novel actually exists.'
    b. *El impresor que quieres ya lo hay en esa tienda.*
       'The printer you want is now available at that store.'

(25) [L DOES NOT CONTAIN THE INDIVIDUAL(S) LABELED AS NPR: IND USED]
    a. *La computadora que yo quiero no existe.*
       'The computer I want does not exist.'
    b. *Ya no hay en la ciudad aquellas tiendecitas donde vendían alfarería.*
       'There are no longer in the city those little stores where they sold pottery.'

(26) [L CONTAINS MEMBERS OF THE CLASS DEFINED BY THE CLAUSE: IND USED][7]
    a. *Hay abogados que cobran barato.*
       'There are still lawyers who charge modest fees.'
    b. *En esa película hay escenas que te va a poner los pelos de punta.*
       [IND]
       'There are scenes in that movie that are going to set your hair on end.'

(27) [L CONTAINS NO MEMBERS OF THE CLASS: SUB USED][8]

    a. *No hay abogados que cobren barato.*
        'There are no lawyers who charge modest fees.'

    b. *Aquí no hay nadie que pueda autorizar eso.*
        'There is no one here who can authorize that.'

(28) [L CONTAINS HARDLY ANY MEMBERS OF THE CLASS: SUB USED]

    a. *Hay muy pocos que entiendan esa teoría.*
        'There are very few who understand that theory.'

    b. *Aquí no hay casi ninguno que quiera competir.*
        'There is almost no one here who wants to compete.'

(29) [DOES L CONTAIN ANY MEMBERS OF THE CLASS?: SUB USED]

    a. *¿Hay computadoras que puedan traducir sin errores?*
        'Are there computers that can translate without error?'

    b. *¿Hay alguien aquí que sepa dónde está Lilian?*
        'Is there anybody here who knows where Lillian is?'

It should be added that when a question constitutes an attempt to verify if indeed L contains members of the class defined by the clause, the indicative is used, as in (30):

(30) *Ah, ¿así que hay computadoras que pueden traducir sin errores?* [IND]
      'Oh, so there are computers that can translate without error?'

5 THE TRUE CRITERIA FOR MOOD CHOICE IN SPANISH RELATIVE CLAUSES

I would now like to summarize what I believe are the true criteria for mood choice in Spanish relative clauses. I believe that any formulation of mood choice in Spanish relative clauses must distinguish between IPs and non-IPs. (R2) is a rule that is accurate only for non-IPs. A better formulation is (R3), which incorporates the distinction between the two types of sentences:

    (R3) a. In IPs, use the indicative to assert that L contains or does not contain the individual(s) labeled NPR and that L contains members of the class defined by the clause, as well as to verify that L does contains members of such a class; use the subjunctive to assert that L contains no members of the class defined by the clause or hardly any members, and to inquire whether it contains any members of such a class;

          b. In Non-IPs, use the indicative when NPR is [+Indiv] and when it is [−Indiv, +Rec, −Fut]; otherwise use the subjunctive.

I believe that (R3) would be a better foundation for a pedagogy of mood in Spanish relative clauses aimed at English-speaking students than the traditional formulation that I described in section 2 of this paper.

6 SUMMARY

In this study I have shown that the criteria for mood choice in Spanish relative clauses are best formulated by always taking into consideration the entire noun phrase of which the relative clause is a part and by regarding the entity to which the clause refers (which I have called NPR) as one or more members of the class defined by the clause. I have shown that the traditional antecedent-based analysis is insufficient, since a sentence containing a relative clause is never exclusively about the entity referred to by the antecedent but is instead about the entity referred to by the NP composed of antecedent plus clause, namely, NPR. I also have shown that the traditional criteria existent/non-existent, known-unknown, and experienced/non-experienced are descriptively inadequate since, contrary to traditional formulations, certain entities that are not existent, or not known, or not experienced are referred to by a clause in the indicative, while certain existing entities are referred to by a clause in the subjunctive.

I have shown that the true criteria for mood choice in sentences that are not inclusion predicates are best formulated by using the features [±Individuated], [±Future], and [±Recurrent], and that there is a need to formulate separate criteria for inclusion predicates since [±Recurrent] plays no role in them.

Notes

1. I am very grateful to Ricardo Maldonado, Peggy Hashemipour, Margaret van Naerssen, and George DeMello for insightful comments on previous versions. I am also very grateful to my students Regina Morin, Susana de los Heros, and Charles Grove for pointing out inconsistencies in my analysis when I presented it in class. I have benefited greatly from discussions with Jorge J.E. Gracia.

2. Henceforth, [SUB] for subjunctive and [IND] for indicative will appear next to the Spanish sentences used in the examples to indicate the mood of the verb in the relative clause that concerns us, with [*IND] or [*SUB] indicating that using that mood would be ungrammatical.

3. By 'entity' I mean here anything that can be named. That is to say, events (e.g., *the concert*, *running out of gas*, etc.) are also entities, along with beings and things (whether abstract or concrete).

4. Incidentally, the examples that Bull offers of experienced vs. non-experienced events show mood contrasts in *noun clauses: Es evidente que han llegado* [IND] 'It is evident that they have arrived', vs. *Es imposible que hayan llegado* [SUB] 'It is impossible for them to have arrived'. Bull apparently did not consider it necessary to say that in the case of events he was no longer speaking of adjectival (i.e., relative) clauses. One serious defect of Bull's analysis is precisely his failure to differentiate between the different types of clauses (noun, relative, adverbial), since they actually follow different criteria for mood choice. For instance, applying the experienced/non-experienced criterion to noun clauses in commentative constructions would yield the wrong results. If I say *Me alegro de que estés aquí*, 'I am glad you are here', I of course have experienced your being here.

5. I owe this example to Regina Morin.

6. It should be understood that it is not *pocos* that triggers the subjunctive but rather the intention of "devaluing" the class NPR by saying that it contains hardly any members.

Compare *En mi clase hay unos pocos que entienden esa teoría y muchos que no la entienden* [IND] 'In my class there are a few who understand that theory and many who don't', where the intention is simply to say that L contains members of the class defined by the clause, though they are few.

7. Notice that in (26) NPR is [+Indiv] since it is equivalent to *Hay ciertos abogados que cobran barato* 'There are certain lawyers that charge modest fees.' The speaker who says this has certain individuals in mind who fit the description.

8. In (27) NPR is of course [-Indiv] since it cannot be matched with any individual. It is instructive to compare (25) and (27): (25) asserts that a certain entity having a certain property is no longer or not yet contained in L (in the latter case it is contained in another L—the speaker's imagination), while (27) asserts that there is no individual in L that has that property. With regard to (27) I would like to suggest that sentences that start *No conozco a nadie que...* 'I don't know anybody that...' or *No sé de nadie/nada que ...* 'I don't know of anybody/anything that...', which call for the subjunctive in the clause, can perhaps be considered cases of "L contains no members of the class defined by the clause," in which L is the private universe of the speaker.

References

Bull, William. 1965. *Spanish for Teachers: Applied Linguistics for Teachers of Spanish.* New York: Ronald Press.

Butt, John, and Carmen Benjamin. 1988. *A New Reference Grammar of Modern Spanish.* London: Edward Arnold.

Gili y Gaya, Samuel. 1961. *Curso superior de sintaxis española.* Barcelona: Vox.

Solé, Yolanda R., and Carlos A. Solé. 1977. *Modern Spanish Syntax: A Study in Contrast.* Lexington, Mass.: D.C. Heath and Company.

Middle-Subjunctive Links

Ricardo Maldonado
University of California, San Diego
Universidad Nacional Autónoma de México

This paper explores the relationship between the clitic *se* and indicative/subjunctive mood choice in Spanish. The Spanish clitic *se* has generally been treated as a marker of detransitivization. Unlike previous analyses, this paper shows that *se* also imposes an increase in transitivity. The participant's level of involvement is increased to exploit fully the properties of the direct object. Transitivity increase is shown to determine mood choice in the complement clause. The notion of *dominion* is proposed to account for the development of what I call *full exploitation middle* constructions which determine the choice of indicative mood in the complement clause.

 ## INTRODUCTION

It is well known in Spanish grammar that there is some type of interaction between indicative/subjunctive mood choice and use of the so-called reflexive pronoun *me/te/se*.[1] Since, in all the cases that I will address, *se* does not have a reflexive function,[2] I will use the term *middle* to refer to the value of this clitic. The details of the middle/mood interaction have not yet been addressed in the current literature. The phenomenon to be observed is whether the use of the middle *se* in the main clause determines the choice of indicative or subjunctive mood in the complement clause. In the examples, I will use the abbreviations (IND) and (SUBJ) to mark the mood of the complement clause. The problem to be analyzed can most obviously be shown in the following contrasting examples:

(1) *Me temo que la policía va a reprimir a los estudiantes.* (IND)
   'I am afraid that the police will repress the students.'

(2) *Temo que la policía vaya a reprimir a los estudiantes.* (SUBJ)
   'I fear that the police may repress the students.'

While the use of the middle marker *me* requires an indicative complement clause, as in (1), its absence allows the occurrence of a subjunctive complement, as in (2). Although the middle/indicative interdependence is clear, the possibility of having a middle/subjunctive combination with a meaning close to the one in (2), but rather different from (1), is also available under very specific circumstances:

(3) *Me temo que la policía vaya a reprimir a los estudiantes.* (SUBJ)
   'I fear that the police may repress the students.'

The analysis of the example in (3) depends crucially on the proper characterization of the first two contrasting examples.

It is more striking that the most common pattern in Spanish does not follow the pattern described above for *temer/temerse*. With a wide variety of verb types, the middle marker *se* determines exactly the opposite results in the complement clause. Instead of taking an indicative complement, as in (1), it favors the use of subjunctive mood:

> (4a)   *Me alegro de que vengas.* (SUBJ)
>   'I'm glad that you are coming.'
> (4b) ??/* *Me alegro de que vienes.* (IND)
>   'I'm glad that you are coming.'

Examples like (4b) depend strongly on context and are rather marginal.[3] The middle/subjunctive combination given in (4a) constitutes the standard use.

The problem to be explained can be summarized in the following manner. While in *alegrarse* and other verb types the use of the middle marker favors a subjunctive complement clause, there is a less common pattern for verbs of the *temer* type where *se* determines indicative mood choice in the complement clause. I propose that the middle marker *se* systematically increases the level of activity of the crucial participant—usually the subject—and that, depending on the meaning of the verb, there can be two very different representations of the experiencer: an *energized undergoer* and a *full exploitation active participant*. Full exploitation *se* corresponds to cases in which the subject is maximally active, as he fully exploits an object located in his dominion. The level of activity of an energized undergoer is much more limited. While active members determine indicative mood choice, less active ones favor subjunctive.

This paper is organized in the following manner. In section 1, I propose the notion of dominion as a crucial one for the proper characterization of active and passive experiencers. In section 2, the notion of dominion is proposed as the proper mechanism to differentiate indicative from subjunctive mood. In section 3, I analyze some notions of activation imposed by middle *se*. In the last section, I link these patterns with the use of indicative/subjunctive mood in Spanish.

1 DOMINION

The notion of *dominion*, as proposed by Langacker (1992), is a component of the *Reference Point Model* (*RPM*). Among other linguistic phenomena, the RPM is intended to capture a wide range of possessive relationships. Since most of the constructions in this paper involve some abstract kind of possession, I will make a few remarks about this issue.

It is well known that the linguistic category of possession does not reduce to a single familiar value, such as ownership. There is a collection of relationships that the thing possessed may hold with respect to the possessor: a part (*my hands*), a relative (*your mother*), an unowned possession (*the baby's crib*), something hosted (*the cat's fleas*), a situation (*his predicament*), a related action (*Maura's misunderstanding*), something that fulfills a particular function (*my bus, her schoolteacher*), and many other possible relationships. Among the wide variety of proposals to account for possession, Seiler (1983) proposes, based on cross-linguistic considerations, that "linguistic possession consists in the relationship between a substance and another substance" where one of them is animate, human, and ego, or close to the speaker. According to this definition the coexistence of two elements in the same domain is sufficient to establish a possessive relationship. While this characterization is abstract and general enough to handle all the data, it may be too general since it doesn't account for the fact that some asymmetries are observable in possessive relationships: the fact that the whole is generally construed as the possessor of a part; and the fundamental fact that, in the association of two objects, the owner—not the owned element—is generally identified as the possessor.

Langacker has proposed a similarly abstract characterization which accounts for such asymmetries. Instead of merely involving the coincidence of two substances in the same domain, it is proposed that possession is a relationship in which one entity is located in relation to another (the reference point). According to the Reference Point Model, certain entities can be more easily located if they are linked to others that are in nature more salient and perceivable. A salient object serves as a reference point to locate a non-salient target object that lies within its vicinity. Each reference point anchors a region, a dominion, in which both the reference point and the target may be located.

All the cases of abstract possession mentioned above are accommodated by the Reference Point Model. The reference point is the possessor and the target is the entity possessed. The asymmetries noted previously are seen as the consequence of construing a salient entity as the reference point for locating a less salient one. A whole is thus the possessor of its (body) parts because the whole is more prominent (e.g., *Brigitte's legs*, not **legs' Brigitte*). Owners are possessors because people are more likely to be recognized individually than are their inanimate possessions (*the boy's knife* not **the knife's boy*). Finally, the cat is the possessor of its fleas (*the cat's fleas*) not only because the cat is more prominent, but also because there is a high level of empathy established with respect to the cat's experience.

The Reference Point Model constitutes an abstract schema that captures the conceptualizer's processing of a wide variety of possessive relationships. This abstract model, however, is based on prototypical cases where possession is established in a concrete sense. The asymmetries of salience suggested above generally correspond to actual differences between the possessor and the possessed element in the objective event. It is actually the case that, in prototypical cases of possession, owning involves a participant establishing concrete control over a specific object located in his dominion. Consequently the possessor is conceptualized as actively interacting with a non-active element. By saying *mi casa* 'my house' or *mis ideas* 'my ideas', *casa* and *ideas* are objects at the possessor's disposal that can be manipulated for different purposes. Since these objects are in my dominion, I can choose to impose changes on them (trade them, destroy them, improve them, and so forth). In a similar manner the possessor is active in the sense that he experiences mental or emotional sensations with respect to objects located in his dominion. Not only can body parts (*mis manos* 'my hands'; *mis ojos* 'my eyes') be manipulated at the possessor's will, but the changes they may undergo also imply an experiential activity by the possessor (*Mis ojos están irritados y no puedo ver* 'My eyes are irritated and I can't see'; *Las pulgas del gato no lo dejan en paz* 'The cat's fleas don't leave it alone' [literally: leave it in peace]). The last example is crucial for the correct understanding of these asymmetries. The cat does not possess the fleas crawling on it. It is only the case that the presence of fleas in the cat's dominion makes the cat experience some sensations. The possession involved here is thus abstract, and the reference point is conceptualized as experientially active.

Indirect object constructions are commonly used to express some of these experiencer-based relationships (e.g., *Me duelen los ojos* 'My eyes hurt'). That the indirect object construction involves some abstract possession can be attested by the fact that the clitic *me* takes over the possessive marker's functions:

(5a) *Duelen   mis   ojos.   >   Me duelen   los   ojos.*
     hurt 3RD-PL   POSS 1ST-PL   eyes   IO-1ST hurt   3RD-PL the-PL   eyes
     'My eyes hurt.'

(5b) *Corté   mi   dedo. >   Me   corté   el dedo.*
     cut 3RD-SG   POSS-1ST-SG   finger   MDDL-1ST   cut-1ST   the finger
     'I cut my finger.'

In standard dialects of Spanish, the indirect object precludes the use of the possessive marker: **Me duelen mis ojos*. It is not the case that the indirect object construction is in itself possessive; rather, the type of activity of the experiencer participant in indirect object constructions implies an *abstract possessive* relationship: (a) the direct object is located with respect to its reference point; (b) it is located in the indirect object's dominion; and (c) the experiencer/recipient establishes contact with the direct object, receiving a concrete or abstract element and undergoing some mental, judgmental, or emotional experience (*tell, send, give*, etc.) as a result of establishing contact with an element located in its dominion. Consider the following examples:

(6) *Arturo le dio un regalo a Blanca.*
    'Arturo gave a gift to Blanca.'

(7) *Juan Carlos por fin le dijo la verdad a Dora.*
    'Juan Carlos finally told the truth to Dora.'

It is clear in these examples that possession of the gift changes from Arturo to Blanca: the gift is first in the sphere of control—the dominion—of the subject and then in that of the indirect object. In a more abstract manner, the truth is located in the dominion of Dora—although not removed from that of Juan Carlos—so that she now establishes mental contact with it. It is due to the fact that the direct object is located in the experiencer's dominion that he may interact with it. In *Le envié una carta a Jorge* 'I sent a letter to Jorge' the letter lands in an area where Jorge has some command and exerts dominion over objects located in his sphere of action/control. Jorge is presumably active not only ensuring the letter's goal (its destination) but also in reading and processing the information conveyed in it.

The Reference Point Model thus involves two levels of abstraction. From the conceptualizer's viewpoint the reference point is a salient entity which is accessed in order to identify an object located in his dominion. From the objective arrangement of the event, the reference point is prototypically an active participant—thus its high level of salience—exerting control over an object located in his sphere of control (his dominion). Both characterizations interact in the construction of abstract possessive relationships.

The connection between level of activity of a participant and dominion is an important one. An experiencer can only be active if an interacting element is within his or her dominion. In the absence of a delimiting dominion the level of activity of the experiencer is limited. Consider the following examples:

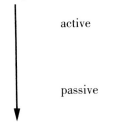

active

passive

(8a) *Le di un regalo al presidente.*
      'I gave a gift to the president.'

(8b) *Le abrí la puerta al presidente.*
      'I opened the door for the president.'

(8c) *Abrí la puerta para el presidente.*
      'I opened the door for the president.'

(8c) *El ruido molestó al presidente.*
      'The noise bothered the president.'

The level of activity of *presidente* is not the same in all the examples. In (8a) *presidente* is a prototypical indirect object, that actively holds dominion over the direct object. *Presidente* is the beneficiary of the subject's action in both (8b) and (8c); they differ, however, in level of activity. While in (8b) it is implied that the president was about to walk through the door, in (8c) such implication is not present. The notion of benefaction is stronger when the action directly enters the dominion of the experiencer who is therefore an active recipient in the development of the event. In (8c) only the subject's intentions are profiled by *para;* whether the president will receive the subject's action remains undecided. In the cases where *le* is used, the coexistence of the experiencer and the object in the same dominion allows the former to interact with the latter. Such coexistence is not evoked by *para.* The consequence of this is that the level of experiencer/object interaction is higher when *le* is used. A handful of examples can be given with the same type of contrast: *Les leí un libro a los niños* 'I read the children a book'/ *Leí un libro para los niños* 'I read a book for the children' where only in the first case can the children be characterized not only as beneficiaries but as active listeners. In the absence of *le* only the subject's activity is foregrounded, while the potential activity of the beneficiary remains in the background.

The final example (8d) is the extreme case where the experiencer is a passive element in object position, as he simply undergoes a change imposed by an external impulse. It is only when the object of benefaction is located in the dominion of the experiencer that the latter can be seen as actively involved with the object. The contrast between active and passive participants is represented in the following diagrams:

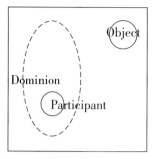

Figure 1. Non-active

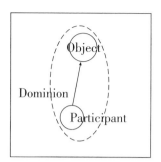

Figure 2. Active

In each figure, the dominion is a dotted oval; interaction is represented with a broken arrow. As represented in Figure 2, participants are active [as in (8a) and (8b)] because an object is located in their dominion. Figure 1 represents the case of passive participants, in which either the object is out the participant's sphere of control [as in (8c)] or no notion of dominion can be appealed to [in (8d)] and with subjects of passive constructions).

In section 3, I will show that the use of the middle marker *se* increases the level of activity of the experiencer participant; depending on the meaning of the verb, this phenomenon has direct consequences with respect to mood choice in Spanish. Before doing so, it is necessary to establish a basic characterization of mood in Spanish. In the following section, I show that the indicative/subjunctive contrast is naturally accommodated by the notion of dominion.

2 MOOD CHOICE

It has been shown from different perspectives that mood choice is dependent upon the level of assertiveness of the proposition as a whole. With respect to Spanish, Terrell and Hooper pointed out that "the choice of mood in Spanish is directly correlated with what the sentence as a whole expresses about the truth of the proposition included in the sentence"(1974:484). One may assert a proposition or presuppose the truth of a proposition in a number of ways: by describing or commenting on a mental or a subjective reaction about something, or simply by pointing out the existence of something as a fact. Common mood choice situations are direct commands: *di/diga la verdad* 'tell the truth' and; *sal/salga de aquí* 'get out of here', which are speech-act dependent (high level of formality triggers subjunctive) and biclausal sentences in which the level of assertion of the main clause with respect to the contents of the complement clause is at issue. I will leave aside the speech-act problem and concentrate on biclausal phenomena. Consider the following examples:

(9) *Es evidente que Susana sólo quiere trabajar.* (IND)
    'It is evident that Susana only wants to work.'

(10) *Los políticos no toman en consideración que a la gente no le interesa votar.* (IND)

'Politicians don't take into consideration that people are not interested in voting.'

Common to these examples is that the complement clause is given as an unquestionable existing fact. On the other hand, complement clauses marked for subjunctive give special prominence to events whose existence is questionable:

(11) *No creo que Susana quiera trabajar.* (SUBJ)
      'I don't think that Susana wants to work.'

(12) *Los políticos quieren que la gente tenga interés en votar.* (SUBJ)
      'Politicians want people to take interest in voting.'

Terrell and Hooper (1974) and Terrell (1976) account for these examples by claiming that in indicative clauses the truth of a proposition is asserted while it is not in clauses marked for the subjunctive. Although to some extent the analysis holds, it has well-known shortcomings: while mental acts pertaining to a presupposed proposition trigger the indicative, emotional reactions and comments take the subjunctive:

(13) *Me he dado cuenta de que miento, siempre he mentido.* (IND) (song by S. Rodríguez)
      'I have realized that I lie, I have always lied.'

(14) *Me molesta que mientas tan cínicamente.* (SUBJ)
      'It bothers me that you lie so cynically.'

In both cases the content of the complement clause is presupposed; however, they behave differently with respect to mood choice. Acknowledging this limitation, Terrell and Hooper claim that mental-act verbs seem more similar to assertions than do comment verbs. However, the assertion/non-assertion contrast offers no explanation as to why some verbs would seem more assertive than others and why the subjunctive would be the mood chosen for only a subclass of presupposed complements. I do not intend to list all the shortcomings of that theory, nor do I want to offer a total explanation of the Spanish mood system. I will limit myself to a basic suggestion that captures in general terms the indicative/subjunctive contrast.

Since the assertion/non-assertion contrast is an insufficient factor for mood choice in Spanish, a more abstract notion is necessary. I propose that the notion of dominion captures all uses of the indicative/subjunctive contrast in a natural manner. The notion implies an abstract possessive relationship between a participant and some entity (be it a thing or a proposition). The notion of dominion is a crucial part of *elaborated reality* (*ER*) (Achard 1993; Langacker 1992). ER is the set of circumstances accepted by a given conceptualizer as being real. Elaborated reality is describable by a set of propositions, which correspond to the meanings of finite clauses. Propositions therefore incorporate *grounding predications:* such elements as tense, modality, and negation, which locate circumstances with respect to the speech event (the locus of *immediate reality*). Hence, the circumstances comprising elaborated reality are not limited to events (and states) that have actually occurred but includes also the notion that certain conceivable events have not in fact occurred or that a future event has some potential to occur. A finite clause describes some facet of elaborated reality, and unless it is grounded, an event has no status (or "address") in this domain.

The notion of dominion refers to the conceptualizer's capacity to control actively and to manipulate a circumstance in order to assess its status with respect to elaborated reality. A clause must be grounded (finite) for this purpose, and finite verb inflection can be identified with indicative (as opposed to subjunctive) mood. The claim can thus be made that indicative mood signals a conceptualizer's dominion over the circumstance described in a clause, implying both grounding and active control. This proposal leads to a general characterization of the indicative/subjunctive contrast: *indicative clauses are located within the crucial participant's dominion, while subjunctive clauses are outside the participant's dominion.* The indicative/subjunctive contrast is schematically represented in the following diagrams:

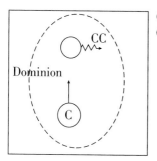

CC = complement clause
C = conceptualizer

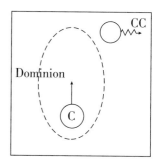

Figure 3. Indicative   *Figure 4.* Subjunctive

The circle C with the straight arrow indicates the crucial participant (generally the subject) and his capacity to interact with other elements. The circle CC with the squiggly arrow represents the complement clause. The contrast is rather evident: while in the indicative cases the complement clause is seen as part of the elements over which the participant has command (since they are located in his dominion), in the subjunctive cases the event in the complement clause is out of his dominion and we can only speculate about his capacity to interact with it.

The conceptualizer is the most immediate participant from whose viewpoint the content of the complement clause is evaluated. The global conceptualization of the sentence as a whole is obviously done by the speaker, yet the value of the complement clause is calculated from the viewpoint of a specific participant for whom the complement clause is relevant. In the case of impersonal *ser* constructions, the most immediate evaluator is the speaker, as can be attested in the following examples:

(15a) *Es evidente que la familia no quiere saber de ti.* (IND)
'It is evident that the family doesn't want to know about you.'

(15b) *Es posible que la familia no quiera saber de ti.* (SUBJ)
'It is possible that the family may not want to know about you.'

In the case of personal constructions, the crucial conceptualizer is a prominent participant most intimately related to the content of the event in the complement clause—in most cases the subject of the main clause. The participant's capacity to interact with the complement is determined by the meaning of the verb. Assertion then is only one of the ways in which the participant might interact with the complement clause. Notice that this accounts for all the data seen so far. In (15a) *evidente* allows for the complement clause to be located in the dominion of the conceptualizer; whereas in (15b) *posible* does not—thus the indicative/subjunctive contrast. The examples in (16) and (17) are likewise accommodated:

(16) *Graciela quiere que Abelardo la acompañe.* (SUBJ)
      'Graciela wants Abelardo to accompany her.'

(17) *Los políticos piensan/creen que la gente es estúpida.* (IND)
      'Politicians think/believe that people are stupid.'

The meaning of the verb will determine whether the content of the complement clause can be located within the participant's dominion: *querer* simply gives information about Graciela's desires, though she has no control of, and no access to, Abelardo's decisions. Whether the act comes true or not is totally out of her command. In contrast, *pensar/creer* designate the dominion over an event or state by a conceptualizer.

The relationship with the complement clause is said to be *local* with respect to the conceptualizer. A number of circumstances in elaborated reality can determine the truth of a proposition, yet the actual way it is seen from the conceptualizer's viewpoint is what determines mood choice. Notice that the notion of dominion accounts for the indicative/subjunctive contrast observed in complement clauses of *saber* 'know':

(18a) *Ya sabía que Antonio era (*fuera) médico.* (IND)
       'I already knew that Antonio was a physician.'

(18b) *No sabía que Antonio fuera médico.* (SUBJ)
       'I didn't know that Antonio was a physician.'

(18c) % *No sabía que Antonio era médico.* (IND)
       'I didn't know that Antonio is a physician'

The affirmative sentence in (18a) is acceptable only in the indicative. The conceptualizer possesses the relevant information to consider the complement clause as a fact. In negative sentences, the subjunctive is the default case while the indicative is more context dependent. Both facts are accounted for by the notion of dominion. In (18b) the content of the complement clause is outside the conceptualizer's dominion, so that the truth of Antonio's being a physician cannot be taken as a fact; thus the complement clause is marked for subjunctive. Now (18c) is the case where the content of the complement clause is in the dominion of a conceptualizer other than the speaker. In the context of a conversation (18c) is perfectly grammatical, although many Spanish speakers would find it awkward (hence the marking %). What makes it questionable is that the speaker does not present himself as the crucial conceptualizer. Actually, he asserts his lack of knowledge with respect to some proposition already seen as true by the hearer. The use of indicative then highlights the fact that the complement clause is in the hearer's dominion and not in that of the speaker. The negative form is imposed on the activity of a conceptualizer that is not the crucial one for the purposes of mood choice. Thus the subjunctive form is ruled out for that particular situation. In an analogous manner, the presupposition cases mentioned above, and repeated here for convenience, are accounted for naturally:

(19) *Me he dado cuenta de que miento, siempre he mentido.* (IND) (song by S. Rodríguez)

'I have realized that I lie, I have always lied.'

(20a) *Me molesta que mientas tan cínicamente.* (SUBJ)
     'It bothers me that you lie so cynically.'

(20b) *Ojalá que puedas venir.* (SUBJ)
     'I hope that you can come'

(20c) *Es una tristeza que no puedas cenar con nosotros.* (SUBJ)
     'It is sad that you can't have dinner with us.'

In the indicative example the participant has enough dominion over the situation to present the complement clause as a fact. In the subjunctive examples the content of the complement clause is out of the participant's dominion: in (20a) *me* is a direct thematic object affected by the clause. Given that the participant is a non-active undergoer he is not seen as capable of establishing any kind of control over any other element. In the other two examples, the speaker manifests his reaction with respect to the possibility of an event coming true. While in (20b) and (20c) the content of the complement clause is not in the dominion of the crucial conceptualizer and is therefore not available to be considered as a fact, in (19) the content of the complement clause precisely enters the participant's awareness so that *de que miento* is seen as an unquestionable fact: Mood choice is thus naturally explained.

Schane (in this volume) proposes the notion of *subject responsibility* to account for the indicative/subjunctive contrast. The notion of dominion is compatible with Schane's proposal, yet it is made more abstract in order to cover other cases (such as temporal sequencing) which can be problematic for the subject-responsibility hypothesis. The well-known temporal phrases introduced by *cuando* and other adverbial markers bear out the dominion analysis. Suppose I say:

(21) *Estoy seguro de que iré/voy a ir.* (IND)
     'I'm sure that I will go/am going to go.'

My actual "going" may or may not take place, yet its occurrence does not determine the selection of indicative mood in the complement clause. Instead it is the dominion I hold over the elements of present reality that allows me to see future events as predictable facts. In contrast with this situation, observe the following case:

(22) *Irá* (IND) *a verlo cuando termine de trabajar.* (SUBJ)
     'She will go to see him when she finishes working.'

Although the act of going constitutes a potential fact, its realization depends on the completion of work. The speaker holds enough information regarding the fact that the participant will go, but the speaker's knowledge of present reality does not allow him/her to tell when the conditioning factor will be under the subject's control so that the event can be seen as true. The contrast with the indicative use illustrates this fact:

(23) *Va* (IND) *a verlo cuando termina de trabajar.* (IND)
     'She goes to see him when she finishes working.'

The subject's completion of work happens iteratively, with this act constituting part of the events that the conceptualizer sees as facts of his everyday reality: it belongs to the set of elements located in his dominion. It is thus expected that the indicative form in the complement clause will combine with the habitual reading imposed by the present tense of the main verb. Things and actions that we control (or that we conclude) are conceptualized as being in our dominion and are therefore marked for indicative, those outside our dominion receive subjunctive marking.

The use of subjunctive with relative clauses exemplifies this contrast clearly:

(24) *Tengo un coche que es lentísimo.* (IND)
'I have a car that is very slow.'

(25) *Quiero un coche que sea más rápido.* (SUBJ)
'I want a car that is faster.'

The qualification of the object as slow in the indicative can only take place due to the fact that the concept of *coche* is in the subject's dominion. Referring to an element extraneous to that dominion can only be conjectural, resulting in the subjunctive marking in (25) Guitart (in this volume) proposes that mood choice in relative clauses depends not on the relationship established with the noun anteceding the relative clause but, rather, on the whole unit composed of the noun and its modifying clause. I shall here use Guitart's abbreviation NPR (Noun Phrase Relative) to refer to the whole unit. In (25), for example, the relationship is not with an abstract *coche* but with a particular car that has the property of running fast. In agreement with Guitart's observation, I propose that if the content of the whole NPR is in the subject's dominion the relative clause is marked for indicative, while subjunctive mood signals NPRs that remain outside the subject's dominion.

Guitart, in the same essay, convincingly rejects Bull's experienced/non-experienced hypothesis and proposes instead that a clause is in the indicative only when the NPR refers to one or more entities that are individuated in the speaker's mind. While a type cannot take indicative, a specific instance of that type can, as will be seen in the contrast between (25) above and (26):

(26) *Quiero el coche que es más rápido.* (SUBJ)
'I want the car that is faster.'

and from the following contrast:

(27a) *Busco un maestro que sepa español.* (SUBJ)
'I'm looking for a teacher who [I hope] knows Spanish.'

(27b) *Busco un maestro que sabe español.* (IND)
'I'm looking for a teacher who knows Spanish.'

The level of individuation of an object constitutes an important part of a conceptualization. A participant interacts better with objects properly defined in his dominion than with those whose level of individuation is low. This phenomenon is also important for the correct understanding of the middle *se*, whose fundamental function is to increase the level of transitivity of the clause, that is, level of interaction of an active participant with respect to an object. Hopper and Thompson (1980) have shown that individuated objects allow for a greater degree of transitivity: *vi un bailarín* 'I saw a dancer' > *vi al bailarín* 'I saw the dancer'. In the following section I show that *se* imposes a transitivity increase and derives constructions in which the participant is more active. I will propose that the *me temo* type of constructions constitute extensions from middle *se* with a high level of transitivity and that this phenomenon correlates with the use of the indicative mood.

3 TRANSITIVITY INCREASE

In section 1, I proposed that when the notion of dominion is called upon, the level of activity of the experiencer is high. I have just noted that there is a high level of transitivity when the object of interaction is clearly individuated in the experiencer's dominion. Indirect object constructions have been characterized as having active experiencers. In the case of the reflexive indirect constructions, the subject and the recipient indirect object are equated with the same participant: *Juan le dio un regalo a María* 'Juan gave a present to María' > *Juan se dio un regalo* 'Juan gave himself a present'. That the subject is the beneficiary and recipient of the gift is marked by the pronoun *se*.

There are other constructions in which self-benefaction or self-orientation of the action is inherent to the meaning of the verb: *conseguir* 'get, obtain', *reservar* 'reserve', and *ahorrar* 'save' are obvious examples.

(28a) *Consiguió un trabajo a dos cuadras de su casa.*
       'She got a job two blocks away from her place.'

(28b) *Ahorre dinero, compre en nuestra gran barata.*
       'Save money, buy in our great sale.'

Since in *conseguir* the recipient and the subject are the same individual, the pronoun *se*—rather than marking coreferentiality—instead strengthens a benefactive meaning already inherent in the meaning of the verb:

(29a) *Se consiguió un trabajo a dos cuadras de su casa.*
       'She got herself a job two blocks away from her place.'

(29b) *Ahórrese el esfuerzo de ir pagar a la oficina, mande su pago por correo.*
       'Save yourself the effort of going to pay at the office, send your payment by mail.'

The clitic *se* emphasizes the fact that the event constitutes a particularly beneficial act in favor of the subject. Ever since Bello (1951) suggested the term *superfluo* to refer to this function of *se*, there has been a general tendency in the Hispanic linguistic tradition to consider this middle marker meaningless. Such an assumption is of course misleading: not only does it miss important information about the emphatic import of *se*, but it also restricts the possibility of observing the wide range of constructions that derive from it. Only a few of those derived patterns will be pointed out in this section. That *se* is not vacuous can be seen from the constrast between the standard construction in (29b) and the marginal use in (30) :

(30) ??/* *Ahorre el esfuerzo de ir pagar a la oficina, mande su pago por correo.*
       'Save the effort of going to pay at the office, send your payment by mail.'

A more obvious example where *se* is clearly meaningful can be observed from the *reservar/reservarse* contrast:

(31a) *Reservamos una mesa para cuatro personas.*
       'We reserved a table for four people.'

(31b) *Nos reservamos el derecho de admisión.*

'We reserve ourselves the right of admittance.'

(31c)   * *Reservamos el derecho de admisión.*

'We reserve ourselves the right of admittance.'

The crucial fact is that *se* imposes a transitivity increase whereby the subject not only interacts with the object but also keeps the object away from any other participant's reach. In a previous work I explained the contrast between the unmarked and the middle-marked use of *reservar* as a consequence of conceptual intimacy between the subject and the direct object: *derecho* is already the subject's belonging, while *mesa* is not (Maldonado 1992). With *reservar* an object extraneous to the participant is located in his sphere of control. With *reservarse* the increase of control over an inherent belonging is taken to the extreme of marking it as exclusive to a specific participant.

An extension from this construction type is constituted by *full exploitation middle* constructions. In this case, the verb implies not only that the object is in (or brought into) the subject's dominion but also that the participant interacts with it in some manner. Obvious examples of this are *comer* 'eat', *tomar* 'drink', and other verbs of ingestion, like *fumar* 'smoke' and *devorar* 'devour':

(32)   *Abelardo fuma paquetes al día.*

'Abelardo smokes packs a day.'

(33)   *Platero no toma alcohol.*

'Platero doesn't drink alcohol.'

Provided that the object constitutes a well-defined and delimited unit, the middle marker *se* imposes a completive interpretation:

(34)   *Abelardo se fuma dos cajetillas diarias.*

'Abelardo smokes two packs a day.'

(35)   *Platero acababa de beberse dos cubos de agua.* (J.R. Jiménez)

'Platero had just drunk up two buckets of water.'

The subject maximally exploits a well-delimited object located in his dominion. What *se* indicates is that the action is done to completion and, consequently, that the whole direct object is affected by the subject's action. This value of *se* also occurs with verbs of mental activity:

(36)   *Tengo allí un primo que se lo conoce todo: teatros, cabarets... ¡Se sabe cada sitio!*

'I have a cousin who knows it all: theaters, cabarets... He knows every place!'

(37)   *Pilar se sabe la canción.*

'Pilar knows the song (by heart).'

Examples (36) and (37) contrast with their unmarked counterparts *conocer todo* 'know everything'and *saber la canción* 'know the song' in that the control of the subject over the direct object is maximal only in the middle constructions. Partial or limited dominion over an object is expressed in plain transitive constructions:

(38a)   *Conoce un poco la ciudad.*

'He knows the city a bit.'

(38b)   * *Se conoce un poco la ciudad.*

'He knows the city a bit.'

Since *se* increases considerably the transitivity effects of the verb, as in the case of relative clauses, the object of full exploitation constructions must constitute delimited units properly contained in the participant's dominion. This can be seen from the following ungrammatical tokens:

(39) * *Abelardo se fuma cajetillas diarias.*
    'Abelardo smokes packs a day.'

(40) * *Platero acababa de beberse cubos de agua.*
    'Platero had just drunk up buckets of water.'

(41) * *Mi primo se conoce lugares.*
    'Mi cousin knows places.'

(42a) *María sabe un poco de francés.*
    'Maria knows a little French.'

(42b) * *María se sabe un poco de francés.*
    'Maria knows a little French.'

Since the verb already implies some interaction between the subject and an object located in his dominion, as in (32) and (33), what *se* does is give special prominence to the subject's action so that the object's attributes are maximally exploited.[4] The point being made here is that, instead of being superfluous, *se* increases the level of interaction between subject and object. When the object constitutes a well-defined unit in the participant's dominion, the transitivity increase leads to a full-exploitation reading. The facts seen so far suggest that such increase is a gradual one:

plain transitive	*reservamos una mesa / conoce un poco la ciudad*
emphatic benefactive	*nos reservamos el derecho de admisión*
full exploitation	*se sabe la canción*

We are now in a position to explain why the use of *se* determines the use of indicative mood in the complement clause. In the following section, I propose that *temerse* and *darse cuenta* constitute extensions from the full-exploitation construction and that this fact determines the choice of the indicative mood in Spanish.

4   MOOD CHOICE AND MIDDLE *SE*

Common to all the middle values of *se* described above is that the clitic produces a new verb giving special prominence to some meaning already present in the verb. Yet the derivative value of *se* follows consistent patterns. In all cases it increases the level of activity/involvement of a participant: it designates a special benefactive reading in inherently benefactive verbs and imposes a full-exploitation reading in verbs in which the subject interacts with objects in his dominion. As will be seen, full-exploitation *se* has produced *temerse* from *temer*, and this new verb prototypically determines the presence of an indicative complement clause:

(43) *Temo que las autoridades tomen represalias en contra de los estudiantes.*
    (SUBJ)
    'I fear that the authorities may take revenge against the students.'

(44) *Me temo que las autoridades van a tomar/tomarán represalias en contra de los estudiantes.* (IND)

'I'm afraid that the authorities will/are going to take revenge against the students.'

With the absence of the middle marker *me*, the complement clause of (43) takes the subjunctive, while in (44) the middle construction takes an indicative complement. The translation is misleading in that it does not reflect the actual contrast between *temer* and *temerse: temo* expresses fear with respect to some potential happening, while *me temo* predicts the happening of a future event. The middle use is a manifestation of full-exploitation *se* where the main clause subject holds enough information and participates in considering the event to a great enough extent that he is able to predict the future existence of some act.

There is a coherent pattern in the development of this construal coming from two different directions. On the one hand, full-exploitation *se* imposes a reading of complete command over an element located in the subject's dominion; on the other, the choice of indicative mood constitutes a level of assertion that depends on the location of an event within the speaker's/participant's dominion. Since full-exploitation *se* implies enough information about elaborated reality that a future event is predicted and even seen as a fact, the choice of indicative mood in the complement clause is explained. Crucially, in (43) the notion of dominion cannot be appealed to since no middle marker is present. The subjunctive use is naturally accounted for in absence of any delimited object located in a specified dominion.

A more difficult question to be addressed is whether the combination of the middle marker and the subjunctive mood will lead to ungrammatical results. The answer is that it does not. This can be seen in the following example:

(45) *Me temo que las autoridades vayan a tomar/tomen represalias en contra de los estudiantes.* (SUBJ)

'I fear that the authorities may take revenge against the students.'

In fact Bello, using a similar example (*Me temo que os engañéis* (SUBJ) 'I fear that you may fool yourselves'), was the first to point out the existence of what he called a *superfluous dative* marker whose value he described in the following manner: "... con él se indica el interés de la persona que habla en el hecho de que se trata [... with it one indicates the interest of the person who speaks about the event at issue]" (1951:218). Bello's description could not be more precise. Notice that the meaning of (45) is closely related to (43), but quite distant from (44). The dative *me* of (45) designates an increase of interest by the participant, in much the same way that it intensifies self-benefaction in *conseguí un trabajo* 'I got a job' > *me conseguí un trabajo* 'I got myself a job'. Two values of *se* seem to be present: an emphatic benefactive *se* and a full-exploitation *se*. These values follow the same graded increase in interaction described in section 3.

With respect to *temer*, three levels of participation can be seen. In the plain transitive construction, the participant's level of involvement is low. As a benefactive marker, *se* increases the level of involvement of the participant. A higher level of participant involvement is developed in full-exploitation *se*. In *temo* the subject fears some remote possibility that an event might come true. The level of involvement increases as *me* is introduced in (45). The participant's fear with respect to the potential occurrence of an event is greater, yet the possibility that it will not happen is still open. While the event in the complement clause is equally remote, the subject's interests play a more prominent role:

(46) *No he podido dormir últimamente, me temo que un ladrón vaya a venir en la noche.*

'I have not been able to sleep—I [myself] am afraid that a thief may come during the night.'

Here *me* emphasizes the speaker's concerns, as recurrent or rather intense. Finally, the predictive reading by which a future event is taken as an almost unquestionable fact emerges when full-involvement *se* is at play. It is the participant's control of facts in his dominion that allows his prediction of a future happening. Under those circumstances, indicative mood in the complement clause is required. This reading is not available for *temer* without *se:*

(47) * *Temo que va a venir.* (IND)
'I fear that he is going to come.'

That the participant's level of control over the elements in his sphere of control is maximal in the middle/indicative combination construction, and that it leads to a predictive reading, can be seen from appended expressions like *Es ya casi un hecho* 'It is almost (already) a fact' that assert the truth of the preceding sentence:

(48a) *Me temo que vas a reprobar/suspender matemáticas. Eso es ya casi un hecho.* (IND)

'I am afraid that you are going to flunk math. That is almost already a fact.'

(48b) * *Me temo que vayas a reprobar matemáticas. Eso es ya casi un hecho.* (SUBJ)

'I am afraid that you may flunk math. That is almost already a fact.'

These facts suggest an organization of the participant's increasing level of activity/involvement in the following manner:

unmarked/subjunctive > low involvement	*Temo que venga.* 'I fear that he may come.'
benefactive/subjunctive > higher involvement	*Me temo que venga.* 'I fear [myself] that he may come.'
middle/indicative > full involvement	*Me temo que va a venir.* 'I'm afraid that he is going to come.'

References to the predictive meaning are not lacking in the relevant literature. As Molina Redondo (1974) has pointed out: "*Temer* tiene dos significados: 'tener miedo' y 'sospechar que pueda producirse algo desfavorable, no deseado, etc.'; *temerse* sólo el segundo' [*Temer* has two meanings: 'have fear' and 'suspect that something disfavorable, unwanted, etc. may happen'; *temerse* has only the second meaning]." It is clear then that the middle *se* marker imposes a special reading not available in the unmarked form of the verb.[5] Molina Redondo treats this phenomenon as a lexical contrast; Alcina and Blecua (1975), Real Academia (1978) suggest that in *temerse* there is an important link between the so-called reflexive marker and the use of the indicative; however, no particular explanation has been offered. Such a link is naturally accommodated as an extension that develops from the full-exploitation middle construction in the way I have proposed here.

The contrast suggested in (48b) is a gradual one. This means that the borderline cases are harder to identify than are those that are maximally opposed. Speakers of Spanish have no problem in recognizing the two polar extremes: the unmarked/subjunctive construction involving low involvement and the middle/indicative construction giving prominence to the maximal involvement predictive reading. However, the recognition of the intermediate stage in examples like *me temo que venga* (SUBJ) not only takes more time to be processed, but also requires a special effort to identify its meaning.

Two polar phenomena can now be explained; first, the fact that *darse cuenta* determines indicative mood choice as in (49a) and, second, that *alegrarse, entristecerse,* and the whole class of verbs of emotional reaction favor subjunctive complement clauses, as in (4a), repeated here as (50a):

(49a)   *Su madre se da cuenta de lo que quieren hacer.* (IND)
         'Their mother realizes what they want to do.'

(49b) * *Su madre se da cuenta de lo que quieran hacer.* (SUBJ)
         'Their mother realizes what they may want to do.'

(50a)   *Me alegro de que vengas.* (SUBJ)
         'I'm glad that you are coming.'

(50b)   ??*Me alegro de que vienes.* (IND)
         'I'm glad that you are coming.'

In both cases middle *se* derives a new verb from an unmarked transitive form. I will show that in both cases the level of involvement of the participant increases via the middle marker. Yet the difference depends on the semantic structure of the verb to which middle *se* applies. In the case of *darse cuenta,* middle *se* applies to an already active participant, whereas in *alegrarse* it operates on a passive one:

(51)   *Su madre da cuenta de lo que quieren hacer.* (IND)
        'Their mother reports on [gives account of] what they want to do.'

(52)   *Me   alegra   que   vengas.* (SUBJ)
        DO-1ST-SING   happy-3RD-SING   that   come-2ND-SING
        'That you are coming makes me happy [gladdens me].'

In (51) the mother has enough knowledge about her children to observe and report about their actions in an objective manner. The indicative mood is accounted for by the fact that the content of the complement clause is one of the elements the mother has dominion over. Since *se* increases the level of interaction of the subject with respect to the object, it is only natural that the derived verb *darse cuenta* 'realize' indicates awareness with respect to a mental object. The subject's relationship to the object is more intimate in the middle construction, as she assumes an experiencer role, than it is with the plain transitive verb, where the subject remains somewhat distant and is limited to observing and reporting about someone else's actions. Whether in the plain transitive or in the middle construction, the content of the complement clause is located in the subject's dominion. The use of the indicative is thus account-ed for.

The notion of dominion includes a reference point from which another object can be located. More concretely, the dominion constitutes the sphere of control/action where some participant is able to interact with some object. The clitic *me* in (52) does not qualify as a reference point. It is a direct object, that is, a passive participant undergoing an emotional change imposed by an external impulse. As a passive mem-ber it can evoke no dominion and no sphere of control. The subjunctive mood of the sentential subject is accounted for by the fact that the content of the clause cannot be located in any participant's dominion. Now the function of middle *se* for this type of verb is to transform a passive participant into a more active one. This function is apparent in the following contrasting examples:

(53a)   *A León lo asusta que grites.*
        'It frightens Leon when you scream.'

(53b)   *León se asusta de que grites.*
        'Leon gets frightened when you scream.'

That León is more involved in experiencing a change of mental state in (53b) than he is in (53a) has widely been acknowledged in the relevant literature (García 1975; Real Academia 1978; Alcina and Blecua 1975; Maldonado 1992). León becomes more active as he changes from a passive undergoer to an experiencer participant. Yet the level of activity does not surpass that of a physical or emotional reaction.[6] Consequently the subject's level of activity is not sufficient to evoke the notion of dominion, where he would interact with some object. His reaction is still provoked by an external cause which he may not control. The lack of interaction within a specific dominion accounts for the use of the subjunctive mood of the oblique clauses of (52) and (53b). All the examples seen here demonstrate that the level of activity of the participant and the notion of dominion work together in determining the mood choice in Spanish.

5 CONCLUSION

We may conclude that the behavior of middle *se* is quite systematic. In all the exam-ples seen in this paper it has always been the case that it increases the level of activ-ity of the most prominent participant in the main clause. Whether the activity increase leads to the use of the indicative or the subjunctive mood in the complement clause depends on the level of activity that the participant has before *se* applies to it. If the participant is already active, as in *dar cuenta*, the activity increase imposed by *se* will determine the indicative mood in the complement clause. If the participant is a passive affected entity, as in *asustar* and *alegrar*, the middle marker *se* will increase his level of activity, although not to the extent of putting him in control of the situa-tion; consequently, this type of middle construction will not determine the use of the indicative in the complementary oblique clause. Intermediate cases like *temer* do not fluctuate randomly. There are two ways in which the participant may increase his level of activity: (a) by augmenting his concerns about a potential event which remains out of his sphere of control, and (b) by establishing control over a specific situation to the extent of being able to predict a future happening. It is only in the second case that a full-exploitation middle construction is at play. It is only then that the level of interaction of an active participant with a (mental) object located in his dominion will require an indicative complement clause.

In explaining mental-act verbs (*Se da cuenta de que* + IND 'He realizes that') versus comment verbs (*Me molesta que* + SUBJ 'It bothers me that'), Terrell and Hooper (1974) and Terrell (1976) suggest that mental-act verbs seem more similar to assertions than comment verbs do. In this paper I have tested the hypotheses of Terrell and Hooper and given finer explanations to their findings with respect to the Spanish mood system. The similarity of mental-act verbs to assertions depends basically on the level of activity of the subject: with respect to an already active participant, full exploitation *se* denotes highly active participants in control of their mental objects. This fact determines indicative mood choice. On the other hand comment verbs are far from being assertive, precisely because their human participants are conceptualized as passive. The activating properties of *se* are insufficient to bring about a full-fledged active participant, and consequently no dominion can be called upon.

The notion of dominion—involving an active participant interacting with an object located in his sphere of control—has been offered here as a justifiable way to explain a set of intricate relationships between the middle marker *se* and mood choice in Spanish. It is my hope that the contents of this paper will shed some light on an area that has heretofore been incompletely examined.

Notes

1. I am indebted to Ronald Langacker for his guidance in this paper. I am also in debt to Michel Achard, Aintzane Doiz-Bienzobas, Errapel Mejías-Bikandi, Sanford Schane, and Maura Velázquez for their insightful comments and to Donna and Valeria for breaking the rules I propose in this paper in their everyday speech.

2. Clear cases in which *se* has a reflexive value are those in which there is a split representation of the participant:
    a. *Era tal su soledad que Alcira se enviaba cartas a sí misma* (Ramírez Heredia, *El Rayo Macoy*)
       'Her loneliness was such that Alcira would send letters to herself'
    b. *Fue frente al espejo que Justine se dijo: ya me tienes harta, judía estúpida* (Durrell, *Justine*)
       'It was in front of the mirror that Justine said to herself: you have me all fed up, you stupid Jew'
    Most uses in Spanish and other Romance languages do not correspond to reflexive split representations but rather to a set of middle meanings in which some internally complex activity is being represented. The examples analyzed in this paper constitute clear examples of middle constructions.

3. The indicative mood may be used for emphatic purposes either to signal that the subject of the complement clause is actually coming at that specific moment or to point out that his coming is an unquestionable fact.

4. Other details and extensions of this construction are given in my thesis (Maldonado 1992), where a detailed study of full exploitation is presented.

5. However, the choice of using *se* with the subjunctive is still possible. In fact, this variation suggests the origins of a quite recent grammaticalization process that has taken place in current Spanish. Although in-depth historical research on this problem is needed, it is possible that in the nineteenth century full-involvement *se* had not yet extended to *temer* and that this pattern has been gaining ground in the course of the last century.

6. No volitional or controlled action is executed by León in the way it would be in constructions with active-subject participants of the type *León se secó la cara con una toalla* 'León dried his face with a towel'.

References

Achard, Michel. 1993. *Complementation in French and Spanish: A Cognitive Grammar Approach*. Ph.D. dissertation, University of California, San Diego.

Alcina, Juan, and José Blecua. 1975. *Gramática española*. Barcelona: Ariel.

Bello, Andrés 1951. *Gramática de la lengua castellana*. Annotated by Rufino J. Cuervo. Caracas: Ministerio de Educación.

García, Erica. 1975. *The Role of Theory in Linguistic Analysis*. Amsterdam: North-Holland.

Hopper, Paul, and Sandra Thompson. 1980. Transitivity in Grammar and Discourse. *Language* 56: 251-299.

Langacker, Ronald. 1987a. *Foundations of Cognitive Grammar*. Vol. 1: *Theoretical Prerequisites*. Stanford: Stanford University Press.

———. 1987b. Nouns and Verbs. *Language* 63:53-94.

———. 1990. Subjectification. *Cognitive Linguistics* 1:5-38.

———. 1992. *Foundations of Cognitive Grammar*. Vol. 2: *Descriptive Application*. Stanford: Stanford University Press.

Maldonado, Ricardo. 1988. Energetic Reflexives in Spanish. *Berkeley Linguistics Society* 14:153-165.

———. 1989. Se gramaticalizó: A Diachronic Account of Energetic Reflexives in Spanish. *Proceedings of the Fourth Pacific Linguistics Conference*. Eugene: University of Oregon.

———. 1992. *Middle Voice: The case of Spanish **se***. Ph.D. dissertation, University of California, San Diego.

Molina Redondo, J.A. 1974. *Usos de se: cuestiones sintácticas y léxicas*. Madrid: Sociedad General Española de Librería.

Real Academia Española. 1978. *Esbozo de una nueva gramática de la lengua española*. Madrid: Espasa Calpe.

Seiler, Hansjakob. 1983. Possessivity. Subject and Object. *Studies in Language* 7:89-117.

Terrell, Tracy D. 1976. Assertion and Presupposition in Spanish Complements. In *Current Studies in Romance Linguistics*, ed. by M. Luján and F. Hensey, 221-245. Washington D.C.: Georgetown University Press. (reprinted in this volume)

Terrell, Tracy, and Joan Hooper. 1974. A Semantically Based Analysis of Mood in Spanish. *Hispania* 57:484-494.

The Painless Subjunctive

Flora Klein-Andreu
SUNY at Stony Brook

Traditionally, the use of the subjunctive in Spanish has been taught as following from (being "governed by") the occurrence of some other item in the context. This paper suggests it is more accurate, and pedagogically much more effective, to explain the use of the subjunctive as following from the fact that it conveys a *different meaning* than the indicative. The occurrence of the subjunctive in certain contexts, as well as its non-occurrence in others, can then be seen as a consequence of whether or not its meaning is coherent with the overall intent of the particular context as a whole.

1 THE SUBJUNCTIVE (AND THE INDICATIVE) AS ARBITRARY OR AS MEANINGFUL

One of the most difficult tasks facing language instructors is teaching distinctions in the target language (L2) that the students' own language (L1) does not make. This problem is aggravated with grammatical distinctions, since teachers—especially when they speak L2 natively—usually are not aware of *why* they use one particular grammatical form, rather than another, just where they do. With lexical differences, on the other hand, the principles that determine actual usage are relatively more accessible. More importantly, it is easier to recognize that different words reflect different meanings.

The suggestions in this paper are based on the view that grammatical differences, like different words, in fact signal different meanings. Grammatical meaning, however, is usually considerably less obvious than lexical meaning; it must be discovered by analysis, based on systematic consideration of the actual usage of the grammatical forms in question. But once the meanings are determined, we have at our disposal a powerful explanatory and predictive tool that can be used, among other ways, to help in teaching the language. For the meanings constitute, in effect, generalizations that *motivate* the actual use, or distribution, of the forms in question. Consequently, grammatical differences need no longer be presented as arbitrary, to be learned by rote, but rather as *following from* their meanings: as ways in which the meanings are exploited to convey different messages in different contexts.

To illustrate, I will discuss the classroom presentation of the use of the subjunctive mood, as opposed to the indicative, in Spanish. Typically, this question is not presented as involving a "distinction" at all, much less one that carries meaning. Rather, at least with English-speaking students, it seems to be assumed that the indicative is "the norm," so to speak, so that what is taught explicitly as a particular "mood" is the subjunctive—or, more precisely, its various "uses" (see Terrell and Hooper 1975:493). Wherever possible, the uses are presented as the automatic consequence of the presence of some other word, said to determine ("govern") the subjunctive's occurrence. For example, it is said that certain expressions that convey doubt, desire, or the speaker's feelings "require" a subjunctive in the dependent clause. Since the connection between these various contexts is not obvious, essentially they must be learned by rote: they become, in effect, exceptions to what the student has come to view as the norm, namely, the indicative. Likewise to be learned by rote, and likewise seemingly unconnected, are various "independent uses," instances where the subjunctive occurs with no particular "governing" word present.

Thus the typical textbook deals with the use of the subjunctive by linking it, wherever possible, to the occurrence of some other word or type of expression. It is relatively rare that examples are given of contexts where *either* the subjunctive *or* the indicative could occur, resulting in a difference in the actual message communicated. Yet it is precisely these contexts that are most useful in illustrating the difference in meaning between the moods themselves.

In this paper I hope to show that learning to use the subjunctive in Spanish is greatly facilitated by presenting the difference between subjunctive and indicative as conveying meaning in itself. Specifically, I have found that the use of one mood or the other is easy to explain, and easy for students to understand and internalize, if it is presented as proposed by Terrell and Hooper. They claimed that the indicative can be characterized as ASSERTING the event's occurrence and the subjunctive as NOT-ASSERTING it—in other words, as non-committal in this regard (Terrell and Hooper 1974; Hooper 1975). In earlier papers I discussed some theoretical differences between my views and the Terrell-Hooper proposal (see Klein 1975 and Klein 1980 for synchronic arguments, and Klein-Andreu 1986 and Klein-Andreu 1991 for diachronic implications). Here I would like to show how the Terrell-Hooper proposal, as I would modify it, can be applied to foreign-language teaching.

2 SOME PRELIMINARY CONSIDERATIONS

Relative Assertiveness: The Future and the Conditional Tenses

If assertiveness and non-assertiveness are regarded simply as meanings expressed by particular verb morphology, as I propose they should be, their opposition sets up a semantic parameter that can accomodate not only the Spanish indicative and subjunctive forms, at either extreme, but also the future and the conditional, as *intermediate* between them.[1] This is diagrammed in Figure 1.

Figure 1. Relative assertiveness of Spanish verb forms[2]

Note that the future tense is usually used to express the relative likelihood of the event *at the time of speaking* itself, with the conditional doing the same in reference to the Past.[3] This is shown in (1) and (2):

   (1) *¿No está en casa?* **Estará** *en la oficina.*
      'He/she isn't at home? He/she **must be** at the office.'

   (2) *¿No estaba en casa?* **Estaría** *en la oficina.*
      'He/she wasn't at the office? He/she **must have been** at the office.'

Moreover, even when the future is used to refer to events expected after the present, this too can be viewed as expressing their relative likelihood—as compared to, say, the relatively higher likelihood of events actually taking place in the present. It seems to be the context, rather than the verb form itself, that determines whether the event's occurrence is to be understood as likely at the time of speaking (as in Example 1), or at some later time (as in Example 3):

   (3) *Acaba de salir.* **Estará** *en la oficina en una hora.*
      'He/she has just gone out. He/she **will be** at the office in an hour.'

Parallel Uses of Past and Non-Past Forms: Past Forms Referring to Past Time

It is easy, too, to see the parallelism claimed between the forms in the upper row in Figure 1, and those in the lower row, in the sense that the lower forms are used in reference to past time just as the upper forms are used for non-past time. This is shown in Examples 4 through 6.

   (4a) **Estudio** *español.*
       '**I'm studying** Spanish.'

   (4b) **Estudiaba** *español cuando conocí a Juan.*
       '**I was studying** Spanish when I met Juan.'

   (4c) **Estudié** *español de pequeña.*
       '**I studied** Spanish as a child.'

   (5a) *Nos* **encontraremos** *en el café.*
       'We **will meet** in the café.'
       Tendrá *unos treinta años.*
       'He **must be** about thirty.'

   (5b) *Decidimos que nos* **encontraríamos** *en el café.*
       'We decided we **would meet** in the café.'

Tendría *unos treinta años.*
'He **must have been** about thirty.'
(6a)   *Mis padres quieren que **estudie** arquitectura.*
'My parents want me to study architecture (now)'.
*Mis padres quisieron/querían que **estudiara** arquitectura.*
'My parents wanted me to study architecture (then).'

Non-Parallel Uses: Past Forms Referring to Non-Past Time

On the other hand, foreign language texts often do not explain that the lower (past) forms can also be used in reference to *non-past time,* and that they then express, quite systematically, a *lesser degree of probability* of the event's occurrence than would the corresponding forms in the upper row—and so, in a sense, lesser assertiveness as well (Bull 1963:61; 1965:194). Yet this is not at all difficult to convey to students since many languages do exactly the same thing, including English (see e.g., Jespersen 1964:255).[4] This can be seen by comparing the English glosses in examples (7) and (8). In reference to past time, the past form in Example (7b) conveys the same degree of likelihood as does the non-past form in (7a) in reference to non-past time. In Example (8), however, the past form refers to non-past time and so conveys a relatively lower degree of likelihood of the event's occurrence:

(7a)   I **have a** vacation (now) (so I'm going skiing).
(7b)   I **had a** vacation (then) (so I went skiing).
(8)   If I **had** a vacation (now), I would go skiing.

In English this difference in likelihood is usually conveyed simply by switching from non-past to past forms, where the verb-form itself is concerned. Spanish, however, has different verb forms that indicate different degrees of assertiveness. Therefore these differences in assertiveness are exploited, among other ways, to distinguish between straightforward reference to past events (which would be made in the preterit or the imperfect) and reference to events as less likely in non-past time. For the latter, the less assertive forms are used (the past subjunctive or the conditional) with the particular form chosen depending, in turn, on the relative degree of assertiveness called for to achieve the desired interpretation. If the lowest degree of assertiveness is needed—as, for example, in conveying conditions as unlikely or even as counterfactual—the form used is the past subjunctive; if the degree of assertiveness called for is slightly higher—as in stating the presumable consequences of such unlikely contingencies—it is the conditional. (Note the Spanish translation of (8): *Si tuviera* (past subjunctive) *vacaciones, iría* (conditional) *a esquiar.*

Expressing Conditions

This last example brings us to another matter that must be made clear as soon as possible, especially to the prospective teacher: namely, usage in "conditional clauses" with *si* 'if'. The fact is that *si* clauses work differently from other dependent clauses: in expressing conditions with *si,* Spanish uses only the extremes of the *de facto* scale of assertiveness proposed here. As we see in Example 9, if a non-past condition is portrayed as relatively unlikely, it is put in the past subjunctive. This is consistent with the meanings proposed, since expressing a condition as unlikely would seem to entail the least amount of commitment on the part of the speaker (as compared to the expressing its possible consequence). The potential problem, then, arises in the case of conditions presented as relatively likely. For likely conditions are not expressed in the corresponding non-past form, the present subjunctive, as the otherwise pervasive time-shift pattern might lead us to expect, but rather in the present indicative, as in Example 10.[5] No other options are possible, if the clause is to be understood as expressing a contingent condition.[6]

(9) Si **ganara** la lotería, me jubilaría.
     (Past Subj.)   (Conditional)
     'If I **won** the lottery, I would retire.'

(10) Si **gano** este partido, quedaré satisfecha.
     (Pres. Ind.)   (Future)
     'If I **win** this game, I will be satisfied.'

Theoretically, use of the present indicative to present conditions as relatively likely may or may not be a counterexample to the claim that it asserts occurrence. After all, it is not implausible that conditions viewed as likely are phrased in the rel-atively more assertive form, precisely to present them as "givens." This use of the indicative would then be similar to its use in questions: Note that questions are never asked in the subjunctive, though they can be in the future or the conditional, under the same conditions as declaratives. It could be argued that this is because questions amount to requests for some degree of assertiveness in response—as opposed, say, to requests for action, which can be in the subjunctive (Terrell and Hooper 1974:486).

For teaching purposes, however, what matters is not so much whether or not these are real counterexamples to the meanings proposed for the moods; it might well be the case that the analysis proposed here could still be improved upon.[7] What matters, rather, is that they might seem like exceptions to language students, which could be confusing and therefore could hinder learning of the more general pattern of exploita-tion of the indicative/subjunctive distinction.

In my experience, students have no more trouble expressing conditions than they have asking questions, provided conditions are taught early enough in the syllabus (i.e., before going into the systematic presentation of the other, more general, exploitations of the indicative-subjunctive opposition; see also Bull 1965:194). Moreover, it is very natural to present conditions early in a course (as traditionally is done with questions). Just as students are taught from the outset how to ask, it is like-wise natural to teach them how to express conditions, and their consequences, fairly early—certainly much earlier than most textbooks do, and, in particular, before other complex utterances. This is because, of all dependent clauses, conditions are the first that students actually seem to need, to discuss expected events, plans, etc. There are always contingencies to consider, always an *if*.

Thus, expressing conditions becomes necessary, and therefore real and under-standable, before other kinds of dependent clauses. For the latter, it is relatively easier to find other ways of conveying the same message. The shrewd teacher will insure that students have a thorough grasp of how conditions and their consequences are expressed before tackling the indicative-subjunctive opposition more generally. Learning to express conditions also gives students the opportunity to learn the past subjunctive form, as well as the conditional. At the same time, they will grasp the difference between referring to non-past events in non-past forms—as relatively likely—and referring to them in past forms—as unlikely.

3 GENERAL USE OF ASSERTION VS. NON-ASSERTION

"Independent" Interpetation of Non-Assertion

Once students have a thorough productive grasp of conditional utterances, then the indicative-subjunctive opposition in other situations presents no problem. It should be presented as reflecting, in various contexts, the difference between asserting an event's occurrence and not asserting it. The first consequence of this difference in assertiveness is that the indicative is especially suited for reference to events that are to be understood without reference to any other event (and so as *independent*), and the subjunctive for the opposite case—for so-called *dependent* clauses. Because it says nothing about the event's occurrence, a subjunctive on its own is interpreted only as expressing the desirability of the event (or its non-desirability, if negated). Whether such expressions of desirability are then interpreted more specifically as suggestions, commands, exhortations, or wishes (optatives), depends only on conditions of the actual situation: principally, on who it is that is expected or called upon to bring about the event (the hearer, or someone else), and on whether or not the speaker is in a position of authority to force this person to do so. Typical interpretations, and the conditions that favor them, are shown in Figure 2.

Note that the hypothesis that the subjunctive is 'non-assertive' also explains why it is the form used for just those commands/requests/suggestions that are intended to be more "formal" (and so presumably more diffident) as well as for requests for non-action (i.e., negative requests). In contrast, requests that are both non-negative and non-formal (that is, positive and familiar) are made in a special form used exclusively for this purpose: *the imperative*. In terms of an analysis based on meaning, it seems reasonable that the more specialized imperative form should "command" more forcefully (since this is all it ever does) and that positive and familiar commands should be expressed more forcefully than negative and/or polite ones. Thus, non-assertion of the event's occurrence is simply a more indirect (and so more diffident and polite) way of suggesting that it would be nice if it were to be brought about (given the appropriate context). Obviously, the common practice of using the term *imperative* to refer to all actual commands/requests/suggestions, regardless of whether they are made in the imperative form or in the subjunctive, obscures the reason for the division of labor between the two forms, making it seem yet another arbitrary quirk of Spanish to be memorized.[8]

	Extralinguistic Situation	Particular Interpretations	Examples
Event Not Asserted (and interpreted without reference to any other event)	and is to be brought by hearer (according to relative authority of speaker)	→ order, request, suggestion, entreaty	*no lo olvides* 'don't forget it' *olvídelo* 'forget it' *siéntese* 'sit down'
General Interpretation:			
Event Is Desirable	and is to be brought about by both the speaker and the hearer	→ exhortation	*olvidémoslo* 'let's forget it *sentémonos* 'let's sit down'
	and is to be brought about by a 3d person (including super- natural or other uncontrollable forces)	→ wish	*que entre/se siente* 'have X come in/sit down' *ojalá no llueva* 'I hope it doesn't rain' *viva el rey* 'long live the king'

Figure 2. Interpretation of non-asserted events as independent verbs (without reference to any other event)

Useful exercises to practice using subjunctives in these independent senses are, for instance, giving directions to strangers or suggesting activities to be done either in common (*Demos una fiesta; encarguemos una pizza; compremos refrescos*) or to be done by someone else (*Que lo traiga él; que lo pague ella*). At this point formulaic expressions can also be presented, of the type *Viva el rey,* or *Que en paz descanse/que en gloria esté,* and of course expressions of wishes with *ojalá,* using either the present or past subjunctive depending on whether or not they are considered likely to be fulfilled.

"Dependent" Uses of Assertion

After this, so-called dependent expressions are very smooth sailing indeed. It can be noted at the outset that, in dependent clauses, it is the subjunctive that is the norm— in other words, that Spanish does not assert a dependent event's occurrence by putting it in the indicative *except* where this claim is required by the interpretation intended for the utterance as a whole. The main instances of this situation are the types of utterances exemplified under A and B below. Those under A are intended precisely to convey the speaker's contention that the dependent event is or is not occurring (or did/did not, will/will not occur), while those under B are intended to indicate on what evidence or authority the speaker believes this to be the case. It is easy for students to see that both require that the dependent event's occurrence be asserted, for the utterance as a whole to be interpreted as either as constituting a claim of occurrence (examples under A), or as involving one (under B). (As will be further explained below, boxed examples are of verbs that also occur with dependent subjunctives, but with a different interpretation. They are only understood as involving a claim of occurrence when the dependent verb is in the indicative.):

A. CLAIMING that the event is occurring/has occurred/will occur:

e.g. *Sostengo que ...*   'I maintain that ...'
    (Te) aseguro que ...   'I assure you that ...'
    Sé que ...   'I know that ...'

Digo que ...	**'I tell you that ...'**
Admito que ...	**'I concede that ...'**
Insisto que ...	**'I maintain that ...'**

B. Indicating BASIS FOR CLAIM:

    Veo que ...   'I see that ...'
    Dicen que ...   'They say that ...'
    Oigo decir que ...   'I hear tell that ...'

Parece que ...	**'It seems that ...'**
Siento que ...	**'I feel that ...'**

As teachers, our aim is to enable students to exploit the indicative-subjunctive opposition productively, to express communications of their own. To this end, it is particularly important that they realize that the message "claim" in the above examples is only an interpretation, and one that is decisively favored by the assertive meaning of the indicative dependent verb. For this reason, I suggest pointing out at soon as possible examples such as those I have boxed off here: main verbs which could also be found with dependent verbs in the subjunctive, but which in that case would not be understood as "claiming." Instead, they would be understood in one of the various ways in which main verbs with non-asserted dependent verbs are interpreted: as expressing desirability, doubt, or indifference with regard to the dependent event's occurrence, or subjective reactions to it. This approach, then, relies heavily on contexts of "contrast," those in which either mood could occur in principle, but where the resulting message would be different in each case. It is contexts such as these that are most effective in bringing across the difference in meaning between the moods, through the effect this difference has on the possible interpretation of the utterance as a whole.

Dependent Uses of Non-Assertion

Students should now understand that the occurrence of dependent events is asserted only when it is clearly necessary to do so, because the utterance as a whole must be interpretable as involving a claim to this effect. They can next be taught that, in all other instances, the dependent event's occurrence is not asserted; thus, it is put in the subjunctive. In the following examples these other instances are broken down in a way I have found very useful pedagogically: It seems to make sense to students (and to me) as reflecting the meanings proposed. Thus, major kinds of interpetations that depend on non-assertion of the dependent event (hence, on its being put in the subjunctive) are those suggesting that, at the time of the main event, (1) the dependent event has not yet happened, or its occurrence is not yet known or experienced by the speaker; (2) its occurrence is denied, or presented as doubtful or questionable; (3) its occurrence/non-occurrence is regarded as immaterial; or (4) the main verb is expressing a comment on the dependent event, rather than a claim about its (actual) occurrence. The following are typical examples:

I. Dependent event is to be understood as NOT YET HAPPENED or NOT KNOWN/EXPERIENCED at the time of the main event.

Its occurrence is DESIRED or PERMITTED:

Quiero que ...	'I want X to ...'
Necesito que ...	'I need X to ...'
Aconsejo que ...	'I advise X to ...'
Conviene que ...	'It's desirable that ...'

Digo que ...	**'I say that X should ...'**
Admito que ...	**'I allow X to ...'**
Insisto que ...	**'I insist that X must ...'**

It is a RESULT SOUGHT:

para que   'in order that ...'
(vs. cause: *porque* + indicative)

It is otherwise placed in FUTURE (e.g., with **cuando** 'when' referring to future, vs. **cuando** referring to habitual situation: indicative).

It describes something NOT YET ENCOUNTERED (vs. describing something already known: indicative)

II. Dependent event's occurrence is DENIED or QUESTIONED:

Niego que ...	'I deny that ...'
Dudo que ...	'I doubt that ...'
Posiblemente ...	'Possibly ...'
Es posible que ...	'It's possible that ...'
No creo que ...	'I don't believe that'
[vs. *creo que* +indicative = 'I believe that ...']	
No es que ...	'It's not that ...'

III. Dependent event's occurrence is treated as IMMATERIAL:

Por mucho/más que ...	'However much X may ...'
Haga lo que haga (type)	'Whatever X may do ...'

| *Aunque ...* | 'Even if ...' |

[vs. ***aunque*** + indicative = 'Even though (it is the case that...')]

IV. Dependent event's occurrence is COMMENTED ON rather than claimed:

Me gusta que ...	'It pleases me that ...'
No me gusta que ...	'It displeases me that ...'
Me extraña/sorprende que ...	'It surprises me that ...'
Es extraño que ...	'It's strange that ...'
Es lástima que ...	'It's a shame that ...'
Siento que ...	'I regret that ...'

4 CONCLUSION

Inasmuch as the approach advocated in this paper is based on a view of language that is different from the traditional view, its categorization of the relevant data is correspondingly different from that usually found in textbooks. Traditional discussions of the use of the subjunctive mood (and of the indicative) are essentially *syntactic* in orientation. Consequently, the various uses typically are classified into different kinds of clauses, as determined by their syntactic function: nominal, adjectival, and adverbial. In contrast, the presentation suggested here is based on an analysis of the difference between the moods as meaningful. It is therefore intended specifically to reinforce the students' grasp of the difference in meaning between the moods, by showing how it affects the kinds of messages each mood will convey, in various kinds of contexts. Thus, for example, we point out that one of the circumstances that leads quite naturally to not asserting a dependent event (and so is a natural interpretation of non-assertion) is that the event *has not yet happened* or has not been encountered. On the other hand, it does not matter whether the event is being used descriptively (in an "adjectival" clause), as part of a "final" or other "adverbial clause" (e.g., following *cuando* when it refers to the future), or is simply presented as desirable (typical "nominal" or independent uses). In other words, the "syntactic function" of the clause, of which so much is made in traditional textbooks, turns out to be quite irrelevant to the use of one mood or the other (see also Bull, 1965:1995).[9]

As noted earlier, traditional discussions of mood usage generally concentrate on those contexts that tend to co-occur with (to "take") one mood or the other but not both. This is because, the choice of a particular mood is presented as an automatic function of the presence some other element, which is said to determine (to "govern") this choice. On the other hand, the present approach gives more emphasis to cases of contrast or near contrast (as suggested by the boxed examples on pages 14 and 16–18), since they illustrate most clearly the effect of the meaning difference between the moods. Once students grasp the implications of asserting vs. not asserting an event's occurrence, it is amazing to see how quickly they themselves come up with possible interpretations of contrastive pairs and even suggest examples of their own.

Of course, students still need ample opportunity and good illustrative contexts to experience and practice the principles they are learning; this would be true whatever approach is taken. The difference between the approach suggested here and the typical textbook presentation, however, is in the ultimate productive value of what the student practices. Traditionally, students must memorize examples of arbitrary "uses" whose relation to one another is not apparent. In this approach, students learn to recognize various manifestations of a single, constant meaning difference, so that practice in any one effectively contributes to a readier understanding of the others.

Notes

1. Among other advantages, hypothesizing a specific meaning for the conditional pre-empts the question of whether it should be regarded as indicative or as subjunctive. In this analysis, all such terms are simply regarded as labels or cover terms for particular verb *forms*, whose actual linguistic value is just the particular meaning posited for each.

2. Since the diagram deals only with differences in assertiveness and in time reference, it does not indicate the aspectual difference between the preterit and the imperfect. At least for teaching purposes, the two may be considered equally assertive in their basic reference to past time; it is apparently the non-perfectivity of the imperfect tense (Bull 1965:167) that makes it the only past form appropriate to suggest lesser likelihood in *non*-past time (Bull 1963:102).

   As for the forms in *-ra* and in *-se*, both termed past subjunctive in grammars of present-day Spanish, I do not consider them equivalent in assertiveness (as explained in Klein-Andreu 1986 and 1991). But since the *-se* form is not used in American Spanish, the difference between the two typically is not an issue in a U.S. classroom.

3. In some dialects this is increasingly the only use of the morphological future tense, as futurity in time tends to be expressed exclusively by periphrasis with *ir a* 'go to' + infinitive.

4. Just why this happens is another matter, which does not seem to have been satisfactorily resolved (see, e.g., Bello and Cuervo 1964: #692; James 1982; Bybee 1987; Fleischman 1989). In reference to past time, the same effect is achieved by use of a form that normally refers to time *anterior to the past* (a Pluperfect); e.g., *If I had known ...* (then). However, if the event is placed in past time, calling it 'less likely' implies that it is counterfactual, whereas if it is still non-past it does not. Compare *If the children had wanted to go to the movies* (then) *I would have taken them* with *If the children wanted to go to the movies* (now) *I would take them*.

5. The abnormality of the pattern used with *si* can be seen by comparing it with usage with other complementizers, such as *cuando* 'when' and *aunque* 'although', which do show the expected time-shift while maintaining the same position on the coordinate of assertiveness:
   > *Aunque **llueva** iremos de paseo.*
   > 'Even if it rains (likely), we'll go for a walk.'
   > *Aunque **lloviera** iríamos de paseo.*
   > 'Even if it rained (less likely), we'd go for a walk.'
   But:
   > *Si **llueve** (not **llueva**), nos quedaremos.*
   > 'If it rains (likely), we'll stay.'
   > *Si **lloviera** nos quedaríamos.*
   > 'If it rained (less likely), we would stay.'

6. *Si* can occur with other verb forms, but then it is not understood as expressing a condition ('if') but usually an option ('whether': *no se si tomaré café hoy* 'I don't know whether I'll take coffee today'). In cases such as *si haría esto por un desconocido, cuanto más por un amigo* 'if he would do this for a stranger, how much more so for a friend' (mentioned in Rojo

1986:184), the *si* clause presents not a hypothetical contingency but rather a situation that must be accepted as fact for the entire sentence to have the desired interpretation.

7. A theoretically reasonable possibility is that the present indicative, and perhaps also the imperfect, do not of themselves express assertiveness at all. That is, they are "unmarked" as to assertiveness, as opposed to the future and the conditional, which are assertive in meaning (for some experimental evidence in this direction, see Klein 1980). For teaching purposes, however, the seemingly simpler (more parallel) analysis presented here turns out to be quite satisfactory and therefore probably is preferable.

8. One of the apparent differences between Terrell and Hooper's proposal and my own (Klein 1975) is that they do not speculate as to the meaning of the imperative form, but rather accept its occurrence in familiar and positive commands (vs. the subjunctive in other commands and requests) as a "formal exception" (Terrell and Hooper 1974:486).

9. A more egregious example of the same thing is the case of so-called impersonal expressions, typically presented as contexts that "require" the subjunctive (e.g., *conviene que estudies, es extraño que te aburras*). It suffices to turn such expressions into the corresponding personal form (*me conviene que estudies, me extraña que te aburras*) to see that it is not "impersonality" that calls for the subjunctive complement but simply the fact that such complementizers either present events as desirable (thus, as events that have not yet happened) or comment on them.

References

Bello, A., and R. J. Cuervo. 1964. *Gramática de la lengua castellana.* 7th Edition. Buenos Aires: Sopena.

Bull, W. 1963. *Time, Tense, and the Verb.* Berkeley: University of California Press.

———. 1965. *Spanish for Teachers.* New York: Ronald.

Bybee, J. 1987. The Semantic Development of Past Tense Modals in English and Other Languages. Paper presented at 8th International Congress on Historical Linguistics.

Diver, W. 1964. The Modal System of the English Verb. *Word* 20: 322-352.

Fleischman, S. 1989. Temporal Distance: A Basic Linguistic Metaphor. *Studies in Language* 13,1: 1-50.

Hooper, J. B. 1975. On Assertive Predicates. In *Syntax and Semantics* 4. New York: Academic Press.

James, D. 1982. Past Tense and Hypothetical: A Cross-Linguistic Study. In *Studies in Language* VI,3: 375-403.

Jespersen, O. 1964. *Essentials of English Grammar.* University, Alabama: University of Alabama Press.

Klein, F. 1975. Pragmatic Constraints on Distribution: The Spanish Subjunctive. In *Papers from the Eleventh Regional Meeting of the Chicago Linguistics Society*, 353-365.

———. 1980. Experimental Verification of Semantic Hypotheses Applied to Mood in Spanish. *Georgetown University Papers on Languages and Linguistics* 17:15-34.

Klein-Andreu, F. 1986. Speaker-Based and Reference-Based Factors in Language: Non-Past Conditional Sentences in Spanish. In *Proceedings of the Linguistic Symposium on Romance Languages* XIV, edited by O. Jaeggli and C. Silva-Corvalán.

———. 1991. *Losing Ground: A Discourse-Pragmatic Solution to the History of -ra in Spanish.* In *Categories of the Verb in Romance: Discourse-Pragmatic Approaches*, edited by S. Fleischman and L. Waugh. London: Routledge.

Rojo, G. 1986. On the Evolution of Conditional Sentences in Old Spanish. In *Studies in Romance Linguistics*, edited by O. Jaeggli and C. Silva-Corvalán. Dordrecht: Foris.

Terrell, T., and J. B. Hooper. 1974. A Semantically-Based Analysis of Mood in Spanish. *Hispania* 57:484-494.

Waugh, L. 1975. A Semantic Analysis of the French Tense System. In *Orbis* 24,2.

A Note on the Spanish Personal 'a'

Ronald W. Langacker
University of California, San Diego

The Spanish personal *a*, which marks human, definite direct objects, is transparently related to the path preposition *a*, meaning 'to'. This paper explores the relationship between the personal and the prepositional *a* from the standpoint of *cognitive grammar*, which claims that all grammatical elements are meaningful. The meanings of the prepositional and the personal *a* are described in terms of the theory, as are the constructions in which they figure. Their similarities are revealed, and their differences are shown to accord with general tendencies observed in semantic shift and grammaticization.

The Spanish personal *a* marks direct objects that are both human and definite, as in Example 1:

1. *Está buscando a su hija.*
   'He is looking for his daughter.'

This object marker is transparently related—at least historically—to the preposition *a*, which in its basic locative sense describes a goal-directed spatial path, as in Example 2:

2. *Corrió a la escuela.*
   'He ran to the school.'

My objective here is to elucidate the nature of this relationship from the perspective of *cognitive grammar* (Langacker 1987a, 1990, 1991). A semantic and grammatical characterization of each element will reveal the similarities that motivate the object marker's evolution from the preposition, as well as the resultant differences. The crucial changes can be observed in many other instances of semantic shift and grammaticization.

Central to cognitive grammar is the claim that grammatical structure is *symbolic,* in the sense that only *symbolic units* (i.e., established form-meaning pairings) figure in its proper characterization. Grammatical elements are therefore claimed to be meaningful, distinguished only in degree from the (generally more contentful) form-meaning pairings that we single out as "lexical items." Grammar resides in patterns for combining simpler symbolic structures to derive progressively more complex ones. These patterns (the theory's equivalent of grammatical "rules") are nothing more than schematizations of complex expressions: abstract templates whose internal organization mirrors that of the expressions from which they are extracted and thus embodies whatever commonality they exhibit. From this perspective, consequently, an account of the personal *a* involves both a semantic characterization and a description of the structural frames in which it occurs. These structural templates are called *constructional schemas*.

This conception of grammar rests on a particular view of linguistic semantics. Meaning is specifically equated with conceptualization (i.e., any kind of mental experience). Moreover, linguistic meaning subsumes not only conceptual "content" but also the ways in which that content is "construed" for expressive purposes. Thus the same objective situation can be described by many expressions that contrast semantically because they embody different ways of conceptualizing it; even when such expressions happen to invoke precisely the same array of conceptual content, they differ in meaning by virtue of construing it in alternate ways. The sentences in Example 3, for instance, can be used with reference to exactly the same objective relationship, yet semantically they are all distinct:

3. a. The statue is on the pedestal.
    b. The statue is sitting on the pedestal.
    c. The statue is standing on the pedestal.
    d. The statue is resting on the pedestal.
    e. The pedestal is supporting the statue.
    f. The statue is being supported by the pedestal.

In deciding to use a particular lexico-grammatical element or construction, a speaker is necessarily making a semantic decision to construe the situation in a certain way representing just one of many possible options.

Of the numerous aspects of construal that must be recognized (Langacker 1988), only a few need concern us here. One aspect is the level of specificity—or conversely, the level of schematicity—at which a situation is characterized. Thus, Example 3a is schematic relative to Examples 3b and 3c, since the latter sentences make contrasting specifications concerning posture, whereas the former is silent on that topic. Lexical illustration is afforded by such hierarchies as *thing* → *creature* → *insect* → *bee* → *killer bee*, each item being schematic for the one that follows (which *elaborates*, or *instantiates*, its schematic specifications). The other relevant aspects of construal pertain to the degree of prominence accorded the various substructures within a conceptualization. For example, the verb *rest* in Example 3d renders the statue's absence of motion more salient than it is in Examples 3a through 3c, though they too imply that the situation is static. Likewise, the verb *support* in Examples 3e and 3f highlights the force dynamics inherent in the situation (Talmy 1988), which the other sentences leave implicit.

Of the several kinds of prominence that can be discerned and distinguished, two hold special significance for grammatical structure. The first I refer to as *profiling*: within the overall conception it evokes (termed its *base*), every expression profiles—

i.e., designates—some substructure. The word *knee,* for instance, evokes as its base the conception of a leg, and within that base it singles out as its profile (*designatum*) the major joint and the immediately surrounding area. *Intermission* evokes the conception of a scheduled event of some duration and profiles a span of time characterized by a temporary suspension of the activity in question. An expression profiles either a *thing* or a *relationship.* These terms are understood in an abstract, inclusive sense (Langacker 1987b). Thus things are not limited to physical objects but also include less tangible entities (like *intermission*) and those arising through conceptual reification (e.g., *procrastination*). By the same token, relationships do not invariably resemble those denoted by *on* or *support,* whose participants are salient, distinct, and explicit. Even "one-place predicates" like *round* and *blue* are considered relational: the relationship designated by *round* resides in the configurational aspects of its single participant, while the one profiled by *blue* holds between its explicitly coded participant and a certain region in color space.

A further type of prominence pertains specifically to the participants in a profiled relationship and is hypothesized to be a matter of figure/ground organization. In most relational expressions, one participant stands out as the figure within the scene. It is this participant—termed the *trajector*—that one is concerned with characterizing, assessing, or locating with respect to other entities. An additional salient participant (secondary figure) is referred to as a *landmark.* In Example 3a, for instance, *the statue* corresponds to *on*'s trajector, and *the pedestal* to its landmark. Observe that two expressions can evoke the same conceptual content, and profile the same relationship, and yet be semantically distinct because they confer the status of trajector (relational figure) on different participants. For example, *before* and *after* profile the same temporal relationship between two events; the difference in their meanings comes down to whether the earlier event is situated with reference to the later one, or conversely. The semantic contrast between an active and a passive is similarly analyzed in terms of figure/ground alignment. Thus in Example 3e *the pedestal* has trajector status at the clausal level of organization, whereas *the statue* enjoys this status in its passive counterpart, Example 3f.

An expression's grammatical class is determined by the nature of its profile. A simple noun (e.g., *statue*) profiles a thing, as do more elaborate nominal expressions such as a modified noun (e.g., *uninspiring statue*) or a full noun phrase (*that uninspiring statue on the pedestal*). Within the class of relational expressions, a fundamental distinction is drawn between those that profile a *process* and those that designate an *atemporal relation.* A processual expression focuses on a situation's evolution through time (regardless of whether it changes or remains constant); examples at different levels of organization are a verb stem (e.g., *be*), a finite verb (*is*), or a full finite clause (*The statue is on the pedestal*). Expressions that designate atemporal relations include such classes as prepositions, adjectives, and adverbs. An atemporal relation can profile either a single configuration or a series of configurations. For example, *on* designates a single locative relationship between its trajector and landmark, whereas *onto* profiles a series of relationships defining the trajector's spatial path vis-à-vis the landmark.

With this much background we can start to characterize both the prepositional and the personal *a* of Spanish, as well as the grammatical constructions in which they occur. The prepositional *a* profiles an atemporal relation. In its basic use, it designates a complex relationship comprising a series of configurations, as in Example 2. This is diagrammed at bottom left in Figure 1. Heavy lines indicate profiling. The trajector (tr) and landmark (lm) are represented by circles, the abbreviation adopted for things. The complex relationship in which they participate is represented by the heavy-line arrow. It consists of an ordered series of component relations, each of which locates the trajector at a certain position with respect to the landmark. Collectively these component relations define a directed spatial path, which takes the landmark as its goal.

a la escuela

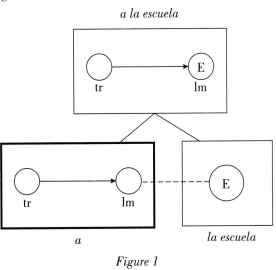

Figure 1

Figure 1 as a whole represents the grammatical construction wherein *a* combines with its object *la escuela* to form the prepositional phrase *a la escuela*. The two *component structures*, shown at the bottom, are *integrated* to form the *composite structure* shown at the top. As noted, the preposition *a* designates a relationship, whose trajector and landmark are characterized only schematically, as things. The other component structure, *la escuela*, profiles a thing (hence the heavy-line circle); its other semantic specifications are not essential here and are simply abbreviated "E." Integration is effected by *correspondences*, indicated by dotted lines. The correspondence line in Figure 1 equates the landmark of *a* with the thing profiled by *la escuela*; it is by virtue of this correspondence that *la escuela* has the status of a prepositional object. The composite structure is obtained by superimposing the specifications of corresponding entities and adopting the profiling of one component structure. Due to the correspondence, consequently, the relational landmark has all the specifications of *la escuela* at the composite-structure level. In this prepositional-object construction, moreover, it is the preposition which functions as the *head*, in the sense that its profile is the one that prevails at the higher level of organization; the box enclosing it is drawn with heavy lines to show this. The result is that the composite structure *a la escuela* has the same relational profile as *a:* it situates its schematic trajector successively at all points along a spatial path directed at its landmark, characterized as a particular school.

The next step is to consider the integration of the prepositional phrase with a verb, such as *corres* in Example 2. The composite structure of the prepositional phrase serves as one component structure at this higher level of organization; hence the upper structure in Figure 1 is identical to the one shown at the lower right in Figure 2. The other component structure is the verb stem (*r* is parenthesized to indicate that the stem in particular—not the more complex infinitive—is the relevant form). *Corres* is a single-participant verb whose trajector exerts volitional control and physical effort to propel itself along a spatial path. The double arrow represents the force thus exerted (both volitional and physical), and the single arrow, the resultant motion. The single arrow contains an ellipsis, whose import is that the trajector's spatial path is specified only schematically by the verb itself. The function of the prepositional phrase is to elaborate these schematic specifications and characterize the path in more precise detail. Two correspondences effect the integration: the verb's trajector is equated with that of the prepositional phrase; and the schematic path evoked by the verb is identified with the specific, goal-directed path of *a la escuela*. The verb is the head, so the composite expression *corre(r) a la escuela* designates an act of running (not a spatial path per se). The verb's trajector/landmark alignment also prevails at the composite-structure level. Observe that *la escuela* has landmark status only within the prepositional phrase, not within the verb, which determines the composite structure's organization. Its role as an object (secondary relational figure) therefore obtains only at the phrasal (not the clausal) level.

corre(r) a la escuela

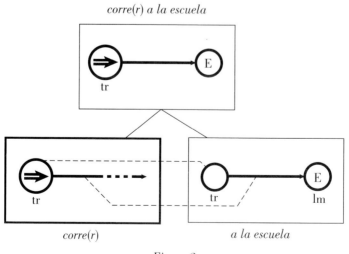

Figure 2

It is important to note that the prepositional phrase corresponds to, and elaborates, only a portion of the overall conception evoked by the verb. Thus *a la escuela* elucidates the spatial path traversed by the verb's trajector, but does not itself invoke or describe the exertions responsible for propelling it along that path. The point is more obvious in Example 4, where the agent and mover are distinct individuals:

   4. *José envió un paquete a la escuela.*
       'José sent a package to the school.'

That portion of *envia(r) un paquete* which *a la escuela* resumes and elaborates is clearly limited to the package and its movement, excluding the actions of the subject (which instantiates the verb's trajector). This construction is diagrammed in Figure 3, where "P" represents the semantic specifications of *un paquete*. Observe that in this case it is the landmark of the verb-object combination that moves and hence corresponds to the trajector of the prepositional phrase. (Recall that the terms trajector and landmark pertain to prominence—primary versus secondary relational figure—so that either one can in principle be the mover.) Once more, the profiling and figure/ground organization of the verbal component prevail at the composite-structure level.

envia(r) un paquete a la escuela

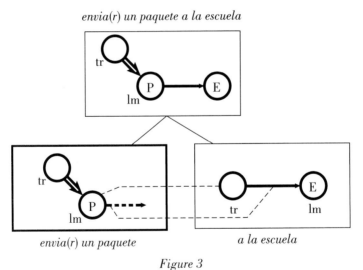

envia(r) un paquete   *a la escuela*

Figure 3

We see, then, that the entity which moves along the spatial path specified by the prepositional phrase complement can be either the verb's trajector (instantiated by the clausal subject) or its landmark (instantiated by the direct object). In other examples the entity that traverses this path cannot be identified with any explicitly coded clausal participant:

   5. *Habló a su hija.*
       'He spoke to his daughter.'
   6. *Tocó a la puerta.*
       'He knocked on the door.'

In Example 5 the moving entity can probably be equated with the words spoken or the information they "contain" (in accordance with the *conduit metaphor* described in Reddy 1979). And if *a* is construed in Example 6 as describing a path (as opposed to a simple location), the entity traversing this path might well be the force transmitted to the door. I will not insist on any particular analysis, since the point is rather that the mover—the trajector of the prepositional phrase—is not invariably discrete, determinate, or singled out for individual mention. In fact, the mover in such examples is hard to distinguish from the verbal action itself (just as the object is hard to distinguish from the verbal action in *cognate object* expressions like *scream a blood-curdling scream* or *sleep a peaceful sleep*); perhaps we ought not try to do so. In this regard examples like 5 and 6 can be seen as intermediate between the expressions diagrammed in Figures 2 and 3 and those involving the personal *a*. The object-marking *a* represents an extreme case in which the goal-directed path is specifically equated with the verbal action, and the goal with the verb's direct object.

What, then, can we posit as the meaning of the personal *a?* Recall that every expression derives its semantic value by invoking some conceptualization as its base and selecting some facet of that base as its profile. The base and profile of the personal *a* reflect its function of marking a clausal direct object. Its base is the schematic conception of a transitive process (since a transitive clause designates such a process). Within that base, *a* profiles the processual landmark (i.e., the participant corresponding to the clausal object), which it characterizes (roughly) as being both human and definite.

A meaning of this sort is straightforwardly describable in the context of cognitive grammar and is fully consistent with the kinds of meanings ascribed to other grammatical elements. Many expressions invoke the conception of a process as their base. For example, the stative-adjectival participle *broken* takes as its base the process *break* and profiles its final, resultant state. Often the base process is highly schematic, being characterized only as a process (or a certain type of process) without any specific detail. A case in point is the stative-adjectival participial morpheme shared (despite its morphological variability) by expressions like *broken, cracked, split, frozen, tired,* and *worn out*. While the participial morpheme invokes as its base the conception of a change-of-state process (and profiles the resultant state), it does not itself describe that process with any degree of specificity. That is the function of the verb stem: the stem (e.g., *break*) elaborates the schematic process evoked by the participial morpheme, which imposes its own (atemporal) profile on the content thus supplied. Further illustration is provided by a nominalizing morpheme such as *-er*, as in *complainer, hiker, painter, designer,* etc. Once more the base comprises a schematic process rendered specific by the verb stem, but in this case the profile is a participant in that process, namely its trajector. Thus, with respect to the specific process supplied by the verb stem, the semantic effect of *-er* is to shift the profile to a processual participant, and since an expression's profile determines its grammatical class, the composite expression (e.g., *complainer*) is categorized as a noun.

The meaning I attribute to the personal *a* represents a variation on this common theme. As shown at the lower left in Figure 4, its base is a schematic transitive process: one involving an asymmetrical relationship between a trajector and a salient nominal landmark (see Rice 1987; Langacker 1990: Ch. 9; Langacker 1991: Part II). The direction of the arrow reflects this asymmetry. Here the arrow does not necessarily indicate a spatial path (as with the prepositional *a*): prototypically the transitive asymmetry resides in the transfer of energy (exertion of force) from the trajector to the landmark (see Figure 3); it may also involve abstract analogs of energy transmission, a perceptual path (as in Example 1), or even—at the extreme—the subjective asymmetry implied by the very act of choosing one participant as the primary figure (trajector) and according the other only a secondary degree of prominence. Within this schematic base, the personal *a* profiles the landmark, the salient participant lying "downstream" in the flow of energy or its abstract analog. It is therefore nominal in character, as befits a case marker, whereas the prepositional *a* is relational. Finally, the personal *a* identifies the profiled entity as being both human and definite. In the diagram, "h/d" represents these specifications.

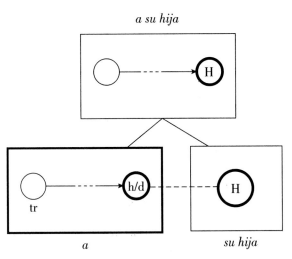

Figure 4

The personal *a* is thus analyzed as a kind of derivational element that combines with a full noun phrase to derive a higher-order nominal expression that portrays the designated thing as having a certain role in a schematically characterized process. Its combination with a noun phrase is sketched in Figure 4, which ought by now to be self-explanatory. Their integration hinges on a correspondence between the schematic thing profiled by *a* and the more elaborately specified thing profiled by the noun phrase, *su hija* in the case of Example 1. The composite structure *a su hija* is obtained by superimposing the specifications of these correspondents. Observe that the description 'human/definite' is subsumed by the more precise characterization 'his daughter' (abbreviated "H"), so it is not separately represented at the composite-structure level. However, *a* does make a semantic contribution: it portrays the referent of the noun phrase against the backdrop of a transitive process in which it functions as the "downstream" participant.

The last step to consider is the integration of the case-marked nominal with a verb. Using *a su hija* with the verb *busca(r)*, this construction is diagrammed in Figure 5, where the dashed arrow represents the process of searching and, more specifically, the perceptual path reaching the landmark which the trajector hopes to establish. As in any direct-object construction, the verb's landmark is put in correspondence with the profile of its noun-phrase complement. The special feature of this particular direct-object construction is that the complement, *a su hija,* already bears a marking signaling its object role in a transitive process. There are consequently two elaborative relationships: *a su hija* of course characterizes in finer detail the landmark that is only schematic within *buscar;* and at the same time, *buscar* renders specific the schematic process evoked by *a su hija.* This latter relationship depends on correspondences between the trajectors of the specific process and the schematic one, and between the two processes overall.

busca(r) a su hija

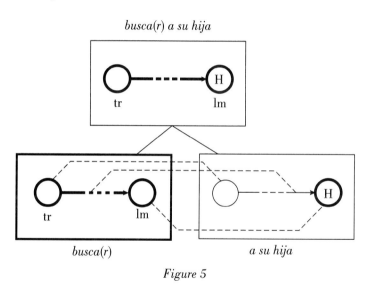

busca(r)   *a su hija*

Figure 5

Let us now compare the prepositional *a,* diagrammed in Figure 1, with the personal *a,* diagrammed in Figure 4. The differences are quite apparent: the former profiles a relation, the latter a thing; only the latter incorporates the specification 'human/definite'; and while arrows are used in each diagram, they have distinct values, representing the trajector's motion through space in the preposition and the asymmetry of a transitive process in the case marker. I will have nothing to say about the 'human/definite' features (although they may indicate that the personal *a* developed via the indirect object use of *a,* as in Example 5). The contrast in profiling is less substantial than it might appear, for it involves not conceptual content per se, but only the relative prominence accorded various substructures. It is in fact quite common for an expression to have basic and extended senses that differ only in the profiles they impose on essentially the same conceptual content. For example, *eye* can designate either the eyeball in particular or else the entire eye region (including lid, lash, and brow). As shown in Example 7, *to* can profile either the complex relation describing a full spatial path, or a simple relation comprising only the final configuration implied by such a path:

  7. a. The prisoner ran to the fence.
     b. The prisoner is already to the fence.

It is also not unusual for the profile to be shifted from a relationship overall to one of its participants. An example is *kill* or *catch* used as a noun designating the landmark of the verbal process (e.g., *They confiscated his catch*).

What about the difference between a spatial path and a transitive process? Although the arrows have distinct values in Figures 1 and 4, I suggest that this common notation for the essential aspects of the prepositional and the personal *a* reflects the same perceived similarity that presumably motivated the latter's evolution from the former. A directed spatial path is part of *source-path-goal*, one of the *image schemas* posited by Johnson (1987) and Lakoff (1987): fundamental concepts, grounded in everyday bodily experience, that provide a basis for metaphorically structuring many other cognitive domains. Among the domains structured by the *source-path-goal* image schema is the notion of transitivity. We certainly find it natural to conceive of prototypical transitive events (involving energetic interaction) in terms of the agent transmitting energy to the patient, either directly or via a path including an instrument and possibly other intermediaries. In the mental sphere, prototypical transitive verbs are probably to be identified with those describing the perception of external objects, particularly visual perception, which we tend to conceptualize in terms of the viewer's gaze following a perceptual path whose goal is the object perceived. This image-schematic commonality (further explored in part II of Langacker 1991) renders quite natural the semantic evolution of a *path-goal* preposition to become the marker for transitive objects.

Concomitant with this semantic shift is a change in grammatical constructions, best seen by comparing Figures 3 and 5. As already noted, a prepositional phrase like *a la escuela* elaborates only part of the scene evoked by the verb or verb-object combination (that pertaining to the mover and its spatial path), and it serves to introduce a participant that would not otherwise be specifically or saliently included in that scene. On the other hand, we see in Figure 5 that the relationship evoked by the case-marked direct object overlaps fully with the process designated by the transitive verb; the two component structures refer to the same process, differing only in which facets of it they profile and which facets they characterize schematically. An object phrase like *a su hija* therefore does not introduce a new participant but merely resumes, and specifies in much finer detail, the downstream participant already implied by the verb. In this way the two component structures display a more intimate semantic association than do a verb and its prepositional-phrase complement.

I conclude by noting that conceptual overlap of this sort tends to be characteristic of highly grammaticized elements. For instance, both the nominalizing suffix *-er* (as in *complainer*) and the stative-adjectival participial morpheme (as in *broken*) evoke as their base a schematic process which coincides exactly with the one profiled by the verb stem they combine with; the grammatical element is meaningful by virtue of the profiling it imposes on this base, not because it provides any additional conceptual content. Similarly, I analyze the auxiliary verb *do* (as in *She DID arrive*) as profiling a fully schematic process equated with the one designated by the accompanying content verb; it appears to be meaningless only because its meaning is fully subsumed by that verb. One last example is the evolution of a motion or posture verb into a progressive auxiliary, e.g., the interpretation of *Anda cantando* to mean not 'He goes along singing' but simply 'He is singing' (see Norwood 1981; Langacker 1990: Ch. 8). On the non-auxiliary interpretation, *andar* profiles spatial motion that occurs in addition to the activity described by the participle, with which it temporally coincides and for which it provides a kind of processual setting. *Andar* approaches the status of a progressive auxiliary to the extent that this conception of spatial movement fades from the scene evoked, so that only the secondary process coded by the participle is left onstage. Once this evolution has run its course, the resulting auxiliary verb resembles *do* or *be*, in that the schematic process it designates is equated with the one profiled by the verbal or participial complement, which fully subsumes it.

References

Johnson, Mark. 1987. *The Body in the Mind: The Bodily Basis of Meaning, Imagination, and Reason.* Chicago: University of Chicago Press.

Lakoff, George. 1987. *Women, Fire, and Dangerous Things: What Categories Reveal About the Mind.* Chicago: University of Chicago Press.

Langacker, Ronald W. 1987a. *Foundations of Cognitive Grammar.* Vol. 1, *Theoretical Prerequisites.* Stanford: Stanford University Press.

———. 1987b. Nouns and Verbs. *Language* 63:53-94.

———. 1988. A View of Linguistic Semantics. In *Topics in Cognitive Linguistics,* ed. by Brygida Rudzka-Ostyn, 49-90. Amsterdam: John Benjamins.

———. 1990. *Concept, Image, and Symbol: The Cognitive Basis of Grammar.* Berlin: Mouton de Gruyter.

———. 1991. *Foundations of Cognitive Grammar.* Vol. 2, *Descriptive Application.* Stanford: Stanford University Press.

Norwood, Susan. 1981. Progressives in Yuman and Romance. Ph.D. diss., University of California, San Diego.

Reddy, Michael J. 1979. The Conduit Metaphor—A Case of Frame Conflict in Our Language About Language. In *Metaphor and Thought,* ed. by Andrew Ortony, 284-324. Cambridge: Cambridge University Press.

Rice, Sally. 1987. Towards a Cognitive Model of Transitivity. Ph.D. diss., University of California, San Diego.

Talmy, Leonard. 1988. Force Dynamics in Language and Cognition. *Cognitive Science* 12:49-100.

Spanish Tense and Aspect from a Typological Perspective

Joan L. Bybee
University of New Mexico

Based on cross-linguistic data discussed by Bybee (1985) and Dahl (1985), this paper presents a sketch of the tense and aspect markers of Spanish as they compare to those most commonly found in the languages of the world. Spanish has a very common type of tripartite system in which aspect is superordinate to tense, and past and present are distinguished only in the imperfective aspect. The special uses of preterite with stative predicates, especially the inchoative use, are paralleled in many other languages; in fact, some languages have taken the reinterpretation of their perfectives with statives much further than Spanish has. The other topic treated is the competition between the older synthetic future and the newer *ir a* future, two forms whose behavior can be predicted from a general theory of grammaticization (which studies the development of grammatical morphemes over time) and from the study of the direction which the development of future morphemes takes in other languages.

Some recent studies of tense and aspect have taken a cross-linguistic perspective and sought to compare the content and form of expression of these grammatical categories in unrelated languages (Comrie 1976; Comrie 1985; Bybee 1985; Dahl 1985; Bybee and Dahl 1989). Bybee (1985) and Dahl (1985) assume that the relevant level for comparison across languages is the semantic category itself—that is, the sense expressed by a marker of present, past, perfective, or imperfective—rather than some more abstract componential features which express the contrasts among categories within a specific language system. In fact, cross-linguistic comparison is very difficult, if not impossible, on the level of language-specific componential features. Rather, the search for similarities and differences among languages is more profitably conducted by considering the sense of a category as an atomic unit and studying its content through its distribution in various contexts.

Dahl (1985) reports on just such a study, an analysis of over 200 questionnaire sentences that were translated into sixty-four languages from around the world. By analyzing the distribution of grammatical markers in these sentences, he was able to find the similarities and differences among the uses and, thus, the meanings of these markers in the languages of his sample. Through his analysis he was able to formulate general definitions for certain commonly occurring cross-linguistic types (*gramtypes*): perfective, imperfective, past, present (default), future, anterior (perfect), and progressive. (The definitions will be presented below.) After comparing the tense and aspect meanings expressed in the languages of his sample, he hypothesized a most typical, or basic, inflectional tense/aspect system. I hope to show that the Spanish system fits this model precisely.

In addition, I compare Spanish with the languages included in two studies I have conducted: one, reported in Bybee 1985, studied the inflectional categories for verbs in a fifty-language sample, and the other, the Gramcats Project, studied all grammatical morphology associated with verbs (including auxiliaries, particles, and clitics) in a seventy-six–language sample (Bybee, Perkins, and Pagliuca 1994). In both studies, access to the languages was through reference grammars. Although I have used a different method than Dahl did, our results are very similar; that is, our independent analyses agree on the identity and definition of the most common tense and aspect categories across languages.

The two studies I have conducted also take a diachronic perspective on tense and aspect. In particular, my colleagues and I have been interested in the cross-linguistic similarities in the diachronic development of grammatical categories from lexical words or phrases. For instance, we have found in the study of morphemes expressing the notion of future in many different languages that there are three primary diachronic sources for future morphemes—verbs meaning 'want' or 'desire', verbs or phrases meaning 'be going to', and verbs or phrases signaling obligation, necessity, or predestination (Bybee and Pagliuca 1987). Further, we have hypothesized semantic paths of development for future morphemes which appear to be similar across languages (Bybee, Pagliuca, and Perkins 1991).

In this article I apply this cross-linguistic and diachronic perspective to certain facts about the inflectional tense and aspect system of Modern Spanish. Before proceeding to that discussion, however, I offer here a brief statement of the definitions of the tense and aspect categories to be discussed. For the most part, these definitions are standard in the recent literature, derived partly from Comrie's 1976 and 1985 works (and the literature upon which these are based) and partly from Dahl (1985). In the following definitions the word *situation* refers to the state, activity, or event described in the proposition of the clause in question.

> *Present:* The situation is in effect at the moment of speech.
>
> *Past:* The situation occurred before the moment of speech.
>
> *Future:* The situation will (or is predicted to) occur after the moment of speech.
>
> *Anterior:* The situation occurred before the moment of speech, but it is relevant at the moment of speech.
>
> *Perfective:* The situation is viewed as a bounded whole.
>
> *Imperfective:* The situation is not viewed as bounded but is rather viewed from an internal perspective, as continuously ongoing or habitually repeated.

My discussion is divided into two main parts. In the first I examine the interaction of the present and past with the perfective and imperfective, and the interaction of the perfective with stative predicates. In the second I discuss the relation of the periphrastic to the synthetic future.

INFLECTIONAL ASPECT

1. The Tripartite Tense/Aspect System

One of the major points made by Dahl (1985) is that the most common basic tense/aspect system in his sample is a tripartite system which contrasts a present, a past imperfective, and a perfective. Such a system is distinct from the derivational system found in Slavic languages, in which perfective and imperfective, being derivational categories, cross-classify with present and past tense completely, and a present perfective is possible, although with a future interpretation. In the tripartite system, as Dahl points out, the perfective is restricted to past time reference, and naturally so, because a situation that is being viewed as bounded cannot also be in effect at the moment of speech. There is a certain inherent asymmetry in such a system, since present and past tense are distinguished only in the imperfective aspect. Of course, this tripartite system is precisely the one found in Spanish (and in other Romance languages), inherited with only minor changes from Latin. The Spanish system corresponds to this cross-linguistic type in the following way:[1]

universal type:	present	past imperfective	perfective
Spanish:	Present	Imperfect	Preterite

The Gramcats database on seventy-six languages (chosen to be maximally unrelated genetically) does not show this tripartite system to be more common than some other possibilities, but this system is certainly one of the major types of languages with inflectional aspect. The Gramcats sample contains only one Italic language, Classical Latin, with the other instances of the tripartite system found in Africa (Kanakuru), Australia (Alawa, Alyawarra, and Maung), the Caucasus (Abkhaz), and Oceania (Tahitian). We can confidently state that it is widespread geographically.

2. The Hierarchical Organization of Tense and Aspect

It is often said of Spanish and other Romance languages that they distinguish aspect only in the past tense. However, Dahl (1985) argues that aspect is not subordinate to tense as this statement implies, but is superordinate, adding that the asymmetry should be phrased as the perfective being restricted to past tense. Thus the hierarchical organization of the tripartite system according to Dahl can be represented by the following diagram:

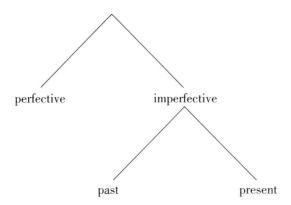

Figure 1. The hierarchical relationship between tense and aspect in Spanish

There are two arguments for the hierarchical arrangement in Figure 1. First, it is not so much that aspect is not distinguished in the present (that is, aspect is not neutralized in the present); it is rather that the present is inherently imperfective. The uses to which a present tense can be put are illustrated by the following three examples: progressive—speaking of situations in progress, as in (1); habitual or generic—speaking of situations that are characteristic of an extended time that includes the present, as in (2); and present stative—an ongoing situation described by a stative predicate, as in (3). All of these uses are imperfective because all of them have their past counterpart in the past imperfective (the imperfect in languages such as Spanish).

(1) *El niño llora.*   'The child is crying.'
(2) *Estudio geografía.*   'I study geography.'
(3) *Juan sabe los nombres.*   'John knows the names.'

The major perfective use of the Present, the so-called historical present in narratives, is not a present tense at all (Silva-Corvalán 1983).

The second argument is a formal one. As Dahl points out for other Indo-European languages, there is no common marker for past tense, but there can often be a great formal similarity between the present and the past imperfective, typically because they are formed from the same stem. I would add that this is not a phenomenon restricted to Indo-European languages: other languages around the world, such as Burushaski and Classical Nahuatl, have stem changes corresponding to perfective versus imperfective stems, so that the present and the past imperfective use the same stem.

This situation is also present in Spanish where there is no single segmental marker of past tense and where the stem differences help to set apart the Preterite from the Present and Imperfect. In fact, the most radical stem changes found anywhere in the Spanish conjugational system are precisely those that correlate with this major aspectual distinction. As is typical in any language, the particular lexical items that manifest these stem changes are among the most common verbs in the language.

(6)

Infinitive	1s Preterite	
andar	*anduve*	'walk'
caber	*cupe*	'fit'
conducir	*conduje*	'conduct'
dar	*di*	'give'
decir	*dije*	'say', 'tell'
estar	*estuve*	'be'
haber	*hube*	'have'
hacer	*hice*	'make', 'do'
ir	*fui*	'go'
poder	*pude*	'be able'
poner	*puse*	'put', 'place'
querer	*quise*	'want'
saber	*supe*	'know'
ser	*fui*	'be'
tener	*tuve*	'have'
traer	*traje*	'bring'
venir	*vine*	'come'
ver	*vi*	'see'

The Imperfect and the Present forms have the same stem as the infinitive for all verbs except the two suppletive verbs, *ir* 'go' and *ser* 'be', whose Present forms are different. Thus for all but two Spanish verbs, the Present and Imperfect have the same stem, while for a significant handful (i.e., those in Example 4 above) the Preterite has a different stem. It is worth noting that the stem differences in the Preterite arose in a variety of ways and at different times in the history of these forms, and yet they demarcate the aspectual line very consistently.

One way in which Spanish might be said to differ from the more typical tripartite system is that it does have a suprasegmental marker of past tense that is consistent across the Preterite and Imperfect. As pointed out by Hooper (1976) and by Hooper and Terrell (1976), stress on the vowel immediately following the stem of the verb is a consistent indicator of past tense in both aspects and both moods.

(5)

Preterite 3s	*cantó*	cf. Present Indicative	*cánta*
Imperfect 3s	*cantába*	Present Subjunctive	*cánte*
Past Subjunctive 3s	*cantára*	Future	*cantaré*

3. The Semantic Relevance of Tense and Aspect

The superordinate position of aspect over tense indicated in Figure 1 may be predicted from the greater semantic relevance of aspect to the verb as compared to tense. In a previous work I defined *relevance* as the extent to which the semantic content of the grammatical marker affects the meaning of the lexical stem (Bybee 1985). Aspect has greater relevance to the verb than tense because aspect affects the way the internal temporal contours of the situation are viewed, while tense takes the situation as a whole and places it in relative time without changing the perspective on the nature of the event described by the verb.

The significance of aspectual meaning should in principle always be examined in the context of the larger discourse. In narrative, as Hopper (1982) has argued, the perfective is used to report discrete events in the main story line, while the imperfective is used to give background information. Silva-Corvalán (1983) has demonstrated the validity of this distributional statement for Spanish narratives as well. The discourse functions of backgrounding and foregrounding have consequences for the semantic interpretation of the verb and its arguments in some cases, so that the choice of aspect affects the meaning of the verb stem itself. The following sentences, given out of context, show the types of implications that can be drawn from perfective versus imperfective sentences.

(6) *Anoche Juan leyó un libro.*   'Last night John read (PRET) a book.'
(7) *Anoche Juan leía un libro.*   'Last night John was reading (IMPF) a book.'

Since (6), using the perfective, would occur in the narrative portions of a discourse, telling "what happened," the implication is that Juan read a whole book last night. In contrast (7), using the imperfective, would occur in the backgrounded or orientation part of the discourse, so the implication is that Juan was reading a book when something else happened, and he may not necessarily have finished reading it.

Some consequences of the greater semantic relevance of aspect to the verb in various unrelated languages are the following: aspectual distinctions can be derivational but tense cannot be; aspect markers usually occur closer to the verb stem than tense markers when the two are separable; and aspect markers tend to have a greater morphophonemic effect on the stem than tense markers (Bybee 1985). The latter criterion applies to Spanish, as we have seen in (4). A further consequence is that even inflectional aspect can sometimes have a rather dramatic semantic effect on the verb's meaning, as evidenced in Spanish by the interaction of perfective meaning with stative predicates, a phenomenon I discuss in the next section.

4. The Meaning of the Preterite with Stative Predicates

An oft-noted peculiarity of the Spanish Preterite is that with stative predicates it can take on a variety of interpretations, including what appear to be opposite poles—a past terminative sense and a past inchoative sense (Bolinger 1963; Guitart 1978). The latter seems most surprising in light of the general meaning of Preterite. However, Spanish is not alone in allowing an inchoative interpretation of a perfective with statives; indeed, some languages have gone much further than Spanish in conventionalizing such interpretations of perfectives and even anteriors.

Since the perfective represents a situation as a bounded entity and is typically used to narrate past discrete events, the application of perfective meaning to stative predicates is intrinsically problematic. Different languages have arrived at different solutions to the equation *perfective + stative = ?*. In some languages, perfective aspect simply does not apply to stative predicates (for instance, in Tojolabal [Mayan] and Chepang [Tibeto-Burman]). In other languages, the perfective applied to stative predicates gives a distinct inchoative (or inceptive) meaning (as in Spanish), while in still others the sense of the perfective with stative predicates is, surprisingly enough, one of present state. Let us examine the way the last two cases arise.

First, it is necessary to know something about the way in which inflectional perfectives develop diachronically. From languages all around the world we have evidence that perfectives arise from *anteriors* (also known as *perfects*), which are markers indicating a past event with relevance for the present moment. Anteriors themselves are formed from various source constructions, the most common of which are constructions using a verb meaning 'finish' (such as *acabar de*) or a main verb meaning 'come from' (such as French *venir de*) as well as constructions using stative auxiliaries, such as *ser* or *haber*, plus a past participle of the main verb.

Anteriors from verbs meaning 'finish' may be found in Bongu (northeast New Guinea), Lao (Kam-Tai), and Temne (Niger-Congo). An anterior from 'finish' which has developed into a perfective is found in Bantu languages such as Mwera. Anteriors from verbs meaning 'have' or 'be' plus a past participle are familiar from modern European languages, such as English and Spanish, but also occur in Buriat (Altaic) and Tigre (Semitic). Anteriors from this source have become perfectives in French, northern Italian, and Rumanian, and are in the process of becoming perfectives or simple pasts in German and Dutch.

Further evidence that anteriors become perfectives is found in the diachronic development of Spanish from Latin, since the Latin Perfect was used both for perfective and for anterior, but the Modern Spanish descendent of the Latin Perfect, the Preterite, is a perfective and no longer has anterior functions in most dialects.

In our data on the seventy-six languages of the Gramcats Project, we have found several cases where a marker of anterior or perfective, when combined with a stative predicate gives an inchoative reading, or signals 'entering into a state'. In Engenni and Island Carib, for instance, the anterior can give an inchoative reading with stative predicates.

Engenni (Kwa, Niger-Congo)
Inchoative
(8)   *o menimeni ni*
      it be-sweet ANT
      'It has become sweet.'
(9)   *adhe bhi ni o*
      day be-black ANT in-fact
      'It has got dark, you know.'
Anterior
(10)   *o ta na te ni akie*
       he go to reach ANT town
       'He had reached the town.'

(Thomas 1978)

Island Carib
   Inchoative (the suffix *ha* is the anterior marker)
   (11)   *saditina*   'I'm ill.'
            sadihadina   'I've become ill.'
            maraotu   'She is childless.'
            maraoharu   'She has become childless.'
   Anterior
   (12)   *colóhadina*   'I have arrived.'

(Taylor 1956: 20,24)

Perfectives can also give inceptive readings with stative predicates in Trukese (Oceanic):

   Inchoative
   (13)   *aa semmwen atewe*
            3s-perf sick fellow
            'That fellow has become sick.'

(Goodenough and Sugita 1980:xlix)

   Perfective
   (14)   *ja a tëëti nee qqyn*
            3s perf descend to ground
            'She descended to the ground.'

(Dyen 1965:27)

This situation arises in these cases and in Spanish in much the same way, I suspect. Use of the anterior treats the situation described by the verb as a past event with current relevance; use of the perfective treats the situation as a past discrete event or, as Bolinger puts it (1963:133), describes "a segment of anteriority." In both cases the situation has to be viewed as an event, that is, as something that happened. Thus with verbs such as *saber, conocer,* and *tener,* a possible inference is that the subject entered into the state.

   (15)   *Supe lo sucedido.*
            'I learned (came to know) what happened.' (Guitart 1978)
            Conocí a su hermano.
            'I met his brother.'
            Tuvimos miedo y nos echamos a correr.
            'We got scared and started to run.'

(Ricardo Maldonado, personal communication)

As Bolinger (1963) argues, in Spanish the inchoative reading of Preterite with stative verbs is the result of inference; it is not part of the inherent meaning of Preterite. Bolinger, as well as Terrell and Salgués (1979) and Guitart (1978), point out that the Preterite with stative predicates can signal the end of a state rather than the beginning, depending upon the verb and the discourse context. The thorough discussion by Guitart (1978) of the different interpretations of the Preterite with different classes of stative predicates, demonstrates that there is not one conventionalized implication for all Preterites with statives, but rather the interpretation varies by verb and by context. In the following example it is the termination of the state that is of interest, because the sentence continues by telling us what happened next (Terrell and Salgués 1979:163):

(16) *Estuvimos allí tres horas y después fuimos al cine.*
      'We were there three hours and then we went to the movies.'

Similarly, Bolinger (1963:131) argues that in the following example the first clause with a Preterite stative predicate is limited at its endpoint, not at its beginning:

(17) *Primero hizo sol y luego llovió.*
      'First it was sunny and then it rained.'

Gili y Gaya (1961:158) offers the following as a non-inchoative example of Preterite with a stative predicate:

(18) *Supe latín.*
      'I knew Latin (but I no longer know it).'

One process of change that has been discussed recently in the literature on grammaticization is the *conventionalization of implicature*, that is, the process by which what was originally a frequently available inference becomes part of the meaning of a grammatical form (Dahl 1985; Bybee 1988; Faltz 1989; Traugott and König 1991). While this apparently has not occurred in Spanish with the inchoative inference (which is available at times for stative predicates in the Preterite), it is certainly a possible development and one that has occurred in some languages. For instance, the Island Carib examples above are a case in point, especially in view of the developments that have taken place in the Island Carib Perfective. The Island Carib Perfective seems to have gone through a stage in which this aspect with stative predicates indicated inception, and this inference has become part of the meaning of the Perfective. A further inference is made from this past inchoative meaning, namely, that the subject is still in the state attained. Thus the Perfective of the stative predicates 'be hungry' and 'be red' in Island Carib have the following meanings:

(19) *lamaali*   'he is hungry'
      funaali   'it has turned red' or 'it is ripe'
                             cf. *funatu* 'it is red'

This situation, in which the Perfective with a stative predicate actually indicates present state, is not uncommon among the languages of the world. It occurs in Slave (Athapaskan), Kanuri (Nilo-Saharan), Mwera (Bantu), Tahitian (Polynesian), and Nakanai (northeast New Guinea), to name a few examples from the random sample of Gramcats languages. Better known examples in Indo-European are the Perfect forms of the verb meaning 'to know', which have a present-tense interpretation in the Greek οιδα, Sanskrit *véda*, and Gothic *wait* (Buck 1933:239), and the Germanic Preterite-Present verbs, such as Old English *witan* 'to know', *agan* 'to own', *cunnan* 'to know', *magan* 'to be able', *sculan* 'to be obliged', and so on.

It would appear, then, that the Spanish Preterite is not unusual for a perfective, and what appears to be a rather special set of uses of the Preterite is actually paralleled elsewhere in the world. However, Spanish has not gone as far as some languages in the incorporation of the inferential meanings into the basic meaning of the grammatical category.

THE TWO FUTURES OF SPANISH

The history of the Spanish synthetic future is well known, for it often serves as a text-book example of the process of grammaticization: lexical morphemes or phrases develop into grammatical morphemes and, in this case, actually give rise to new inflectional affixes. The development of a construction signaling destiny or obligation (as the Latin source construction did [Benveniste 1968]) is also attested in the languages of the world, although it is not as common as some other sources. Examples occur in English (*shall*) and other Germanic languages. Examples of auxiliaries of possession (such as *haber*), which probably had a sense of destiny or obligation, becoming futures occur in the eastern Kru languages and Ukrainian.

If grammatical morphemes can be viewed as having life cycles, the Spanish synthetic future must be regarded as an "old" future morpheme. It is well known that the periphrastic *ir a* future is replacing the synthetic future in spoken Spanish, especially among the less educated (Grimes 1967-68). Futures from verbs indicating movement toward a goal are quite frequent throughout the world. Besides English and French, in the following Gramcats-sample languages we find futures derived from a verb meaning 'go': Margi (Chadic), Cocama (Equatorial), Maung (Australian), Atchin (Oceanic), Abipon (Ge-Pano-Carib), Mano (Niger-Congo), Zuni (Penutian), and Nung (Tibeto-Burman). In addition to these eight, nine languages use a verb glossed as 'come' (Bybee, Pagliuca, and Perkins 1991).

It is also common for a language to have more than one future morpheme. Given that the grammaticization process is ongoing at all times, it is not surprising that new grammatical morphemes develop while older ones are still in use. In the Gramcats sample, thirty-one of the fifty-five languages that have future morphemes have more than one.

The various uses of future morphemes correlate to a large extent with the degree of grammaticization that they have undergone (Bybee and Pagliuca 1987; Bybee, Pagliuca, and Perkins 1991). Thus certain uses, such as the expression of intention, are characteristic of future morphemes in early stages of development, while others, such as the expression of epistemic meanings, are characteristic of futures that have undergone a long period of development. In this regard it is interesting to note the distribution of the Spanish synthetic future as the periphrastic one grows more frequent. While in many dialects the two futures still serve many of the same functions (Moreno de Alba 1977), such as the expression of intention and prediction, reports from all over the Spanish-speaking world indicate that the synthetic future is more and more associated with what might be termed *modal* functions. Consider the following examples from Moreno de Alba (1977) for Mexican Spanish (Examples 20, 24, 26, and 29) and from Silva-Corvalán and Terrell (1989) for Caribbean and Chilean Spanish (Example 21, 22, 23, 25, 27, and 28) as illustrative of the uses of futures:

Intention
(20)   *Tú cena y acuéstate; yo **hablaré** con él.*
       'You eat and go to bed; I'll speak with him.'

(21)   *Les **voy a decir** ahora que estoy aquí.*
'I'm going to tell them now that I'm here.'

Prediction

(22)   *... y por eso queda y **quedará** siempre una profecía que no se realizará.*
'... and therefore it is and will remain always a prophecy that will never be fulfilled.'

(23)   *La realidad es que todo el problema de urbanismo de Caracas parece que **va a ser** gravísimo.*
'The reality is that the whole problem of urbanism in Caracas is going to become very grave.'

General truth

(24)   *La pedagogía, como ciencia de la educación, **tendrá** varias ramas.*
'Pedagogy, as the science of education, has various branches.'

(25)   *Después que usted tenga el muchacho ocupado en el deporte, el muchacho no se le **va a ir** para otra cosa.*
'After you get a boy involved in sports, he's not going to go for other things.'

Supposition

(26)   *Ya tú **comprenderás** cómo nos reímos.*
'Now you might understand how we laughed.'

(27)   ***Hará** un año y medio pues.*
'It must be about a year and a half.'

(28)   *No sé si **será** que ellos eran tímidos.*
'I don't know if it might be that they were shy.'

Concessive

(29)   *Con palabras se **podrán** decir cosas muy hermosas ... pero muchas veces se tiene que llegar a la acción.*
'With words you might be able to say pretty things ... but many times one has to take some action.'

By comparing the uses of future forms from many different languages, each of these uses can be shown to occur in a relative sequence in the semantic development of future morphemes. We have presented evidence that the intention use of future morphemes is associated with the diachronically early stages of development of future morphemes (Bybee and Pagliuca 1987; Bybee, Pagliuca, and Perkins 1991). In particular, *go*-futures and futures from modal sources (desire and obligation) are used to express first-person intentions even before any of their more temporal uses develop. It appears that the more prototypical use of future, that of prediction about future time, develops from the intention use when that use is applied to a third person. That is, if we change Examples 20 and 21 so that they have third-person subjects for the future verb, then we find that from the statement of the third person's intention we can infer a prediction about his future action:

(30)   *Tú cena y acuéstate; él **hablará** con ellos.*

(31)   *Les **va a decir** ahora que estoy aquí.*

When this sense of prediction becomes conventionalized as part of the meaning of the construction, it can be used without any intention sense, as in Examples 24 and 25, where abstract nouns serve as the subjects of the future verb.

We argue in the two works cited above that the prototypical meaning of future is not simply reference to a time after the moment of speech, but rather "prediction"— the speaker's assertion that the situation will come to pass. The evidence for this is the fact that typical futures across languages fail to occur in certain adverbial clauses despite clear future-time reference. The following clause types, for example, take the future in neither Spanish nor English:

(32) *Pasará mucho tiempo antes de que puedas (*podrás) medir la importancia de esas fuerzas.*

'It will take a long time before you can (?will be able to) judge the importance of these forces.'

(33) *Si llegas (*llegarás) a la verdad absoluta, será por pura casualidad.*

'If you (*will) arrive at the absolute truth, it will be by pure chance.'

Here the content of the adverbial clause is not being predicted, that is, asserted to be true in the future.

We further argue that the general truth and the supposition sense derive from the prediction use: assertions of general truth are predictions that are not restricted to the future but are good for all time; suppositions are predictions about what will turn out to be true if more were known. For instance, if the phone rings, one can say *Será María* knowing that the prediction will be confirmed when the phone is answered. Since these are predictions about the present rather than the future, the resulting sense is one of probability: the speaker is asserting that the proposition is probably true. From here the future of supposition can move into questions and embedded questions that indicate uncertainty or supposition.

Gili Gaya (1961) argues that the concessive sense (as illustrated in Example 29) derives directly from the supposition sense in interactional contexts in which the speaker wants to concede to the opinion of the interlocutor while at the same time asserting something that might appear contrary, as in the following (Gili Gaya 1961:166):

(34) —*Fulano es un sabio.*

—*Lo será; sin embargo, se ha equivocado algunas veces.*

'Fulano is a wise man.'

'He may be; nevertheless, he has been mistaken at times.'

While the supposition use indicates reservations about the truth of the proposition, the concessive use expresses reservations about unconditionally accepting the consequences of the truth of the proposition in view of the possibly contradictory assertion in the next clause. This hypothesized diachronic progression from supposition, which has a single clause in its scope, to concessive, which expresses a relation among clauses, is an example of the commonly occurring progression in grammaticization toward the expression of functions at the discourse or textual level and the expressive or speaker-attitude level (Traugott 1982).

Combining findings for other languages with the specific facts about Spanish, we find that the path of development for futures includes at least the stages indicated in Figure 2. This diagram also shows how the two futures of Spanish map onto the stages on this path. The solid line underscores the uses for which the synthetic or periphrastic future is the main exponent, and the dotted line underscores the uses for which the future in question is a possible, but not frequent, choice.

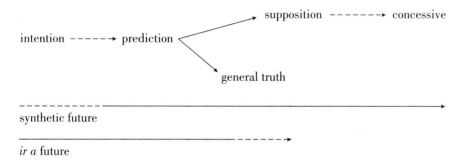

Figure 2. Progression of the synthetic future and the *ir a* future along the universal path of development for futures

The quantitative data that Figure 2 reflects is presented by Moreno de Alba (1977) for Mexican Spanish and Silva-Corvalán and Terrell (1989) for Caribbean and Chilean Spanish. In their data, intention and prediction uses (which are not distinguished) have the periphrastic future in 80% or more of the examples.[2] The general truth use in Moreno de Alba's data is more often expressed by the synthetic future (in twenty-three cases out of thirty), while similar counts for Silva-Corvalán and Terrell are not available. For supposition, the *ir a* periphrasis is simply not an option: Silva-Corvalán and Terrell report 100% synthetic futures in these uses, and Moreno de Alba reports twenty-five cases of the synthetic future and six cases of the *haber de +* infinitive periphrasis.

The distribution of the two futures, then, can be understood in terms of how far each one has progressed on this grammaticization path. The older synthetic future has undergone semantic developments that have allowed it to extend into uses that are no longer considered temporal, while the newer periphrastic future is taking over the early sections of the path, particularly those uses that are more associated with "future" meaning cross-linguistically.

My argument, then, is that the distribution of the two Spanish futures (and, indeed, any two coexisting futures) is in large measure predictable given their relative age and the universal path of development for future morphemes.

However, there is another possible explanation for part of the distributional picture, an explanation which is also compatible with all that is known about grammaticization. The supposition sense was hypothesized to have developed from the prediction sense, since this seems to occur in other languages with futures of various sources. For example, in English this sense may be obtained from either the *will* future or the *go* future, as in *That'll be Mary now* or *That's gonna be Mary now*. But because the Spanish synthetic future comes from a construction originally used for obligation, it is possible that the supposition use developed even earlier, since obligation can give rise to a sense of supposition even in the absence of the prediction use. Thus *haber de* + infinitive can be used for supposition, just as *should* and *must* can in English (e.g., *John should be home by now*). I do not have information about when this use developed for the synthetic future. Even if this is the source of the supposition sense, it is still true that the reason the periphrastic future cannot be used in the supposition or concessive senses is because it has not progressed far enough in its semantic development.

We can predict the continued attrition of the synthetic future in the intention and prediction uses as the periphrastic future becomes more frequent. The resulting distribution of the synthetic future then is of considerable interest. Its most prominent use (in terms of text frequency) is in the epistemic sense of probability or supposition. It is also used in certain kinds of subordinate clauses, notably concessives, and increasingly in the complement to *no sé* (see Example 28). If the synthetic future survives at all, and if we were to look at its distribution with an objective eye, we might be inclined to call it a type of subjunctive or at least a kind of mood marker (Bybee 1985: Chapters 8&9). And we might watch its development for an increased use in subordinate clauses which are not asserted, but rather whose truth value is somewhat in doubt. In other words, the current and future distribution of the synthetic future in Spanish may give us some indication of the path along which subjunctives develop.

 ## CONCLUSION

In this short discussion I hope to have shed some light on the core tense and aspect system of Spanish by comparing it with recent findings in cross-linguistic research. The major claims that I have made are that the perfective/imperfective distinction is hierarchically superordinate to the present/past distinction in Spanish; that the inceptive use of the Preterite with stative predicates is paralleled in other languages, although Spanish has not gone so far as some languages in conventionalizing the implications of this combination of meanings; and that the distribution of the uses of the two futures in Spanish is in part predictable from the cross-linguistically established diachronic path of development of future morphemes.

Notes

1. In the text I will follow Comrie's 1976 convention of writing universal meaning labels in all lower-case letters (perfective) and language-specific names of grammatical categories with an initial capital letter (Spanish Preterite).
2. If intention and prediction were distinguished in these counts, some differences in usage might emerge. In particular, on the basis of developments in other languages, we can predict a higher percentage of use of the periphrastic future for intention over prediction.

References

Benveniste, E. 1968. Mutations of Linguistic Categories. In *Directions for Historical Linguistics*, ed. by W. P. Lehmann and Y. Malkiel, 83-94. Austin, Texas: University of Texas Press.

Bolinger, D. 1963. Reference and Inference: Inceptiveness in the Spanish Preterite. *Hispania* 46:128-135.

Buck, C. D. 1933. *Comparative Grammar of Greek and Latin.* Chicago: University of Chicago Press.

Bybee, J. L. 1985. *Morphology: a Study of the Relation Between Meaning and Form.* Amsterdam: John Benjamins.

———. 1988. Semantic Substance vs. Contrast in the Development of Grammatical Meaning. *Proceedings of the Fourteenth Annual Meeting of the Berkeley Linguistics Society*, pp. 247-264.

Bybee, J. L., W. Pagliuca, and R. Perkins. 1991. Back to the Future. In *Approaches to Grammaticalization*, ed. by E. Traugott and B. Heine. Amsterdam: John Benjamins.

Bybee, J. L., R. Perkins, and W. Pagliuca. 1994. *The Evolution of Grammar.* Chicago: University of Chicago Press.

Bybee, J. L., and Ö. Dahl. 1989. The Creation of Tense and Aspect Systems in the Languages of the World. *Studies in Language* 13:51-103.

Bybee, J. L., and W. Pagliuca. 1987. The Evolution of Future Meaning. In *Papers from the VIIth International Conference on Historical Linguistics*, ed. by A. G. Ramat, O. Carruba, and G. Bernini, 109-22. Amsterdam: John Benjamins.

Comrie, B. 1976. *Aspect.* Cambridge: Cambridge University Press.

———. 1985. *Tense.* Cambridge: Cambridge University Press.

Dahl, Ö. 1985. *Tense and Aspect Systems.* Oxford: Basil Blackwell.

Dyen, I. 1965. *A Sketch of Trukese Grammar.* American Oriental Essay, no. 4. New Haven: American Oriental Society.

Faltz, L. M. 1989. A Role for Inference in Meaning Change. *Studies in Language* 13:317-31.

Gili y Gaya, S. 1961. *Curso superior de sintaxis española.* Barcelona: Bibliograf.

Goodenough, W. H., and H. Sugita. 1980. *Trukese-English Dictionary.* Philadelphia: American Philosophical Society.

Grimes, L. 1967-68. Sintaxis de 'futuridad' en dos representaciones del habla popular mexicano. *Archiv für das Studium der neuren Sprachen und Literaturen* 204: 349-52.

Guitart, J. M. 1978. Aspects of Spanish Aspect: A New Look at the Preterit/Imperfect Distinction. In *Contemporary Studies in Romance Linguistics*, ed. by Margarita Suñer, 132-168. Washington, D. C.: Georgetown University Press.

Hooper, J. B. 1976. *An Introduction to Natural Generative Phonology.* New York: Academic Press.

Hooper, J. B., and T. D. Terrell. 1976. Stress Assignment in Spanish: A Natural Generative Analysis. *Glossa* 10:64-110.

Hopper, P. J. 1982. Aspect Between Discourse and Grammar: An Introductory Essay for the Volume. In *Tense-Aspect: Between Semantics and Pragmatics*, ed. by P. J. Hopper, 3-18. Amsterdam: John Benjamins.

Moreno de Alba, J. G. 1977. Vitalidad del futuro del indicativo en la norma culta del español hablado en México. *Anuario de Letras* 8:81-102.

Silva-Corvalán, C. 1983. Tense and Aspect in Oral Spanish Narrative. *Language* 59:760-780.

Silva-Corvalán, C., and T. D. Terrell. 1989. Notas sobre la expresión de futuridad en el español del caribe. *Hispanic Linguistics* 2:191-208.

Taylor, D. 1956. Island Carib II: Word-classes, Affixes, Nouns and Verbs. *International Journal of American Linguistics* 22:1-44.

Terrell, T. D., and M. Salgués. 1979. *Lingüística aplicada*. New York: John Wiley & Sons.

Thomas, E. 1978. *A Grammatical Description of the Engenni Language*. Arlington: Summer Institute of Linguistics.

Traugott, E. C. 1982. From Propositional to Textual and Expressive Meanings: Some Semantic-Pragmatic Aspects of Grammaticalization. In *Perspectives on Historical Linguistics*, ed. by W. Lehmann, and Y. Malkiel, 245-71. Amsterdam: John Benjamins.

Traugott, E. C., and E. König. 1991. The Semantics-Pragmatics of Grammaticalization Revisited. In *Approaches to Grammaticalization*, ed. by E. C. Traugott and B. Heine. Amsterdam: John Benjamins.

The Future of the Future in Spanish Foreign Language Textbooks

Margaret van Naerssen
University of Pennsylvania

Prior to the advent of communicative language teaching for Spanish as a foreign language, beginning textbooks, in general, treated the periphrastic future (*ir* + *a* + infinitive) as a note. It has received second-class treatment even though there is sufficient evidence from language acquisition, sociolinguistics, and historical linguistics to suggest it is a natural form in conversation for expressing the future. With the shift toward communicative teaching, textbooks are beginning to organize language around the communicative needs of students and around functions and are introducing more natural language. An example is the elevation of the periphrastic future to greater importance.

 INTRODUCTION

Before the spread of communicative language teaching in foreign languages in the United States, beginning students somehow discovered, despite the textbook focus on the inflected future tense, that the easiest way to talk about the future was to use *ir* + *a* + infinitive—the *periphrastic future*. It is convenient to speculate that students might have been influenced by their first languages, especially if the languages have a similar construction (such as *going to* + verb in English). However, when we examine this usage in more depth, evidence suggests that this form is also "natural" in conversation for even native speakers of Spanish. Some textbook writers, shifting toward more communicative teaching, have focused on the actual communication needs of the learner, organizing content around functions of the language rather than around structures. This shift has introduced the language that is needed for specific functions, which might include several different structures or constructions for a particular function. As a result, the importance of the periphrastic future has been emphasized over the inflected future. This is a hopeful sign that communicative teaching can bring about more natural language use, although all textbooks, irrespective of their approaches, should reflect natural language.

In my 1979–80 study on the use of the periphrastic and inflected futures in beginning Spanish textbooks (van Naerssen 1983) I found that they ignored the reality of natural language in teaching the future. While the study pointed out this particular incongruity for Spanish, it had broader objectives: (1) to support, in general, approaches of teaching natural language, and (2) to illustrate how linguistic research can benefit foreign language textbook developers and classroom teachers. The purpose of this paper, ten years later, is to update that study by expanding the survey of research, and to examine recent textbooks to determine the possible effect of changes in methodology.

The inflected and periphrastic futures are contrasted below.

Inflected future:		*cantare*		
	VB	1st P.S. FUTURE		
	will	sing		
Periphrastic future:		*voy*	*a*	*cantar*
	VB	1st P.S.	PREP	INF
	PRESENT			
	going		to	sing

While both the periphrastic and the inflected forms can express various modalities and functions, the focus of this study is on the expression of future action with the following meanings: the immediate, near, easily imagined, or known future.[1] This general category of meaning will henceforth be referred to as the *definite future*. Learners are frequently taught that the inflected future is the proper verb form expressing all future actions, including the types just mentioned. However, as will be seen in this paper, in natural language the inflected future is, in fact, not generally used in these ways.

Summary of Linguistic Research

While it is important to heed the warning by Tarone, Swain, and Fathman (1976) not to proceed too rapidly with the interpretation of research results, such results are at least worth considering when various disciplines such as psycholinguistics, sociolinguistics, and historical linguistics report converging tendencies. There appears to be such a convergence for the periphrastic future in Spanish. The research will only be summarized here; the reader is referred to the earlier study (van Naerssen 1983) for a more in-depth analysis of the research from linguistics.

1. Psycholinguistics: Language Acquisition

In first-language acquisition research, oral evidence of young children being able to distinguish between the *present* and *future* appears as early as age 2:6 (Gonzalez

1970) and at age 2:11 (Peronard 1977). In both studies only the periphrastic future appeared. The "official" or inflected future does not appear in first language studies until about age four. Gili y Gaya (1972) reports it at 4:0 and Gonzalez at 4:6, with only one instance in each study; Brisk (1972) finds no evidence at all even at age 5:0.

At the primary grade level Gili y Gaya reports only five cases of the inflected future, denoting future action, in the first grade, and only a few more in the fourth grade. (The inflected future represented only 2.1% of the expressions involving tense.) According to Gili y Gaya, children normally express the future by means of the present indicative or subjunctive along with the periphrastic construction, which is inflected in the present. For Kernan and Blount (1966) the inflected future is not established until the age of 11 to 12 years.

Thus, cognitively the child can distinguish very early between present and future time and finds a form to express this through means other than the "official" grammatical or inflected future. Vidal de Battini (1964), making recommendations for Spanish language arts for native speakers in Argentina, provides indirect evidence of the dominant use of the periphrastic future by children. She recommends teaching the use of inflected forms in place of all periphrastic forms commonly used by children. Anecdotal evidence of the early use of the periphrastic by children is given by a Spanish language professor to a university student of Spanish as a foreign language: "You really must use the inflected future more so you won't sound like a child." [2]

In analyses of foreign and second language learners of Spanish, both college-age students (van Naerssen 1981) and primary-grade immersion students (Boyd 1975) show a definite preference for the periphrastic future by second language learners. Perhaps the preference by both first and second language speakers for the periphrastic is, in part, related to meaning conveyed by *voy a*. Learners will already have been exposed to this form, which conveys a sense of movement from "here." In the periphrastic future it conveys a sense of movement from "now."

2. Sociolinguistics: General Language Usage

While the periphrastic form is very frequently found in the language around the child (in older sibling speech, in caregiver speech, and in adult speech in general), the teaching recommendation by Vidal de Battini and evidence from a sampling of older foreign language texts indicate, for the most part, that the inflected future is considered the more educated of the two forms. The preference for the periphrastic by adults is not merely an impressionistic observation. Data from adult speech indicates that the inflected future is indeed not the most common form. It is, therefore, not surprising that the child learning Spanish as a first language should acquire it so late.

Dialect studies from Argentina (Vidal de Battini 1964), Chile (Oroz 1964), Colombia (Flores 1964), Mexico (Lope Blanch 1964; Morena de Alba 1977), Venezuela (Iuliano 1976), and Chile, the Dominican Republic, Puerto Rico, and Venezuela (Corvalán and Terrell 1989), and in more general descriptions (Kany 1969) also indicate that, in the Spanish of the Americas, the inflected future is not the preferred oral form. A study of four modern authors from Colombia, Mexico, and Uruguay

(Myhill 1988) also supports a strong preference for the periphrastic when the features of volitionality, imminence, and present relevance are considered.

A very detailed analysis of the uses of the periphrastic future in the educated speech of Caracas, Venezuela, was made by Iuliano (1976). Of the 627 occurrences of the future, 77 percent were of the periphrastic form, using this construction to express an immediate or more probable or real future. The remaining 23 percent were of the inflected future form, which conveyed a certain hypothetical meaning. An examination of Iuliano's data by age group reveals a greater frequency in the use of the periphrastic future among the younger adult speakers. This could be interpreted as evidence of a trend for the periphrastic future to replace the inflected.

The more recent study by Corvalán and Terrell (1989) on oral Spanish in four countries confirms the wider use of the periphrastic future to express the definite or known future, with the inflected form reserved for an indefinite and usually more distant future, conveying a sense of doubt or probability. The inflected future was used for the definite or known future in some instances, but Corvalán and Terrell suggest these might be related to a particularly formal interview style used by highly educated informants.

3. Sociolinguistics: Conversation Management

Perhaps human interaction also influences the choice of forms that dominate in a particular language context. Ochs has proposed that the linguistic community give greater status to social processes as constraints on grammatical structures. She discusses the effect of human interaction on word order and finds that word order, particularly an item in the initial position, is sensitive to social interaction. Word order is a *shaper of subsequent social interaction*. The initial item in an utterance can determine who will speak next, who will occupy the next turn. These functions of word order can be as important and, in some cases, more important than the functions of encoding inherently salient information (Ochs 1978:20).

Applying word order analysis to verb form choice may provide evidence of social processes at work in the widespread preference for the periphrastic future to express the definite future. This approach was taken by van Naerssen (1983), who examined the choice between the periphrastic and inflected future. It was proposed that the periphrastic future construction is, in current Spanish, easier to use in conversations than the inflected future as it can better fill a gap as the speaker plans his/her thoughts, thus allowing the speaker to hold the floor.[3] That is, the speaker can begin in the present time, conceptually the easiest position (the "here and now"), with the *ir* + *a* + **infinitive** as this expression of the future is inflected for the present tense. In addition, speakers do not have to commit themselves immediately to a specific verb complement, the infinitive. With the inflected future it would be necessary both to choose a specific verb and to inflect for the future almost simultaneously.

Sociolinguistics provides another hypothesis by Ochs, which seems applicable here. She proposes (Ochs Keenan 1977) that "adult speech behavior takes on many of the characteristics of child language when communication is spontaneous and relatively unpredictable." This hypothesis includes reliance more on earlier acquired structures than on the later acquired ones. And, as has been mentioned previously, the periphrastic future is acquired much earlier than the inflected future. This might also explain the variation Corvalan and Terrell found in the more formal interview styles.

4. Historical Linguistics

Meier (1965, cited in Houston 1980) reminds us that the Romance languages throughout history have demonstrated a range of ways to express the future through verbs from which the speaker may select. There has been no single future construction, although specific forms have reflected the definite future and a probable future.

Givon (1971) suggests that the periphrastic form is now replacing the inflected future and that this is more than an isolated tendency when observed from a historical perspective. He further suggests that this tendency is part of a larger cycle that Spanish and certain other languages are experiencing. In this cycle (noted by other linguists as well), the language changes from a primarily synthetic language to a predominantly analytic language and, eventually, back to a synthetic one. Givon hypothesize an endless cycle which can be best understood if one looks at the syntactic order and the transformation structure of a language at various periods. One of his many examples is the expression of the future in Spanish. He points out that the syntactic order of verba phrases in early Latin, as well as in all early Indo-European dialects, was *complement:verb*. It is well known that many modality morphemes in Romance languages that appear as *verb suffixes* had their origins as *main verbs*. The Spanish inflected future had its origins as *infinitive + haber*, as illustrated below using the verb *cantar* (to sing):

Infinitive complement	+	Inflected verb *haber*		
cantar	+	*he* (1st P.S. FUTURE)	$\rightarrow$	*cantaré*

Gradually the **Subject : Complement : Verb** word order of Romance languages evolved into a primarily Subject:Verb:Complement order, which is currently a controlling force in Romance languages. The recently developed modals in these languages appear as prefixed to the verb, as with, for example, the future marker *ir* (to go) in the Spanish periphrastic future. This holds true for other auxiliaries as well: *andar, llegar*, and *haber*. Textbooks need to reflect this change.

 ## THE FIT BETWEEN TEXTBOOKS AND REALITY

The reality of oral conversational Spanish, as illustrated by research in language acquisition, sociolinguistics, and historical linguistics, is one in which the periphrastic future is preferred over the inflected for the expression of a simple future event. This reality was not, however, reflected in most texts prior to the advent of communicative language teaching. The periphrastic future was generally ignored in such texts. It was, for the most part, treated in grammar texts as a "second-class citizen," a footnote, or an aside, and it sometimes has been totally ignored (van Naerssen 1983).

In my first study (carried out in 1979–80 and reported in 1983), the second-class-citizen treatment of the periphrastic future was apparent after an examination of sixteen textbooks for the ways in which students were taught to express the simple future concept.[4] These textbooks had been (with the exception of one) widely used in the United States for teaching Spanish as a foreign language, at least through the 1970s, and reflected a variety of teaching methodologies. In my second study (carried out in 1990 and reported in this paper), I found that with a shift to a more communicative approach to foreign language teaching, textbooks had begun to focus more on the communicative needs of the learner: language is organized more around functions, introducing the language construction (sometimes more than one construction) for expressing a particular function. The intent is to assist the student in communicating more naturally. In the more communicatively oriented textbooks, the periphrastic future has in fact been given first-class-citizen treatment. The results from both the previous study and the more recent study are now summarized.

Table 1

A summary comparison of the treatment of the inflected and periphrastic futures in 16 university Spanish foreign language texts (1979–80) study.

When Inflected Introduced		When Periphrastic Introduced		Formal Lesson on Inflected	Formal Lesson on Periphrastic
Early 2 (13%)	Late 13 (81%)	Early 12 (75%)	Late 2 (13%)	15 (94%)	4 (25%)
Never 1 (.06%)		Never 2 (13%) Sometimes note on periphrastic repeated under lesson on Inflected			
Periphrastic Only as a Note 10 (63%)		Exercises on Inflected 15 (94%)		Exercises on Periphrastic 10 (63%) In one case it was only in a dialogue; frequently mixed with other constructions and used in only a few sentences.	

Note: "Formal lesson" is a separate section devoted to the tense, construction, or function. The section was not a note under another tense, verb forms, or other construction. Such sections give the contents equal status to other forms or functions in the organization of the text.

1. Textbooks in the 1970s

No specific rationale was adopted for the selection of the sixteen textbooks for my 1979–80 study. As coordinator of introductory Spanish courses, Terrell had the most complete collection I could find.

Seventy-six percent (thirteen) of the texts introduced the expression of the future early,[5] simultaneously with or shortly after the present indicative and before the preterite. In almost all cases it was in the periphrastic form but was introduced only as a note, sometimes a one-liner, under some other morphological or syntactic category. In two texts it was never mentioned at all.

In contrast, the inflected future was formally introduced as a separate lesson on the future in all but one text (in which it was entirely omitted). In general its introduction was late in the text or text series. Thus, formal recognition was given to the less preferred, less frequent, more difficult, and more semantically complex structure as the acceptable form of the future.

The allocation of the periphrastic future to brief notations suggested that one of the most frequent and easiest means of expressing the simple future was really not acceptable, and, thus, not worth much notice. That the periphrastic seems to be easier might have justified giving it less space and time for explanation and practice, but does not then justify lowering its level of acceptability by not formally recognizing it.

Since my earlier study, an older textbook from Barcelona (Alcoba) was examined and found to give moderately early (lesson 11 out of 28) and strong emphasis to the periphrastic future with a formal lesson, even though the text's methodology was not communicative. As in the other texts, the inflected future was also introduced quite late in the text. One might speculate that this special attention to the periphrastic might have been because the textbook was written for foreigners studying in Spain, for second language students as opposed to foreign language students. Perhaps Alcoba recognized the daily life needs of the students and tried to provide the appropriate language to meet those needs.

Table 2

A summary comparison of the treatment of the inflected and periphrastic futures in 13 university Spanish foreign language texts (1990 study).

When Inflected Introduced		When Periphrastic Introduced		Formal Lesson on Inflected	Formal Lesson on Periphrastic
Early	Late	Early	Late	16 (100%)	10 (62.5%) Includes one that is ranked as more than "only a note" but not quite as formal as a separate section
0 (0%)	14 (87.5%)	16 (100%)	0 (0%)		
Mid-way 2 (12.2%) Never 0 (0%)		Never 0 (0%) Sometimes note on periphrastic repeated under lesson on Inflected			
Periphrastic Only as a Note 6 (37.5%)		Exercises on Inflected 16 (100%)		Exercises on Periphrastic 15 (93.75%)	

2. Textbooks in the Late 1980s

The results of my 1990 study are reflected in Table 2, a summary of the treatment of the future in eighteen textbooks published since 1985.[6] An attempt was made to locate as many textbooks, including the same or most recent editions, as those covered in Terrell's own 1990 study of trends in methodology in textbooks. Suggestions were also made by a publisher of foreign language texts who knew of the current market and use of Spanish textbooks.[7] Thus, a more specific rationale was developed for selecting textbooks for this second analysis.

At the time of the first study, communicative teaching had not yet begun in any significant way to penetrate the foreign language classroom in the United States, nor had textbooks been designed with this approach in mind. Nevertheless, there were some teachers, such as Terrell (with his Natural Approach), who were teaching Spanish communicatively and developing their own materials. In 1990, by the time of second study, there were already a number of texts with a communicative approach, including Tracy Terrell's own. As can be seen in Table 2, there has been a significant change in the treatment of the periphrastic future:

    a. 100% of the texts introduce it early;

    b. 100% have exercises on it;

    c. the number introducing it only as a note has been reduced from 10 to 6; and

    d. the number having a formal section on it has increased from 4 to 10.

It is proposed here that this change is due to the change in the overall approach to foreign language teaching: a shift toward a communicative approach, with the use of more natural language.

3. Discussion

It was not my objective in either of these studies of the future actually to analyze the textbooks for methodology. Terrell, however, in "Trends in the Teaching of Grammar in Spanish Language Textbooks" (1990) provides a useful analysis of seventeen elementary college and four elementary high school texts, as well as a chronological study of six editions of the same text (from 1963 to 1987). In my study I was not able to make a match with all of the texts in Terrell's study; however, enough correlation was possible to make some useful observations. Three other textbooks, published after Terrell's study, also were examined in my study: *En camino*, Fourth edition (Nicholas, Swietlicki, Dominicis, and Neale-Silva 1990), *Puertas*, Third edition (Copeland, Kite, Sandstedt, and Vargas 1990) and *¡Ya comprendo!* (Castells 1990).

Terrell (1990:201) used the following parameters to evaluate the degree to which textbooks reflect communicative principles:

    a. communicative activities/grammar exercises

    b. contextualization/non-contextualization

    c. meaningful/rote

    d. open/closed (divergent/convergent)

    e. interactive/non-interactive

Using these five parameters, Terrell ranked four university level textbooks Above Average on three or more of the points: *Dos mundos* (Terrell, Andrade, Egasse, and Muñoz 1986), *¡En directo!* (Boylan, Rissel, and Lett 1988), *Charlando* (Inman 1988) and *Entradas* (Higgs, Liskin-Gasparro, and Medley 1989). Although I was unable to examine *Charlando*, the three other textbooks took a functional approach to introducing the periphrastic future as one of several ways of "talking about the future," "making plans," or "talking about going places." All assigned it a formal section, introduced it early, and provided exercises for using it. *Puntos de partida* and *Poco a poco* also treated the periphrastic future in this way; these had been ranked either "above average" or "average" on Terrell's scale of communicability.

While *¡Ya comprendo!* was not examined by Terrell nor did I examine its methodology in depth, it appears to be a very communicatively oriented textbook and organized by functions. It treats the periphrastic in the same way as described for those texts Terrell judged "communicative" in approach. It also gives the least status to the inflected future. First, it introduces the inflected form by reminding the student that both the present tense and the periphrastic future can express the future. Second, it suggests that the inflected future is not very useful, and even ignores its use for expressing probability: "You do not have to use this future tense in order to communicate in Spanish, but you should be able to recognize it when reading or listening." (Castells 1990:331).

The textbook that treated the periphrastic future most obscurely was DaSilva's *Beginning Spanish: A Concept Approach*, introducing it under special uses of the preposition *a;* no exercises were included at all. This text (the 6th edition) was rated as "average" on four out of five of the parameters and "above average" on one. Terrell's chronological analysis of all six of DaSilva's editions shows that after the 1978 edition there was a dramatic change in the textbook toward becoming more communicative. However, the language is not organized around functions, thus the periphrastic remained relegated to a less than even second-class treatment.

All but one of the high school textbooks examined by Terrell were also part of my present study. The *Spanish for Mastery* series (Valette et al. 1989) was ranked by Terrell "as above average" on three out of the five parameters, while *Pasos y puentes* and *Voces y vistas* (Reynolds et al. 1989) was ranked "average" on all five. *¿Y tú?* (G. Jarvis, et al. 1986) was ranked "above average" on only one parameter, with two parameters ranked "average" and two "below average."

Voces y vistas and *Pasos y puentes*, (books 1 and 2 of the Scott, Foresman three-book series) and *Entre nosotros* and *¿Qué tal?* (books 1 and 2 of the *Spanish for Mastery* series), were the two high school textbooks series examined in my 1990 study. In both series the periphrastic is introduced relatively early in book 1, but the inflected is delayed until late in book 2. In the *Spanish for Mastery* series the periphrastic is introduced in a formal section. In the Reynolds et al. series and *¿Y tú?* it is not introduced formally in a separate section, but it is elevated to more than just a note, as evidenced by the space allocated to it in the note and exercises, and the way in which it is used to introduce the inflected future.

 IMPLICATIONS

In the 1979–80 study (van Naerssen 1983), I called for an "equal rights" treatment in textbooks based on a convergence of data supporting use of the periphrastic as a primary means of expression. The data came from research on language acquisition, on historical distribution and tendencies for change, on actual language usage by both adult and child native speakers, and on the influence of human interaction on language usage. With all the research pointing to the same conclusions, a strong argument existed for teaching early in the instructional process the language that is most natural and frequent and therefore, most useful to second and foreign language learners' needs.

Recent trends in foreign language teaching methodology indicate that a communicative approach to language teaching (in which the language needed is organized around functions rather than structures) may promote selection of more natural language forms. This is encouraging. But two notes of caution are needed here. First, it is not known how much research and how much native-speaker intuitions affect the choice of language for specific functions. In some instances it appears that writers have ended up understating the rather specific role of the inflected future, perhaps without reference to research. Second, there should not be a rigid correlation between the approach and the language that is taught. All textbooks, irrespective of their approaches, should reflect shifts in language use.

Similar cross-disciplinary research on other controversial constructions in Spanish (and in other languages) can provide useful insights and further support for textbook writers and contribute to theoretical concerns in language acquisition and to the search for universal tendencies in linguistics.[8]

Notes

1. The frequent use of the present tense with an adverb indicating future time to express the future is beyond the scope of this paper.
2. Vicki Lynn Smith, personal communication, spring 1990.
3. In addition, the periphrastic future, by its construction, offers another advantage over the inflected future for helping the speaker to keep his/her turn. It is a longer construction than the synthetic, inflected future, and thus does not offer a transitionally relevant space (trs) as quickly: (trs) *ir + a + **infinitive*** (trs).
4. The texts examined were Allen, Sandstedt, and Wegmann 1976, Angel and Dixson 1954, Castells and Lionetti 1978, Christensen and Wolfe 1977, Crow 1979, Dalbor 1972, DaSilva 1978, 1980, Jarrett and McManus 1953, Keller, Sebastini and Jimenez Maqueo 1978, Modern Language Materials Development Center 1961 and later levels, Turk, Espinosa and Sole 1978, and Valencia and Melonghi 1980.
5. "Early" and "late" were not defined precisely in terms of a percentage of material or number of pages, as the texts were not comparable in size or organization. "Early" refers roughly to the first third and "late" to the last third of the content of the text.
6. This number does not include the various editions of *A Concept Approach*.
7. Thalia Dorwick (Publisher of Foreign Languages and ESL, McGraw-Hill, Inc.), personal communication.
8. I am grateful to Stephen Krashen and Tracy Terrell for their comments on an earlier version of the 1979–80 study and the other editors of this collection for their comments. However, I am, of course, responsible for any errors that may still persist.

References

Alcoba, Santiago. 1974. *Vox: módulos de español para extranjeros.* Barcelona: Bibliograf.

Allen, D., L. Sandstedt, and B. Wegmann. 1976. *¿Habla español?* 3d ed, New York: Holt, Rinehart and Winston.

Allen, David A., Ronald A. Freeman, Teresa Mendez-Faith, and Luis Gonzalez de Valle. 1985. *¿Habla español?* New York: Holt, Rinehart and Winston.

Boyd, Patricia. 1975. The Development of Grammatical Categories in Spanish by Anglo Children Learning a Second Language. *TESOL Quarterly* 9, 2.

Boylan, Patricia, Dorothy Rissel, and John Lett, Jr. 1988. *¡En directo!* New York: Random House.

Brisk, Maria E. 1972. The Spanish Syntax of the Preschool Spanish American: The Case of New Mexican Five-year-old Children. Ph.D. dissertation, University of Mexico.

Burt, M. D., H. Dulay, and E. Hernandez-Chavez. 1976. *Bilingual Syntax Measure: Technical Handbook.* New York: Harcourt Brace Jovanovich.

Castells, Matilde Orvilla de. 1990. *¡Ya comprendo!* New York: Macmillan.

Castells, Matilde Orvilla de, and H. E. Lionetti. 1978. *La lengua española: gramática y cultura.* 2d ed. New York: Scribners.

Christensen, C. B., and D. E. Wolfe. 1977. *Vistas hispánicas.* New York: Rand McNally.

Clark, Herbert H., and Eve V. Clark. 1977. *Psychology and Language: An Introduction to Psycholinguistics.* New York: Harcourt Brace Jovanovich.

Copeland, John G., Ralph Kite, Lynn A. Sandstedt, and Vivian Vargas. 1990. *Puertas.* 3d ed. New York: McGraw-Hill.

Corvalán, Carmen S., and Tracy D. Terrell. 1989. La expresión de futuridad en el español del Caribe. *Hispanic Linguistics* 22 (Spring).

Crow, J. A. 1979. *Se habla español.* New York: Harper and Row.

Dalbor, J. B. 1972. *Beginning College Spanish.* New York: Random House.

DaSilva, Zenia Sacks. 1978. *Beginning Spanish: A Concept Approach.* 4th ed. New York: Harper and Row.

———. 1980. *Spanish: A Short Course.* New York: Harper and Row.

———. 1987. *Beginning Spanish: A Concept Approach.* 6th ed. New York: Harper and Row.

Dawson, Albert C., and Laila Dawson. 1985. *Dicho y hecho.* 2d ed. New York: Wiley.

Dorwick, Thalia, Martha A. Marks, Bill VanPatten, and Theodore Higgs. 1987. *¿Qué tal?* 2d ed. New York: McGraw-Hill.

Flores, Luis. 1964. El español hablado en Colombia y su altas. In *Presente y futuro de la lengua española* Vol. 1 Actas de la asemblea de filología del I Congreso de Instituciones Hispánicas. Madrid: Oficina Internacional de Información y Observación de Español.

Gili y Gaya, Samuel. 1972. *Estudios de lenguaje infantil.* Barcelona: Bibliograf, S. A.

Givon, Talmy. 1971. Historical Syntax and Synchronic Morphology: An Archaeologist's Field Trip. *Papers from the Seventh Regional Meeting of the Chicago Linguistic Society,* April 16-18, 394-415.

Gonzalez, Gustavo. 1970. The Acquisition of Spanish Grammar by Native Spanish Speakers. Ph.D. dissertation, University of Texas, Austin.

Harley, B., and M. Swain. 1978. An Analysis of the Verb System Used by Young Learners of French. *Interlanguage Studies Bulletin* 3,1.

Hendrickson, James. 1986. *Poco a poco.* Boston: Heinle and Heinle.

Higgs, T., J. Liskin-Gasparro, and F. Medley. 1989. *Entradas* 1st ed. Boston, Mass.: Heinle and Heinle.

Houston, Dorine S. 1980. Forma y función del futuro en Lope de Rueda. Master's thesis, Temple University, Philadelphia.

Iuliano, Rosalba. 1976. La perifrasis ir + a (infinitivo) en el habla culta de Caracas. In *1975 Colloquium on Hispanic Linguistics* ed. by F. M. Aid, M.C. Resnick, and B. Sacink, M. C. Resnick, and B. Sacink, 59-66.

Jarrett, Edith M., and Beryl J. McManus. 1953. *El camino real.* Books 1 and 2. Boston: Houghton Mifflin.

Jarvis, Ana C., Raquel Lebredo, and Francesco Mena. 1986. *¿Cómo se dice...?* 3d ed. Lexington, Mass.: D. C. Heath and Co.

Jarvis, Gilbert A., Therese M. Bonin, Diane W. Birckbichler, and Linita C. Shih. 1986. *¿Y tú?* Teacher's ed. New York: Holt, Rinehart & Winston.

Johnson, Teresa H. de. 1976. Temporal Analysis of English and Spanish. Ph.D. dissertation, St. Louis University. University Microfilms 77-12, 106.

Kany, Charles E. 1969. *Sintaxis Hispanoamericana*. Madrid: Editorial Gredos, S. A. Translated from *American-Spanish Syntax*. 1963. Chicago: University of Chicago Press.

Keller, G. D., N. A. Sebastiani, and F. Jimenez. 1978. *Spanish Here and Now*. New York: Harcourt Brace Jovanovich.

Kernan, Keigh, and Benjamin Blount. 1966. The Acquisition of Spanish Grammar by Mexican Children. *Anthropological Linguistics* (December).

Knorre, Marty, Thalia Dorwick, Bill VanPatten, Francisco R. Ferran, and Walter Lusetti. 1989. *Puntos de partida*. 2d ed. New York: McGraw-Hill.

La Grone, G. G., A. S. Midenberger, and P. O'Connor. 1970. *Primeros pasos*. New York: Holt, Rinehart and Winston.

Lamadrid, E. E., W. E. Bull, and L. A. Briscoe. 1974. *Communicating in Spanish*, Level 1. Boston: Houghton Mifflin.

Lope Blanch, Juan M. 1964. Estado actual del español en México. In *Presente y futuro de la lengua española*, Vol. 1. Actas de la asemblea de filología del I Congreso de Instituciones Hispánicas. Madrid: Oficina Internacional de Información y Observación de Español.

Maqueo, Ana M. 1979. *Español uno: la lengua y la vida en México*. Mexico City: privately published.

Meier, H. 1965. Futuro y futuridad. *Revista de filología española* XLIII: 61-77. Modern Language Materials Development Center. 1961. A-LM: Spanish, Levels 2 and 4. New York: Harcourt, Brace and World.

Morena De Alba, Jose. 1977. Vitalidad del futuro de indicativo en la norma culta del español hablado en México. In *Estudios sobre el español hablado en las principales ciudades de América*, ed. by Juan M. Lope Blanch, 129-46. Mexico City: Universidad Autónoma de México, 129-46.

Myhill, John. 1988. A Quantitative Study of Future Tense Marking in Spanish. In *Linguistic Change and Contact*, ed. by Kathleen Ferrara, Becky Brown, Keith Walter, and John Baugh. Proceedings of the 16th New Ways of Analyzing Variation in English (and Other Languages). Austin: University of Texas, Department of Linguistics.

Nicholas, Robert L., Alain Swietlicki, Maria Canteli Dominicis, and Eduardo Neale-Silva. 1990. *¡En camino!* 4th ed. New York: McGraw-Hill.

Ochs, Elinor. 1978. Social Foundations of Language. Earlier versions were presented at Johns Hopkins University, Department of Anthropology, March 1978, and at the meeting of the California Linguistics Association, May 1978. Manuscript.

Ochs Keenan, Elinor. 1977. Why Look at Planned and Unplanned Discourse? In *Discourse across Time*. SCOPIL no. 5. ed. by E. Ochs Keenan and B. Kroll, 1-41. Los Angeles: University of Southern California, Department of Linguistics.

Oroz, Rudolfo. 1964. El Español de Chile. In *Presente y futuro de la lengua española*, Vol 1. Actas de la asemblea de filología del I Congreso de Instituciones Hispánicas. Madrid: Oficina Internacional de Información y Observación de Español.

Peronard, Marianne. 1977. Aquisición del lenguaje en un niño atípico: retardo o desviación. *Boletin de Filología* 28:139-152.

Reynolds, Bernadette M., Carol Eubanks Rodriguez, and Rudolfo L. Schonfeld. 1989. *Pasos y puentes*. Glenview, Ill.: Scott, Foresman and Company.

———. 1989. *Voces y vistas*. Glenview, Ill.: Scott, Foresman and Company.

Rietmann, Kearney. 1977. Temporal Sequencing and Organization in Planned and Unplanned Narratives. Los Angeles: University of Southern California, Department of Linguistics. Manuscript.

Samaniego, Fabian, Thomas Blommers, Magaly Lagunas-Carvacho, Tina Castillo, Vivianne Sardan, and Emma Sepulveda-Pulvirenti. 1989. *¡Dímelo tú!* Fort Worth, Tex.: Holt, Rinehart and Winston.

Spinelli, Emily, and Marta Rosso-O'Laughlin. 1988. *Encuentros.* New York: Holt, Rinehart and Winston.

Tapia-Hernandez, Rafael. 1978. Correlation between Knowledge of Grammar Rules and Performance in Spanish as a Foreign Language. Ph.D. dissertation, University of Texas, Austin. University Microfilms 7911038.

Tarone, E., M. Swain, and A. Fathman. 1976. Some Limitations to the Classroom Application of Current Second Language Research. *TESOL Quarterly* 10, 1 (March).

Terrell, Tracy D. 1990. Trends in the Teaching of Grammar in Spanish Language Textbooks. *Hispania 73:201-211.*

Terrell, Tracy D., Magdelena Andrade, Jeanne Egasse, and Elías Miguel Muñoz. 1986. *Dos mundos.* New York: Random House.

Turk, L. H., A. M. Espinosa, and C. A. Sole. 1978. *Foundation Course in Spanish.* 4th ed. Boston: D.C. Heath and Co.

Turner, D. 1978. The Effect of Instruction on Second Language Learning and Second Language Acquisition. Paper presented at the TESOL Convention, Mexico City.

Valencia, Pablo, and Franca Melonghi. 1980. *En contacto.* Boston: Houghton Mifflin.

Valencia, Pablo, Franca Melonghi, and Maureen Weissenrider. 1988. *En contacto.* 3d ed. Boston: Houghton Mifflin.

Valette, Jean-Paul, Gene S. Kuperschmid, and Rebecca Valette. 1984. *Con mucho gusto.* 2d ed. New York: Holt, Rinehart and Winston.

Valette, Jean-Paul, and Rebecca Valette. 1989. *Spanish for Mastery: Entre nosotros.* Lexington, Mass.: D. C. Heath and Co.

———. 1989. *Spanish for Mastery: ¿Qué tal?* Lexington, Mass.: D. C. Heath and Co.

van Naerssen, Margaret. 1981. Generalizing Second Language Acquisition Hypotheses Across Languages: A Test Case in Spanish as a Second Language. Ph.D. dissertation, University of Southern California, Los Angeles.

———. 1983. Ignoring the Reality of the Future in Spanish. In *Second Language Acquisition Studies* ed. by K. Bailey, M. Long, and S. Peck, 56-67. Rowley, Mass.: Newbury House.

Vidal de Battini, Berta E. 1964. El español de la Argentina: Presente y futuro de la lengua española, Vol. 1. Actas de la asemblea de filología del I Congreso de Instituciones Hispánicas. Madrid: Oficina Internacional de Información y Observación de Español.

REFLECTIONS ON THE LIFE AND WORK OF TRACY D. TERRELL

4

People who met or knew Tracy Terrell have very distinct memories of his personality and his high academic standards. It was with enthusiasm and a spirit of cooperation that he inspired many to embark upon research in his areas of expertise. The encouragement and collegiality that he offered to students and established scholars alike are evident in the personal reminiscences included in this section.

Richard Barrutia

My relationship with Tracy lasted many years. We both did our graduate work in linguistics at the University of Texas at Austin. I graduated a few years before he did and was already established as chairman of the linguistics program at the University of California, Irvine, when Tracy began searching for his first teaching position. I remember well interviewing him at the AATSP annual conference in Denver in 1969. His responses during the interview were quick and brilliant—characteristics that would be his trademark in everything he did. Tracy joined us at Irvine just in time to take over some of my courses and duties as language coordinator when I went to Mexico City as director of our Education Abroad program. When I returned, Tracy had things in better shape than I had left them. He made a great success in that position, which he kept until 1986 when he moved to UC San Diego. It was during Tracy's UCI years that he became an associate editor of *Hispania*, in charge first of "Shop Talk" then of the linguistics sections. It was at UCI also where he conceived and completed the books *The Natural Approach, Dos mundos, Lingüística aplicada*, and *Fonética y fonología españolas*. He published numerous articles on supposition and Caribbean dialectology at UCI, where he became an internationally renowned scholar of applied linguistics.

Tracy's move to UCSD was a great loss to Irvine and to me personally. I missed our animated discussions about all manner of topics in linguistics and language acquisition. But on the level of our lasting friendship and cooperation, little changed that we couldn't handle by phone, fax, or MCI plus our frequent meetings at conferences. His work will undoubtedly continue to have a strong impact on all of us in the language teaching profession for years to come.

Joan Bybee

I met Tracy in 1971 at UCLA, where I was a graduate student in linguistics. It was his first year at UC Irvine, and he came up regularly to UCLA to sit in on Barbara Partee's syntax class, which I was taking. Naïve as I was, I chose the Spanish subjunctive as a paper topic. When I sent Tracy a copy of my paper, he suggested working on the subjunctive together. We also talked a great deal about phonology, and I felt that we were kindred spirits on that subject as well. Tracy's creativity proved just as successful on theoretical topics as on applied ones. I think that, if he had continued to pursue linguistic theory, he would have achieved as much as he did by concentrating on language teaching. In fact, the success of his teaching methods and textbooks may be due largely to the validity of his implicit theory of grammar.

Marianne Celce-Murcia

I have many fond memories of Tracy, but the one that really stands out in my mind is the first time I saw him demonstrate the Natural Approach. We had met before at various meetings and, on this occasion, were both attending a CATESOL conference in

San Diego in the late 1970s. I had just presented a talk on motivating the study of grammar in ESL classes by using personal information about the students themselves.

Satisfied with my presentation and relieved that it was over, I went to hear Tracy do his NA demonstration. It was one of the most exciting experiences I had ever witnessed. Using only Dutch, Tracy very quickly got us to answer "Yes" or "No" and to respond with one-word responses to his "who-what-where" questions. He walked energetically around the group of 200-or-so observers and gave us a barrage of comprehensible input in Dutch while eliciting our names and words for articles of our clothing and their colors. After a while, he introduced some large pictures, which enabled him to give us additional input and questions. Everyone remained incredibly attentive and involved.

I was fortunate to have a chance to speak with Tracy after his demonstration, and I confessed that it was he who had truly used class information to teach language. My own talk had been dry and professorial by comparison. He told me not to be overly concerned: my topic (practicing grammar) had been more focused than his (listening comprehension as the basis for all other language teaching) and my target students had been more advanced than his. He felt there was room for different foci as long as listening comprehension and comprehensible input were given primacy. I didn't disagree, and Tracy and I remained fast friends—personally and professionally—after this particular conversation.

Jorge M. Guitart

The first time I met Tracy in person was in San Juan, Puerto Rico, in April 1976 on the occasion of our being invited to speak at the first Symposium on Caribbean Spanish Dialectology. I had been corresponding with him for several years, since he was one of the contributors to an anthology I was editing. It was the era of the controversy between abstractness and concreteness in phonology. Tracy favored concreteness and I abstractness, and we had been arguing ad infinitum by letter. Then in San Juan we kept arguing. I remember the very first afternoon we got there, sitting in the sun on the patio of the Convento Hotel with Tracy, having a drink and arguing, both of us writing furiously on napkins, oblivious to our surroundings. We both were dressed inappropriately for the weather: I had on a turtleneck since I had come from Buffalo, and Tracy was wearing a long-sleeved shirt. The other invited guests changed into shorts and t-shirts and went out sightseeing, but Tracy and I remained on that patio, writing on our napkins.

The argument continued at the symposium and extended to other symposia in other years. People were expecting us always to argue. The wonderful thing was that our disputes were strictly academic. We came to be very good friends, even as we continued trying to convince each other of the folly of the other's position. Throughout the years I learned a great deal from Tracy, about dialectology and second-language acquisition and language teaching, even about phonology—he had not been all that wrong after all. Stealing a bit from John Berryman, I remember the young man, alive with surplus energy and enthusiasm and bonhomie.

Peggy Hashemipour

When I became acquainted with Tracy Terrell in 1984, I was a graduate student in the Language Program at UC San Diego. Like many of the other Teaching Assistants, I was initially somewhat skeptical of Tracy. He was very energetic, self-motivated, on the run, and somewhat demanding. We wanted to finish our graduate careers, had established our own system of teaching, and were not really enthusiastic about Tracy changing the status quo. Did he ever—and it was great! Through twice-weekly meetings, Tracy provided us with an understanding of the how and why of teaching language effectively. He showed us through multiple examples: videos, role play, visiting our classes, all in a very non-threatening fashion. It didn't take long before I was convinced. From then on, Tracy and I developed a special bond that was central in my graduate years. Although I never took a class with him, he taught me so much. We talked the business of the language program, he mentored me, he supported my candidacy (even though he knew nothing about Persian and really disliked the GB theory on which I worked—and he did try on many occasions to switch over to it), and he advised me on my career.

I was even more honored when Tracy asked me to be his assistant in a large introductory linguistics class, in addition to my regular duties as a Spanish T.A. We worked closely, Tracy giving large lectures while I ran the problem-solving sessions. In their evaluations of our course, students commented that they had never observed such a complementary teaching duo. Again, I felt honored. In that class, Tracy taught me how to teach. For me, it is my personal experience with his work and his contributions that allows me to keep Tracy Terrell in my heart and continue to honor him by offering knowledge to others, as he so loved to do.

Ann M. Johns

Two important features of Tracy's personality were mentioned several times at his memorial service: his egalitarianism and his generosity. In the elitist academic world whose initiates are so concerned with their own professional successes, Tracy was a rare individual indeed. Perhaps one of several stories from my own experience will illustrate how I benefited from these qualities of his.

We San Diegans in the second/foreign language business were very pleased when Tracy moved down from Irvine to UCSD. Now he could be asked to give his famous Natural Approach demonstrations (I particularly liked the one on Greek) on my campus, at adult schools, or in public school classrooms. For his generosity was not confined to his academic peers but was available to all of us, regardless of the prestige of our schools and of our students. So I soon invited him over to San Diego State, and my students and visiting scholars were thrilled. When I offered him an honorarium, he refused, saying that it was his professional duty to be available to teachers everywhere.

Then one fall, I got a phone call from Tracy, who apparently was gradually being assigned the responsibilities on his campus for everything related to second and foreign language teaching. Just the previous week, he had been asked to direct the ESL writing program and supervise the teaching assistants. "And, Ann," he said, "I don't know (expletive) about writing, as you can imagine!" So I did a session for him (and, incidentally, was given an honorarium that very evening). Both he and the TAs seemed appreciative, and when I saw Tracy for the last time, he again mentioned how important that session had been to his thinking and to the ESL writing instruction in his TAs' classes.

When I think about this and other experiences with Tracy, it gives me hope. His life provided a constant example for us all of how a person can be famous without cant and generous to a fault. We miss him.

Karen Judd (Managing Editor, McGraw-Hill)

At least once a year, every book publisher has a sales meeting at which forthcoming new books are presented to the sales staff. Selected authors are often invited to make presentations in the hope that salespeople will become enthusiastic about the prospect of selling exciting new titles. The publisher crosses its fingers that the author won't be a dud in front of hundreds of sales representatives: some authors are boring presenters, and the sales staff is left to wonder how interesting the book could possibly be.

Along came the first edition of *Dos mundos* in 1986, a book not only unreadable by most of our salespeople but unlike any first-year Spanish text that potential adopting instructors had ever seen. Tracy was asked to present his book so that the sales force could understand its important new features. With more than 100 people held captive in a large room, Tracy proceeded to do a lesson using the Natural Approach— in Dutch. First he had us stand (the direction came in Dutch, along with a healthy dose of Total Physical Response). I can still see him, almost ten years later, arm extended, wrist down, twirling his index finger and saying, "Draai je om!" And, amazed, we all turned around!

Then there was the picture file. In Dutch he would ask, Is this a man? And we would shake our heads because the picture was that of a woman or a cat or a locomotive. Or we would nod and respond, "Ja" (as he had already taught us), because it was indeed a man. He explained that we would not be able to speak yet but that we could, with the help of some cognates and a little body language, understand everything he said. With sufficient practice, we knew that we would eventually be able to produce as well. We were sold on the Natural Approach and we were prepared to sell it to the world.

Tracy's presentation was enormously successful, and the sales force responded by selling thousands and thousands more copies than we had hoped. I wouldn't be surprised if he even inspired a few salespeople to learn, if not Dutch, at least some other language.

Thalia Dorwick

At the 1986 sales meeting at which we introduced *Dos mundos* to our sales staff, another author was "on" to present a book just before Tracy. Tracy asked if he could watch that presentation (of a chemistry book) with me. He listened for a few minutes, then started to make notes on the back of a large envelope that contained some of the Natural Approach props that he intended to use. I glanced over at his notes and realized in horror that he was in the process of outlining the entire presentation that he was scheduled to give in about fifteen minutes!

I knew how important the presentation would be to the success of *Dos mundos*, and I was terrified that Tracy would not "play well" to our audience of sales representatives. I thought that I had done my job a few weeks earlier by carefully talking him through the points he should cover, but I realized at that moment that I had not explicitly told him to prepare ahead of time.

That day I learned that I didn't need to worry about Tracy's presentations. He had done so many of them that he didn't really need to prepare the way most of us do for a large audience. As many times as Tracy did the Natural Approach demonstration, he never seemed to tire of it, and audiences always responded with the enthusiasm our salespeople showed.

Barbara A. Lafford

One of my memorable experiences with Tracy occurred the day we first met. As a graduate student working on my dissertation, I was attending the 1978 ALFAL conference in Caracas, Venezuela. At the time, I was collecting data in Colombia from informants of various social classes in Cartagena de Indias for a sociolinguistic study of the variable /s/. Tracy was already a well-known, established scholar in the field, but he took the time at the conference to sit with me and give me valuable advice about how to proceed with gathering, transcribing, and analyzing my data. I was attending the conference as a lowly, unknown graduate student; I was not even on the program. And yet Tracy spent almost three hours with me giving me invaluable guidance and encouragement because he found my work interesting.

After our first meeting, Tracy continued to give me feedback on my dissertation and my other research. This willingness on his part to encourage younger scholars, critique their work, and help open "windows" of opportunity for them to share their research with other scholars in the field impressed me greatly. I have made it a point in my career as a professor to carry on this tradition of mentoring that Tracy so gracefully established.

Ricardo Maldonado

I began my Ph.D. studies in linguistics at UCSD in 1985, the year in which Tracy started directing our old language-teaching program with new ideas. I was overwhelmed by Tracy's speed and skills in managing about 60 TAs. No, I didn't admire him—I feared him. As a good member of a Hispanic group, I was always ready with a sly retort in Spanish about Tracy's instructions. Soon enough, Tracy was answering me with the fastest native-Caribbean accent I had ever heard. The game was over. From that moment I was with him, not against him.

At UCSD, we were required to write one syntax paper and one phonology paper, both for publication. When the time came to write the second paper, I asked Tracy to be my advisor on a sociolinguistic/phonology problem. He was unique. Not only did he have his door open for consultation without restriction and spend time telling me how to use a complex statistics program, but he also allowed me to use his home computer. His attitude contrasted with the ten minutes of impersonal discussion granted by other professors in the department. One day, early in the morning, Tracy called to tell me excitedly that he had been working for over four hours running the data for my paper and they were finally yielding good results. How could I forget such a giving person?

Joseph H. Matluck

I was one of Tracy's Spanish linguistics professors at the University of Texas at Austin during the 1960s when he did his graduate work with us. I was his advising professor in that area and also a member of his dissertation committee on Romance linguistics, which was chaired by Ernest Haden. Tracy was the most brilliant student we have ever had in that program and is certainly one of the most illustrious professionals that this University has ever produced. That is not all: he has surpassed all his professors, not only in the excellence of his teaching and in the virtuosity of his unparalleled achievements in Hispanic dialect studies but also in his innovative thinking about language pedagogy, language acquisition, and general linguistics. For myself, I can think of no more crowning achievement in my own professional life than that of having contributed to the linguistic formation and professional growth of Tracy Terrell and—together with my wife, Dr. Betty Mace-Matluck—of having given him moral support and encouragement in the very early, difficult days of his work with the Natural Approach.

Patricia A. Richard-Amato

I feel very fortunate to have met Tracy, however briefly, and to have been exposed to his work. Although I have no personal anecdote to relate, I would like to share a few thoughts. I have always admired (with some envy) his immense energy and his courage. I mention courage because he dared to challenge forces in the field committed to reducing language learning to sets of rules and drills, as though language learning were simply a matter of conscious rule application and practice. He was among those who reminded us that second-language development is, for the most part, a creative, active process. But he did not stop there. He gave us one very important way to promote such development—the Natural Approach—that has made a difference in the way many teachers and learners approach the learning process. I feel certain that second-language students and their teachers will remain grateful in the years to come for the contributions that Tracy made to what happens in language classrooms.

Diane Ringer Uber

I first began corresponding with Tracy in 1979, while I was working on my dissertation on Puerto Rican Spanish at the University of Wisconsin. Tracy was very helpful, sending me copies of the recordings from the Norma Culta project to use in making the demonstration tape for my fieldwork. It was not until 1982, at the seventh Symposium on Caribbean Spanish Dialectology in San Juan, Puerto Rico, that we finally met. Upon returning from the symposium, I proceeded to tell a colleague about meeting Tracy. Apparently I talked about him for some time, because my colleague said, "You make this person sound just wonderful!" I thought for a minute and replied, "Well, I can't think of anything about him that I don't like."

Tracy was extremely supportive of my work over the years. Although I have always lived in the eastern United States and Tracy lived in the West, much of our work has been complementary and I tried to keep in touch with him. Whenever I finished a paper, Tracy was the first person on my mailing list. When I visited San Diego a few years ago, he took time from his busy schedule to invite me to dinner to discuss our mutual interests in Spanish linguistics and language teaching, which I greatly appreciated.

My last communication from Tracy was a note from him in May 1991 in which he wrote, "I must say I had a wonderful life; I've had nothing but warm support from colleagues." Nobody was more deserving of such love and respect.

Wilga M. Rivers

I first met Tracy in the early 1970s when I was lecturing at UCLA soon after my arrival in the United States from Australia. I distinctly remember his slender figure and alert, lively face. Our paths crossed again not long afterward at Brigham Young University. We had begun to be known in the same circles, and soon after our second meeting I asked him to conduct a workshop at our orientation for Harvard foreign-language TAs. Tracy gave his very impressive demonstration of the Natural Approach using Dutch, to the delight of our neophyte teaching fellows. By this time, we had become professional friends, and Tracy kept a WMR file with the various manuscript-stage articles I sent him, as I kept a TDD file. His insights into the problems of language learning were always stimulating, firmly based in his long experience as an excellent teacher of Spanish: they were always intuitively sensible and applicable to the regular foreign-language classroom situation. Intellectually honest, he was always ready to rethink and readjust his theoretical positions according to his observation of what actually takes place in the real instructional context in college or high school.

On one occasion, he mentioned to me that he was a little sorry that he had opted so early in the game for the label "Natural Approach" (for the methodology that he had, of course, elaborated himself before he met and collaborated with Stephen

Krashen). I immediately reacted playfully with the rejoinder: "Then link up with the Interactive Approach!" At this, he smiled that gentle smile of his, knowing as he did that we were very much on the same wavelength. It is very important to me that we continue to emphasize that the Natural Approach was Tracy's, and I am continually correcting errors in this regard in articles I review for journals and in manuscripts that people send me for advice and evaluation. Tracy made a great and solid contribution to our work in the foreign-language teaching field, and we must see that it is not forgotten.

Carmen Silva-Corvalán

I met Tracy in 1978. He was then very actively working on phonological variation in Spanish within a sociolinguistic perspective. Because I was planning to write a dissertation on syntactic variation and sociolinguistics for my Ph.D. at UCLA, I asked Tracy to serve on my committee. He agreed. This initial professor-student relationship soon turned into friendship. Tracy was perhaps the most crucial person in enabling me to start and develop a career in linguistics in the United States. In 1979, he was offered the position I now hold in the Department of Spanish and Portuguese at the University of Southern California. Because he could not accept it, and with his strong support, the position was offered to me.

I later had the opportunity to work with Tracy on a joint project that examined the expression of futurity in Spanish. My sons and I still remember the hot dogs, American-style, that he prepared when he came to our house! Tracy was very encouraging, supportive, and helpful to me. He was always an excellent colleague and friend—a model to follow.

Margaret van Naerssen

I met Tracy when, starting on my Ph.D. research, I needed a population of college students studying first-year Spanish with an instructor willing to cooperate with me. Steve Krashen, who was directing my dissertation, suggested Tracy and his students at UC Irvine. Over the next year I watched him teach, picked his brain, came to understand the Natural Approach, gathered data from his class, and received valuable feedback on my results. I saw how involved he was in his teaching, writing, and research and realized how fortunate I was that he was taking the time to work with me. Eventually, Tracy also became a member of my dissertation committee.

I'd like to pass on a teaching/testing technique I learned from him that saved hours of initial transcription in my data collection and that I've modified for use in my own classes. Periodically he had students tape, under timed conditions in the language lab, their personal responses to open-ended questions designed to elicit the language patterns he had been emphasizing in class. After the recording, they would rewind and transcribe their own recording, writing on every other line and including all errors. In the final step, with time to focus on the "rules," students added corrections of their own speech. Tracy would then listen to individual tapes and check the transcriptions, focusing on the patterns stressed in class.

As a teaching tool, this procedure gave students the opportunity to express their own ideas and to become aware of their own language. It was also a manageable testing tool, allowing Tracy to check on individual progress. As a research tool, the benefits are clear. Tracy allowed me to add open-ended questions to elicit the data I needed and, eventually, I had the tapes and first drafts of transcriptions to work with. Of course, I had to verify the transcriptions and revise them further. But anyone who has transcribed data can appreciate the time that was saved!

Working as an editor on this collection has been like taking an independent study course, reading about topics I might not have read on my own and further exploring Tracy's world. I have valued this experience of getting to know Tracy even better through the work of his friends and colleagues.

Bill VanPatten

I would like to add a personal note about Tracy David Terrell. Tracy possessed the capacity for listening to and thinking about positions on acquisition and teaching that differed from his own. While in a technical sense we all have this capacity, Tracy always impressed me because he consistently exercised it more than anyone else I know. I recall a Second Language Research Forum several years ago at which I first presented the research I published in 1989 and 1990. After my presentation Tracy said (and this is a paraphrase and not a direct quote): "You know, Bill, your data are very interesting. They are causing me to rethink this thing about grammar as an advanced organizer that I have been talking about." This is classic Tracy, and those of us who over the years have read his publications on language teaching and acquisition have been witnesses to a progression of thought, to an evolution of ideas, to a continued process of analysis and reanalysis, evaluation and re-evaluation. I think that this is important. Given a profession in which debate often prevails over dialogue, in which rhetoric often wins out over empiricism, in which camps line up on opposite sides of some invisible line, Tracy's willingness to consider issues and to rethink his own position as other theories and research presented themselves served as a model for all academics.

Tracy, many thanks ...

Dolly J. Young

Humorous, energetic, dynamic, bright, articulate, warm, friendly, young, fun, enthusiastic, knowledgeable, professional, personable ... These are only some of the rich qualities that I associate with Tracy. I remember being extremely impressed the first time I met him. It was the AATSP conference in Spain in 1986, and a group of us "novices" were meeting for lunch at a restaurant across from the conference hotel. He recognized one of the graduate students among us and invited all of us to sit with him for lunch. In that hour, I developed an impression of Tracy that never changed. As the years passed, his accomplishments multiplied but Tracy remained accessible, friendly, warm, supportive, and enthusiastic. His down-to-earth nature was a pleasant welcome and surprise. He became a model for many young, aspiring applied linguists.

I was also fortunate enough to know Tracy in his final years during the times he stayed with his sister in Austin and had so little energy that he could barely cut an apple. On a number of occasions, I would call him for information regarding our recent interview or some other topic. It was during these hour-long conversations that Tracy gave to me something I shall forever remember. He shared with me his thoughts and feelings about what he was going through with AIDS. I gained an insight that has since seeped into the very marrow of my bones.

Not only am I grateful for his incredible contributions to my particular field and to the profession, but he made a lasting impression on me at a very personal level. For all this and more, I can only say: Thank you, Tracy.

Stephen D. Krashen

Tracy Terrell died on December 2, 1991, at the age of 48 after a long illness. We have lost a fine scholar and a good friend.

A graduate of the University of Texas, Tracy Terrell was a professor of linguistics at the University of California, Irvine, and at the University of California, San Diego. A respected sociolinguist, he was best known as the originator of the Natural Approach. The Natural Approach was initially designed for foreign language instruction and has had wide acceptance at the university level. Natural Approach–oriented texts (*Dos mundos, Deux mondes,* and *Kontakte*), developed by Tracy and colleagues, are widely used throughout North America. At the time of his death, Tracy was developing a high school Spanish series, *¡Bravo!,* which has now been published.

Soon after its debut as a foreign language teaching method, the Natural Approach was used in ESL and EFL classes around the world. In the United States, many public school systems, including those in Los Angeles, San Diego, and El Paso, adopted the Natural Approach for ESL. Tracy was a major contributor to the California Theoretical Framework in Bilingual Education, and in January 1990 the California Bilingual Association honored him for his contributions to the education of language-minority students.

Tracy was the most enthusiastic supporter of his method as well as its best critic. He was a phenomenal presenter, and his lectures and demonstrations brought the Natural Approach to many school districts and colleges. He was also constantly refining the method and examining its linguistic and affective impact on students.

Although Tracy lived with AIDS for several years before his death, he nevertheless continued to devote himself to his work. He revised and extended his textbook series and wrote several outstanding scholarly papers in the last few years of his life. The latter include "The Role of Grammar Instruction in a Communicative Approach," from 1991; "Affective Reactions of Foreign Language Students to Natural Approach Activities and Teaching Techniques," coauthored with April Koch, from 1991; and "Foreigner Talk as Comprehensible Input," his last publicly presented paper at a major conference, given at the Georgetown University Round Table in 1990. He also continued to devote himself to his friends.

Tracy Terrell's work has greatly facilitated language acquisition for foreign language and second language students around the world, and it will continue to affect the lives of students and language educators for years to come. He has earned an honored place in the history of foreign and second language pedagogy.

Goodbye, my friend. Thank you for your enthusiasm, your honesty, and your good humor.

[adapted from an obituary notice originally written
for *TESOL Matters,* Spring 1992]